PHILIP'S

STREET

Suffolk

Bury St Edmunds, Felixstowe, Ipswich, Lowestoft, Newmarket

C000142779

www.philips-maps.co.uk

First published in 2003 by
Philip's, a division of
Octopus Publishing Group Ltd
www.octopusbooks.co.uk
Endeavour House, 189 Shaftesbury Avenue
London WC2H 8JY
An Hachette UK Company
www.hachette.co.uk

Third edition with interim revision 2012
Second impression 2014
SUFCA

ISBN 978-1-84907-246-5 (spiral)

© Philip's 2012

Ordnance Survey®

This product includes mapping data licensed
from Ordnance Survey® with the permission
of the Controller of Her Majesty's Stationery
Office. © Crown copyright 2012. All rights
reserved. Licence number 100011710.

Contents

II	**Key to map pages**	
IV	**Route planning**	
VIII	Administrative and Postcode boundaries	
1	**Key to map symbols**	
2	**Street maps** at 1¾ inches to 1 mile	
109	**Street maps** at 3½ inches to 1 mile	
154	**Street maps** of centres of Bury St Edmunds and Ipswich at 7 inches to 1 mile	
156	**Index** of towns and villages, streets, hospitals, industrial estates, railway stations, schools, shopping centres, universities and places of interest	

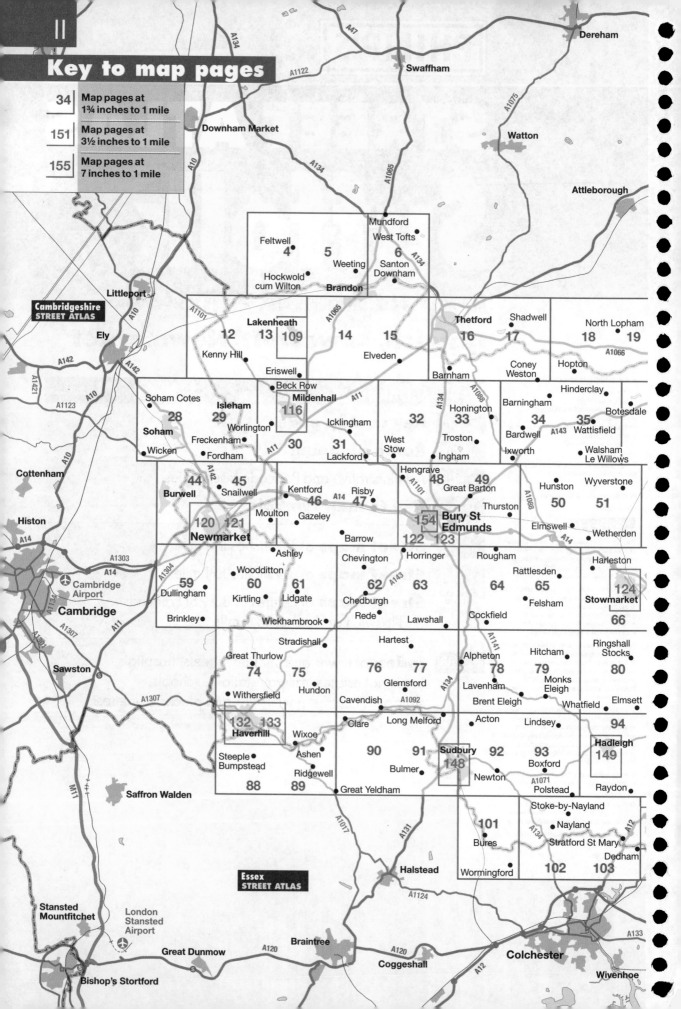

Key to map pages

34	Map pages at 1¾ inches to 1 mile
151	Map pages at 3½ inches to 1 mile
155	Map pages at 7 inches to 1 mile

Dereham

Swaffham

Downham Market

Watton

Attleborough

Littleport

Cambridgeshire STREET ATLAS

Ely

Feltwell
4
5
Weeting
Mundford
West Tofts
Santon Downham
6

Hockwold cum Wilton
Brandon

Lakenheath
12 **13** **109**
14
15
Thetford
16
Shadwell
17
North Lopham
18 **19**

Kenny Hill
Elveden
Barnham
Coney Weston
Hopton

Eriswell

Soham Cotes
28
Isleham
29
Beck Row
Mildenhall
116
Icklingham
30 **31**
Lackford
West Stow
Ingham
32
Honington
33
Troston
Barningham
34
Bardwell
Ixworth
Hinderclay
35
Wattisfield
Botesdale
Walsham Le Willows

Soham
Worlington
Freckenham
Fordham
Wicken

Burwell
44 **45**
Snailwell
Kentford
46 **47**
Risby
Hengrave
48
Great Barton
49
Thurston
Hunston
50
Wyverstone
51

120 **121**
Newmarket
Moulton
Gazeley
154
Bury St Edmunds
122 **123**
Elmswell
Wetherden

Barrow

Cambridge Airport
Ashley
Wooddity
59 **60** **61**
Kirtling
Lidgate
Chevington
62 **63**
Horringer
Rougham
64
Rattlesden
65
Harleston
Stowmarket
124

Cambridge
Dullingham
Brinkley
Chedburgh
Rede
Lawshall
Cockfield
Felsham
66

Sawston
Great Thurlow
74 **75**
Stradishall
Hundon
Hartest
76 **77**
Glemsford
Alpheton
78
Lavenham
Hitcham
79
Monks Eleigh
Ringshall Stocks
80

Withersfield
Cavendish
Brent Eleigh
Whatfield
Elmsett

132 **133**
Haverhill
Wixoe
Ashen
Clare
Long Melford
Acton
Lindsey
94
Hadleigh
149

Steeple Bumpstead
Ridgewell
90 **91**
Bulmer
Sudbury
148
Newton
92
Boxford
93
Raydon

88 **89**
Great Yeldham
Polstead
Stoke-by-Nayland
Nayland
101
Bures
Stratford St Mary
Dedham
102 **103**

Saffron Walden
Halstead
Wormingford

Essex STREET ATLAS

Stansted Mountfitchet
London Stansted Airport
Colchester

Great Dunmow
Braintree
Coggeshall
Wivenhoe

Bishop's Stortford

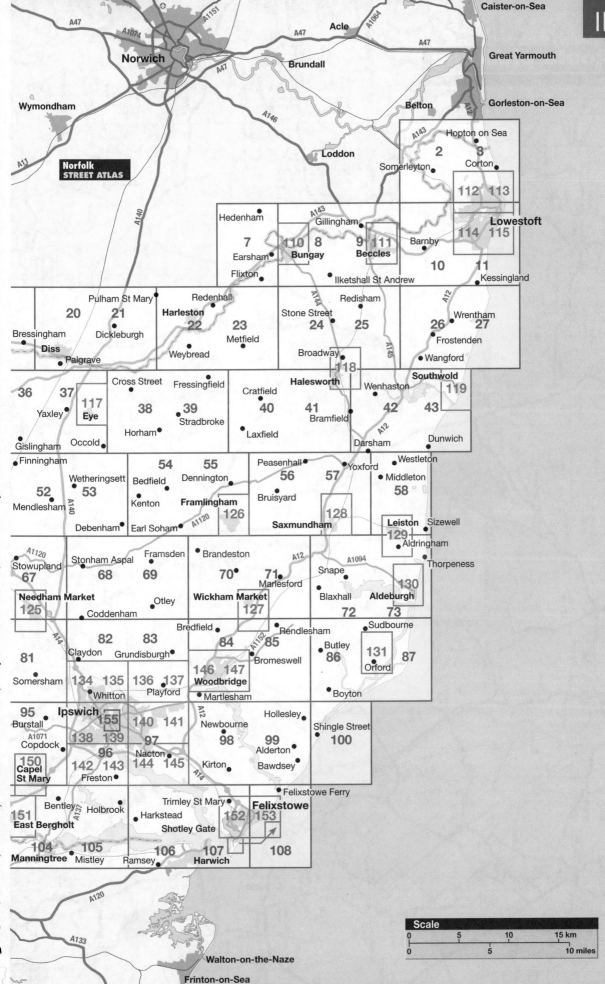

Caister-on-Sea
Great Yarmouth
Gorleston-on-Sea

Acle
Brundall
Norwich
Wymondham
Belton
Hopton on Sea
Somerleyton
Corton

Norfolk STREET ATLAS

Loddon

2
3
112 **113**

114 **115**
Lowestoft
Barnby
10 **11**
Kessingland

Hedenham
Gillingham
7 **110** **8** **9** **111**
Earsham
Bungay
Beccles
Flixton
Ilketshall St Andrew

Pulham St Mary
Redenhall
Redisham
Wrentham
20 **21** **Harleston** **22** **23** **24** **25** **26** **27**
Bressingham
Dickleburgh
Metfield
Stone Street
Frostenden
Diss
Weybread
Broadway
Wangford
Palgrave

Cross Street
Fressingfield
Cratfield
Halesworth
Wenhaston
Southwold
36 **37** **117** **38** **39** **40** **41** **42** **43** **119**
Yaxley
Eye
Stradbroke
Bramfield
Gislingham
Horham
Laxfield
Darsham
Dunwich
Occold

Finningham
Westleton
54 **55** Peasenhall Yoxford
52 **53** Wetheringsett Bedfield Dennington **56** **57** Middleton **58**
Mendlesham Kenton **Framlingham** Bruisyard
Debenham Earl Soham **126** **128** **Leiston** Sizewell
Saxmundham **129** Aldringham

Stonham Aspal Framsden Brandeston Snape Thorpeness
67 **68** **69** **70** **71** **130**
Stowupland Marlesford Blaxhall **Aldeburgh**
Needham Market Otley Wickham Market **72** **73**
125 Coddenham **127**

Bredfield Rendlesham Sudbourne
82 **83** **84** **85** Butley **131** **87**
81 Claydon Grundisburgh Bromeswell **86** Orford
Somersham **134** **135** **136** **137** **146** **147** Boyton
Whitton Playford **Woodbridge**
Martlesham

95 **Ipswich** **155** **140** **141** Hollesley
Burstall **138** **139** Newbourne Shingle Street
Copdock **97** **98** **99** **100**
96 Nacton Alderton
150 **142** **143** **144** **145** Kirton Bawdsey
Capel St Mary Freston
Felixstowe Ferry
151 Bentley Holbrook Trimley St Mary **Felixstowe**
East Bergholt Harkstead **152** **153**
Shotley Gate
104 **105** **106** **107** **108**
Manningtree Mistley Ramsey **Harwich**

Walton-on-the-Naze
Frinton-on-Sea

Scale
0   5   10   15 km
0   5   10 miles

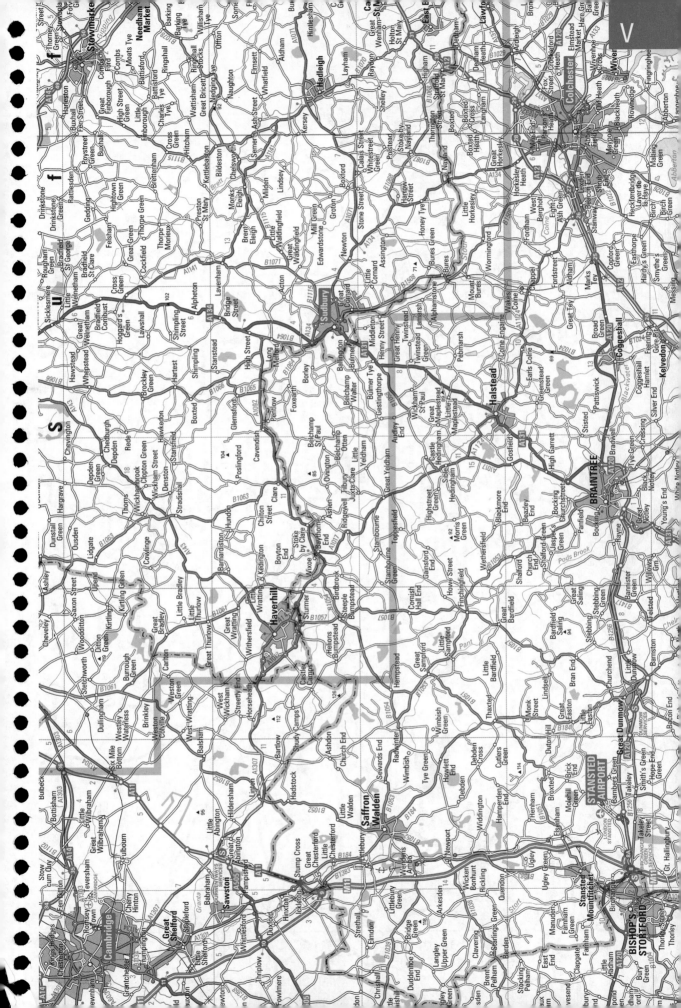

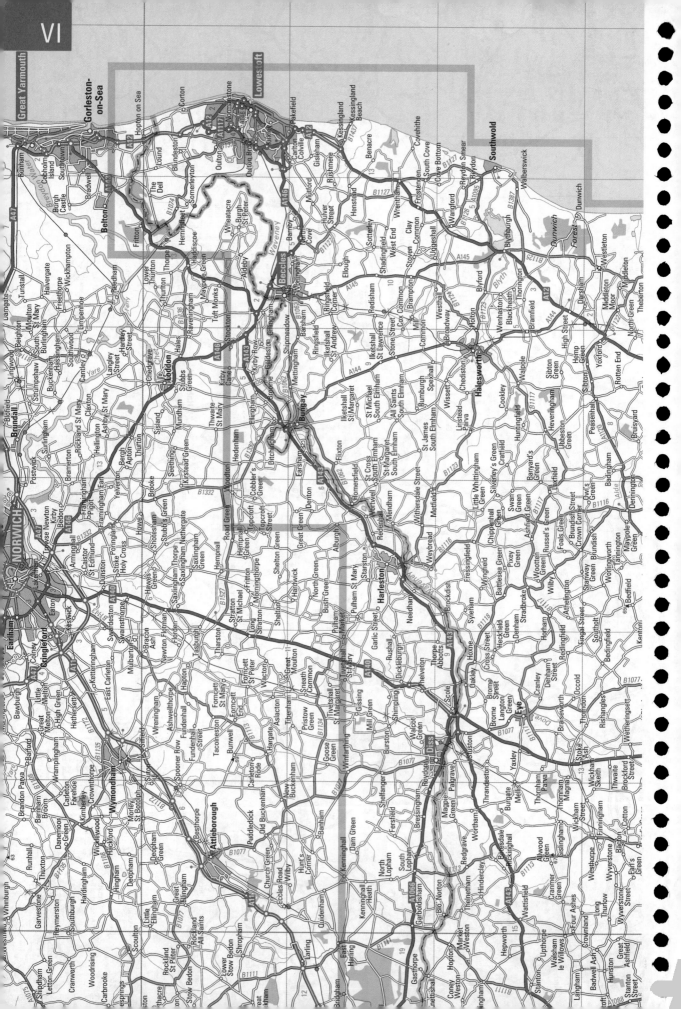

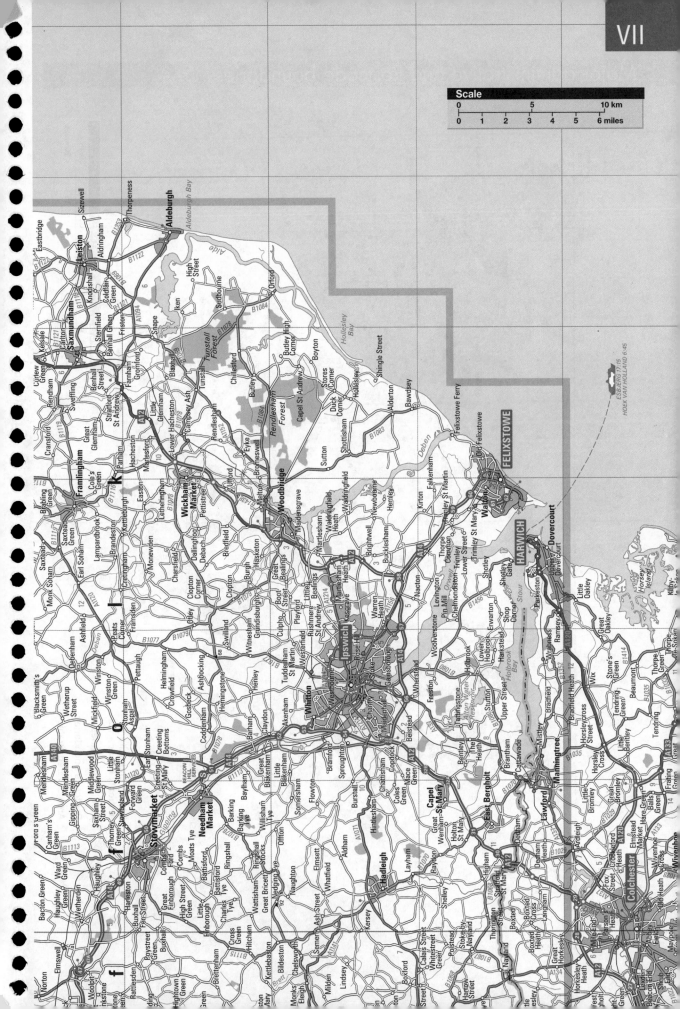

Scale

0   5   10 km
0   1   2   3   4   5   6 miles

Major administrative and Postcode boundaries

TG
TM
TF | TG
TF | TL

Hopton on Sea
Corton
Lowestoft
Kessingland
NR32
NR33
Wheatacre
Barnby
NR31
NR14
Wrentham
Waveney
Southwold
IP18
NR34
Kirby Row
NR35
Beccles
Bungay
Halesworth
Wangford
IP19
Westleton
Thorpeness
IP15
Aldeburgh
Pulham St Mary
NR20
Metfield
Cratfield
Bramfield
Yoxford
IP16
Leiston
Orford
Harleston
Fressingfield
Laxfield
Badingham
IP17
Saxmundham
Rendlesham
Suffolk Coastal
IP21
Stradbroke
Framlingham
IP13
Wickham Market
Woodbridge
IP12
Waldringfield
NR15
Scole
Occold
Debenham
Grundisburgh
Kesgrave
Kirton
IP11
Felixstowe
Harwich
CO12
Diss
Eye
IP23
Mendlesham
Mid Suffolk
IP14
Needham Market
IP6
Claydon
Ipswich
IP1 IP4 IP5
IP8 IP2 IP3
IP10
Holbrook
IP9
CO11
North Lopham
IP22
Rickinghall
Gislingham
Haughley
Stowmarket
Somersham
Hintlesham
Capel St Mary
Mistley
Manningtree
Stanton
IP31
Ixworth
Great Barton
Elmswell
Sicklesmere
IP30
Felsham
Suffolk
IP7
Hadleigh
East Bergholt
CO7
Langham
Lawford
TL | TM
Norfolk
NR16
Thetford
IP24
Barnham
Honington
IP32
Brockley Green
IP33
Bury St Edmunds
Barrow
St Edmundsbury
IP29
Bildeston
Lavenham
Acton
Babergh
Boxford
Nayland
Bures
CO6
CO8
Weeting
Brandon
IP27
Lackford
Risby
Hundon
Clare
Glemsford
Sudbury
Great Yeldham
CO10
Essex
Feltwell
Lakenheath
Mildenhall
IP28
Newmarket
Lidgate
CB9
Haverhill
CM7
CO9
IP26
Beck Row
Fordham
Cheveley
CB8
Dullingham
Steeple Bumpstead
CB10
Cambridgeshire
Isleham
Burwell
Soham
CB7
CB5

Scale
0 5 10 15 20 25 30km
0 5 10 15 20 miles

County and unitary authority boundaries
District boundaries
Postcode boundaries
Area covered by this atlas

Key to map symbols

—22—	Motorway with junction number
	Primary route – dual/single carriageway
	A road – dual/single carriageway
	B road – dual/single carriageway
	Minor road – dual/single carriageway
	Other minor road – dual/single carriageway
	Road under construction
	Tunnel, covered road
	Rural track, private road or narrow road in urban area
	Gate or obstruction to traffic – may not apply at all times or to all vehicles
	Path, bridleway, byway open to all traffic, restricted byway
	Pedestrianised area
BS22	Postcode boundaries
	County and unitary authority boundaries
	Railway with station
	Tunnel
	Railway under construction
	Metro station
	Private railway station
	Miniature railway
	Tramway, tram stop
	Tramway, tram stop under construction
	Bus, coach station

◆	Ambulance station
◆	Coastguard station
◆	Fire station
◆	Police station
✚	Accident and Emergency entrance to hospital
H	Hospital
+	Place of worship
i	Information centre – open all year
P	Shopping centre, parking
P&R PO	Park and Ride, Post Office
⚐ ⚑	Camping site, caravan site
⚑ ✕	Golf course, picnic site
Church ROMAN FORT	Non-Roman antiquity, Roman antiquity
Univ	Important buildings, schools, colleges, universities and hospitals
	Woods, built-up area
River Medway	Water name
	River, weir
	Stream
<	Canal, lock, tunnel
	Water
	Tidal water
58 87 246	Adjoining page indicators and overlap bands – the colour of the arrow and band indicates the scale of the adjoining or overlapping page (see scales below)

The dark grey border on the inside edge of some pages indicates that the mapping does not continue onto the adjacent page

The small numbers around the edges of the maps identify the 1-kilometre National Grid lines

Enlarged maps only

	Railway or bus station building
	Place of interest
	Parkland

Abbreviations

Acad	Academy	Meml	Memorial
Allot Gdns	Allotments	Mon	Monument
Cemy	Cemetery	Mus	Museum
C Ctr	Civic centre	Obsy	Observatory
CH	Club house	Pal	Royal palace
Coll	College	PH	Public house
Crem	Crematorium	Recn Gd	Recreation ground
Ent	Enterprise		
Ex H	Exhibition hall	Resr	Reservoir
Ind Est	Industrial Estate	Ret Pk	Retail park
IRB Sta	Inshore rescue boat station	Sch	School
		Sh Ctr	Shopping centre
Inst	Institute	TH	Town hall / house
Ct	Law court	Trad Est	Trading estate
L Ctr	Leisure centre	Univ	University
LC	Level crossing	W Twr	Water tower
Liby	Library	Wks	Works
Mkt	Market	YH	Youth hostel

The map scale on the pages numbered in green is 1¾ inches to 1 mile
2.76 cm to 1 km • 1:36206

0	½ mile	1 mile	1½ miles	2 miles
0	500m 1 km	1½ km	2km	

The map scale on the pages numbered in blue is 3½ inches to 1 mile
5.52 cm to 1 km • 1:18103

0	¼ mile	½ mile	¾ mile	1 mile
0	250m 500m	750m	1km	

The map scale on the pages numbered in red is 7 inches to 1 mile
11.04 cm to 1 km • 1:9051

0	220yds	440yds	660yds	½ mile
0	125m 250m	375m	500m	

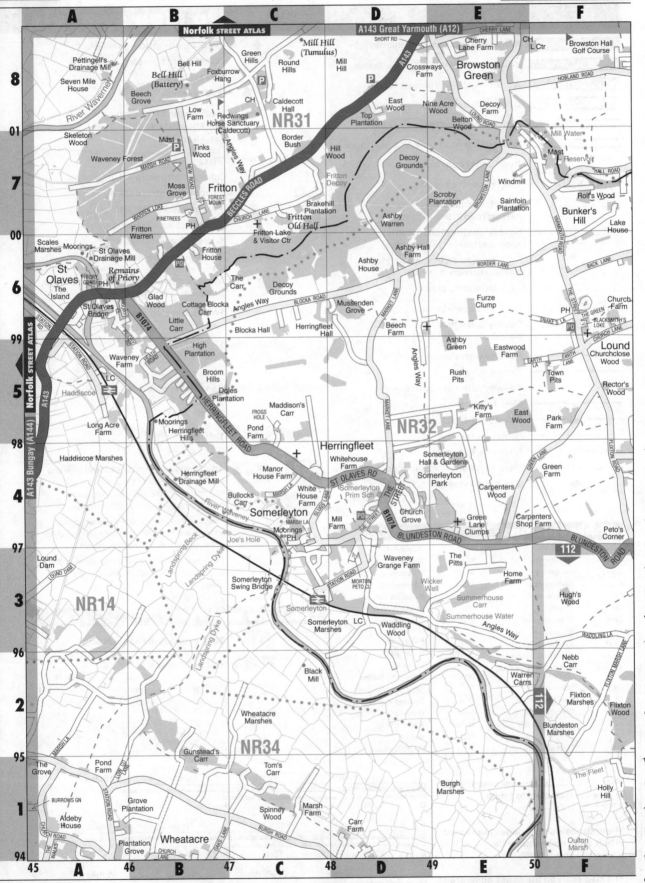

Scale: 1¾ inches to 1 mile

0   ¼   ½ mile
0 250m 500m 750m 1 km

A143 Great Yarmouth (A12)

NR31

NR32

NR14

NR34

Pettingell's Drainage Mill
Seven Mile House
Bell Hill
Bell Hill (Battery)
Foxburrow Hang
Green Hills
Mill Hill (Tumulus)
Mill Hill
Browston Hall Golf Course
CHERRY LANE
Cherry Lane Farm
CH L Ctr
Browston Green
River Waveney
Beech Grove
Low Farm
Redwings Horse Sanctuary (Caldecott)
CH
Caldecott Hall
Round Hills
Crossways Farm
SHORT RD
HOBLAND ROAD
Skeleton Wood
Mast
Tinks Wood
Border Bush
East Wood
Top Plantation
Nine Acre Wood
Decoy Farm
Belton Wood
Mill Water
Reservoir
Mast
Waveney Forest
MARSH ROAD
NEW ROAD
Moss Grove
FOREST MOUNT
Fritton
BECCLES ROAD
ANGLES WAY
Hill Wood
Fritton Decoy
Decoy Grounds
Scroby Plantation
Windmill
BROWSTON LANE
Rolf's Wood
HALL ROAD
Bunker's Hill
Lake House
WARREN LOKE
PINETREES
PH
CHURCH LANE
Brakehill Plantation
Fritton Old Hall
Ashby Warren
Sainfoin Plantation
YARMOUTH ROAD
Fritton Warren
Fritton Lake & Visitor Ctr
Ashby Hall Farm
BORDER LANE
BACK LANE
Scales Marshes Moorings
St Olaves Drainage Mill
P0
Fritton House
The Carr
Decoy Grounds
Ashby House
Furze Clump
THE STREET
PH
Church
SNAKE'S LA
P0
The Green
BLACKSMITH'S LOKE
CHURCH LANE
St Olaves
PRIORY GDNS
PH
Remains of Priory
Glad Wood
ANGLES WAY
BLOCKA ROAD
Mussenden Grove
MARKET LANE
Beech Farm
Ashby Green
Eastwood Farm
EARTH LA
EARTH LANE
Town Pits
Lound Churchclose Wood
The Island
St Olaves Bridge
B1074
Cottage Blocka Carr
Herringfleet Hall
Ashby House
Rush Pits
Rector's Wood
Little Carr
Blocka Hall
STATION RD
Norfolk STREET ATLAS
Waveney Farm
High Plantation
ANGLES WAY
Kitty's Farm
East Wood
Park Farm
STATION ROAD
LC
Broom Hills
Doles Plantation
FROGS HOLE
Maddison's Carr
Herringfleet
NR32
Somerleyton Hall & Gardens
GREEN LANE
Green Farm
Haddiscoe
MARSH LA
Pond Farm
Whitehouse Farm
Somerleyton Park
Carpenters Wood
FLIXTON ROAD
A143
Long Acre Farm
Moorings Herringfleet Hills
HERRINGFLEET ROAD
Manor House Farm
White House Farm
St Olaves RD
Somerleyton Prim Sch
THE STREET
Carpenters Shop Farm
A143 Bungay (A144)
Haddiscoe Marshes
Herringfleet Drainage Mill
Bullocks Carr
MARSH LA
SLUGS LANE
P0
B1074
Church Grove
Green Lane Clumps
Peto's Corner
River Waveney
Somerleyton
Moorings PH
Mill Farm
THE STREET
BLUNDESTON ROAD
BLUNDESTON ROAD
Joe's Hole
Waveney Grange Farm
The Pitts
Home Farm
112
Lound Dam
LOUND DAM
Landspring Beck
Landspring Dyke
Somerleyton Swing Bridge
Somerleyton
STATION ROAD
MORTON PETO CL
Wicker Well
Summerhouse Carr
Hugh's Wood
Somerleyton Marshes
LC
Waddling Wood
Summerhouse Water
ANGLES WAY
WADDLING LA
Black Mill
Nebb Carr
112
Wheatacre Marshes
Warren Carrs
Flixton Marshes
Flixton Wood
FLIXTON MARSH LANE
Blundeston Marshes
MARSH LA
Gunstead's Carr
Tom's Carr
Burgh Marshes
The Fleet
The Grove
Pond Farm
LOW LA
Spinney Wood
Marsh Farm
Holly Hill
BURROWS GN
STATION ROAD
Grove Plantation
BURGH ROAD
Carr Farm
Aldeby House
CHURCH ROAD
Plantation Grove
Wheatacre
GAS LANE
CHURCH LANE
THE WALKS
Oulton Marsh

For full street detail of the highlighted area see pages 112 and 113

112

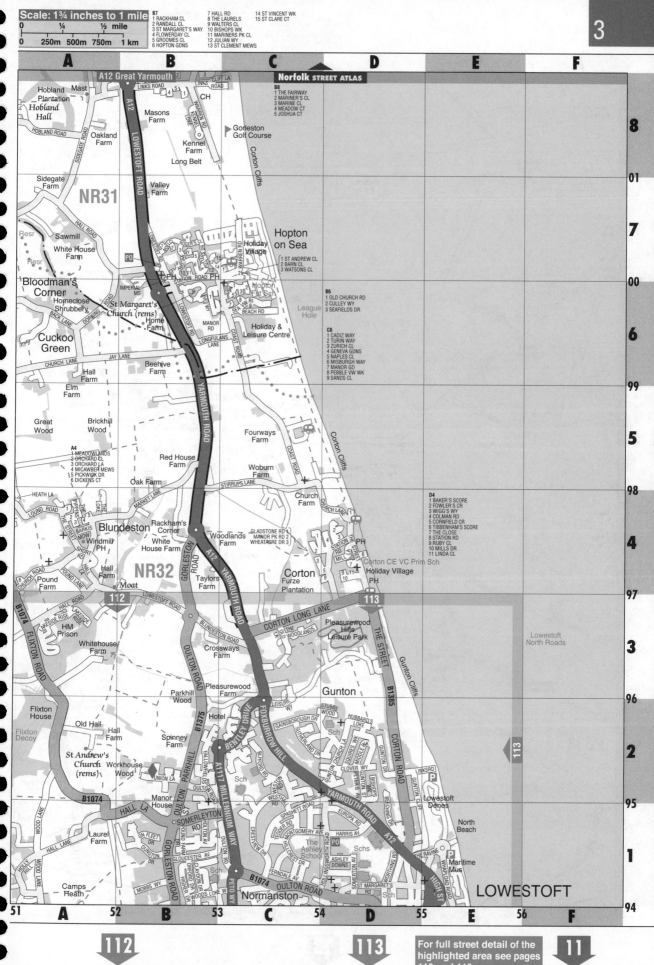

Scale: 1¾ inches to 1 mile

0   ¼   ½   mile
0 250m 500m 750m 1 km

Norfolk STREET ATLAS

B7
1 RACKHAM CL
2 RANDALL CL
3 ST MARGARET'S WAY
4 FLOWERDAY CL
5 GROOMES CL
6 HOPTON GDNS
7 HALL RD
8 THE LAURELS
9 WALTERS CL
10 BISHOPS WK
11 MARINERS PK CL
12 JULIAN WY
13 ST CLEMENT MEWS
14 ST VINCENT WK
15 ST CLARE CT

B8
1 THE FAIRWAY
2 MARINER'S CL
3 MARINE CL
4 MEADOW CT
5 JOSHUA CT

B6
1 OLD CHURCH RD
2 CULLEY WY
3 SEAFIELDS DR

C6
1 CADIZ WAY
2 TURIN WAY
3 ZURICH CL
4 GENEVA GDNS
5 NAPLES CL
6 MISBURGH WAY
7 MANOR GD
8 PEBBLE VW WK
9 SANDS CL

D4
1 BAKER'S SCORE
2 FOWLER'S CR
3 WIGG'S WY
4 COLMAN RD
5 CORNFIELD CR
6 TIBBENHAM'S SCORE
7 THE CLOSE
8 STATION RD
9 RUBY CL
10 MILLS DR
11 LINDA CL

A4
1 MEADOWLANDS
2 ORCHARD CL
3 ORCHARD LA
4 MICAWBER MEWS
5 PICKWICK DR
6 DICKENS CT

LOWESTOFT

112

113

11

For full street detail of the highlighted area see pages 112 and 113

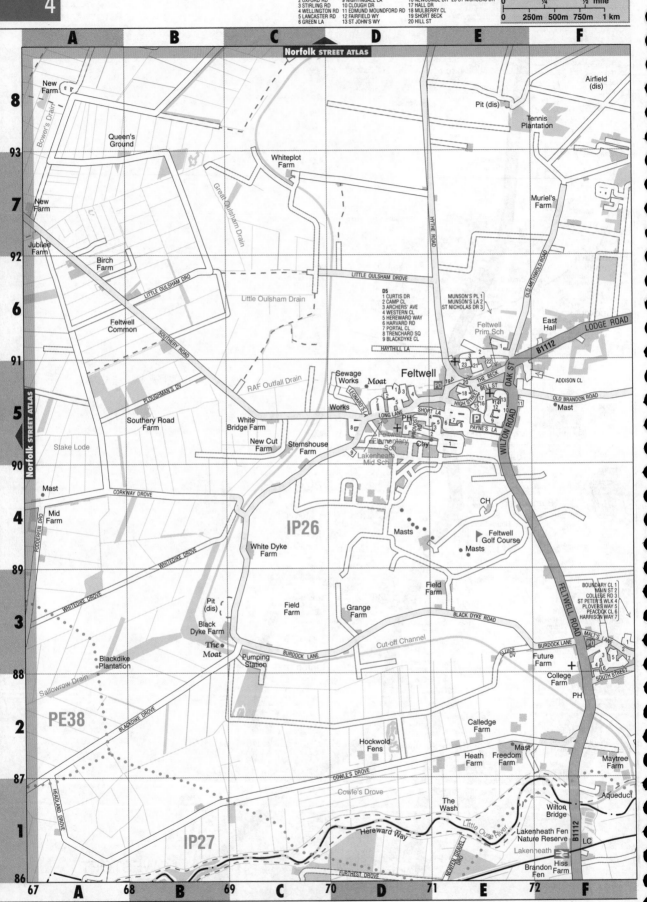

Scale: 1¾ inches to 1 mile

E5
1 BIRD VIEW SQ
2 OXFORD RD
3 STIRLING RD
4 WELLINGTON RD
5 LANCASTER RD
6 GREEN LA
7 VINCENT CL
8 CRABBE'S CL
9 NIGHTINGALE LA
10 CLOUGH DR
11 EDMUND MOUNDFORD RD
12 FAIRFIELD WY
13 ST JOHN'S WY
14 FAIR CL
15 FALCON RD
16 NEWCOMBE DR
17 HALL DR
18 MULBERRY CL
19 SHORT BECK
20 HILL ST
21 LAMBERTS CL
22 RAWLINGS WY
23 ST NICHOLAS DR

D5
1 CURTIS DR
2 CAMP CL
3 ARCHERS' AVE
4 WESTERN CL
5 HEREWARD WAY
6 HARVARD RD
7 PORTAL CL
8 TRENCHARD SQ
9 BLACKDYKE CL

Norfolk STREET ATLAS

BOUNDARY CL 1
MAIN ST 2
COLLEGE RD 3
ST PETER'S WLK 4
PLOVERS WAY 5
PEACOCK CL 6
HARRISON WAY 7

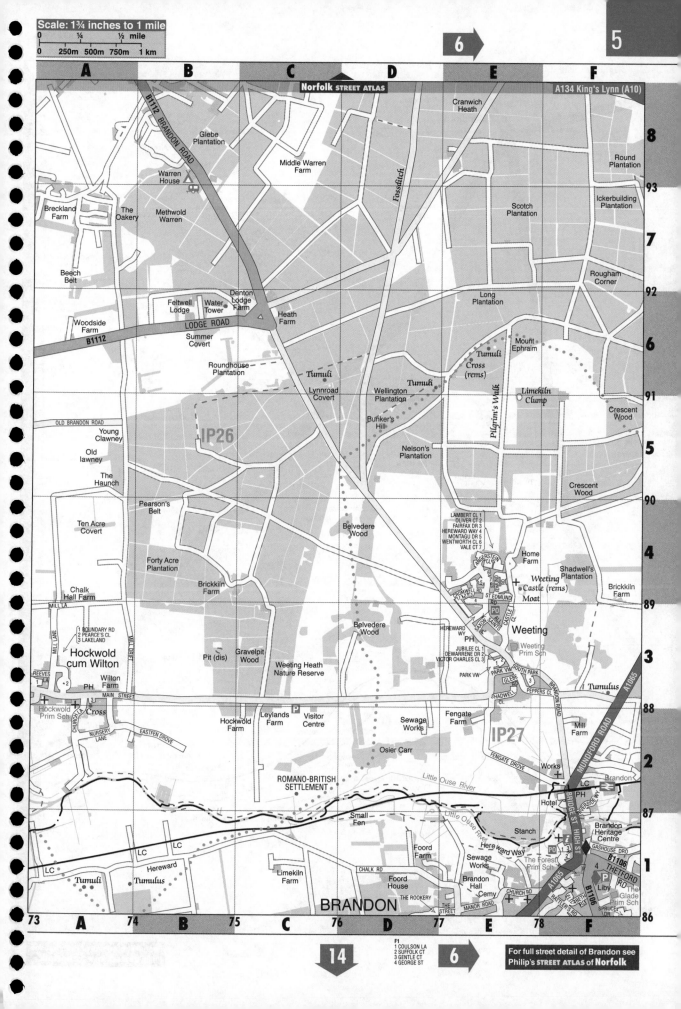

A B C D E F

8
93
7
92
6
91
5
90
4
89
3
88
2
87
1
86

B1112 BRANDON ROAD

Cranwich
Heath

Glebe
Plantation

Middle Warren
Farm

Fossditch

Round
Plantation

Warren
House

Scotch
Plantation

Ickerbuilding
Plantation

Breckland
Farm

The
Oakery

Methwold
Warren

Rougham
Corner

Long
Plantation

Beech
Belt

Feltwell
Lodge

Water
Tower

Denton
Lodge
Farm

LODGE ROAD

Heath
Farm

Mount
Ephraim

Tumuli
Cross
(rems)

Woodside
Farm

B1112

Summer
Covert

Limekiln
Clump

Crescent
Wood

Roundhouse
Plantation

Tumuli

Lynnroad
Covert

Tumuli

Wellington
Plantation

Bunker's
Hill

Pilgrim's Walk

OLD BRANDON ROAD

Young
Clawney

Nelson's
Plantation

Old
lawney

IP26

The
Haunch

Crescent
Wood

Pearson's
Belt

Ten Acre
Covert

Belvedere
Wood

LAMBERT CL 1
OLIVER CT 2
FAIRFAX DR 3
HEREWARD WAY 4
MONTAGU DR 5
WENTWORTH CL 6
VALE CT 7

Forty Acre
Plantation

Home
Farm

Shadwell's
Plantation

Brickkiln
Farm

Chalk
Hall Farm

ANGERSTEIN
CL 5

Weeting
Castle (rems)

Brickkiln
Farm

MILL LA

MILL LANE

1 BOUNDARY RD
2 PEARCE'S CL
3 LAKELAND

MILL DRIFT

Belvedere
Wood

CROMWELL RD

ST EDMUND

Moat

Pit (dis)

Gravelpit
Wood

SAXON
SAINTS

CASTLE
CL

PO

Weeting

Weeting
Prim Sch

Hockwold
cum Wilton

Weeting Heath
Nature Reserve

HEREWARD
WY

PH

Tumulus

A1065

REEVES
LA

PH

Wilton
Farm

MAIN STREET

JUBILEE CL 1
DEWARRENE DR 2
VICTOR CHARLES CL 3

PARK VW

SOUTH PARK

PARK VW

GLEBE
RD

PEPPERS CL

BRANDON ROAD

Tumulus

Hockwold
Prim Sch

Cross

CHURCH LA

NURSERY
LANE

EASTFEN DROVE

Hockwold
Farm

Leylands
Farm

P

Visitor
Centre

SHADWELL
CL

Sewage
Works

Fengate
Farm

Mill
Farm

MUNDFORD ROAD

Osier Carr

IP27

FENGATE DROVE

Works

Brandon

LC

Little Ouse River

ROMANO-BRITISH
SETTLEMENT

Small
Fen

Little Ouse River

Hotel

PH

BRIDGE ST

HIGH ST

Brandon
Heritage
Centre

Stanch

GASHOUSE DRO

B1106

Hereward Way

PO

THETFORD
RD

Tumuli

Tumulus

Hereward

LC

LC

LC

Foord
Farm

Limekiln
Farm

CHALK RD

Sewage
Works

Brandon
Hall
Cemy

The Forest
Prim Sch

A1065

B1106

Liby

P

The
Glade
Prim Sch

Foord
House

THE ROOKERY

MANOR ROAD

CHURCH RD

RATTLER'S RD

SPRUCE
DR

BRANDON

A B C D E F

73 74 75 76 77 78

14 ↓

6 →

F1
1 COULSON LA
2 SUFFOLK CT
3 GENTLE CT
4 GEORGE ST

For full street detail of Brandon see
Philip's STREET ATLAS of Norfolk

Scale: 1¾ inches to 1 mile

B8
1 WEST HALL RD
2 WISSEY VW
3 CHURCH LA
4 LONDON LA
5 BRECKLANDS

Norfolk STREET ATLAS

A1065 Swaffham

Mundford

Wellington
Plantation

Ash
Carr

Iron
Carr

Buckenham Tofts
Plantation

West Tofts
Covert

Doublebank
Covert

SAXON WK 1
CHERRY TREE CL 2
IMPSON WY 3

Water
Tower

East Hall
Farm

Zigzag
Covert

Pumphouse
Plantation

Archer's
Covert

Horseshoe
Covert

Round Covert
Farm

Mundford
Prim Sch

Glebe
Covert

Marly
Covert

Lynford Home
Farm

DANGER
AREA

Moat

Barn
Covert

Great
Carr

West
Tofts

Ickerbuilding
Plantation

Attleborough
Covert

Dixon's
Covert

Brick Kiln
Covert

Young Salamanca
Covert

WEST TOFTS ROAD

Great
Covert

Foxtail
Farm

Sewage
Works

Heath
Covert

Big
Wood

IP26

Camp

Watering
Carr

West Tofts
Mere

Mundford
Covert

Twenty Acre
Plantation

Water
Tower

Foxtail
Covert

Gravelpit
Plantation

Evergreen
Covert

Lynford

Oak
Covert

DANGER
AREA

Snake
Wood

Oak
Farm

Crescent
Wood

Tumuli

Flint Mines

DANGER
AREA

Youngoak
Covert

West Tofts
Heath

Emily's
Wood

Visitor Centre

Grimshoe

Lynford
Point

Grime's Graves
(Flint Mines)

Tumuli

Bromehill
Cott

IP27

Field Barn
Farm

HARLING DROVE

MUNDFORD ROAD

Santon
Warren

The
Brecks

LC

Blood
Hill

Blood Hill
(Tumulus)

Jubilee
Wood

St Edmund Way

HALL LANE
MARK LANE

Sewage
Works

Water
Tower

St Helen's
Oratory
(site of)

Santon Road
Plantation

Santon
Downham

Hereward Way

Moat

Hereward Way

Santon
House

Little Ouse River

Little
Lodge Farm

Two Mile
Bottom

PHEASANT
WY

WOODCOCK
RI

Mayes
Plantation

Tumulus

Tumulus

IP24

Thetford Forest

Reed
Fen

GASHOUSE DRO
ST BENEDICTS RD

Chalk
Pit

Warren
Wood

B1107

THETFORD ROAD

B1107

BRANDON

1 MALLARD WAY
2 MARTIN CL

For full street detail of Brandon see
Philip's STREET ATLAS of Norfolk

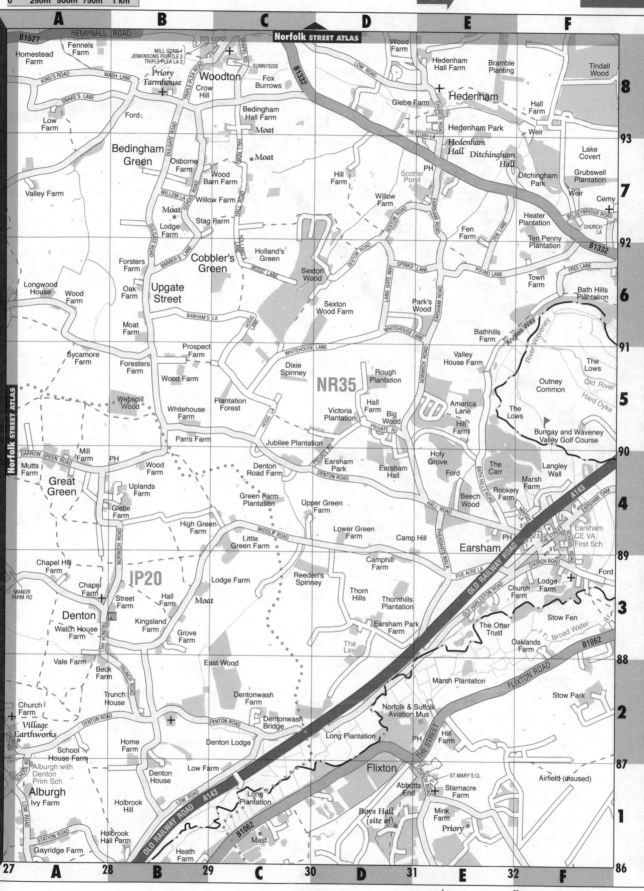

Norfolk STREET ATLAS

Norfolk STREET ATLAS

B1527
HEMPNALL ROAD

A   B   C   D   E   F

8

Homestead Farm
Fennels Farm
KING'S ROAD
WASH LANE
SNAKE'S LANE
Low Farm
Valley Farm
Longwood House
Wood Farm
Sycamore Farm

Priory Farmhouse
MILL GDNS 1
JENKINSONS PIGHTLE 2
TRIPLE-PLEA LA 3
TRIPLE-PLEA ROAD
Woodton
Crow Hill
Bedingham Green
Osborne Farm
WILLOW LA
Willow Farm
DALGATE ROAD
Moat
Lodge Farm
BARBER'S LA
DALGATE ROAD
SCHOOL ROAD
Stag Farm
Forsters Farm
Oak Farm
Upgate Street
Moat Farm
BANHAM'S LA
Foresters Farm
Prospect Farm
Wood Farm
Websdill Wood
Whitehouse Farm
HOGG LANE
Plantation Forest
Parrs Farm

Sunnyside
Fox Burrows
Bedingham Hall Farm
Moat
Moat
HALL ROAD
OLD TREE ROAD
HOLLAND'S
Holland's Green
WOOD LANE
Cobbler's Green
Dixie Spinney
NR35
Victoria Plantation

Wood Farm
Glebe Farm
Hill Farm
Willow Farm
Sexton Wood
SEXTON ROAD
Sexton Wood Farm
LANG GATE WAY
SPINKS LANE
Park's Wood
WHITEHOUSE LANE
WHITEHOUSE LANE
Rough Plantation
Hall Farm
Big Wood
PRIVATE RD
PRIVATE RD

B1332
LOW ROAD
Wood Farm
Hedenham Hall Farm
Bramble Planting
Tindall Wood
Hedenham
CHURCH ROAD
RECTORY LA
Hedenham Park
Hall Farm
Weir
Hedenham Hall
Ditchingham Hall
Ditchingham Park
Lake Covert
Grubswell Plantation
Weir
Cemy
CHURCH LA
B1332
PH
Scotter Pond
EARSHAM ROAD
Fen Farm
FEN LANE
Ten Penny Plantation
Heater Plantation
BELSEYBRIDGE ROAD
Town Farm
POUND LANE
FREE LANE
Bath Hills Plantation
Bathhills Farm
Angles Way
River Waveney
Valley House Farm
NORWICH ROAD
EARSHAM ROAD
America Lane
Hill Farm
The Lows
Old River
Hard Dyke
The Lows
Outney Common
Bungay and Waveney Valley Golf Course

93

7

92

6

91

5

90

Jubilee Plantation
Mill Farm
DARROW GREEN ROAD
PH
Mutts Farm
Great Green
Glebe Farm
Uplands Farm
Wood Farm
NORWICH ROAD
High Green Farm
MIDDLE ROAD
Little Green Farm
Denton Road Farm
DENTON ROAD
Green Farm Plantation
Upper Green Farm
Earsham Park
Lower Green Farm
Earsham Hall
HALL ROAD
Holy Grove
Ford
Beech Wood
BATH HILLS ROAD
The Carr
Rookery Farm
MARSH LA
Marsh Farm
Langley Wall
A143
EARSHAM DAM
Earsham
PH
THE STREET
SCHOOL ROAD
Earsham CE VA First Sch
CHURCH ROAD

4

89

Chapel Hill Farm
MANOR FARM RD
Chapel Farm
IP20
Street Farm
PO
Denton
Watch House Farm
TRUNCH HILL
Kingsland Farm
Hall Farm
Grove Farm
Moat
Lodge Farm
High Green Farm
Camp Hill
Camphill Farm
PHEASANTS WALK
Reeden's Spinney
Thorn Hills
Thornhills Plantation
Earsham Park Farm
FIVE ACRE LA
Church Farm
OLD HARLESTON ROAD
Lodge Farm
Ford
Stow Fen
Broad Water
Oaklands Farm
B1062
Stow Park
The Otter Trust
OLD RAILWAY ROAD

3

88

Vale Farm
Beck Farm
TRUNCH ROAD
Trunch House
DENTON ROAD
East Wood
Dentonwash Farm
Dentonwash Bridge
The Lay
Marsh Plantation
FLIXTON ROAD
Stow Park

2

87

Church Farm
Village Earthworks
CHURCH ROAD
School House Farm
Alburgh with Denton Prim Sch
Home Farm
DENTON ROAD
Denton House
Denton Lodge
Low Farm
Long Plantation
OLD RAILWAY ROAD
Norfolk & Suffolk Aviation Mus
PH
THE STREET
Hill Farm
Flixton
CHURCH ROAD
Abbotts End
ST MARY'S CL
Starnacre Farm
Airfield (disused)

1

86

Alburgh
Ivy Farm
LOW ROAD
Holbrook Hill
STATION ROAD
Gayridge Farm
Holbrook Hall Farm
Heath Farm
A143
B1062
Long Plantation
Mast
Boys Hall (site of)
Mink Farm
Priory

27   A   28   B   29   C   30   D   31   E   32   F   86

F4
1 DUKESWAY
2 STATION RD
3 MARSH LA
4 KINGSWAY
5 PRINCESS WAY
6 ELMS CL
7 QUEENSWAY
8 THE GREEN
9 BEECH TREE WAY

Scale: 1¾ inches to 1 mile

0   ¼   ½   mile
0   250m   500m   750m   1 km

A   B   C   D   E   F

Norfolk STREET ATLAS

Kirby Cane
The Shrub
Hungry Hill
Old Bungay Road
RAYNER'S LANE
LODDON RD
SCHOOL ROAD
BUNGAY ROAD
The Hall
BUNGAY ROAD

8
Wood Farm
BRICK KILN ROAD
Pewter Hill
CHURCH ROAD
Sheepwalk Farm
Manor Farm

Moat
Tindall Hall
Spion Kop Plantation
Wardly Hill
A143
Kirby Hill
Gravel Pit

93
Spink's Hill
BUNGAY ROAD
Ellingham Hall
YARMOUTH RD 1
LOCKHART RD 2
CRISP RD 3
OLD POST OFFICE LA 4
CHAPEL LA 5
WOODLAND DR 6
PH
Kirby Row
YARMOUTH ROAD
Leet Hill
RECTORY ROAD
Old Hall Farm
Lodge Plantation
Leet Hill Farm
West End
Geldeston
KELL'S ACRES

7
Cerny
BELSEYBRIDGE ROAD
Belsey Bridge
Broome Fruit Farm
CHURCH LANE
Ivy House Farm
New Covert
HOME FARM ROAD
WILLOW LANE
Ellingham
Broome Place
STATION RD
MILL ROAD
Ellingham VC FLORENCE WAY Prim Sch
MILL CL
Main Run
Henry's Plantation
Florence Way

DRAPERS LANE
Hollybush Farm
Lengford Bridge
Stonewall Plantation
Osier Carr
Church Road
CHURCH ROAD
MILL LA
Church Farm
Boon's Plantation
KELL'S WY
PO
PH

92
All Hallows Farm
BAKERS LANE
110
Sewage Works
SUN LANE
YARMOUTH ROAD
Station Farm
Old Station Road
STATION ROAD
MILL POOL
GELDESTON ROAD
Sewage Works
BRACES LANE
Ellingham Marshes
Willow Farm
GREEN LA
STATION RD
BIG ROW
Dockeney
PO

6
Home Farm
NORWICH ROAD
WILDFLOWER WY
HOLLOW HL
LODDON ROAD
WAVENEY RD
STANLEY CL
PH
A143
Broome Common
New Dyke
River Waveney
Benstead Marshes

Ditchingham
GREEN LA
Tumuli
Street Farm
Broome
Benstead's Farm
Alder Farm
Geldeston Marshes

91
B1332
PH
STATION RD
H
Broome Marshes
Prospect Farm
Benstead's Farm
White House Farm
Shipmeadow Marshes
Geldeston Lock

Old River
A143
P
Sports Gd
PINNOCK STREET
Valley Farm
LOW ROAD
MILL HILL
By Road Farm
Cherry Tree Farm
Manor Farm
Sewage Works

5
NR35
Wainford
WAINFORD
Low Fell
DEER ROW
PH
THE HILL
Nunnery Farm
B1062

NEWGATE LA
BROAD ST
FALCON
River Waveney
WATCH HO HL
PH
Mettingham
Top Farm
The Hall Moat
ANGLES WAY
Church Farm
Shipmeadow

90
110
DUTNEY RD
PO
B1435
CASTLE LA
Sch
Liby
BECCLES RD
Grove Farm
RECTORY LANE
NR34
Laurels Farm

4
Castle (rems)
CASTLE LA
Sch
GARDEN DR
BECCLES ROAD
HILLSIDE RD E
VICARAGE LANE
ANGLES WAY
High Common

BUNGAY
B1345
UPPER OLLAND STREET
ST JOHN'S ROAD
WAVENEY RD
Sch
Annis Hill
ANNIS HILL
NEW RD
Castle Farm
CASTLE ROAD
Crow's Nest Wood
Highfields Farm
Shipmeadow Common
CLARKE'S LANE
Boundary Farm

89
HILLSIDE RD W
PYNNEE'S RD
KINGS RD
MEADOW
Trinity Farm
Moats
Round Wood
MANOR FARM ROAD
Low Farm

3
FLIXTON ROAD
MOUNTWATTEN DR
ST MARGARET'S ROAD
WOODLAND DR
Sch
ST MARGARET'S
Mettingham Wood
The Mount
Orchard Farm
HALL RD
B1062

110

88
St Margaret's Plantation
Manor Farm
St Johns Lodge Farm
LODGE ROAD
Manor Farm
Birchams Farm
Tithe Farm

2
Three Ash Farm
St John's Hall
Ilketshall St Andrew
CLARKE'S LANE
CHAPEL RD
BANTERS LANE

87
Uplandhall Farm
ST MARGARET'S ROAD
MILL LANE
LOW ROAD
SCHOOL RD
Great Common
Glebe Farm
Green Farm
GREAT COMMON LANE
COOKS COMMON LANE
Moat Farm
St Andrew's Hall

1
Angles Way
Hill Farm
Hill Farm
Grove Farm
Church Farm
TOP ROAD
Willow Farm
Water Tower
Willow Tree Farm
Hanna Barn Farm

86
Shadowbarn Farm
The Elms
MOLES LANE
A144

33   34   35   36   37   38
A   B   C   D   E   F

For full street detail of the highlighted area see page 110

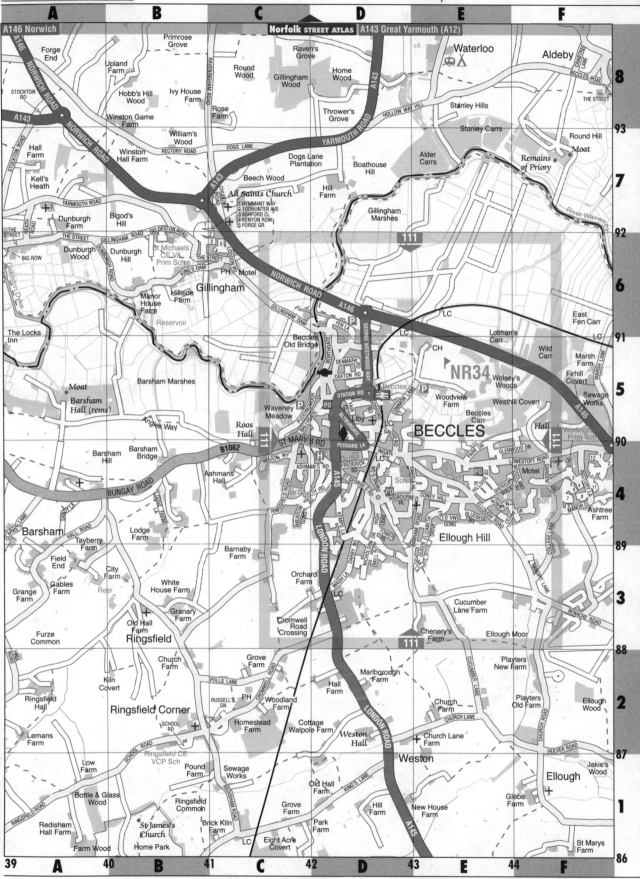

Norfolk STREET ATLAS

A146 Norwich

A143 Great Yarmouth (A12)

Grid columns: A B C D E F
Grid rows: 8 93 7 92 6 91 5 90 4 89 88 3 2 87 1 86

Forge End
Primrose Grove
Waterloo
Aldeby

STOCKTON RD
Upland Farm
Round Wood
Raven's Grove
Home Wood

Hobb's Hill Wood
Ivy House Farm
Gillingham Wood
Stanley Hills

Winston Game Farm
Rose Farm
Thrower's Grove
Stanley Carrs

Hall Farm
William's Wood
Round Hill Moat

Kell's Heath
RECTORY ROAD
DOGS LANE
Dogs Lane Plantation
Boathouse Hill
Alder Carrs
Remains of Priory

YARMOUTH ROAD
Winston Hall Farm
Beech Wood
Hill Farm
Gillingham Marshes

Dunburgh Farm
Bigod's Hill
All Saints Church
1 HEMMANT WAY
2 TODHUNTER AVE
3 ASHFORD CL
4 KENYON ROW
5 FORGE GR

111

THE STREET
Big Row
Dunburgh Wood
Dunburgh Hill
St Michaels CE VA Prim Sch
Motel

The Locks Inn
Manor House Farm
Hillside Farm
Gillingham
NORWICH ROAD
East Fen Carr

Reservoir
GILLINGHAM DAM
Beccles Old Bridge
Lotman's Carr
Wild Carr
Marsh Lane

Moat
Barsham Marshes
NR34
Wolsey's Woods
Firhill Covert

Barsham Hall (rems)
Angles Way
DENMARK RD
CAXTON RD
Westhill Covert
Sewage Works

Roos Hall
Waveney Meadow
STATION RD
Beccles
Woodview Farm
Beccles Carr

Barsham Hill
Barsham Bridge
B1062
ST MARY'S RD
Liby
BECCLES
Hall
Worlingham Prim Sch

Barsham
Ashmans Hall
ASHMAN'S RD
FREDERICK RD
Sch
PARK DR
GLENWOOD DR
LOWESTOFT ROAD
Motel

Barnaby Farm
Orchard Farm
SOUTH RD
ST GEORGE'S RD
RIGBOURNE HL
Coney Hill
Ellough Hill

Lodge Farm
White House Farm
Granary Farm
LONDON ROAD
Cucumber Lane Farm

Grange Farm
Gables Farm
Old Hall Farm
Ringsfield
Cromwell Road Crossing
Chenery's Farm
Ellough Moor

Furze Common
111
Playters New Farm

Field End
City Farm
Church Farm
Grove Farm
Marlborough Farm
Church Farm
Playters Old Farm
Ellough Wood

Ringsfield Hall
Kiln Covert
POLLS LANE
Hall Farm
CHURCH LANE

Lemans Farm
Ringsfield Corner
RUSSELL'S GN
PH
Woodland Farm
Church Lane Farm
Weston

Low Farm
SCHOOL RD
Ringsfield CE VCP Sch
Pound Farm
Homestead Farm
Cottage Walpole Farm
Weston Hall
HULVER ROAD
Jakie's Wood

Bottle & Glass Wood
Sewage Works
REDISHAM ROAD
Old Hall Farm
KING'S LANE
New House Farm
Glebe Farm
Ellough

Redisham Hall Farm
St James's Church
Home Park
Brick Kiln Farm
Grove Farm
Park Farm
Hill Farm
A145
St Marys Farm

Farm Wood
Eight Acre Covert

F4
1 PEPYS AVE
2 PAINS CL
3 ALL SAINTS GN
4 HOLM CL
5 WAINFORD CL
6 MIRBECK'S CL
7 BROOKWOOD CL
8 ASH TREE CL
9 MANOR CL
10 SUTTONS RD
11 JANET HADENHAM CL
12 COPPLESTONE CL

For full street detail of the highlighted area see page 111

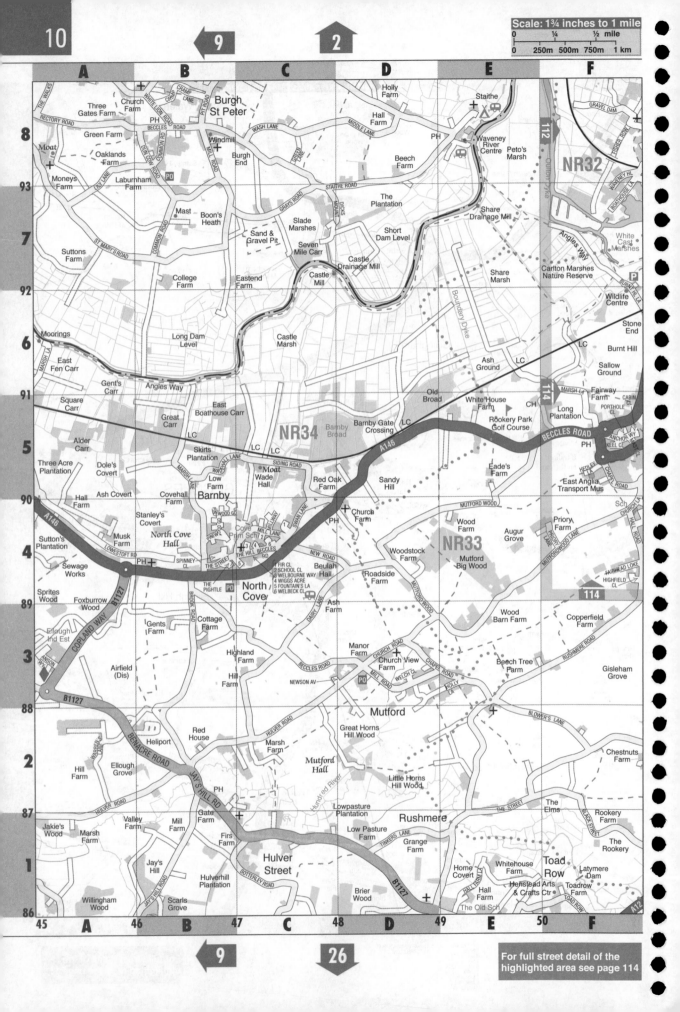

Scale: 1¾ inches to 1 mile

For full street detail of the
highlighted area see page 114

A   B   C   D   E   F

8
93
7
92
6
91
5
90
4
89
3
88
2
87
1
86

Roman Hill
Euroscope
Ness Point

NR32
Cemy

Oulton Broad North

Lowestoft Mus
Liby
Mutford Bridges
NR33
Sports Gd
Riverside Business Park
Commercial Rd
Lowestoft
East Point Pavilion

Oulton Broad South

Victoria Rd
Waveney Dr
Kimberley Rd
Suffolk Coast & Heaths Path

Beccles Road
Bridge Rd
Cotmer Rd
B1531
Acad
Claremont Pier
South Beach

A146
Elm Tree Rd
A1117
Tom Crisp Way
Kirkley
Cemy
St Mary's RC Prim Sch
Kirkley Cliff Road

Castleton Ave
A1145
A12
Stradbroke Road
Pakefield
Recn Gd
Lowestoft South Roads
LOWESTOFT

Carlton Colville
Bell Farm
South Lowestoft Industrial Est
Bloodmoor Rd
Cooke Rd
Jubilee Rd
Pakefield Cliffs

Gisleham Mid Sch
Bloodmoor Hill
Hadenham Rd
Grange Farm
Tower Road
London Road

114   115

Gisleham
Lodge Farm
Church Farm
Glebe Farm
Solar Mink Farm
Heath Farm
Pakefield Hall
Moat
Crazy Mary's Hole
Lighthouse

White House Farm
Moats
ROMANY LA
A12
London Road

NR33
Hall Farm
Laurel Farm
Pond Farm
B1437
Kessingland
Suffolk Coast & Heaths Path
Kessingland CE VCP Sch
Kessingland Cliffs

Black Street
Briar End
BLACK STREET
HIGH
Liby

Africa Alive!
B1437
Manor Farm
War Memorial

51   52   53   54   55   56

For full street detail of the highlighted area see pages 112, 113, 114 and 115

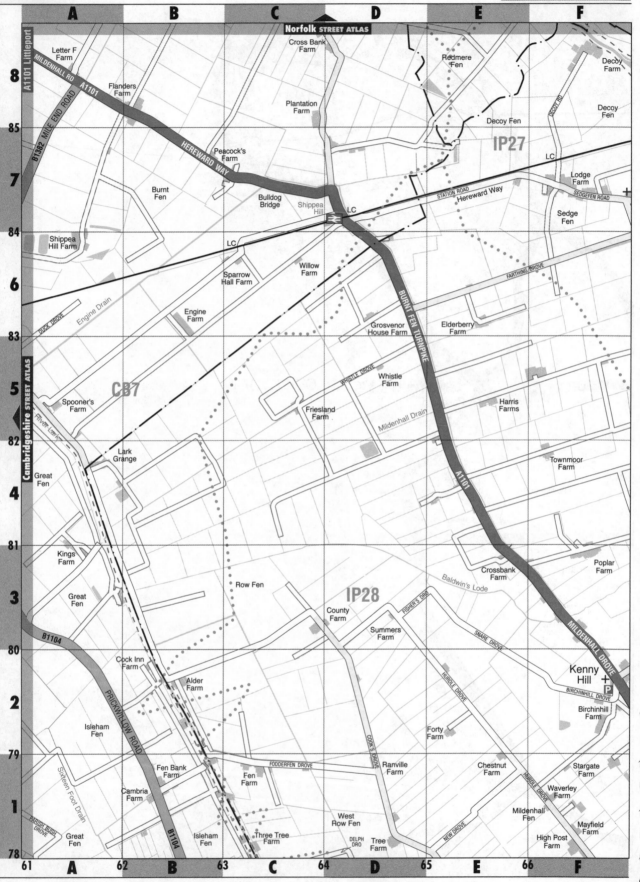

Scale: 1¾ inches to 1 mile
0   ¼   ½ mile
0   250m 500m 750m 1 km

Norfolk STREET ATLAS

Cambridgeshire STREET ATLAS

A11101 Littleport

MILDENHALL RD A1101
B1382 MILE END ROAD
A1101
HEREWARD WAY

Letter F Farm
Flanders Farm
Cross Bank Farm
Redmere Fen
Decoy Farm

Plantation Farm
Decoy Fen
Decoy Fen

IP27

Peacock's Farm
Burnt Fen
Bulldog Bridge
Shippea Hill
LC
Hereward Way
STATION ROAD
LC
Lodge Farm
SEDGEFEN ROAD
Sedge Fen

Shippea Hill Farm
LC
Sparrow Hall Farm
Willow Farm
FARTHING DROVE

DUCK DROVE
Engine Drain
Engine Farm
Grosvenor House Farm
Elderberry Farm
BURNT FEN TURNPIKE

CB7
Spooner's Farm
WHISTLE DROVE
Whistle Farm
Harris Farms

River Lark
Friesland Farm
Mildenhall Drain

Lark Grange
Townmoor Farm

Great Fen
A1101

Kings Farm
Crossbank Farm
Poplar Farm

Great Fen
Row Fen
IP28
Baldwin's Lode

B1104
County Farm
FISHER'S DRO
SNARE DROVE
MILDENHALL DROVE

Cock Inn Farm
Summers Farm
Kenny Hill
P

PRICKWILLOW ROAD
Alder Farm
NURBLE DROVE
BIRCHINHILL DROVE
Birchinhill Farm

Isleham Fen
COOK'S DROVE
Forty Farm

Fen Bank Farm
FODDERFEN DROVE
Ranville Farm
Chestnut Farm
Stargate Farm

Sixteen Foot Drain
Cambria Farm
Fen Farm
Waverley Farm

B1104
Mildenhall Fen
NEW DROVE
NURDLE DROVE
Mayfield Farm

PARISH BUSH DROVE
Great Fen
Isleham Fen
Three Tree Farm
West Row Fen
DELPH DRO
Tree Farm
High Post Farm

28 29

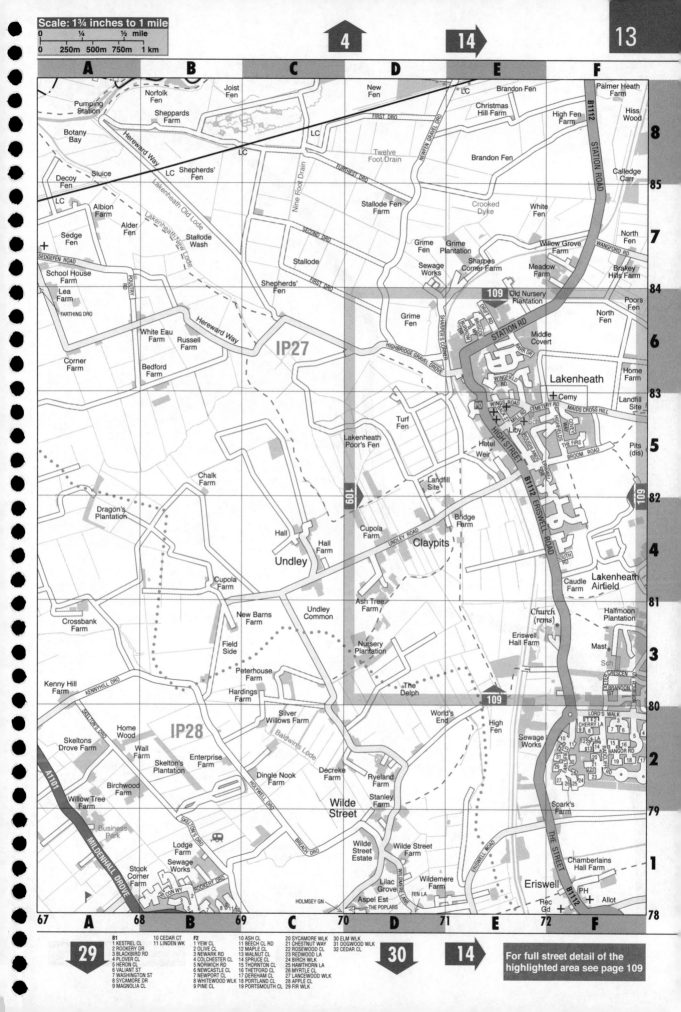

A   B   C   D   E   F

8
85
7
84
6
83
5
82
4
81
3
80
2
79
1
78

67   68   69   70   71   72

Pumping Station
Norfolk Fen
Joist Fen
New Fen
LC
Brandon Fen
Palmer Heath Farm
Sheppards Farm
Christmas Hill Farm
High Fen Farm
Hiss Wood
Botany Bay
FIRST DRO
Twelve Foot Drain
Calledge Carr
Decoy Fen
Sluice
Shepherds' Fen
LC
LC
Brandon Fen
White Fen
North Fen
LC
Hereward Way
Albion Farm
Stallode Fen Farm
Crooked Dyke
Willow Grove Farm
WANGFORD RD
Sedge Fen
Alder Fen
Stallode Wash
Grime Fen
Grime Plantation
Sharpes Corner Farm
Meadow Farm
Brakey Hills Farm
SEDGEFEN ROAD
Nine Foot Drain
Stallode
Sewage Works
109
Old Nursery Plantation
Poors Fen
School House Farm
Lea Farm
SECOND DRO
Shepherds' Fen
STATION RD
Middle Covert
North Fen
FARTHING DRO
Hereward Way
Grime Fen
BRISCOE WY
BURROW
Lakenheath
Home Farm
White Eau Farm
Russell Farm
FIRST DRO
IP27
HIGHBRIDGE GRAVEL DROVE
SHARPER'S CORNER
WINGFIELD RD.
BARR DR.
Cemy
Landfill Site
Corner Farm
Bedford Farm
Turf Fen
WINGS ROAD
CEMETERY RD
MILL RD
HIGHFIELDS
MAIDS CROSS HILL
Lakenheath Poor's Fen
PO
Liby
SCH
THE FIRS
BROOM ROAD
Pits (dis)
Chalk Farm
Hotel
Weir
Landfill Site
HIGH STREET
BROUGHAM DRIVE
COVEY WAY
Dragon's Plantation
109
Cupola Farm
Bridge Farm
B1112 ERISWELL ROAD
109
Hall
Hall Farm
Claypits
SOUTH RD
Undley
Cupola Farm
UNDLEY ROAD
Caudle Farm
Lakenheath Airfield
New Barns Farm
Undley Common
Ash Tree Farm
Church (rems)
Halfmoon Plantation
Crossbank Farm
Field Side
Nursery Plantation
Eriswell Hall Farm
Mast
Sch
Kenny Hill Farm
KENNYHILL DRO
Peterhouse Farm
The Delph
World's End
CRESCENT
BRANDON ST
Hardings Farm
109
High Fen
LORD'S WALK
IP28
Silver Willows Farm
Sewage Works
CHERRY LA
Skeltons Drove Farm
Home Wood
Baldwins Lode
CARLISFIELD
BANGOR RD
RADCLIFFE RD
SKELTONS DRO
Wall Farm
Enterprise Farm
Decreke Farm
Ryeland Farm
Skelton's Plantation
HOLWELL DRO
Dingle Nook Farm
Spark's Farm
A1101
Birchwood Farm
Stanley Farm
Wilde Street
Chamberlains Hall Farm
Willow Tree Farm
SKELTON'S DRO
BREACY DRO
Wilde Street Estate
Wilde Street Farm
ERISWELL ROAD
THE STREET
Eriswell
PH
B1112
Business Park
Lodge Farm
Sewage Works
FALCON WY
ROOKERY DRO
Lilac Grove
WILDEMERE LANE
Wildemere Farm
Rec Gd
Allot
MILDENHALL DROVE
Stock Corner Farm
HOLMSEY GN
Aspel Est
THE POPLARS
FEN LA

B1
1 KESTREL CL
2 ROOKERY DR
3 BLACKBIRD RD
4 PLOVER CL
5 HERON CL
6 VALIANT ST
7 WASHINGTON ST
8 SYCAMORE DR
9 MAGNOLIA CL
10 CEDAR CT
11 LINDEN WK

F2
1 YEW CL
2 OLIVE CL
3 NEWARK RD
4 COLCHESTER CL
5 NORWICH RD
6 NEWCASTLE CL
7 NEWPORT CL
8 WHITEWOOD WLK
9 PINE CL
10 ASH CL
11 BEECH CL RD
12 MAPLE CL
13 WALNUT CL
14 SPRUCE CL
15 THORNTON CL
16 THETFORD CL
17 DEREHAM CL
18 PORTLAND CL
19 PORTSMOUTH CL
20 SYCAMORE WLK
21 CHESTNUT WAY
22 ROSEWOOD CL
23 REDWOOD LA
24 BIRCH WLK
25 HAWTHORN LA
26 MYRTLE CL
27 LANCEWOOD WLK
28 APPLE CL
29 FIR WLK
30 ELM WLK
31 DOGWOOD WLK
32 CEDAR CL

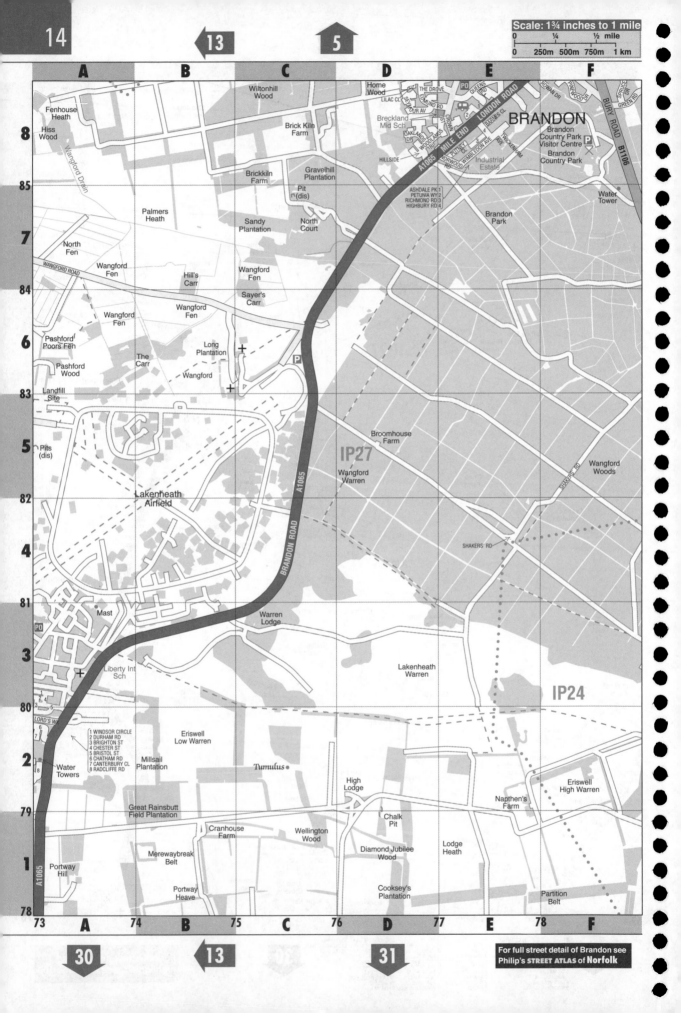

A   B   C   D   E   F

8
Fenhouse Heath
Hiss Wood
Wiltonhill Wood
Brick Kiln Farm
Home Wood
THE DROVE
PO
QUEENS
LILAC CL
EDMUND RD
FOUR AV
OAKLANDS
WOODLANDS
MILE END
LONDON ROAD
ROWAN DR
PINKWOODS
BRANDON
BURY ROAD
SPRUCE DR
GREEN RD
B1106
Breckland Mid Sch
HILLSIDE
A1065
NORWOOD RD
WIMBLEDON AVE
PUTNEY
BARNES CL
CROWN
FRECKENHAM
Brandon Country Park Visitor Centre
Brandon Country Park
P

85
Brickkiln Farm
Gravelhill Plantation
Pit (dis)
ASHDALE PK   1
PETUNIA WY   2
RICHMOND RD   3
HIGHBURY RD   4
Water Tower

7
Palmers Heath
Sandy Plantation
North Court
Brandon Park

North Fen
WANGFORD ROAD
Wangford Fen
Wangford Fen
Hill's Carr

84
Wangford Fen
Sayer's Carr

6
Pashford Poors Fen
Wangford Fen
The Carr
Long Plantation
Pashford Wood
Wangford

83
Landfill Site

5
Pits (dis)
Lakenheath Airfield
IP27
Wangford Warren
Broomhouse Farm
P
A1065
BRANDON ROAD
Wangford Woods

82

4
SHAKERS RD
SHAKERS RD

81
Mast
Warren Lodge

3
PO
Liberty Int Sch
Lakenheath Warren
IP24

80
LORD'S WK
1 WINDSOR CIRCLE
2 DURHAM RD
3 BRIGHTON ST
4 CHESTER ST
5 BRISTOL ST
6 CHATHAM RD
7 CANTERBURY CL
8 RADCLIFFE RD

2
1
2 4
3
5
8
6
7
8
Water Towers
Eriswell Low Warren
Millsail Plantation
Tumulus
High Lodge
Napthen's Farm
Eriswell High Warren

79
Great Rainsbutt Field Plantation
Cranhouse Farm
Wellington Wood
Chalk Pit
Diamond Jubilee Wood
Lodge Heath

1
A1065
Portway Hill
Merewaybreak Belt
Portway Heave
Cooksey's Plantation
Partition Belt

78
73   A   74   B   75   C   76   D   77   E   78   F

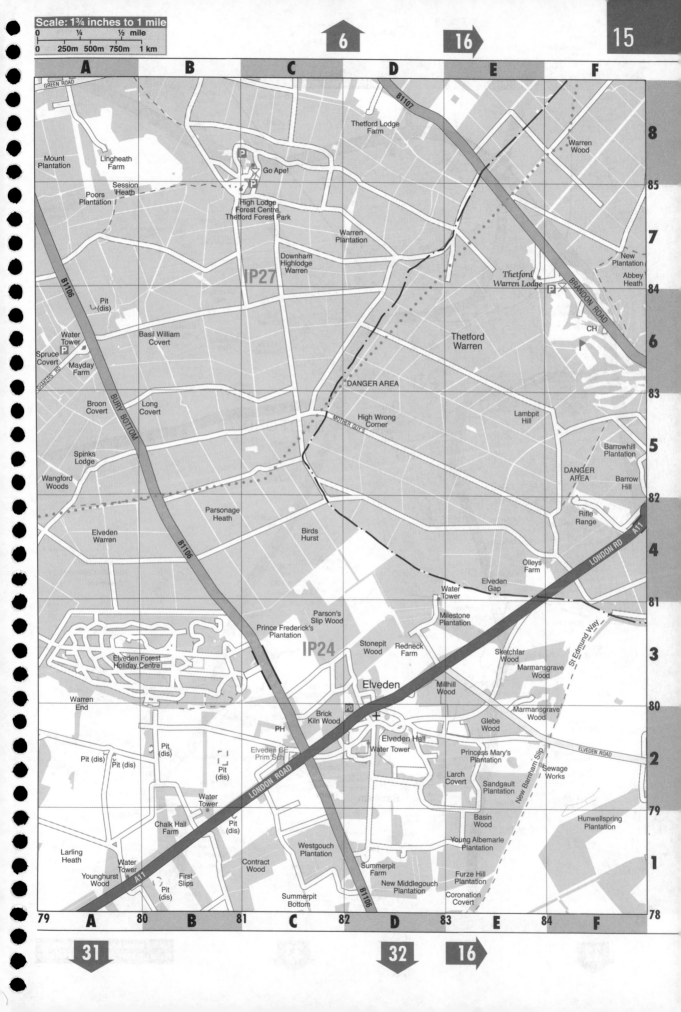

A B C D E F

8
85
7
84
6
83
5
82
4
81
3
80
2
79
1
78

GREEN ROAD

B1107

Mount Plantation
Lingheath Farm
Session Heath
Poors Plantation
Go Ape!
High Lodge Forest Centre, Thetford Forest Park
Thetford Lodge Farm
Warren Wood
IP27
Downham Highlodge Warren
Warren Plantation
New Plantation
Abbey Heath
B1106
Thetford Warren Lodge
CH
Water Tower
Spruce Covert
Mayday Farm
Basil William Covert
Thetford Warren
SHAKERS RD
BRANDON ROAD
Broon Covert
Long Covert
DANGER AREA
High Wrong Corner
MOTHER QUY'S
Lambpit Hill
Barrowhill Plantation
BURY BOTTOM
Spinks Lodge
Wangford Woods
DANGER AREA
Barrow Hill
B1106
Elveden Warren
Parsonage Heath
Birds Hurst
Rifle Range
LONDON RD
A11
Olleys Farm
Elveden Gap
Water Tower
Milestone Plantation
Parson's Slip Wood
Prince Frederick's Plantation
IP24
Stonepit Wood
Redneck Farm
Sketchfar Wood
Marmansgrave Wood
St Edmund Way
Elveden Forest Holiday Centre
Elveden
Millhill Wood
Glebe Wood
Marmansgrave Wood
ELVEDEN ROAD
Warren End
PH
Brick Kiln Wood
PO
Elveden Hall Water Tower
Princess Mary's Plantation
New Barnham Slip
Sewage Works
Pit (dis)
Pit (dis)
Elveden CE Prim Sch
Pit (dis)
Larch Covert
Sandgault Plantation
Hunwellspring Plantation
Water Tower
Pit (dis)
Basin Wood
Chalk Hall Farm
Westgouch Plantation
Young Albemarle Plantation
Larling Heath
Younghurst Wood
Water Tower
A11
First Slips
Pit (dis)
Contract Wood
Summerpit Bottom
Summerpit Farm
New Middlegouch Plantation
Furze Hill Plantation
Coronation Covert
B1106
LONDON ROAD

79 80 81 82 83 84

A B C D E F

A5
1 MONTPELIER DR
2 NEW ENGLAND WAY
3 PORTLAND PL
4 MAINE ST
5 NEW HAMPSHIRE WAY
6 BOSTON END

15

Scale: 1¾ inches to 1 mile

0 ¼ ½ mile
0 250m 500m 750m 1 km

Norfolk STREET ATLAS

A B C D E F

A134 King's Lynn (A10) A1075 Watton A11 Norwich

8 85 7 84 6 83 5 82 4 81 3 80 2 79 1 78

Chisley Vale
Little Ouse River
St Edmund Way
New Plantation
Abbey Heath
Sewage Works
Breck Plantation
Box Covert
Lodge Farm
Gallows Hill
WYATT WY
LODGE WY
Depot
BRUNEL WY
HOWLETT WY
ANNE BARTHOLOMEW
CROXTON ROAD
Croxton End
Thetford
EXETER WY
CANTERBURY WY
MOYNES GATE
STATION ROAD
LONDON ROAD
Weir
CONEY CL
HALING WY
CANTERBURY WY
BRIDGES
Thetford Gram Sch
BRANDON ROAD
MCKENZIE RD
ST JOHN'S
ST MARTIN'S
PO
Church
Ind Est
Cemy
Queensway Inf Sch
Superstore
Forest Retail Park
BURRELL WY
LONDON RD
STEPHENSON WY
NAPIER PL
FULMERSTON RD
QUEENSWAY
ELM ROAD
ASH
KELVIN PL
ALMOND GR
Charles Burrell High Sch
Playing Field
Barnhamcross Common
Nature Reserve
St Edmund Way
Boundary Belt
Aughton Spinney
Barnham Camp
Gorse Industrial Estate
Water Tower
Thetford Heath National Nature Reserve
ELVEDEN ROAD
North Farm
STATION ROAD
Works
Triangle Plantation
A11
A1066
A134
MUNDFORD ROAD
B1107 BRANDON RD
BURY ROAD

Dreadnought
Landfill Site
Tollgate Wood
Ladyship Wood
LC
Hockham Belt
Waterloo Wood
Milestone Plantation
Diamond Plantation
Field Barn Farm
Blakeney Farm
Jane's Wood
Rosemary Musker County High Sch
TENNYSON WY
WOODLANDS
THE GLADE
STURGEON WY
RICHARD FAIRHEAD
EASTER
HARWOOD CL
Norwich Road Sch
VICARAGE RD
Thetford Cottage
NORWICH ROAD
Mus
H
PO
Mus
Lib y
CASTLE STREET
RAMPART
CAST
Motte and Bailey
Church
Church
Nuns Bridges
MONS BRIDGES ROAD
ARLINGTON WY
ASTLE CL
Pig Farm
St Martin's (rems)
Low Wood
WATER LA
THE STREET
Tumulus
Barnham CE Prim Sch
ST MARTIN'S LA 1
BLACKSMITH LA 2
East Farm
Barnham
CHURCH LA
THE STREET
Tumulus
Pit (dis)
Blackbird Spinney

D7
1 ETHELREDA DR
2 LAWRENCE RD
3 PETER DRIVE
4 PENNYCRESS DR
5 CHARLOCK RD

War Memorial
Superstore
Kilverstone Hall
Spruce Covert
Broom Covert
Mount Plantation
Snarehill Hall
BECKHAM
SKELER WY
BRYANT
GREEN LA
CHURCH RD
MALLOW RD
RINSEN
BRICK KILN
CARAWAY
FOXGLOVE
Weir
Limekiln Plantation
Square Covert
Church (rems)
THETFORD
IP24
HURTH WY
A1088
A1066
The Slough
Snarehill Farm
Snarehill Wood
Oak Wood
Nunnery Stud
Tutt Hill
Tutt Hill (Tumulus)
Elder Hill
Great Snare Hill
Little Ouse River
MILL LA
Pit (dis)
Pit (dis)
County Hole
Weir
Warren Plantation
Warren Cott
Barnham Heath
Pit (dis)
Tumulus
Barnham Carr
Severals Plantation
Quarry
Gravelhill Plantation
Icknield Way Path
Barnham Spinney
Barnham Road
Decoy Covert
Icewell Plantation
Home Farm
Seven Hills (Barrow Cemetery)
Seven Hills
Seven Hills Plantation
Ashfen Carr
Black Carr
Gravelpit Plantation
RUSHFORD ROAD
THETFORD ROAD
Rushfordroad Belts
Long Spinney
Long Spinney
Euston
Euston Hall
Tap Basin
Euston Hall
The Temple
Broad Water
A1088

D6
1 MALLOW RD
2 CUTHBERT CL
3 GEORGE RD
4 HAZEL COVERT
5 COVERT SYCAMORE
6 ALDER COVERT
7 VALERIAN RISE
8 CHERVIL WALK

C6
1 HIGHLANDS
2 GLEBE CL
3 CHALK CL
4 WHITEACRES
5 THE SIDINGS
6 BEN CURLEY DR

B5
1 SAXON PL
2 NELSON DR
3 ST MARGARET'S CR
4 JUBILEE CL
5 Thetford Adult Ed Ctr
6 Redcastle Furze Prim Sch
7 Queensway Com Jun Sch

C2
1 ELLINGTON RD
2 NEWALL RD
3 TEDDER CL
4 PORTAL CL
5 SALMOND DR
6 EDINBURGH CL
7 WINDSOR CL

For full street detail of Thetford see
Philip's STREET ATLAS of Norfolk

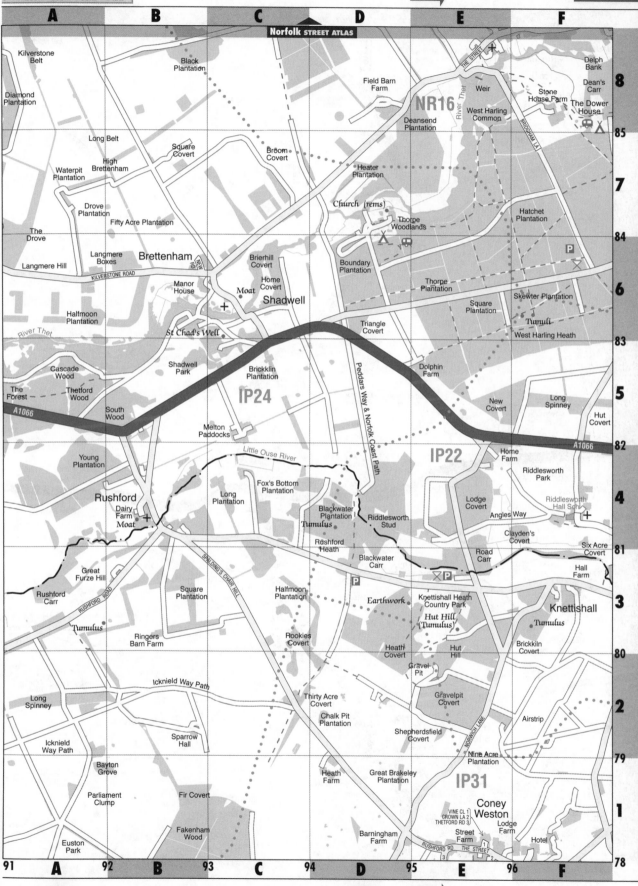

Norfolk STREET ATLAS

Kilverstone Belt

Diamond Plantation

Field Barn Farm

NR16

Weir

West Harling Common

THE STREET

River Thet

BRIDGHAM LA

Delph Bank

Dean's Carr

Stone House Farm

The Dower House

8

85

Long Belt

Square Covert

Broom Covert

Deansend Plantation

Heater Plantation

Hatchet Plantation

7

Waterpit Plantation

High Brettenham

Drove Plantation

Fifty Acre Plantation

Church (rems)

Thorpe Woodlands

Boundary Plantation

Thorpe Plantation

Square Plantation

Skewter Plantation

Tumuli

P

84

The Drove

Langmere Hill

Langmere Boxes

Brettenham

NEW RD

KILVERSTONE ROAD

Manor House

Brierhill Covert

Home Covert

Moat

Shadwell

+

Triangle Covert

West Harling Heath

6

83

Halfmoon Plantation

River Thet

St Chad's Well

Cascade Wood

Thetford Wood

Shadwell Park

Brickklin Plantation

Dolphin Farm

New Covert

Long Spinney

Hut Covert

5

The Forest

A1066

South Wood

IP24

Melton Paddocks

A1066

82

Young Plantation

Little Ouse River

Fox's Bottom Plantation

Long Plantation

Peddars Way & Norfolk Coast Path

IP22

Home Farm

Riddlesworth Park

Riddlesworth Hall Sch

+

4

Rushford

Dairy Farm

Moat

+

Blackwater Plantation

Tumulus

Rushford Heath

Riddlesworth Stud

Lodge Covert

Angles Way

Clayden's Covert

Six Acre Covert

81

Great Furze Hill

RUSHFORD ROAD

SPALDING'S CHAIR HILL

Square Plantation

Halfmoon Plantation

Blackwater Carr

P

Earthwork

Road Carr

X P

Knettishall Heath Country Park

Hut Hill (Tumulus)

Tumulus

Knettishall

Hall Farm

3

Rushford Carr

Tumulus

Ringers Barn Farm

Rookies Covert

Heath Covert

Hut Hill

Brickklin Covert

80

Long Spinney

Icknield Way Path

Thirty Acre Covert

Chalk Pit Plantation

Gravel Pit

Gravelpit Covert

NORWICH LANE

Airstrip

2

Icknield Way Path

Sparrow Hall

Shepherdsfield Covert

Nine Acre Plantation

79

Bayton Grove

Parliament Clump

Fir Covert

Heath Farm

Great Brakeley Plantation

IP31

Coney Weston

VINE CL 1
CROWN LA 2
THETFORD RD 3

Lodge Farm

1

Euston Park

Fakenham Wood

Barningham Farm

RUSHFORD RD

THE STREET

Street Farm

1

2

3

Hotel

78

17

A   B   C   D   E   F

Norfolk STREET ATLAS

EAST HARLING ROAD

8
85
7
84
6
83
5
82
4
81
3
80
2
79
1
78

Micklemoor Hill
Settlement
Black Carr
Berdewell Hall Farm
West Harling
Big Wood
Lodge Plantation
Privet Plantation
Twenty Acre Plantation
West Harlinghill Plantation
Hut Covert
Fir Covert
Seventeen Acre Plantation
Twelve Acre Plantation
St John's Covert
Gasthorpe
St Nicholas's Church (rems of)
Six Acre Covert
THE STREET
Alder Carr
LODGE LA
Lodge Farm
All Saints Church
Wall Covert
Wall Covert
Dairy Farm
Fen Street
Broom Covert
IP31
HOLLOW LA

Middle Harling
WEST HARLING RD
Mauleys Farm
Middle Harling Farm
Town Farm
Allot
GARBOLDISHAM ROAD
Ten Acre Plantation
East Harling Heath
Tumulus
Devil's Ditch
Garboldisham Heath
Tumulus
Hill Plantation
Oldoak Plantation
Lodge Farm
Angles Way
Garboldisham Common
Hopton Fen
NETHERGATE STREET
Dairy Farm
SHICKLE PL 1
LEWIS CL 2
HOLME CL 3
PINE TREE CT 4
Hopton
HIGH STREET
PH
2 3 4
Robsons Farm
PO
GREYHOUND LA
WALNUT CL
Hillside Farm
BURY ROAD
Church Farm
Hopton End Farm
B1111
Cinque Farm
CHURCH ROAD

KERRIDGES RD
HAMBLING'S PIECE
B1111
Cemy
Mauleys Farm
Allot
Triangle Covert
Tumulus
Old Sheep Pen Plantation
Hall Farm
Sandy Betty's Plantation
Georgiana Plantation
IP22
Long Furlong Plantation
Home Covert
Tumulus
THETFORD ROAD
Fen Farm
Old Fen
FEN LA
MILL LA
MILL LA
Common Farm
COMMON ROAD
Manor Farm
Angles Way
THELNETHAM ROAD
Hopton CE VC Prim Sch

Hill Harling Farm
Hill Harling
NR16
LOPHAM ROAD
Flint Hall Farm
HARLING ROAD
Cranespond Plantation
Garboldisham Manor
Wilderness Plantation
The Hall
B1111
Garboldisham VC Prim Sch
BACK ST
WATER LA
CHURCH RD
Garboldisham
POND RD
FORGE RD
ELM LA
HOPTON ROAD
Church Farm
CHAPEL CL
THOMAS BOLE CL
HARBOUR LANE
DISS ROAD
Windmill
Rec Gd
Smallworth
Boundary Farm
Broomscot Common
MILL LA
Hotel
Fir Covert
Raydon Common
Spring Farm
Hall Farm
Moat
Hilldrop Farm
BUGGS HOLE LA
Thelnetham Windmill
Thelnetham
HOPTON ROAD
Kays Farm
WATER LA
Cross Green Farm
Moat
HINDERCLAY LA
PH
SCHOOL LA
FEN LANE
MILL RD
HIGH ST
CHURCH LA
LOGGERS LA

Grove Farm
Uphall Farm
Guiltcross Farm
GARBOLDISHAM ROAD
Dairy Farm
Finchams Farm
Dickersons Farm
Stubbings's Farm
Fir Tree Farm
Whitebreads Farm
Ling Farm
LYNG LA
Orchard Farm
HIGH COMMON ROAD
Gables Farm
Allotments Farm
THETFORD ROAD
A1066
Mill Pond Farm
Smallworth Farm
SMALLWORTH LA
Three Wells Farm
Willow Farm
SELFS LA
THE STREET
White House Farm
BLO NORTON RD
Lodge Farm
MIDDLE ROAD
Church Farm
MEADOWSIDE
CHURCH LA
Manor Farm
Ash Tree Farm
THELNETHAM RD
Blo' Norton
Fen Farm
FEN ROAD
Willow Farm
The Banks
Little Ouse River
Hinderclay Fen
Blo Norton Fen
(Nature Reserve) Thelnetham Fen
St Mary's Well (Spring)
Holiday Farm
FEN STREET

A1066

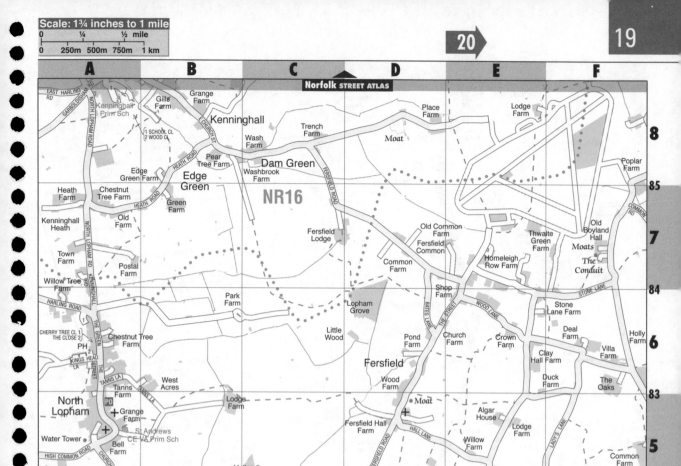

Norfolk STREET ATLAS

A | B | C | D | E | F

East Harling Rd
GARBOLDISHAM RD
NORTH LOPHAM ROAD

Kenninghall Prim Sch

Gills Farm

Grange Farm

Kenninghall

E CHURCH ST

Wash Farm

Trench Farm

Place Farm

Lodge Farm

8

Pear Tree Farm

Dam Green

Washbrook Farm

Moat

Poplar Farm

Edge Green Farm

Edge Green

FERSFIELD ROAD

85

Heath Farm

Chestnut Tree Farm

HEATH ROAD

Green Farm

NR16

Fersfield Lodge

Old Common Farm

Thwaite Green Farm

Old Boyland Hall

Moats

COMMON RD

7

Old Farm

Fersfield Common

Homeleigh Row Farm

Stone Lane Farm

The Conduit

Kenninghall Heath

Postal Farm

Common Farm

STONE LANE

84

Willow Tree Farm

Park Farm

Lopham Grove

Shop Farm

BATES LANE

THE STREET

WOOD LANE

Deal Farm

Holly Farm

HARLING ROAD

Little Wood

Church Farm

Crown Farm

Clay Hall Farm

Stone Lane Farm

Villa Farm

6

CHERRY TREE CL 1
THE CLOSE 2
PH

THE GREEN

Chestnut Tree Farm

Fersfield

Pond Farm

Duck Farm

The Oaks

KINGS HEAD LA
KINGS LA

TANNS LA
ANNS LA

West Acres

Wood Farm

83

North Lopham

PO

Tanns Farm

Grange Farm

Lodge Farm

Moat

HALL LANE

Algar House

Lodge Farm

5

Water Tower

St Andrews CE VA Prim Sch

Bell Farm

Fersfield Hall Farm

Willow Farm

Bressingham Common

HIGH COMMON RD

CHURCH ROAD

Holland's Wood

FERSFIELD ROAD

Duke's Plantation

Folly Farm

Common Farm

82

Common Farm

South Lopham

Lodge Farm

Hill Farm

Wilney Green

Fenner's Farm

FOLLY LANE

LADY'S LANE

Fysons Farm

Hall Farm

Valley Farm

High House

COMMON RD 1
BRESSINGHAM RD 2

4

Primrose Farm

THE STREET

PH

Bridge Farm

Ashes Farm

Poplar Farm

Bressingham Prim Sch

HIGH RD

PO

Works

Loke Farm

THETFORD RD

DISS ROAD

Wood Farm

Bressingham

SAMSON'S LA

Pearces Farm

Oxfootstone Farm

Pooley Street

The Spinney

81

Villa Farm

REDGRAVE ROAD

BRICKKILN LANE

POOLEY ST

SILVER ST

Corner Farm

Old Hall Farm

PH

Blue Pump Farm

HIGH RD A1066

OLD NORTON RD

LNR DRAG WY

Deal Farm

Bottle Hall Farm

Fen Farm

HALFORD LANE

CHEQUERS LA

CHURCH LA

FELL LA

Malting Farm

Fen Farm

Fen Street

Three Gates Farm

Church Farm

Bressingham Steam Mus & Gardens

3

Waveney Farm

LOW COMMON

Redgrave & Lopham Fen National Nature Reserve

Visitor Centre

IP22

HALFORD LANE

Bressingham Fen

Waveney Valley Railway

P

THE DITT

Grange Farm

Walnut Tree Farm

LOW COMMON ROAD

P

Lang Fen

Great Fen

Dashes Farm

LOW ROAD

Manor House Farm

Wortham Manor

P

80

Poplar Farm

Chequers Farm

Middle Fen

Angles Way

River Waveney

Musks Meadows Farm

Low Road

Long Gardens Plantation

Wortham Ling Nature Reserve

B1113

Elm Tree Farm

Pine Farm

Redgrave Fen

Pond Farm

Fen Street

Woodhouse Farm

SLADE LA

Angles Way

2

MIDDLE ROAD

Little Fen

Grove House Farm

Monument

Watch Tower

FEN ROAD

Source of Little Ouse River

Source of River Waveney

Fen Street

Farm

BIER LA

The Grove

MAGPIE HILL

WIGWAM HILL

RECTORY RD

MILLWAY LA

CHURCH ROAD

79

1 WEST HERNE LA
2 SOUTHERN LA

FEN STREET

Fir Tree Farm

Moneypot Hill Farm

Holly Farm

REDGRAVE ROAD

Magpie Green

Beech Tree Farm

1

Bridge Farm

HINDERCLAY LANE

MILL LA

MONEYPOT LA

Moneypot Hill

Street Farm

Sewage Works

Pond Farm

Low Farm

WASH LANE

Sewage Works

THE STREET

PH

CHURCHWAY

WASH LANE

78

Crackthorn Corner

03 | A | 04 | B | 05 | C | 06 | D | 07 | E | 08 | F

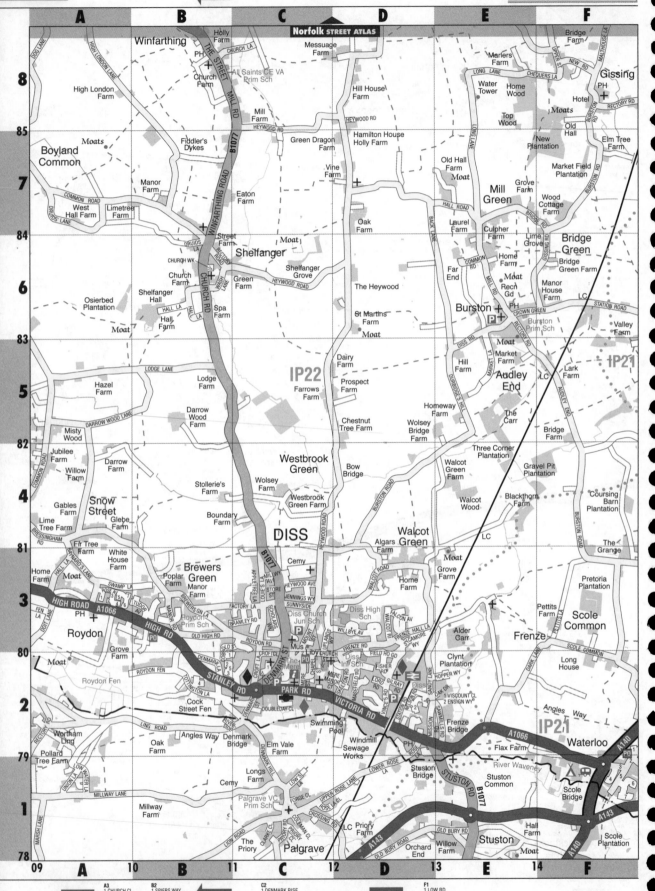

Scale: 1¾ inches to 1 mile
0   ¼   ½   mile
0   250m   500m   750m   1 km

Norfolk STREET ATLAS

A   B   C   D   E   F

Winfarthing
Holly Farm
Messuage Farm
Marlers Farm
Long Lane
Chequers La
Gissing
PH
Bridge Farm
Upper St
New Rd
Malthouse La

High London Farm
Church La
All Saints CE VA Prim Sch
Hill House Farm
Water Tower
Home Wood
Hotel
Moats
Top Wood
Old Hall
Rectory Rd

Moats
Mill Farm
Heywood Rd
Green Dragon Farm
Hamilton House Holly Farm
Old Hall Farm Moat
New Plantation
Elm Tree Farm
Market Field Plantation

Boyland Common
Fiddler's Dykes
Vine Farm
Mill Green
Grove Farm
Wood Cottage Farm
Bridge Green

Manor Farm
Eaton Farm
Oak Farm
Hall Road
Laurel Farm
Culpher Farm
Lime Grove
Bridge Green Farm

West Hall Farm
Limetree Farm
Street Farm
Druids La
Rectory Road
Shelfanger
Shelfanger Grove
Heywood Road
The Heywood
Far End
Home Farm
Moat
Rectn Gd
Manor House Farm
LC

Church Wk
Church Farm
Green Farm
St Martins Farm
Burston
PH
Burston Prim Sch
Station Road
Valley Farm

Osierbed Plantation
Shelfanger Hall
Spa Farm
Moat
Moat
Hill Farm
Moat
Market Farm
IP21

Hazel Farm
Lodge Lane
Lodge Farm
IP22
Dairy Farm
Prospect Farm
Audley End
Lark Farm
LC

Misty Wood
Darrow Wood Farm
Farrows Farm
Chestnut Tree Farm
Homeway Farm
Wolsey Bridge Farm
The Carr
Bridge Farm

Jubilee Farm
Darrow Farm
Darrow Wood Lane
Three Corner Plantation
Gravel Pit Plantation
Coursing Barn Plantation

Willow Farm
Stollerie's Farm
Westbrook Green
Bow Bridge
Walcot Green Farm
Walcot Wood
Blackthorn Farm

Gables Farm
Snow Street
Glebe Farm
Boundary Farm
Wolsey Farm
Westbrook Green Farm
DISS
Walcot Green
LC
The Grange

Lime Tree Farm
Fir Tree Farm
White House Farm
Brewers Green
Cemy
Algars Farm
Moat
Grove Farm
Pretoria Plantation

Home Farm
Moat
Poplar Farm
Manor Farm
Mill Wy
Store
Heywood Ave
Home Farm
Pettits Farm
Scole Common

HIGH ROAD
A1066
PH
Swamp La
Brewers Gn La
Factory La
Sunnyside
Diss Church Jun Sch
Diss High Sch
Falcon Av
Alder Carr
Frenze
Long House

Roydon
HIGH RD
Roydon Prim Sch
Old High Rd
Roydon Rd
Mus
Church
Diss Inf Sch
Frenze Rd
Clynt Plantation

Moat
Roydon Fen
Stanley Rd
The Mere
P
Victoria Rd
Diss
1 Viscount Wy
2 Ensign Wy
Waterloo
A1066
IP21

Cock Street Fen
Park Rd
Doubleday Cl
Frenze Bridge
Angles Way

Wortham Ling
Ling Road
Angles Way
Denmark Bridge
Swimming Pool
Windmill Sewage Works
PH
Flax Farm
Waterloo

Pollard Tree Farm
Oak Farm
Elm Vale Farm
River Waveney
A140

Millway Lane
Longs Farm
Stuston Bridge
Stuston Common
Scole Bridge

Millway Farm
Cemy
Palgrave VC Prim Sch
Forge Cl
Lower Rose La
Stuston
Stuston Rd
B1077
Hall Farm
Scole Plantation

The Priory
Palgrave
LC
Priory Farm
A143
Old Bury Road
Orchard End
Willow Farm
Moat

09   A   10   B   11   C   12   D   13   E   14   F

A3
1 CHURCH CL
2 BLENHEIM WAY
3 COPEMAN RD
4 WATERLOO AVE
5 TWISS CL
6 OLD RECTORY CL
7 FRERE CR

B2
1 SPIERS WAY
2 GOSTLING CL
3 TAYLOR RD
4 TOTTINGTON LA
5 BUXTON RD

C2
1 DENMARK RISE
2 NICHOLAS'S ST

F1
1 LOW RD
2 THE STREET
3 DISS RD
4 KAREN CL
5 BRIDGE RD
6 ROBINSON RD
7 CLEMENTS CL

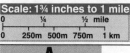

Scale: 1¾ inches to 1 mile

22

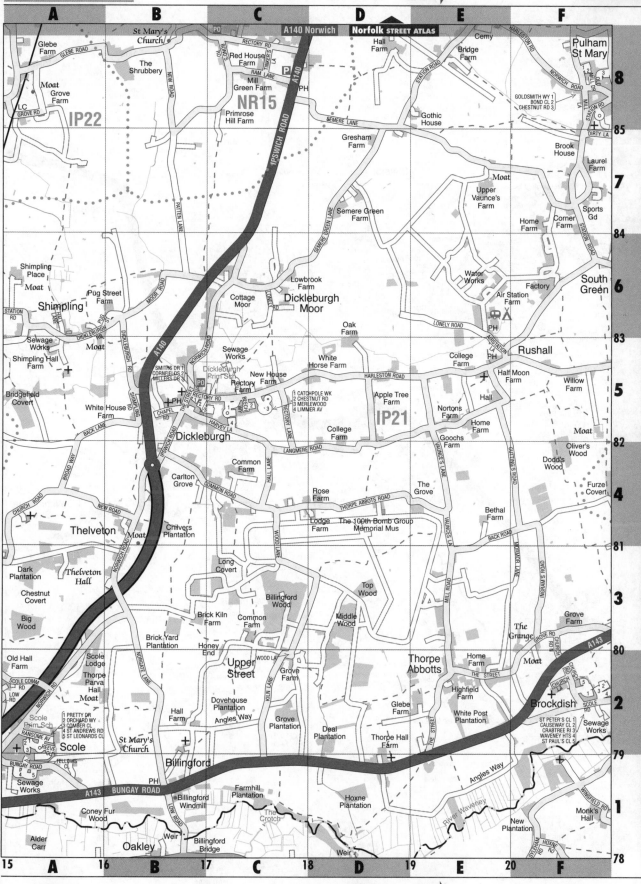

Norfolk STREET ATLAS

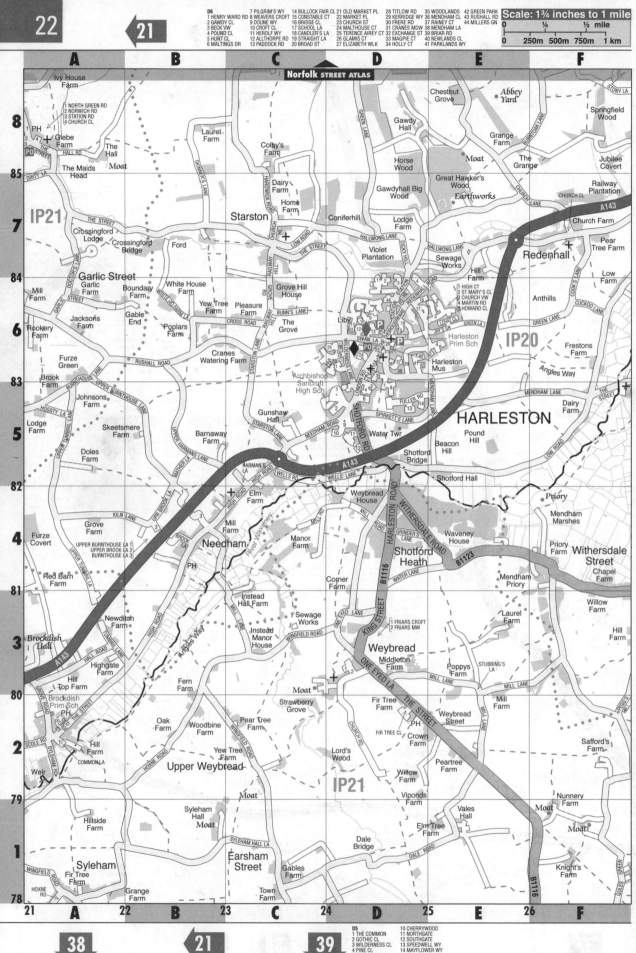

D6
1 HENRY WARD RD
2 GAWDY CL
3 BECK VW
4 POUND CL
5 HUNT CL
6 MALTINGS DR
7 PILGRIM'S WY
8 WEAVERS CROFT
9 DOUNE WY
10 CROFT CL
11 HEROLF WY
12 ALLTHORPE RD
13 PADDOCK RD
14 BULLOCK FAIR CL
15 CONSTABLE CT
16 BRIDGE CL
17 SCHOOL LA
18 CANDLER'S LA
19 STRAIGHT LA
20 BROAD ST
21 OLD MARKET PL
22 MARKET PL
23 CHURCH ST
24 MALTHOUSE CT
25 TERENCE AIREY CT
26 GLAMIS CT
27 ELIZABETH WLK
28 TITLOW RD
29 KERRIDGE WY
30 FRERE RD
31 CRANES MDW
32 EXCHANGE ST
33 MAGPIE CT
34 HOLLY CT
35 WOODLANDS
36 MENDHAM CL
37 RAINEY CT
38 MENDHAM LA
39 BRIAR RD
40 NEWLANDS CL
41 PARKLANDS WY
42 GREEN PARK
43 RUSHALL CT
44 MILLERS GN

D5
1 THE COMMON
2 GOTHIC CL
3 WILDERNESS CL
4 PINE CL
5 WILLOW WLK
6 PEMBERTON RD
7 LIME CL
8 OAK TREE WY
9 DOVE CL
10 CHERRYWOOD
11 NORTHGATE
12 SOUTHGATE
13 SPEEDWELL WY
14 MAYFLOWER WY

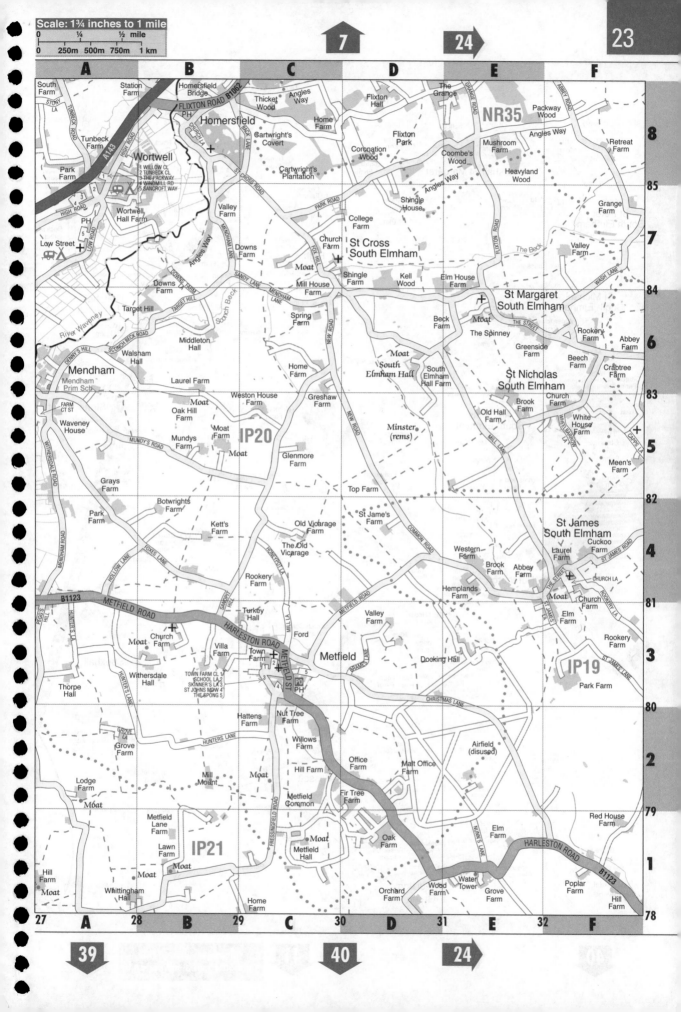

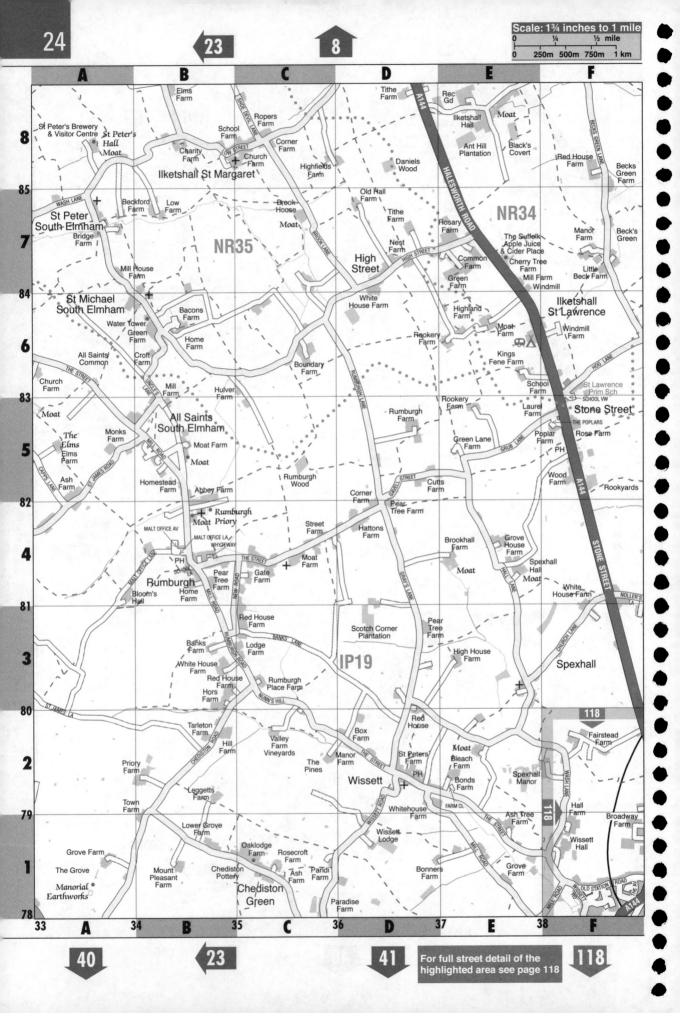

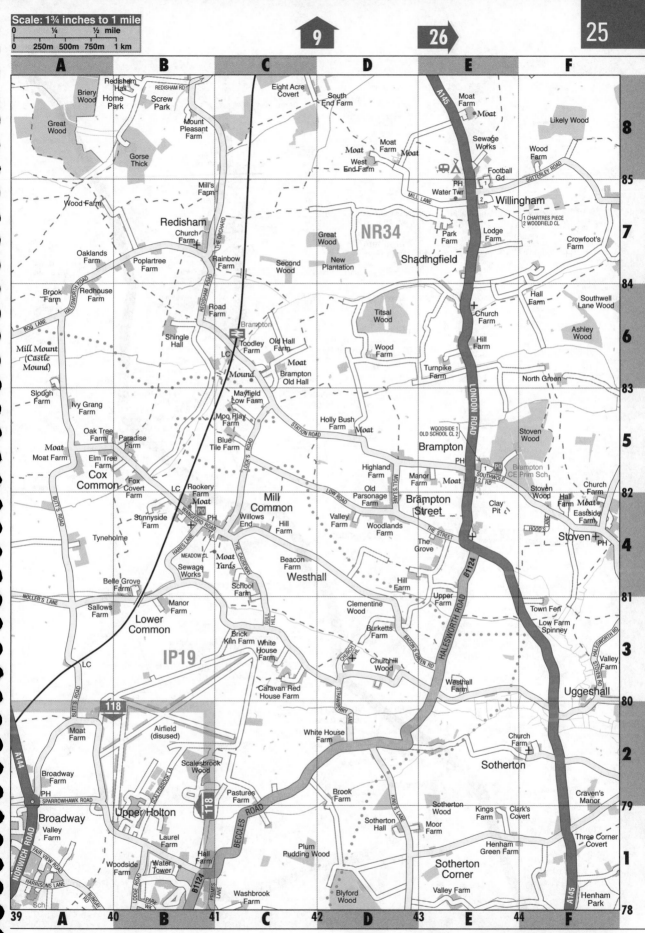

A B C D E F

Briery Wood
Redisham Hall
Home Park
REDISHAM RD
Screw Park
Mount Pleasant Farm
Eight Acre Covert
South End Farm
Moat Farm
Moat
Sewage Works
Likely Wood
Wood Farm

Great Wood
Gorse Thick
Mill's Farm
Moat
Moat Farm
Moat
Football Gd
SOTTERLEY ROAD
8

85

Wood Farm
Redisham
Church Farm
THE ORCHARD
Rainbow Farm
NR34
MILL LANE
Willingham
PH
Water Twr
1 CHARTRES PIECE
2 WOODFIELD CL
7

Oaklands Farm
Poplartree Farm
Great Wood
New Plantation
Shadingfield
Park Farm
Lodge Farm
Crowfoot's Farm
84

Brook Farm
Redhouse Farm
HALESWORTH ROAD
REDISHAM ROAD
Road Farm
Second Wood
Titsal Wood
Church Farm
Hall Farm
Southwell Lane Wood
6

HOG LANE
Shingle Hall
Brampton
Toodley Farm
Old Hall Farm
Moat
Wood Farm
Hill Farm
Turnpike Farm
North Green
Ashley Wood
83

Mill Mount (Castle Mound)
LC
Mound
Brampton Old Hall
LONDON ROAD
5

Slough Farm
Ivy Grang Farm
STATION ROAD
Mayfield Low Farm
Mog Play Farm
Holly Bush Farm
Moat
WOODSIDE 1
OLD SCHOOL CL 2
Brampton
Stoven Wood
82

Oak Tree Farm
Paradise Farm
Blue Tile Farm
LOCK'S ROAD
Highland Farm
Old Parsonage Farm
PH
SOUTHWOLD RD
PO
Brampton CE Prim Sch
Stoven Wood
Church Farm
Moat
Moat Farm
Elm Tree Farm
LC
Rookery Farm
Moat
LOW ROAD
Manor Farm
Moat
Brampton Street
Hall Farm
Eastside Farm
4

BUTT'S ROAD
Cox Common
Fox Covert Farm
WANGFORD ROAD
PO
PH
Willows End
Hill Farm
Valley Farm
Woodlands Farm
The Grove
THE STREET
Clay Pit
HOOD'S LANE
Stoven
PH
81

Sunnyside Farm
HARES LANE
MEADOW CL
Moat Yards
THE CAUSEWAY
Beacon Farm
Westhall
Hill Farm
Upper Farm
B1124
Town Fen
Low Farm Spinney
HALESWORTH RD
Tyneholme
Sewage Works
School Farm

Belle Grove Farm
NOLLER'S LANE
Sallows Farm
Manor Farm
Lower Common
IP19
Brick Kiln Farm
GULL HILL
White House Farm
Clementine Wood
Burketts Farm
CHURCH RL
Churchill Wood
Westhall Farm
HALESWORTH ROAD
Uggeshall
3

A144
118
LC
Moat Farm
Airfield (disused)
Caravan Red House Farm
STRAWBERRY LANE
BACON'S GREEN RD
80

118
SCALESBROOK LA
Scalesbrook Wood
118
Pastures Farm
BECCLES ROAD
White House Farm
Brook Farm
KING'S LANE
Church Farm
Sotherton
2

NORWICH ROAD
Broadway Farm
PH
SPARROWHAWK ROAD
Laurel Farm
Plum Pudding Wood
Sotherton Hall
Sotherton Wood
Kings Farm
Clark's Covert
Craven's Manor
Three Corner Covert
79

Broadway
Valley Farm
FAIR VIEW ROAD
Upper Holton
Woodside Farm
Water Tower
LODGE ROAD
PARK WK
Hall Farm
B1124
PRIMES LANE
Washbrook Farm
Blyford Wood
Moor Farm
Sotherton Corner
Valley Farm
Henham Green Farm
A145
Henham Park
1

HARRISONS LANE
BUNGAY RD
Sch
78

39 A 40 B 41 C 42 D 43 E 44 F

For full street detail of the highlighted area see page 118

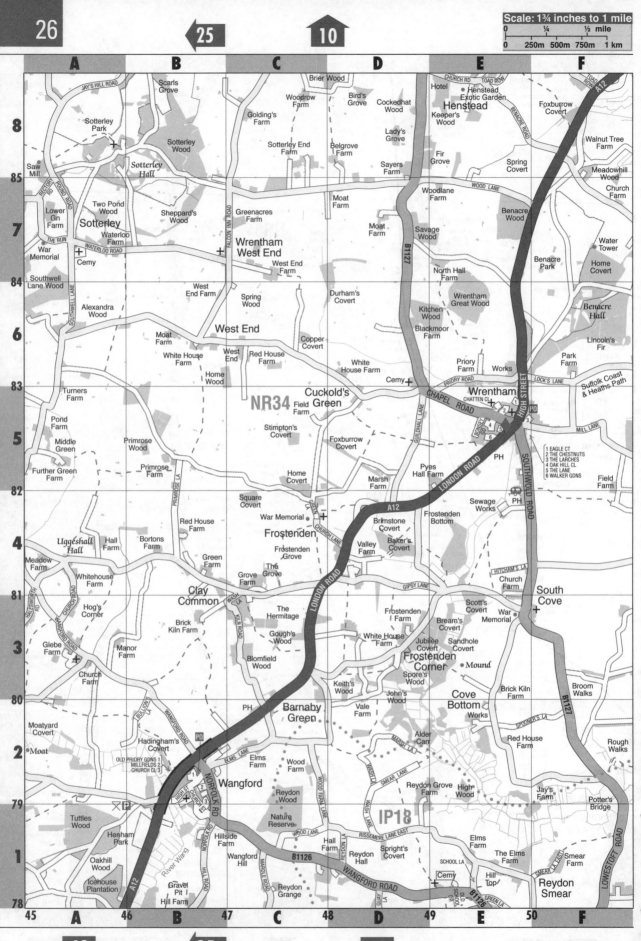

Scale: 1¾ inches to 1 mile

0   ¼   ½ mile

0   250m 500m 750m 1 km

A   B   C   D   E   F

Kessingland
Beach

NR33

COOPERS LA.

Blackcap
Wood

Churchfarm
Marshes

Sewage
Works

MARSH LA.

HOLLY GRANGE
ROAD

BEACH RD

PH
CHURCH
RD

Kessingland
Level

Suffolk Coast & Heaths Path

8

85

Benacre

War
Memorial

Church Covert

THE STREET

Beachfarm
Marshes

Northwalk
Plantation

Pumping
Station

The
Denes

Beach
Farm

7

84

Hall
Farm

Blackwater
Covert

Alder
Carr

Coney
Hill

Wood
Farm

Holly Hang

Craft
Plantation

Boathouse
Covert

Benacre National
Nature Reserve

6

83

NR34

Benacre
Broad

Holly
Grove

North
Common Wood

Chancel
Covert

Long
Covert

5

82

Ausgates

St Andrew's
Church

Church
Farm

Covehithe

Covehithe Cliffs

4

81

Porter's
Farm

Green
Heath

Covehithe
Broad

Warren
House

The
Warren

Suffolk Coast
& Heaths Path

Easton
Wood

3

80

Benacre National
Nature Reserve

Easton Home
Covert

Easton
Broad

Pottersbridge
Marshes

Easton
Marshes

2

79

IP18

Easton
Bavents

Easton Cliffs

EASTON LA.

1

78

51   A   52   B   53   C   54   D   55   E   56   F

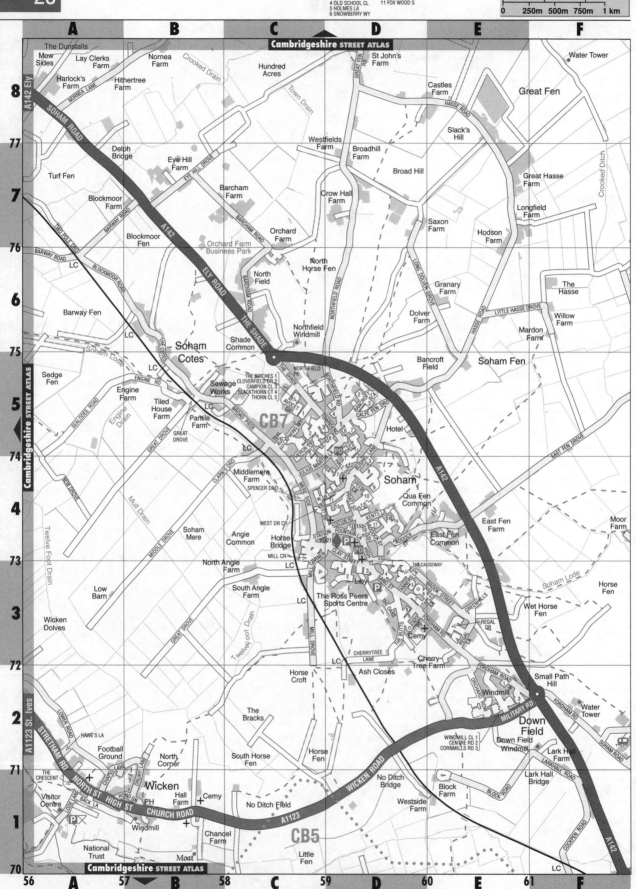

Scale: 1¾ inches to 1 mile

0   ¼   ½ mile
0   250m   500m   750m   1 km

D5
1 NORTH DR
2 ST FELIX CL
3 CALFE FEN CL
4 OLD SCHOOL CL
5 HOLMES LA
6 SNOWBERRY WY
7 FOX WOOD N
8 MARTIN CL
9 POPPY FIELDS
10 PRIMROSE LA
11 FOX WOOD S

D3
1 LODE CL
2 COLLEGE RD
3 REGENT PL
4 FRANK BRIDGES CL
5 REDHOUSE GDNS
6 THE CRESCENT
7 FORDHAM RD
8 MEADOW CL
9 MILL CFT

D4
1 ROSEBAY GDNS
2 BLUEBELL WK
3 HERBERT HUMAN CL
4 HONEYSUCKLE CL
5 NIGHTALL RD
6 CHESTNUT DR
7 GIMBERT RD
8 QUEENSWAY
9 WEATHERALLS CL

10 TEN BELL LA
11 BERRYCROFT
12 GUNTONS CL
13 BELL GDNS
14 FREDERICK TALBOT CL
15 CHURCHGATE ST
16 MARKET ST
17 ADELAIDE CL
18 EASTERN AV
19 BREWHOUSE LA

20 WHITE HART LA
21 GARDENERS LA
22 BROOK DAM LA

44

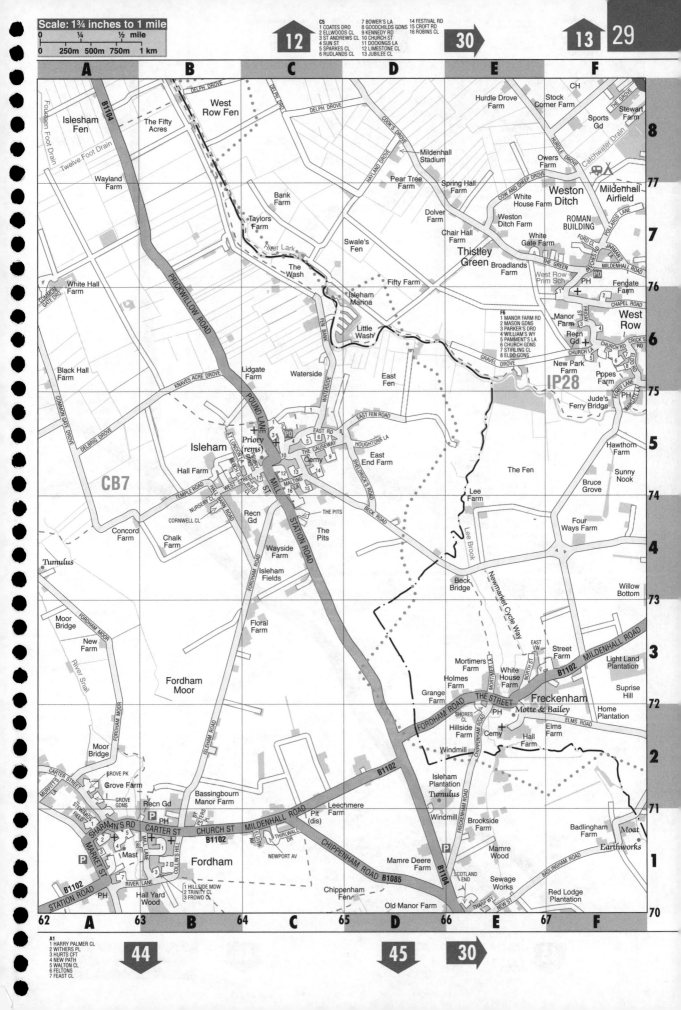

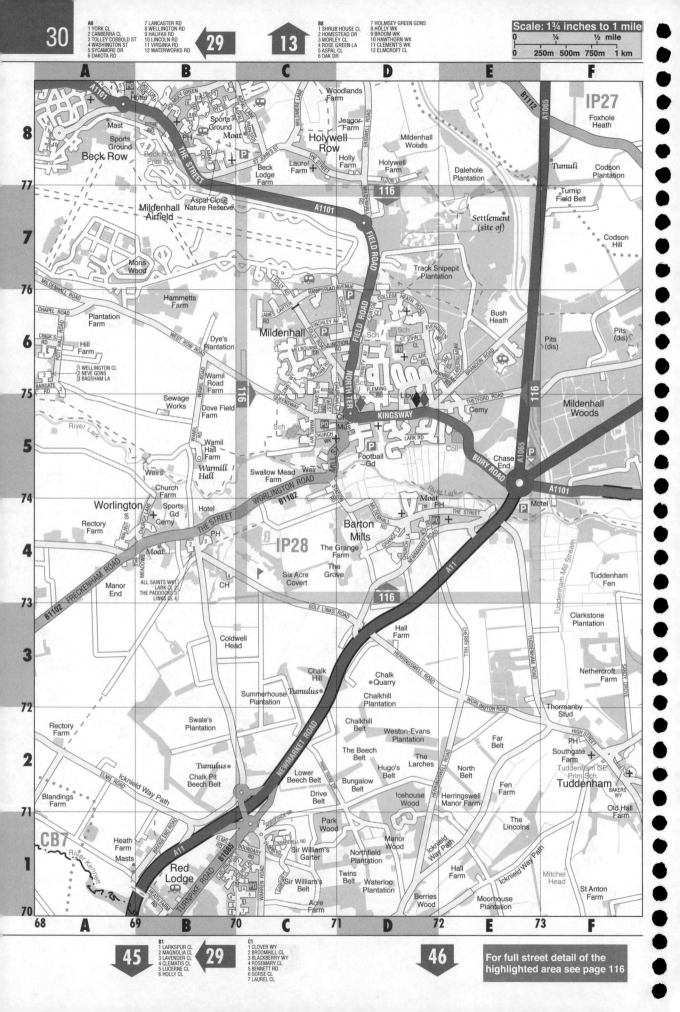

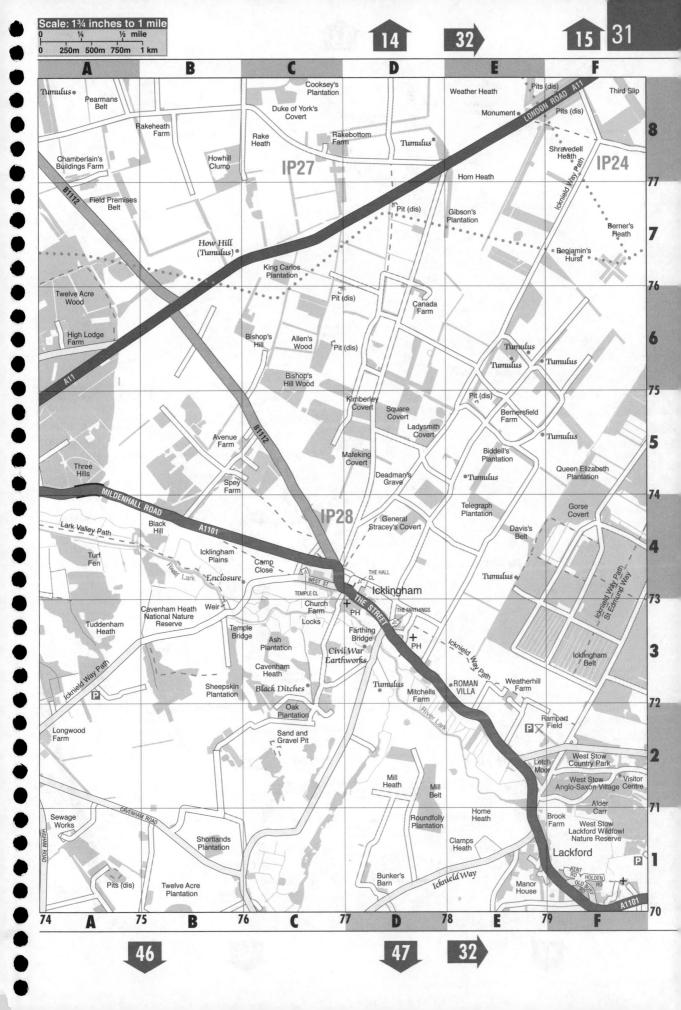

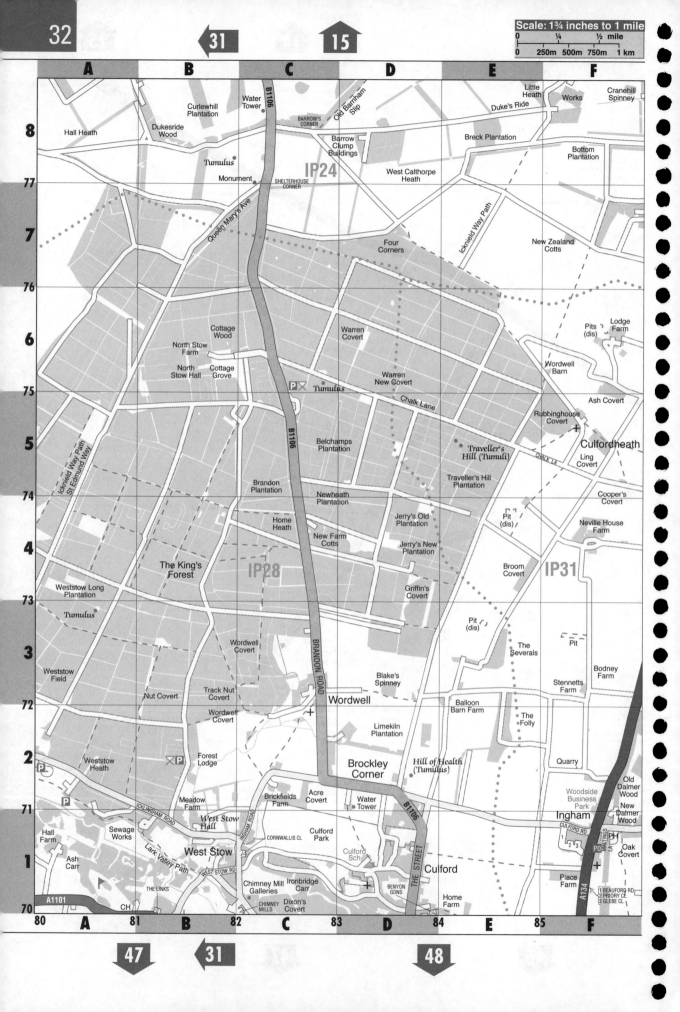

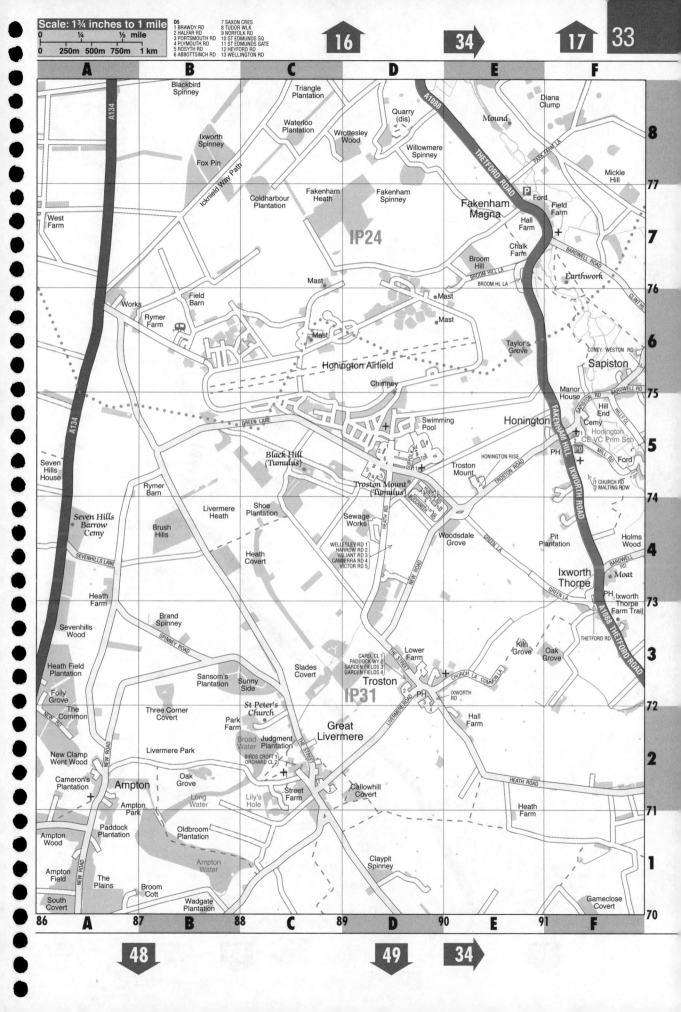

33
17

Scale: 1¾ inches to 1 mile
0 ¼ ½ mile
0 250m 500m 750m 1 km

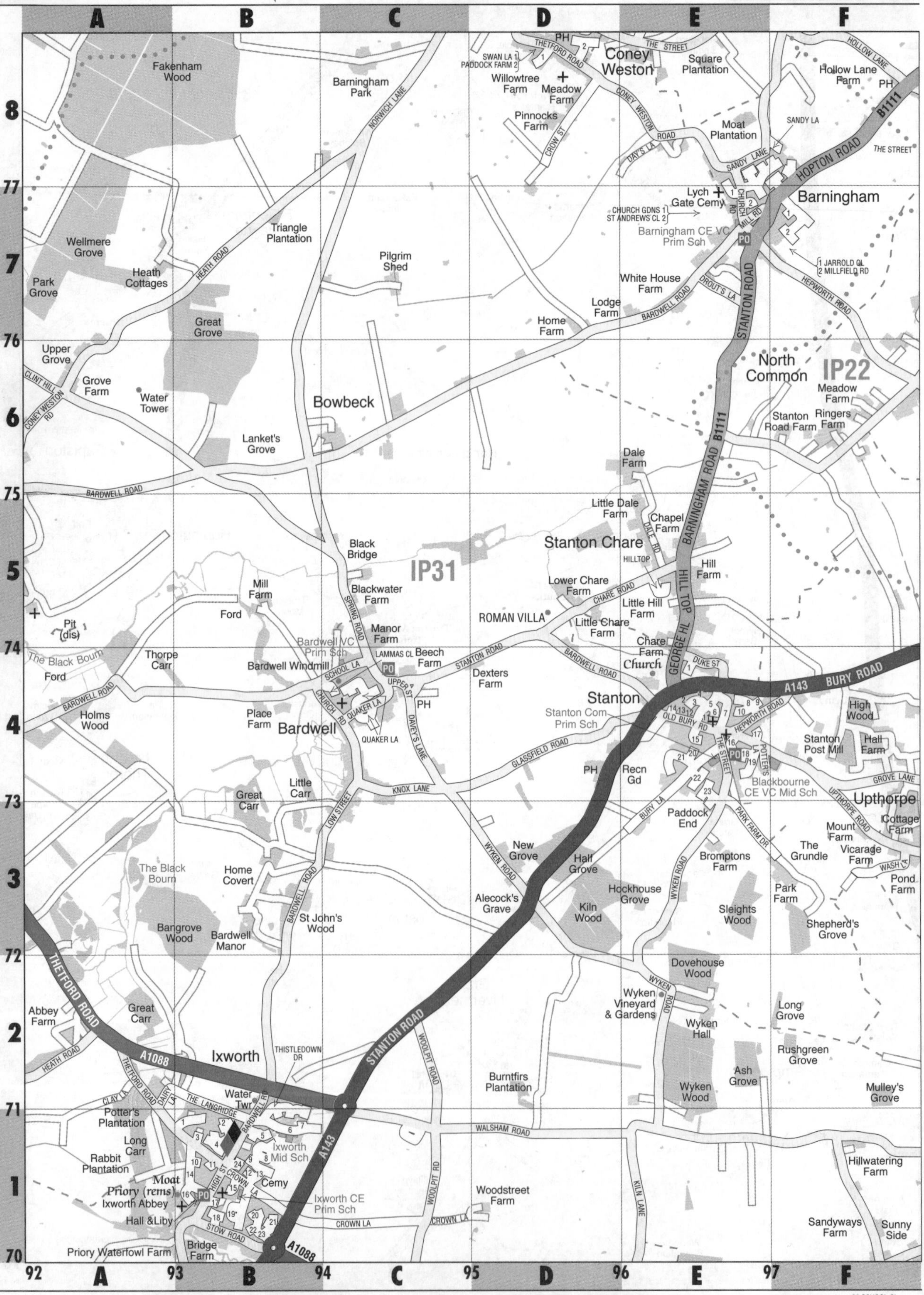
A
B
C
D
E
F
8
77
7
76
6
75
5
74
4
73
3
72
2
71
1
70
92
93
94
95
96
97
Fakenham Wood
Barningham Park
NORWICH LANE
SWAN LA 1
PADDOCK FARM 2
THETFORD ROAD
PH
Willowtree Farm
Meadow Farm
Pinnocks Farm
CROW ST
THE STREET
Coney Weston
CONEY WESTON ROAD
DAY'S LA
Square Plantation
Moat Plantation
SANDY LANE
SANDY LA
Hollow Lane Farm
HOLLOW LANE
PH
B1111
HOPTON ROAD
THE STREET
Lych Gate Cemy
CHURCH GDNS 1
ST ANDREWS CL 2
CHURCH RD
MILL RD
Barningham
Barningham CE VC Prim Sch
PO
1 JARROLD CL
2 MILLFIELD RD
HEPWORTH ROAD
Triangle Plantation
Wellmere Grove
Pilgrim Shed
HEATH ROAD
Heath Cottages
Park Grove
Great Grove
White House Farm
Lodge Farm
DROUT'S LA
STANTON ROAD
BARDWELL ROAD
Home Farm
Upper Grove
CLINT HILL
CONEY WESTON RD
Grove Farm
Water Tower
Bowbeck
North Common
IP22
Meadow Farm
Stanton Road Farm
Ringers Farm
Lanket's Grove
BARDWELL ROAD
Dale Farm
BARNINGHAM ROAD
B1111
Little Dale Farm
Chapel Farm
DALE RD
Stanton Chare
Black Bridge
IP31
HILLTOP
Hill Farm
Mill Farm
Blackwater Farm
SPRING ROAD
Lower Chare Farm
CHARE ROAD
HILL TOP
Little Hill Farm
Ford
ROMAN VILLA
Little Chare Farm
Pit (dis)
Manor Farm
Bardwell VC Prim Sch
LAMMAS CL
Beech Farm
Chare Farm
Church
GEORGE HL
DUKE ST
The Black Bourn
Thorpe Carr
Bardwell Windmill
SCHOOL LA
PO
STANTON ROAD
BARDWELL ROAD
Ford
UPPER ST
Dexters Farm
A143
BURY ROAD
BARDWELL ROAD
CHURCH LA
QUAKER LA
PH
Stanton
Holms Wood
Place Farm
Bardwell
QUAKER LA
DAVEY'S LANE
Stanton Com Prim Sch
OLD BURY RD
HEPWORTH ROAD
High Wood
Stanton Post Mill
Hall Farm
GLASSFIELD ROAD
THE STREET
POTTER'S LA
PO
PH
Recn Gd
Little Carr
KNOX LANE
Blackbourne CE VC Mid Sch
GROVE LANE
Great Carr
LOW STREET
BURY LA
PARK FARM DR
UPTHORPE ROAD
Upthorpe
Paddock End
Cottage Farm
Mount Farm
New Grove
The Grundle
Vicarage Farm
Half Grove
Bromptons Farm
WASH LA
The Black Bourn
Home Covert
BARDWELL ROAD
WYKEN ROAD
WYKEN ROAD
Pond Farm
Hockhouse Grove
Park Farm
Alecock's Grave
Kiln Wood
Sleights Wood
St John's Wood
Shepherd's Grove
Bangrove Wood
Bardwell Manor
THETFORD ROAD
Dovehouse Wood
WYKEN ROAD
Great Carr
Wyken Vineyard & Gardens
Long Grove
Abbey Farm
Wyken Hall
STANTON ROAD
HEATH ROAD
A1088
Ixworth
THISTLEDOWN DR
WOOLPIT ROAD
Rushgreen Grove
Ash Grove
Burntfirs Plantation
CLAY LA
THETFORD ROAD
DAIRY LA
Water Twr
BARDWELL RD
Wyken Wood
Mulley's Grove
THE LANGRIDGE
Potter's Plantation
WALSHAM ROAD
Long Carr
Ixworth Mid Sch
A143
Hillwatering Farm
Rabbit Plantation
HIGH ST
CROWN LA
Cemy
WOOLPIT ROAD
KILN LANE
Moat
Priory (rems)
Ixworth Abbey
PO
Ixworth CE Prim Sch
Woodstreet Farm
Hall & Liby
STOW ROAD
CROWN LA
CROWN LA
Sandyways Farm
Sunny Side
Priory Waterfowl Farm
Bridge Farm
A1088

49
33
50

B1
1 PEDDARS CL
2 CHALK LA
3 PEASECROFT RD
4 STREET FARM LA
5 ST EDMUND CL
6 WALSHAM RD
7 COLTSFOOT CL
8 CODDINGTON WY
9 GOUGH PL
10 ABBEY CL
11 BEECHES CL
12 GARRARD PL
13 SCOTT RD
14 COMMISTER LA
15 CROWN CRES
16 THE PADDOCK
17 SADDLERS YARD
18 PEACOCK RISE
19 NEW RD
20 THOMAS CL
21 KETTLEBORROW CL
22 PLUMMER CL
23 MICKLESMERE DR
24 FORDHAM PL

E4
1 OLD BARNINGHAM RD
2 CAPELL WLK
3 PARKSIDE
4 CULVERS MDW
5 THE CHASE
6 GRUNDLE CL
7 DUKE ST
8 BUCKLES FIELD
9 NORTH CL
10 CATCHPOLE WY
11 LOFFT CL
12 MICHAELHOUSE WY
13 SHETLANDS
14 JACOBS CL
15 CHURCH CL
16 MEADOW CT
17 THE KNOWLE
18 FIELD WY
19 WINDMILL GN
20 SCHOOL CL
21 FORDHAMS CL
22 STURGEON WY
23 HONEYMEADE CL

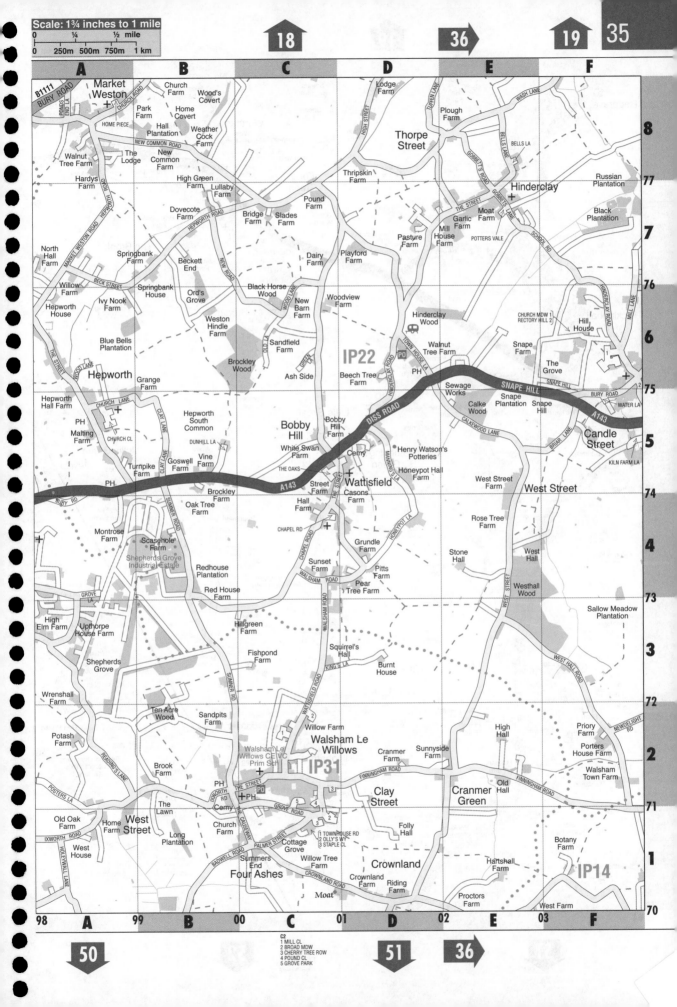

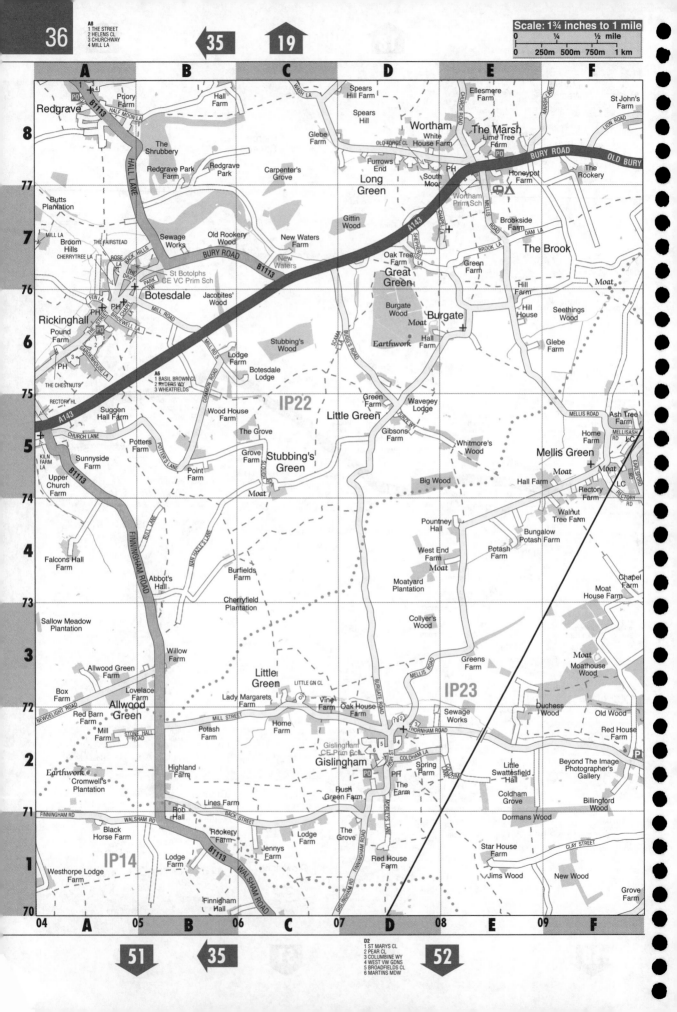

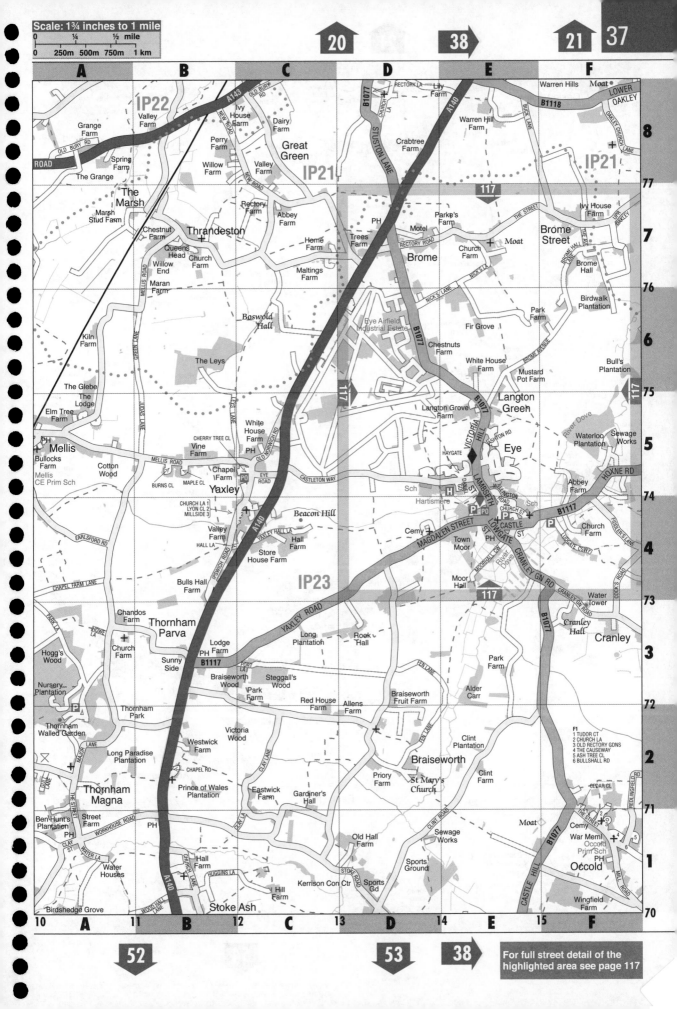

37 21

Scale: 1¾ inches to 1 mile
0   ¼   ½   mile
0   250m 500m 750m 1 km

A | B | C | D | E | F

Row 8:
LOWER OAKLEY, Oakley, Street Farm, The Grove, Red Bridge, Nuttery Plantation, B1118, Moor Bridge, WATER MILL LANE, Waveney Farm, Park Farm, Glebe Farm, HOXNE ROAD, Walnut Tree Farm, Windmill, WINGFIELD RD, WINDMILL LA, Etheridges Farm, Well Plantation, Hoxne, CHURCH HL, SYLEHAM ROAD, Dairy Farm, Red House Farm, Town Farm, Wingfield Green, Green Hill, Keeleys Farm

Row 77:
OAKLEY CHURCH LA, UPPER OAKLEY, Oakley Park, Oakley House, Swan Bridge, LOW STREET, Bridge Farm, PO, GREEN STREET, Green Street, Corner Farm, Gate House Farm, Sewage Works, Wingfield Green Farm, Corner Green Farm

Row 7:
Capon's Farm, White Bridge, Weir, ABBEY HILL, St Edmund's Mon, Moat, Abbey Farm, Moat, WITTONS LANE, Heckfield Green, White House Farm, Spin River's Bridge, Chickering Corner Farm, Chickering Corner, Chickering, B1118, Cross Street, Foxborough Plantation, RED LION CL, Big Carr

Row 76:
Little Carr, CROSS STREET, EVELYN CL, St Edmunds Prim Sch, Castle Farm, CHICKERING ROAD, Chickering Bridge, The Depperhaugh, Stud Farm, The Slades

Row 6:
Pit Wood, NUTTERY VALE, Bungalow Farm, Shreeves Farm, DENHAM ROAD, Hoxne Wood, PARK FARM LANE, The Grove, Depperhaugh Wood, Rookery Farm, Moat, Gissing Farm, Fir Plantation

Row 75:
New Plantation, Oak Plantation, South Green Farm, Moat, College Farm, Town Farm, Park Farm, Barnes Farm, Oak Lawn, Red House Farm, Home Farm

Row 5:
Oaklawn Farm, South Green, CHURCH ROAD, East Anglian Fruit Farm, Vicarage Farm, Denham, Broome Farm, Reading Green Farm, IP21, Grove Wood, HOXNE RD, Burnt House Farm, Mill Farm, Reading Green, Gardeners Farm, B1117, COOKLEY ROAD, COOKLEY LA, DENHAM LOW ROAD, PO, READING GREEN, Maggots Farm, Thorpe Hall, Moat, Valley Farm, Moat, Cookley Farm, Meadow End, Standwell Farm, WATERING ROAD, REDLINGFIELD CR, Locks Farm

Row 74:
Denham Hall Farm, Deal Plantation, Denham Green, Post Office Farm, THORPE HALL ROAD

Row 4:
Uplands Farm, COCK'S ROAD, Cranley Farm, Flimworth Hall, Moat, SHINGLE HL, Goldham Wood, Coney Wood, Hoxne Place Farm, B1117, CRANLEY LA, Greenlands Farm, HORHAM ROAD, HOXNE ROAD, Hall Farm

Row 73:
Cranley Manor, Fuffolk Farm, THE STREET, Denham Street, 95th Bomb Group Hospl Mus, Low Farm, Redlingfield Wood, DENHAM CORNER, Lodge Farm, Church Farm

Row 3:
Gate Farm, CRANLEY GN RD, Grove Farm, Cottage Grove, White House Farm, THE STREET, Horham, Recn Gd, PO, 1 CHURCH FARM CL, 2 ST MARY'S CL, Manor Farm, WORLINGWORTH ROAD, Thick Thorn Farm

Row 72:
King's Farm, IP23, Kiln Farm, LOW ROAD, CHURCH ROAD

Row 2:
Stanaway Cottages, REDLINGFIELD ROAD, Mill Farm, Hill Farm, Green Farm, REDLINGFIELD ROAD, Meadow Farm, Moat Farm, Moat, Oak Farm, Athelington, Moat, ATHELINGTON RD, Rose Farm, Chapel Farm

Row 71:
Benningham Hall, Moat, OCCOLD ROAD, MILL ROAD, Redlingfield, Sewage Works, Athelington Wood, HORHAM ROAD, Church Farm, SOUTHOLT ROAD, Walnut Tree Farm

Row 1:
BULL'S HALL ROAD, Ash Tree Farm, Benningham Green Farm, The Leys, CHURCH ROAD, Priory, WOODLANE ROAD, Red House Farm, White House Farm, Grove Farm, WATER LANE

Row 70:
Benningham Grange, Rookery Farm, Little Wood, Southolt Hall, Ford, IP13, Poplar Farm

A | 16 | B | 17 | C | 18 | D | 19 | E | 20 | F | 21

53 37 54

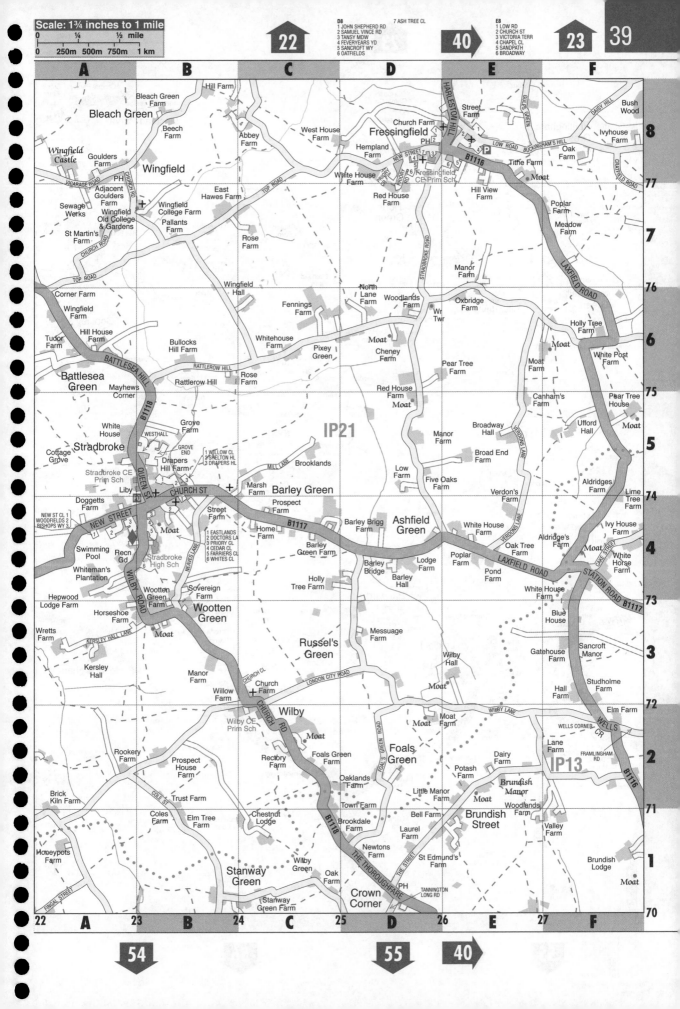

39 23

A B C D E F

8
Home Farm
Moat
Little Whittingham Green
Tink's Wood
Barbers Farm
Gissing's Farm
Oasis Camel Ctr
Morsenet Farm
Catkin Farm
Banes Farm
Mast
Littletown Farm
Chapel Farm
Brook Farm
Vicarage Farm
Bridge Farm
Linstead Parva
HALESWORTH ROAD
B1123
GODFREY'S HL

77
WOOD LANE
Woodside Farm
CRATFIELD ROAD
Watson's Farm
Mill Farm
Cratfield Hall
North Green
Magna Farm
Wind Pump
Abbey Farm
Valley Farm
LINSTEAD ROAD

7
Apricot Farm
Yew Tree Farm
IP21
Old Hall Farm
Town Farm
Church Farm
St Peter's Church
Lower Hall Farm
Newall Hall Farm
Green Farm

76
Mill Farm
Chippenhall Green
Willow Farm
Elder Farm
Moat House Farm
North Green Farm
Silverley's Green
Spong Farm
Larters Farm
Linstead Farm
Linstead Hall
Moat
MARY'S LANE
Corner Farm
Cookley Green

6
Common Farm
Rookery Farm
Elm Lodge
Poplar Farm
Grove Farm
Holly Tree Farm
Oemy
BELL GREEN
Bell Farm
Cratfield
PH
Manor Farm
Towranna Farm
Whitechurch Covert

75
Moat
Moat Farm
The Firs
MANSE LANE
Rookery Farm
School Farm
THE STREET
Baltic Farm
Cantley Farm
Bates's Covert
Sandpit Plantation

5
Swan Green
White House Farm
Rose Farm
SWAN GN LA
Church Farm
IP19
HUNTINGFIELD ROAD
CRATFIELD ROAD
Whitehouse Farm
Clover Forge Farm
CAUSEWAY

74
Lodge Farm
Moat
Moat
Red House Farm
HEVENINGHAM ROAD
Dunnett's Farm
Low Farm
Moat
Hill Farm
BRICK KILN LANE
PH

4
Moat
CAKE STREET
Dowsing Farm
Moat
Moat
Stadhaugh Manor Farm
CRATFIELD LANE
Manor Farm
High House Farm
Hill Farm
BAREL'S HILL

73
Yew Tree Farm
B1117
Moat
Chestnuts Farm
Surlinside Farm
Corner Farm
Banyard's Green
Oakes Farm
Hill Farm
Turkey Hall
Allans Farm
Wood Farm
Ubbeston Wood
Ubbeston
Packway Farm
THE STREET
HALESWORTH ROAD

3
STATION ROAD
Cemy
Jubilee Farm
PO
PH
Laxfield
MARKET ST
BICKERS HL RD
FRAMS MILL
Valley Farm
LOW ROAD
Church Farm
St Peter's Church
Gothic Farm
Heveningham
White House Farm
CHURCH ROAD

72
All Saints CE VA Prim Sch
Chestnut Tree Farm
FRAMLINGHAM ROAD
HIGH STREET
NOYES AV
Recn Gd
Hill Farm Laxfield & District Museum
P
Ubbeston Green
Green Farm
CLAY HILL
Hill Farm
Poplars Farm
B1117

2
Burnt House
Scogging's Farm
Fishers Farm
IP13
Street Farm
DENNINGTON ROAD
Rookery Farm
VICARAGE ROAD
Noyes Farm
ROWE'S HILL
Grove Farm
Greenvalley
Blackberry Farm
Irongate Farm
Moat Farm

71
Mills Farmhouse
GIN LANE
St Jacob's Hall
BADINGHAM ROAD
Manor Farm
Boats Hall
Moat
White House Farm
Low Grange Farm
River Yox
Moat
Moat

1
B1116
Laxfield House
Park Field Farm
IP17

70
Potash Farm
Wood Farm
LAXFIELD ROAD

28 A 29 B 30 C 31 D 32 E 33 F

B3
1 THE ORCHARDS
2 JUBILEE CL
3 CHURCH WK
4 HOME MDW
5 MALT CL
6 THE LINX
7 ELM LODGE RD

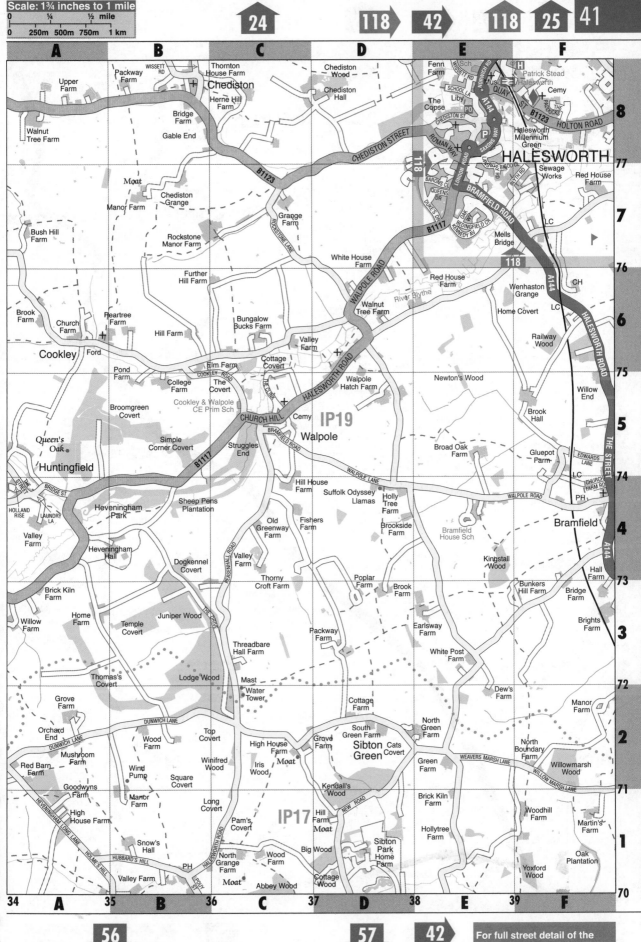

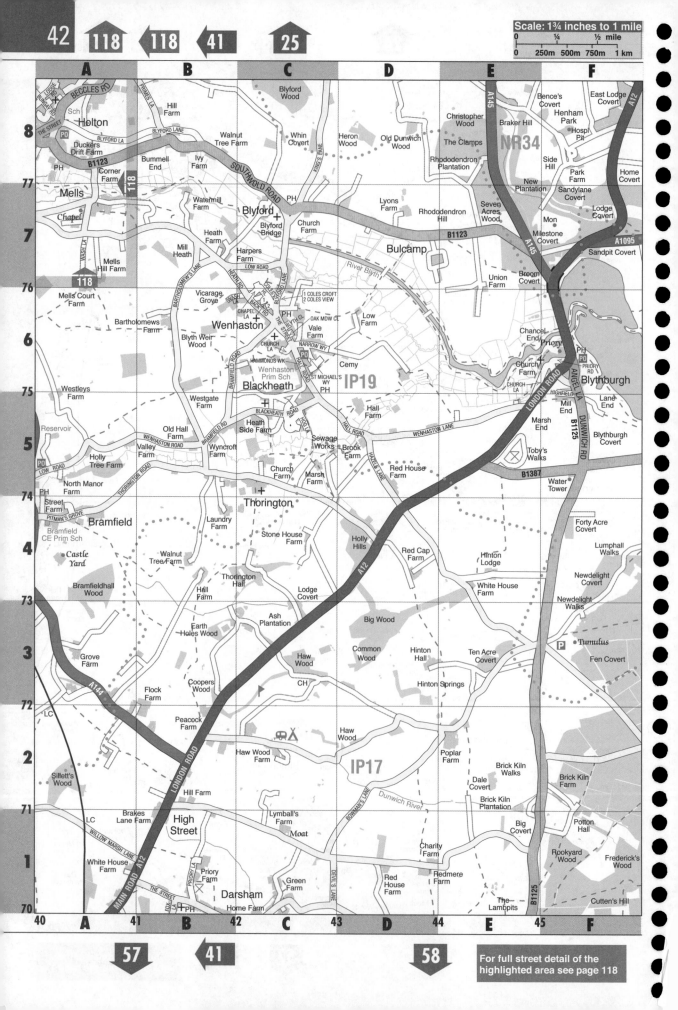

Scale: 1¾ inches to 1 mile

0   ¼   ½   mile
0 250m 500m 750m 1 km

Grid columns: A B C D E F (top and bottom)
Grid rows: 8 77 7 76 6 75 5 74 4 73 3 72 2 71 1 70

Holton
Sch
BURGH RD
LODGE RD
BECCLES RD
The Street
PO
PH
B1123
Corner Farm
Mells
Chapel
Mells Hill Farm
WASH LA
118
Mells Court Farm
Bartholomews Farm
Westleys Farm
Reservoir
PO
LOW ROAD
Holly Tree Farm
North Manor Farm
PH
Street Farm
PITMAN'S GROVE
Bramfield
Bramfield CE Prim Sch
Castle Yard
Bramfieldhall Wood
Grove Farm
A144
LC
LC
Sillett's Wood
White House Farm
WILLOW MARSH LANE
MAIN ROAD
A12
LC
Brakes Lane Farm
Hill Farm
THE STREET
Priory Farm
Darsham
Home Farm
PH

PRIMES LA
Hill Farm
BLYFORD LANE
Walnut Tree Farm
Bummell End
Ivy Farm
Watermill Farm
SOUTHWOLD ROAD
Blyford
Blyford Bridge
Heath Farm
Mill Heath
Harpers Farm
LOW ROAD
BARTHOLOMEW'S LANE
HEATH ROAD
Vicarage Grove
CHAPEL LA
BLYFORD LANE
Wenhaston
Blyth Weir Wood
CHURCH LA
HAMMONDS WK
Wenhaston Prim Sch
Blackheath
BRAMFIELD ROAD
Westgate Farm
Old Hall Farm
Wyncroft Farm
WENHASTON ROAD
THORINGTON ROAD
Valley Farm
BRAMFIELD RD
BLACKHEATH ROAD
Heath Side Farm
HOG LA
Church Farm
Marsh Farm
Thorington
Laundry Farm
Walnut Tree Farm
Thorington Hall
Hall Farm
Ash Plantation
Earth Holes Wood
Coopers Wood
Flock Farm
Peacock Farm
LONDON ROAD
Hill Farm
High Street
Lymball's Farm
Moat
Green Farm
PRIORY LA

Blyford Wood
Whin Covert
KING'S LANE
Heron Wood
Old Dunwich Wood
PH
Church Farm
1 COLES CROFT
2 COLES VIEW
OAK MDW CL
Vale Farm
NARROW WY
St Michael's WY
PH
Cemy
IP19
Hall Farm
Sewage Works
Brook Farm
Red House Farm
HALL ROAD
HAZEL'S LANE
WENHASTON LANE
Low Road
Lyons Farm
River Blyth
Bulcamp
B1123
Union Farm
Stone House Farm
Holly Hills
Red Cap Farm
A12
Lodge Covert
Haw Wood
CH
Big Wood
Common Wood
Hinton Hall
Hinton Springs
Haw Wood Farm
Haw Wood
IP17
BOWMAN'S LANE
Dunwich River
DEVIL'S LANE
Charity Farm
Red House Farm
Redmere Farm

Christopher Wood
The Clamps
Rhododendron Plantation
Rhododendron Hill
Seven Acres Wood
Mon
A145
NR34
Bence's Covert
East Lodge Covert
Henham Park
Braker Hill
Hosp Pit
Side Hill
Park Farm
New Plantation
Sandylane Covert
Home Covert
A12
Lodge Covert
Milestone Covert
A1095
Sandpit Covert
Broom Covert
Chancel End
Priory
PH
PO
PRIORY RD
Blythburgh
CHURCH LA
Church Farm
HIGHFIELD
Mill End
Lane End
Blythburgh Covert
Marsh End
ANGEL LA
LONDON ROAD
DUNWICH RD
B1125
Toby's Walks
B1387
Water Tower
Hinton Lodge
White House Farm
Ten Acre Covert
Forty Acre Covert
Lumphall Walks
Newdelight Covert
Newdelight Walks
P
Tumulus
Fen Covert
Poplar Farm
Dale Covert
Brick Kiln Walks
Brick Kiln Plantation
Brick Kiln Farm
Big Covert
Potton Hall
Rookyard Wood
Frederick's Wood
B1125
The Lampits
Cutten's Hill

For full street detail of the highlighted area see page 118

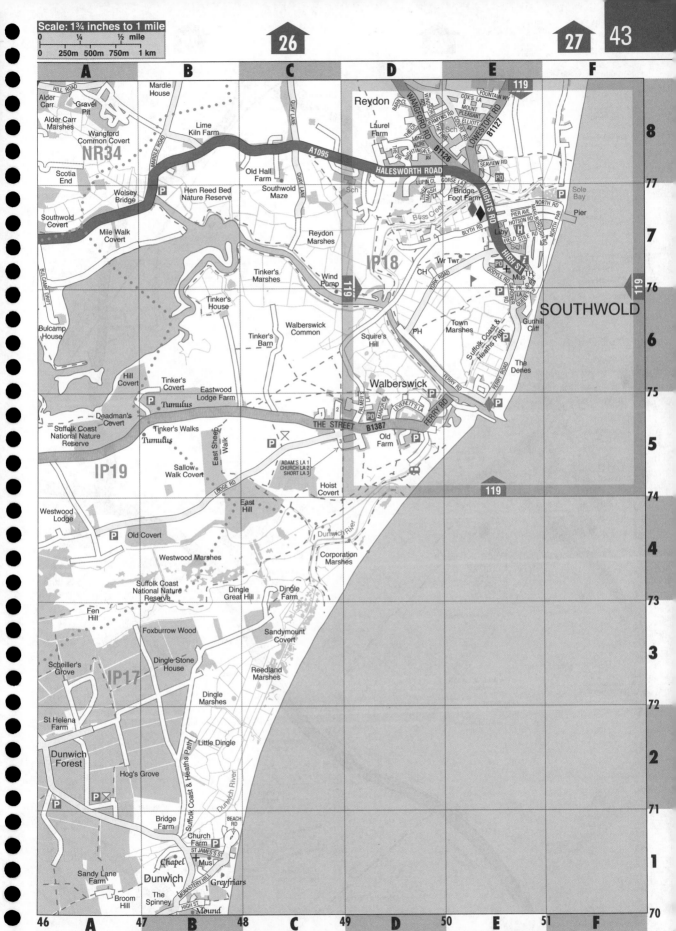

Scale: 1¾ inches to 1 mile

0   ¼   ½ mile
0   250m 500m 750m 1 km

26   27

A   B   C   D   E   F

HILL ROAD
Alder Carr
Gravel Pit
Alder Carr Marshes
Wangford Common Covert
NR34
Scotia End
Wolsey Bridge
Southwold Covert
Mile Walk Covert

Mardle House
Lime Kiln Farm
MARDLE ROAD
QUAY LANE
Old Hall Farm
Hen Reed Bed Nature Reserve
Southwold Maze
QUAY LANE

A1095

Reydon
Laurel Farm
HALESWORTH ROAD
WANGFORD RD
WINDSOR RD
JERMYNS RD
COX'S LA
MOUNT PLEASANT
FOUNTAIN WY
119
Sch
ELLIOTT AV
B1126
LOWESTOFT RD
B1127
SEAVIEW RD
PO
8
77

Reydon Marshes
Tinker's Marshes
Wind Pump
119
IP18
Buss Creek
Sch
LUPIN CL GORSE LA
THREE MARSH
MARSH LA
Bridge Foot Farm
Libry
BLYTH RD
PIER AVE
NORTH RD
HOTSON RD
MARLBOROUGH RD
NORTH PAR
Sole Bay
Pier
77
7

Tinker's House
Walberswick Common
Tinker's Barn
Squire's Hill
Wr Twr
CH
WORK ROAD
PH
HIGH ST
PO
TH
Mus
GODYLL RD
GARDNER QUEEN
Wr Twr
SOUTHWOLD
119
76

Bulcamp House
BULCAMP DRIFT
Hill Covert
Tinker's Covert
Eastwood Lodge Farm
Town Marshes
Suffolk Coast & Heaths Path
Gunhill Cliff
The Denes
6
75

Deadman's Covert
Tumulus
Suffolk Coast National Nature Reserve
Tinker's Walks
Tumulus
IP19
East Sheep Walk
Sallow Walk Covert
THE STREET
PALMER'S
PO MANOR
EVERETT'S LA
FERRY RD
B1387
Old Farm
Walberswick
FERRY RD
5
74

1 ADAM'S LA 1
CHURCH LA 2
3 SHORT LA 3
Hoist Covert

Westwood Lodge
Old Covert
LODGE RD
East Hill
Dunwich River
Corporation Marshes
119
4
73

Westwood Marshes
Suffolk Coast National Nature Reserve
Dingle Great Hill
Dingle Farm

Fen Hill
Foxburrow Wood
Sandymount Covert
Reedland Marshes
3
72

Scheiller's Grove
IP17
Dingle Stone House
Dingle Marshes

St Helena Farm
Dunwich Forest
Hog's Grove
Suffolk Coast & Heaths Path
Little Dingle
Dunwich River
2
71

P
Bridge Farm
Church Farm
BEACH RD
ST JAMES'S ST
Chapel
Mus
MONASTERY HILL
Sandy Lane Farm
Dunwich
Greyfriars
The Spinney
HIGH ST
Broom Hill
Mound
1
70

46   A   47   B   48   C   49   D   50   E   51   F

58

For full street detail of the highlighted area see page 119

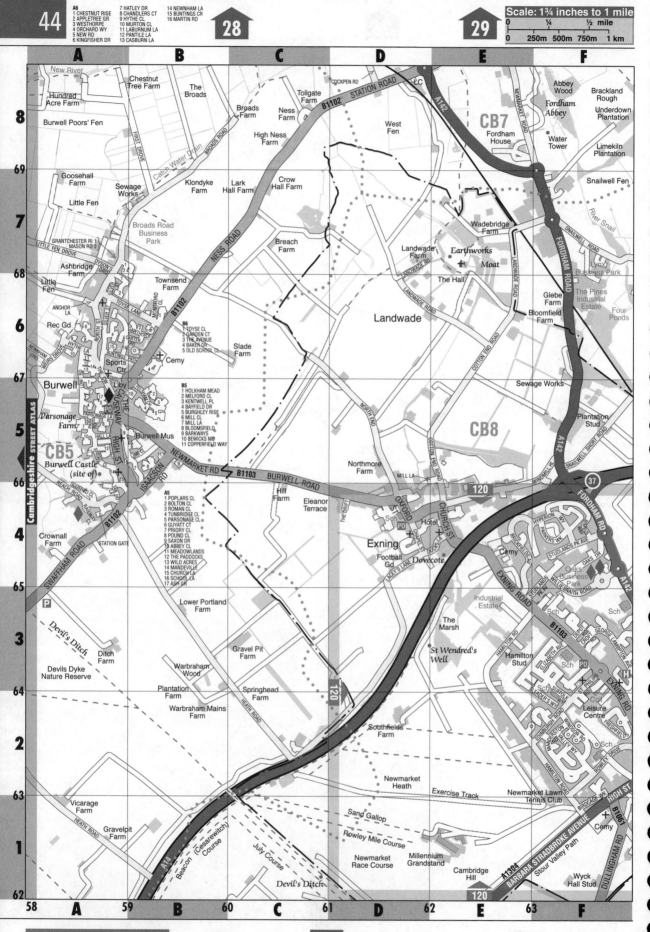

A6
1 CHESTNUT RISE
2 APPLETREE GR
3 WESTHORPE
4 ORCHARD WY
5 NEW RD
6 KINGFISHER DR

7 HATLEY DR
8 CHANDLERS CT
9 HYTHE CL
10 MURTON CL
11 LABURNUM LA
12 PANTILE LA
13 CASBURN LA

14 NEWNHAM LA
15 BUNTINGS CR
16 MARTIN RD

Scale: 1¾ inches to 1 mile
0   ¼   ½ mile
0 250m 500m 750m 1 km

Cambridgeshire Street Atlas

For full street detail of the highlighted area see page 120

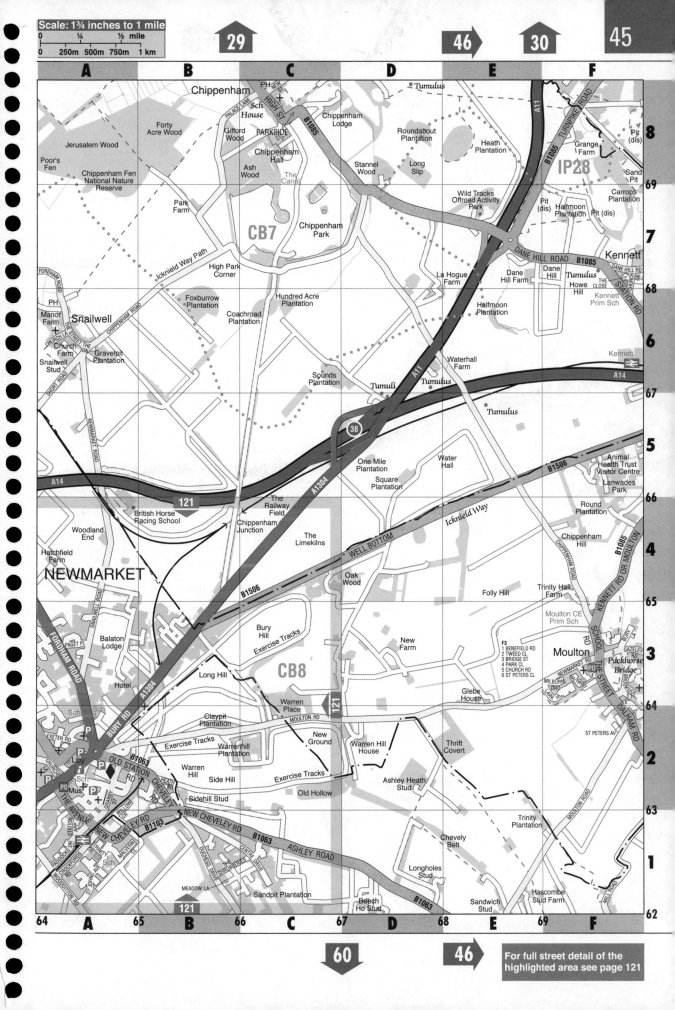

A   B   C   D   E   F

Chippenham

PH

Palace Lane

Sch House

PARKSIDE

Chippenham Lodge

Tumulus

8

Forty Acre Wood

Gifford Wood

Chippenham Hall

Roundabout Plantation

Heath Plantation

Grange Farm

Pit (dis)

Jerusalem Wood

Ash Wood

Stannel Wood

Long Slip

Sand Pit

Poor's Fen

The Canal

IP28

69

Chippenham Fen National Nature Reserve

Park Farm

CB7

Chippenham Park

Wild Tracks Offroad Activity Park

Pit (dis)

Halfmoon Plantation

Pit (dis)

Carrops Plantation

7

Icknield Way Path

High Park Corner

La Hogue Farm

Dane Hill Road

B1085

Kennett

Snailwell

Foxburrow Plantation

Hundred Acre Plantation

Dane Hill Farm

Dane Hill

Tumulus Howe Hill

THE CLOSE

Kennett Prim Sch

STATION RD

DANE HILL RD

68

PH

Manor Farm

Church Farm

Gravelpit Plantation

Coachroad Plantation

Halfmoon Plantation

6

Snailwell Stud

Sounds Plantation

Waterhall Farm

Kennett

Tumuli

Tumulus

Tumulus

A11

A14

67

NEWMARKET

121

A14

38

Tumulus

5

British Horse Racing School

One Mile Plantation

Water Hall

A1304

Square Plantation

B1506

Animal Health Trust Visitor Centre

Lanwades Park

Woodland End

The Railway Field

Chippenham Junction

Icknield Way

Round Plantation

66

Hatchfield Farm

The Limekilns

WELL BOTTOM

Chippenham Hill

B1085

KENNETT RD OR MOULTON

4

B1506

Oak Wood

Folly Hill

Trinity Hall Farm

65

FORDHAM ROAD

SNAILWELL ROAD

Balaton Lodge

Bury Hill Exercise Tracks

CB8

New Farm

Moulton CE Prim Sch

Moulton

SCHOOL RD

THE STREET

GAZELEY RD

Packhorse Bridge

3

Hotel

A1304

Long Hill

121

Glebe House

F3
1 BENEFIELD RD
2 TWEED ST
3 BRIDGE ST
4 PARK CL
5 CHURCH RD
6 ST PETERS CL

NEWMARKET RD

PO

BROOK

DALHAM RD

Sch

Claypit Plantation

Warren Place

MOULTON RD

New Ground

Warren Hill House

Thrift Covert

ST PETERS AV

64

P

Liby

BURY RD

B1063

Exercise Tracks

Warrenhill Plantation

Warren Hill

Side Hill

Exercise Tracks

Ashley Heath Stud

MOULTON ROAD

2

P

Sch

PO

Mus

OLD STATION RD

CHEVELEY RD

Sidehill Stud

Old Hollow

THE AVENUE

NEW CHEVELEY RD

B1103

New Cheveley Rd

B1063

ASHLEY ROAD

B1063

Chevely Belt

Trinity Plantation

63

MEADOW LA

CENTRE DRIVE

DUCHESS DRIVE

Sandpit Plantation

Beech Ho Stud

Longholes Stud

Sandwich Stud

Hascombe Stud Farm

MILL ROAD

1

121

64   65   66   67   68   69

62

A   B   C   D   E   F

For full street detail of the highlighted area see page 121

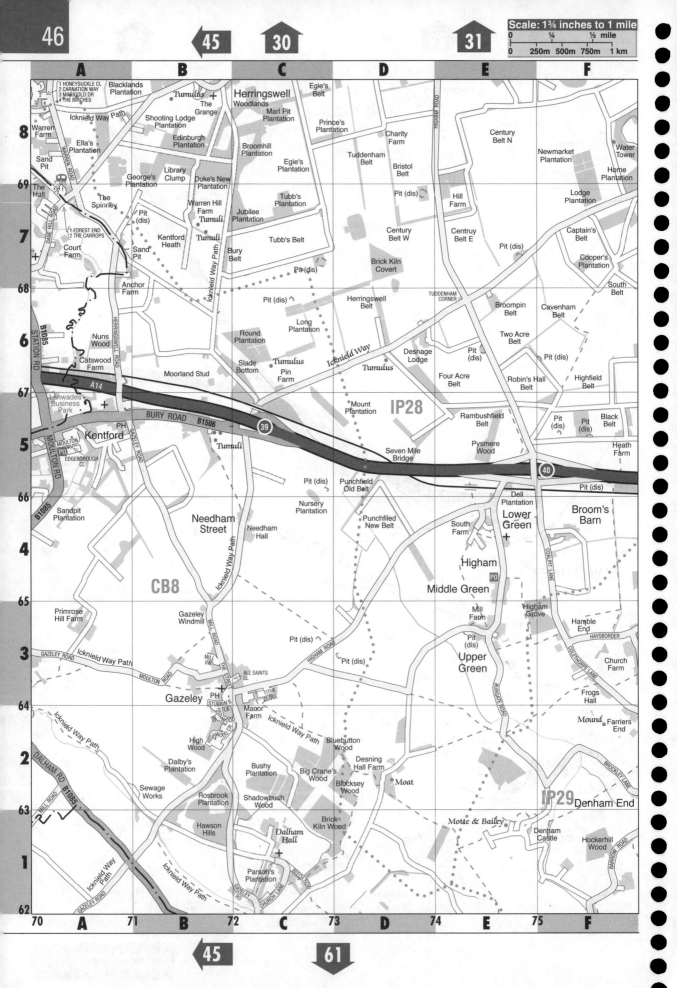

A   B   C   D   E   F

8

1 HONEYSUCKLE CL
2 CARNATION WAY
3 MARIGOLD DR
4 THE BIRCHES

Blacklands
Plantation

Tumulus   The
            Grange

Herringswell
Woodlands

Egie's
Belt

Warren
Farm

Icknield Way Path

Shooting Lodge
Plantation

Edinburgh
Plantation

Broomhill
Plantation

Marl Pit
Plantation

Prince's
Plantation

Charity
Farm

Century
Belt N

Newmarket
Plantation

Water
Tower

Ella's
Plantation

Egie's
Plantation

Tuddenham
Belt

Bristol
Belt

Home
Plantation

Sand
Pit

69

The Hall

George's
Plantation

Library
Clump

Duke's New
Plantation

Hill
Farm

Lodge
Plantation

The
Spinney

7

1 FOREST END
2 THE CARROPS

Pit
(dis)

Warren Hill
Farm

Tumuli

Jubilee
Plantation

Tubb's
Plantation

Pit (dis)

Century
Belt W

Centruy
Belt E

Captain's
Belt

Cooper's
Plantation

Court
Farm

Kentford
Heath

Sand
Pit

Tumuli

Tubb's Belt

Bury
Belt

Pit (dis)

South
Belt

68

Anchor
Farm

Pit (dis)

Herringswell
Belt

TUDDENHAM
CORNER

Broompin
Belt

Cavenham
Belt

6

Nuns
Wood

Herringswell Road

Round
Plantation

Long
Plantation

Desnage
Lodge

Two Acre
Belt

Pit (dis)

Highfield
Belt

Catswood
Farm

Moorland Stud

Slade
Bottom

Tumulus

Pin
Farm

Icknield Way

Tumulus

Pit
(dis)

Four Acre
Belt

Robin's Hall
Belt

Highfield
Belt

67

A14

Lanwades
Business
Park

Mount
Plantation

IP28

Rambushfield
Belt

Pit
(dis)

Pit
(dis)

Black
Belt

5

B1085

STATION RD

MOULTON DR

Kentford

BURY ROAD B1506

39

Tumuli

Seven Mile
Bridge

Pysmere
Wood

40

Heath
Farm

MOULTON RD

PO

EDGEBOROUGH
CL

Pit (dis)

Punchfield
Old Belt

Dell
Plantation

Pit (dis)

66

B1085

Sandpit
Plantation

Nursery
Plantation

Punchfiled
New Belt

Lower
Green

Broom's
Barn

4

Needham
Street

Needham
Hall

South
Farm

Higham

PO

CB8

Icknield Way Path

Middle Green

COALPIT LANE

65

Primrose
Hill Farm

Gazeley
Windmill

Mill
Farm

Higham
Grove

Hamble
End

HAYSBORDER

3

GAZELEY ROAD

Icknield Way Path

MOULTON ROAD

MILL ROAD

THE STREET

MILL
VW

Pit (dis)

HIGHAM ROAD

Pit (dis)

Pit
(dis)

Upper
Green

BURGATE ROAD

Church
Farm

COLTHORPE LANE

ALL SAINTS
CL

Gazeley

PH

STUBBIN'S
LA

HIGHWOOD DR

Manor
Farm

Icknield Way Path

Frogs
Hall

64

HIGHWOOD DR

TITHE
CLOSE

Mound

Farriers
End

2

DALHAM RD B1085

MILL RD

High
Wood

Dalby's
Plantation

Bushy
Plantation

Bluebutton
Wood

Desning
Hall Farm

BROCKLEY LANE

Sewage
Works

Rosbrook
Plantation

Big Crane's
Wood

Moat

IP29

Denham End

63

Shadowbush
Wood

Blocksey
Wood

Motte & Bailey

Denham
Castle

Hockerhill
Wood

Hawson
Hills

Brick
Kiln Wood

1

Icknield Way
Path

Dalham
Hall

BARROW ROAD

Parson's
Plantation

BEECH RD

62

GAZELEY ROAD

Icknield Way Path

GAZELEY
RD

CHURCH LANE

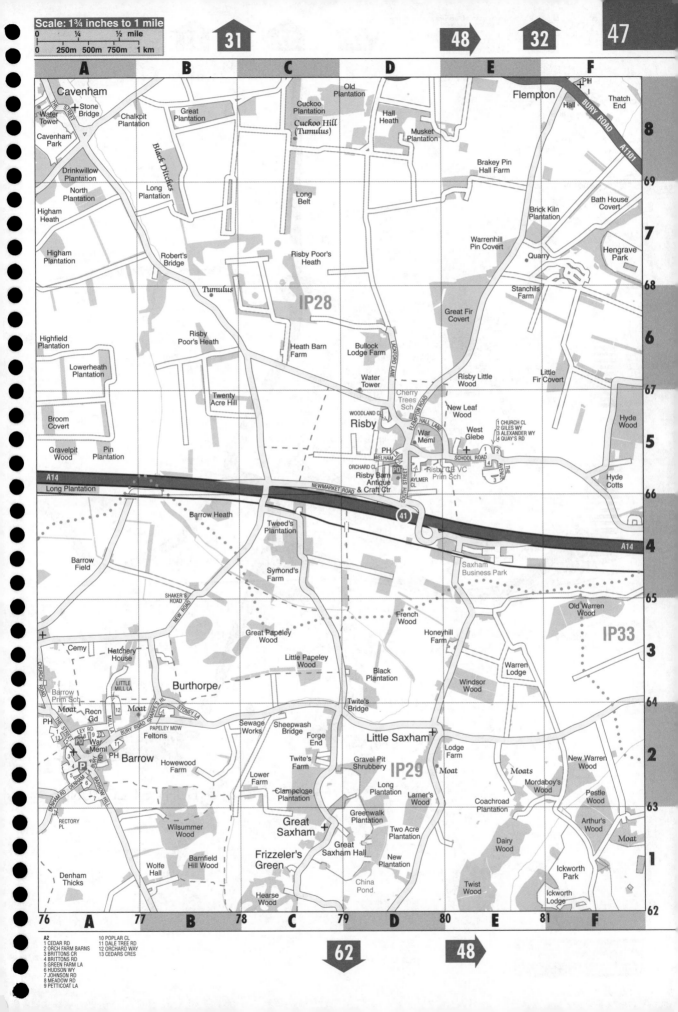

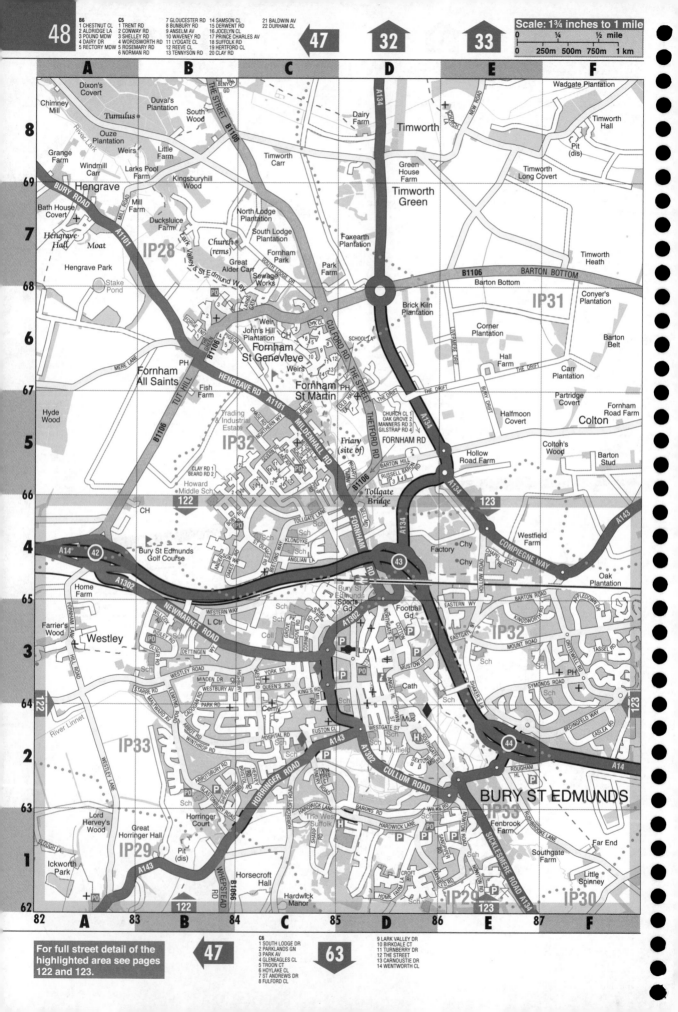

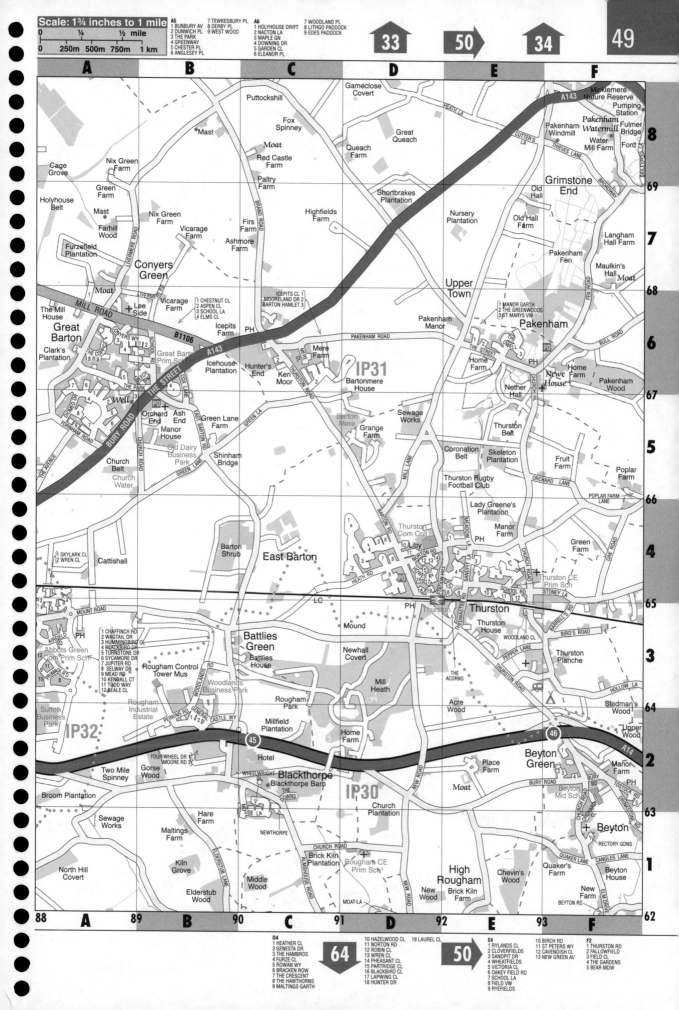

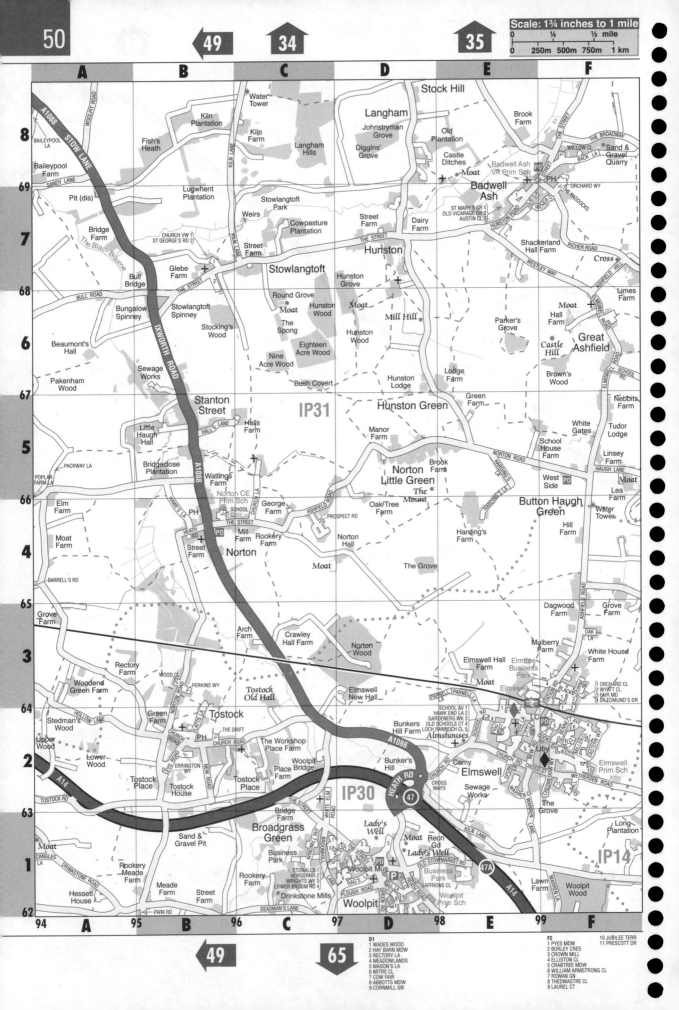

Scale: 1¾ inches to 1 mile

0 ¼ ½ mile
0 250m 500m 750m 1 km

A   B   C   D   E   F

8
69
7
68
6
67
5
66
4
65
3
64
2
63
1
62

Stock Hill
Langham
Johnstryman Grove
Diggins' Grove
Old Plantation
Castle Ditches
Brook Farm
THE STREET
THE BROADWAY
WILLOW CL
Sand & Gravel Quarry
BACK CL
Badwell Ash VA Prim Sch
P.O.
PH
ORCHARD WY
Badwell Ash
Moat
RICHER CL

Water Tower
Kiln Plantation
Kiln Farm
Langham Hills
KILN LANE

Fish's Heath

BAILEYPOOL LA
A1088 STOW LANE
Baileypool Farm
SANDY LANE
Pit (dis)
Lugwhent Plantation
Weirs
Stowlangtoft Park
Cowpasture Plantation
Street Farm
Street Farm
Dairy Farm
Hunston
St MARY'S CR 1
OLD VICARAGE DR 2
AUSTIN CL 3
HUNSTON ROAD
Shackerland Hall Farm
WESTLEY WAY
RICHER ROAD
ASHFIELD HILL
Cross

Bridge Farm
The Black Bourne
CHURCH VW 1
St GEORGE'S RD 2
Glebe Farm
THE STREET
Bull Bridge
BULL ROAD
IXWORTH ROAD
Stowlangtoft
Round Grove
Moat
Hunston Wood
The Spong
Hunston Grove
Moat
Mill Hill
Parker's Grove
Castle Hill
Great Ashfield
Limes Farm
Hall Farm
Moat
ELMSWELL ROAD

Beaumont's Hall
Pakenham Wood
Bungalow Spinney
Stowlangtoft Spinney
Stocking's Wood
Nine Acre Wood
Eighteen Acre Wood
Bush Covert
Hunston Wood
Hunston Lodge
Lodge Farm
Brown's Wood
Castle Hill
Nebbits Farm
White Gates
Tudor Lodge
Linsey Farm
SCHOOL LANE

Sewage Works
IP31
Hunston Green
Green Farm
School House Farm
HAUGH LANE
Moat
Lea Farm

Stanton Street
HALL'S LANE
Halls Farm
Manor Farm
Brook Farm
Norton Little Green
The Mount
NORTON ROAD
West Side
P.O.
Button Haugh Green
Hill Farm
Water Tower

Little Haugh Hall
PACKWAY LA
POPLAR FARM LA
Bridgeclose Plantation
A1088
Watlings Farm
Norton CE Prim Sch
SCHOOL CL
George Farm
Oak Tree Farm
HARDING'S LA
Harding's Farm
ASHFIELD RD

Elm Farm
Moat Farm
BARRELL'S RD
PH
THE STREET
CHURCH LA
Mill Farm
Rookery Farm
PROSPECT RD
Norton Hall
HEATH RD
P.O.
Street Farm
Norton
Moat
The Grove
Dagwood Farm
Grove Farm
White House Farm
OAK LA

Grove Farm
Arch Farm
Crawley Hall Farm
Norton Wood
Mulberry Farm
Elmswell Hall Farm
Elmtree Business Park
Moat
Elmswell
1 ORCHARD CL
2 WYATT CL
3 FAIR MD
4 St EDMUND'S DR

Rectory Farm
WOOD CL
PERKINS WY
Tostock Old Hall
Elmswell New Hall
PARNELL'S
PARNELL
STATION RD
BLACKBOURN
SCHOOL AV 1
HAWK END LA 2
GARDENERS WK 3
OLD SCHOOLS CT 4
LOCH RANNOCH CL 5

Woodend Green Farm
Green Farm
RATTS LA
Tostock
THE DRIFT
Bunkers Hill Farm
Almshouses
CHURCH RD
NEW RD
CROSS ST
Elmswell Prim Sch
WETHERDEN ROAD

Stedman's Wood
HOLLOW LANE
LEYS ROAD
NORTON ROAD
PH
CHURCH ROAD
The Workshop
Place Farm
Woolpit Place Farm
Woolpit Place Bridge Farm
HEATH RD
CROSS WAYS
Cemy
Elmswell
Libry
WARREN CL
WARREN LA
EASTERN WY
Elmswell Prim Sch

A14
Upper Wood
Lower Wood
ERRINGTON WY
NEW ROAD
Tostock Place
Tostock House
Bridge Farm
THE STREET
WHITE ELM RD
IP30
47
Bunker's Hill
Sewage Works
The Grove

TOSTOCK RD
Moat
CANGLES LA
DRINKSTONE ROAD
Rookery Meade Farm
Meade Farm
Sand & Gravel Pit
Street Farm
Broadgrass Green
Business Park
Rookery Farm
WINDMILL LANE
THIMBLEROW
Lady's Well
Moat
Lady's Well
Recn Gd
OLD STOWMARKET RD
Business Park
SAFFRONS CL
47A
A14
Long Plantation
IP14
Lawn Farm
Woolpit Wood

Hessett House
PARK RD
Drinkstone Mills
DEADMAN'S LANE
STONALLS 1
HORSEFAIR 2
WRIGHTS WY 3
LOWER BROOM RD 4
Woolpit Mus
P
RAG'S LA
PLOUGH ROAD
Woolpit
Woolpit Prim Sch

49   34   35   49   65

94   95   96   97   98   99
A   B   C   D   E   F

D1
1 WADES WOOD
2 HAY BARN MDW
3 RECTORY LA
4 MEADOWLANDS
5 MASON'S LA
6 MITRE CL
7 COW FAIR
8 ABBOTTS MDW
9 CORNMILL GN

F2
1 PYES MDW
2 BORLEY CRES
3 CROWN MILL
4 ELLISTON CL
5 CRABTREE MDW
6 WILLIAM ARMSTRONG CL
7 ROWAN GN
8 THEDWASTRE CL
9 LAUREL CT
10 JUBILEE TERR
11 PRESCOTT DR

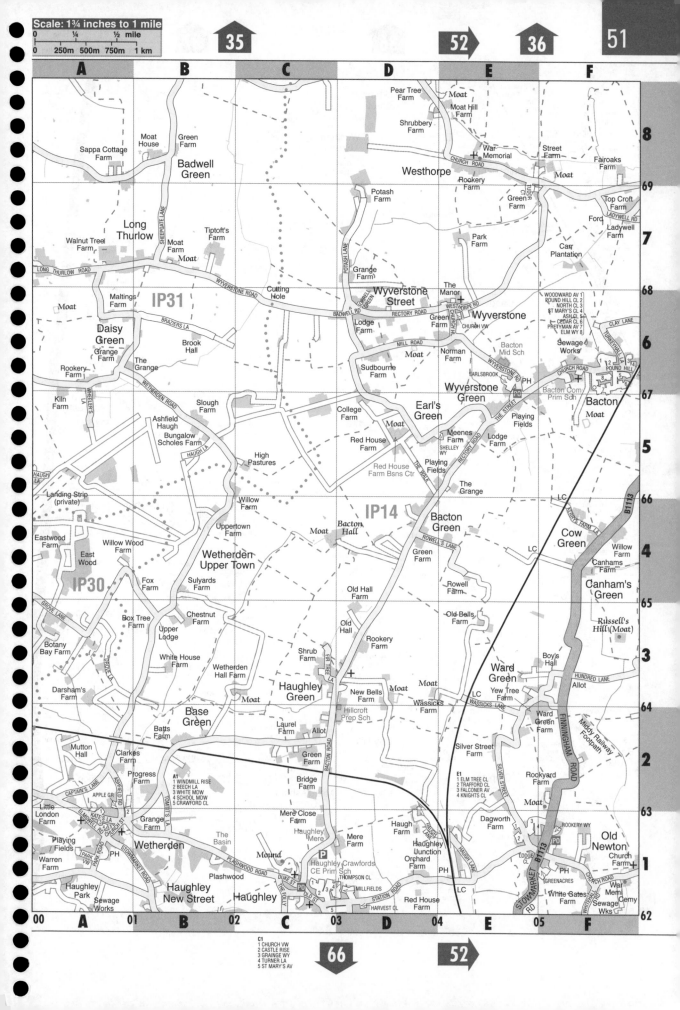

A B C D E F

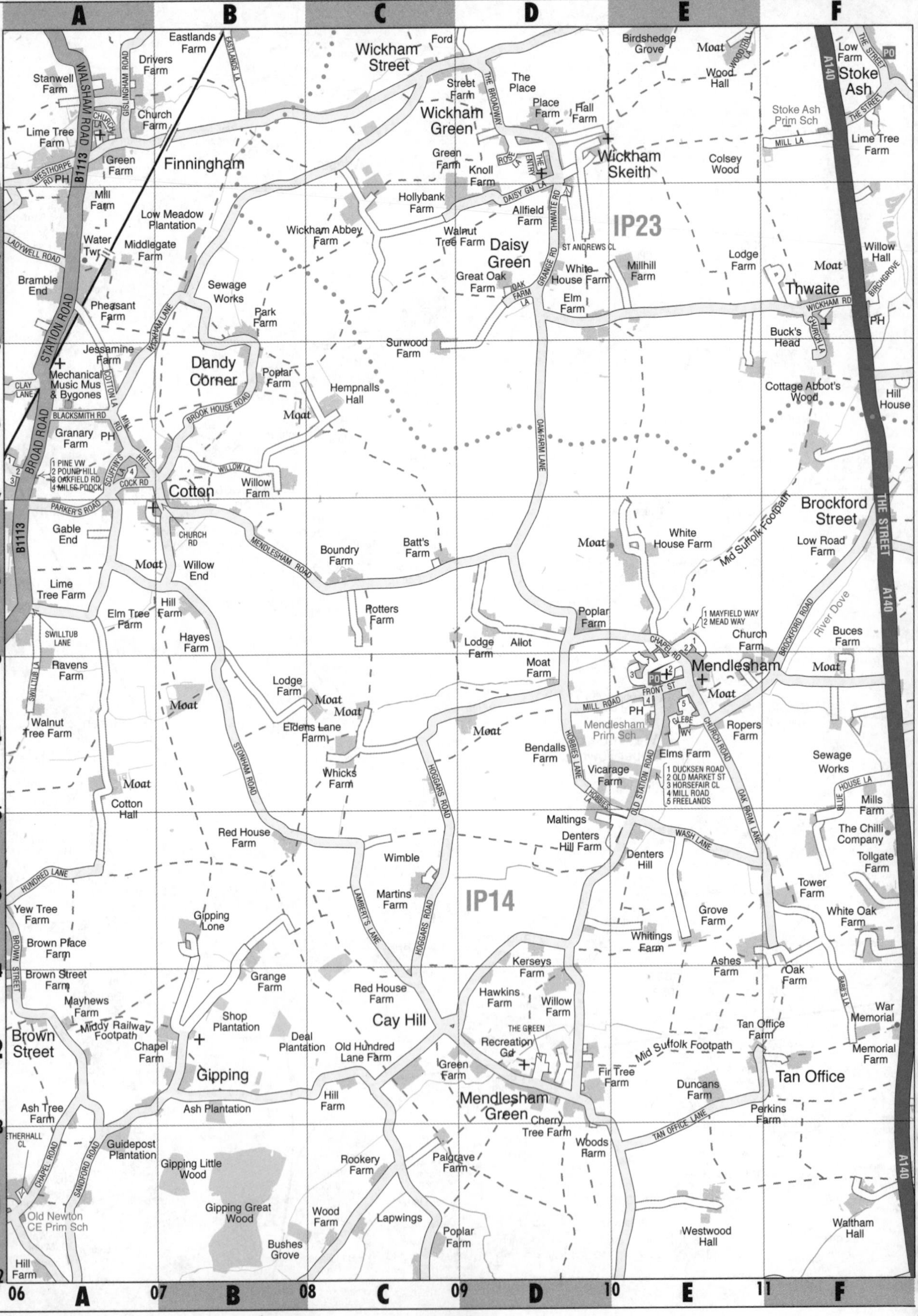

8
7
69
68
67
66
65
64
63
62
6
5
4
3
2
1

IP23

IP14

Stanwell Farm
Lime Tree Farm
Finningham
Eastlands Farm
Drivers Farm
Church Farm
Green Farm
Mill Farm
Water Twr
Middlegate Farm
Low Meadow Plantation
Sewage Works
Park Farm
Pheasant Farm
Jessamine Farm
Dandy Corner
Poplar Farm
Hempnalls Hall
Moat
Bramble End
Mechanical Music Mus & Bygones
Granary Farm
Cotton
Willow End
Willow La
Gable End
Lime Tree Farm
Elm Tree Farm
Hill Farm
Hayes Farm
Moat
Ravens Farm
Walnut Tree Farm
Moat
Cotton Hall
Lodge Farm
Moat
Eldens Lane Farm
Whicks Farm
Red House Farm
Wimble
Martins Farm
Gipping Lone
Grange Farm
Shop Plantation
Deal Plantation
Red House Farm
Cay Hill
Yew Tree Farm
Brown Place Farm
Brown Street Farm
Mayhews Farm
Middy Railway Footpath
Chapel Farm
Gipping
Hill Farm
Ash Plantation
Brown Street
Ash Tree Farm
Guidepost Plantation
Gipping Little Wood
Rookery Farm
Gipping Great Wood
Wood Farm
Lapwings
Bushes Grove
Palgrave Farm
Poplar Farm
Old Newton CE Prim Sch
Hill Farm

Wickham Street
Ford
Wickham Green
Street Farm
The Broadway
The Place
Place Farm
Hall Farm
Wickham Skeith
Birdshedge Grove
Moat
Wood Hall
Green Farm
Knoll Farm
Hollybank Farm
Walnut Tree Farm
Allfield Farm
Daisy Green
Great Oak Farm
White House Farm
Elm Farm
Millhill Farm
Colsey Wood
Lodge Farm
Stoke Ash
Low Farm
Lime Tree Farm
Willow Hall
Thwaite
Moat
Buck's Head
Cottage Abbot's Wood
Hill House
Wickham Abbey Farm
Surwood Farm
Batt's Farm
Moat
White House Farm
Brockford Street
Low Road Farm
Boundry Farm
Rotters Farm
Lodge Farm
Allot
Poplar Farm
Moat Farm
Moat
Mendlesham
Church Farm
Buces Farm
River Dove
Moat
Bendalls Farm
Vicarage Farm
Elms Farm
Ropers Farm
Mendlesham Prim Sch
Sewage Works
Maltings
Denters Hill Farm
Denters Hill
Grove Farm
Whitings Farm
Mills Farm
The Chilli Company
Tollgate Farm
Tower Farm
White Oak Farm
Ashes Farm
Oak Farm
War Memorial
Memorial Farm
Kerseys Farm
Hawkins Farm
Willow Farm
The Green Recreation Gd
Fir Tree Farm
Duncans Farm
Tan Office Farm
Tan Office
Green Farm
Mendlesham Green
Cherry Tree Farm
Woods Farm
Perkins Farm
Westwood Hall
Waltham Hall

51 67

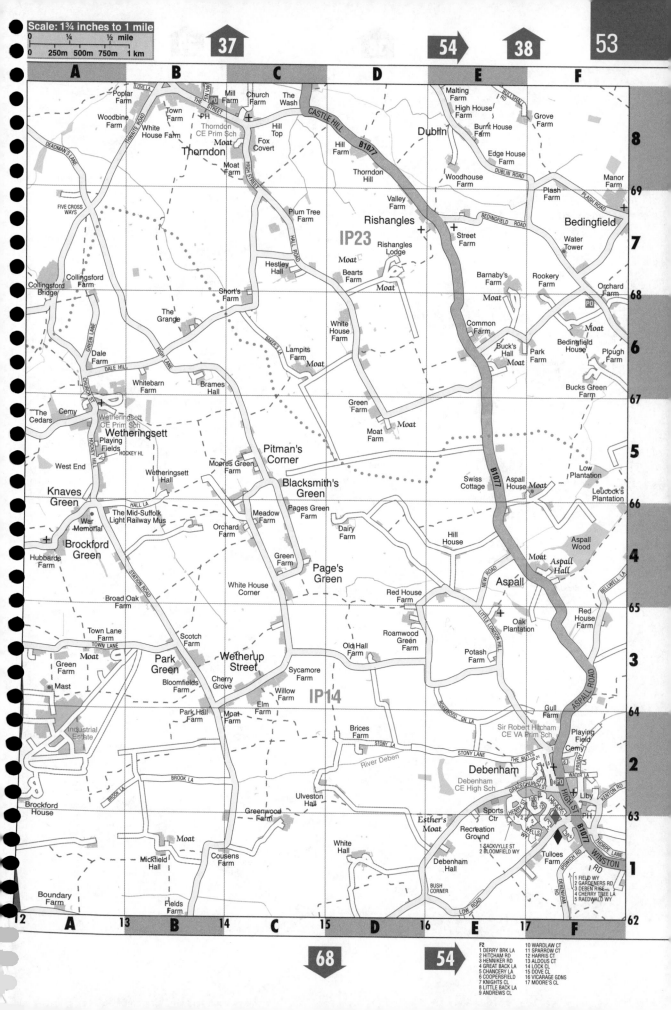

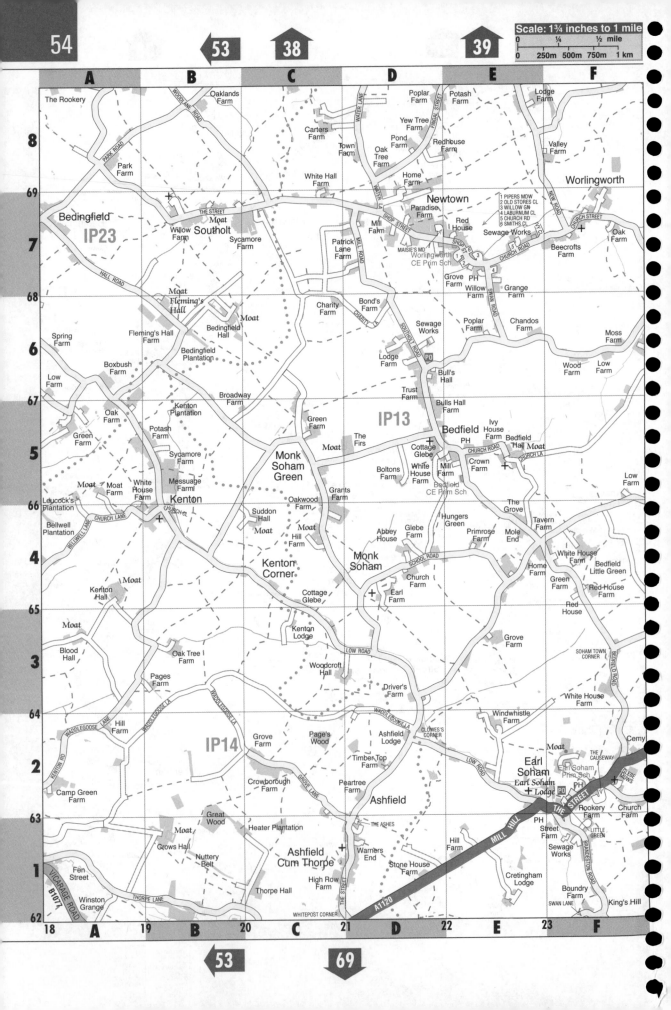

A B C D E F

The Rookery

Oaklands Farm

Poplar Farm Potash Farm Lodge Farm

8

Park Farm

Carters Farm

Yew Tree Farm Valley Farm

Town Farm

Pond Farm Redhouse Farm

Oak Tree Farm

69

White Hall Farm

Home Farm

Newtown

Worlingworth

Bedingfield IP23

Moat Willow Farm Southolt

The Street

Paradise Farm

Red House

7

Sycamore Farm

Mill Farm

Patrick Lane Farm

1 PIPERS MDW
2 OLD STORES CL
3 WILLOW GN
4 LABURNUM CL
5 CHURCH RD
6 SMITHS CL

Worlingworth CE Prim Sch

Sewage Works

Beecrofts Farm

Oak Farm

MAISIE'S MD

Grove Farm Willow Farm PH Grange Farm

Hall Road

68

Moat Fleming's Hall

Charity Farm Bond's Farm

Sewage Works

Poplar Farm Chandos Farm

Moss Farm

Spring Farm

Moat Bedingfield Hall

Fleming's Hall Farm

Lodge Farm PO

Wood Farm Low Farm

6

Boxbush Farm

Bedingfield Plantation

Bull's Hall

Trust Farm

Low Farm

Green Farm

Oak Farm

Broadway Farm

Kenton Plantation

Green Farm

IP13

Bulls Hall Farm

Ivy House Farm

Bedfield

67

5

Potash Farm

Sycamore Farm

Moat

The Firs

Cottage Glebe

PH

Crown Farm Bedfield Hall Moat

Church Road CHURCH LA

Green Farm

Messuage Farm

Monk Soham Green

Boltons Farm

White House Farm

Mill Farm

Low Farm

White House Farm

Bedfield CE Prim Sch

66

Moat Moat

Kenton

Suddon Hall

Oakwood Farm

Grants Farm

Hungers Green

The Grove

Tavern Farm

Leucock's Plantation

CHURCH CL

Moat Moat Hill Farm

Abbey House

Glebe Farm

Primrose Farm

Mole End

White House Farm Bedfield Little Green

Bellwell Plantation

CHURCH LANE BELLWELL LANE

Kenton Corner

Monk Soham

SCHOOL ROAD

Home Farm

Green Farm Red House Farm

4

Moat

Cottage Glebe

Earl Farm

Church Farm

Red House

Kenton Hall

Moat

65

Blood Hall

Kenton Lodge

LOW ROAD

Grove Farm

SOHAM TOWN CORNER

Oak Tree Farm

Woodcroft Hall

White House Farm

3

Pages Farm

Driver's Farm

Windwhistle Farm

WADDLEGOOSE LANE WADDLEGOOSE LA

WADDLEGOOSE LA

Moat Cemy

64

Hill Farm

Grove Farm

Page's Wood

Ashfield Lodge

CLOWES'S CORNER

THE CAUSEWAY

WADDLEGOOSE LANE KENTON RD

IP14

GROVE LANE

Timber Top Farm

LOW ROAD

Earl Soham

Earl Soham Prim Sch PH

2

Camp Green Farm

Crowborough Farm

Peartree Farm

Ashfield

Earl Soham Lodge GLEBE MDWS

Rookery Farm Church Farm

Great Wood

Heater Plantation

THE ASHES

Hill Farm

PH Street Farm LITTLE GREEN

63

Crows Hall

Moat

Warners End

Sewage Works

Fen Street

Nuttery Belt

Ashfield Cum Thorpe

Stone House Farm

MILL HILL

Cretingham Lodge

Boundry Farm

King's Hill

1

VICARAGE ROAD B1077

Winston Grange

THORPE LANE

Thorpe Hall

High Row Farm

THE STREET

A1120

SWAN LANE

BRANDESTON ROAD

62

WHITEPOST CORNER

18 A 19 B 20 C 21 D 22 E 23 F

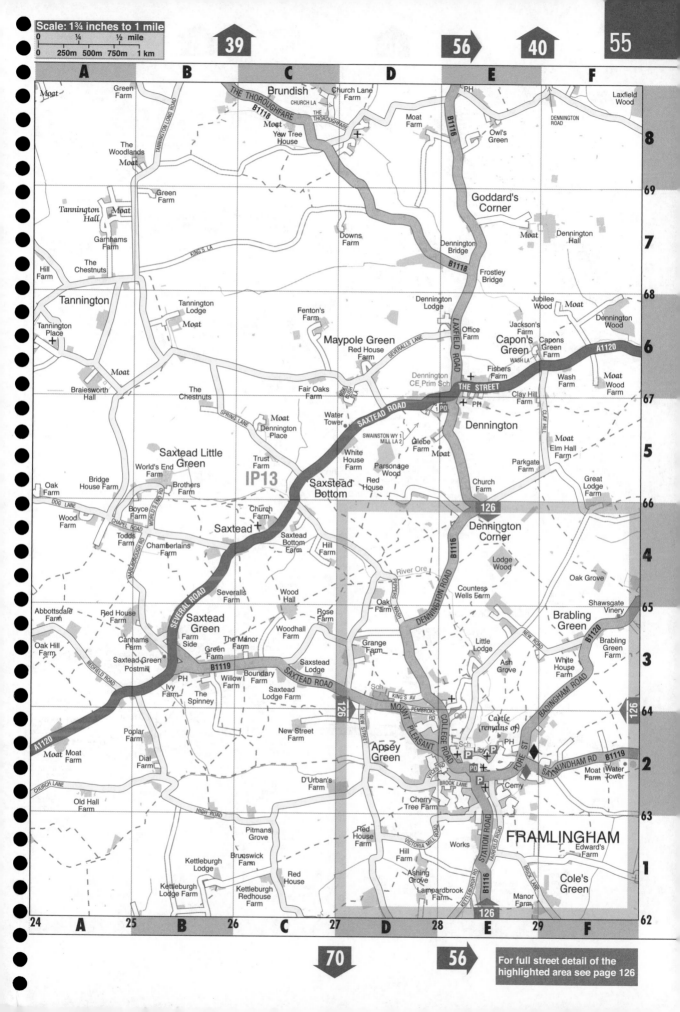

A   B   C   D   E   F

Moat
Green Farm
The Woodlands
Moat

Brundish
THE THOROUGHFARE
B1118
CHURCH LA
Church Lane Farm
THE THOROUGHFARE
Moat
Yew Tree House

PH
B1118
Moat Farm
DENNINGTON ROAD
Owl's Green
Laxfield Wood

8

Tannington Hall
Moat
Green Farm
KING'S LA

Downs Farm

Goddard's Corner

Moat
Dennington Hall

69

7

Garnhams Farm
Hill Farm
The Chestnuts

Dennington Bridge
B1118
Frostley Bridge

Jubilee Wood
Moat
Dennington Wood

68

Tannington
Tannington Lodge
Moat

Fenton's Farm
Maypole Green
Red House Farm
SEVERALLS LANE

Dennington Lodge
Office Farm

Jackson's Farm
Capon's Green
Capons Green Farm
A1120

6

Tannington Place
Moat
Braiesworth Hall
The Chestnuts
SPRING LANE
BOX BUSH LA

Fair Oaks Farm

LAXFIELD ROAD
Dennington CE Prim Sch
THE STREET
PH
PO

Fishers Farm
WASH LA
Clay Hill Farm
CLAY HILL
Wash Farm
Moat Wood Farm

67

Saxstead Little Green
World's End Farm
Brothers Farm
Trust Farm

Moat
Dennington Place
Water Tower
White House Farm
SWAINSTON WY 1
MILL LA 2
Glebe Farm
SAXTEAD ROAD
Parsonage Wood
Red House

Dennington
Moat
Moat
Elm Hall Farm
Parkgate Farm
Great Lodge Farm

5

Oak Farm
DOG LANE
Bridge House Farm
Boyce Farm
CHAPEL ROAD
WORLD'S END RD
Saxstead Bottom
Saxtead
Church Farm

Church Farm

126
Dennington Corner

66

Wood Farm
Todds Farm
Chamberlains Farm
MARLBOROUGH RD
Saxtead Bottom Farm
Hill Farm

River Ore
PEPPERS WASH
Oak Farm
B1116
DENNINGTON ROAD
Lodge Wood
Countess Wells Farm
Oak Grove
Shawsgate Vinery

4

65

Abbottsdale Farm
Red House Farm
SEVERALL ROAD
Severalls Farm
Saxtead Green
Wood Hall
Rose Farm
Woodhall Farm
Grange Farm
Little Lodge
Ash Grove
NEW ROAD
Brabling Green
White House Farm
B1120
Brabling Green Farm

Oak Hill Farm
BEDFIELD ROAD
Canhams Farm
Saxtead Green Postmill
Farm Side
Green Farm
The Manor Farm
B1119
Willow Farm
Boundary Farm
SAXTEAD ROAD
Saxtead Lodge
New Street Farm
126
NEW STREET
Sch
KING'S AV
MOUNT PLEASANT
COLLEGE ROAD
PEMBROKE RD
Coll
Castle (remains of)
Sch
BADINGHAM ROAD
126

3

A1120
Moat
Moat Farm
Dial Farm
PH
Ivy Farm
The Spinney
Saxtead Lodge Farm
Apsey Green
Liby
P
P
PO
Fore St
PH
SAXMUNDHAM RD
Moat Farm
B1119
Water Tower

2

CHURCH LANE
Old Hall Farm
HIGH ROAD
D'Urban's Farm
Cerny
Cherry Tree Farm
BROOK LANE
P
FRAMLINGHAM
Edward's Farm

63

Pitmans Grove
Brunswick Farm
Red House
Red House Farm
Hill Farm
Ashing Grove
VICTORIA MILL ROAD
Works
STATION ROAD
FAIRFIELD ROAD
BRICK LANE
Cole's Green

1

Kettleburgh Lodge
Kettleburgh Lodge Farm
Kettleburgh Redhouse Farm
KETTLEBURGH RD
Lampardbrook Farm
B1116
126
Manor Farm

62

24   A   25   B   26   C   27   D   28   E   29   F

For full street detail of the highlighted area see page 126

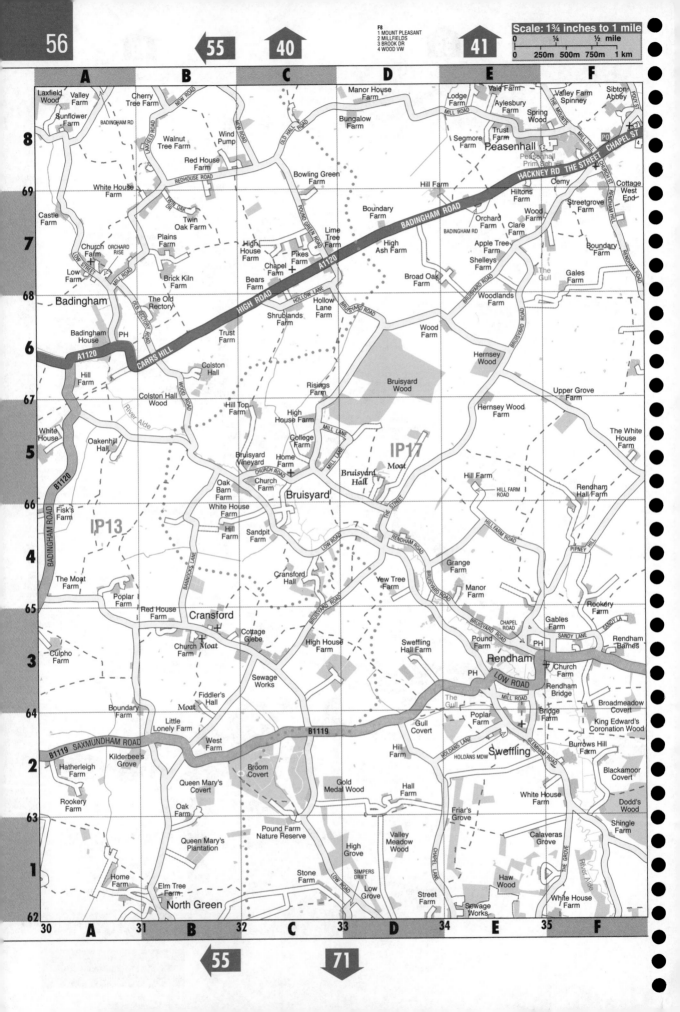

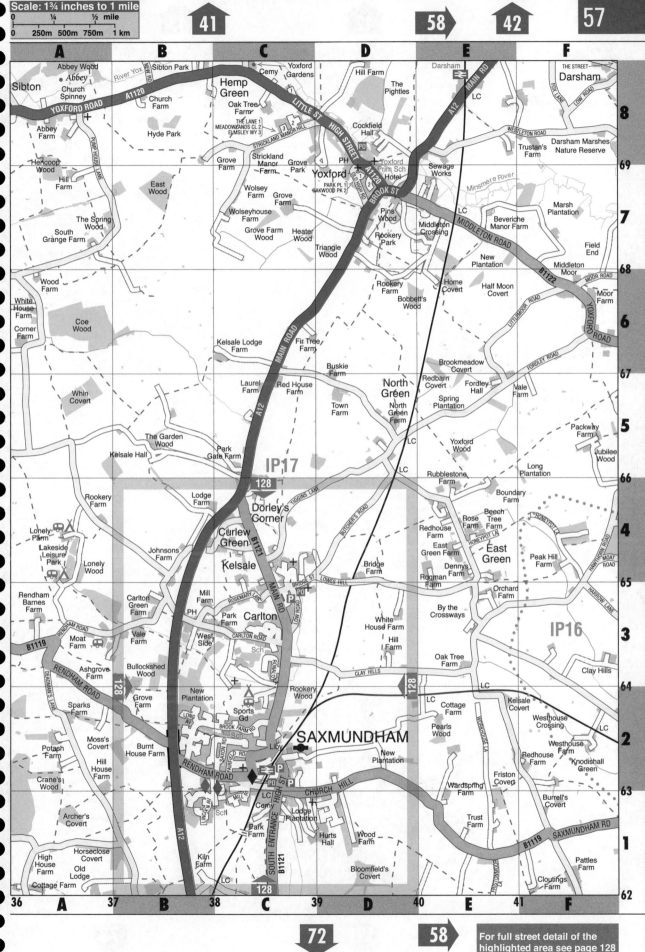

For full street detail of the highlighted area see page 128

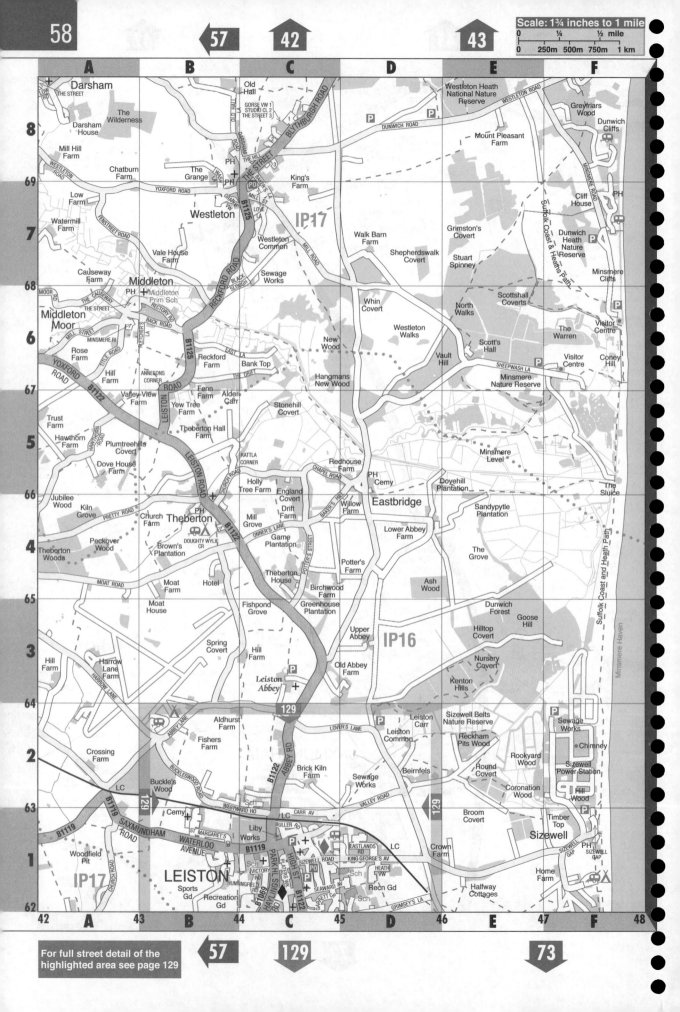

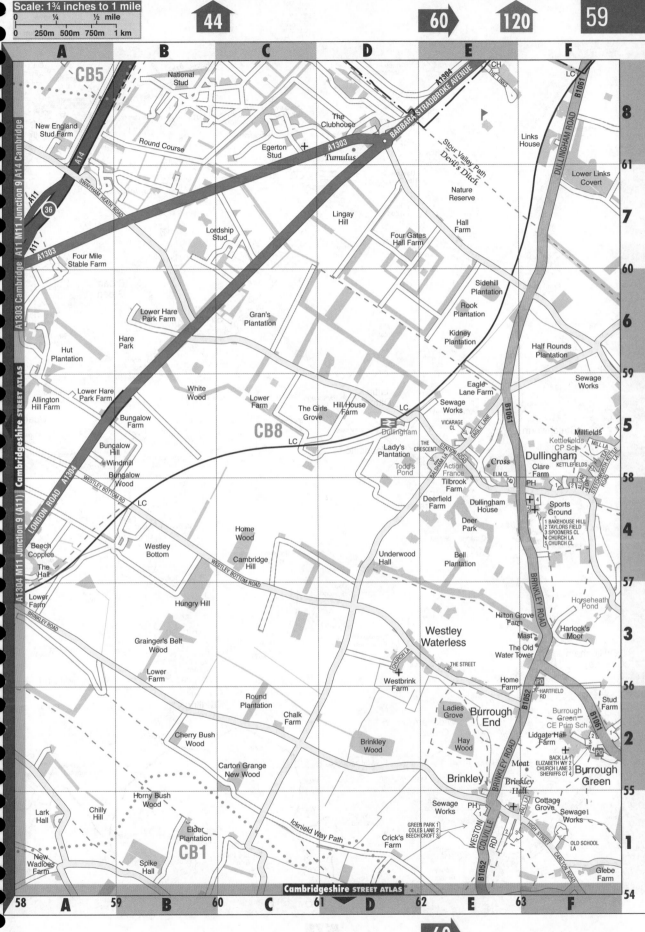

A   B   C   D   E   F

CB5

National Stud

New England Stud Farm

The Clubhouse

A14

SWAFFHAM HEATH ROAD

Round Course

Egerton Stud

Tumulus

A1303

BARBARA STRADBROKE AVENUE

A1304

THE LINKS

CH

LC

B1061

DULLINGHAM ROAD

Stour Valley Path
Devil's Ditch

Links House

Lower Links Covert

8

61

A11 M11 Junction 9 A14 Cambridge

36

A11

A1303 Cambridge

A1303

Four Mile Stable Farm

Lordship Stud

Lingay Hill

Four Gates Hall Farm

Nature Reserve

Hall Farm

7

60

Lower Hare Park Farm

Gran's Plantation

Sidehill Plantation

Rook Plantation

Kidney Plantation

Half Rounds Plantation

6

Hare Park

Hut Plantation

Cambridgeshire STREET ATLAS

Allington Hill Farm

Lower Hare Park Farm

White Wood

Lower Farm

The Girls Grove

Hill House Farm

LC

Eagle Lane Farm

Sewage Works

Sewage Works

59

5

Bungalow Farm

CB8

Dullingham

LC

Lady's Plantation

VICARAGE CL

EAGLE LANE

B1061

Millfields

Kettlefields

Dullingham

MILL LA

Clare Farm

PH

STETCHWORTH KETTLE

KETTLEFIELDS

Bungalow Hill

Windmill

Bungalow Wood

A1304

LONDON ROAD

WESTLEY BOTTOM RD

LC

Todd's Pond

THE CRESCENT

STATION ROAD

BALSHAM LA

Action France

Tilbrook Farm

Cross

ELM CL

Sports Ground

58

4

A1304 M11 Junction 9 (A11)

Beech Coppice

The Hall

Westley Bottom

Home Wood

Cambridge Hill

WESTLEY BOTTOM ROAD

Deerfield Farm

Dullingham House

Deer Park

Bell Plantation

1 BAKEHOUSE HILL
2 TAYLORS FIELD
3 SPOONERS CL
4 CHURCH LA
5 CHURCH CL

57

Lower Farm

Hungry Hill

Underwood Hall

Hilton Grove Farm

Mast

Horseheath Pond

Harlock's Moor

BRINKLEY ROAD

3

Grainger's Belt Wood

Lower Farm

Westley Waterless

CHURCH LA

Westbrink Farm

THE STREET

The Old Water Tower

Home Farm

HARTFIELD RD

PO

Stud Farm

56

Round Plantation

Chalk Farm

Brinkley Wood

Ladies Grove

Burrough End

Hay Wood

B1052

Burrough Green CE Prim Sch

Lidgate Hall Farm

B1061

2

Cherry Bush Wood

Carton Grange New Wood

Horny Bush Wood

Lark Hall

Chilly Hill

Elder Plantation

CB1

Spike Hall

Icknield Way Path

Crick's Farm

GREEN PARK 1
COLES LANE 2
BEECH CROFT 3

Brinkley

Sewage Works

PH

Moat

Brinkley Hall

BRINKLEY ROAD

BACK LA 1
ELIZABETH WY 2
CHURCH LANE 3
SHERIFFS CT 4

Burrough Green

Cottage Grove

HIGH STREET

HALL LA

OLD SCHOOL LA

CARLTON ROAD

Sewage Works

55

New Wadloes Farm

WESTON COLVILLE RD

B1052

Sewage Works

Glebe Farm

1

58   A   59   B   60   C   61   D   62   E   63   F   54

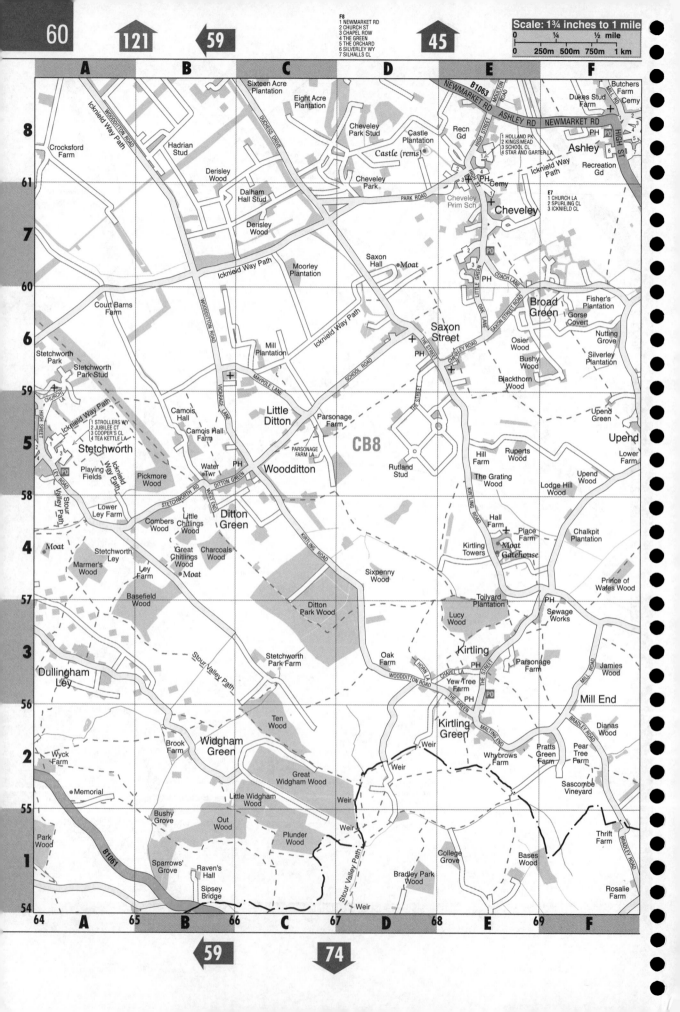

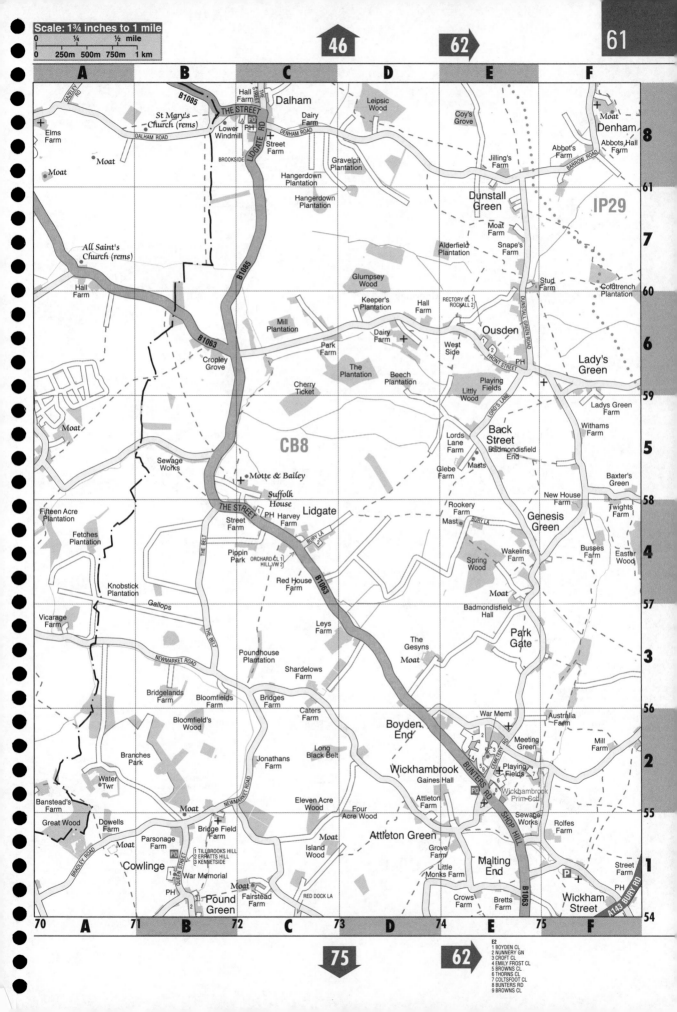

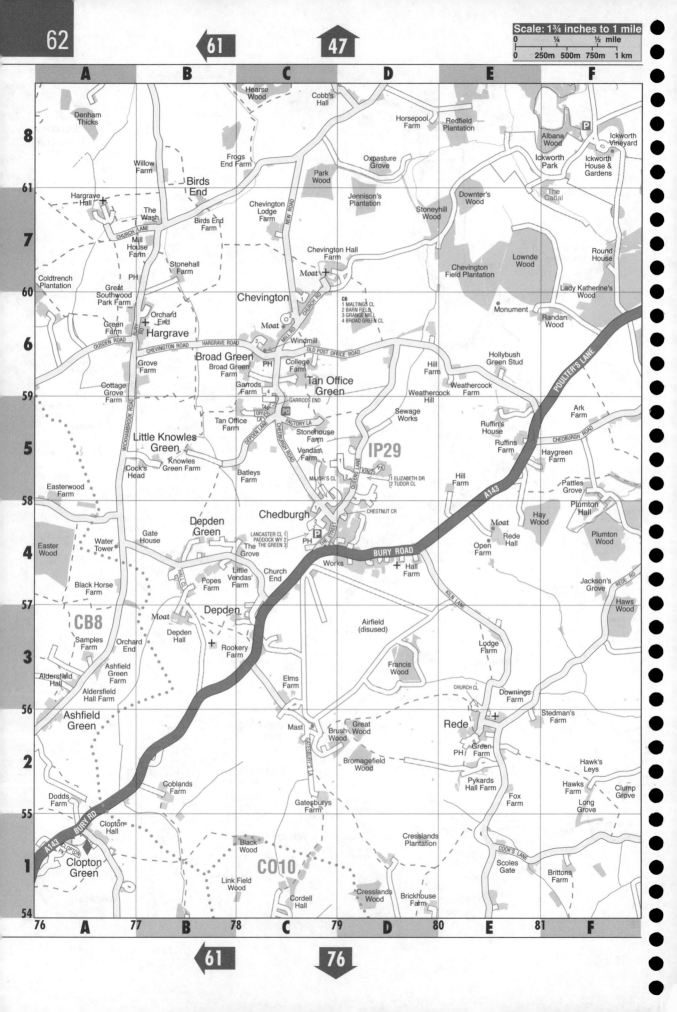

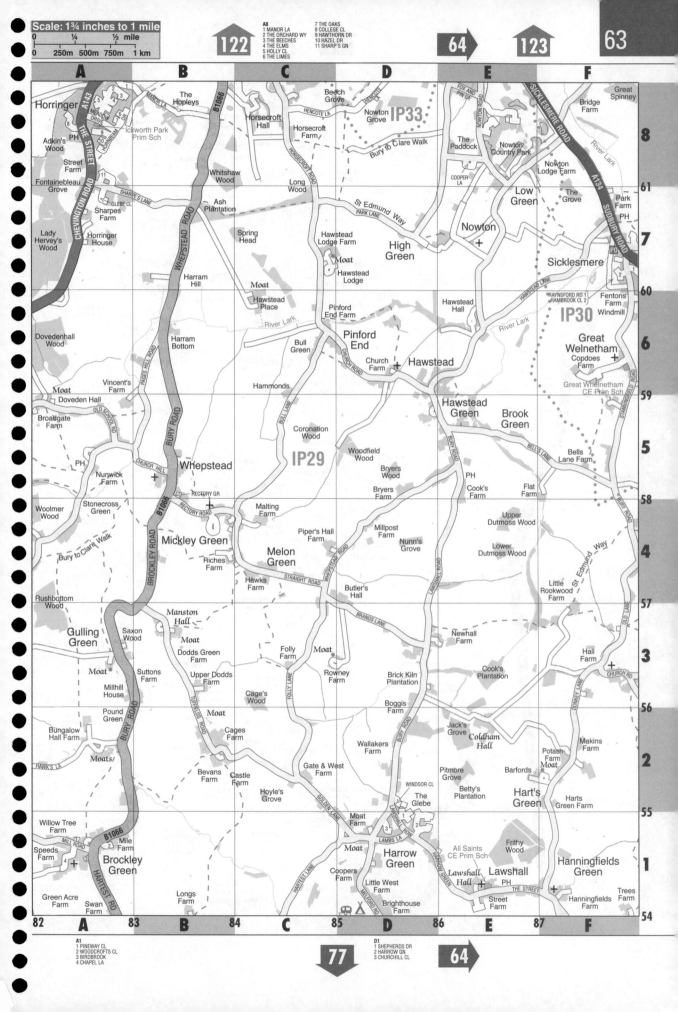

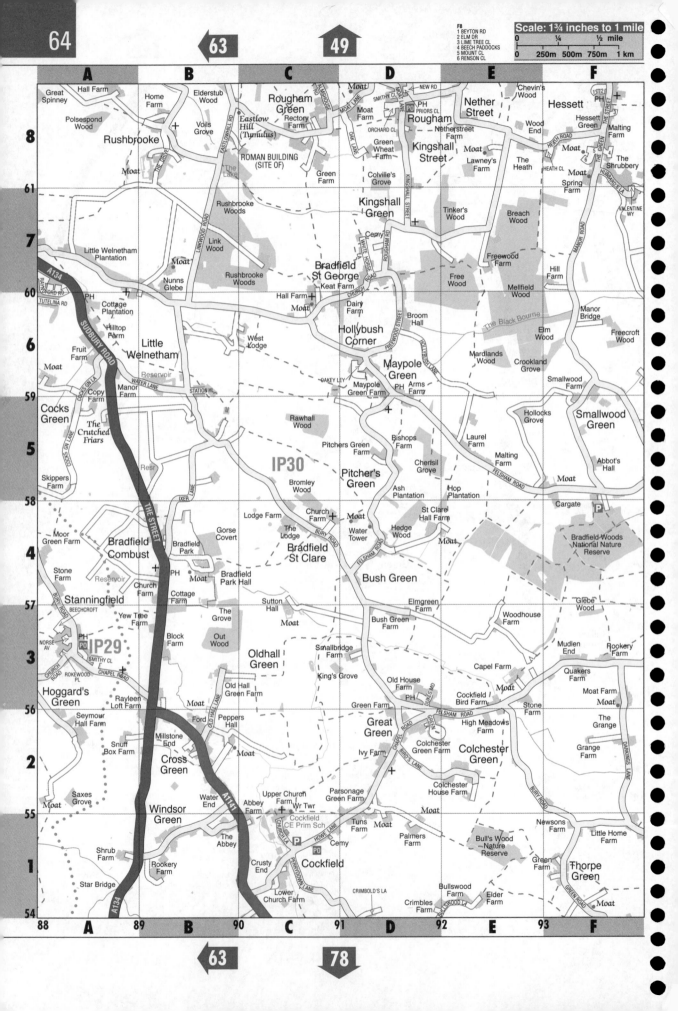

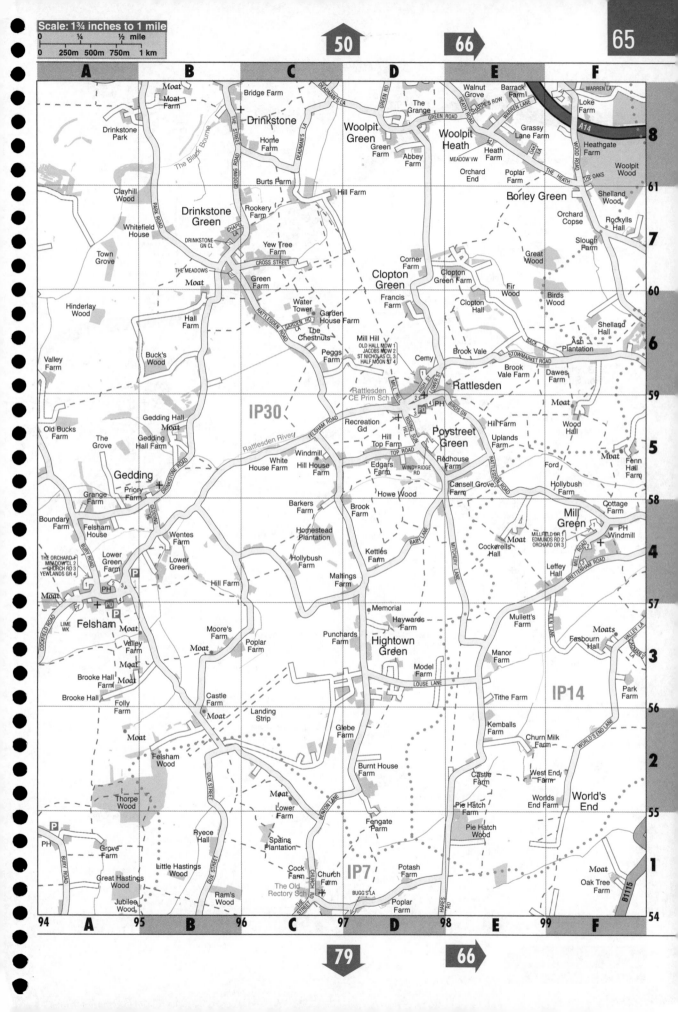

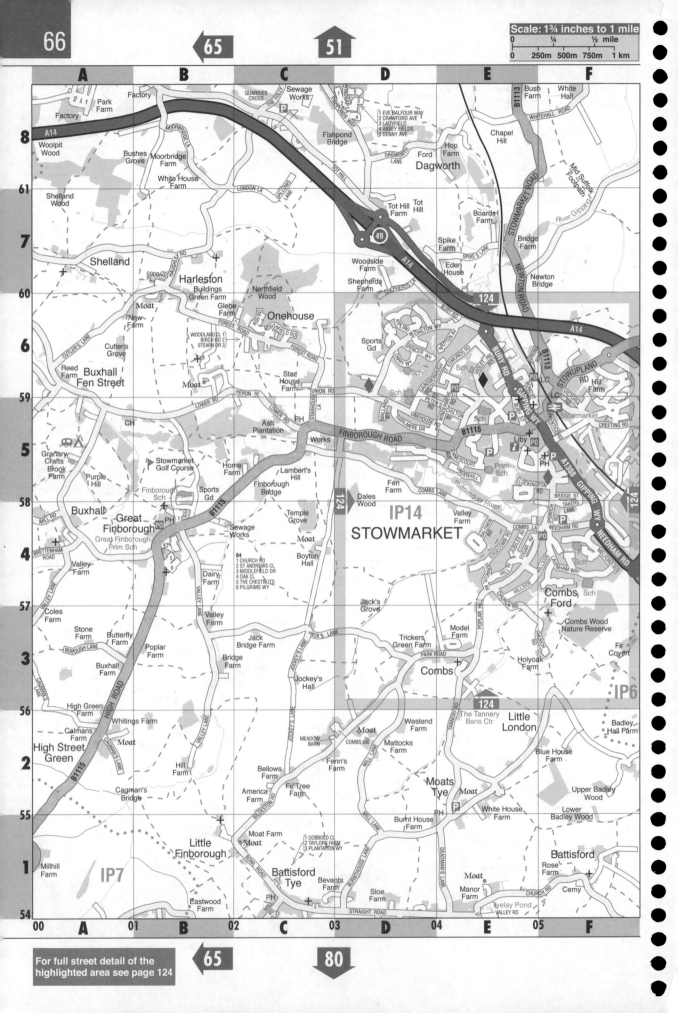

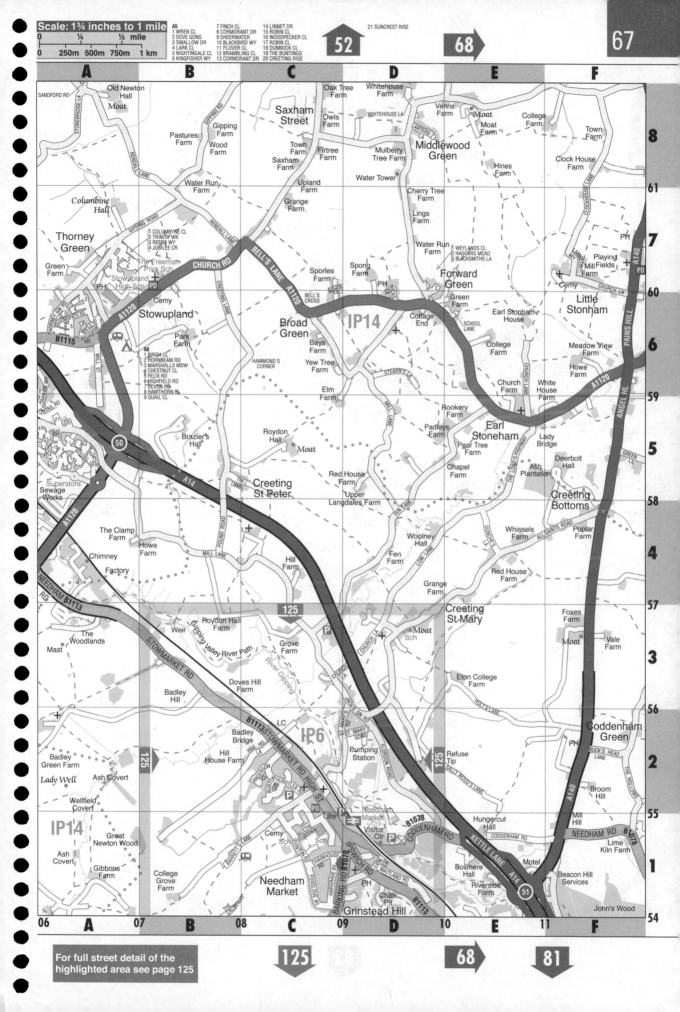

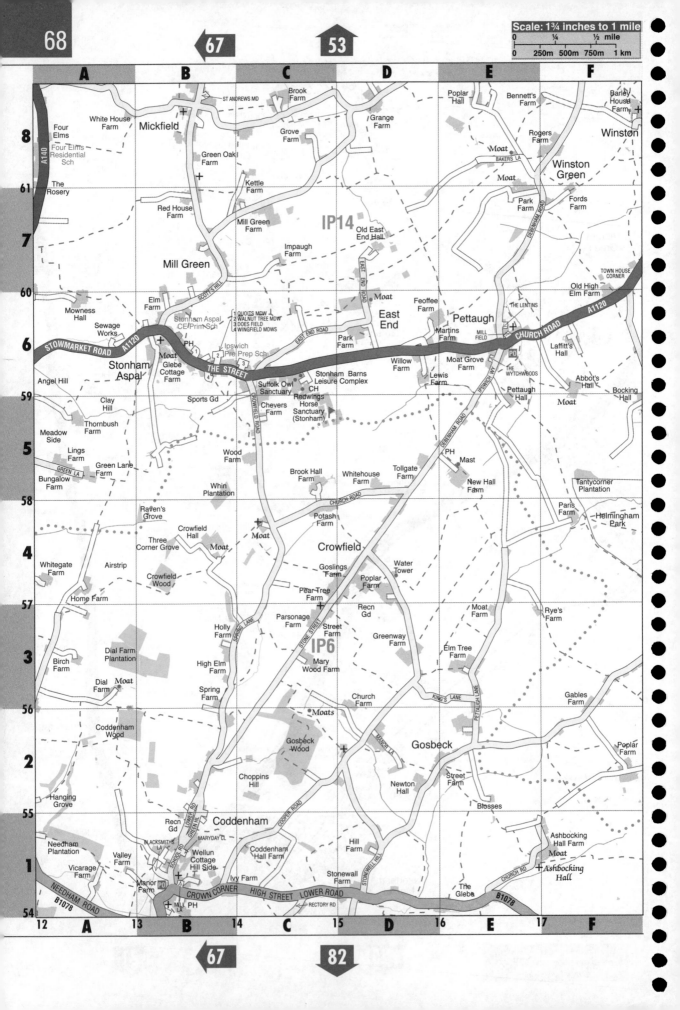

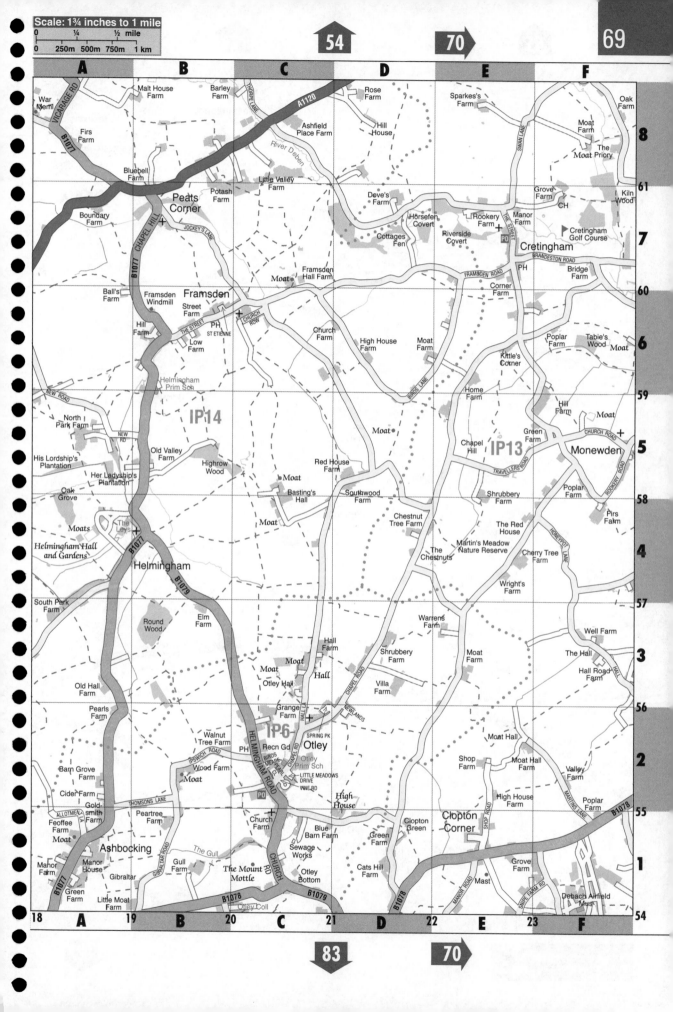

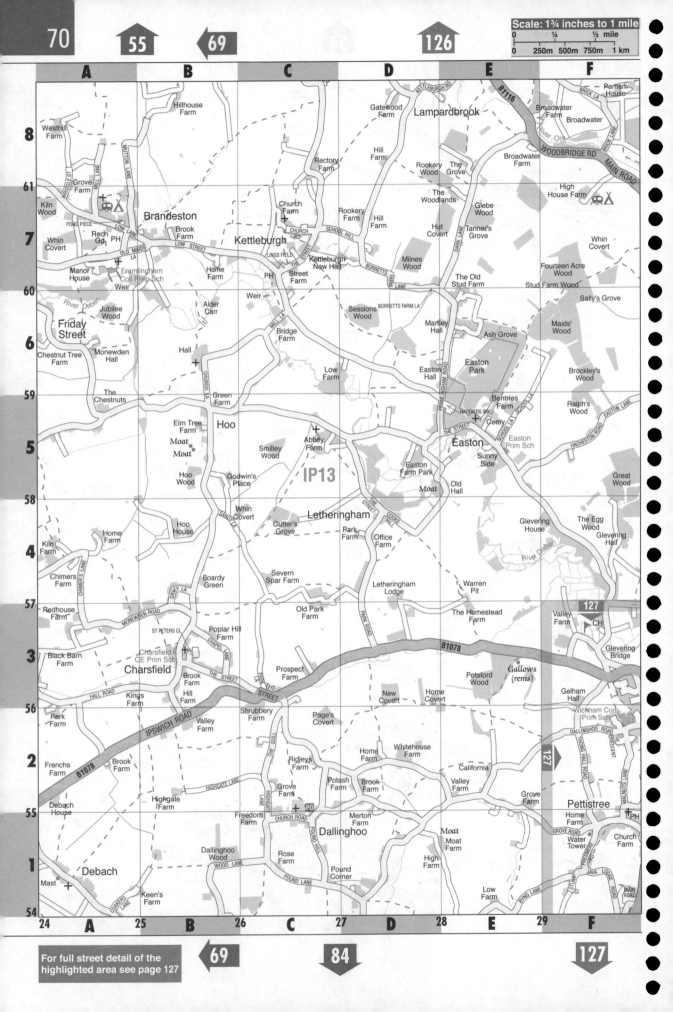

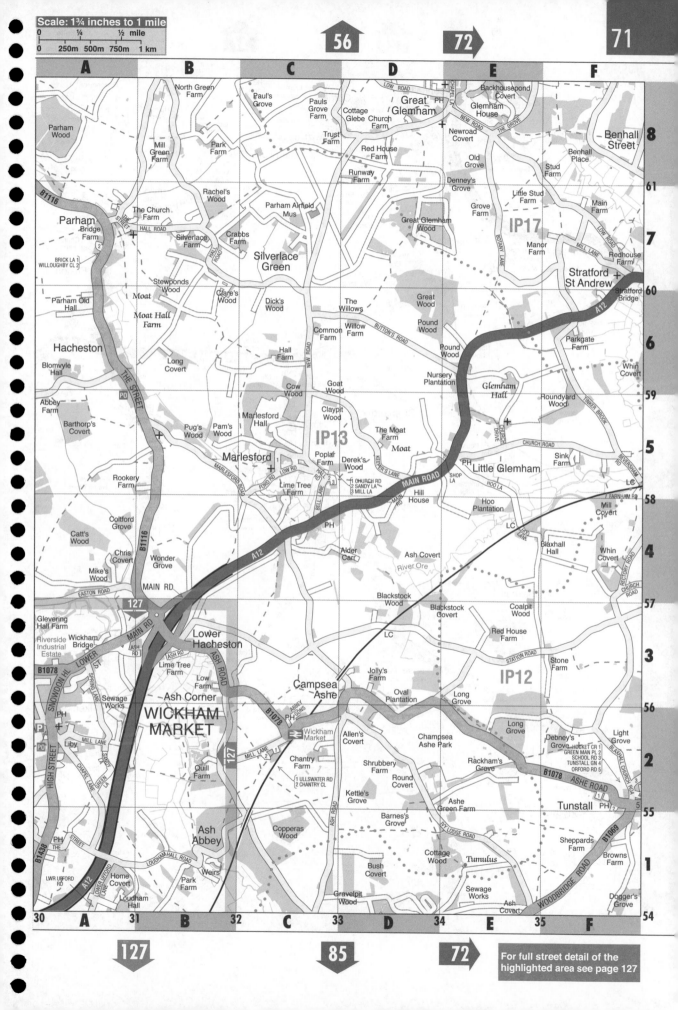

C8
1 CHALFONT DR
2 FORGE CL
3 MEADOW WK
4 FESTIVAL CL

Scale: 1¾ inches to 1 mile
0   ¼   ½ mile
0   250m 500m 750m 1 km

A B C D E F

8 7 61 7 60 6 59 5 58 4 57 3 56 2 55 1 54

Winding Covert
Cemy
Kilkeni Walnut Tree Farm
High Wood
Stewart's Covert
Home Farm
The Walled Garden
Benhall Lodge
Benhall Green
LC
MAIN ROAD
CHURCH HILL
Bigsby's Corner
Leekhill Plantation
Hill Farm
Willow Side
Start Farm
Glebe Farm
Benhall St Marys CE Prim Sch
Smokehouse Farm
THE ST
Sternfield
B1121
Redhouse Farm
High House Farm
Fristonmoor
Fristonmoor Covert
Little Moor Farm
Pear Tree Farm
Laurel Covert
Old World Wood
Grove Wood

White House Farm
Green Farm
Marsh Farm
Brook Farm
Sewage Works
RED LANE
Rudley's Grove
New Covert
SAXMUNDHAM ROAD
Moor Farm
Friston House
Friston House Wood
CHURCH ROAD
Church Farm
Friston
PH
ALDEBURGH ROAD

Friday Street Farm Maize Maze
Farnham
THE STREET
Street Farm
A12
Elm Tree Farm
Molletts Farm
Friday Street
Watering Farm
Watering End
Snape Watering
Hill Farm
A1094
The Spinney
IP17
Valley Farm
Church Common
DONKEY LA
CHASE'S
PO
Knodishall Whin
Firs Farm
Oakyard Covert
MILL ROAD

Recn Gd
Foxburrow Wood
Palant's Grove
Rose Hill House
Racewalk Covert
Pond Wood
Whin Covert
Hill Farm
Burnter's Covert
Croft Farm
Green Heys
Church Farm
Tumulus
Farnham Road
FARNHAM ROAD
A1094
The Priory
Rookery Farm
Decoy Farm
Decoy Wood

Botany Farm
Botany Wood
Gromford
HULVER LANE
WADD LANE
GROMFORD LANE
Snape Hall Farm
CHURCH ROAD
Snape Com Prim Sch
SAXONFIELDS 1
THE GLEBES 2
STANHOPE CL 3
DRURY PK 4
GARRETT CL 5
PO
THE TERR
Black Heath Wood
Snape Warren

Burnt House Farm
Langham Bridge
River Alde
CANDLE GN LA
Willow Farm
Street Farm
B1069
Abbey Farm
PH
Snape
BRIDGE ROAD
Trundlers End
Snape Marshes Nature Reserve
New England Farm
Sand Point

Glebe Farm
RECTORY ROAD
FARNHAM ROAD
Firtree Farm
Grove Farm
LANGHAM ROAD
Snape Bridge
PH
Dunningworth Hall
Concert Hall
Snape Maltings
Suffolk Coast & Heaths Path
Cliff Reach

Church Road
STATION ROAD
SCHOOL ROAD
Blaxhall
PH
YH
OLD POST OFFICE LA
HEATH WK
Blaxhall Common or Blaxhall Heath
P
Iken Wood
Nature Reserve
Ikencliff
The Anchorage
CHURCH LANE
Church Carr
Iken

School Hill
Scarecrow Covert
Blaxhall Heath Nature Reserve
P
Sheepyard Covert
Alde House Farm
Church Farm
Pratt's Carr
Iken Common

Lime Tree Farm
The Knolls
SNAPE ROAD
SCHOOL ROAD
Sandgalls Plantation
P
IP12
Middle Covert
Valley Farm
SANDY LANE
The Carr

Old Hall Farm
B1069
White Cross Farm
Walk Farm
TUNSTALL GN
Tunstall
Granary Church Farm
ORFORD ROAD
Gable Farm
P
MILL LA
B1078
Tunstall Common
Tunstall Forest
Iken Heath
Oak Covert
Iken Boot
Alder Carr
Wood Farm

Cat's Barn
P
Bracken Farm
Facons Bottom Farm
Fazeboons Forest Farm
Sudbourne Great Wood

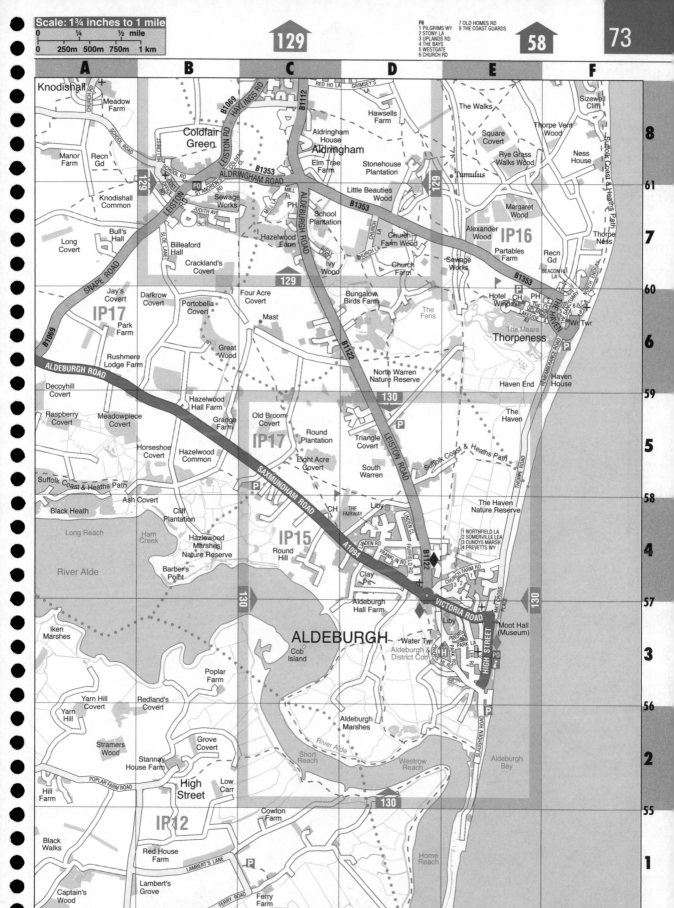

F6
1 PILGRIMS WY
2 STONY LA
3 UPLANDS RD
4 THE BAYS
5 WESTGATE
6 CHURCH RD
7 OLD HOMES RD
8 THE COAST GUARDS

A   B   C   D   E   F

8
61
7
60
6
59
5
58
4
57
3
56
2
55
1
54

Knodishall
Meadow Farm
Manor Farm
Recn Gd
Coldfair Green
Knodishall Common
Bull's Hall
Long Covert
School Road
Leiston Rd
Hazlings Rd
B1069
Aldringham House
Aldringham
Hawsells Farm
The Walks
Square Covert
Sizewell Cliff
Thorpe Vent Wood
Rye Grass Walks Wood
Ness House
Elm Tree Farm
Stonehouse Plantation
Tumulus
Aldringham Road
B1353
Sewage Works
Billeaford Hall
Crackland's Covert
Hazelwood Farm
Little Beauties Wood
School Plantation
Church La
Church Farm Wood
B1353
Alexander Wood
Margaret Wood
IP16
Partables Farm
Recn Gd
Thorpe Ness
Snape Road
Jay's Covert
Park Farm
Darkrow Covert
Portobella Covert
Four Acre Covert
Mast
Church Farm
Bungalow Birds Farm
Sewage Works
The Fens
Hotel Windmill
PH
Thorpeness
The Maare
Haven End
Haven House
B1069
IP17
Rushmere Lodge Farm
Great Wood
North Warren Nature Reserve
130
Aldeburgh Road
Decoyhill Covert
Hazelwood Hall Farm
Grange Farm
Old Broom Covert
Round Plantation
Triangle Covert
Suffolk Coast & Heaths Path
The Haven
Raspberry Covert
Meadowpiece Covert
IP17
South Warren
The Haven Nature Reserve
Horseshoe Covert
Hazelwood Common
Eight Acre Covert
Leiston Road
Thorpe Road
Suffolk Coast & Heaths Path
Ash Covert
Cliff Plantation
CH
Liby
The Fairway
1 NORTHFIELD LA
2 SOMERVILLE LEA
3 CUNDYS MARSH
4 PREVETTS WY
Black Heath
Long Reach
Ham Creek
Hazelwood Marshes Nature Reserve
IP15
Round Hill
Linden Cl
Linden Rd
Franklin Rd
Fairfield Rd
B1122
Church Farm Rd
130
River Alde
Barber's Point
Clay Pit
Aldeburgh Hall Farm
Victoria Road
MKT CROSS PLACE
Iken Marshes
Cob Island
ALDEBURGH
Water Twr
Aldeburgh & District Com
Liby
Moot Hall (Museum)
High Street
PO
Poplar Farm
Yarn Hill Covert
Redland's Covert
Aldeburgh Marshes
Slaughden Road
Yarn Hill
Stramers Wood
Grove Covert
Short Reach
Westrow Reach
Aldeburgh Bay
Hill Farm
Stannay House Farm
Poplar Farm Road
High Street
Low Carr
130
Black Walks
IP12
Red House Farm
Cowton Farm
Lambert's Lane
Home Reach
Captain's Wood
Lambert's Grove
Ferry Road
Ferry Farm

87

For full street detail of the highlighted areas see pages 129 and 130

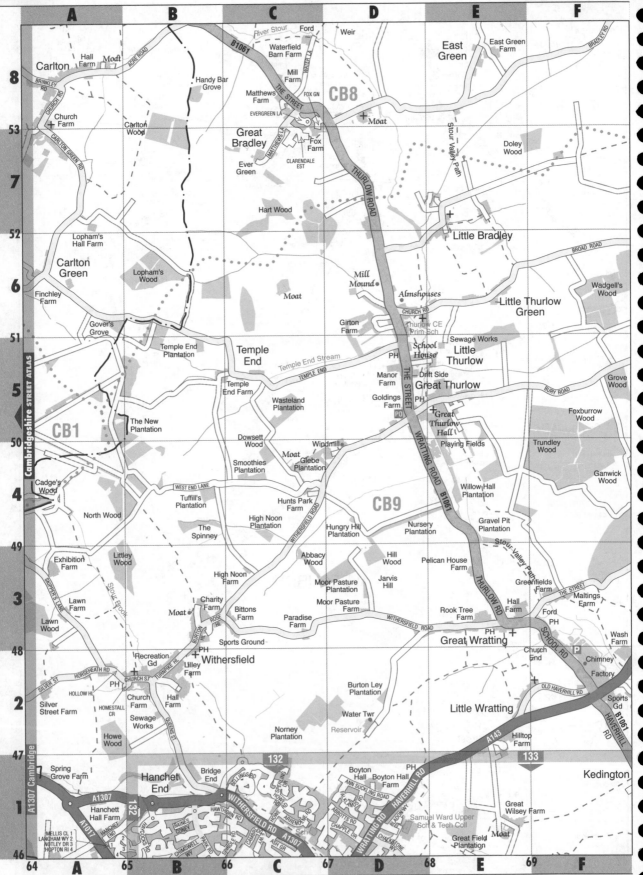

Scale: 1¾ inches to 1 mile

60

Carlton
Hall Farm
Moat
ACRE ROAD
BRINKLEY RD
CHURCH RD
Church Farm
CARLTON GREEN RD
Carlton Wood

River Stour
Ford
Weir
Waterfield Barn Farm
B1061
Mill Farm
Handy Bar Grove
Matthews Farm
THE STREET
EVERGREEN LA
FOX GN
CB8
Moat
East Green
East Green Farm
BRADLEY RD

Great Bradley
MATTHEWS LA
Fox Farm
CLARENDALE EST
Ever Green
THURLOW ROAD
Stour Valley Path
Doley Wood

Lopham's Hall Farm
Hart Wood
Little Bradley
BROAD ROAD

Carlton Green
Lopham's Wood
Moat
Mill Mound
Almshouses
CHURCH RD
Little Thurlow Green
Wadgell's Wood

Finchley Farm
Gover's Grove
Girton Farm
Thurlow CE Prim Sch
School House
Sewage Works
Little Thurlow
Grove Wood

Temple End Plantation
Temple End
Temple End Stream
TEMPLE END
PH
THE STREET
Manor Farm
Drift Side
Great Thurlow
BURY ROAD

The New Plantation
CB1
Temple End Farm
Wasteland Plantation
Dowsett Wood
Smoothies Plantation
Moat
Glebe Plantation
Windmill
Goldings Farm
PO
PH
Great Thurlow Hall
Playing Fields
Foxburrow Wood
Trundley Wood

Cadge's Wood
WEST END LANE
Tuffill's Plantation
Hunts Park Farm
WITHERSFIELD ROAD
CB9
B1061
Willow Hall Plantation
Gravel Pit Plantation
Ganwick Wood

North Wood
The Spinney
High Noon Plantation
Hungry Hill Plantation
Nursery Plantation
Stour Valley Path
Greenfields Farm
THE STREET

Exhibition Farm
Littley Wood
High Noon Farm
Abbacy Wood
Hill Wood
Pelican House Farm
THURLOW RD
Hall Farm
Maltings Farm

SKIPPER'S LANE
Stour Brook
Charity Farm
Moor Pasture Plantation
Jarvis Hill
Rook Tree Farm
Ford
PH
Wash Farm

Lawn Farm
Lawn Wood
Moat
Bittons Farm
Moor Pasture Farm
Paradise Farm
WITHERSFIELD ROAD
Great Wratting
SCHOOL RD
Chimney Factory

BURTON HL
ROSE HL
Sports Ground
PH
Recreation Gd
Lilley Farm
Withersfield
Church End
OLD HAVERHILL RD

HORSEHEATH RD
SILVER ST
HOLLOW HL
PH
Church Farm
HOMESTALL CR
Hall Farm
TURNPIKE RD
CHURCH ST
Burton Ley Plantation
Little Wratting
HAVERHILL RD
B1061

Silver Street Farm
Sewage Works
QUEEN'S ST
Howe Wood
Norney Plantation
Water Twr
Reservoir
A143
Hilltop Farm
Sports Gd

Spring Grove Farm
Hanchet End
Bridge End
132
Boyton Hall
Boyton Hall Farm
PH
133
Kedington

A1307 Cambridge
A1307
Hanchett Hall Farm
HANCHET END
132
BILLINGS RD
WITHERSFIELD ROAD
HAWTHORN RD
ANN SUCKLING ROAD
HAVERHILL RD
WRATTING ROAD
Samuel Ward Upper Sch & Tech Coll
Great Wilsey Farm
Great Field Plantation
Moat

MELLIS CL 1
LANGHAM WY 2
NOTLEY DR 3
HOPTON RI 3
A1017
BAINES CONEY
CHIMSWELL WY
PAPER RD
SCHOOL RD
CAMDEN WY
ASH GR
A1307
ABBOTTS RD
CHAPPLE DR
CHACKSTONE
BLOOM WY

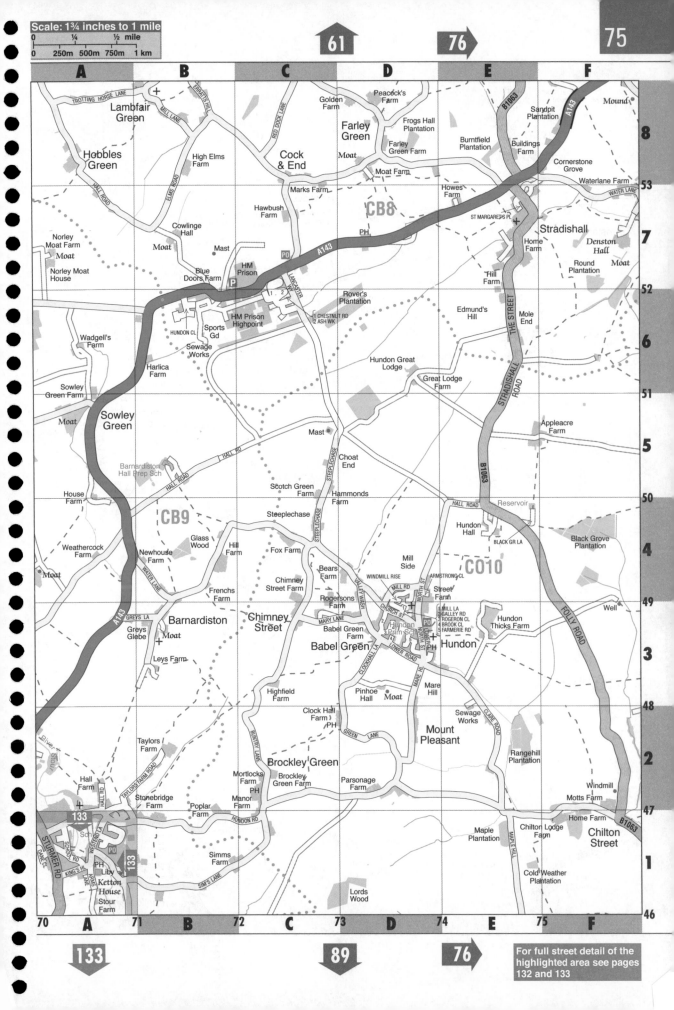

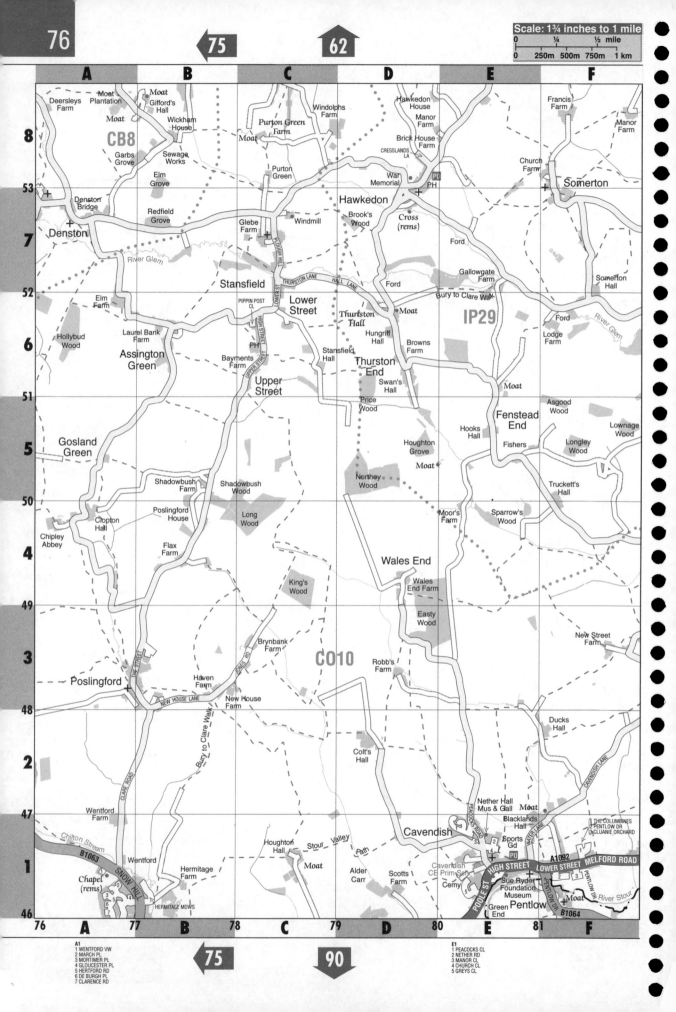

A B C D E F

8

Deersleys Farm
Moat Plantation
Moat
Gifford's Hall
Wickham House
Moat
Garbs Grove
Elm Grove
Sewage Works
CB8

Windolphs Farm
Purton Green Farm
Moat
Purton Green

Hawkedon House
Manor Farm
Brick House Farm
CRESSLANDS LA
PO
PH
Francis Farm
Manor Farm
Church Farm

53

Denston Bridge
Redfield Grove
Glebe Farm
Windmill
Brook's Wood
War Memorial
Cross (rems)
Somerton

7

Denston
River Glem
Stansfield
PLOUGH HILL
Ford
Ford
Gallowgate Farm
Somerton Hall

52

Elm Farm
THURSTON LANE
HALL LANE
Lower Street
Thurston Hall
Moat
Bury to Clare Walk
Ford
IP29
Ford
Lodge Farm
River Glem

6

Hollybud Wood
Laurel Bank Farm
PIPPIN POST CL
HIGH STREET
PH
Bayments Farm
UPPER STREET
Upper Street
Hungriff Hall
Stansfield Hall
Thurston End
Browns Hall
Moat

Assington Green

51

Price Wood
Swan's Hall
Hooks Hall
Fenstead End
Fishers
Asgood Wood
Lownage Wood

5

Gosland Green
Houghton Grove
Moat
Longley Wood
Truckett's Hall

50

Shadowbush Farm
Shadowbush Wood
Long Wood
Northey Wood
Moor's Farm
Sparrow's Wood

Clopton Hall
Poslingford House
Chipley Abbey
Flax Farm

4

King's Wood
Wales End
Wales End Farm
New Street Farm

49

Easty Wood

3

THE STREET
Brynbank Farm
JONES RD
CO10
Robb's Farm

Poslingford
Haven Farm
New House Farm

48

NEW HOUSE LANE
Bury to Clare Walk
Ducks Hall

2

CLARE ROAD
Colt's Hall
Nether Hall Mus & Gall
PEACOCKS ROAD
Blacklands Hall
Sports Gd
1 THE COLUMBINES
2 PENTLOW DR
3 CLUANIE ORCHARD

47

Wentford Farm
Chilton Stream
B1063
SNOW HILL
Wentford
Hermitage Farm
Houghton Hall
Stour Valley
Path
Moat
Cavendish
PO
Cavendish CE Prim Sch
WATER LANE
HIGH STREET
A1092
LOWER STREET
MELFORD ROAD

1

Chapel (rems)
HERMITAGE MDWS
Alder Carr
Scotts Farm
Cemy
Sue Ryder Foundation Museum
Green End
Pentlow
PODLEST
PENTLOW DR
Moat
River Stour
B1064

46

A1
1 WENTFORD VW
2 MARCH PL
3 MORTIMER PL
4 GLOUCESTER PL
5 HERTFORD RD
6 DE BURGH PL
7 CLARENCE RD

E1
1 PEACOCKS CL
2 NETHER RD
3 MANOR CL
4 CHURCH CL
5 GREYS CL

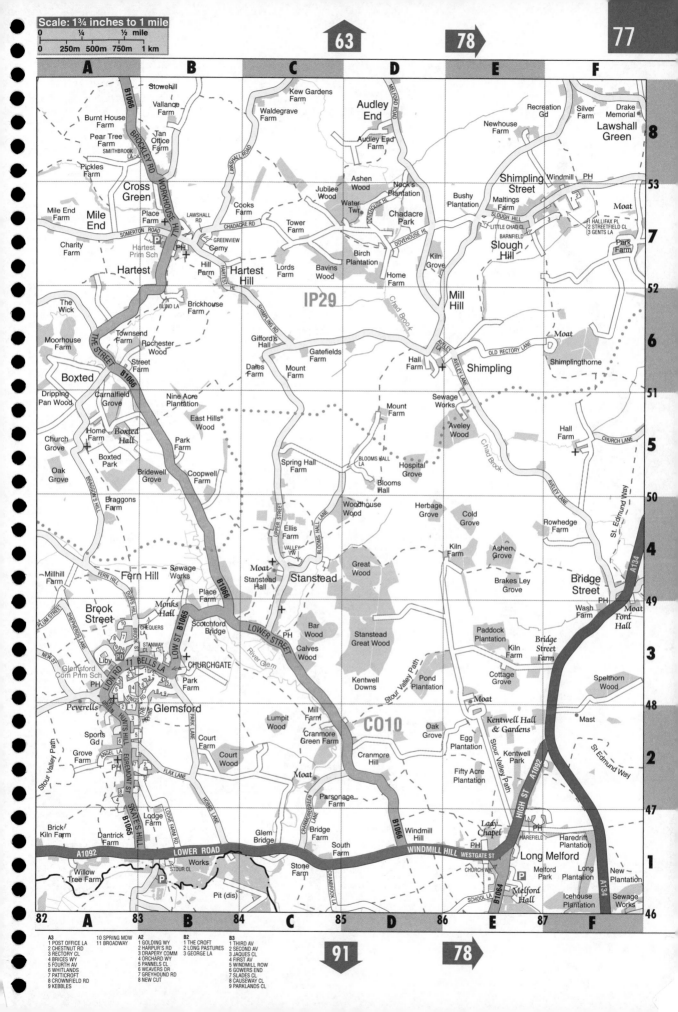

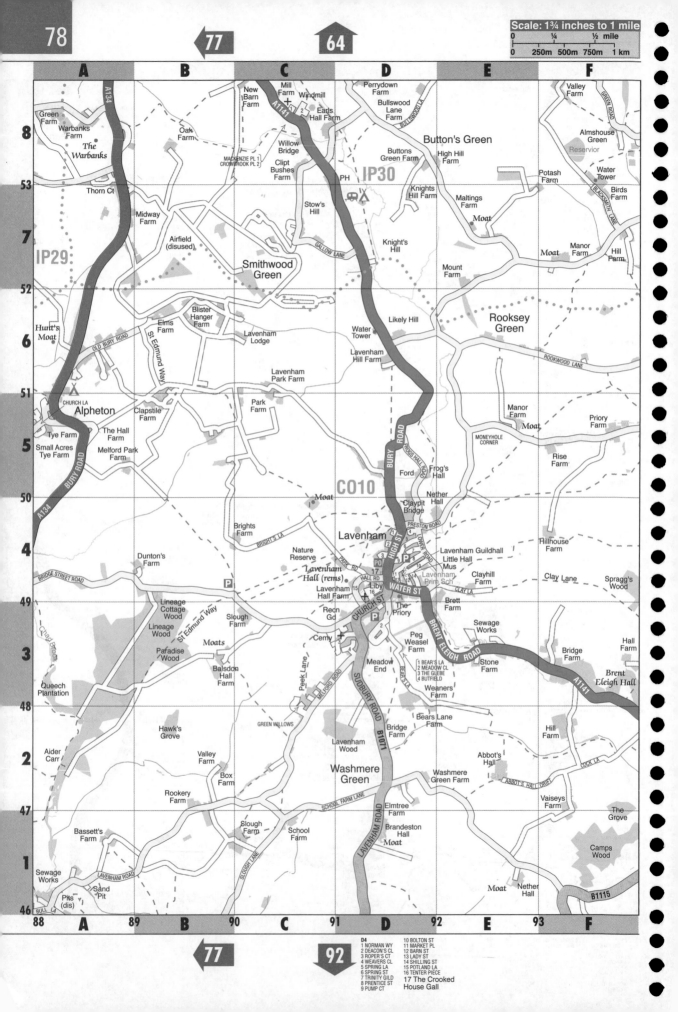

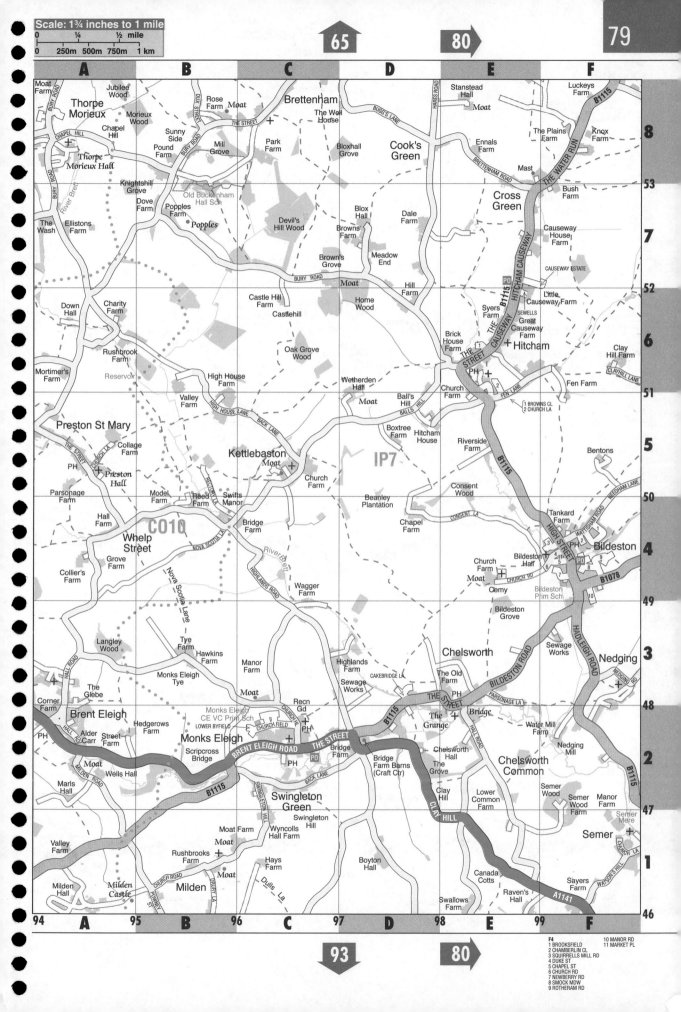

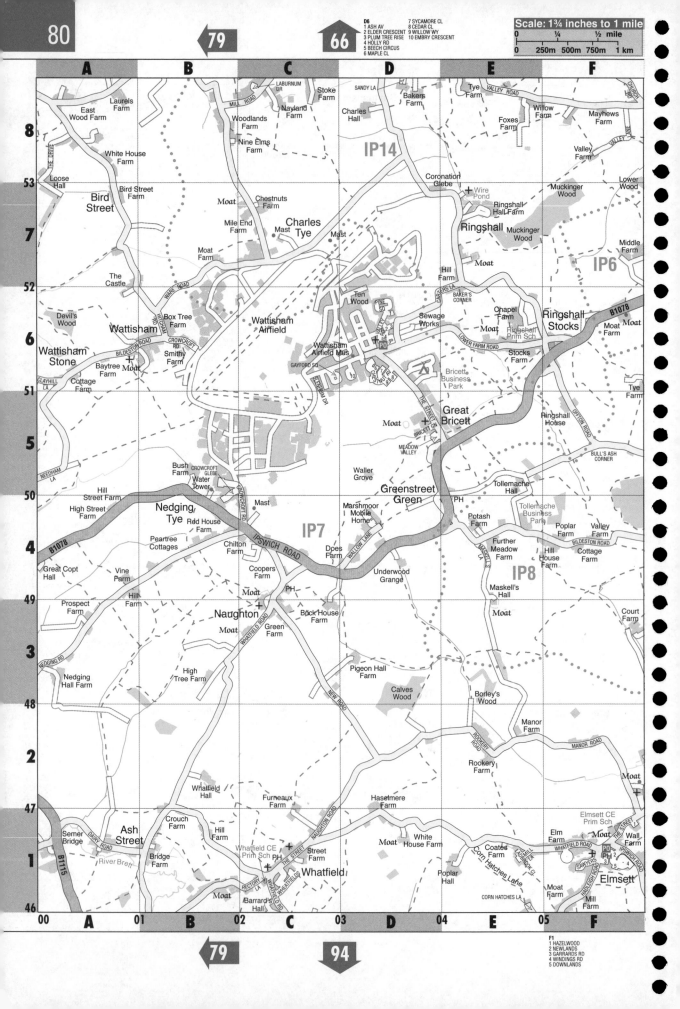

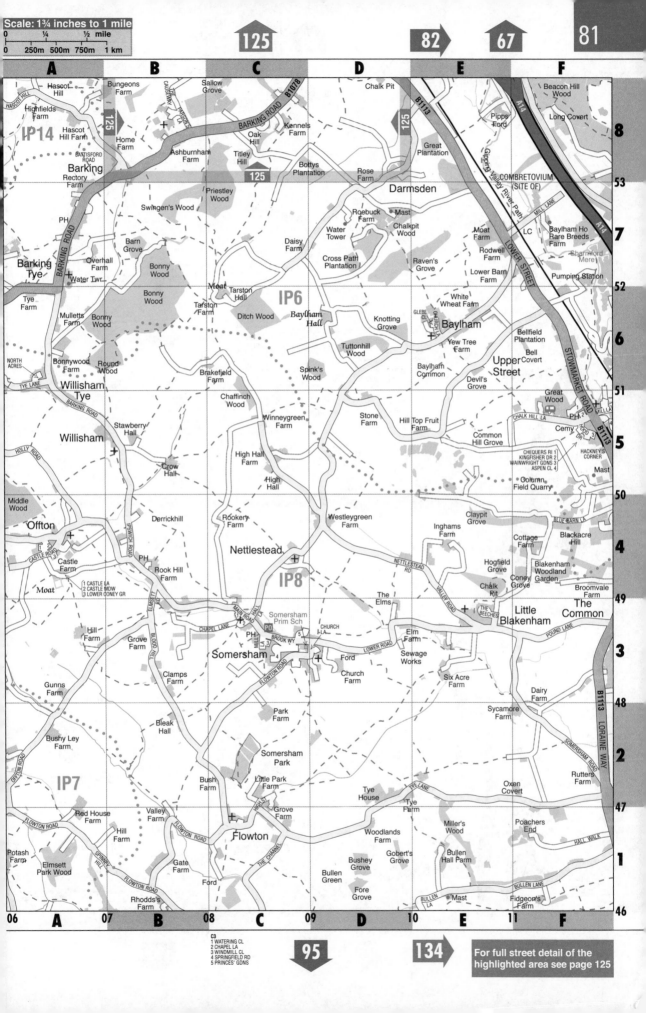

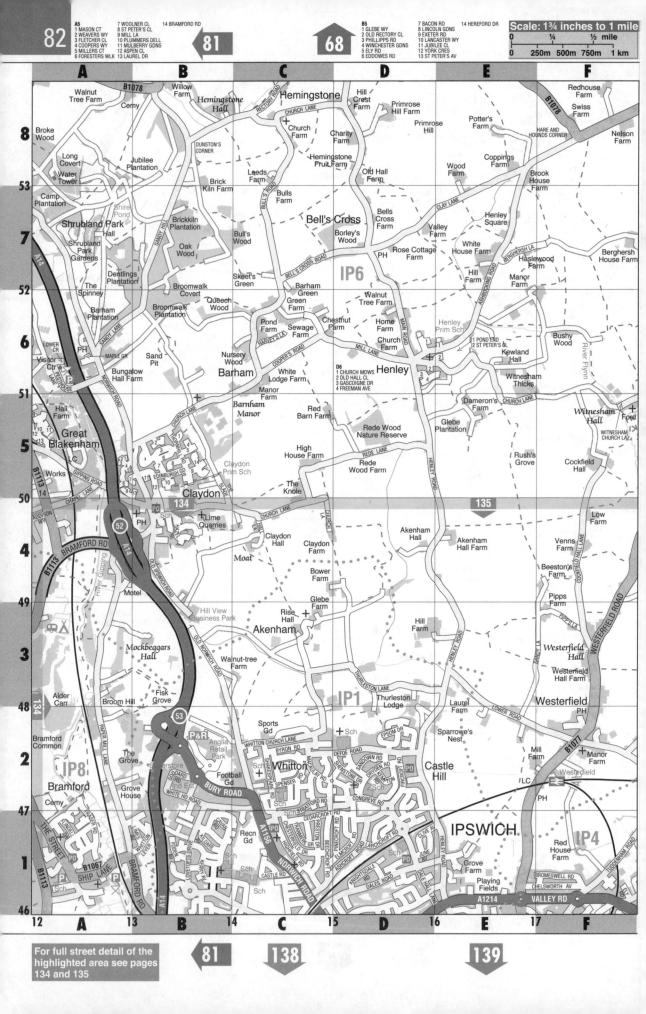

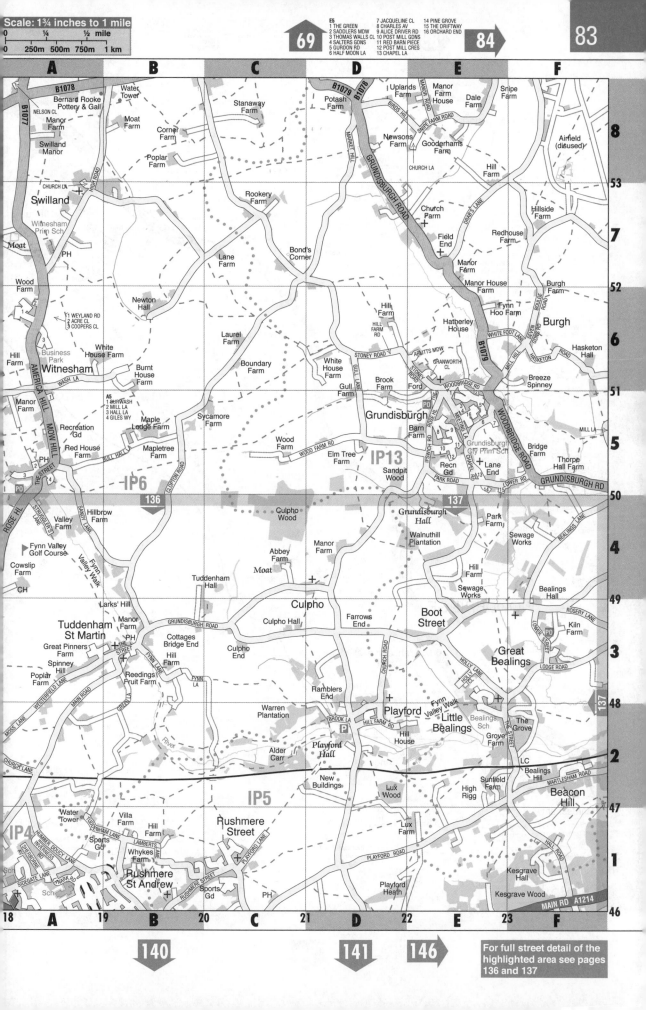

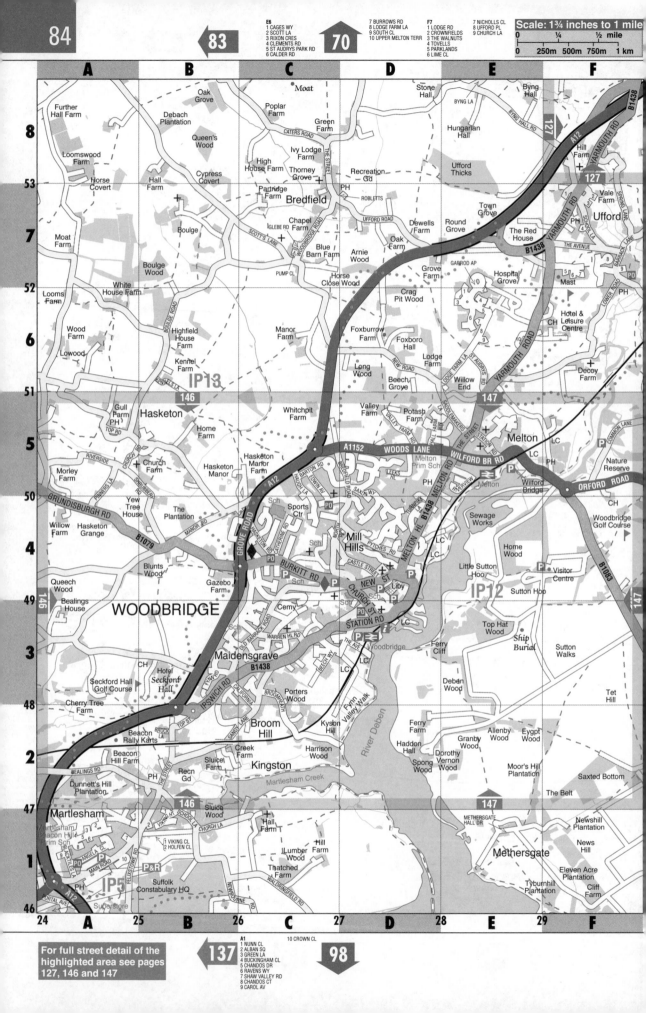

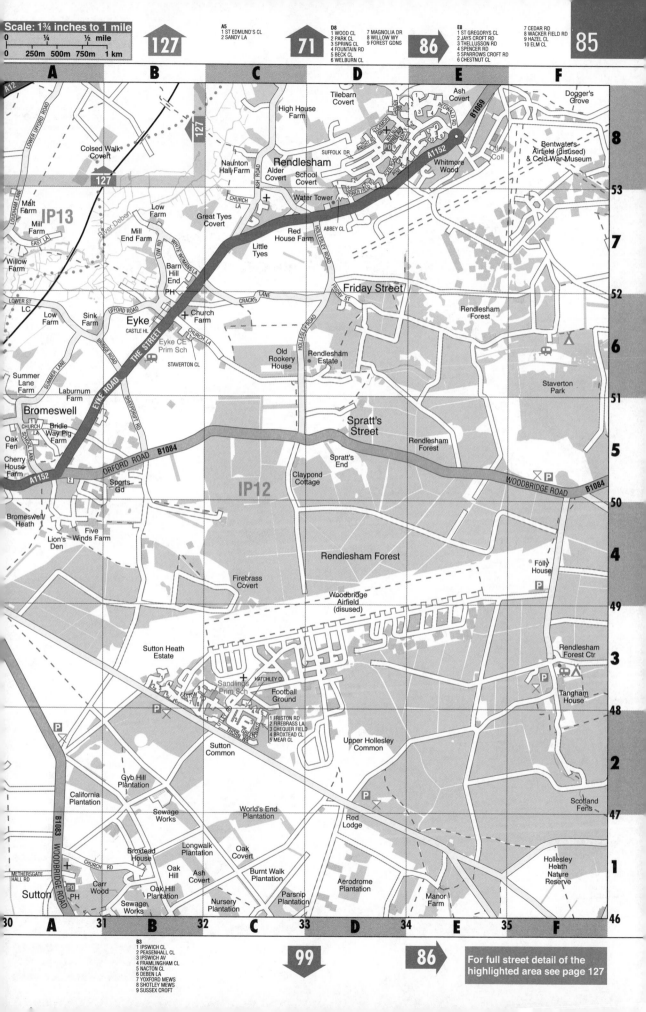

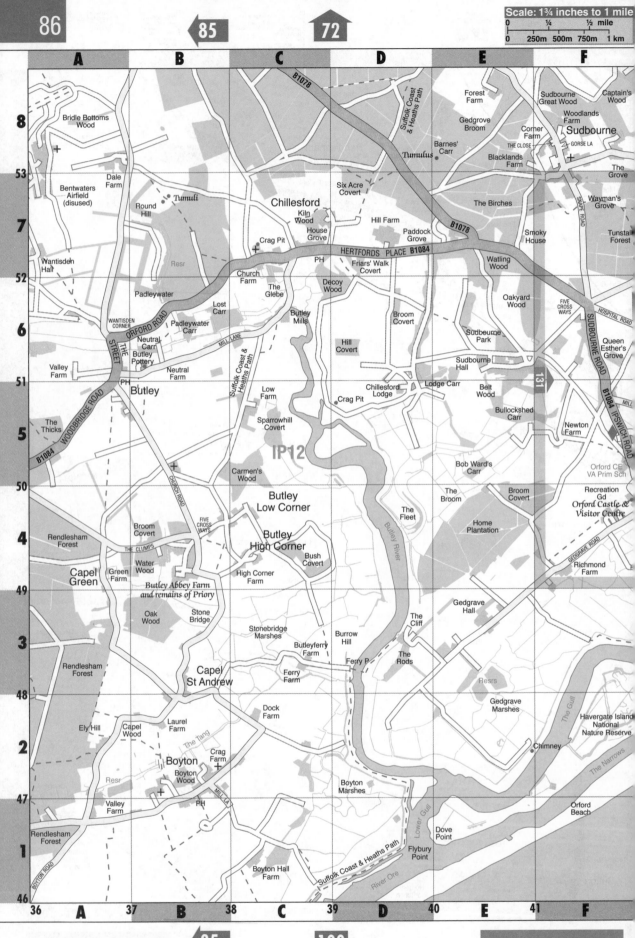

Scale: 1¾ inches to 1 mile

0   ¼   ½   mile
0   250m 500m 750m 1 km

Aldeburgh Bay

IP15

River Alde

Sudbourne Beach

Firs Farm

The Firs

The White House

SCHOOL ROAD

Longdrift Carr

Sudbourne Marshes

Valley Farm

131

High House Farm

HIGH HOUSE FARM ROAD

Elm Covert

Crag Pit

Crag Farm

FERRY ROAD

CRAG FARM ROAD

Chaplin's Carr

Church Farm

Moss' Carr

Ox Carr

Blackstakes Reach

Lantern Marshes

Masts

Prettyman's Whin

FERRY ROAD

Lodge Farm

IP12

Cobbins Farm

Masts

Bullockshed Grove

BROADWAY

BULLOCKSHED LA

Ash Carr

131

Raydon Hall

RAYDON LANE

Wireless Station

Town Marshes

Pig Pail Bridge

Orford

RECTORY RD

HIGH ST

CHANTRY RD

PO

King's Marshes

Town Hall

BROAD ST

QUAY ST

P   P

PH

Chantry Farm

FRONT ST

Orfordness

River Ore

Sewage Works

131

Orford Ness

Chantry Point

Orford Ness National Nature Reserve

Orfordness Lighthouse

Stony Ditch

Stonyditch Point

Cuckold's Point

Orford Beach

8
53
7
52
6
51
5
50
4
49
3
48
2
47
1
46

42   A   43   B   44   C   45   D   46   E   47   F   46

For full street detail of the highlighted area see page 131

Scale: 1¾ inches to 1 mile

0   ¼   ½ mile
0   250m 500m 750m 1 km

HAVERHILL

Hanchet End

Duncey Plantation

A1017

Hazel Stub Farm

Hazel Stub

CB1

Nosterfield Farm

Goodwoods Farm

Poplar Wood

Ladygate Wood

Moat

Horseham Hall

Copy Farm

Copse Hall Farm

Greatley Wood

Hilltop Farm

Garland's Wood

Bex Grove

Moat

PH

Abbott's Grove

The Spinney

Parkway Mid Sch

Recn Gd

Cemy

Chy

Sch

Liby

TH

Woodland Green

Eagles Farm

Mary Cole's Grove

Ruses Farm

Eastcotts Farm

STURMER

Sports Gd

P

CH

Pope Mill Farm

Sturmer

Coupals Rd

Tumulus

A143

STURMER RD

ROWLEY HL

A1017

BUMPSTEAD RD

B1057

Homefield Road Ind Est

Homefield Road

Piperell Way

132

133

Board Barn Farm

Draper's Farm

DRAPERS LA

Lancelots Farm

Catherines Wood

CAMPS ROAD

Pale Green

PO

Haven Farm

HAVERHILL ROAD

Wiggens Green

Whites Farm

Jacobs Farm

Wiggins Farm

Gable End

CB9

HAVERHILL RD

Garlands Farm

Lower House Farm

Yew Tree Farm

Upper House Farm

Waltons Farm

COPY HILL

132

Wash Bridge

Sewage Works

Ford

B1054

BLOIS ROAD

Rylands Farm

Devil's Grove

Rookery Wood

Meadow Side

Rolls Farm

Moss Farm

SAGES END RD

CHURCH HILL

PH

Helions Bumpstead

Rec Gd

WATER

Helions Farm

Moat

Helions

STEEPLE BUMPSTEAD RD

Bumpstead Hall

New House Farm

Balance Wood

Boblow

Bulls Bridge Farm

Little Smith Green Farm

Smith's Green

NORTH CR 1
THE CHASE 2
LION MDW 3

Freezes Farm

Steeple Bumpstead

PO

NORTH ST

CHAPEL ST

PH

CHURCH

Steeple Bumstead Pottery

EDITH CAVELL WY

Cemy

Blois Farm

HOME CL
SUCKLINGS YD

B1057

THE ENDWAY

Dock Plantation

Moyn's Park

CO9

Sycamore Wood

Maze Plantation

Arbour Grove

Brook End

Rec Gd

QUEEN EDITH

Bower Hall

WATER LA

HELIONS ROAD

ANN COLES CL

Bower Hall Farm

FINCHINGFIELD ROAD

Old Hall Farm

Old Hall

Moat

Cootes Farm

Round Wood

Whitehouse Farm

Mill Farm

MILL CL

Wildings Farm

Old Hall Wood

Moat

Hillside Farm

CB10

Hempstead Hall

Moat

B1054

Ruses Farm

BOYTONS LA

Hophouse Farm

Hempstead Wood

Latchley's Farm

Little Bulls Farm

Wakeland's Farm

EGGSHELL LANE

Lakehouse Grove

Moat

CM7

Martin's Farm

Prouds Farm

Green Farm

B1057

Messings Farm

Revels Farm

Lakehouse Farm

Moat

Herkstead Hall Farm

Moat

Mast

ESSEX STREET ATLAS

64   A   65   B   66   C   67   D   68   E   69   F

For full street detail of the highlighted area see pages 132 and 133

D3
1 CHURCHFIELDS DR
2 ST MARY'S WK
3 BARKER CL
4 JOHN TIBAULD CT
5 BORRADALE CT
6 WOOLNOUGH CL
7 GEORGE GENT CL
8 Stanley Drapkin Prim Sch

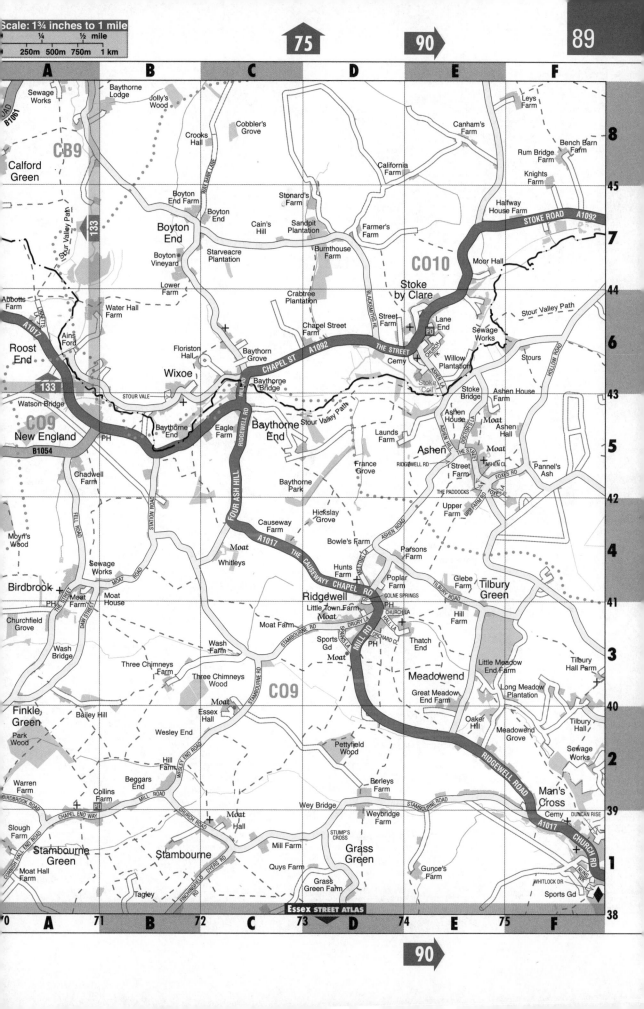

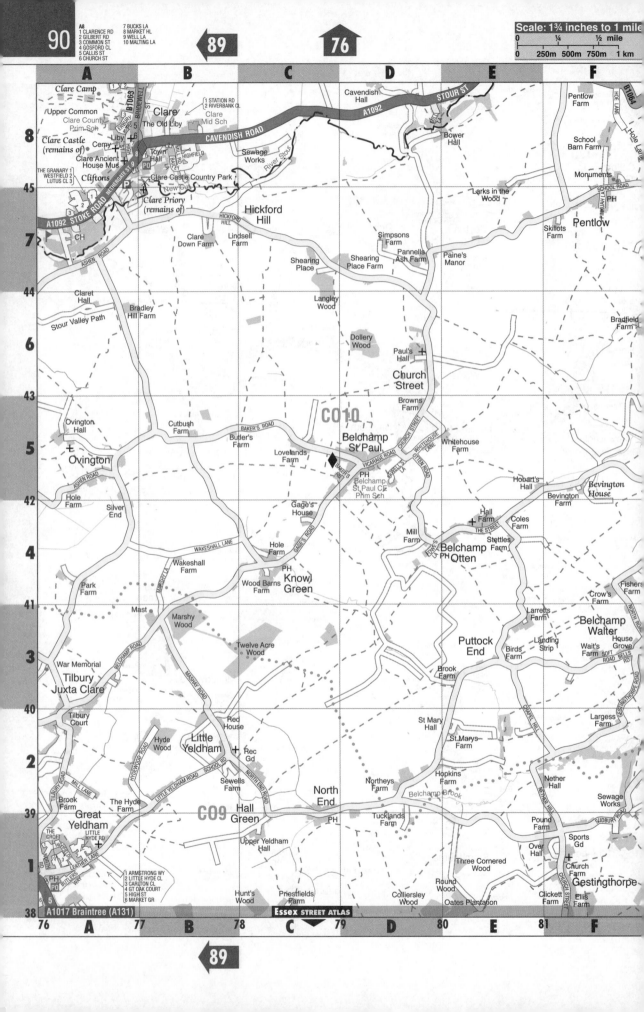

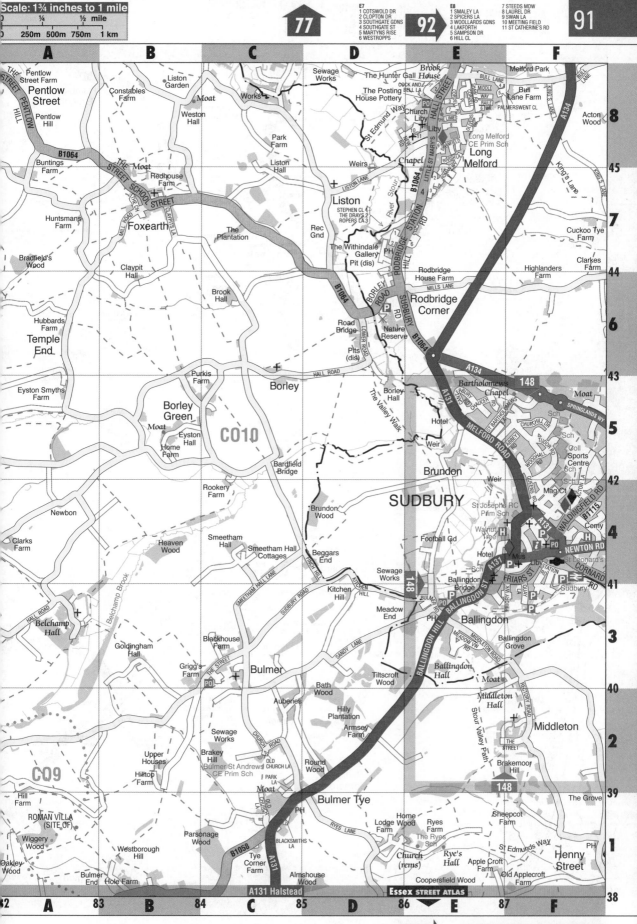

E7
1 COTSWOLD DR
2 CLOPTON DR
3 SOUTHGATE GDNS
4 SOUTHGATE ST
5 MARTYNS RISE
6 WESTROPPS

E8
1 SMALEY LA
2 SPICERS LA
3 WOOLLARDS GDNS
4 LAKFORTH
5 SAMPSON DR
6 HILL CL

7 STEEDS MDW
8 LAUREL DR
9 SWAN LA
10 MEETING FIELD
11 ST CATHERINE'S RD

B7
1 GOTSFIELD CL
2 GOTSFIELD CL
3 COBLERS WY
4 QUEENSWAY
5 BROWNS CL
6 CANON PUGH DR

7 KINGS CL
8 DANIELS CL
9 BABERGH CL
10 WALDINGFIELD RD

91

C6
1 CORONATION RI
2 GREEN ACRE
3 CHESTNUT CL
4 CHAPEL CL
5 GARRISON LA
6 BADLEYS CL

7 BRAITHWAITE DR
8 GREEN ACRE
9 KENYON DR
10 BRANDESTON CL
11 HOLBROOK CL
12 CARBONELS

78

Scale: 1¾ inches to 1 mile
0   ¼   ½ mile
0   250m 500m 750m   1 km

CO10

91

B3
1 HARTEST WY
2 SHEEPSHEAD HL
3 OAK RD
4 ASH GR
5 FARFORD FIELD
6 CARSONS DR
7 KEMPSON DR
8 DE GREYS CL
9 CAUSTONS CL

10 PECOCKES CL
11 WALSINGHAM CL
12 BRANDS CL
13 PARMENTER DR
14 TURKENTINE CL
15 LIONEL HURST CL
16 CHAPLIN WK
17 CARSONS DR

101

For full street detail of the highlighted area see page 148

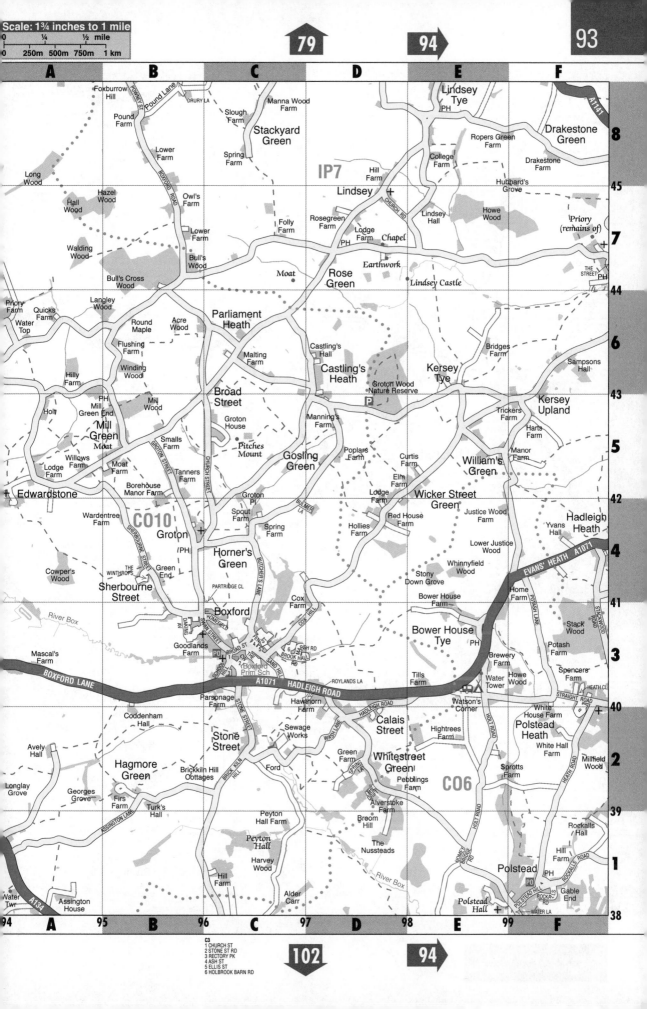

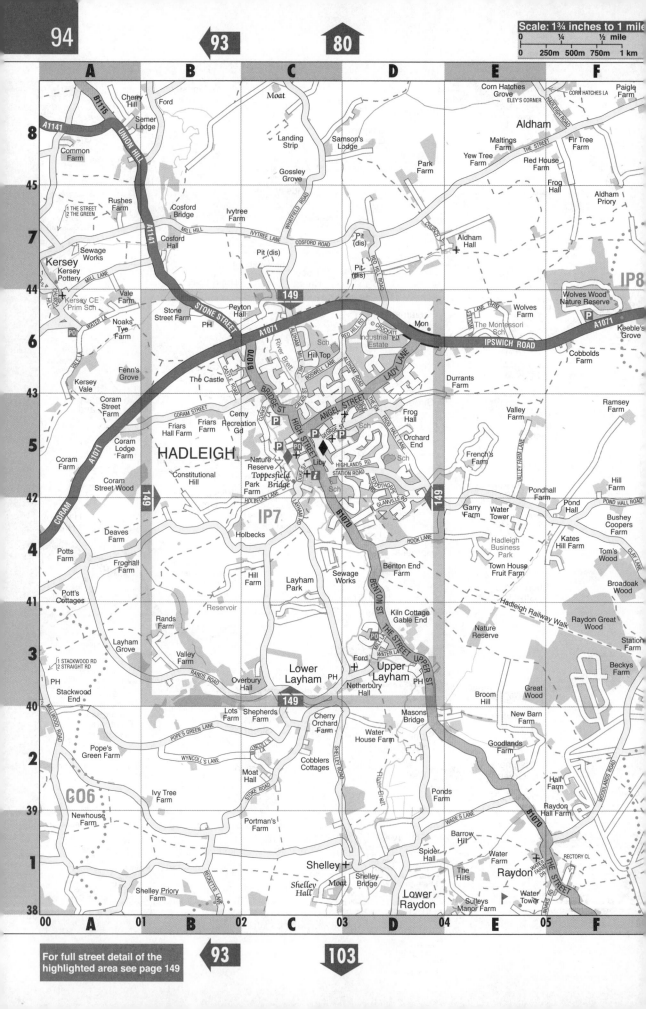

A B C D E F

8

Common Farm
Cherry Hill
Ford
Semer Lodge
Moat
Landing Strip
Samson's Lodge
Park Farm
Corn Hatches Grove
ELEY'S CORNER
CORN HATCHES LA
Paigle Farm
Aldham
Maltings Farm
THE STREET
Fir Tree Farm
Yew Tree Farm
Red House Farm
Frog Hall

45

Gossley Grove

7

Rushes Farm
1 THE STREET
2 THE GREEN
Cosford Bridge
Ivytree Farm
MILL HILL
Cosford Hall
IVYTREE LANE
COSFORD ROAD
Pit (dis)
Pit (dis)
CHURCH
Aldham Hall
Aldham Priory
IP8

44

Kersey
Kersey Pottery
Sewage Works
MILL LANE
Stone Street Farm
STONE STREET
Peyton Hall
PH
149
Pit (dis)
RED HILL RD
Wolves Farm
LANE FARM
The Montessori Sch
Wolves Wood Nature Reserve
P
A1071
Keeble's Grove

6

Kersey CE Prim Sch
CHURCH HILL
WATER LA
PO
Vale Farm
Noaks Tye Farm
A1141
A1071
The Castle
CORAM STREET
CASTLE ROAD
B1070
River Brett
ALDHAM MILL
Hill Top
Sch
CROCKATT RD
Industrial Estate
RED HILL RD
Mon
IPSWICH ROAD
Cobbolds Farm

43

Fenn's Grove
Kersey Vale
Coram Street Farm
Friars Hall Farm
Friars Farm
Cemy Recreation Gd
BRIDGE ST
CALAIS ST
CORKS LANE
HIGH STREET
ANGEL STREET
GEORGE ST
THE GT
Frog Hall
Durrants Farm
Valley Farm
Ramsey Farm

5

Coram Farm
A1071
Coram Lodge Farm
HADLEIGH
Constitutional Hill
Nature Reserve
Toppesfield Bridge
Park Farm
PO
P
P
P
DUKE ST
Liby
i
HIGHLANDS RD
STATION ROAD
Sch
Sch
WOODHOPE RD
FROG HALL LANE
Orchard End
LADY LANE
Sch
French's Farm
VALLEY FARM LANE
Pondhall Farm
Hill Farm

42

Coram Street Wood
149
HOLBECKS LANE
IP7
Holbecks
LAYHAM RD
B1070
GLANVILLE RD
149
Garry Farm
Water Tower
Pond Hall
POND HALL ROAD
Bushey Coopers Farm

4

Coram
A1071
Potts Farm
Deaves Farm
Froghall Farm
Hill Farm
Layham Park
Sewage Works
HOOK LANE
Benton End Farm
BENTON ST
Hadleigh Business Park
Town House Fruit Farm
Kates Hill Farm
Tom's Wood
Broadoak Wood

41

Pott's Cottages
Layham Grove
Rands Farm
Reservoir
Kiln Cottage Gable End
Nature Reserve
Hadleigh Railway Walk
Raydon Great Wood
Station Farm

3

1 STACKWOOD RD
2 STRAIGHT RD
Layham Grove
Valley Farm
RANDS ROAD
Overbury Hall
Lower Layham
PH
POTT
WATER LANE
THE STREET
Ford
Upper Layham
UPPER ST
PH
Netherbury Hall
Broom Hill
Great Wood
Beckys Farm

40

1 STACKWOOD END
PH
Stackwood End
MILLWOOD ROAD
Lots Farm
Shepherds Farm
149
Cherry Orchard Farm
Water House Farm
Masons Bridge
Goodlands Farm
New Barn Farm

CO6

2

Pope's Green Farm
POPE'S GREEN LANE
WYNCOLL'S LANE
WINCOLL'S LA
Moat Hall
Cobblers Cottages
SHELLEY ROAD
River Brett
Ponds Farm
Hall Farm
WOODLANDS ROAD

39

Newhouse Farm
Ivy Tree Farm
STOKE ROAD
Portman's Farm
WADE'S LANE
Raydon Hall Farm
B1070

1

PH
BECKETTS LANE
Shelley
Shelley Bridge
Spider Hall
Barrow Hill
The Hills
Water Farm
Raydon
WATER FARM DRY
RECTORY CL
THE STREET
SWAN RD

38

Shelley Priory Farm
Shelley Hall
Moat
Shelley Bridge
Lower Raydon
Sulleys Manor Farm
Water Tower

00 A 01 B 02 C 03 D 04 E 05 F

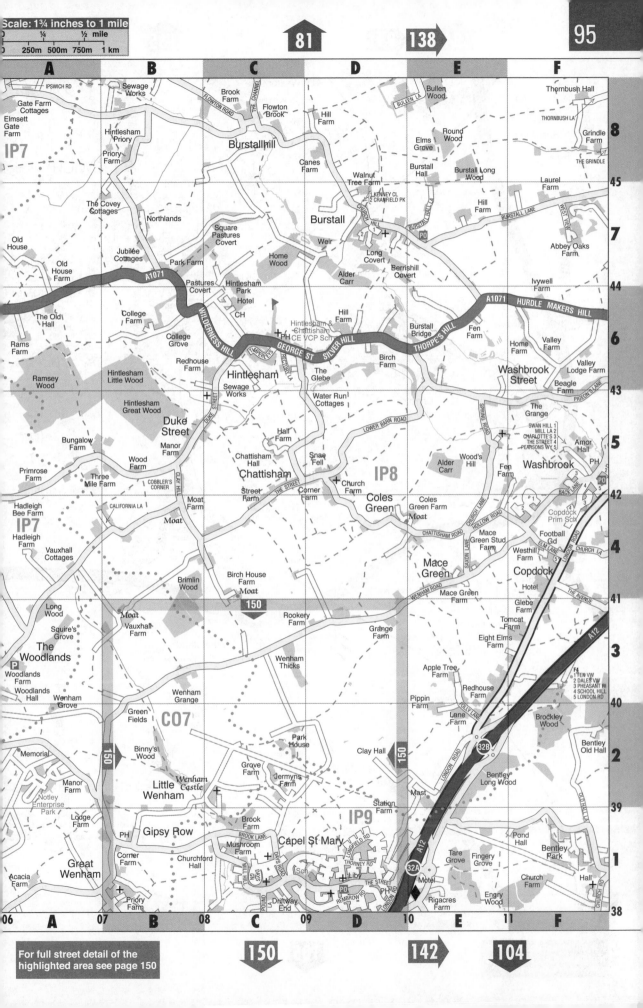

A **B** **C** **D** **E** **F**

IPSWICH RD

Gate Farm Cottages

Elmsett Gate Farm

Sewage Works

Sewage Works

Brook Farm

THE CHANNEL

Flowton Brook

FLOWTON ROAD

Hill Farm

Bullen Wood

BULLEN LA

Thornbush Hall

THORNBUSH LA

8

IP7

Hintlesham Priory

Priory Farm

Burstallhill

Canes Farm

Walnut Tree Farm

Elms Grove

Round Wood

Burstall Long Wood

Grindle Farm

THE GRINDLE

The Covey Cottages

Northlands

Square Pastures Covert

Burstall

CHURCH HILL

Burstall Hall

Hill Farm

Laurel Farm

WEST VIEW

BURSTALL LANE

45

Old House

Jubilee Cottages

Park Farm

Weir

Home Wood

2 1

1 KENNEY CL
2 CRANFIELD PK

PO

BURSTALL LA

Abbey Oaks Farm

7

Old House Farm

A1071

Pastures Covert

Hintlesham Park Hotel

CH

Alder Carr

Long Covert

Berrishill Covert

Burstall Bridge

Ivywell Farm

A1071 HURDLE MAKERS HILL

44

The Old Hall

Rams Farm

College Farm

College Grove

WILDERNESS HILL

LIMPERLEYS

GEORGE ST

Hintlesham & Chattisham CE VCP Sch

PH

SILVER HILL

Hill Farm

The Glebe

THORPE'S HILL

Fen Farm

Home Farm

Valley Farm

Washbrook Street

Valley Lodge Farm

Beagle Lane

PIGEON'S LANE

6

Ramsey Wood

Hintlesham Little Wood

Redhouse Farm

Hintlesham

Sewage Works

DUKE STREET

PRIORY LA

Birch Farm

Water Run Cottages

The Grange

SWAN HILL 1
MILL LA 2
CHARLOTTE'S 3
THE STREET 4
PEARSONS WY 5

43

Hintlesham Great Wood

Bungalow Farm

Duke Street

Hall Farm

LOWER BARN ROAD

SPRING ROAD

Amor Hall

PH

5

Primrose Farm

Three Mile Farm

Wood Farm

Manor Farm

COBBLER'S CORNER

CLAY HILL

Chattisham Hall

Chattisham

Street Farm

THE STREET

Snae Fell

Corner Farm

Church Farm

IP8

Alder Carr

Wood's Hill

Fen Farm

Washbrook

PO

42

IP7

Hadleigh Bee Farm

Hadleigh Farm

CALIFORNIA LA

Moat Farm

Moat

Moat

Coles Green

Coles Green Farm

Moat

CHATTISHAM ROAD

HOLLOW ROAD

CHURCH LANE

Mace Green Stud Farm

Copdock Prim Sch

BACK LANE

Football Gd

LONDON ROAD

CHURCH LA

4

Vauxhall Cottages

Birch House Farm

Moat

Brimlin Wood

150

Rookery Farm

WENHAM ROAD

Mace Green

Mace Green Farm

SAXON LANE

Westhill Farm

ELM LANE

Copdock

Hotel

THE AVENUE

A12

41

Long Wood

Squire's Grove

Moat

Vauxhall Farm

150

Grange Farm

Apple Tree Farm

Eight Elms Farm

Tomcat Farm

Glebe Farm

3

The Woodlands

P

Woodlands Farm

Woodlands Hall

Wenham Grove

Wenham Grange

Wenham Thicks

Pippin Farm

Redhouse Farm

Lane Farm

FOLLY LANE

32B

Brockley Wood

Bentley Old Hall

1 FEN VW
2 DALES VW
3 PHEASANT RI
4 SCHOOL HILL
5 LONDON RD

2

Memorial

Manor Farm

Notley Enterprise Park

Lodge Farm

150

Green Fields

CO7

Binny's Wood

Little Wenham

Wenham Castle

Grove Farm

Park House

Jermyns Farm

Clay Hall

150

Station Farm

Mast

Bentley Long Wood

A12

39

Acacia Farm

Great Wenham

PH

Corner Farm

Gipsy Row

Churchford Hall

Brook Farm

BROOK LANE

DAYS ROAD

Mushroom Farm

Sch

Capel St Mary

IP9

THORNEY RD

LOWFIELD RD

Liby

PO

PH

THE STREET

REMBROW RD

32A

A12

Motel

Tare Grove

Fingery Grove

Pond Hall

Church Farm

Bentley Park

Hall

CHURCH LA

1

Priory Farm

POUND LA

Driftway End

Rigacres Farm

Engry Wood

38

A 07 **B** 08 **C** 09 **D** 10 **E** 11 **F**

06

For full street detail of the highlighted area see page 150

150

142

104

A   B   C   D   E   F

8
45
7
44
6
43
5
42
4
41
3
40
2
39
1
38

18   A   19   B   20   C   21   D   22   E   23   F

144   145

106   98 ▶

For full street detail of the
highlighted area see pages
140, 141, 144 and 145

A1214   COLCHESTER ROAD
Rushmere
St Andrew
Sports Gd
WOODBRIDGE ROAD
Humber Doucy Sports Ctr
High Sch
WOODBRIDGE RD
A1214
PO
IP4
California
Ipswich
Sch
Rushmere Heath
Water Twr
Heathside Specl Sch
Broke Hall Prim Sch
Kiln Farm
Kesgrave High Sch
MAIN ROAD   A1214
Prim Sch
Kesgrave
IP5
Tumuli
Cedarwood Prim Sch
Tumulus
Foxhall Heath
Pote Hill (Tumulus)
FOXHALL ROAD
141
Broadlands Wy
Foxhall Stadium
Black Walk Plantation
Brookhill Wood
Hill Wood
Foxhall Hall
Valley Farm
Liby
Derby Rd
St Clement's
Broke Hall
IP3
Racecourse
Broke Hall
Brook Hill
Suffolk Nuffield
Monument
Springbank Farm
Lodge Farm
Decoypond Wood
Ipswich Golf Course
Purdis Hall Farm
Monument Farm
PURDIS ROAD
KENNELS RD
Warren Heath
Ash Grove
Purdis Farm La
Wood House
Priory Heath
FELIXSTOWE ROAD
Murrills Rd
Superstore
Suffolk Showground
Rook Wood
Hightree Covert
Hollies Farm
Beeches End
A12
MAIN ROAD
Sports Centre
Ravenswood Community Prim Sch
Brazier's Wood
A14
Morland Prim Sch
NACTON RD
Hotel
57
Ret Pk
Bus Pk
Ransomes Europark
Round Plantation
Whitehouse Farm
PH
IP10
Straightroad Covert
LC
Bucklesham Wood
Knight's Wood
Porter's Covert
58
A1156
A14
Tumuli
Pond Hall Farm
Robert's Grove
Square Covert
Nactonheath Plantation
Craigagh Wood
Seven Hills
Hobbin's Walk
Orwell Ctry Park
Bridge Wood
Alnesbourn Priory
Fox's Carr
Deals Carr
Foxes Farm
Sorrel Grove
Home Farm
Amberfield School
Decoy Wood
Manor Ponds
145
Mulberry Middle
Mansbrook Grove
Goldsmith's Covert
Ipswich Road
Lady Wood
Rec Gd
Wood End
Nacton
Nacton CE VC Prim Sch
White House Farm
Park Farm
Water Tower
Lower Farm
Levington
Red House Farm
Toweralder Carr
Whinnyfield Wood
Downham Reach
River Orwell
Woolverstone Marina
Cathouse Point
Deer Park
Water Twr
Orwell Park Sch
Broke Hall Woods
Walnut Tree Farm
Corners House
IP9
Hall Pt
Cat House
Ipswich High Sch
Suffolk Coast & Heaths Path
Porter's Reach
Playing Field
Broke Hall
Rackhams Farm
CHURCH LANE
PH
Water Tower
MAIN ROAD   B1456
Woolverstone
Woolverstone Park
Sewage Works
Butterman's Bay
Home Wood
Suffolk Coast & Heaths Path
Sewage Works

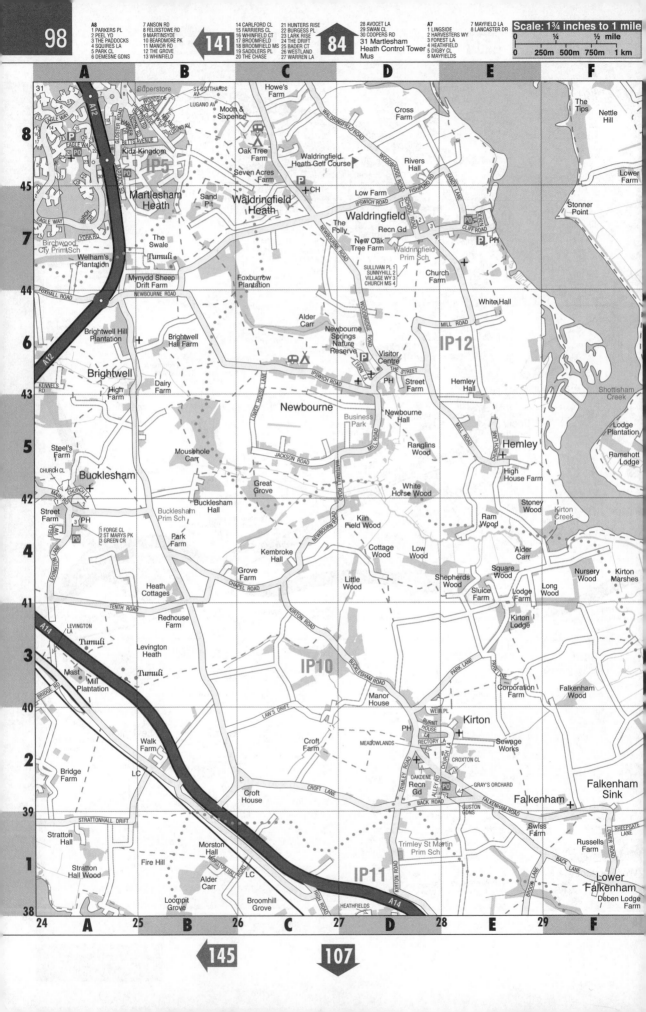

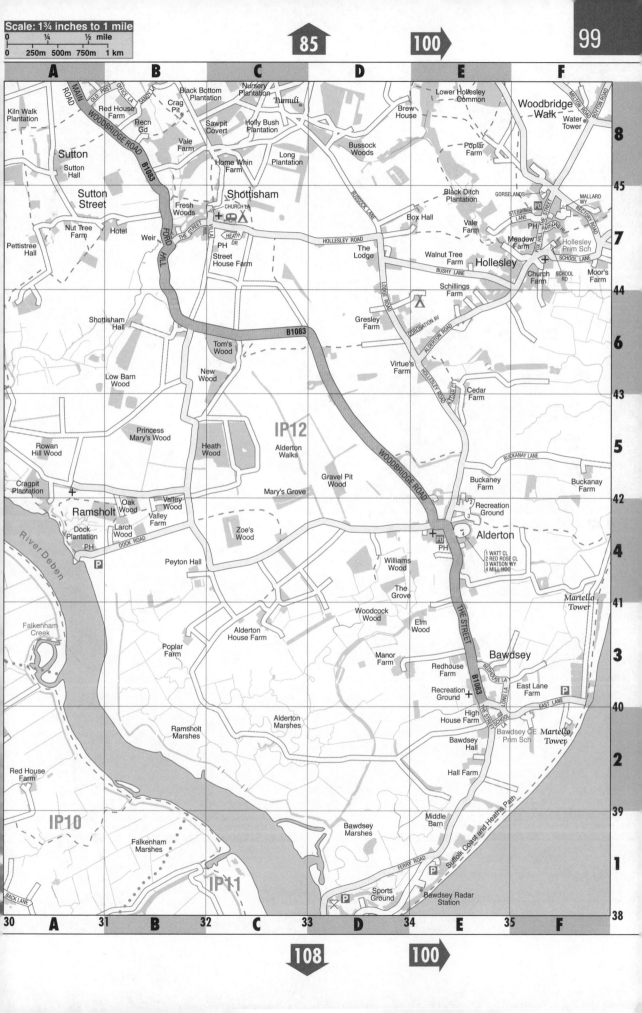

Scale: 1¾ inches to 1 mile

| 0 | ¼ | ½ | mile |
| 0 | 250m | 500m | 750m | 1 km |

A **B** **C** **D** **E** **F**

Oak Hill

Sports Ground

HM Prison

Grove House

The Grove

IP12

The Suffolk Punch Trust Colony Stud

✚

Hollesley Bay Colony
(HM Young Offender Institution)

River Ore

Hollesley Bay

Orford Haven

Sewage Works

Oxley Dairy

Oxley Marshes

North Weir Point

P

Shingle Street

Martello Tower

Suffolk Coast & Heaths Path

8
45
7
44
6
43
5
42
4
41
3
40
2
39
1
38

36 **A** 37 **B** 38 **C** 39 **D** 40 **E** 41 **F**

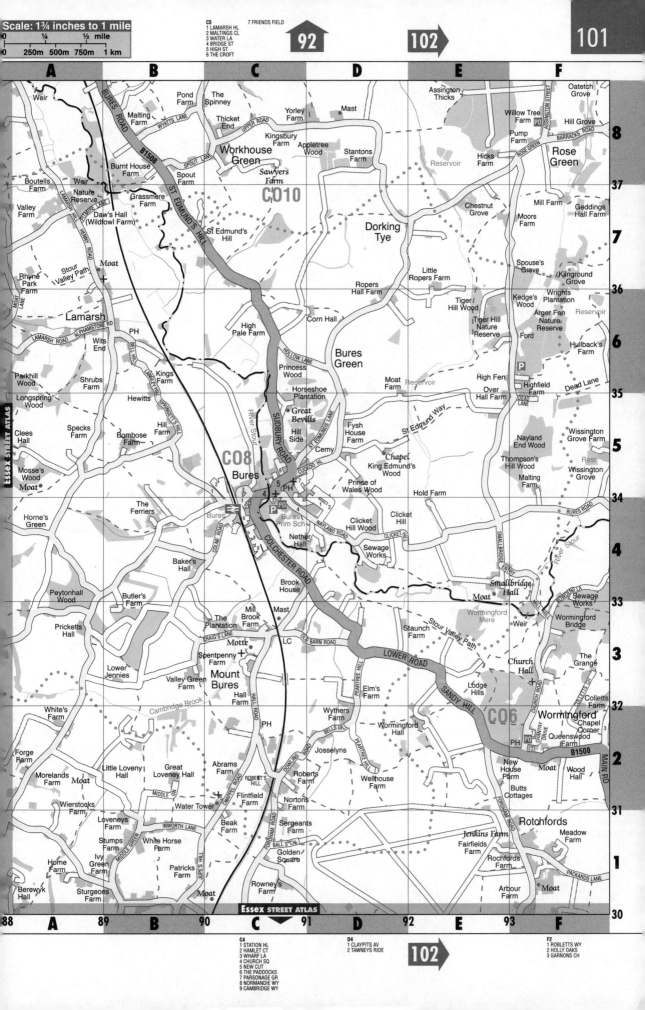

C5
1 LAMARSH HL
2 MALTINGS CL
3 WATER LA
4 BRIDGE ST
5 HIGH ST
6 THE CROFT
7 FRIENDS FIELD

Weir

Pond Farm
The Spinney
Malting Farm
WYATTS LANE
Thicket End
UPPER ROAD
Yorley Farm
Mast

Kingsbury Farm
Appletree Wood
Stantons Farm

Assington Thicks
Willow Tree Farm
Oatetch Grove
Hill Grove
BARRACKS ROAD
ASSINGTON STREET

Burnt House Farm
Spout LANE
Workhouse Green
SPOUT LANE
Sawyers Farm

Reservoir
Hicks Farm
Pump Farm
ROSE GREEN
Rose Green

Boutells Farm
Weir
Nature Reserve
EXTMITE LANE
Grassmere Farm
Daw's Hall (Wildfowl Farm)
ST EDMUND'S HILL

CO10

Chestnut Grove
Mill Farm
Moors Farm
Geddings Hall Farm

Valley Farm
LAMARSH HILL
HENRY ROAD
Moat

St Edmund's Hill

Dorking Tye

Little Ropers Farm
Spouse's Grove
Kilnground Grove

Rhyne Park Farm
Stour Valley Path

Ropers Hall Farm
Tiger Hill Wood
Kedge's Wood
Wrights Plantation
Reservoir

Lamarsh
LAMARSH ROAD
ALPHAMSTONE RD
Wits End
PH
BELL HILL
Kings Farm
High Pale Farm
HOLLOW LANE
Corn Hall
Bures Green
Tiger Hill Nature Reserve
Arger Fen Nature Reserve
Hullback's Farm

Parkhill Wood
Shrubs Farm
LANGE HILL
SPRINGETT'S HILL
Hewitts
Hill Farm
Princess Wood
Horseshoe Plantation
Moat Farm
Reservoir
High Fen
Over Hall Farm
Highfield Farm
Dead Lane
DEAD LANE

Longspring Wood
Specks Farm
Bombose Farm
River Stour
SUDBURY ROAD
Great Bevills
Hill Side
ST EDMUNDS LANE
Fysh House Farm
St Edmund Way
Nayland End Wood
Wissington Grove Farm

Clees Hall
CO8
Bures
Cemy
CUCKOO HL
Chapel
King Edmund's Wood
Thompson's Hill Wood
Malting Farm
Resr
Wissington Grove

Mosse's Wood
Moat
Bures
4
5
PH
Prince of Wales Wood
Hold Farm

Horne's Green
The Ferriers
2
3
PO
Bures Prim Sch
NAYLAND ROAD
Clicket Hill Wood
Clicket Hill
BURES ROAD

Baker's Hall
Nether Hall
CLICKET
Sewage Works
SMALLBRIDGE ENTRY
River Stour
RYWDENS LA
Sewage Works

Peytonhall Wood
Butler's Farm
COLNE ROAD
Brook House
Smallbridge Hall
Moat
MILL HILL
Wormingford Bridge

Pricketts Hall
The Plantation
CRAIG'S LANE
Mill Brook Farm
Mast
OLD BARN ROAD
Staunch Farm
Stour Valley Path
Wormingford Mere
Weir
Church Hall
CHURCH ROAD
The Grange

Lower Jennies
Motte
Spentpenny Farm
LC
LOWER ROAD
SANDY HILL
Lodge Hills
CO6
Colletts CH
COLLETTS CH
Wormingford

White's Farm
Valley Green Farm
Mount Bures
HALL ROAD
PEARTREE HILL
Elm's Farm
Wormingford Hall
PH
PO
CHERRY DRIVE
Queenswood Farm
Chapel Corner
B1508
MAIN RD

Forge Farm
Morelands Farm
Moat
Little Loveny Hall
Great Loveney Hall
Abrams Farm
DOWLING ROAD
BELLS HILL
Wythers Farm
Josselyns
Wellhouse Farm
New House Farm
Butts Cottages
Moat
Wood Hall
FORDHAM ROAD

Wierstocks Farm
CAMBRIDGE BROOK
Flintfield Farm
ROBERT'S HILL
CHAPEL ROAD
Roberts Farm
Nortons Farm

Loveneys Farm
Water Tower
MIDDLE GREEN
INWORTH LANE
Beak Farm
Sergeants Farm
Golden Square
Jenkins Farm
Fairfields Farm
Rochfords Farm
Rotchfords
Meadow Farm

Stumps Farm
White Horse Farm
THE SPEER
JUPER'S LANE
Rowney's Farm
PACKARDS LANE
Arbour Farm
Moat

Home Farm
Ivy Green Farm
Patricks Farm
Sturgeons Farm
Moat

Berewyk Hall

Essex STREET ATLAS

88   A   89   B   90   C   91   D   92   E   93   F   30

C4
1 STATION HL
2 HAMLET CT
3 WHARF LA
4 CHURCH SQ
5 NEW CUT
6 THE PADDOCKS
7 PARSONAGE GR
8 NORMANDIE WY
9 CAMBRIDGE WY

D4
1 CLAYPITS AV
2 TAWNEYS RIDE

F2
1 ROBLETTS WY
2 HOLLY OAKS
3 GARNONS CH

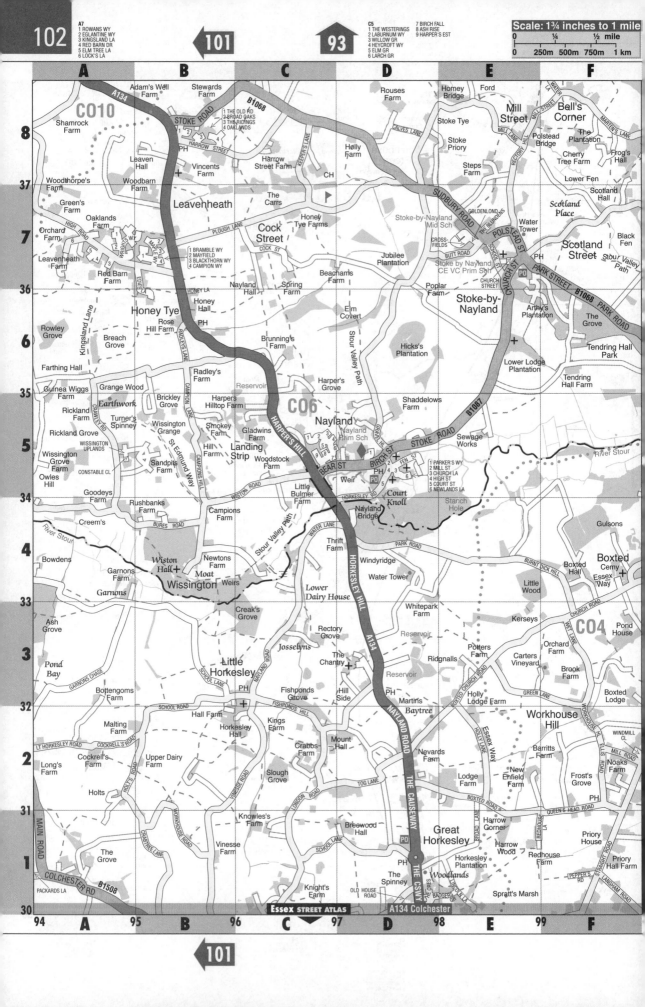

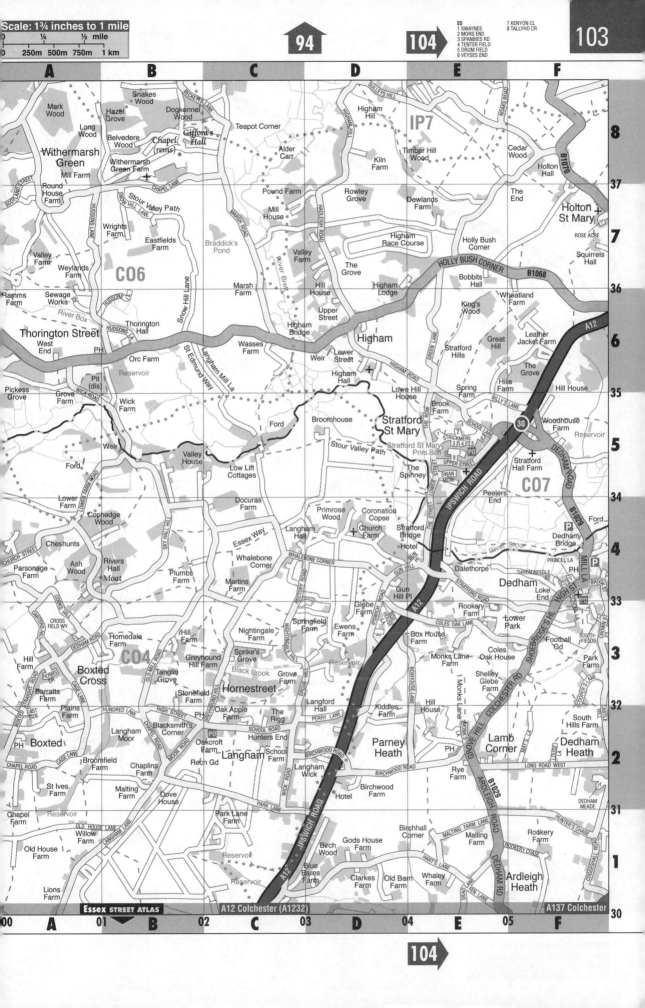

Scale: 1¾ inches to 1 mile

0   ¼   ½ mile
0 250m 500m 750m 1 km

94

104

E5
1 SWAYNES
2 MORS END
3 SPANBIES RD
4 TENTER FIELD
5 DRUM FIELD
6 VEYSES END

7 KENYON CL
8 TALLYHO CR

103

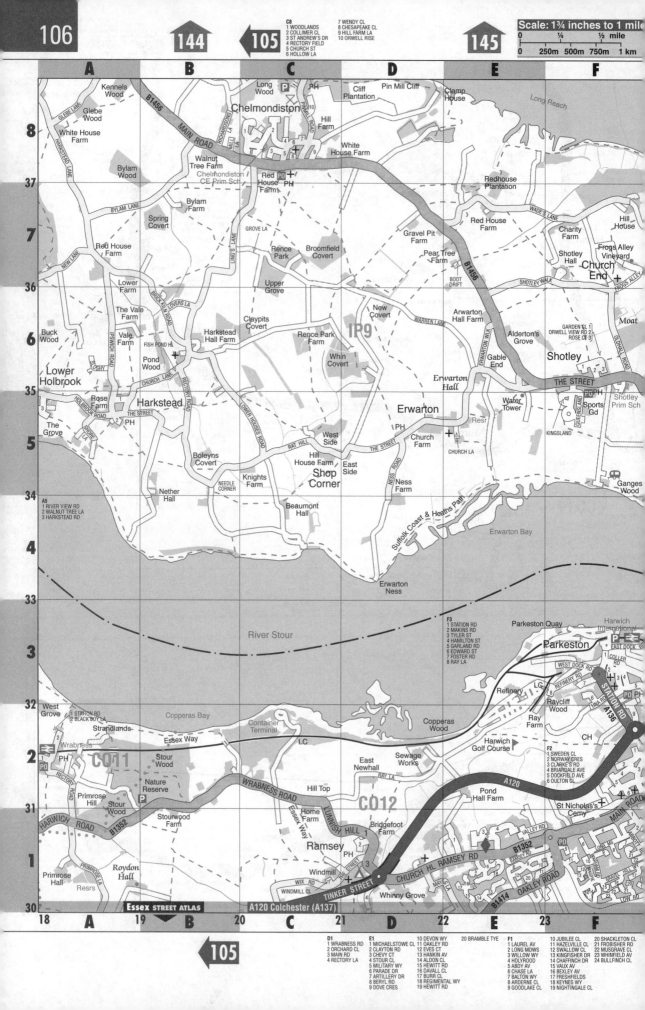

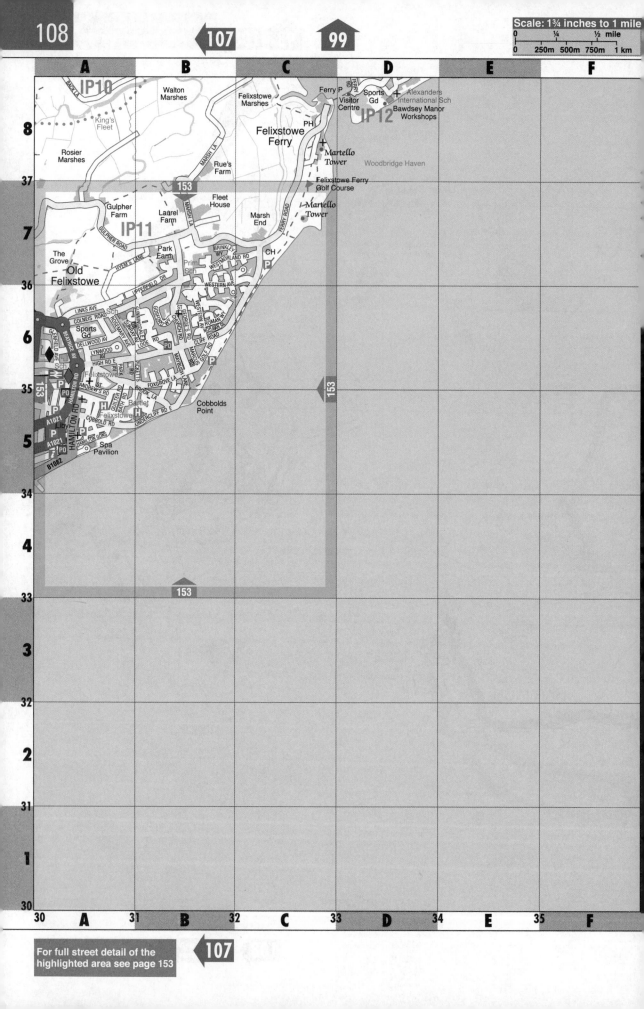

107
99

Scale: 1¾ inches to 1 mile

0   ¼   ½   mile
0   250m 500m 750m 1 km

IP10

Walton Marshes

King's Fleet

Felixstowe Marshes

Ferry P

Sports Gd

Visitor Centre

Alexanders International Sch

Bawdsey Manor Workshops

IP12

Rosier Marshes

Felixstowe Ferry

Marsh LA

Rue's Farm

PH

Martello Tower

Woodbridge Haven

153

Gulpher Farm

Laurel Farm

Fleet House

Marsh End

Felixstowe Ferry Golf Course

IP11

The Grove

Old Felixstowe

GULPHER ROAD

HYEM'S LANE

Park Farm

LIPPERFIELD DR

MARSH LA

BRINKLEY WY

WESTMORLAND RD

Prim Sch

WESTERN AVE

CH

Martello Tower

FERRY ROAD

LINKS AVE

COLNEIS ROAD

Sch

ROSEMARY AVE

SUNNINGDALE

Sports Gd

DELLWOOD AV

LYNWOOD AV

HIGH RD E

GORSON WY

ST CHURCH RD

ST GEORGE'S RD

MORGAN RD

ROMAN RD

WESTERN AV

CLIFF RD

GOLF ROAD

LOOE RD

MAYBUSH LANE

MARIN

GLENFIELD AVE

BEATRICE AV

HAMILTON RD

SUMRAYAN

PICKETTS

PARK DR

BROOK LA

QUILTER RD

BATH RD

COBBOLD RD

HAMILTON GDNS

Felixstowe

ST ANDREW'S RD

FOXGROVE LA

UNDERCLIFF RD E

Cobbolds Point

153

153

A1021

P

PO

P

Library

A1021

PO

Bartlet

Felixstowe

Spa Pavilion

B1082

153

107

For full street detail of the highlighted area see page 153

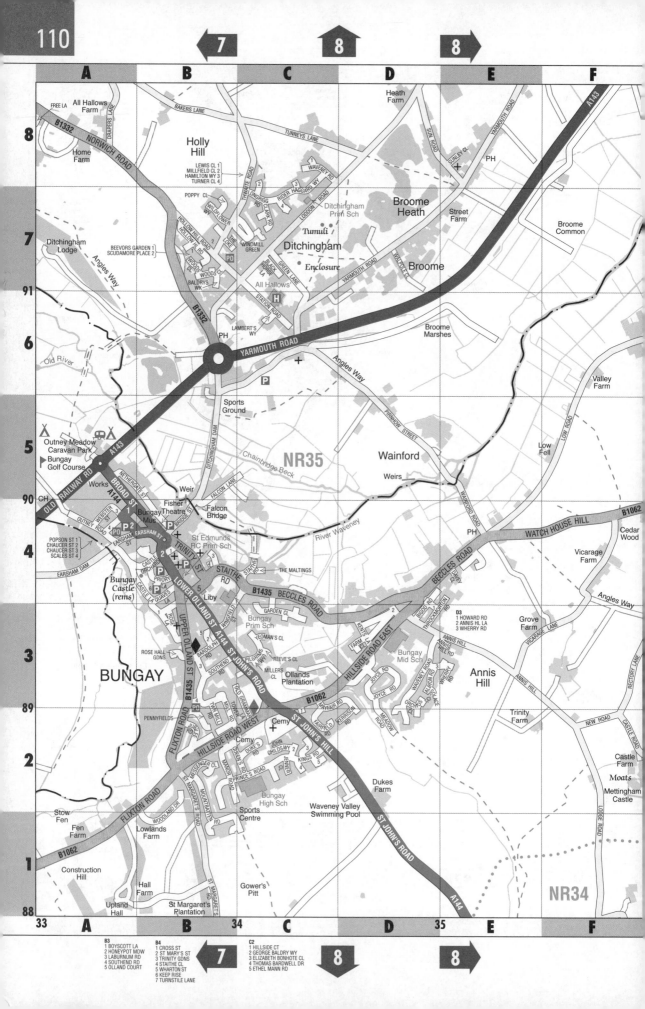

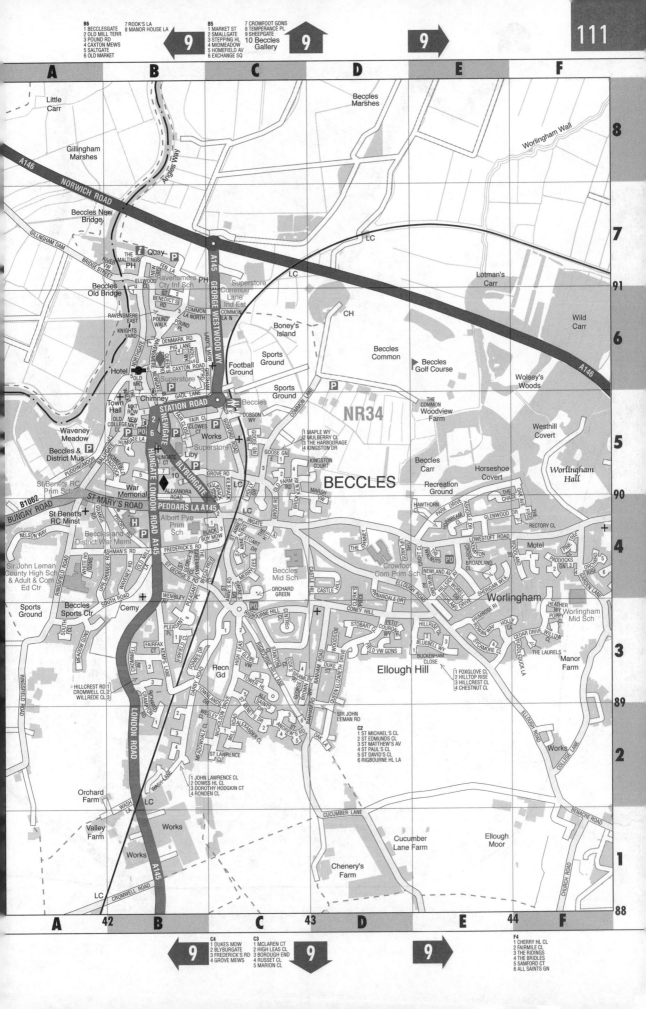

A   B   C   D   E   F

8

BLUNDESTON ROAD B1074

FLIXTON ROAD

B1375
GORLESTON ROAD

Hugh's Wood

HALL ROAD

LAKESIDE RISE

P HM Prison Chy

LAKESIDE RISE

Lowestoft Road

BLUNDESTON ROAD

7

Decoy Farm

Angles Way

WADDLING LA

FLIXTON MARSH LA

Whitehouse Farm

Crossways Farm

OULTON ROAD

96

Flixton Wood

Flixton House

Parkhill Wood

B1375

Newholme Farm

Hotel

6

Nebb Carr

Flixton Decoy

Old Hall

Hall Farm

F6
1 MAPLE COVERT
2 ASPEN COPPICE

F5
1 BOSQUET CL
2 VERDURE CL
3 NORTH FIELD CL
4 SANCTUARY GDNS

Spinney Farm

Parkhill

B1375

THE PASTURES

PARK MDWS

WILLOWTALE

Flixton Marshes

Flixton Wood

B1074

St Andrew's Church (rems)

Workhouse Wood

Oulton

THE RELEAS

LAWN GR

RED CH RD

AIREY CL

TUBBY WALK

FALLOWFIELDS

FIELD GRANGE

5

Blundeston Marshes

NR32

F4
1 CRANWORTH GDNS
2 SANDERS CL
3 AMBERLEY CT
4 BLAKENHAM CL
5 FARNHAM CL
6 SOTHERLEY RD
7 POUND FARM PAR
8 DARSHAM VALE
9 BRAMPTON GROVE
10 ROYDON WAY
11 DUNWICH WAY
12 FRITTON CLOSE

LOTHINGLAND CL

OULTON ROAD

MEADOW RD

MELROSE C

STIRLING CL

95

Flixton Wood

The Fleet

WOOD LA

HALL LANE

B1074

Manor House

UNION LA

PARKHILL

OULTON STREET

B1375

B1074

SOMERLEYTON ROAD

4

Holly Hill

Holly Farm

HALL LANE

E4
1 FERN GREEN CL
2 BROAD FLEET CL
3 HOLLOWELL CL
4 SOUTH LEET CL
5 VALLIBUS CL
6 HERIVAN GDNS
7 STAYNGATE WK

KEMPSHORNE

HOLSTON

GREEN FLEET DR

OULTON COURT BLOOMSBURY

STAFFORD CT

INVER

DINSTON DR

POUND FARM DR

HOLTON AV

GLEMSFORD RD

TUNSTALL DR

HOLBROOK RD

10

8

7

11

GLOUCESTER AVE

Woods Loke Prim Sch

3

Garden Farm

ANGLES WAY

HOLLY HILL

Camps Heath

D2
1 THE TROSSACHS
2 CAMBRIAN CRES
3 CHEVIOT RD
4 HOLLYDENE CL
5 CUTLER RD
6 LONGFIELD WY
7 WHISKIN CL
8 PLUMTREES
9 DESMOND CL

HOBART WY

HOBART CL

Oulton Ind Est

MOBBS WY

Mast

ORPFORD RD

CLAXTON DR

WOODS LOKE W

KESSING DR

94

Oulton Marshes Nature Reserve

NR34

Dairy Farm

WOOD LANE

QUEEN'S HIGHWAY

Copperfield End

Willow's End

CHURCH LANE

BIRCH CL

LIME AVE

WHITING RD

GRAMPIAN WY

SANDS LANE

BRENDON

MENDIP RD

CAMBRIAN DR

COTSWOLD

CHILTERN

HIGHER RD

HODLEIGH DR

PO

GRESHAM RD

2

GRAVEL DAM

Annabel's Spinney

Oulton Broad Prim Sch

Glebe Farm

ANGLES WAY

QUEEN'S HIGHWAY

CHURCH LANE

EDENDALE

KEVINGTON DR

FOXGLADE

THE GLADES

LONGFIELD WY

FERN AVE

GRANGE RD

HERONS LA

BLACKBERRY WY 1
PENNINE WY 2
THE WEALD 3

RONDS MDW

ELMHURST AV

THE DRIVE

LONGDEN AV

MARLBOROUGH RD

Marlborough

CONSTABLE CL

1

Oulton Drive

TESSBEY ROW

BOATSWAIN LA

WAVENEY HILL

ST MICHAEL'S CL

NOEL RD

CURLEW GN

CHRISTMAS LANE

HALL DR

PROSPECT RD

BLINCO RD

HOLTON RD

ALLEN RD

CLARKSON RD

BROAD RD

ROCK RD

MOYES RD

GILPIN RD

CHESTNUT AV

PATRICIA

HARRISON RD 1
HARBOUR RD 2
GEORGE CL 3

HALL ROAD

PO

The Spinney

HOLLY LN

BERRY

RED LN

BRIDGE RD

A1117 NORMANSTON DRIVE

Oulton Broad North

MARLBOROUGH RD

LEATHES CL

MUTFORD

LAKES

LEATHES WY

93

BORROW RD

CALDECOTT RD

COMMODORE RD

P

LC

LOTHING ST

HARBOUR

50   A   B   51   C   D   52   E   F

D1
1 PEGASUS MEWS
2 SWONNELL'S WLK
3 MALTSTERS' WY

F2
1 MILL BANK
2 GRESHAM AV
3 MONCKTON AV
4 MONCKTON CRES
5 BURGESS CL

F3
1 ORWELL DR
2 WENHASTON DR
3 BUTLEY DR
4 DEDHAM DR
5 LAVENHAM WY

3   3

A   B   C   D   E   F

8
7
96
6
5
95
4
94
3
2
93

B5
1 MONET SQ
2 RENOIR WY
3 KNIGHTSWOOD
4 VILLAGE WY
5 PLEASUREWOOD CL
6 ASTBURY RD

A6
1 GREENWOOD WY
2 LEONARD DR
3 STIMPSON CL
4 WAINWRIGHT CL
5 QUINNELL WY
6 ROWNTREE CL
7 SOTTERLEY CL

B6
1 DEGAS GDNS
2 HOLBEIN WY
3 COTMAN CL
4 CANALETTO CL
5 VERMEER CL
6 ROMNEY PL
7 BURWOOD PL
8 HOGARTH WLK
9 VAN DYCK CL
10 RAPHAEL WALK

C6
1 MURILLO DR
2 HUBBARD'S AV
3 REMBRANDT CL
4 TURNER CL

E3
1 CART SCORE
2 LIGHTHOUSE SCORE
3 ST MARGARET'S RD
4 OSBORNE ST
5 CAMDEN ST

E2
1 ALBANY RD
2 MARINERS ST
3 COMPASS ST
4 WHITE HORSE ST
5 CROWN ST EAST
6 DUKES HEAD ST
7 HIGH ST
8 OLD MARKET PLAIN
9 TRIANGLE YARD
10 ST PETER'S ST
11 ARTILLERY WY
12 SPURGEON SCORE
13 CUMBERLAND PLACE
14 MANOR CT
15 GODFREY'S COURT

E1
1 CHRIST CHURCH SQ
2 HERRING FISHERY SCORE
3 ARNOLD ST
4 OLD NELSON ST
5 BATTERY GREEN RD
6 MARINA
7 BATTERY GN

A3
1 PEMBROOKE WY
2 COLLEGE MDWS
3 MAGDALEN CL
4 FASTOLT CL
5 CHATSWORTH CL
6 RINGSFIELD CL
7 CAVENDISH CL
8 WALBERSWICK WY

A4
1 CULZEAN GDNS
2 ASHNESS CL
3 PATTERDALE GDNS
4 KIRKSTONE WY
5 DERWENT GDNS
6 SNAPE DR
7 WORLINGHAM WY
8 LULWORTH PK
9 PENTLAND WLK

B2
1 GREENACRE CRES
2 BROOM RD
3 MAGNOLIA CL
4 MARHAM RD
5 NORMANSTON DR
6 MYRTLE CL
7 NORMANSTON DR
8 SOUTH VIEW CL

B4
1 FROSTENDEN CRES
2 SPASHETT RD
3 CRISP CL
4 HOPELYN CL
5 CASTLETON CL
6 GODETIA CL

C2
1 NEWSON'S MDW
2 NICHOLSON SQ
3 CROWN MEADOW WLK
4 LATTENS SQ
5 VIBURNUM GREEN

C1
1 THE CROFT
2 UNION RD
3 STANFORD ST
4 TRAFALGAR ST

D1
1 ETHEL RD
2 RAGLAN RD
3 CLAPHAM RD CENTRAL
4 LEISTON RD
5 POLICE STATION RD
6 SURREY ST
7 RISHTON RD
8 SUMMER RD
9 CAMP RD

10 MILTON RD WEST
11 Marina Theatre

D2
1 CLARENCE RD
2 THE HEMPLANDS
3 THURSTON RD
4 ST PETER'S ST
5 ARNOLD ST
6 ADRIAN RD
7 JACOBS ST
8 CATHCART ST
9 CHAPEL ST
10 CHAPEL ST
11 ELIM TERR
12 GODFREY'S CT

LOWESTOFT

NR32

Gunton
Normanston
Roman Hill

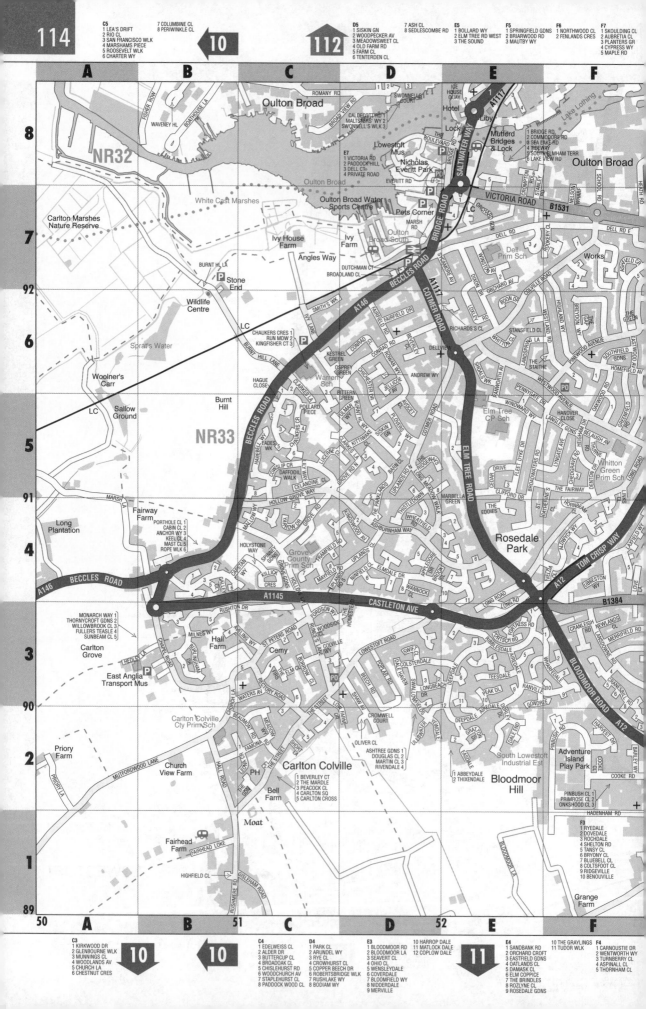

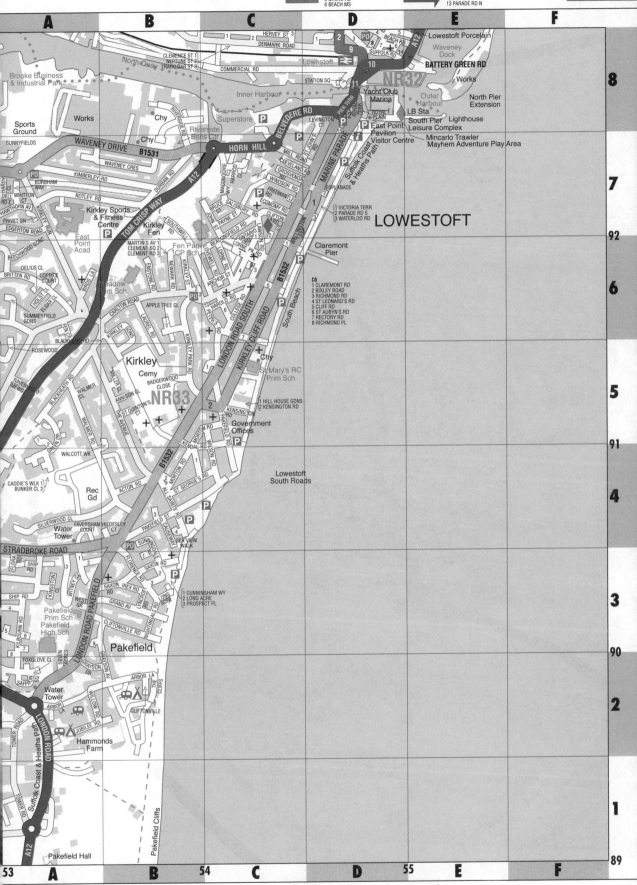

C7
1 ST LEONARD'S RD
2 LAWSON CT
3 UNION PL
4 ORCHARD TERR

D8
1 FLENSBURGH ST
2 KATWIJK WY
3 BEVAN ST E
4 SURREY ST
5 GROVE RD
6 BEACH MS

7 BON MARCHE
8 LONDON RD N
9 DENMARK RD
10 WAVENEY RD
11 STATION SQ
12 FYFFE WY
13 PARADE RD N

14 HERRING MARKET

113
11

A3
1 NELSON RD
2 WELLINGTON RD
3 WITNEY RD
4 CRANFIELD CL
5 MARSDEN CL
6 KILBOURN RD
7 SPEEDWELL CL
8 HONEYSUCKLE CL

B4
1 ROCHESTER RD
2 SHORT ST
3 DOLPHIN CL
4 KIRKDALE CT

11
11

Fairstead Farm

Spexhall Manor

Hall Farm

Wissett Hall

Fenn Farm

HALESWORTH

Halesworth Gall

The Copse

Red House Farm

WASH LANE

MILL ROAD

WALPOLE RD

B1111

LONDON RD

ROMAN WAY

B1123

SAXONS WAY

Trewens Farm

Dairy Farm

Moat Farm

Hightrees Farm

Airfield (disused)

Scalesbrook Wood

Upper Holton

Laurel Farm

Orchard End

Hall Farm

Water Tower

B1124

Oak Tree Farm

Broadway Farm

PH

SPARROWHAWK ROAD

STONE STREET

A144

Broadway Farm

Fairview Farm

Works

Valley Farm

Broadway

Halesworth (Holton) Airfield Mus

IP19

Brick Kiln Farm

Woodside Farm

NORWICH ROAD

BROADWAY DR

FAIR VIEW RD

GREEN BANK

HENTLEY CRESCENT

Douglas CL

WAPWICK AV

HARRISONS LA

Halesworth Mid Sch

Patrick Stead

Town Farm

BECCLES ROAD

St Peters Church Wood

Valley Farm

LODGE ROAD

BUNGAY RD

PARK WK

ST PETERS PATH

Holton St Peter Prim Sch

Holton

The Street

Holton St Peter Postmill

LOWER PK WK

SANDY LA

CHURCH VIEW

BLYFORD LANE

MILL RD

PO PH

B1124

ORCHARD VALLEY

VALLEY CL

Edgar Sewter Prim Sch

HILLSIDE WY 1
UPLANDS WY 2
CHURCHILL RD 3
UPPER AV 4

OLD STATION RD

THE AVENUE

PLEASANT

PARRY CLOSE

WISSETT RD

FENN CL

Park Rd

CHICHESTER RD

MILL HLR DR

RECTORY ST

RECTORY GREEN

SCHOOL LANE

Wr Twr

H

Sports Gd

1 ORCHID CL
2 BRAMBLEWOOD WY
3 BRIAR CL

A144

STATION RD

P

Halesworth & District Mus

Dairy Hl

LOAM PIT LANE

QUAY ST

Halesworth

Cemy

1 BENSLY'S DRIFT
2 THE PADDOCKS
3 SARSEN CL
4 CASTLE HL

HILL FARM RD

HOLTON TERR

LARKS RD

Hill Farm

HOLTON ROAD

B1123

Avondale Farm

PH

B1123

SOUTHWOLD ROAD

Corner Farm

Dairy Farm

Liby

P

BRIDGE ST

SAXONS WAY

P

PO

Angel Link

RIVER DR

Leisure Club

CHEDISTON STREET

OLD BREWERY YD

BEECH

NEW

HOLMERE DR

HOLDBERGH DR

STEEPLE END

SWAN LANE

LONDON RD

THOROUGHFARE

1 BENTON WY
2 NEW CUT
3 MALTINGS CL

Halesworth Millennium Green

POUND

SWAN CL

LANSBURY RD

BIGOD CL

1 ANDREW JOHNSTON WY
2 CRABTREE CL
3 LAMBERT CL

BABINGTON DR

HIGHFIELD RD

BLYTH ROAD

Sewage Works

Red House Farm

Mells

Chapel

St Margarets Farm

Old Chapel Farm

Gravel Pit

DUKE'S DRIVE

JERMYN WY

CONSTABLE CL

BARONS CL

DUKE'S DR

QUEENS DR

PRINCES

CARL CL

QUEENS DR

ORCHARD

GAINSBOROUGH DR

LONDON RD

DURBAN CLOSE

BRAMFIELD RD

BEDINGFIELD CR

KENNEDY AV

KENNEDY CL

Mells Bridge

LC

A144

Mells Hill Farm

WASH LANE

A3
1 BOUCHAIN CT
2 MARKET PL
3 CHURCH FARM LA
4 HAREPARK CL
5 BARLEY MDW
6 DAKING'S DRIFT
7 ALLINGTON RD
8 CLAYHILLS
9 THE LIMES

Parking £1 - 2 hrs

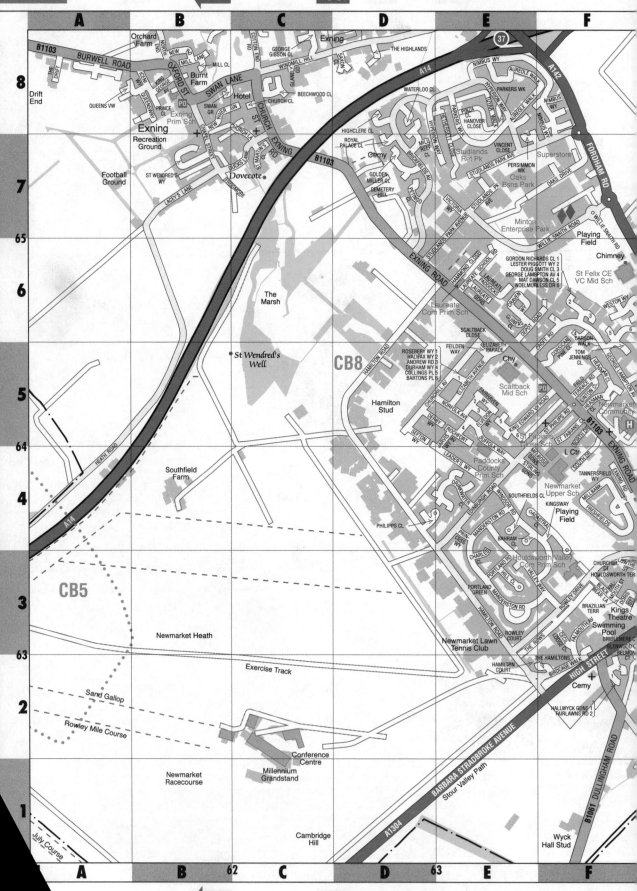

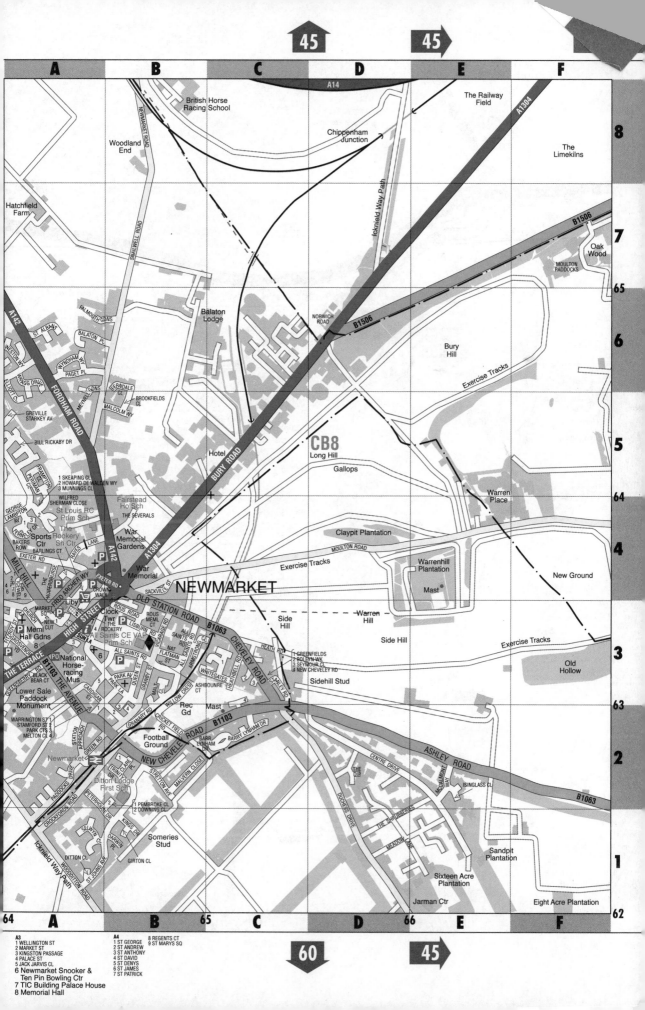

A B C D E F

8 7 65 6 5 64 4 3 63 2 1 62

A14

British Horse
Racing School

The Railway
Field

The Limekilns

Chippenham
Junction

Woodland
End

Icknield Way Path

A1304

Hatchfield
Farm

B1506

Oak
Wood

Balaton
Lodge

MOULTON
PADDOCKS

Norwich
Road

B1506

Bury
Hill

FALMOUTH GDNS

BALATON PL.

Exercise Tracks

ST ALBANS

WYNDHAM WY

WRAGG DRIVE

ELLIOTT CL

PAGET PL

FERNDALE CL

BROOKFIELDS CL

MALCOLM WY

GREVILLE STARKEY AV

BILL RICKABY DR

FORDHAM ROAD

BURY ROAD

A142

CB8

Long Hill

Gallops

Hotel

Warren
Place

1 SKEAPING CL
2 HOWARD DE WALDEN WY
3 MUNNINGS CL

WILFRED SHERMAN CLOSE

St Louis RC
Prim Sch

Fairstead
Ho Sch

THE SEVERALS

FRAMPTON

PETTITTS

GEORGE LAMPTON AV

FERNE

BAKERS ROW

The
Rookery
Sh Ctr

Sports
Ctr

BARLINGS CT

War
Memorial
Gardens

Claypit Plantation

Warrenhill
Plantation

Mast

New Ground

A1304

MOULTON ROAD

Exercise Tracks

EXETER RD

THE WATERHOUSE

FRED ARCHER WY

TRAVERS LANE

War
Memorial

CROWN WALK

NEWMARKET

MILL HILL

CROMWELL

Liby

MARKET SQ

THE

ROUS ROAD

LISBURN RD

OLD STATION ROAD

B1063

Side
Hill

Warren
Hill

NEW.1 CUT

THE ROOKERY

Clock
Twr

MEML CT

VICARAGE RD

CHEVELEY ROAD

Side Hill

Exercise Tracks

Old
Hollow

Mem'l
Hall Gdns

All Saints CE VA
Prim Sch

ALL SAINTS RD

ST
SAINTS RD

NAT
FLATMAN
ST

ARMSTRONG

HEATHERBELL RD

HEATH RD

1 GREENFIELDS
2 BOLEYN WK
3 SEYMOUR CL
4 NEW CHEVELEY RD

THE TERRACE

B1103

National
Horse-
racing Mus

BLACK
BEAR CT

WHITEGATES

ASHBOURNE CT

ASHLEY RD

Sidehill Stud

QUEENSBERRY RD

Lower Sale
Paddock
Monument

Park Av

PARK LA

ALL SAINTS RD

CARDIGAN

WILLOW CRES

Rec
Gd

Mast

CRICKET FIELD

B1103

B1103

ASHLEY ROAD

B1063

WARRINGTON ST 1
STAMFORD ST 2
PARK CTS 3
MELTON CL 4

STATION
APPROACH

GREEN RD

GRANARY RD

Football
Ground

NEW CHEVELEY ROAD

BARR
LYNHAM
DR

Barry Lynham Dr

CENTRE DRIVE

THE DIB

MEDERMONT WAY

ISINGLASS CL

Newmarket

PADDOCKS ROAD

CROCKFORDS ROAD

TRINITY

CLARE

STRETTON AVE

MALVERN CLOSE

DUCHESS DRIVE

THE SHRUBBERIES

Icknield Way Path

PETERHOUSE DR

KINGS DR

SELWYN CL

DARWIN

DITTON CL

Ditton Lodge
First Sch

1 PEMBROKE CL
2 DOWNING CL

Someries
Stud

GIRTON CL

ST JOHNS AVE

WOODDITTON ROAD

MEADOW LANE

Sandpit
Plantation

Sixteen Acre
Plantation

Jarman Ctr

Eight Acre Plantation

A3
1 WELLINGTON ST
2 MARKET ST
3 KINGSTON PASSAGE
4 PALACE ST
5 JACK JARVIS CL
6 Newmarket Snooker &
   Ten Pin Bowling Ctr
7 TIC Building Palace House
8 Memorial Hall

A4
1 ST GEORGE
2 ST ANDREW
3 ST ANTHONY
4 ST DAVID
5 ST DENYS
6 ST JAMES
7 ST PATRICK

8 REGENTS CT
9 ST MARYS SQ

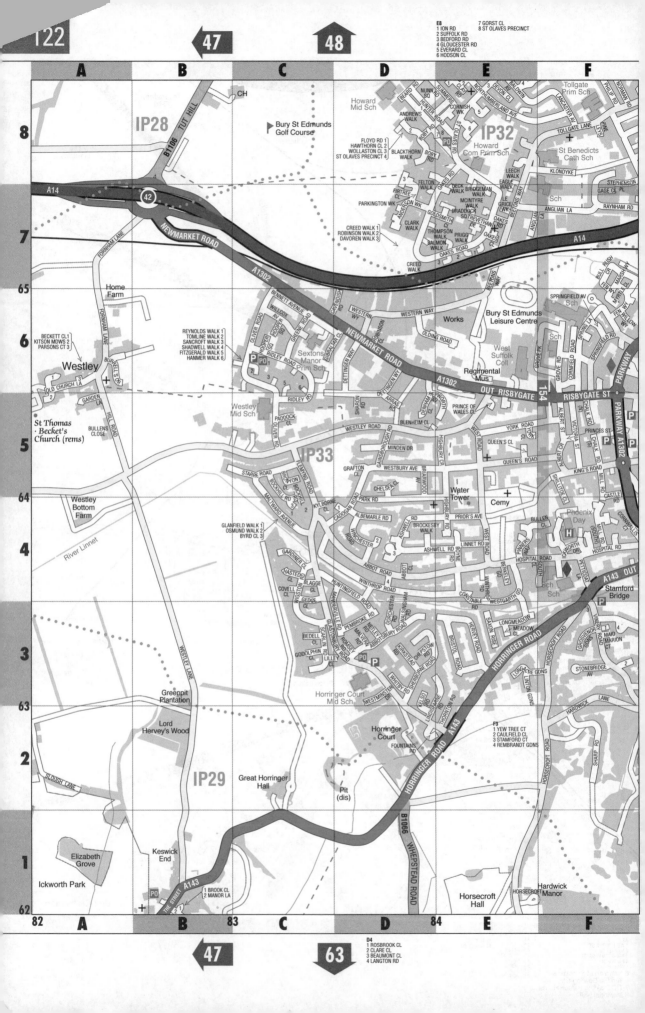

47

48

E8
1 ION RD
2 SUFFOLK RD
3 BEDFORD RD
4 GLOUCESTER RD
5 EVERARD CL
6 HODSON CL
7 GORST CL
8 ST OLAVES PRECINCT

Map labels

IP28
TUT HILL
B1106
CH
Bury St Edmunds Golf Course
Howard Mid Sch
NUNN SQ
SUMMERS RD
BEARD RD
NUNN SQ
HUNTER ROAD
ANDREWS WALK
POST RD
CORNISH WK
NORTHUMBERLAND AVE
DEVON CL
BALDWIN
IP32
Howard Com Prim Sch
FLOYD RD 1
HAWTHORN CL 2
WOLLASTON CL 3
ST OLAVES PRECINCT 4
BLACKTHORN WALK
BORY RD
FELTON WK
FIRTREE WK
OAKES RD
DECK WALK
BRIDGEMAN WALK
McINTYRE WALK
BRADDOCK
GOLDSMITH SQ
GRICE CL
TREVETHAN RD
LE GRICE CL
EAGLE WALK
LEECH WALK
KLONDYKE
St Benedicts Cath Sch
Tollgate Prim Sch
PHILIP RD
NORMAN RD
LANCASTER AV
PINE LEYS
TOLLGATE LANE
STEPHENSON
GAGE CL
PL
RAYNHAM RD
ANGLIAN LA
PARKINGTON WK
ANDERSON WK
CLARK WALK
GOLDSMITH SQ
THOMPSON WALK
PRIGG WALK
SALMON WALK
PRIGG WALK
OAKES CL
OAKES RD
OAKES CL
CREED WALK 1
ROBINSON WALK 2
DAVOREN WALK 3
CREED WALK
NEWMARKET ROAD
A1302
A14
42
NEWMARKET ROAD
FORNHAM LANE
Home Farm
BENNETT AVENUE
CATHEDRAL CT
WESTERN WY
ROBINSON WY
WESTERN WY
Western Way
Works
OLDING ROAD
Bury St Edmunds Leisure Centre
BEETONS WAY
SPRINGFIELD AV
Sch
BULL BUSH
KELWAY
MARSHWAY
TEN BELLS WY
A14
65
BECKETT CL 1
KITSON MDWS 2
PARSONS CT 3
Westley
FORNHAM LANE
REYNOLDS WALK 1
TOMLINE WALK 2
SANCROFT WALK 3
SHADWELL WALK 4
FITZGERALD WALK 5
HANMER WALK 6
OLIVER ROAD
WILLCOX
HOPPER
GREENE RD
RIDLEY ROAD
PO
Sextons Manor Prim Sch
DETTINGEN WAY
NEWMARKET ROAD
A1302
OUT RISBYGATE
Regimental Mus
West Suffolk Coll
CROFT RD
SPRINGFIELD RD
CORNFIELD ROAD
RISBYGATE ST
PARKWAY
6
St Thomas Becket's Church (rems)
BURRELL'S RD
Old Church La
GARDEN LA
HILL ROAD
BULLENS CLOSE
Westley Mid Sch
PADDOCK
OLIVER ROAD
RIDLEY RD
DETTINGEN WAY
SHARON RD
ARRAS RD
DERHAM
HEPWORTH
BLENHEIM CL
PRINCE OF WALES CL
WEST ROAD
York Road
A1302
OUT RISBYGATE
A14
CROFT RD
ALBERT ST
VICTORIA RD
PRINCES ST
CHALK RD
CHALK RD
5
STARRE ROAD
BOCKILL RD
LYON
BOCKILL
FLEMING ROAD
GAINSBOROUGH RD
WESTLEY ROAD
MINDEN DR
GRAFTON CL
WESTBURY AVE
CHELSEA CL
BRIARWOOD AV
PARK RD
HIGHBURY CR
Water Tower
QUEEN'S CL
Queen's Road
QUEEN'S CL
KING'S ROAD
SHILLITOE CL
CASTLE RD
IP33
64
Westley Bottom Farm
River Linnet
MALTWARD AVENUE
GLANFIELD WALK 1
OSMUND WALK 2
BYRD CL 3
CADOGAN RD
KYLBORNE
ALBEMARLE RD
ASHWELL RD
BROCKESBY WALK
PRIOR'S AVE
BOYNE
LINNET ROAD
WEST ROAD
Cemy
BULLEN CL
Phoenix Day
CORNWALLIS
MILL RD SOUTH
MILL RD NORTH
4
GARDINER CL
HASTED CL
BLAGGE CL
COVELL CL
WISTON
GEDGE CL
HUNTINGFIELD ROAD
WINCHESTER ROAD
ABBOT ROAD
WINTHROP ROAD
ABBOT RD
CONSTABLE RD
WESTGARTH RD
WINTHROP RD
BERKELEY CL
Sch
HOSPITAL ROAD
ICKNORTH DR
Hospital Rd
PETTICOAT LA
A143 OUT
Stamford Bridge
STARE RD
3
Greeppit Plantation
WESTLEY LANE
BEDELL CL
GODOLPHIN CL
MANDEVILLE RD
GLASTONBURY RD
LILLEY CL
PEMBROKE RD
WHITBY RD
SHERBORNE RD
KIRKSTEAD
CHEPSTOW RD
MALTBY RD
ABBOTSBURY RD
CORCHESTER RD
WALSINGHAM
PO
BRISTOL ROAD
KELSO
HENLEY ROAD
SAXON RISE
MEADOW CL
LONGMEADOW
HORRINGER ROAD
A143
LINTON GDNS
LONGCASTLE GDNS
HARDWICK LANE
Stonebridge
GROSVENOR AV
MAID MARION CT
F3
1 YEW TREE CT
2 CAULFIELD CL
3 STAMFORD CT
4 REMBRANDT GDNS
63
Lord Hervey's Wood
Horringer Court Mid Sch
WESTMINSTER DR
THORNTON RD
LINDISFARNE RD
Horringer Court
FOUNTAINS RD
HORRINGER ROAD
A143
HORSECROFT ROAD
SHARP RD
HARDWICK LANE
2
IP29
Great Horringer Hall
Pit (dis)
B1066
WHEPSTEAD ROAD
Horsecroft Hall
HORSECROFT
Hardwick Manor
SLOUGH LANE
1
Elizabeth Grove
Ickworth Park
Keswick End
PO
THE STREET
A143
1 BROOK CL
2 MANOR LA
62
82
83
84

47

63

D4
1 ROSBROOK CL
2 CLARE CL
3 BEAUMONT CL
4 LANGTON RD

A B C D E F

IP31

IP31

Westfield Farm

1 FORNHAM RD
2 MILDENHALL RD
3 TOLLGATE LA
4 LAYHAM DR
5 HANOVER CL

154

A143 COMPIEGNE WAY

COMPIEGNE WAY

A1101 FORDHAM ROAD

MERMAID CLOSE

RIVERSIDE CT

AVENUE APP

43

A143

1 SOUTHERN BELLE CL
2 MAULKIN CL
3 HOLLIDAY CL
4 MANNING RD
5 KINGFISHER CL
6 WAGTAIL DR
7 NORTHERN ROSE CL

THINGOE HL

Bury St Edmunds

Superstore

Factory

Chimney

Chimney

HOLDERNESS RD

CHAPEL POND HL

A14

A31X

COMPIEGNE WY

NORTHGATE

The Original Factory Shop

RUSSET CL

APPLEDOWN DR

7

Works

EASTERN WAY

Eastern Way

St Nicholas Cl

BARTON ROAD

BRAFIELD

GREENWAY

POND GR

MANOR EAST

BRAMLEY CL

SHEERWATER

65

EASTERN WY

LEABROOK

KINGSWORTH

ORTTEWELL ROAD

SWAN DR

6

Football Ground

MARK JENNINGS LA

COTTON LANE

UNICORN

EASTGATE ST PL

EAST

St Stephens Cl

IP32

MOUNT ROAD

MANOR AST

RAINOR

WINSFORD

CARDINAL

DOWNING

MOUNT ROAD

DARBY CL

CALA

HOPE CL

BRUNWIN

TASSEL CL

LIBERTY

JERMYN AV

Gov Off

Liby

Mus

St Andrew's St S

BARN LA

MINDEN CL

MUSTOW STREET

PICKWICK CRES

PUMP LA

LOOMS LA

ANGEL LA

Priory Specl Sch

D6
1 LAYWOOD CL
2 EMSWORTH CL
3 MIDHURST CL
4 ARUNDEL CL
5 HASELMERE CL
6 LYMINGSTER CL

Moreton Hall Prep Sch

DOWNING CL

ORTTEWELL ROAD

E6
1 BRACKENWOOD CR
2 PIPPIN CL
3 LAMBOURNE CL
4 HONEYSUCKLE WY
5 WORCESTER CL
6 BOURNE AV

MARKANT

FISKE

BLUEBELL AV

COLTSFOOT

BITTERCUP

DAISY AV

COWSLIP CV

5

St Edmundsbury Cath

ATHENAEUM LA

154

St James Mid Sch

SHAKER'S LANE

Sebert Wood County Prim Sch

SYMONDS ROAD

REDGOLD

SUTTON CL

SWAYNE

CAMOMILE DR

DROVERS AVE

Chapel (rems)

Manor House Mus

CHEQUER SQ

HONEY HL

SPARHAWK ST

River Lark

SYMONDS RD

BIGORIC RD

OSWYN RD

Layhill

BERNHAM

RAGWALD DR

DARCY

BROWSE

CROPLEY

64

BURY ST EDMUNDS

GUILDHALL ST

WESTGATE ST

GATNDE ST

SWAN LA

Layhill Covert

MYLFORD

SALTER CL

BEDINGFELD WAY

GREYFRIARS

CHAMBERLAYNE

BUNTING RD

BULFORD ROAD

KEMPSON WAY

4

PARKWAY

Nuffield

Sch

FRIAR'S LANE

COPPERS CL

MAYNEWATER LANE

BAKER

RAINGATE ST

Sports Ground

No Man's Meadows

Southgate Bridge

44

ATKINS

EASLEA RD

Moreton Hall Ret Pk

St Edmundsbury Retail Park

Suffolk Business Park

KEMPSON WY

A14

WESTGATE

Holywater Meadows

154

St Edmund Way

CULLUM ROAD

A1302

Government Offices

TANNERY DRVE

SEXTONS MD

Football Ground

ROUGHAM ROAD

ROUGHAM HILL

RUSHBROOKE LANE

Lorry Park

3

MBRANDT WY

HOLYWELL CL

RUNNYMEDE LN

LAUNDRY LA

CHICHESTER CL

GRINDLE GDN

BEECH

VALE LANE

BOTANY WY

SHAKER'S LA

63

Broom Plantation

Puthawks Bush Plantation

1 CULLUM RD
2 SOUTHGATE ST
3 SOUTHGATE GDNS
4 THE GATEWAY
5 BYFIELD WY
6 NOWTON RD

GOVERNORS MEWS

IP33

Fenbrook Farm

RUSHBROOKE LANE

2

SAMUEL STREET WK 1
GRANGE WK 2
PEMBERTON WK 3
THE SEWELLS 4

Hardwick Heath

Hardwick Prim Sch

FAIERS CL

HERON RD

Hardwick Shopping Centre

MAYFIELD RD

NOWTON ROAD

BURY RD DR

VICTORY RD

STEWARD RD

BRIGHT CL

JARMAN

Sports Ground

South Lee Sch

Sports Gd

Southgate Farm

SICKLESMERE ROAD

Far End

H

Hardwick Lane

HARDWICK LANE

WATSON CL

KESTREL RD

OLLE

THE CURLEWS

PLOVERS WY

1 SMITH WALK
2 CAIE WALK
3 BEVIS WALK
4 FULCHER CL
5 MAYFIELD RD

North Hill Covert

Little Spinney

1

he West Suffolk

FALLOWFIELD WALK

HACKLING DR

CROFT RD

COPSE

TOWNLANE

CODSIDE

OLD TOWN LN

REDWING

1 BANKS WALK
2 RAVEN RD

A134

IP30

Great Spinney

RISEWAY CL

Hardwick Mid Sch

IP29

Nowton Park

62

A B 86 C D 87 E F

B8
1 WALTON CL
2 WORDSWORTH RD
3 RUSKIN CL
4 ELIOT WY

66

C7
1 DELIUS CL
2 MARGARET RD
3 KINGSMEAD CL
4 WOLSEY RD

66

D6
1 TYDEMANS CT
2 THURLOW CT
3 BURY ST
4 MILTON RD N
5 MARRIOTT'S WK

67

E5
1 STRICKLANDS RD
2 CHESTNUT GR
3 HOLLINGSWORTH RD
4 LOCKINGTON CL

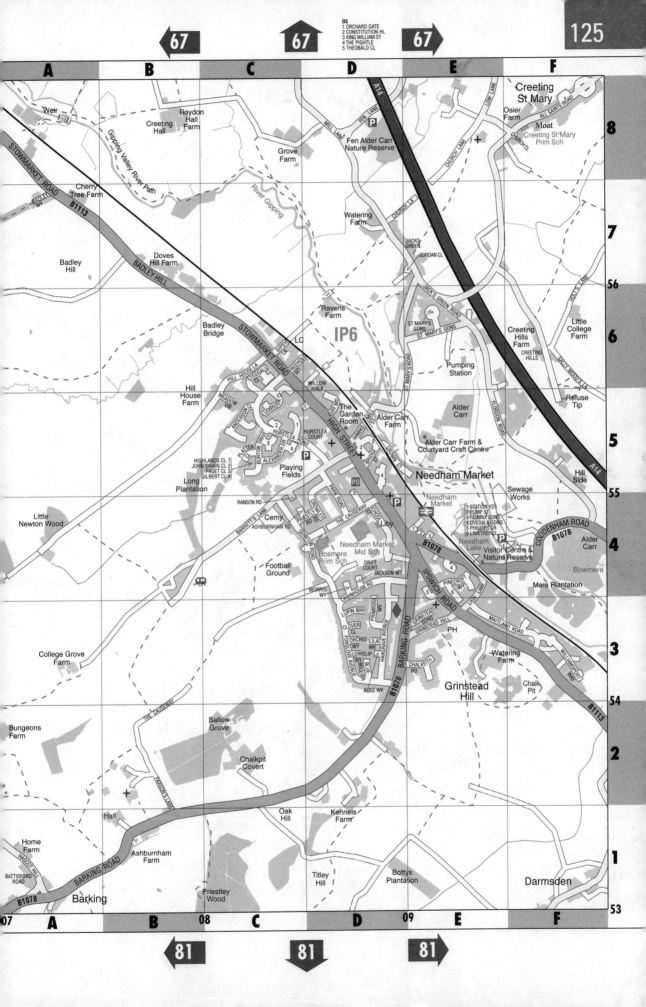

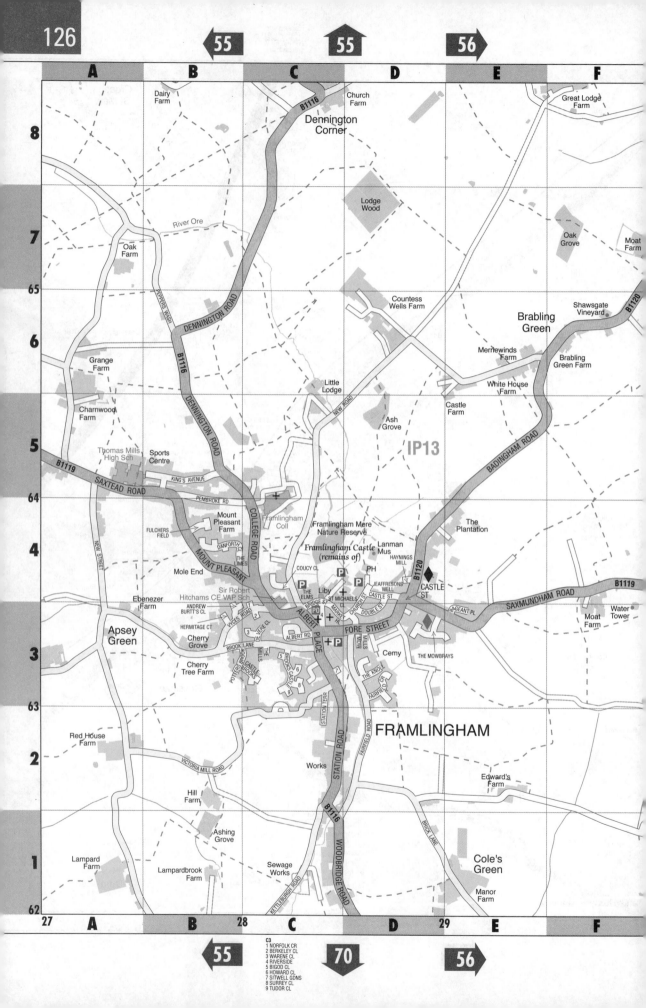

A   B   C   D   E   F

8

Dairy
Farm

B1116

Church
Farm

Dennington
Corner

Great Lodge
Farm

7

River Ore

Lodge
Wood

Oak
Grove

Moat
Farm

65

Oak
Farm

PEPPER'S WASH

DENNINGTON ROAD

Countess
Wells Farm

Shawsgate
Vineyard

B1120

6

B1116

Grange
Farm

Brabling
Green

Merriewinds
Farm

Brabling
Green Farm

Little
Lodge

New Road

White House
Farm

Charnwood
Farm

DENNINGTON ROAD

BADINGHAM ROAD

Castle
Farm

Ash
Grove

IP13

5

B1119

SAXTEAD ROAD

Thomas Mills
High Sch

Sports
Centre

KING'S AVENUE

The
Plantation

64

PEMBROKE RD

Framlingham
Coll

Framlingham Mere
Nature Reserve

COLLEGE ROAD

Mount
Pleasant
Farm

4

NEW STREET

FULCHERS
FIELD

DANFORTH

THE
LIMES

MOUNT PLEASANT

Mole End

Framlingham Castle
(remains of)

Lanman
Mus

HAYNINGS
MILL

B1120

B1119

SAXMUNDHAM ROAD

COUCY CL

PH

Ebenezer
Farm

Sir Robert
Hitchams CE VAP Sch

ANDREW
BURTT'S CL

P

THE
ELMS

Liby

ST MICHAELS

JEAFFRESONS
WELL

CASTLE
ST

Water
Tower

Apsey
Green

HERMITAGE CT

VYCES ROAD

VERE CL

BRIDGE ST

ST MARK'S
HL

CASTLE ST

CHURCH ST

PAGEANT PL

Moat
Farm

Cherry
Grove

ALBERT PLACE

PO

DOUBLE ST

BROOK LANE

ALBERT RD

FORE STREET

3

Cherry
Tree Farm

POTTER'S BROOK

BROOKS CL

CASTLE BROOKS

THE MILLS

Cemy

THE KNOLL

MILLS MDW

THE MOWBRAYS

FAIRFIELD CR

Fairfield

63

STATION TERR

FRAMLINGHAM

2

Red House
Farm

VICTORIA MILL ROAD

STATION ROAD

FAIRFIELD ROAD

Works

Edward's
Farm

Hill
Farm

Ashing
Grove

B1116

WOODBRIDGE ROAD

BRICK LANE

1

Lampard
Farm

Lampardbrook
Farm

Sewage
Works

KETTLEBURGH ROAD

Cole's
Green

Manor
Farm

62

27   A   B   28   C   D   29   E   F

C3
1 NORFOLK CR
2 BERKELEY CL
3 WARENE CL
4 RIVERSIDE
5 BIGOD CL
6 HOWARD CL
7 SITWELL GDNS
8 SURREY CL
9 TUDOR CL

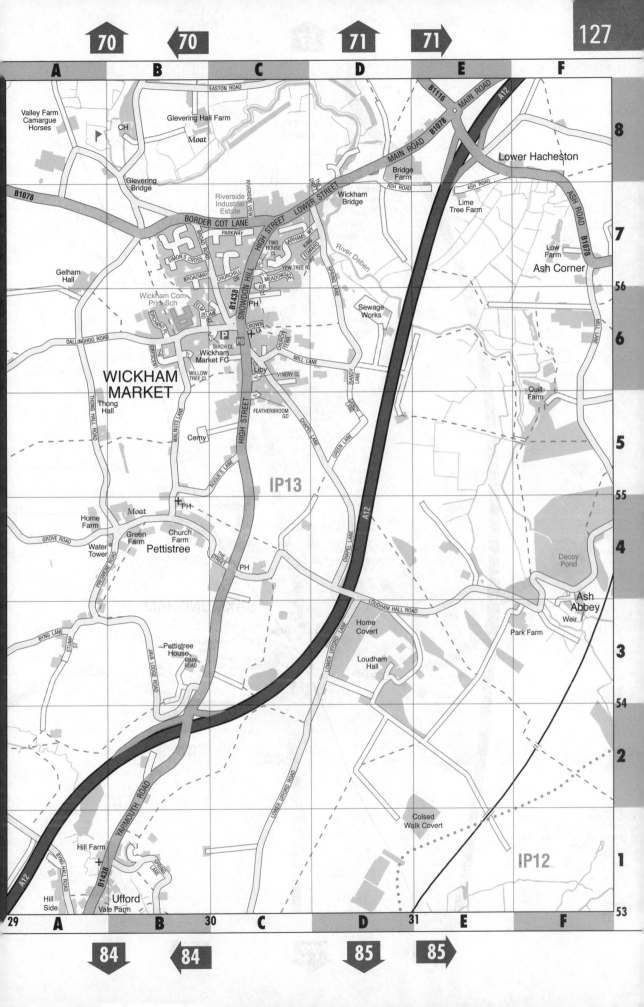

DS
1 PAXTON CDK CL
2 SEAWARD AVE
3 QUAKERS WY
4 HANCOCKS CL

58 ← 58 ↑ 58 →

129

A B C D E F

8

Leiston Carr

Aldhurst Farm

Leiston Common

Buckle's Wood

Beirnfels

THE COMMON

7

Brick Kiln Farm

BUCKLESWOOD ROAD

Common Farm

Sewage Works

House I Farm

IP16

Wood Farm

Summerhill Sch

Valley Road

63

Cemy

1 NEALE CL
2 FARROW CL

Football Ground

WESTWARD HO

CARR AVE

LC

6

B1119 SAXMUNDHAM ROAD

ST MARGARET'S CRES

WATERLOO AVENUE

HIGH GREEN 1
OLD SCHOOL CLOSE 2
OLD FOUNDRY PL 3

Masterlord Ind Est

Long Shop Mus

STATION RD

B1122

BULLER RD

DINSMIL

ROBERT'S RD

KITCHENER RD

CROWN

Eastlands Rd

KING GEORGE'S AVENUE

LC

CHURCH VW

Recn Gd

KING EDWARD

PLATERS WK

Leiston Mid Sch

MAIN ST

HIGH STREET

MAFEKING PL

LONG ROW

PROSPECT

URBAN

SIZEWELL ROAD

GRIMSEY RD

CHARLES ADAMS

Heath View

Leiston Prim Sch

Recn Gd

Sports Ground

5

The Cupola

Sports Ground

SYCAMORE CL

LIME TREE AV

BEECH

ASHFIELD DR

HUNTINGFIELD RD

HAYLINGS ROAD

VICTORY RD

CROSS ST

PARK HL

B1069

CENTRAL RD

ORCHARD RD

UPTON PLACE

KINGS RD

HAVEN RD

CHARLES MILLER CT

EASTWARD HO

PO

SOUTH

SYLVESTER RD

ARNHEM RD

GARRETT CR

Leiston High Sch

Leiston Leisure Centre

LEISTON

62

FRIDAY'S ORCH

PARADISE PL

JOHN

SOUTHFIELD OR

MINDEN DR

SEAWARD AVE

ANDREW RD

RED HOUSE LA

GRIMSEY'S LA

Hawsells Farm

4

Water Twr

WOODLANDS

GOLDING'S LANE

HAYLINGS GR 1
DANEWAY GDNS 2
QUEEN ELIZABETH CL 3

B1122

ALDEBURGH ROAD

Red House Farm

Holly Wood

3

HILLCREST

SCHOOL ROAD

IP17

LEISTON ROAD

COLDFAIR CL

ALDRINGHAM PK

Aldringham House

Aldringham

Elm Tree Farm

Stonehouse Plantation

Recreation Ground

POST OFFICE ROAD

MILL RD

ST ANDREW'S RD

Cherry Tree Farm

ALDRINGHAM ROAD

B1353

Aldringham Craft Market

CHANDLERS WAY

WEST HILL

MILL HL

MEADOW RISE

PH

THORPE ROAD

Little Beauties Wood

61

THE COMMON

PH

Coldfair Green

Sewage Works

JUDITH AVENUE

BUXLOW

MILL HILL ESTATE

MILL LA

School Plantation

CHURCH LANE

Square Plantation

Church Farm Wood

B1353

2

Knodishall Common

SNAPE ROAD

1
2

Coldfair Green Prim Sch

HAWTHORN CL

1 BURCH'S CL
2 THE FITCHES

School Plantation

Hundred River

GIPSY LA

CHURCH LA

Church Farm

Sewage Works

1

B1069

SLOE LA

Billeaford Hall

Long Covert

Crackland's Covert

FITCHES LANE

Hazelwood Farm

B1122

Darkrow Covert

Four Acre Covert

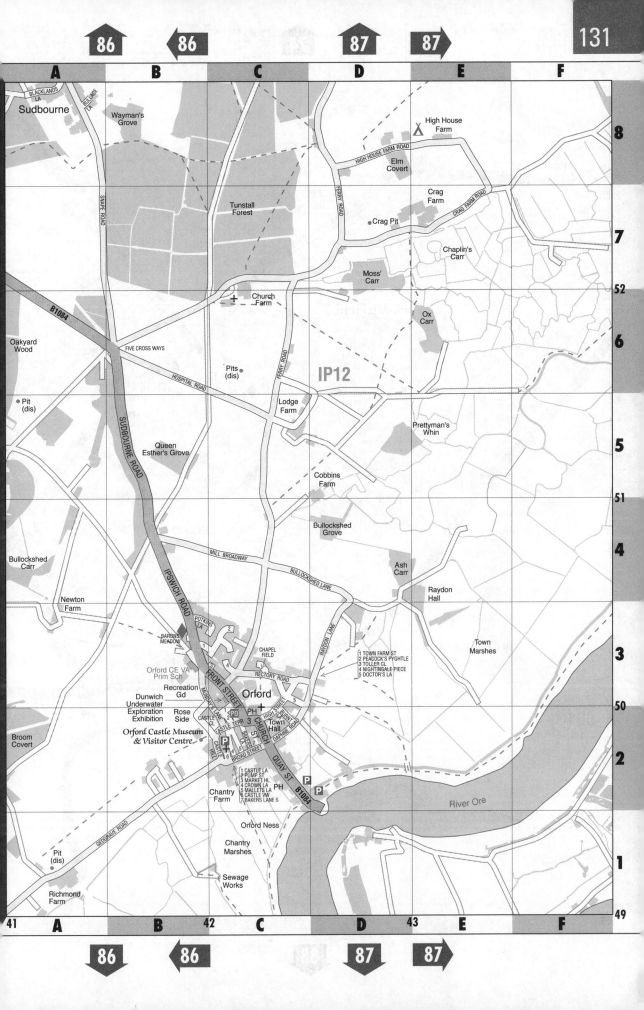

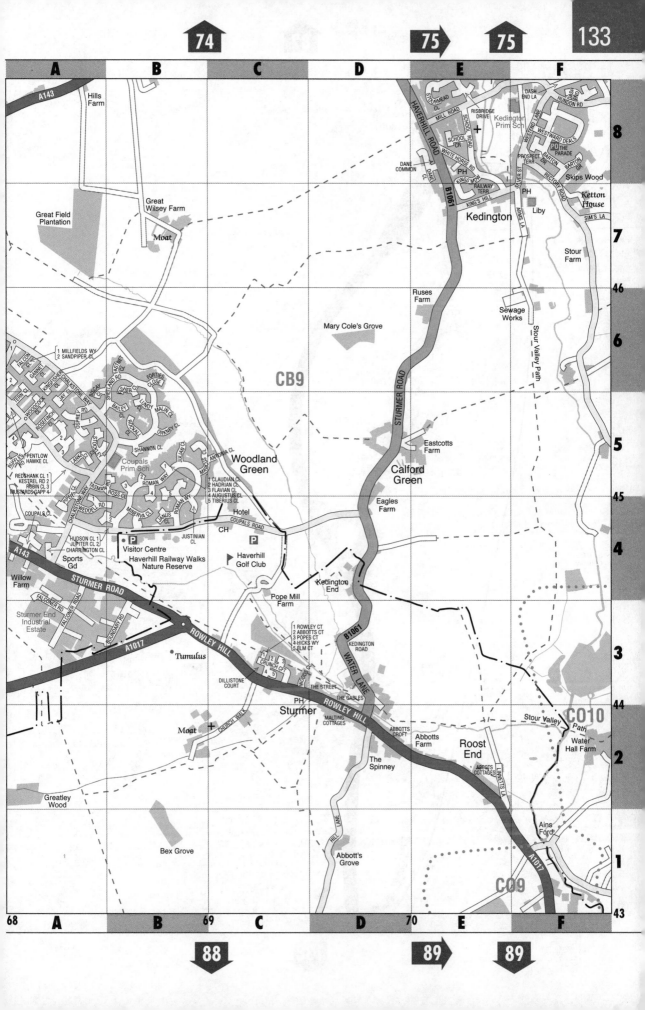

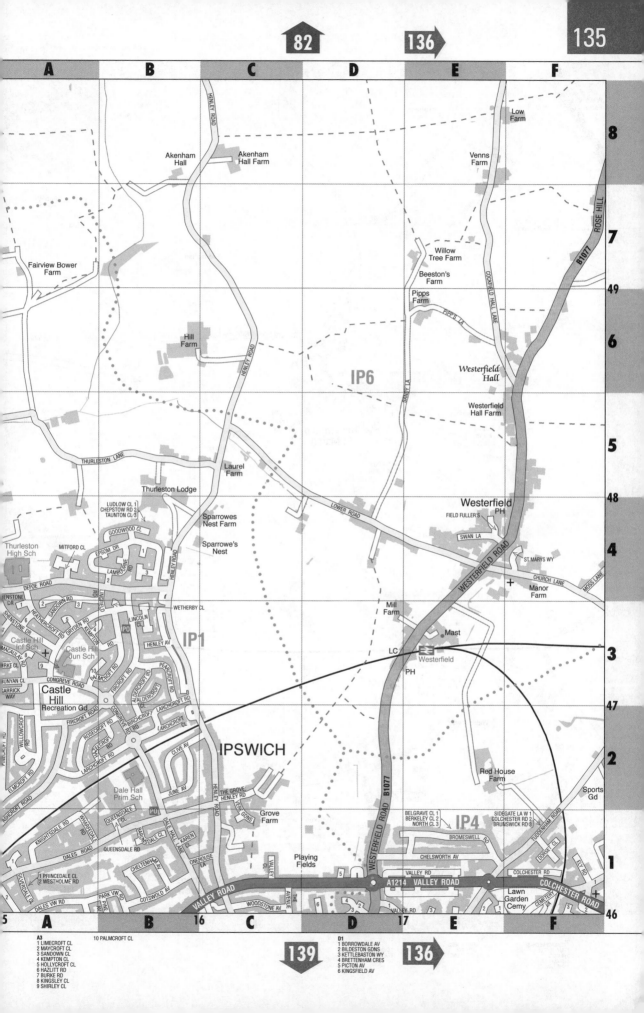

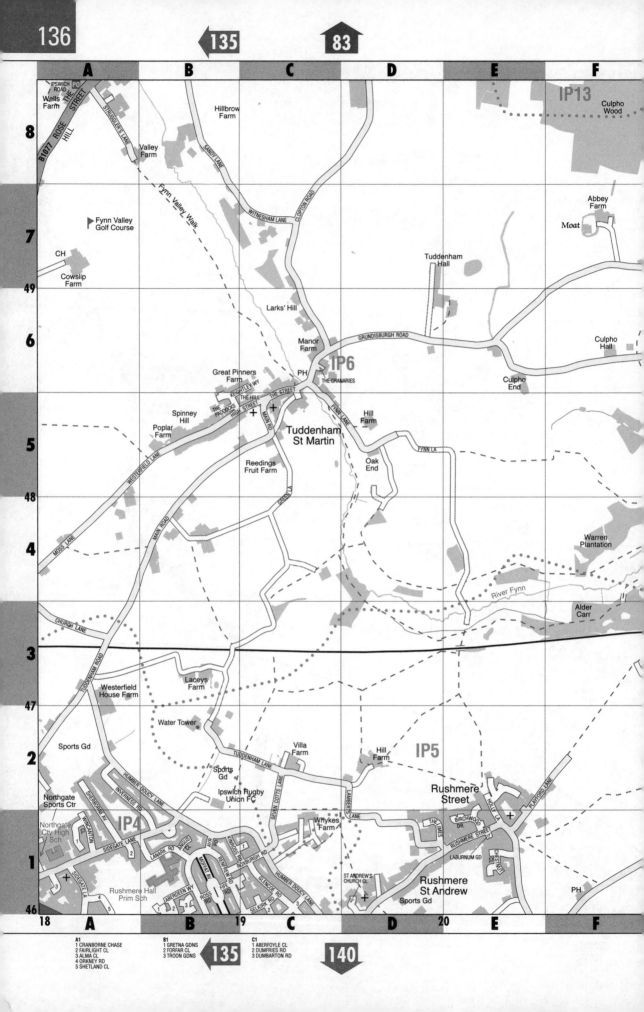

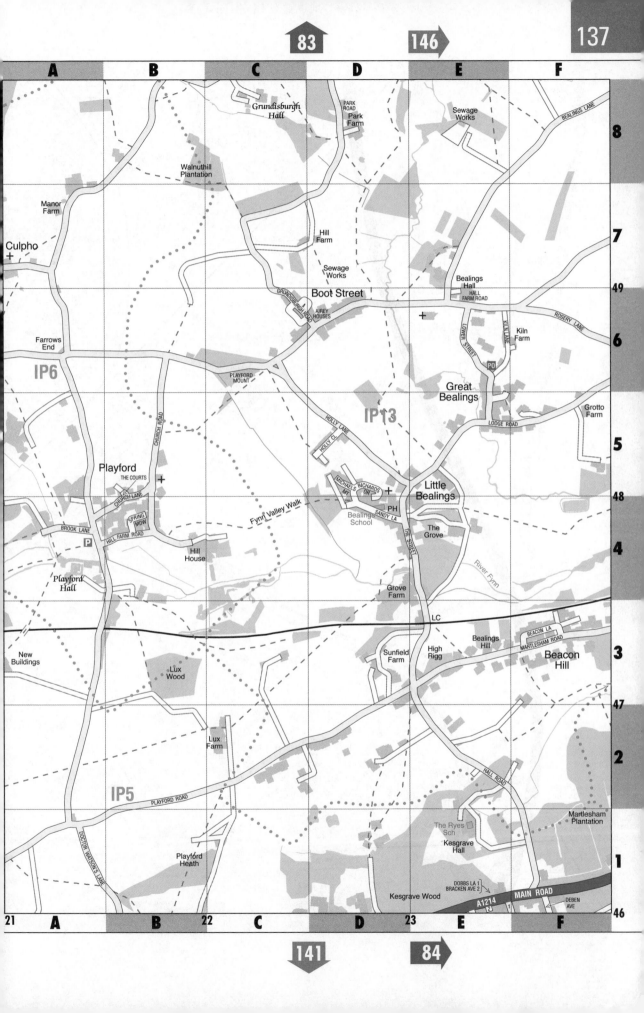

A B C D E F

8
7
49
6
5
48
4
3
47
2
1
46

Grundisburgh Hall
Park Road
Park Farm
Sewage Works
BEALINGS LANE

Manor Farm

Walnuthill Plantation

Culpho

Hill Farm

Sewage Works

Bealings Hall
HALL FARM ROAD

Farrows End

IP6

Boot Street

GRUNDISBURGH ROAD
AIREY HOUSES

ROSERY LANE

LOWER STREET
KILN LANE
Kiln Farm

PO

PLAYFORD MOUNT

Great Bealings

HOLLY LANE
HOLLY CL

IP13

LODGE ROAD

Grotto Farm

CHURCH ROAD

Playford
THE COURTS

MICHAELS
RICHARDS
DR
MT
PH
SANDY LA

Little Bealings

Bealings School

THE STREET

The Grove

CHURCH LANE
SPRING MOW

Fynn Valley Walk

BROOK LANE
HILL FARM ROAD

Hill House

Grove Farm

River Fynn

LC

Playford Hall

New Buildings

Lux Wood

Sunfield Farm

High Rigg

Bealings Hill

BEACON LA
MARTLESHAM ROAD

Beacon Hill

Lux Farm

IP5
PLAYFORD ROAD

HALL ROAD

Martlesham Plantation

DOCTOR WATSON'S LANE

Playford Heath

The Ryes Sch

Kesgrave Hall

DOBBS LA 1
BRACKEN AVE 2

Kesgrave Wood

A1214

MAIN ROAD

DEBEN AVE

C2
1 BRAMBLEWOOD
2 BROAD MDW
3 LABURNUM CL
4 INNES END
5 PEACOCK CL
6 HALFORD CT
7 WENTWORTH DR
8 MAGPIE CL
9 ACORN CL
10 MILNROW
11 THE CHESTNUTS
12 MERRION CL
13 MATLOCK CL
14 MOTTRAM CL

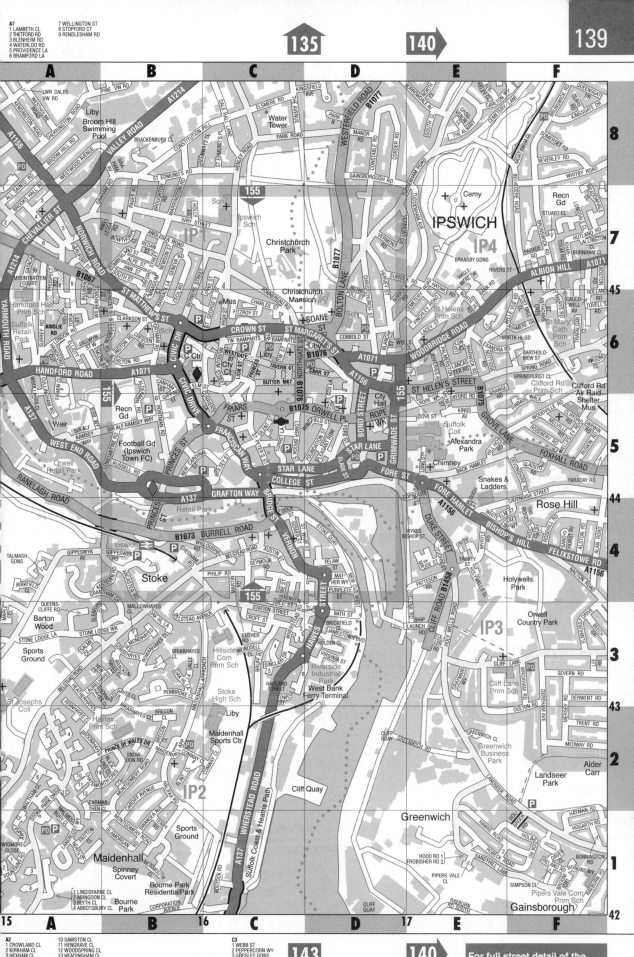

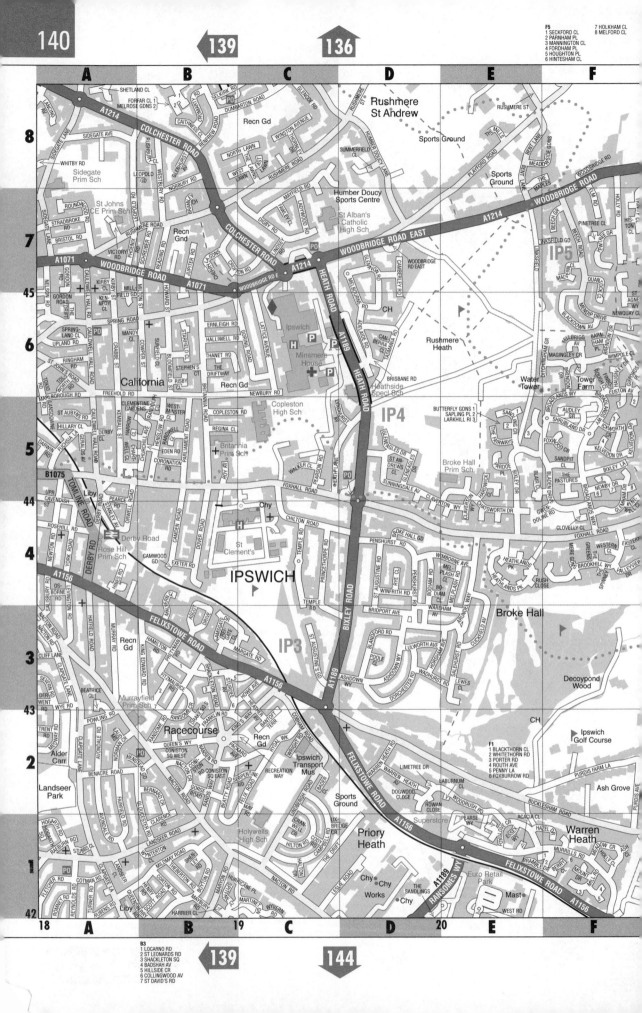

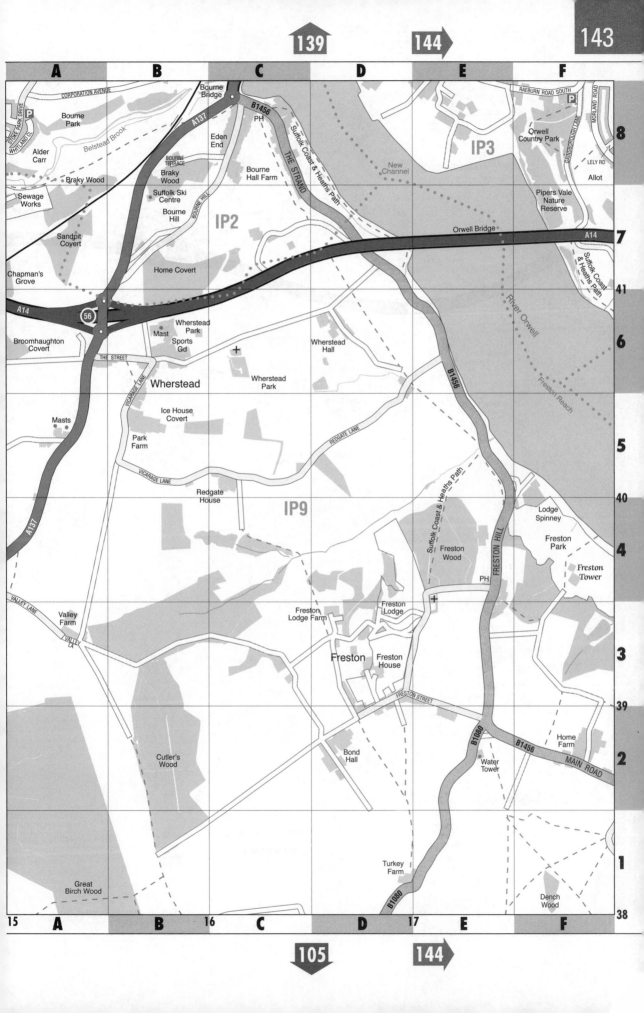

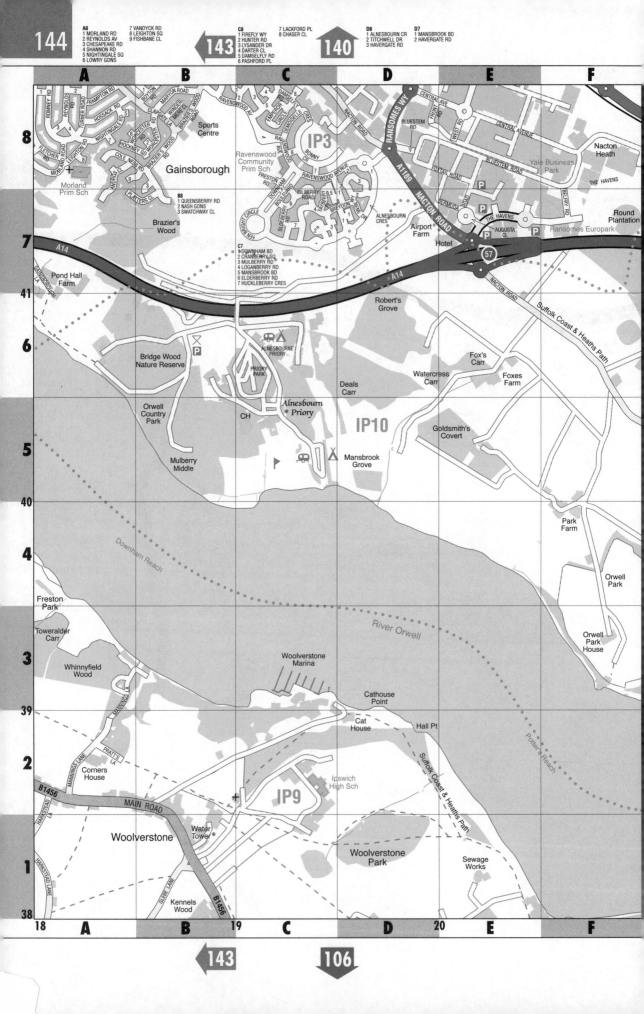

143
140

A8
1 MORLAND RD
2 REYNOLDS AV
3 CHESAPEAKE RD
4 SHANNON RD
5 NIGHTINGALE SQ
6 LOWRY GDNS
7 VANDYCK RD
8 LEIGHTON SQ
9 FISHBANE CL

C8
1 FIREFLY WY
2 HUNTER RD
3 LYSANDER DR
4 DARTER CL
5 DAMSELFLY RD
6 PASHFORD PL
7 LACKFORD PL
8 CHASER CL

D6
1 ALNESBOURN CR
2 TITCHWELL DR
3 HAVERGATE RD

D7
1 MANSBROOK BD
2 HAVERGATE RD

B8
1 QUEENSBERRY RD
2 NASH GDNS
3 SWATCHWAY CL

C7
1 DOWNHAM BD
2 CRANBERRY SQ
3 MULBERRY RD
4 LOGANBERRY RD
5 MANSBROOK BD
6 ELDERBERRY RD
7 HUCKLEBERRY CRES

8
41
7
6
5
40
4
39
3
2
1
38

A   B   C   D   E   F

IP3
Sports Centre
Gainsborough
Morland Prim Sch
Brazier's Wood
Ravenswood Community Prim Sch
Pond Hall Farm
Bridge Wood Nature Reserve
Orwell Country Park
Mulberry Middle
ALNESBOURNE PRIORY
PRIORY PARK
CH
Alnesbourn Priory
Deals Carr
Mansbrook Grove
IP10
Airport Farm
Hotel
Robert's Grove
Fox's Carr
Watercress Carr
Foxes Farm
Goldsmith's Covert
Nacton Heath
THE HAVENS
Round Plantation
Ransomes Europark
Yale Business Park
Park Farm
Orwell Park
Orwell Park House
Downham Reach
River Orwell
Potter's Reach
Freston Park
Toweralder Carr
Whinnyfield Wood
Corners House
Woolverstone
Water Tower
Kennels Wood
IP9
Ipswich High Sch
Woolverstone Marina
Cathouse Point
Cat House
Hall Pt
Woolverstone Park
Sewage Works
Suffolk Coast & Heaths Path
A14
A1189
RANSOMES WY
NACTON ROAD
CENTRAL AVE
CENTRAL AVENUE
BLUESTEM RD
BLUESTEM ROAD
BERMUDA ROAD
AUGUSTA CL
THE HAVENS
BELFRY RD
FOXTAIL ROAD
FRONT RD
WEST RD
57
B1456
MAIN ROAD
MANNINGS LANE
HARKSTEAD LANE
GLEBE LANE
B1456
PRATT'S LA

18   A   B   19   C   D   20   E   F

143
106

83
84

A B C D E F

8

7

50

6

5

49

4

3

48

2

1

47

Gull Farm

Whitchpit Farm

Home Farm

PH

LOW RD   TOP RD

BOULGE ROAD

Hasketon

TYMMES PL

TYMMES PL

FARLINGAYES 1
COLLINGWOOD RD 2
RODNEY CT 3
NELSON WY 4

A12

Morley Farm

MILL LA   WATERY LANE

MILL LANE

Riverside

CHURCH RD

Church Farm

SHRUBBERY ROAD

PINNERS LANE

Hasketon Manor

Moat

Hasketon Manor Farm

BARTON RD

HAUGH LA

COLLING WOOD

BERESFORD DR

EDWIN AVENUE

ADMIRALS WALK

CORFLD RD

LACHLAN GR

MISTLEY WAY

HAUGH LANE

EDWIN TERR

WARWICK AVE

HAUGHGATE CLOSE

PO

B1079

BEALINGS LA

GRUNDISBURGH ROAD

Willow Farm

Hasketon Grange

Grange Farm

Yew Tree House

Shrubbery Farm

The Plantation

MANOR ROAD

HASKETON RD

RUSSELL CL

PRENTICES LANE

GROVE ROAD

Sports Centre

Farlingaye High Sch

WOOLNOUGH RD

WOODBRIDGE

HAUGH LANE

NORTH HI

Woodbridge Ssh

Queech Wood

Bealings House

Rosery Farm

ROSERY LA

LODGE RD

Blunt's Wood

IP13

Gazebo Farm

GRUNDISBURGH ROAD

B1079

GRUNDISBURGH RD

GROVE ROAD

OLD BARRACK RD

WILMSLOW AV

HAMILTON RD

EDWARD FITZGERALD CT

RANSOM ROAD

CATHERINE ROAD

UPPER MOORFIELD

MOORFIELD

Buttrum's Mill

P

WAGGONERS CT

BURKITT ROAD

THEATRE ST

B1079

BREDFIELD ST

SECKFORD ST

SECKFORD ALMSHOUSES

St Marys CE Aided Prim Sch

MILL VW CL

COLLETT'S WLK

BRIDGEWOOD RD

DRYWOOD HI

Queen's Head La

P

MARKET HILL

Woodbridge Gallery

Woodbridge Cemy

CEMETERY LA

FEN WALK

PORTLAND CRES

Wood Farm Cottages

LADY MARGARET GDNS 1
GREYFRIARS 2
ST PETER'S CL 3

A12

PETERHOUSE DR

NEWNHAM AVE

PEMBROKE AV

Kyson Prim Sch

CLARE AVENUE

KINGS CLOSE

OXFORD RD

GIRTON CL

THROUGH DUNCANS

The LANCERS

HILLY FIELDS

WARREN HILL RD

MORLEY AV

WESTHOLME CL

CHERRY TREE RD

BIRCH CL

BEECH WAY

SNT CL

Bealings House

CH

Hotel Seckford Hall

Seckford Hall Golf Course

ST ANNES CL 1
TRINITY CL 2
CHRISTCHURCH DR 3
BORRETT PLACE 4
TURNER GDNS 5
CLAYTON CT 6

BALLIOL CL

MAGDALEN DR

SECKFORD HALL RD

LYTTON RD

CRANE CL

IPSWICH RD

PINEWOOD

IPSWICH ROAD

B1438

DUKE'S MDW

DUNCANS

California

ORWELL CT

BRINKWORTH RD

Maidensgrave

Porters Wood

IP12

Cherry Tree Farm

Football Ground

DUKE'S PK

High Grove

Broom Hill

Kyson Hill

River Fynn

TOP STREET

BROCK LA

SANDY LANE

BROOMHEATH

Kingston

Harrison Wood

Martlesham Creek

MARTLESHAM RD

BEALINGS ROAD

Beacon Hill Farm

Gorse Fell

THE STREET

COST LANE

TOP ST

PH

RENDOLL RD

MAIN ROAD

SCHOOL LA

Recreation Ground

Creek Farm

Sluice Farm

Sewage Works

Dunnett's Hill Plantation

A12

Sluice Wood

24   25   26

137
84

E4
1 GONVILLE CL
2 DOWNING CL
3 ST EDMUNDS CL
4 PORTLAND CR
5 QUEENS AV
6 FITZWILLIAM CL
7 CHURCHILL CL
8 ANDERSON'S WY

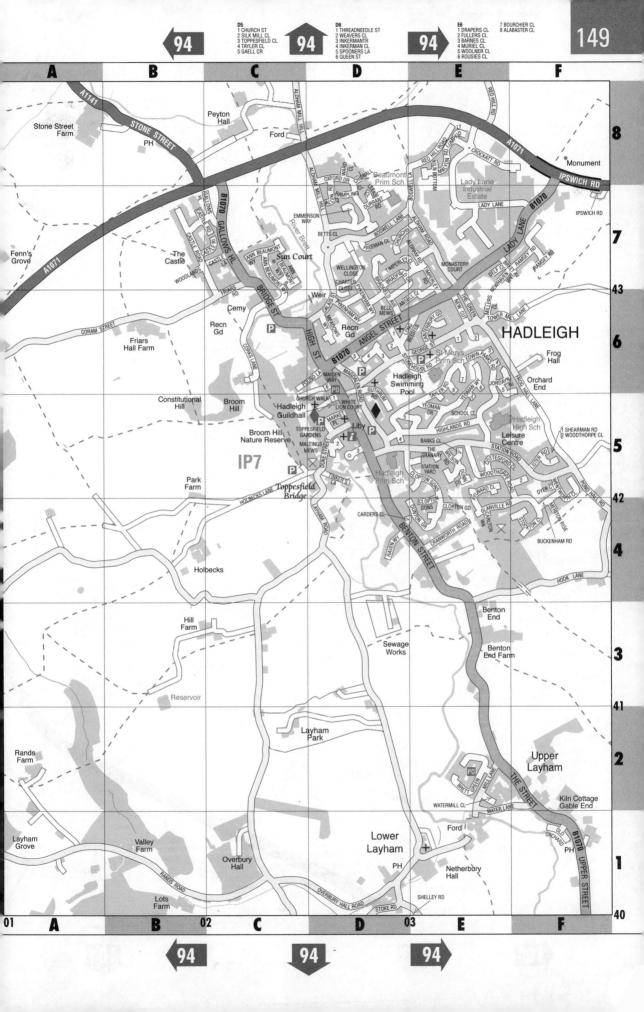

D5
1 CHURCH ST
2 SILK MILL CL
3 TOPPESFIELD CL
4 TAYLER CL
5 GAELL CR

D6
1 THREADNEEDLE ST
2 WEAVERS CL
3 INKERMANTR
4 INKERMAN CL
5 SPOONERS LA
6 QUEEN ST

E6
1 DRAPERS CL
2 FULLERS CL
3 BARNES CL
4 MURIEL CL
5 WOOLNER CL
6 ROUSIES CL

7 BOURCHIER CL
8 ALABASTER CL

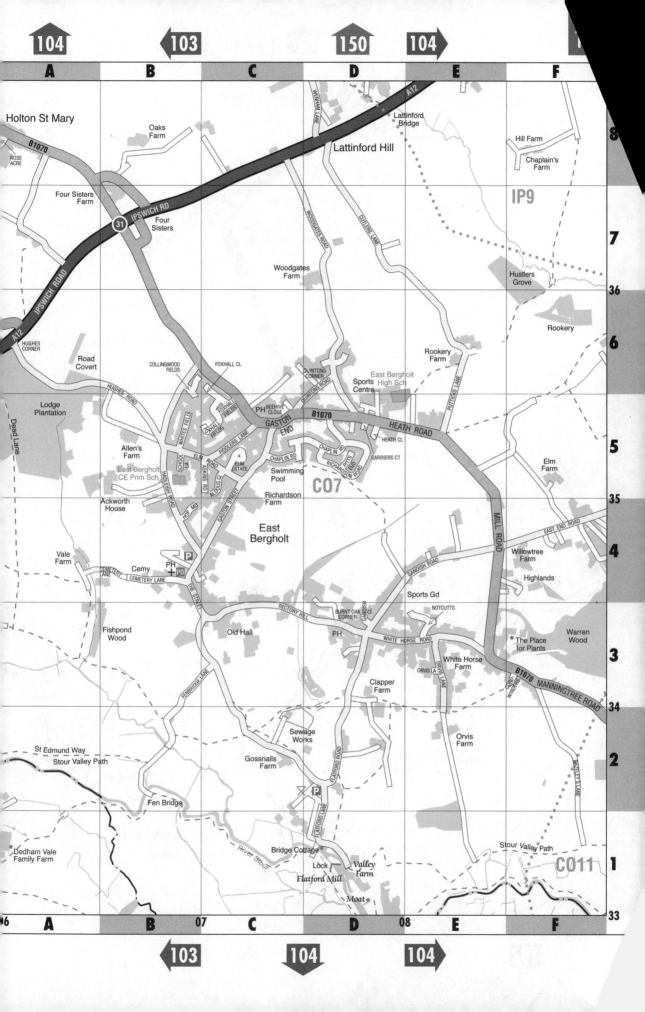

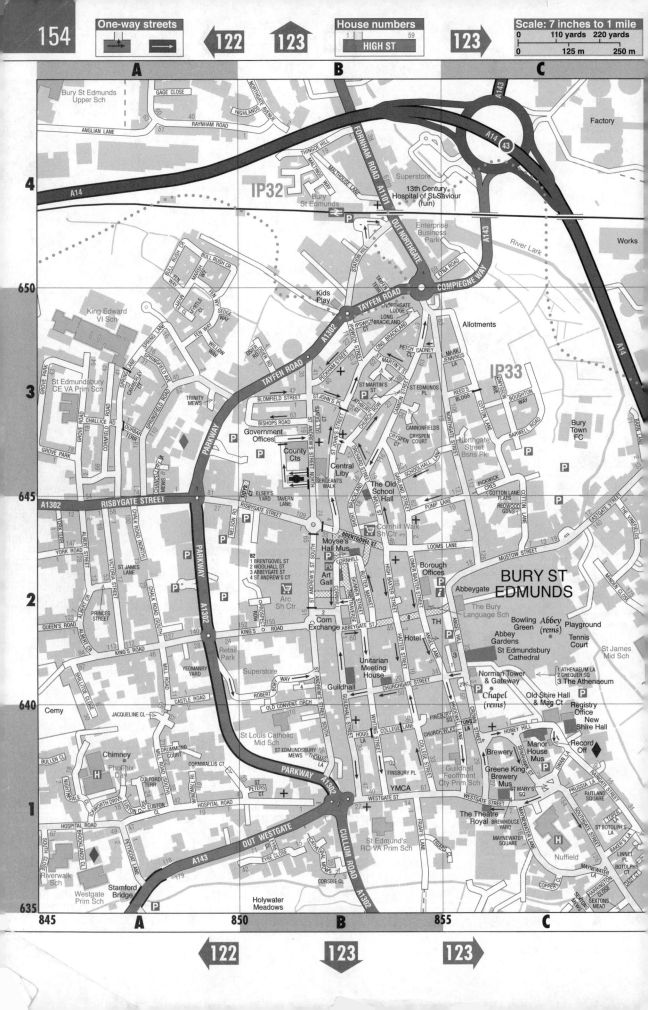

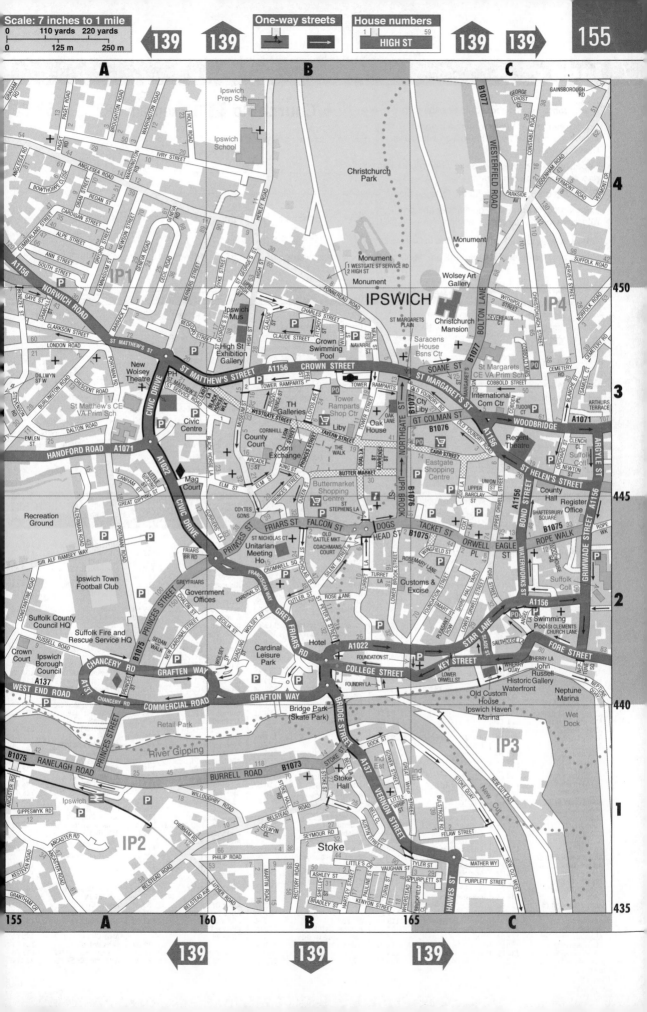

Index

	Church Rd **6** Beckenham BR2..........**53** C6
Place name May be abbreviated on the map	
Location number Present when a number indicates the place's position in a crowded area of mapping	
Locality, town or village Shown when more than one place has the same name	
Postcode district District for the indexed place	
Page and grid square Page number and grid reference for the standard mapping	

Cities, towns and villages are listed in CAPITAL LETTERS

Public and commercial buildings are highlighted in magenta   **Places of interest** are highlighted in blue with a star ★

Abbreviations used in the index

Acad	Academy	Comm	Common	Gd	Ground	L	Leisure	Prom	Promenade
App	Approach	Cott	Cottage	Gdn	Garden	La	Lane	Rd	Road
Arc	Arcade	Cres	Crescent	Gn	Green	Liby	Library	Recn	Recreation
Ave	Avenue	Cswy	Causeway	Gr	Grove	Mdw	Meadow	Ret	Retail
Bglw	Bungalow	Ct	Court	H	Hall	Meml	Memorial	Sh	Shopping
Bldg	Building	Ctr	Centre	Ho	House	Mkt	Market	Sq	Square
Bsns, Bus	Business	Ctry	Country	Hospl	Hospital	Mus	Museum	St	Street
Bvd	Boulevard	Cty	County	HQ	Headquarters	Orch	Orchard	Sta	Station
Cath	Cathedral	Dr	Drive	Hts	Heights	Pal	Palace	Terr	Terrace
Cir	Circus	Dro	Drove	Ind	Industrial	Par	Parade	TH	Town Hall
Cl	Close	Ed	Education	Inst	Institute	Pas	Passage	Univ	University
Cnr	Corner	Emb	Embankment	Int	International	Pk	Park	Wk, Wlk	Walk
Coll	College	Est	Estate	Intc	Interchange	Pl	Place	Wr	Water
Com	Community	Ex	Exhibition	Junc	Junction	Prec	Precinct	Yd	Yard

Index of towns, villages, streets, hospitals, industrial estates, railway stations, schools, shopping centres, universities and places of interest

13t–Amb

13th Century Hospl of St Saviour★ IP32.......154 B4
95th Bomb Group Hospl Museum★ IP21....38 C4
100th Bomb Group Meml Mus The★ IP21........21 D4

A

Abbey Cl
　10 Burwell CB5........44 A5
　10 Ixworth IP31........34 B1
　Rendlesham IP12........85 D7
Abbeydale NR32........114 E2
Abbey Farm Jun Sch **1**
　IP24.............16 B6
Abbey Fields IP14......66 D8
Abbeygate St **3** IP33..154 B2
Abbey Gdns IP13........71 C2
Abbey Hill IP21.........38 C7
Abbey La IP16.........129 B8
Abbey Rd
　Flixton NR35............23 F8
　Leiston IP16...........129 C7
　Sudbury CO10.........148 C2
Abbey Sch The IP12...147 A4
Abbot Cl IP33..........122 D4
Abbot Rd IP33..........122 D4
Abbotsbury Cl IP2.....139 A1
Abbotsbury Rd IP33....122 D3
Abbots Cotts CB9......133 E2
Abbots Hall★ IP14.....124 D5
Abbot's Hall Drift CO10..78 E2
Abbot's Hall Prim Sch
　IP14................124 C5
Abbot's Hall Rd IP14...124 D5
Abbott Rd CO12.........106 F1
Abbotts Croft CB9......133 D2
Abbotts Ct CB9.........133 C3
Abbotts Gn Com Prim Sch
　IP32.................49 A3
Abbottsinch Rd **6** IP31..33 D5
Abbotts Meadow **8** IP30.50 D1
Abbotts Rd CB9........132 E2
Abdy Ave **5** CO12......106 F1
Abercorn Ct **2** CB9....132 D4
Aberdeen Way IP4......136 B1
Aberfoyle Cl **1** IP4....136 C1
Abingdon Cl IP2........139 A1

Abington Pl CB9........132 E7
Ablitts Meadow IP13....83 E6
Acacia Ave IP32........48 C5
Acacia Cl IP3..........140 E1
Acer Gr IP8............138 C1
Acer Rd IP12...........85 D8
Acheson Way **7** IP15...130 E5
Acorn Cl **9** IP8........138 C2
Acorns The IP30........49 E3
Acorn Way IP5..........98 B8
Acre Cl IP6............83 A6
Acre Rd CB8............74 B8
Action France CB8......59 E5
ACTON................92 B7
Acton CE Prim Sch CO10..92 B7
Acton Cl
　Bramford IP8.........134 A2
　Sudbury CO10.........148 D6
Acton Gdns **1** IP8....134 A2
Acton Gn **3** CO10......148 C5
Acton La
　Acton CO10............92 A6
　Sudbury CO10.........148 D6
ACTON PLACE...........92 B8
Acton Pl Ind Est CO10..92 A8
Acton Rd
　Bramford IP8.........134 A2
　Lowestoft NR33.......115 B4
Adair Rd IP1...........138 D8
Adam's La IP18.........43 C5
Adamson Rd IP18.......119 B8
Adams Pl IP5...........141 C7
Adastral Cl
　Felixstowe IP11......153 H11
　Newmarket CB8........120 E4
Addington Rd IP11......152 C7
Addison Cl IP26........4 F5
Addison Rd CO10.......148 E2
Addison Way IP8.......134 A8
Adeane Meadow IP26....6 A8
Adelaide Cl **17** CB7...28 D4
Adelaide Rd IP4........140 D6
Admiral Rd **2** IP8.....142 E8
Admirals Jun Sch **2** IP24..16 C7
Admirals Wlk IP12.....146 F7
Adnams Brewery★ **22**
　IP18................119 D5
Adrian Rd **6** NR32....113 D2
Adventure Island Play Park★
　NR33................114 F2
Africa Alive!★ NR33....11 A1
Agate Cl **2** IP1......134 D1
Ailwin Rd IP32.........123 E4

Ainslie Rd IP1.........139 A6
Airedale NR33.........114 E2
Airey Cl
　Lowestoft NR32.......112 F5
　Newton CO10..........92 E3
Airey Houses IP13.....137 D6
Airfield Rd IP32........49 A3
Airstation La IP21.....21 E6
Aisthorpe IP9.........150 D3
AKENHAM..............134 F6
Akethorpe Way NR32...113 A6
Alabaster Cl **8** IP7...149 E6
Alandale Dr **25** NR33...11 C1
Alan Rd IP3...........139 F4
Alasdair Pl **9** IP6....134 C8
Alban Sq **2** IP12.....84 A1
Albany Rd **1** NR32....113 E2
Albany The IP4.........139 E8
Albemarle Rd IP33.....122 D4
Albemarle St **6** CO12..107 B3
Alberta Cl IP3.........141 A8
Albert Cres IP33.......154 A2
Albert Pl IP13.........126 C3
Albert Pye Prim Sch
　NR34................111 B4
Albert Rd IP13.........126 C3
Albert Rd **9** IP6......134 C8
Albert Rolph Dr IP27...109 E4
Albert St IP33.........154 A2
Albert Wlk IP11........153 B3
Albion Hill IP4........139 F4
Albion Rd NR35........110 D3
Albion St IP17.........128 C3
ALBURGH..............7 A1
Alburgh with Denton Prim
　Sch IP20.............7 A1
ALDEBURGH............130 D4
Aldeburgh Cl CB9......132 C5
Aldeburgh & District Com
　Hospl IP15..........130 D4
Aldeburgh Lodge Gdns
　IP15................130 E5
Aldeburgh Mus★ IP15..130 F4
Aldeburgh Prim Sch
　IP15................130 E3
Aldeburgh Rd
　Friston IP17..........72 F7
　Leiston IP16.........129 D4
ALDEBY...............9 F8
Aldecar La IP17........72 C7
Alde House Dr IP15....130 E4
Alde La IP15...........130 E4
Alder Carr Farm & Ctyd Craft
　Ctr★ IP6............125 E5

Alder Covert **6** IP24...16 D6
Aldercroft Cl IP1......135 B3
Aldercroft Rd IP1......135 B3
Alde Rd CB9...........132 E7
Alder Dr **2** NR33......114 C4
Aldergrove Cl IP19.....118 A3
Alderlee IP2...........142 F8
Alderman Rd IP1.......155 A2
ALDERTON.............99 E4
Alderton Cl CB9........132 C8
Alderton Rd IP12.......99 E6
Alder Way CO10........148 D6
ALDHAM..............94 E8
Aldham Ct **1** CB9.....132 C5
Aldham Gdns IP14......124 E4
Aldham Mill Hill IP7...149 C8
Aldham Rd IP7.........149 E7
Aldis Ave IP14.........124 D4
Aldon Cl **14** CO12.....106 E1
Aldous Cl CO7.........151 C5
Aldous Ct **13** IP14....53 F2
Aldridge La **2** IP28...48 B6
ALDRINGHAM..........129 D3
Aldringham Craft Mkt★
　IP16................129 C3
Aldringham Mews **13**
　IP11................152 D5
Aldringham Pk IP16....129 D3
Aldringham Rd IP17....129 B3
Aldwyck Way NR33.....114 F4
Alexander Cl NR34.....111 C2
Alexander Dr
　8 Great Waldingfield
　CO10................92 C6
　Needham Market IP6..125 C5
Alexanders Int Sch IP12..108 D8
Alexander Way IP28....47 E5
Alexandra Rd
　Beccles NR34........111 B5
　Felixstowe IP11......152 E6
　Ipswich IP4..........139 E6
　Lowestoft NR32......113 D1
　Sudbury CO10........148 E5
Alexandra St **8** CO12..107 B3
Alfred Corry Mus★ IP18..119 C2
Algar Dr CB8...........59 F4
Alice Driver Rd **9** IP13..83 E5
Alicia Ct IP33.........123 C3
Allenby Rd IP2.........138 F6
Allen Rd
　Hadleigh IP7.........149 D7
　Lowestoft NR32......112 D1
Alley Rd IP10..........98 D2

Allfields **3** CO12......107 A1
All Hallows' Hospl NR35..110 C7
Allington Cl IP4........139 F7
Allington Rd **7** IP19...118 A3
Allington Wlk CB9......132 C6
Allotment La IP6........69 A1
All Saints IP27.........5 E3
All Saints CE Mid Sch
　CO10................148 E8
All Saints CE Prim Sch
　IP29.................63 E1
All Saints CE VA Prim Sch
　Laxfield IP13.........40 A3
　Newmarket CB8.......121 B3
　Winfarthing IP22.....20 C8
All Saints Cl CB8.......46 C3
All Saints Ct IP33......154 B3
All Saints Dr NR34......111 C3
All Saints Gn **6** NR34..111 F4
All Saints Rd
　Creeting St Mary IP6..125 F8
　Newmarket CB8.......121 B3
All Saints' Rd
　Ipswich IP1..........139 A7
　Lowestoft NR33.......115 B4
ALL SAINTS SOUTH
　ELMHAM.............24 B5
All Saints Wlk IP28.....30 B4
Allthorpe Rd **12** IP20..22 C6
ALLWOOD GREEN.......36 A4
Alma Cl **3** IP4........136 A1
Alma Pl IP17...........128 C3
Alma Rd NR32..........113 C1
Almond Gr IP24........16 A4
Almondhayes IP2.......139 B3
Almshouse Rd IP30.....49 C1
Alnesbourn Cres
　1 Gainsborough IP2..144 D8
　Ipswich IP3..........144 D7
Alnesbourne Priory
　IP10................144 A4
Alpe St IP1............155 A4
Alpha Bsns Pk IP1.....134 D3
Alphamstone Rd CO8...101 A6
ALPHETON.............78 A5
Alston Cl CO10.........92 D3
Alston Rd IP3..........139 F4
Alton Hall La IP9.......105 C6
Alton Wr Sports Ctr IP9..105 B6
Alvis Cl IP32..........123 F5
Alvis Wlk IP1..........134 C1
Amberfield Sch IP10....145 C6
Amberley Ct **8** NR32...112 F4

Amber Mus The★ IP18 119 D5
Ambleside Gdns NR32 113 A4
America Hill IP6 83 A6
Amis Ct IP27 109 D4
AMPTON 33 A2
Amy Johnson Ct 6 IP28 116 B5
Ancaster Rd IP2 155 A1
Anchor End 2 CO11 105 A2
Anchor La
Burwell CB5 44 A6
Dedham CO7 104 A2
Lakenheath IP27 109 C6
1 Mistley CO11 105 A2
Anchor St NR33 115 C6
Anchor Way NR33 114 B4
Ancient House Museum of Thetford Life★ IP24 16 C6
Anderson Cl IP6 125 C5
Anderson's Way 8 IP12 146 E4
Anderson Wlk IP32 122 D7
Andrew Burtt's Cl IP13 126 B3
Andrew Cl
Felixstowe IP11 152 E3
Leiston IP16 129 D5
Andrew Johnston Way IP19 118 B3
Andrew Rd CB8 120 E5
Andrews Cl 9 IP14 53 F2
Andrews Wlk IP32 122 D8
Andrew Way NR33 114 D6
Andros Cl IP3 144 A7
Angela Cl IP12 84 A1
Angelgate Espl 4 CO12 107 C3
Angel Hill
Bury St Edmunds IP33 154 C2
Stonham Earl IP14 67 F5
Angel La
Blythburgh IP19 42 F6
Bury St Edmunds IP33 154 B2
Glemsford CO10 77 A2
Ipswich IP4 155 C2
2 Woodbridge IP12 147 A5
Angel Link IP19 118 B3
Angel Rd IP8 134 A2
Angel St IP7 149 D6
Angerstein Cl IP27 5 E4
Anglesea Rd IP1 155 A4
Anglesey Pl 6 IP31 49 A5
Anglian La IP32 154 A4
Anglian Way NR31 3 B7
Anglia Parkway N IP1 134 D4
Anglia Parkway S IP1 134 D3
Anglia Ret Pk IP1 134 D4
Angus Cl IP4 136 B1
Animal Health Trust Visitor Ctr★ CB8 45 F5
Anita Cl E IP2 138 E5
Anita Cl W IP2 138 E5
Annandale Dr NR34 111 D4
Ann Beaumont Way IP7 149 C7
Annbrook Rd IP2 138 E1
Ann Coles Cl CB9 88 E3
Anne Bartholomew Rd IP24 16 C7
Annesons Cnr IP17 58 B6
Anne St IP11 152 E3
ANNIS HILL 110 E3
Annis Hill NR35 110 E3
Annis Hill La 2 NR35 110 D3
Annis Hill Rd NR35 110 D3
Annison Cl NR33 115 B5
Ann St IP1 155 A4
Ann Suckling Rd CB9 132 E8
Ansell Cl IP7 149 D6
Anselm Ave 9 IP32 48 C5
Anson Rd 7 IP5 98 A8
Anson Way NR34 10 A3
Antonia Cl CB9 133 C5
Antrim Rd IP1 134 D1
Anzani Ave IP11 152 C4
Apple Acre Rd CB9 132 A7
Appleby Cl IP8 138 C1
Apple Cl 28 IP27 13 F2
Appledore Dr NR33 114 D4
Appledown Dr IP30 123 E7
Apple Gr IP14 51 A2
Apple Tree Cl NR33 115 B6
Appletree Gr 2 CB5 44 A6
Appletree La IP22 20 C3
Approach Cotts CB9 132 B8
APSEY GREEN 126 A3
Aragon Rd CB9 132 B4
Arbor La NR33 115 A2
Arcade St IP1 155 B3
Archangel Gdns IP2 138 E4
Archbishop Sancroft High Sch IP20 22 C6
Archers' Ave 3 IP26 4 D5
Arc Sh Ctr IP33 154 B2
Arderne Cl 8 CO12 106 F1
ARDLEIGH HEATH 103 F1
Ardleigh Rd CO7 103 E2
Arger Fen Nature Reserve★ CO10 101 F6
Argyle St IP4 155 C3
Argyll Ct 7 CB9 132 D5
Ark Cl 7 NR33 11 B1
Arkle Ct IP5 141 D7
Arkwright Rd IP2 138 E6
Arlington Way IP24 16 C5
Arms La CB9 133 F7
Armstrong Cl
Hundon CO10 75 D4
Newmarket CB8 121 B3
Armstrong Way CO9 90 A1
Arnhem Ct NR32 113 C4
Arnhem Rd IP16 129 D5
Arnold Cl IP1 134 F3
Arnold St 3 NR32 113 E1
Arras Rd IP33 122 D5
Arrendene Rd CB9 132 D7
Arrowhead Dr IP27 109 C7
Arthurs Terr IP4 155 C3
Artillery Dr 7 CO12 106 E1
Artillery Way 11 NR32 113 E2
Arundel Cl 4 IP32 123 D6
Arundel Way
Ipswich IP3 140 E3
2 Lowestoft NR33 114 D4
Arundel Wlk 11 CB9 132 C6
Arwela Rd IP11 152 F2
Ascot Dr
Felixstowe IP11 152 E6
Ipswich IP3 140 B3
ASH ABBEY 127 F3
Ash Ave 1 IP7 80 D6
ASHBOCKING 69 A1
Ashbocking Rd IP6 82 E6
Ashbourne Ct CB8 121 B3
Ashburnham Rd IP6 125 C4
Ashburnham Way NR33 114 D4
Ashby Rd NR32 113 C1
Ash Cl
Bacton IP14 51 F6
10 Lakenheath IP27 13 F2
7 Lowestoft NR33 114 D5
Thetford IP24 16 A4
Warren Heath IP3 140 F1
Woodbridge IP12 146 F4
ASH CORNER 127 F7
Ashcroft Rd IP1 135 A1
Ashdale Dr NR34 111 E4
Ashdale Pk IP27 14 E8
Ashdale Rd IP5 141 D8
Ashdown Way IP3 140 D3
Ash Dr IP23 117 D3
ASHEN 89 E5
Ashen Cl CO10 89 E5
Ashen Hill CO10 89 E5
Ashen La CO10 89 E6
Ashen Rd
Ashen CO10 90 A7
Ridgewell CO9 89 D4
Ashe Rd IP12 71 F2
Ashes The IP14 54 D1
ASHFIELD 54 D2
Ashfield Cres NR33 114 F7
ASHFIELD CUM THORPE 54 C1
Ashfield Dr IP16 129 C5
ASHFIELD GREEN
Stradbroke 39 D4
Wickhambrook 62 A2
Ashfield Hill IP31 50 F6
Ashfield Rd
Elmswell IP30 50 F3
Norton IP31 50 C4
Wetherden IP14 51 A2
Ashford Cl NR34 9 B6
Ashfords Cl IP17 128 B4
Ash Gd Cl
3 Brantham CO11 104 E4
10 Felixstowe IP11 107 D8
Ash Gr
17 Burwell CB5 44 A5
Capel St Mary IP9 150 E3
Haverhill CB9 132 C7
4 Sudbury CO10 92 B3
Ashlea Cl CB9 132 F4
Ashlea Rd CB9 132 F4
ASHLEY 60 F8
Ashley Downs NR32 113 C3
Ashley Rd
Cheveley CB8 60 E8
Harwich CO12 107 A2
Newmarket CB8 121 E2
Ashley Sch The NR32 113 C4
Ashley St IP2 155 B1
Ashman's Rd NR34 111 A4
Ashmere Gr IP4 139 F6
Ashmere Rise CO10 148 E6
Ashness Cl 2 NR32 113 A4
Ash Rd
Campsey Ash IP12 71 C1
Hacheston IP13 127 F7
Onehouse IP14 66 C6
Rendlesham IP12 85 C7
Ash Rise 8 CO6 102 C5
Ash St 4 CO10 93 C3
ASH STREET 80 A1
Ashton Cl IP2 138 C2
Ashton Rd IP23 117 C3
Ash Tree Cl
8 Beccles NR34 9 F4
7 Fessingfield IP21 39 D8
5 Occold IP23 37 F1
Ashtree Gdns NR33 114 D3
Ashwell Rd IP33 122 D4
Ash Wlk CB8 75 C6
Askins Rd CO7 151 C5
Aspal Cl 5 IP28 30 B8
Aspal Close Nature Reserve★ IP28 30 B7
Aspal Hall Rd IP28 30 B8
ASPALL 53 E4
Aspal La IP28 30 C8
Aspall Rd IP14 53 F3
Aspal Pk IP28 30 B8
Aspel Est IP28 13 D1
Aspen Cl
Claydon IP6 134 D8
Great Barton IP31 49 B6
Haverhill CB9 132 C7
Ipswich IP6 82 A5
3 Woodbridge IP12 147 B6
Aspen Coppice 6 NR32 112 F5
Aspinall Cl 4 NR33 114 F4
ASSINGTON 92 F1
ASSINGTON GREEN 76 B6
Assington La CO6 93 A1
Assington Rd CO10 92 D3
Assington St CO10 101 F8
Astbury Rd 6 NR32 113 B5
Aster Rd IP2 138 E4
Aston Cl IP1 134 C1
Ataka Rd IP11 152 F6
ATHELINGTON 38 E2
Athelington Rd IP21 38 F2
Athenaeum La IP33 154 C2
Athenaeum The★ IP33 154 C2
Atherton Rd IP2 138 D2
Atterton Rd CB9 132 B7
ATTLETON GREEN 61 D1
Aubretia Cl 2 NR33 114 F7
AUDLEY END
Burston and Shimpling 20 E5
Lawshall 77 D8
Audley End IP21 20 F5
Audley Gr IP4 140 F5
Augusta Cl IP10 144 E7
Augustus Cl CB9 133 B5
Aureole Wlk CB8 120 E8
Austin Cl IP31 50 E7
Austin St IP2 155 B1
Aveley La IP29 77 D6
Aveling Way NR33 114 B3
Avenue App IP32 123 A8
Avenue Rd IP27 109 E4
Avenue The
Brome & Oakley IP23 117 E8
3 Burwell CB5 44 B6
Copdock & Washbrook IP8 95 F4
Felixstowe IP11 152 B7
Great Barton IP31 123 F8
Halesworth IP19 118 B5
Ipswich IP1 135 C1
4 Kessingland NR33 11 B1
Lowestoft NR33 115 B5
Newmarket CB8 121 A3
Risby IP28 47 E5
Ufford IP13 84 F7
Woodbridge IP12 147 A4
Aves Cl CB7 29 C5
Avocet Cl NR33 114 D5
Avocet Gr 12 CB7 28 D5
Avocet La 28 IP5 98 A8
Avondale Rd
Ipswich IP3 140 A2
Lowestoft NR32 113 C1
Aylmer Cl IP28 47 D5
Aylward Cl IP7 149 E4
Ayr Rd IP4 136 B1

B

Babb's La IP14 52 F2
BABEL GREEN 75 D3
Babergh Cl 9 CO10 92 B7
Babington Dr IP19 118 B2
Baby La IP30 65 D4
Back Hamlet IP3 139 E5
Back Hill IP9 105 F6
Back Hills IP22 36 A7
Back La
Badwell Ash IP31 50 F8
Burrough Green CB8 59 F2
Claydon IP6 134 C8
Copdock & Washbrook IP8 95 F5
Diss IP22 20 D7
Falkenham IP10 98 F1
Felixstowe IP11 152 F5
Kettlebaston IP7 79 C5
Lound NR32 2 F6
Monks Eleigh IP7 79 C2
Scole IP21 21 A5
St Mary, South Elmham otherwise Homersfield IP20 23 C8
Tattingstone IP9 105 B7
Wicken CB7 28 A1
Back Rd
Brockdish IP21 21 E4
Middleton IP17 58 B6
Rattlesden IP30 65 E6
Trimley St Martin IP10 98 D2
Wenhaston with Mells Hamlet IP19 42 C6
Back St
Garboldisham IP22 18 D5
Gislingham IP23 36 B1
Lakenheath IP27 109 D6
BACK STREET 61 E5
Bacon Rd 7 IP6 82 B5
Bacon's Gn Rd IP19 25 D3
BACTON 51 F5
Bacton Com Prim Sch IP14 51 F6
BACTON GREEN 51 E4
Bacton Mid Sch IP14 51 E6
Bacton Rd
Felixstowe IP11 152 F3
Haughley IP14 51 C2
Baden Powell Wlk IP5 141 E7
Bader Cl IP3 140 C2
Bader Ct 25 IP5 98 A8
Badgers Bank IP2 138 E1
Badgers Gr CO6 102 D1
Badger's Holt 10 NR33 11 B1
Badgerwood Cl NR33 115 B5
BADINGHAM 56 A6
Badingham Rd
Badingham IP13 56 A4
Framlingham IP13 126 E5
Laxfield IP13 40 C1
Badingham Rd *continued*
Peasenhall IP17 56 D7
Badley Hill IP6 125 B7
Badleys Cl 6 CO10 92 C6
Badley Wlk IP6 125 A7
Badlingham Rd CB7 29 E1
Badshah Ave 4 IP3 140 B3
BADWELL ASH 50 E7
Badwell Ash VA Prim Sch IP31 50 E8
BADWELL GREEN 51 B8
Badwell Rd
Walsham le Willows IP31 35 B1
Wyverstone IP14 51 C6
Bagsham La IP28 30 A6
Bahram Cl CB8 120 E4
Bailey Ave IP5 141 E7
Bailey Cl
Haverhill CB9 133 B5
Ipswich IP2 138 E6
Bailey La CO10 90 B8
Baileypool La IP31 49 F8
Baines Coney CB9 132 A7
Baird Cl IP2 138 F7
Baird Gr IP5 141 B6
Bakehouse Hill CB8 59 F4
Baker Dr 4 CB5 44 B6
Baker Rd 2 IP9 107 A4
Baker's Cnr IP14 80 E6
Baker's Hill IP16 58 C4
Bakers La
Ditchingham NR35 110 B8
Orford IP12 131 C2
Winston IP14 68 E8
1 Woodbridge IP12 147 A4
Baker's La
Bury St Edmunds IP33 154 C1
Thorndon IP23 53 C6
Westleton IP17 58 C8
Bakers La S IP12 131 C2
Baker's Rd CO10 90 D5
Bakers Row CB8 121 A4
Baker's Score 1 NR32 3 D4
Bakers Way IP28 30 F2
Balaton Pl CB8 121 A6
Baldry Cl IP8 138 C1
Baldrys Wlk NR35 110 B7
Baldwin Ave IP32 122 E8
Baldwin Rd IP14 124 C4
Ballater Cl IP1 134 E4
BALLINGDON 148 B4
Ballingdon Hill CO10 148 A3
Ballingdon St CO10 148 A4
Balliol Cl IP12 146 D3
Ball's Chace CO6 101 C1
Balls Hill IP7 79 D5
Ballygate NR34 111 A5
Balmoral Cl IP2 138 F1
Balmoral Dr 9 CB9 132 C6
Balton Way 7 CO12 106 F1
Bancroft La CB7 28 D5
Bangor Rd IP27 13 F2
Banham Dr 3 CO10 148 D6
Banham Rd NR34 111 C2
Banham's La NR35 7 B6
Bank Alley 8 IP18 119 D5
Bank Bldgs 14 CO10 148 C5
Bank Rd IP4 139 E6
Banks Cl IP7 149 E5
Banks' La IP19 24 C3
Banks Wlk IP33 123 C1
Bannocks La IP13 56 B4
Banters La NR34 8 F2
Bantocks Rd CO10 92 C5
Bantoft Terr IP3 140 C2
Banyard Cl 4 IP5 141 D7
BANYARD'S GREEN 40 C4
Barbara Stradbroke Ave CB8 120 D1
Barber Cl 3 NR33 11 B1
Barber's La NR35 7 B6
Barcham Rd CB7 28 C7
Bardolph Rd NR35 110 B3
BARDWELL 34 C4
Bardwell Rd IP31 33 F5
Bardwell VC Prim Sch IP31 34 C5
Bardwell Windmill★ IP31 34 B4
Barell's Hill IP19 40 F4
Bargate La
Beck Row, Holywell Row & Kenny Hill IP28 29 F5
Dedham CO7 104 A2
Bargate Rd IP28 30 A6
BARHAM 82 C6
Barham Picnic Site Visitor Ctr★ IP6 82 A6
Barhams Way IP13 127 C7
Barker Cl
Ipswich IP2 138 D5
6 Manningtree CO11 104 D2
3 Steeple Bumpstead CB9 88 D3
Barker Rd CO10 148 C8
BARKING 125 A1
Barking Rd
Barking IP6 125 A1
Willisham IP8 81 A5
BARKING TYE 81 A7
Barkis Meadow NR32 3 A4
Barkways 9 CB5 44 B5
BARLEY GREEN 39 C5
Barley Lands IP15 130 E5
Barley Meadow 5 IP19 118 A3
Barley Way NR33 114 F2
Barlings Ct CB8 121 A4
Barnaby Gn IP18 119 C5
BARNABY GREEN 26 C2
BARNARDISTON 75 B3
Barnardiston Hall Prep Sch CB9 75 A5
Barnards Way NR32 113 B1
BARNBY 10 B5
Barnby & N Cove Prim Sch NR34 10 C4
Barn Cl
2 Hopton on Sea NR31 3 C7
Lowestoft NR33 114 D5
Southwold IP18 119 B8
Barnes Cl
Brandon IP27 14 E8
3 Hadleigh IP7 149 E6
Barnfield
Capel St Mary IP9 150 F3
Felixstowe IP11 152 D6
26 Manningtree CO11 104 E2
Barn Field 2 IP29 62 C6
BARNHAM 16 C2
Barnham CE Prim Sch IP24 16 B1
Barnham Pl IP5 140 F6
Barnham Rd IP24 16 E2
BARNINGHAM 34 F7
Barningham CE VC Prim Sch IP31 34 E7
Barningham Rd IP31 34 E5
Barn La IP33 154 C3
Barn St 12 CO10 78 D4
Barons Cl
9 Felixstowe IP11 153 D6
Halesworth IP19 118 A2
Barons Ct 17 CB9 132 C5
Baronsdale Cl IP1 135 B1
Barons Meadow IP12 131 B3
Barons Rd IP33 123 A2
Barrack La
Harwich CO12 107 C2
Ipswich IP1 155 A3
Ufford IP13 84 F7
Barrack Sq IP5 98 A8
Barracks Rd CO10 101 F8
Barr Dr IP27 109 D7
Barrell's Rd IP31 49 F3
Barrett's La IP6 125 C4
BARROW 47 A2
Barrow Hill
Acton CO10 92 B8
Barrow IP29 47 A2
Barrow Prim Sch IP29 47 A3
Barrow Rd IP29 46 F1
Barrow's Cnr IP24 32 C8
Barry Lynham Dr CB8 121 B2
Barsey Cl CB9 132 A7
BARSHAM 9 A4
Bartholomew Gn IP18 119 D5
Bartholomew's La IP19 42 B6
Bartholomew St IP4 139 F6
Bartlet Hospl IP11 153 C4
Bartlow Pl CB9 132 F7
Barton Bottom IP31 48 E7
Barton Dr CB9 133 F8
Barton Gr CB9 133 F8
Barton Hamlet IP31 49 C6
Barton Hill IP31 48 D5
BARTON MILLS 116 D2
Barton Rd
Bury St Edmunds IP32 123 D6
Felixstowe IP11 153 B4
Thurston IP31 49 D4
Woodbridge IP12 146 F7
Bartons Pl CB8 120 E5
Bartrum La 7 IP5 141 C7
Barvens The IP8 138 A1
Barway Rd CB7 28 A6
Barwell Rd IP33 154 C3
BASE GREEN 51 B2
Basil Brown Cl 1 IP22 36 A6
Bates La IP22 19 D6
Bath Ct CB9 132 D4
Bath Hill IP11 153 B4
Bath Hills Rd NR35 7 E4
Bath Rd IP11 153 B4
BATH SIDE 107 B3
Bath St IP2 139 D3
Battery Gn 7 NR32 113 E1
Battery Gn Rd 5 NR32 113 E1
Battery La 10 IP9 107 A4
BATTISFORD 66 F1
Battisford Rd IP6 125 A1
BATTISFORD TYE 66 C1
BATTLESEA GREEN 39 A6
Battlesea Hill IP21 39 A6
Battles La IP5 141 D7
BATTLIES GREEN 49 C3
BAWDSEY 99 E3
Bawdsey CE Prim Sch IP12 99 E2
Bawdsey Cl IP11 153 D7
Bawdsey Manor Workshops★ IP12 108 D8
Bawdsey Radar Sta★ IP12 99 E1
Bayfield Dr 4 CB5 44 B5
BAYLHAM 81 E6
Baylham House Rare Breeds Farm★ IP6 81 F7
Baynard's La IP22 20 A3
Bay Rd 11 CO12 107 B2
Bays The 4 IP16 73 F6
BAYTHORNE END 89 C5
Beach Mews 6 NR32 115 D8
Beach Rd
Dunwich IP17 43 B1
1 Harwich CO12 107 B1

Beach Rd continued
Hopton on Sea NR31 . . . . 3 C6
Kessingland NR33 . . . . 27 C8
Lowestoft NR32 . . . . 115 D8
Beach Rd E IP11 . . . . 153 C4
Beach Rd W IP11 . . . . 152 F2
Beach Sta Rd IP11 . . . . 152 E1
Beacon Field 4 IP11 . . . . . . 152 E5
BEACON HILL 137 F3
Beacon Hill Ave CO12 . . . . . 107 C2
Beacon Hill La IP16 . . . . 73 F7
Beacon Hill Specl Sch
IP2 . . . . 138 F2
Beacon La IP13 . . . . 137 F3
Beacon Rally Karts★ IP5 . 84 A2
Beaconsfield Ct CO10 . . . . 148 C6
Beaconsfield Ct 9 CB9 . . 132 D5
Beaconsfield Rd
Aldeburgh IP15 . . . . 130 E3
Ipswich IP1 . . . . 138 F7
21 Kessingland NR33 . . . 11 C1
Lowestoft NR33 . . . . 115 C6
Sudbury CO10 . . . . 148 C6
3 Woodbridge IP12 . . . . 147 A5
Beale Cl IP32 . . . . 49 A3
Bealings La IP13 . . . . 137 F8
Bealings Rd IP12 . . . . 146 A1
Bealings Sch IP13 . . . . 137 D4
Beardmore Pk 10 IP5 . . . . . . 98 A8
Beard Rd IP32 . . . . 49 A3
Bear Meadow 5 IP30 . . . . . 49 F2
Bear's La CO10 . . . . 78 D3
Bear St CO6 . . . . 102 C5
Beatrice Ave IP11 . . . . 153 A5
Beatrice Cl IP3 . . . . 140 A3
Beatty Rd
Ipswich IP3 . . . . 140 B2
Sudbury CO10 . . . . 148 E7
Beaufort Rd IP31 . . . . 32 F1
Beaufort Ct 10 CB9 . . . . . . 132 D5
Beaufort St IP1 . . . . 139 A7
Beaumont Cl 3 IP33 . . . . 122 D4
Beaumont Cotts IP17 . . . . 128 C6
Beaumont Ct CB9 . . . . 132 F4
Beaumont Prim Sch IP7 149 D8
Beaumont Rd NR33 . . . . . . 114 B2
Beaumont Vale CB9 . . . . . 132 F4
Beaumont Way IP14 . . . . . 124 B5
BECCLES 111 D5
Beccles & District Mus★
NR34 . . . . 111 A5
Beccles & District War Meml
Hospl NR34 . . . . 111 B4
Becclesgate 1 NR34 . . . . 111 B6
Beccles Gall★ 10 NR34 . . 111 B5
Beccles Mid Sch NR34 . . 111 C4
Beccles Rd
Aldeby NR34 . . . . 9 F8
Aldeby/Wheatacre/Burgh St
Peter NR34 . . . . 10 B8
Blyford IP19 . . . . 25 C1
Bungay NR35 . . . . 110 C4
Carlton Colville NR33 . . . . 114 A4
Fritton & St Olaves NR31 . . . 2 C7
Holton IP19 . . . . 118 F4
Lowestoft NR33 . . . . 114 D7
Mutford NR34 . . . . 10 C3
Beccles Sports Ctr NR34 111 A3
Beccles Sta NR34 . . . . 111 C5
Beck Cl 5 IP12 . . . . 85 D8
Beckett Cl IP33 . . . . 122 A6
Becketts La IP7 . . . . 94 B1
Becketts The IP14 . . . . . . 124 B8
Beckford Rd 17 CO11 . . . . 105 A2
Beckham Rd NR32 . . . . . . 113 C1
Beck Rd CB7 . . . . 29 D4
BECK ROW 30 A8
Beck Row Prim Sch IP28. 30 B8
Becks Gn La NR34 . . . . 24 F8
Beck St IP22 . . . . 35 A7
Beck The IP26 . . . . 4 E5
Beck View 3 IP20 . . . . 22 D6
Bedell Cl IP33 . . . . 122 C3
Bederic Cl IP32 . . . . 123 D4
BEDFIELD 54 E5
Bedfield CE Prim Sch
IP13 . . . . 54 D5
Bedfield Rd IP13 . . . . 55 A3
Bedford Rd 3 IP32 . . . . . 122 E8
Bedford St IP1 . . . . 155 A3
Bedingfield Way IP32 . . . 123 E4
BEDINGFIELD 53 F7
Bedingfield Cres IP19 . . . 118 A1
Bedingfield Rd IP23 . . . . . 53 E7
BEDINGHAM GREEN 7 B7
Beech Circus 5 IP7 . . . . . 80 D6
Beech Cl
Halesworth IP19 . . . . . . 118 A3
Isleham CB7 . . . . 29 B5
11 Lakenheath IP27 . . . . 13 F2
Sproughton IP8 . . . . 138 A6
Beechcroft IP29 . . . . 64 A3
Beech Croft CB8 . . . . 59 E1
Beechcroft Rd IP31 . . . . . 134 F2
Beeches Cl 11 IP31 . . . . . . 34 B1
Beeches Rd IP28 . . . . 29 F7
Beeches The
Benhall Green IP17 . . . . . . 72 C8
Claydon IP6 . . . . 134 C8
Horringer IP29 . . . . 63 A8
Ipswich IP3 . . . . 139 F4
31 Lawford CO11 . . . . . . 104 E2
Little Blakenham IP8 . . . . . 81 E3
Beech Gr
Haverhill CB9 . . . . 132 C7

Beech Gr continued
Ipswich IP3 . . . . 139 F3
Beeching Dr NR32 . . . . . . 113 D4
Beech La IP14 . . . . 51 A1
Beech Paddocks 4 IP30 . 64 F8
Beech Pk IP31 . . . . 49 B6
Beech Rd
Ipswich IP5 . . . . 140 F7
Lowestoft NR33 . . . . 114 D3
Sudbury CO10 . . . . 148 F4
Beech Rise IP33 . . . . 123 C3
Beech Row CB8 . . . . 46 C1
Beech Terr IP14 . . . . 124 D7
Beech Tree Cl NR34 . . . . . 111 B4
Beech Tree Way 9 NR35 . .7 F4
Beech Way
Dickleburgh IP21 . . . . 21 C5
Woodbridge IP12 . . . . . . 146 F3
Beech Wlk IP16 . . . . 129 C5
Beechwood Cl CB8 . . . . . 120 C8
Beechwood Gdns NR33 . 115 A6
Beehive Cl CO7 . . . . 151 C5
Beetons Way IP32 . . . . . . 122 E7
Beevors Gdn NR35 . . . . . 110 B7
Belaugh Ave NR33 . . . . . 114 F5
Belcham Hall★ CO10 . . . . 91 A3
Belchamp Rd CO9 . . . . 90 A3
BELCHAMP OTTEN 90 E4
Belchamp Rd CO9 . . . . 90 A3
BELCHAMP ST PAUL 90 D5
Belchamp St Paul CE Prim
Sch CO10 . . . . 90 D5
BELCHAMP WALTER 90 F3
Belcher Gn IP18 . . . . 119 C8
Belfry Rd IP3 . . . . 144 F7
Belgrave Cl IP4 . . . . 135 E1
Bellands Way IP23 . . . . . 117 C3
Bell Cl IP2 . . . . 155 B1
Belle Vue Rd
Ipswich IP4 . . . . 139 F6
Sudbury CO10 . . . . 148 D5
Bell Gdns 13 CB7 . . . . 28 D4
Bell Gn IP19 . . . . 40 C6
Bell Hill CO8 . . . . 101 B6
Bellings Rd CB9 . . . . 132 C8
Bell La
Barton Mills IP28 . . . . . . 116 D2
Ipswich IP3 . . . . 155 B1
Marlesford IP13 . . . . 71 C4
Bell Meadow IP32 . . . . . . 123 A8
Bell Mews IP7 . . . . 149 D6
BELL'S CORNER 102 F8
BELL'S CROSS 82 D7
Bell's Cross IP14 . . . . 67 C6
Bell's Cross Rd IP6 . . . . . 82 C7
Bells Hill CO8 . . . . 101 D2
Bells La
Glemsford CO10 . . . . 77 A3
Hinderclay IP22 . . . . 35 E8
Bell's La
Hawstead IP29 . . . . 63 E5
Stowupland IP14 . . . . 67 C7
Bells Rd CO10 . . . . 90 F3
Bell St IP26 . . . . 4 E5
Bellwell La
Debenham IP14 . . . . 53 F4
Kenton IP14 . . . . 54 A4
Belmont Ct
8 Haverhill CB9 . . . . . . 132 D5
Newmarket CB8 . . . . 120 F3
Belmont Gdns NR32 . . . . 113 B3
Belmont Rd IP8 . . . . 138 C1
Belsay Ct CB9 . . . . 132 B6
Belseybridge Rd NR35 . . . .7 F7
BELSTEAD 142 C7
Belstead Ave IP2 . . . . 155 A1
Belstead Rd IP2 . . . . 155 A1
Belstead Sch IP8 . . . . 138 C2
Belt The CB8 . . . . 61 B4
Belvedere Dr 23 NR33 . . 11 C1
Belvedere Rd
Ipswich IP4 . . . . 139 F8
Lowestoft NR33 . . . . 115 C7
Belvoir Ct 7 CB9 . . . . . . 132 C6
BENACRE 27 A7
Benacre National Nature
Reserve★ NR34 . . . . . . 27 B6
Benacre Rd
Ellough NR34 . . . . 111 F1
Henstead with Hulver Street
NR34 . . . . 26 B8
Ipswich IP3 . . . . 140 A2
Ben Curley Dr 6 IP24 . . . 16 C6
Benefield Rd 1 CB8 . . . . . 45 F3
Benezet St IP1 . . . . 155 A3
Benouville 10 NR33 . . . . 114 F3
Bensly's Drift IP19 . . . . . 118 C4
Bent La IP4 . . . . 140 E8
BENTLEY 104 F8
Bentley Dr NR32 . . . . 113 A6
Bentley La
Belstead IP8 . . . . 142 C5
Stutton IP9 . . . . 105 B6
Bentley Prim Sch IP9 . . . 104 F8
Bentley Rd IP1 . . . . 134 C2
Benton La IP7 . . . . 65 C1
Benton St IP7 . . . . 149 D4

Benton Way IP19 . . . . 118 B4
Bentwaters Cold War
Museum★ IP12 . . . . 85 F8
Benyon Gdns IP28 . . . . . . 32 D1
Beresford Dr IP12 . . . . . . 146 F7
Beresford Rd NR32 . . . . . 113 D2
Bergamot Rd CB9 . . . . . . 132 A6
Berghersh La IP6 . . . . 82 E7
Bergholt Rd CO11 . . . . . . 104 D4
Berkeley Cl
2 Framlingham IP13 . . . 126 C3
Ipswich IP4 . . . . 135 E1
Berkeley Gdns
Bury St Edmunds IP33 . . 122 E4
Lowestoft NR33 . . . . 113 A4
Bermuda Rd IP10 . . . . . . 144 D7
Bernard Cres IP3 . . . . 140 B2
Bernard Rooke Pottery &
Gall★ IP6 . . . . 83 A8
Berners Rd IP11 . . . . 153 C4
Berners St IP1 . . . . 155 A3
Bernham Cl IP32 . . . . 123 D5
Berry Cl
Ipswich IP3 . . . . 140 F1
Lowestoft NR32 . . . . 112 E1
Berrycroft 11 CB7 . . . . 28 D4
Beryl Rd 8 CO12 . . . . 106 E1
Bethel Dr 24 NR33 . . . . . . 11 C1
Betjeman Cl IP24 . . . . 16 C7
Betony Wlk CB9 . . . . 132 B6
Betts Ave IP5 . . . . 98 A8
Betts Cl IP7 . . . . 149 D7
Betty Cocker Gr CO10 . . 148 F5
Bevan St E 3 NR32 . . . . . 115 D8
Bevan St W NR32 . . . . . . 113 C1
Beverley Ct NR33 . . . . . . 114 D6
Beverley Ct NR33 . . . . . . 114 C2
Beverley Rd IP4 . . . . 139 F8
Beversham Rd IP13 . . . . . 71 F5
Bevis Wlk IP33 . . . . 123 D2
Bewicks Mead 10 CB5 . . 44 B5
Bexley Ave 16 CO12 . . . . 106 F1
Beyond the Image
Photographers Gall★
IP23 . . . . 36 F2
BEYTON 49 F1
BEYTON GREEN 49 F2
Beyton Mid Sch IP30 . . . . 49 F2
Beyton Rd IP30 . . . . 49 F1
Bibb Way IP1 . . . . 139 A5
Bickers Hill Rd IP13 . . . . . 40 B3
Bier La IP22 . . . . 19 C1
Bigod Cl
5 Framlingham IP13 . . . 126 C3
Halesworth IP19 . . . . . . 118 B2
Bigod Rd NR35 . . . . 110 D3
Big Row NR34 . . . . .8 F6
BIGSBY'S CORNER 72 D8
Bilberry Rd IP3 . . . . 144 C1
BILDESTON 79 F4
Bildeston Gdns 2 IP1 . . 135 D1
Bildeston Prim Sch IP7 . 79 E4
Bildeston Rd
Chelsworth IP7 . . . . 79 E3
Combs IP14 . . . . 124 A1
Offton IP7 . . . . 80 F4
BILLINGFORD 21 B1
Billings Cl IP3 . . . . 132 D8
Bill Rickaby Dr CB8 . . . . 121 A5
Billy's La CO7 . . . . 103 E5
Bilney Rd IP12 . . . . 146 E5
Birch Ave CO12 . . . . 107 A2
Birch Cl
Lowestoft NR32 . . . . 112 D2
1 Stowupland IP14 . . . . 67 A6
Wickham Market IP13 . . 127 C6
Woodbridge IP12 . . . . . . 146 F3
Birch Covert IP24 . . . . 16 D6
Birch Cres IP27 . . . . 109 D7
Birchcroft Rd IP1 . . . . . . 135 B2
Birch Dr 8 CO11 . . . . 104 E5
Birches The
Kennett IP28 . . . . 46 A8
Soham CB7 . . . . 28 C5
Birch Fall 7 CO6 . . . . . . 102 C5
Birch Gr IP5 . . . . 98 A7
Birchgrove 23 IP12 . . . . . 147 B6
Birchinhill Dro IP28 . . . . . 12 F2
Birch Rd
Onehouse IP14 . . . . 66 C6
10 Thurstow IP31 . . . . . 49 E4
Birch St CO6 . . . . 102 D5
Birch Wlk 24 IP27 . . . . . . 13 F2
Birchwood Cty Prim Sch
IP5 . . . . 98 A8
Birchwood Dr IP5 . . . . . . 136 E1
Birchwood Rd CO7 . . . . . 103 D2
BIRDBROOK 89 A4
Birdbrook 3 IP29 . . . . 63 A1
Birdbrook Rd CO9 . . . . . . 89 A2
Birdcage Wlk CB8 . . . . . . 120 F2
Birds Croft IP31 . . . . 33 C2
BIRDS END 62 B7
Birds Gn IP30 . . . . 65 E5
Birds Hill IP13 . . . . 83 D8
Birds La
Framsden IP14 . . . . 69 D5
Lowestoft NR33 . . . . 115 B6
Bird's La IP30 . . . . 64 D2
Birds Meare IP6 . . . . 69 C2
Bird's Rd IP31 . . . . 49 F3
BIRD STREET 80 A7
Bird View Sq 1 IP26 . . . . .4 E5
Birkdale Ave IP28 . . . . . . 116 B5
Birkdale Ct 10 IP28 . . . . . 48 C6
Birkfield Cl IP2 . . . . 139 A4
Birkfield Dr IP2 . . . . 138 E1
Biscay Cl CB9 . . . . 133 A5

Bishop Mews IP8 . . . . . . 138 B2
Bishops Cl
6 Felixstowe IP11 . . . . . 153 D6
Haverhill CB9 . . . . 132 C6
Sudbury CO10 . . . . 148 C8
Bishops Ct 1 CB9 . . . . . . 132 C6
Bishop's Hill IP3 . . . . 139 E4
Bishops Rd IP33 . . . . 154 B3
Bishops Way IP21 . . . . . . 39 A4
Bishops Wlk
10 Hopton on Sea NR31 . . . 3 B7
Lowestoft NR32 . . . . 113 D5
Bittern Cl IP2 . . . . 138 E3
Bittern Gn NR33 . . . . 114 C6
Bittern Rd IP17 . . . . 128 B3
Bixley Dr IP4 . . . . 140 E5
Bixley La IP4 . . . . 140 F5
Bixley Rd
Ipswich IP3 . . . . 140 D3
2 Lowestoft NR33 . . . . . 115 C6
Black Barns IP11 . . . . 152 C7
Black Bear Ct CB8 . . . . . . 121 A3
Black Bear La CB8 . . . . . . 120 F3
Blackberry Way
Lowestoft NR32 . . . . 112 E2
3 Red Lodge IP28 . . . . . 30 C1
Blackbird Ave IP27 . . . . . . .6 A1
Blackbird Cl 16 IP31 . . . . 49 D4
Blackbird Dr IP28 . . . . 49 A3
Blackbird Rd 3 IP28 . . . . 13 B1
Blackbird Way 10 IP4 . . . . .2 F6
Blackbourne CE VC Mid Sch
IP31 . . . . 34 F4
Blackbourne Rd IP30 . . . . 50 F3
Black Boy La CO11 . . . . . 106 A2
Black Boy Meadow NR34 111 B4
Blackdike Dro IP26 . . . . . . .4 A2
Blackdown Ave IP5 . . . . . 140 F6
Blackdyke Cl 9 IP26 . . . . . .4 D5
Black Dyke Rd IP26 . . . . . .4 E3
Blackfriars CO10 . . . . 148 B4
Black Gr La CO10 . . . . 75 E4
BLACKHEATH 42 C5
Blackheath Rd
Lowestoft NR33 . . . . 115 A5
Wenhaston with Mells Hamlet
IP19 . . . . 42 C5
Black Hill (Tumulus)★
IP31 . . . . 33 C5
Black Horse La
Ditchingham NR35 . . . . . 110 C7
Ipswich IP1 . . . . 155 A3
Black Horse Wlk IP1 . . . . 155 B3
Blackhouse La CO10 . . . . 148 F1
Blacklands La IP12 . . . . . 131 A8
Black Mill Rd IP18 . . . . . . 119 C5
Blackmore Cl CB9 . . . . . . 132 D7
Black Slough IP17 . . . . . . 58 B7
Blacksmith La
Barnham IP24 . . . . 16 B2
Thorpe Morieux IP30 . . . . 78 F7
Blacksmith Rd IP14 . . . . . 52 A6
Blacksmith's Cnr IP8 . . . 142 C6
BLACKSMITH'S GREEN . . 53 C5
Blacksmiths Hill CO10 . . 89 D6
Blacksmiths La
Bulmer CO10 . . . . 91 C1
Coddenham IP6 . . . . 68 B1
Stonham Earl IP14 . . . . . 67 D6
Blacksmith's Loke NR32 . .2 F6
BLACK STREET 11 A2
Blackthorn Cl 1 IP3 . . . 140 F1
Blackthorn Ct CB7 . . . . . . 28 C5
Blackthorn Way CO6 . . . 102 B7
Blackthorn Wlk IP3 . . . . . 122 D8
BLACKTHORPE 49 C2
Blackthorpe Barn★ IP30 . 49 C2
Blacktiles La IP12 . . . . 84 A1
Bladen Dr IP4 . . . . 140 F5
Bladon Way CB9 . . . . 132 C4
Blagge Cl IP33 . . . . 122 C4
Blair Cl IP4 . . . . 140 E5
Blair Par 6 CB9 . . . . 132 C6
Blake Ave 4 IP9 . . . . 107 A5
Blake Cl 7 CO11 . . . . 104 D2
Blakenham Cl 4 NR32 . . 112 F4
Blakenham Woodland Gdn★
IP6 . . . . 81 F4
Blake Rd
Ipswich IP1 . . . . 134 F3
Stowmarket IP14 . . . . . . 124 B7
Blakes Cl IP12 . . . . 147 C7
Blanche St IP4 . . . . 155 C3
Blandford Rd IP3 . . . . . . 140 D3
BLAXHALL 72 B4
Blaxhall Church Rd IP12 . 71 F2
Blaxhall Ct 2 CB9 . . . . . 132 C5
Blaxhall Heath Nature
Reserve★ IP12 . . . . 72 C3
BLEACH GREEN 39 A8
Blenheim Cl
10 Brantham CO11 . . . . 104 E5
Bury St Edmunds IP33 . . 122 D5
Haverhill CB9 . . . . 132 F7
Blenheim Dr IP7 . . . . 80 C6
Blenheim Rd 3 IP1 . . . . . 139 A7
Blenheim Way 2 IP22 . . . 20 A3
Blickling Cl IP2 . . . . 139 B2
Blinco Rd NR32 . . . . 112 C1
Blind La IP29 . . . . 77 B6
Blocka Rd NR32 . . . . .2 C6
Blockmoor Rd CB7 . . . . . . 28 A6
Block Rd CB7 . . . . 28 A6
Blofield Rd IP11 . . . . 152 B4
Blois Rd CB9 . . . . 88 F4
Blomfield St IP33 . . . . . . 154 B3
BLO' NORTON 18 E2

Blo' Norton Rd
Blo' Norton IP22 . . . . 18 F3
South Lopham IP22 . . . . . 19 A4
Blood Hill IP8 . . . . 81 B3
BLOODMAN'S CORNER . . . 3 A6
BLOODMOOR HILL 114 E2
Bloodmoor La 2 NR33 . . 114 E3
Bloodmoor Rd 1 NR33 . 114 E3
Bloomfield St IP4 . . . . . . 140 B6
Bloomfield Way
Debenham IP14 . . . . 53 E1
7 Lowestoft NR33 . . . . . 114 E3
Bloomsbury Cl NR32 . . . 112 E4
Blooms Ct IP28 . . . . 116 D5
Bloomsfield 8 CB5 . . . . . 44 B5
Blooms Hall La CO10 . . . . 77 D5
Blower's La NR33 . . . . 10 E2
Blue Barn Cl 13 IP11 . . . 107 D8
Blue Barn La IP8 . . . . 134 A8
Bluebell Ave IP32 . . . . . . 123 F5
Bluebell Cl
Ipswich IP3 . . . . 138 E4
7 Lowestoft NR33 . . . . . 114 E3
Bluebell Gr IP6 . . . . 125 D3
Bluebell Way NR34 . . . . . 111 E3
Bluebell Wlk 2 CB7 . . . . 28 D4
Bluegate La IP9 . . . . 150 F1
Blue House La IP14 . . . . . 52 F3
Bluestem Rd IP3 . . . . 144 D8
BLUNDESTON 3 A4
Blundeston Rd
Corton NR32 . . . . 112 F8
Somerleyton, Ashby &
Herringfleet NR32 . . . 112 B8
Blyburgate 2 NR34 . . . . 111 C4
BLYFORD 42 C7
Blyford La
Blyford IP19 . . . . 42 B8
Holton IP19 . . . . 118 E3
Wenhaston with Mells Hamlet
IP19 . . . . 42 C6
Blyford Rd NR32 . . . . 113 A5
Blyford Way IP11 . . . . . . 152 C4
BLYTHBURGH 42 F6
Blythburgh Rd IP17 . . . . . 58 C8
Blyth Cl
Ipswich IP2 . . . . 139 A1
Wenhaston IP19 . . . . 42 C6
Blyth Rd
Halesworth IP19 . . . . . . 118 C2
Southwold IP18 . . . . 119 B5
Boathouse La
Carlton Colville NR32 . . . 114 B8
Lowestoft NR32 . . . . 112 B1
Boatman Cl 16 IP8 . . . . . 142 E8
Bobbits La
Pinewood IP9 . . . . 142 E8
Wherstead IP9 . . . . 143 A7
BOBBY HILL 35 C5
Boby Rd IP32 . . . . 122 D8
Bockhill Rd IP33 . . . . 122 C5
Bodiam Cl IP3 . . . . 140 D4
Bodiam Rd IP3 . . . . 140 D4
Bodiam Way 8 NR33 . . . 114 D4
Bodian Wlk 8 CB9 . . . . . 132 C6
Bodmin Cl IP5 . . . . 141 A6
Boeing Way IP28 . . . . . . 116 B5
Boldero Rd IP32 . . . . 123 F4
Boleyn Way CB9 . . . . 132 B5
Boleyn Wlk CB8 . . . . 121 C3
Bollard Way NR33 . . . . . . 114 E5
Bolton Cl 2 CB5 . . . . 44 A5
Bolton La IP1 . . . . 155 C3
Bolton St 10 CO10 . . . . . . 78 D4
Bond Cl IP21 . . . . 21 F8
Bonds Meadow NR32 . . . 112 E2
Bond's Rd NR15 . . . . 21 C8
Bond St
Ipswich IP4 . . . . 155 C2
Stowmarket IP14 . . . . . . 124 D7
Bon Marche 7 NR32 . . . . 115 D8
Bonnington Rd IP3 . . . . . 139 F1
Bonny Cres IP3 . . . . 144 C8
Bonsey Gdns NR34 . . . . . 26 C8
Boon Cl IP33 . . . . 123 A3
Boon Dr NR33 . . . . 114 E6
Boot Drift IP9 . . . . 106 E7
Booth La IP5 . . . . 141 E8
BOOT STREET 137 D6
Border Cot La IP13 . . . . . 127 B7
Border La NR32 . . . . .2 E6
Borehamgate Prec 5
CO10 . . . . 148 C6
Borehamgate Sh Ctr 21
CO10 . . . . 148 C5
BORLEY 91 C5
Borley Cres 2 IP30 . . . . . 50 F2
BORLEY GREEN
Borley 91 B5
Woolpit 65 E7
Borley Rd CO10 . . . . 91 D6
Borough End 3 NR34 . . . 111 C3
Borough La IP14 . . . . 66 A3
Borradale Ct 5 CB9 . . . . . 88 D3
Borradale Rd IP32 . . . . . . 123 F5
Borrett Pl IP12 . . . . 146 D3
Borretts Farm La IP13 . . . 70 D6
Borrow Cl NR33 . . . . 114 C3
Borrowdale Ave 1 IP4 . . 135 D1
Borrow Rd NR32 . . . . 112 C1
Bosmere Prim Sch IP6 . . 125 D4
Bosquet Cl 1 NR32 . . . . 112 F5
Boss Hall Ind Est IP1 . . . 138 C7
Boss Hall Rd IP1 . . . . 138 E7
Bostock Rd IP2 . . . . 139 C1
Boston End 6 IP24 . . . . . 16 A5

Boston Rd
Ipswich IP4 139 F7
Lowestoft NR32 113 D2
Boswell La IP7 149 D7
Botany La IP17 71 E7
BOTESDALE 36 B6
Botolphs Ct IP33 154 C1
Bouchain Ct 1 IP19 118 A3
Boughton Way IP33 154 C3
Boulevard The NR32 114 D8
Boulge Rd
Burgh IP13 83 F6
Hasketon IP13 146 B8
Boulters Cl IP14 124 B6
Boulters Way IP14 124 B6
Boundary Cl IP26 4 F3
Boundary Rd
Haverhill CB9 133 B3
1 Hockwood cum Wilton IP26 5 A3
Red Lodge IP28 30 C1
Bourchier Cl 7 IP7 149 E6
Bourne Ave 6 IP32 123 E6
Bourne Hill IP2 143 B7
Bourne Pk Residential Park IP2 139 B1
Bourne Rd
Haverhill CB9 132 F6
Lowestoft NR32 113 B3
Bourne Terr IP2 143 B8
BOWBECK 34 C6
Bowdens La CO6 101 F3
BOWER HOUSE TYE 93 E3
Bower's La 7 CB7 29 C5
Bowland Dr IP8 138 C1
Bowl Rd IP14 66 C1
Bowman's La IP17 42 D1
Bowthorpe Cl IP1 155 A4
Box Bush La IP13 55 D5
BOXFORD 93 C3
Boxford Cl 2 IP14 124 E3
Boxford Ct
7 Felixstowe IP11 152 C4
3 Haverhill CB9 132 C5
Boxford La CO10 93 A3
Boxford Prim Sch CO10 93 C3
Boxford Rd IP7 93 B8
Boxhouse La CO7 103 D3
BOXTED
Colchester 77 A6
Glemsford 102 F4
Boxted Church Rd CO6 102 E2
BOXTED CROSS 103 A3
Boxted Rd CO6 102 E2
Boxted Straight Rd CO4 103 A2
Boyden Cl 1 CB8 61 E2
BOYDEN END 61 D2
Boydlands IP9 150 E3
BOYLAND COMMON 20 A7
Boyne Rd IP33 122 E4
Boyscott La 1 NR35 110 B3
BOYTON 86 B2
Boyton Cl CB9 132 E8
BOYTON END 89 B7
Boyton Rd
Hollesley IP12 86 A1
Ipswich IP3 140 B1
Boyton's La CB10 88 A1
Boyton Vineyard★ CO9 89 B7
BRABLING GREEN 126 E6
Braces La NR35 8 E7
Bracken Ave IP5 137 E1
Brackenbury Cl IP1 139 B8
Brackenbury Sports Ctr IP11 153 C5
Brackenhayes Cl IP2 139 B3
Bracken Rise IP26 6 A8
Bracken Row 6 IP31 49 D4
Brackenwood Cres 1 IP32 123 E6
Brackley Cl 8 IP11 152 D5
Bradbrook Cl IP32 123 F6
Braddock Sq IP32 122 E7
BRADFIELD 105 C1
Bradfield Ave IP7 149 D7
BRADFIELD COMBUST 64 A4
Bradfield Cres IP7 149 D7
BRADFIELD ST CLARE 64 C4
BRADFIELD ST GEORGE 64 D7
Bradfield Woods National Nature Reserve★ IP30 64 F4
Bradley Rd
Cowlinge CB8 60 F1
Great Bradley CB8 74 F8
Kirtling CB8 60 F2
Bradley St IP2 155 B1
Braggon's Hill IP29 77 A5
BRAISEWORTH 37 D2
Braithwaite Dr 7 CO10 92 C6
Bramble Cl CB9 132 B7
Bramble Dr IP3 140 E1
Bramble Gn NR32 113 B3
Brambles The IP15 130 C6
Bramble Tye 20 CO12 106 E1
Bramble Way CO6 102 B7
Bramblewood 1 IP8 138 C2
Bramblewood Way IP19 118 C4
Brambling Cl 12 IP14 67 A5
Brames La IP20 23 D3
BRAMFIELD 41 F4
Bramfield CE Prim Sch IP19 42 A4
Bramfield House Sch IP19 41 E4
Bramfield Rd
Halesworth IP19 118 B2
Lowestoft NR32 113 A3
Walpole IP19 41 C5
Bramfield Rd *continued*
Wenhaston with Mells Hamlet IP19 42 B5
BRAMFORD 134 A2
Bramford CE Prim Sch IP8 134 A1
Bramford Ct IP14 124 E4
Bramford La 6 IP1 139 A7
Bramford Meadows Nature Reserve★ IP1 134 B3
Bramford Rd
Bramford IP8 134 B1
Claydon IP8 134 A8
Great Blakenham IP6 134 A8
Ipswich IP1 138 E8
Bramhall Cl IP2 138 D1
Bramley Chase IP4 140 B7
Bramley Cl IP32 123 F6
Bramley Rd
Diss IP22 20 B3
Haverhill CB9 132 A5
Bramley Rise NR34 111 C3
BRAMPTON 25 E5
Brampton CE Prim Sch NR34 25 E5
Brampton Gr 9 NR32 112 F4
Brampton Sta NR34 25 C6
BRAMPTON STREET 25 E4
BRANDESTON 70 B7
Brandeston Cl 10 CO10 92 C6
Brandeston Rd
Cretingham IP13 69 E7
Earl Soham IP13 54 F1
BRANDON 6 A1
Brandon Ctry Pk Visitor Ctr★ IP27 14 F8
Brandon Her Ctr★ IP27 5 F1
Brandon Rd
Felixstowe IP11 152 C4
Lakenheath IP27 14 C4
Methwold IP26 5 B8
Mildenhall IP28 116 E5
Thetford IP24 15 F6
Weeting IP27 5 F3
Wordwell IP28 32 C3
Brandon St IP27 109 F1
Brandon Sta IP27 5 F2
Brand Rd IP31 49 C7
Brands Cl 12 CO10 92 B3
Brands La IP29 63 D3
Bransby Gdns IP4 139 E7
BRANTHAM 104 F4
Brantham Hill CO11 104 E4
Brawdy Rd 1 IP31 33 D5
Brayfield Cl IP32 123 D6
Braziers La IP31 51 B6
Brazier's Wood Rd IP3 144 B8
Brazilian Terr CB8 120 F3
Breach Dro IP28 13 C1
Breckland Ave IP27 109 D7
Breckland Mid Sch IP27 14 D8
Brecklands 5 IP26 6 B8
Breckland Way
Lowestoft NR32 113 A3
Mildenhall IP28 116 C5
Brecon Cl IP2 139 B2
BREDFIELD 84 C7
Bredfield Cl 7 IP11 152 D5
Bredfield Rd IP12 147 A7
Bredfield St IP12 146 F5
Brendon Cl NR32 112 E2
Brendon Dr IP5 140 F6
Brent Cl IP28 116 D4
BRENT ELEIGH 79 A2
Brent Eleigh Rd
Lavenham CO10 78 D3
Monks Eleigh IP7 79 B2
Brentgovel St 1 IP33 154 B2
BRESSINGHAM 19 F4
BRESSINGHAM COMMON 19 F5
Bressingham Prim Sch IP22 19 E4
Bressingham Rd IP22 19 F4
Bressingham Steam Mus & Gdns★ IP22 19 E3
Brett Ave IP7 149 E7
Brett Cl IP1 138 E8
BRETTENHAM
Stowmarket 79 C8
Thetford 17 B6
Brettenham Cres 4 IP1 135 D1
Brettenham Rd
Buxhall IP14 65 F4
Hitcham IP7 79 E8
Brett Gn IP7 149 E2
Bretts The IP5 141 E8
Brewers Cl IP27 109 C6
Brewers Gn La IP22 20 B3
BREWERS GREEN 20 B3
Brewhouse La 19 CB7 28 D4
Breydon Way
Gainsborough IP3 144 C7
Lowestoft NR33 114 F6
Briar Cl
Halesworth IP19 118 C4
Lowestoft NR32 113 B5
Briardale Ave 4 CO12 106 F2
Briarhayes Cl IP2 139 B3
Briar Hill IP30 50 D1
Briar La IP22 35 F5
Briar Rd 39 IP20 22 D6
Briarwood Ave IP33 122 D5
Briarwood Rd
Lowestoft NR33 114 F5
Woodbridge IP12 146 E3
Brices Way 4 CO10 77 A3
Bricett Bsns Pk IP7 80 E6
Bricett Gn IP7 80 D5
Brickfield Cl IP2 155 C1
Brickfields Ave CB8 120 D7
Brickfields Dr CB9 132 C8
Brickfields The IP14 124 C6
Brick Kiln Ave NR34 111 C4
Brick Kiln Cl 15 IP11 107 D8
Brick Kiln Hill CO6 93 C2
Brickkiln La IP22 19 C3
Brick Kiln La
Huntingfield IP19 40 F4
Melton IP12 147 E7
Brick Kiln Rd
Ellingham NR35 8 C8
Harkstead IP9 106 B6
Mildenhall IP28 116 D5
Brick La
Framlingham IP13 126 D1
Parham IP13 71 A7
Brickman's Hill CO11 105 B2
Bridewell Cl IP28 116 B4
Bridewell La
Botesdale IP22 36 A6
Bury St Edmunds IP33 154 C2
Bridewell St CO10 90 B8
Bridge Cl 16 IP20 22 D6
Bridge Cottage★ CO7 151 D1
Bridge End Rd IP28 30 B1
Bridge Farm Barns (Craft Ctr)★ IP2 79 D2
Bridge Foot Cnr IP18 119 C7
BRIDGE GREEN 20 F6
Bridgeman Wlk IP32 122 E7
Bridge Pk (Skate Park)★ IP1 155 B1
Bridge Rd
Bromeswell IP12 85 A6
Burston & Shimpling IP22 20 E7
Felixstowe IP11 153 A5
Levington IP10 145 E4
Lowestoft NR32 112 E1
Reydon IP18 119 C7
6 Scole IP21 20 F1
Snape IP17 72 D4
Bridge St Rd CO10 78 A4
Bridge St
Beccles NR34 111 A7
Brandon IP27 5 F2
Bungay NR35 110 B4
4 Bures Hamlet CO8 101 C5
Carlton IP17 128 D6
Framlingham IP13 126 C3
Hadleigh IP7 149 C7
Halesworth IP19 118 B4
Huntingfield IP19 41 A4
Ipswich IP1 155 B2
Moulton CB8 45 F3
Needham Market IP6 125 D5
Stowmarket IP14 124 F5
Thetford IP24 16 B5
BRIDGE STREET 77 F4
Bridge Terr 7 CO10 148 D6
Bridge Wood Nature Reserve★ IP3 144 B6
Bridgewood Rd IP12 146 E5
Bridgham La NR16 17 F8
Bridgwater Rd IP2 138 D2
Bridlemere Ct CB8 120 F3
Bridles The 4 NR34 111 F4
Bridport Ave IP3 140 D3
Bright Cl
Bury St Edmunds IP33 123 C3
Saxmundham IP17 128 B4
Brighton St IP27 14 A3
Bright's La CO10 78 C4
Brights Wlk IP5 141 E7
BRIGHTWELL 98 A6
Brightwell Cl IP11 152 C4
Brimstone Rd IP8 142 E8
Brindles The 7 NR33 114 E4
BRINKLEY 59 E2
Brinkley Rd
Brinkley CB8 59 E1
Carlton CB8 74 A8
Dullingham CB8 59 F4
Brinkley Way IP11 153 D7
Brisbane Rd IP4 140 D6
Briscoe Way IP27 109 C8
Bristol Hill IP9 107 A4
Bristol Rd
Bury St Edmunds IP33 122 E3
Ipswich IP4 140 A7
Bristol St IP27 14 A2
Britannia Prim Sch IP4 140 B5
Britannia Rd IP4 140 B6
Britten Ave IP14 124 C7
Britten Cl IP15 130 D5
Britten Ctr The NR32 113 D1
Britten Rd NR33 115 A6
Brittons Cres 3 IP29 47 A2
Brittons Rd 4 IP29 47 A2
Broadcroft Cres CB9 132 C6
Broadfields Rd 5 IP23 36 D2
Broad Fleet Cl 2 NR32 112 E4
Broad Gn Cl 4 IP29 62 C6
BROADGRASS GREEN 50 C1
BROAD GREEN
Cheveley 60 F6
Chevington 62 B6
Creeting St Peter or West Creeting 67 C6
Broad La CO6 102 E1
Broadland Cl
Beccles NR34 111 E4
Lowestoft NR33 114 C7
Broadland Rd IP33 123 B1
Broadlands Way IP4 140 F5
Broad Meadow
2 Ipswich IP8 138 C2
2 Walsham le Willows IP31 35 C2
Broadmere Rd IP1 138 E8
Broadoak Cl 4 NR33 114 C4
Broad Oaks CO6 102 B8
Broad Piece CB7 28 C5
Broad Rd
Cotton IP14 52 A6
Little Thurlow CB9 74 F6
Lowestoft NR32 112 D1
Wickham Market IP13 127 B7
Broads Rd CB5 44 B8
Broads Rd Bsns Pk CB5 44 B7
Broad St
Boxford CO10 93 C3
Bungay NR35 110 A5
Eye IP23 117 C2
20 Harleston IP20 22 D6
Haverhill CB9 132 D6
Orford IP12 131 C2
BROAD STREET 93 C5
Broad View Rd NR32 114 C8
Broadwater Gdns 6 IP9 107 A4
Broadwaters Rd NR33 114 E5
BROADWAY 118 C6
Broadway
6 Fressingfield IP21 39 E8
11 Glemsford CO10 77 A3
Pakenham IP31 49 F8
Wickham Market IP13 127 B7
Broad Way IP21 21 A4
Broadway Dr IP19 118 C6
Broadway The
Badwell Ash IP31 50 F8
Wickham Skeith IP23 52 D8
BROCKDISH 21 F2
Brockdish Prim Sch IP21 22 A2
Brockesby Wlk IP33 122 D4
BROCKFORD GREEN 53 A4
Brockford Rd IP14 52 F4
BROCKFORD STREET 52 F5
Brock La IP13 146 C2
BROCKLEY CORNER 32 D2
Brockley Cres IP1 134 D1
BROCKLEY GREEN
Hartest 63 A1
Hundon 75 C2
Brockley La IP29 46 F2
Brockley Rd
Hartest IP29 77 A8
Whepstead IP29 63 B4
Brocks Bsns Ctr CB9 132 C3
Broke Ave IP8 134 B2
BROKE HALL 140 E3
Broke Hall Gdns IP3 140 D4
Broke Hall Prim Sch IP4 140 E5
BROME 117 B7
Brome Ave IP23 117 D5
Brome Hall La IP23 117 E7
Bromelands IP23 117 E8
BROME STREET 117 E8
BROMESWELL 85 A5
Bromeswell Gn Nature Reserve★ IP12 147 F7
Bromeswell Rd IP4 135 E1
Bromley Cl 4 IP2 139 C3
Bromley Rd CO11 104 D1
Bronyon Cl IP33 122 C5
Brook Cl
Horringer IP29 122 B1
Hundon CO10 75 D3
Lowestoft NR33 114 D4
Stowmarket IP14 124 B7
Brook Dam La 22 CB7 28 D4
Brook Dr 3 IP17 56 F8
Brooke Bsns & Ind Pk NR33 115 A8
Brook Farm La 4 IP9 105 E7
Brook Farm Rd IP17 128 B4
Brookfield Rd IP1 138 F8
Brookfields Cl CB8 121 B5
BROOK GREEN 63 E5
Brook Hall Rd CO10 93 C3
Brookhill Way IP4 140 F4
Brookhouse Bsns Pk IP2 138 F6
Brook House Rd IP14 52 B6
Brook La
Burgate IP22 36 E7
Capel St Mary IP9 150 C4
Felixstowe IP11 153 B5
Framlingham IP13 126 B3
Mickfield IP14 53 A2
Needham IP20 22 B4
Playford IP6 137 A4
St Margaret, Ilketshall NR35 24 C7
Trimley St Martin IP10 98 E1
Brooklands Cl IP33 154 A1
Brooklands Rd CO11 104 E4
Brooklands Rise CO11 104 E4
Brooklyn Rd 14 CO12 107 B2
Brook Rd NR34 10 B4
Brooks Castle IP13 126 C3
Brook Service Rd 1 CB9 132 E5
Brooksfield 1 IP7 79 F4
Brooks Hall Rd IP1 139 A7
Brookside
Dalham CB8 61 C8
Moulton CB8 45 F3
Brook St
Dedham CO7 103 F4
Glemsford CO10 77 A3
Soham CB7 28 D3
Woodbridge IP12 147 A5
Yoxford IP17 57 D7
BROOK STREET 77 A3
Brookview
6 Ipswich IP2 142 E8
Pinewood IP2 138 E1
Brook Way IP8 81 C3
Brookwood Cl 7 NR34 9 F4
Broom Cres IP3 139 F1
BROOME 110 D7
BROOME HEATH 110 D7
Broomfield
17 Martlesham Heath IP5 98 A8
Martlesham IP5 141 F7
Broom Field 5 IP11 152 E5
Broomfield Comm IP8 138 B6
Broomfield Mews 18 IP5 98 A8
Broomhayes IP2 139 A2
Broomheath IP12 146 F2
BROOM HILL 146 E2
Broomhill Cl 2 IP28 30 C1
Broomhill La IP30 50 C1
Broom Hill La IP24 33 E7
Broom Hill Nature Reserve★ IP7 149 C5
Broom Hill Rd IP1 139 A8
Broom Hill Swimming Pool IP1 139 A8
Broom Knoll 1 CO11 104 E5
Broomley Gn Rd IP32 123 F6
Broom Rd
Lakenheath IP27 109 E5
2 Lowestoft NR32 113 B2
Broom Rd Cl IP27 109 E5
BROOM'S BARN 46 F4
Broomspath Rd IP14 67 A6
Broom St CO10 148 F3
Broom Way IP9 150 E4
Broom Wlk 9 IP28 30 B8
Brotherton Ave IP11 152 B8
Broughton Rd IP1 155 A4
Browning Rd
10 Brantham CO11 104 E4
Ipswich IP1 134 F3
Brownlow Rd IP11 153 A4
Browns Cl
5 Acton CO10 92 B7
Hitcham IP7 79 E6
5 Wickhambrook CB8 61 E2
Browns Gr IP5 141 D7
Brown St IP14 52 A3
BROWN STREET 52 A2
Browse Cl IP32 123 E4
BROWSTON GREEN 2 E8
Browston La NR32 2 E7
Broxtead Cl IP12 85 C2
Bruce St NR33 115 C7
Brudenell St IP15 130 E3
Bruff Rd IP2 139 C3
Bruges Cl 14 CO12 107 A1
BRUISYARD 56 C5
Bruisyard Rd IP13 56 C3
Bruisyard Vineyard★ IP17 56 C5
BRUNDISH 55 C8
BRUNDISH STREET 39 E1
BRUNDON 148 A7
Brundon La CO10 148 A5
Brunel Rd IP2 138 E6
Brunel Way IP24 16 B7
Brunswick House Cut 13 CO11 105 A2
Brunswick Rd IP4 135 F1
Brunwyn Cl IP32 123 F6
Brussels Cl 15 CO12 107 A1
Brybank Rd CB9 132 A7
Bryon Ave IP11 152 B2
Bryony Cl
Haverhill CB9 132 C7
6 Lowestoft NR33 114 F3
Buccaneer Rd IP31 33 D5
Buckanay La IP12 99 E5
Buckenham Ct 17 IP18 119 D5
Buckenham Rd IP7 149 F4
Buckfast Cl 4 IP2 139 A2
Buckingham Cl 4 IP12 84 A1
Buckingham Rd CB9 132 C4
Buckingham's Hill IP21 39 E8
Buck La IP23 117 E8
Buckles Field 8 IP31 34 E4
BUCKLESHAM 98 A5
Bucklesham Prim Sch IP10 98 B4
Bucklesham Rd
Ipswich IP3 140 E2
Kirton IP10 98 D3
Buckleswood Rd IP16 129 A7
Bucknam Cl 14 NR33 11 C1
Buck's Head La IP6 67 F2
Buckshorn La IP23 117 D2
Buck's Horns La IP8 142 B6
Bucks La 7 CO10 90 A8
Buddleia Cl IP2 138 E4
Bude Cl IP5 141 A6
Buggs Hole La IP22 18 D2
Bugg's La
Brettenham IP7 65 D1
Hitcham IP7 79 D8
Bugg's Rd IP22 36 D6
Bugsby Way IP5 141 E7
BULCAMP 42 D7
Bulcamp Drift IP19 43 A7
Bullace La IP12 131 A8
Bullard's La IP12 146 E5
Bull Dr IP5 141 C6
Bullen Cl
Bramford IP8 134 A2

Bullen Cl continued
Bury St Edmunds IP33 . . . . 154 A1
Bullen La 5 IP8 . . . . 134 A2
Bullens Cl IP33 . . . . 122 A5
Buller Rd IP16 . . . . 129 C6
Bullfinch Cl 24 CO12 . . . . 106 F1
Bull Hall La IP6 . . . . 83 A5
Bullion's La NR34 . . . . 26 B2
Bull La
  Acton CO10 . . . . 78 A1
  Hawstead IP29 . . . . 63 C5
  Long Melford CO10 . . . . 91 E8
  Rickinghall Superior IP22 . . 36 B4
Bullock Fair Cl 14 IP20 . . . 22 D6
Bullockshed La IP12 . . . . . 131 C4
Bullocks La CO10 . . . . 148 C5
Bull Rd IP31 . . . . 49 F6
Bull Rush Cres IP33 . . . . . 154 A4
Bull's Ash Cnr IP7 . . . . 80 F5
Bullshall Rd 6 IP23 . . . . . . 37 F1
Bull's Rd IP6 . . . . 82 C7
Bullswood La IP30 . . . . 64 D1
Bull's Wood Nature
  Reserve★ IP30 . . . . 64 E1
BULMER 91 C3
Bulmer La CO10 . . . . 93 C4
Bulmer Rd CO10 . . . . 148 A4
Bulmer Rd Ind Est CO10 . 148 A4
Bulmer St Andrews CE Prim
  Sch CO10 . . . . 91 C2
BULMER TYE 91 D1
Bulstrode Rd IP2 . . . . 155 C1
Bulwer Rd IP1 . . . . 139 A6
Bumpstead Rd CB9 . . . . . 132 F3
Bunbury Ave
  1 Great Barton IP31 . . . . . 49 A5
  Mildenhall IP28 . . . . 116 C5
Bunbury Rd 8 IP32 . . . . . . 48 C5
BUNGAY 110 B3
Bungay Castle (rems)★
  NR35 . . . . 110 A4
Bungay High Sch NR35 . . 110 C2
Bungay Mid Sch NR35 . . . 110 D3
Bungay Mus★ NR35 . . . . . 110 B4
Bungay Prim Sch NR35 . . 110 C3
Bungay Rd
  Barsham NR34 . . . . 9 B4
  Beccles NR34 . . . . 110 A1
  Dickleburgh & Rushall IP21 . 21 B1
  Ellingham NR35 . . . . 8 C8
  Halesworth IP19 . . . . 118 B4
  Scole IP21 . . . . 21 A1
  Stockton NR34 . . . . 8 F8
Bunker Cl NR33 . . . . 115 A5
Bunn's La IP20 . . . . 22 C6
Bunters Rd 8 CB8 . . . . 61 E2
Bunting Rd
  Bury St Edmunds IP32 . . . 123 F4
  Ipswich IP2 . . . . 138 D3
Buntings Cres 15 CB5 . . . . 44 A6
Buntings Path CB5 . . . . . . 44 A6
Buntry La CO10 . . . . 75 C2
Bunyan Cl IP1 . . . . 135 A3
Burch's Cl IP17 . . . . 129 A2
Burdock La IP26 . . . . 4 C3
Buregate Rd IP11 . . . . . . 152 F2
BURES 101 C5
Bures Cl IP14 . . . . 124 E4
Bures Ct 6 CB9 . . . . 132 C5
BURES GREEN 101 D6
Bures Prim Sch CO8 . . . . . 101 C4
Bures Rd
  Little Cornard CO10 . . . . . 101 A8
  Nayland-with-Wissington
   CO6 . . . . 101 F4
  Sudbury CO10 . . . . 148 E2
Bures Sta CO8 . . . . 101 C4
BURGATE 36 E6
Burgate Rd
  Gislingham IP23 . . . . 36 D3
  Higham IP28 . . . . 46 E3
Burgess Cl 14 IP2 . . . . . . 139 A2
Burgess Pl 22 IP5 . . . . 98 A8
BURGH 83 F6
Burghley Cl 14 IP2 . . . . . . 139 A2
Burghley Rise 5 CB5 . . . . 44 B5
Burgh Rd NR34 . . . . 2 C1
BURGH ST PETER 10 B8
Burke Cl IP1 . . . . 135 A3
Burke Rd 7 IP1 . . . . 135 A3
Burkitt Rd IP12 . . . . 146 E5
Burkitts La CO10 . . . . 148 C5
Burlingham Dr NR33 . . . . 114 B3
Burlington Rd IP1 . . . . . . 155 A3
Burnet Cl IP8 . . . . 142 D8
Burnham Cl
  Felixstowe IP11 . . . . 152 C7
  Ipswich IP4 . . . . 139 F7
Burnham Way NR33 . . . . . 115 A7
Burns Cl IP23 . . . . 37 B5
Burns Dr IP14 . . . . 124 C8
Burns Rd IP1 . . . . 134 E3
Burnt Dick Hill CO4 . . . . . 102 E4
Burnt Fen Turnpike IP28 . 12 D6
Burnt Hill La NR33 . . . . . . 114 B7
Burnt Hill Way NR33 . . . . 114 D5
Burnt House Cl 3 CB9 . . . 132 B4
Burnthouse La
  Battisford IP14 . . . . 66 D1
  Needham IP20 . . . . 22 B4
Burnt House La IP10 . . . . . 98 D2
Burnt La IP12 . . . . 131 C2
Burnt Oak Cnr CO7 . . . . . . 151 D3
Burntoak La IP20 . . . . 22 E8
Burr Cl 17 CO12 . . . . 106 E1

Burrell Cres IP28 . . . . 116 D2
Burrell Rd IP2 . . . . 155 B1
Burrell's Orch IP33 . . . . . 122 A6
Burrell Way IP24 . . . . 16 A5
BURROUGH END 59 E2
Burrough Gn CE Prim Sch
  CB8 . . . . 59 F2
BURROUGH GREEN 59 F2
Burroughs Piece Rd 2
  CO10 . . . . 148 D5
Burrow Dr IP27 . . . . 109 C8
Burrows Cl 5 CO11 . . . . . 104 D2
Burrows Gn NR34 . . . . 2 A1
Burrows Rd 7 IP12 . . . . . . 84 E6
BURSTALL 95 D7
Burstall Hall La IP8 . . . . . . 95 E7
BURSTALL HILL 95 C8
Burstall La IP8 . . . . 95 E7
BURSTON 20 E6
Burston Com Prim Sch
  IP22 . . . . 20 E6
Burston Rd
  Dickleburgh & Rushall
   IP21 . . . . 20 F4
  Diss IP22 . . . . 20 D4
  Gissing IP22 . . . . 20 F7
BURTHORPE 47 B3
Burton Cl CB9 . . . . 132 C5
Burton Dr IP6 . . . . 125 C5
Burton End CB9 . . . . 132 C5
Burton End Com Prim Sch
  CB9 . . . . 132 B5
Burton Hill CB9 . . . . 74 B3
Burton St NR32 . . . . 113 D2
Burwash 1 IP6 . . . . 83 A5
BURWELL 44 A5
Burwell Mus★ CB5 . . . . . . 44 B5
Burwell Rd CB8 . . . . 120 A8
Burwood Pl
  7 Lowestoft NR32 . . . . . 113 B6
  Trimley St Mary IP11 . . . . 152 C8
Bury Bottom IP27 . . . . 15 A5
Bury Drift IP31 . . . . 48 E6
Bury Hill IP12 . . . . 147 A7
Bury Hill Cl IP12 . . . . 147 A7
Bury La
  Lidgate CB8 . . . . 61 C4
  Moulton CB8 . . . . 45 F3
  Stanton IP31 . . . . 34 E3
  Wickhambrook CB8 . . . . . . 61 E4
Bury Language Sch The
  IP33 . . . . 154 C2
Bury Pk Dr IP33 . . . . 123 C2
Bury Rd
  Alpheton CO10 . . . . 78 A5
  Barrow IP29 . . . . 47 A2
  Beyton IP30 . . . . 49 E2
  Botesdale IP22 . . . . 36 B7
  Bradfield St Clare IP30 . . . . 64 C4
  Brandon IP27 . . . . 14 F8
  Brettenham IP7 . . . . 79 C7
  Brockley IP29 . . . . 63 A2
  Chedburgh IP29 . . . . 62 D4
  Felsham IP30 . . . . 65 A4
  Flempton IP28 . . . . 47 F8
  Great Barton IP31 . . . . 49 A5
  Great Thurlow CB9 . . . . . . 74 F5
  Great Whelnetham IP30 . . . 63 F4
  Haughley IP14 . . . . 66 D7
  Hengrave IP28 . . . . 48 A7
  Hepworth IP22 . . . . 35 A4
  Ipswich IP1 . . . . 134 D4
  Kentford CB8 . . . . 46 B5
  Lavenham CO10 . . . . 78 D5
  Lawshall IP29 . . . . 63 D2
  Market Weston IP22 . . . . . 18 B1
  Mildenhall IP28 . . . . 116 E4
  Newmarket CB8 . . . . 121 C5
  Rickinghall Inferior IP22 . . 35 F5
  Stanton IP31 . . . . 34 F4
  Stowmarket IP14 . . . . . . 124 C2
  Thetford IP24 . . . . 16 B3
  Thorpe Morieux IP30 . . . . 64 E2
  Wickhambrook CB8 . . . . . . 61 F1
  Wortham IP22 . . . . 36 E8
BURY ST EDMUNDS 154 C2
Bury St Edmunds Abbey★
  IP33 . . . . 154 C2
Bury St Edmunds Abbey
  Gdns★ IP33 . . . . 154 C2
Bury St Edmunds Art Gall★
  IP33 . . . . 154 B2
Bury St Edmunds Leisure Ctr
  IP33 . . . . 122 C6
Bury St Edmunds Sta
  IP32 . . . . 154 A4
Bury St Edmunds Upper Sch
  IP32 . . . . 154 A4
Bury St 3 IP14 . . . . 124 D6
Bush Cnr IP14 . . . . 53 E1
Bushel La CB7 . . . . 28 D4
Bushey Cl IP9 . . . . 150 E3
Bush Gr CO10 . . . . 148 A4
BUSH GREEN 64 D4
Bushman Gdns 3 IP8 . . . 134 A2
Bushy La IP12 . . . . 99 E7
Bussock La IP12 . . . . 99 D7
Buston Rd 5 IP22 . . . . 20 B2
Butchers La IP14 . . . . 80 E6
Butcher's La CO10 . . . . . . 93 C4
Butcher's Rd IP17 . . . . . . 128 C7
Bute Ct CB9 . . . . 132 D4
Butfield CO10 . . . . 78 D3
Butler's La CO11 . . . . 105 F1
Butler Smith Gdns 6
  IP5 . . . . 141 C7
Butlers Way CO9 . . . . 90 A1
BUTLEY 86 B5

Butley Cl IP2 . . . . 142 F8
Butley Ct 3 CB9 . . . . 132 C3
Butley Dr 3 NR32 . . . . . . 112 F3
BUTLEY HIGH CORNER . . . 86 C4
BUTLEY LOW CORNER 86 C4
Butley Pottery★ IP12 . . . 86 B6
Butley Rd IP11 . . . . 152 E3
Buttercup Cl
  Bury St Edmunds IP32 . . . 123 F5
  Ipswich IP5 . . . . 138 C1
  3 Lowestoft NR33 . . . . . 114 C4
Butterfly Gdns IP4 . . . . . . 140 E5
Buttermarket Sh Ctr IP1 . 155 B3
Buttermere Gn IP11 . . . . . 153 D6
Butter Mkt
  Bury St Edmunds IP33 . . . 154 B2
  Ipswich IP1 . . . . 155 B3
BUTTON HAUGH GREEN . . 50 F4
BUTTON'S GREEN 78 E8
Button's Rd IP13 . . . . 71 D6
Butt Rd
  Stoke-by-Nayland CO6 . . . 102 A4
  Sudbury CO10 . . . . 148 F4
Buttrum's Mill★ IP12 . . . 146 E5
Butt's Rd
  Holton IP19 . . . . 118 D8
  Spexhall IP19 . . . . 25 A4
Butts The
  Debenham IP14 . . . . 53 E2
  Soham CB7 . . . . 28 D3
BUXHALL 66 A4
BUXHALL FEN STREET . . . 66 A6
Buxlow Cl IP17 . . . . 129 B2
Byfield Way IP33 . . . . 123 C3
Byford Rd CO10 . . . . 148 E7
Bylam La IP9 . . . . 106 A7
Byland Cl 8 IP2 . . . . 139 A2
Byng Hall Rd
  Pettistree IP13 . . . . 84 E8
  Ufford IP13 . . . . 127 A1
Byng La IP13 . . . . 127 A3
Byrd Cl IP33 . . . . 122 C4
Byron Pl IP14 . . . . 124 C8
Byron Rd IP1 . . . . 134 E4

C

Cabin Cl NR33 . . . . 114 B4
Cable La IP15 . . . . 130 C5
Caddie's Wlk NR33 . . . . . . 115 A5
Cadiz Way 1 NR31 . . . . 3 C6
Cadmus Rd IP1 . . . . 138 D7
Cadney La IP33 . . . . 154 B3
Cadogan Rd IP33 . . . . 122 C4
Caernarvon Wlk CB9 . . . . 132 C6
Cage La
  Boxted CO4 . . . . 103 A3
  Felixstowe IP11 . . . . 152 E5
Cages Way 1 IP12 . . . . . . 84 E6
Cagman's La IP14 . . . . 65 F3
Caie Wlk IP33 . . . . 123 A3
Caithness Cl IP4 . . . . 140 B8
Cakebridge La IP7 . . . . . . 79 D3
Cake St IP13 . . . . 39 F4
Calais St IP7 . . . . 149 D6
CALAIS STREET 93 D2
Caldecott Rd NR32 . . . . . 112 D1
Calder Rd 6 IP12 . . . . 84 E6
Caledonia Rd 8 IP9 . . . . . 107 A4
Calfe Fen Cl 3 CB7 . . . . . 28 D5
Calfe Fen Dro CB7 . . . . . . 28 D5
Calford Dr CB9 . . . . 132 A6
CALFORD GREEN 133 D5
CALIFORNIA 140 B6
California Cl IP12 . . . . 146 D3
California La IP8 . . . . 95 B4
California Rd 14 CO11 . . . 105 A2
Calkewood La IP22 . . . . . . 35 E5
Callis St 5 CO10 . . . . 90 A8
Calves La CO6 . . . . 102 D8
Calthorpe Cl IP32 . . . . . . 123 E6
Calves La CO6 . . . . 102 D8
Camberley Ct IP33 . . . . . . 154 A3
Camberley Rd IP4 . . . . . . 140 D7
Camborne Rd IP5 . . . . 141 B7
Cambria Cl 9 CO11 . . . . . 105 A2
Cambrian Cres 2 NR32 . . 112 D2
Cambridge Cl CB9 . . . . . . 132 C7
Cambridge Dr IP2 . . . . . . 138 F2
Cambridge Rd
  Felixstowe IP11 . . . . 153 B4
  Ipswich IP5 . . . . 141 A7
  Lowestoft NR32 . . . . 113 D3
Cambridge Way
  9 Bures CO8 . . . . 101 C4
  Haverhill CB9 . . . . 132 C7
Camden Rd IP3 . . . . 140 B4
Camden St 5 NR32 . . . . . 113 E3
Campbell Cl 11 IP28 . . . . 116 B5
Campbell Rd IP3 . . . . 140 C1
Camp Cl 2 IP26 . . . . 4 D5
Campion Cl CB7 . . . . 28 C5
Campion Cres IP14 . . . . . 124 C4
Campion La CO6 . . . . 102 B6
Campion Rd IP2 . . . . 138 F4
Campions Hill CO6 . . . . . 102 B5
Campion Way CO6 . . . . . . 102 B6
Camp Rd NR32 . . . . 113 D1
CAMPSEA ASHE 71 C3
CAMPS HEATH 112 D3
Camps Rd
  Haverhill CB9 . . . . 132 D5
  Helions Bumpstead CB9 . . . 88 A5
Camwood Gdns IP3 . . . . . 140 B4
Canaletto Cl 4 NR32 . . . . 113 B6
Canberra Cl
  Ipswich IP4 . . . . 140 D6
  2 Mildenhall IP28 . . . . . . 30 A8

Canberra Rd IP31 . . . . 33 D4
Candler's La 18 IP20 . . . . . 22 D6
CANDLE STREET 35 F5
Candlet Gr IP11 . . . . 152 F5
Candlet Rd IP11 . . . . 152 E7
Cangle Junc 8 CB9 . . . . . 132 E6
Cangles La IP30 . . . . 49 F1
CANHAM'S GREEN 51 F4
Canhams Rd CO10 . . . . . . 148 F3
Canham St IP1 . . . . 155 A3
Cann Cl CO10 . . . . 148 C8
Cannonfields IP33 . . . . . . 154 B3
Cannon St IP33 . . . . 154 B3
Canon Cl CB9 . . . . 132 D7
Canon Pugh Dr 6 CO10 . . 92 B7
Canterbury Cl
  Ipswich IP2 . . . . 142 F8
  Lakenheath IP27 . . . . 14 A2
Canterbury Gdns IP7 . . . . 149 E6
Canterbury Gn IP33 . . . . . 123 A3
Canterbury Inf Sch 2
  IP24 . . . . 16 B6
Canterbury Rd CO10 . . . . 148 B8
Canterbury Way IP24 . . . . 16 B6
Capel Cl
  4 Felixstowe IP11 . . . . . 107 D8
  Troston IP31 . . . . 33 D3
Capel Dr IP11 . . . . 152 C4
CAPEL GREEN 86 A4
Capel Hall La IP11 . . . . . . 107 E8
Capell Wlk 2 IP31 . . . . 34 E4
CAPEL ST ANDREW 86 B3
CAPEL ST MARY 150 E4
Capel St Mary CE Prim Sch
  Capel St Mary IP9 . . . . . . 150 E3
  Copdock IP7 . . . . 95 F4
CAPON'S GREEN 55 E6
Capps La IP19 . . . . 23 F5
Capstan Way NR33 . . . . . 114 B4
Captain's La IP14 . . . . 51 A2
Caraway Rd IP24 . . . . 16 D6
Carbonels 12 CO10 . . . . . . 92 C6
Carders Cl IP7 . . . . 149 D4
Cardew Drift IP5 . . . . 141 D8
Cardiff Ave IP4 . . . . 139 B1
Cardigan St
  Ipswich IP1 . . . . 155 A4
  Newmarket CB8 . . . . 121 A3
Cardinal Cl IP32 . . . . 123 E6
Cardinalls Rd IP14 . . . . . . 124 D7
Cardinal Pk IP1 . . . . 155 B2
Cardinal Cl 14 IP5 . . . . 98 A8
Cardinal St IP1 . . . . 155 B2
Cardinal Way CB9 . . . . . . 132 D7
Carlford Cl 14 IP5 . . . . 98 A8
Carlow Mews 13 IP12 . . . 147 A5
CARLTON
  Kelsale cum Carlton 128 C6
  Carlton 74 A8
Carlton Cl
  Great Yeldham CO9 . . . . . . 90 A1
  Haverhill CB9 . . . . 132 D8
CARLTON COLVILLE 114 C2
Carlton Colville Cty Prim Sch
  NR33 . . . . 114 C2
Carlton Cross NR33 . . . . . 114 C2
Carlton Gn Rd CB8 . . . . . . 74 A7
CARLTON GREEN 74 A6
Carlton Marshes Nature
  Reserve★ NR33 . . . . . . 114 A7
Carlton Pk Ind Est IP17 . . 128 C5
Carlton Rd
  Brinkley CB8 . . . . 59 F1
  Carlton IP17 . . . . 128 C5
  Ipswich IP5 . . . . 141 A7
  Lowestoft NR33 . . . . 115 B6
Carlton Sq NR33 . . . . 114 C2
Carlton Way IP4 . . . . 139 E8
Carlton Wlk IP7 . . . . 149 E4
Carlyle Cl IP1 . . . . 134 F4
Carmarthen Cl IP2 . . . . . . 139 A2
Carmelite Pl 14 IP12 . . . . 147 A5
Carnation Way 2 IP28 . . . 46 A8
Carnoustie Dr
  13 Fornham St Martin
   IP28 . . . . 48 C6
  1 Lowestoft NR33 . . . . . 114 F4
Carol Ave 9 IP4 . . . . 84 A1
Carolbrook Rd IP2 . . . . . . 138 E1
Carol Cl IP11 . . . . 153 C5
Carr Ave IP16 . . . . 129 D6
Carriage Cl IP11 . . . . 152 C8
Carriers Cl CO7 . . . . 151 D5
Carrops The CB8 . . . . 46 A7
Carr Rd IP11 . . . . 152 E1
Carrs Hill IP13 . . . . 56 B6
Carr St IP4 . . . . 155 C3
Carsons Dr 6 CO10 . . . . . . 92 B3
Carson Wlk CB8 . . . . 120 F6
Carter Rd CB5 . . . . 44 A6
Carters Hill CO4 . . . . 103 A3
Carters La IP14 . . . . 80 E6
Carter St CB7 . . . . 29 B1
Carters Teapot Pottery★
  IP14 . . . . 53 F1
Carters Vineyard★ CO4 . . 102 F3
Cart Score NR32 . . . . 113 E3
Casburn La 13 CB5 . . . . . . 44 A6
Case La IP9 . . . . 104 E8
Castle Ave CB9 . . . . 132 C6
Castle Brooks IP6 . . . . . . 126 B3
Castle Cl
  Felixstowe IP11 . . . . 153 D6
  Orford IP12 . . . . 131 B2
  Weeting-with-Broomhill IP27 5 E3
CASTLE HILL 135 A3
Castle Hill
  Beccles NR34 . . . . 111 C4
  Dedham CO7 . . . . 103 F2

Castle Hill continued
  Eye IP23 . . . . 117 D2
  Eyke IP12 . . . . 85 B6
  Halesworth IP19 . . . . 118 C3
  Orford IP12 . . . . 131 C2
  Thorndon IP23 . . . . 37 E1
Castle Hill Inf Sch IP1 . . . 135 A3
Castle Hill Jun Sch IP1 . . . 135 A3
Castle Hill Mid Sch CB9 . . 132 B6
Castle La
  Bungay NR35 . . . . 110 A4
  Hadleigh IP7 . . . . 149 C7
  Haverhill CB9 . . . . 132 C6
  Offton IP8 . . . . 81 A4
  Orford IP12 . . . . 131 C2
  Thetford IP24 . . . . 16 C5
Castle Manor Bsns &
  Enterprise Coll CB9 . . . 132 C6
Castle Meadow IP8 . . . . . . 81 A4
Castle Orch NR35 . . . . 110 B4
Castle Rd
  Bury St Edmunds IP33 . . . 154 A1
  Hadleigh IP7 . . . . 149 B7
  Ipswich IP1 . . . . 134 E1
  Mettingham NR35 . . . . . . 110 F2
  Offton IP8 . . . . 81 A4
Castle Rise
  Hadleigh IP7 . . . . 149 B7
  2 Haughley IP14 . . . . . . 51 C1
Castle St
  Eye IP23 . . . . 117 D2
  Framlingham IP13 . . . . . . 126 D4
  Thetford IP24 . . . . 16 C5
  Woodbridge IP12 . . . . 147 A5
Castle Terr IP12 . . . . 131 C2
Castleton Ave NR33 . . . . . 114 B4
Castleton Cl 5 NR32 . . . . 113 B4
Castleton Way
  Eye IP23 . . . . 117 D2
  Yaxley IP23 . . . . 37 C5
Castle View IP12 . . . . 131 C2
CASTLING'S HEATH 93 D6
Catchpole Cl 19 NR33 . . . 11 B1
Catchpole Ct CO10 . . . . . 148 B5
Catchpole Way 10 IP31 . . 34 E4
Catchpole Wlk IP21 . . . . . 21 C5
Caters Rd IP13 . . . . 84 C8
Catesbray IP9 . . . . 150 D3
Catesby Meadow CO10 . . 148 B4
Cathcart St 8 NR32 . . . . . 113 D2
Cathedral Meadows
  IP33 . . . . 154 B1
Catherine Rd IP12 . . . . . . 146 E6
Catkin Cl CB9 . . . . 132 B7
Cat's La CO10 . . . . 148 E5
CATTAWADE 104 E4
Cattawade St 12 CO11 . . 104 E4
Catts Cl IP9 . . . . 105 C5
Cattsfield IP9 . . . . 105 C5
Caudle Ave IP27 . . . . 109 C4
Cauldwell Ave IP4 . . . . . . 139 F6
Cauldwell Hall Rd IP4 . . . 140 A5
Caulfield Cl 2 IP33 . . . . . 122 F3
Causeway
  Brockdish IP21 . . . . 21 F2
  8 Glemsford CO10 . . . . . 77 B3
Causeway End CO11 . . . . 104 D3
Causeway Est IP7 . . . . 79 F7
Causeway The
  Barking IP6 . . . . 125 B2
  Boxford CO10 . . . . 93 C3
  Burwell CB5 . . . . 44 A5
  Earl Soham IP13 . . . . 54 F2
  Great Horkesley CO6 . . . . 102 A3
  Hitcham IP7 . . . . 79 E6
  Isleham CB7 . . . . 29 C5
  Middleton IP17 . . . . 58 A6
  Needham Market IP6 . . . . 125 D4
  4 Occold IP23 . . . . 37 F1
  Ridgewell CO9 . . . . 89 C4
  Soham CB7 . . . . 28 D3
  Walsham le Willows IP31 . . 35 B2
  Westhall IP19 . . . . 25 C4
Causton Jun Sch IP11 . . . 152 E6
Caustons Cl 9 CO10 . . . . . 92 B3
Cautley Rd IP18 . . . . 119 D6
Cavan Rd IP1 . . . . 134 D2
CAVENDISH 76 D1
Cavendish CE Prim Sch
  CO10 . . . . 76 E1
Cavendish Cl
  7 Lowestoft NR32 . . . . . 113 A3
  12 Thurstow IP31 . . . . . . 49 E4
Cavendish Ct 2 CB9 . . . . 132 C4
Cavendish Dr 21 CO11 . . 104 D2
Cavendish La CO10 . . . . . . 76 F2
Cavendish Rd
  Bury St Edmunds IP33 . . . 122 C6
  Clare CO10 . . . . 90 B8
  Felixstowe IP11 . . . . 152 F3
  Stowmarket IP14 . . . . . . 124 B6
Cavendish St IP3 . . . . 139 F4
Cavendish Way 1 CO10 . . 148 D5
CAVENHAM 47 A8
Cavenham Heath National
  Nature Reserve★ IP28 . 31 C3
Cavenham Rd IP28 . . . . . . 31 A1
Caville White CB9 . . . . . . 132 A6
Cawley Rd CO6 . . . . 102 A5
Caxton Mews 4 NR34 . . . 111 B6
Caxton Rd NR34 . . . . 111 B6
CAY HILL 52 C2
Cecilia St IP1 . . . . 155 B2
Cecil Lodge Cl CB8 . . . . . 120 F3

Cecil Rd IP1 . . . . 155 A4
Cedar Ave IP5 . . . . 141 A6
Cedar Cl
  Bacton IP14 . . . . 51 F6
  7 Brantham CO11 . . . . . . 104 E5
  8 Great Brickett IP7 . . . . 80 D6
  32 Lakenheath IP27 . . . . . . 13 F2
  Occold IP23 . . . . 37 F2
  Stradbroke IP21 . . . . 39 B4
Cedar Cres
  13 Barrow IP29 . . . . 47 A2
  30 Manningtree CO11 . . . . 104 E2
Cedarcroft Rd IP1 . . . . . . 134 F2
Cedar Ct
  Alderton IP12 . . . . 99 E5
  10 Beck Row, Holywell Row &
  Kenny Hill IP28 . . . . . . 13 B1
Cedar Dr
  Lowestoft NR33 . . . . 114 C5
  Worlingham NR34 . . . . . 111 F3
Cedar Rd
  1 Barrow IP29 . . . . 47 A2
  7 Bentwaters Airfield IP12 85 E8
Cedars La IP9 . . . . 150 D3
Cedars The IP27 . . . . 109 E5
Cedarwood Prim Sch
  IP5 . . . . 141 C6
Celandine Cl NR33 . . . . . 114 C5
Cemetery Hill CB8 . . . . . 120 D7
Cemetery La
  East Bergholt CO7 . . . . . . 151 A4
  Ipswich IP4 . . . . 135 F1
  Woodbridge IP12 . . . . 146 E4
Cemetery Rd
  Ipswich IP4 . . . . 155 C3
  Lakenheath IP27 . . . . 109 D6
  Wickhambrook CB8 . . . . . . 61 E2
Central Ave IP3 . . . . 144 D8
Central Rd IP16 . . . . 129 C5
Centre Cl NR34 . . . . 111 C3
Centre Cliff IP18 . . . . . . 119 D5
Centre Dr CB8 . . . . 121 D2
Centre Rd CB7 . . . . 28 E2
Century Cl IP5 . . . . 141 E7
Century Rd IP23 . . . . . . 117 C4
Chadacre Rd IP29 . . . . . . 77 B7
Chaffinch Dr **14** CO12 . . 106 F1
Chaffinch Rd IP32 . . . . . . 49 A3
Chaffinch Way IP14 . . . . 124 F7
Chainey Pieces CB9 . . . . 132 D5
Chainhouse Rd IP6 . . . . . 125 D3
Chalfont Dr **1** IP17 . . . . . 72 C8
Chalk Cl **3** IP24 . . . . 16 C6
Chalkeith Rd IP6 . . . . . . 125 E3
Chalk Hill La IP6 . . . . 81 F5
Chalk La
  Culford IP31 . . . . 32 E5
  2 Ixworth IP31 . . . . 34 B1
Chalkners Cl **7** IP9 . . . . 150 E3
Chalk Rd IP27 . . . . 5 D1
Chalk Rd (North) IP33 . . 154 A2
Chalk Rd (South) IP33 . . 154 A2
Chalkstone Mid Sch CB9 132 E2
Chalkstone Way CB9 . . . 133 A6
Challice Rd IP33 . . . . 154 A3
Chalon St IP1 . . . . 155 A2
Chamberlain Way IP8 . . . 138 C2
Chamberlayne Rd IP32 . . 123 E4
Champion Rd IP15 . . . . . 130 E3
Chancellery Mews IP33 . 154 A3
Chancery La **5** IP14 . . . . 53 F2
Chancery Rd IP1 . . . . 155 A2
Chandlers Ct **8** CB5 . . . . 44 A6
Chandlers Way IP16 . . . . 129 C3
Chandlers Wlk IP14 . . . . 124 D4
Chandos Ct **8** IP12 . . . . . 84 A1
Chandos Dr **5** IP12 . . . . . 84 A1
Channel The IP8 . . . . 81 C1
CHANTRY 138 D2
Chantry Cl IP13 . . . . 71 C2
Chantry Dr CO6 . . . . 101 F2
Chantry Gn IP2 . . . . 138 D3
Chantry High Sch IP2 . . . 138 D3
Chantry Rd IP17 . . . . 128 C3
Chapel Cl
  Capel St Mary IP9 . . . . . . 150 E3
  4 Fressingfield IP21 . . . . 39 E8
  Garboldisham IP22 . . . . . . 18 D4
  4 Great Waldingfield CO10 92 C6
Chapel Ct **10** CO10 . . . . 113 D2
Chapel Cut **16** CO11 . . . 105 A2
Chapel End Way CO9 . . . . 89 A1
Chapel Farm La IP23 . . . . 37 A4
Chapelfield IP12 . . . . 131 C3
Chapel Field IP8 . . . . 134 E4
Chapel Hill
  Belchamp Walter CO10 . . . 90 E3
  Framsden IP14 . . . . 69 B7
  Thorpe Morieux IP30 . . . . . 79 A8
Chapel La
  Belstead IP8 . . . . 142 C7
  Botesdale IP22 . . . . 36 A6
  4 Brockley IP29 . . . . 63 A1
  Claydon IP6 . . . . 134 B8
  Copdock & Washbrook IP8 138 A1
  Drinkstone IP30 . . . . 65 B7
  Great Glemham IP17 . . . . . 56 D1
  13 Grundisburgh IP13 . . . 83 E5
  Horham IP21 . . . . 38 F2
  Kirby Row NR35 . . . . 8 E7
  Kirtling CB8 . . . . 60 E3
  Little Cornard CO10 . . . . . 92 B1
  3 Somersham IP8 . . . . . . 81 C3
  Stoke-by-Nayland CO6 . . 103 B7
  Wenhaston with Mells Hamlet
  IP19 . . . . 42 C6
  Wicken CB7 . . . . 28 A1

Chapel La continued
  Wickham Market IP13 . . . 127 C5
  Wortham IP22 . . . . 36 D7
Chapel Pond Hill IP32 . . 123 C8
Chapel Rd
  Beck Row, Holywell Row &
  Kenny Hill IP28 . . . . . . 29 F6
  Bedingham NR35 . . . . 7 C8
  Boxted CO4 . . . . 103 A2
  Bradfield Combust with
  Stanningfield IP29 . . . . 64 A3
  Bucklesham IP10 . . . . 98 B4
  Cockfield IP30 . . . . 64 D2
  Grundisburgh IP13 . . . . . . 83 E5
  Langham CO4 . . . . 103 B2
  Lowestoft NR33 . . . . 114 B3
  Mendlesham IP14 . . . . 52 E5
  Mutford NR34 . . . . 10 D3
  Old Newton with Dagworth
  IP14 . . . . 52 A1
  Otley IP6 . . . . 69 D3
  Rendham IP17 . . . . 56 E3
  Ridgewell CO9 . . . . 89 D4
  Saxmundham IP17 . . . . . 128 C3
  Saxtead IP13 . . . . 55 A4
  Scole IP21 . . . . 21 B5
  St Andrew, Ilketshall NR34 . . 8 F2
  Stoke Ash IP23 . . . . 37 B2
  Theberton IP16 . . . . 58 C5
  Wattisfield IP22 . . . . 35 C4
  Wrentham NR34 . . . . 26 D5
Chapel Row **3** CB8 . . . . . 60 F8
Chapel St
  5 Bildeston IP7 . . . . 79 F4
  Diss IP22 . . . . 20 C2
  Exning CB8 . . . . 120 B8
  9 Lowestoft NR32 . . . . . 113 D2
  Peasenhall IP17 . . . . 56 F8
  Steeple Bumpstead CB9 . . 88 E4
  Stoke-by-Clare CO9 . . . . . 89 C6
  Woodbridge IP12 . . . . . . 147 A5
Chapelwent Rd CB9 . . . . 132 C8
Chaplains Cl CB9 . . . . . . 132 D7
Chaplin Rd CO7 . . . . 151 C5
Chaplin Wlk **16** CO10 . . . 92 B3
Chappel Rd CO6 . . . . 101 C2
Chapple Dr CB9 . . . . 132 E7
Chare Rd IP31 . . . . 34 D5
Charity La IP13 . . . . 54 D6
Charles Adams Cl IP16 . . 129 D6
Charles Ave **8** IP13 . . . . . 83 E5
Charles Burrell High Sch
  IP24 . . . . 16 B4
Charles Cl CB8 . . . . 120 E3
Charles Ind Est IP14 . . . 124 E7
Charles Melrose Cl **1**
  IP28 . . . . 116 B4
Charles Miller Ct IP16 . . 129 D5
Charles Rd IP11 . . . . 152 E3
Charles St IP1 . . . . 155 B3
CHARLES TYE 80 C7
Charlock Rd **5** IP24 . . . . 16 C7
Charlotte's IP8 . . . . 95 F5
Charlton Ave IP1 . . . . . . 134 F2
Charrington Cl CB9 . . . . 133 A4
CHARSFIELD 70 B3
Charsfield CE Prim Sch
  IP13 . . . . 70 B3
Charter Cl IP7 . . . . 149 D7
Charter Way **6** NR33 . . 114 C5
Chartres Piece NR34 . . . . 25 E7
Chartwell Cl IP4 . . . . . . 140 A5
Chase Cl CB9 . . . . 132 E7
Chase La **6** CO12 . . . . . 106 F1
Chaser Cl **8** IP3 . . . . . . 144 C8
Chase Rd IP28 . . . . 48 C5
Chase's La IP17 . . . . 72 F6
Chase The
  Beccles NR34 . . . . 111 E5
  Brandon IP27 . . . . 6 A1
  Brantham CO11 . . . . 104 F5
  Dedham CO7 . . . . 104 A2
  Felixstowe IP11 . . . . 152 F4
  Foxearth CO10 . . . . 91 B7
  27 Manningtree CO11 . . 104 E2
  20 Manningtree Heath IP5 . 98 A8
  5 Stanton IP31 . . . . 34 E4
  Steeple Bumpstead CB9 . . 88 D4
Chatham Rd IP1 . . . . 134 F3
Chatsworth Cl **5** NR32 . 113 A3
Chatsworth Cres
  Felixstowe IP11 . . . . 152 C7
  Ipswich IP2 . . . . 139 A2
Chatsworth Dr IP4 . . . . . 140 E4
Chatten Cl NR34 . . . . 26 E5
Chattisham Cl IP10 . . . . 124 E3
Chattisham Rd IP8 . . . . . 95 E4
Chaucer Cl IP14 . . . . 124 C8
Chaucer Rd
  Felixstowe IP11 . . . . 152 F3
  Ipswich IP1 . . . . 134 F3
  Sudbury CO10 . . . . 148 B8
Chaucer St NR35 . . . . . . 110 A4
Chaukers Cres NR33 . . . 114 C5
Chauntry Rd CB9 . . . . . . 132 D5
CHEDBURGH 62 C4
Chedburgh Pl **8** CB9 . . . 132 F6
Chedburgh Rd
  Chevington IP29 . . . . 62 D5
  Whepstead IP29 . . . . 62 F5
Chedgrave Rd NR33 . . . . 114 F5
CHEDISTON 41 C8
CHEDISTON GREEN 41 B8
Chediston Pottery * IP19 . 24 B1
Chediston Rd IP19 . . . . . 24 B2
Chediston St
  Chediston IP19 . . . . 41 D8

Chediston St continued
  Halesworth IP19 . . . . . . 118 A3
Chelmer Rd CB9 . . . . . . 132 F6
CHELMONDISTON 106 C8
Chelmondiston CE Prim Sch
  IP9 . . . . 106 B8
Chelsea Cl
  Bury St Edmunds IP33 . . 122 D5
  Ipswich IP1 . . . . 134 F1
Chelsea Ct **4** CO10 . . . 148 D5
Chelsea Rd **3** CO10 . . . 148 D5
CHELSWORTH 79 E3
Chelsworth Ave
  Ipswich IP4 . . . . 135 E1
  Sudbury CO10 . . . . 148 F4
CHELSWORTH COMMON . . 79 E2
Chelsworth Rd IP11 . . . . 152 D5
Chelsworth Way IP14 . . 124 E3
Cheltenham Ave IP1 . . . 135 B1
Chepstow Rd
  Bury St Edmunds IP33 . . 122 D3
  Felixstowe IP11 . . . . 152 F5
  Ipswich IP1 . . . . 135 B4
Chequer Field IP12 . . . . . 85 C2
Chequers La
  Bressingham IP22 . . . . . . 19 E3
  Burston & Shimpling IP22 . . 20 E8
  Glemsford CO10 . . . . 77 B3
Chequer Sq IP33 . . . . . . 154 C2
Chequers Rd CO11 . . . . . 104 E1
Chequers Rise IP6 . . . . . . 81 F5
Cherry Blossom Cl IP8 . . 138 B2
Cherryfields IP8 . . . . 134 A1
Cherry Hill IP28 . . . . 30 E3
Cherry Hill Cl **1** NR34 . . 111 F4
Cherry La
  Aldeburgh IP15 . . . . 130 D5
  Belton with Browston NR31 . 2 E8
  Lakenheath IP27 . . . . 13 F2
Cherry La Gdns IP4 . . . . 140 B7
Cherry Tree Cl
  Mundford IP26 . . . . 6 A8
  North Lopham IP22 . . . . . . 19 A6
  Yaxley IP23 . . . . 37 B5
Cherrytree La
  Rickinghall Inferior IP22 . . 36 A7
  Soham CB7 . . . . 28 D3
Cherry Tree La IP14 . . . . . 53 F4
Cherrytree Rd CO10 . . . . 148 F5
Cherry Tree Rd
  Stowmarket IP14 . . . . . . 124 C8
  Woodbridge IP12 . . . . . . 146 F4
Cherry Tree Row **3** IP31 . 35 C2
Cherry Tress Sch IP28 . . . 47 D5
Cherrywood **10** IP20 . . . 22 D5
Chervil Wlk **8** IP14 . . . . 16 D6
Chesapeake Cl **8** IP9 . . . 106 C8
Chesapeake Rd **8** IP3 . . 144 A8
Chesham Rd IP2 . . . . 155 A1
Chessington Gdns IP1 . . 138 F8
Chester Cl **8** CB9 . . . . . 132 C4
Chesterfield Dr IP1 . . . . 134 F2
Chester Pl **5** IP31 . . . . . 49 A5
Chester Rd
  Felixstowe IP11 . . . . 152 F5
  6 Southwold IP18 . . . . . 119 D5
Chester St IP27 . . . . 14 A3
Chesterton Cl IP2 . . . . . 138 F1
Chestnut Ave
  Great Brickett IP7 . . . . . . 80 D6
  Lowestoft NR32 . . . . 112 E2
Chestnut Cl
  4 Beccles NR34 . . . . . . 111 E3
  6 Bentwaters Airfield IP12 85 E8
  1 Fornham All Saints IP28 48 B6
  Great Barton IP31 . . . . . . 49 B6
  3 Great Waldingfield CO10 92 C6
  Haverhill IP9 . . . . 132 D6
  1 Mildenhall IP28 . . . . . 116 D4
  Rushmere St Andrew IP5 . 136 E1
  4 Stowupland IP14 . . . . . 67 A6
Chestnut Cres
  Chedburgh IP29 . . . . 62 D4
  6 Lowestoft NR33 . . . . 114 C3
Chestnut Dr
  Claydon IP6 . . . . 134 C8
  6 Soham CB7 . . . . 28 D4
Chestnut Gr **2** IP14 . . . . 124 E5
Chestnut Mews **17** CO10 . 148 C5
Chestnut Rd
  Dickleburgh IP21 . . . . 21 C5
  Glemsford CO10 . . . . 77 A3
  Pulham St Mary IP21 . . . . 21 F8
  Stradishall CB8 . . . . 75 C6
Chestnut Rise **1** CB5 . . . 44 A6
Chestnuts The
  5 Great Finborough IP14 . 66 B4
  11 Ipswich IP2 . . . . 138 C2
  Rickinghall Superior IP22 . . 36 A4
  Wrentham NR34 . . . . 26 E5
Chestnut Way **21** IP27 . . 13 F2
Chevalier Rd IP11 . . . . . . 153 B4
Chevalier St IP1 . . . . 139 A7
CHEVELEY 60 E7
Cheveley Prim Sch CB8 . . 60 E7
Cheveley Rd
  Newmarket CB8 . . . . 121 C3
  Woodditton CB8 . . . . 60 E6
CHEVINGTON 62 C6
Chevington Rd
  Hargrave IP29 . . . . 62 B6
  Horringer IP29 . . . . 63 A7
Cheviot Rd **3** NR32 . . . 112 D2
Chevy Ct **3** CO10 . . . . . 148 C5
Cheyne Ct **10** CO10 . . . 148 C5
Chichester Cl IP33 . . . . . 123 B3
Chichester Dr NR33 . . . . 114 D6
Chichester Rd IP19 . . . . 118 A5

CHICKERING 38 F7
Chickering Rd IP21 . . . . . 38 D6
Childer Rd IP14 . . . . 124 D6
Childers Cl **1** IP9 . . . . . 107 A5
Childers Field **2** IP11 . . 152 D5
CHILLESFORD 86 C7
Chilli Company The *
  IP14 . . . . 52 F3
Chiltern Cres NR32 . . . . 112 E2
CHILTON 92 B5
Chilton Ave IP14 . . . . . . 124 C6
Chilton Com Prim Sch
  IP14 . . . . 124 C7
Chilton Ct CO10 . . . . 148 E5
Chilton Ind Est CO10 . . . 148 F6
Chilton Lodge Rd CO10 . 148 E5
Chilton Rd IP3 . . . . 140 C4
CHILTON STREET 75 F1
Chilton Way IP12 . . . . . . 146 D3
Chilton Way Sports Club
  IP19 . . . . 24 C1
Chimer's La IP13 . . . . 70 A4
Chimney Mill Galleries *
  IP19 . . . . 24 C1
Chimney Mills IP28 . . . . . 32 C1
CHIMNEY STREET 75 C3
Chimswell Way CB9 . . . 132 A6
CHIPPENHALL GREEN 40 A5
CHIPPENHAM 45 C8
Chippenham Fen National
  Nature Reserve * CB7 . . 45 A8
Chippenham Rd
  Chippenham IP28 . . . . . . 29 E2
  Fordham CB7 . . . . 29 C1
  Moulton CB8 . . . . 45 F3
Chipperfield Rd **20** NR33 . 11 C1
Chippings The IP15 . . . . 130 E4
Chislehurst Rd **5** NR33 . 114 C4
Chisnall Cl IP7 . . . . 149 D8
Chiswick Ave IP28 . . . . . 116 C6
Chivers Rd CB9 . . . . 132 B5
Christchurch Ct **15** CO10 . 148 C5
Christchurch Mansion *
  IP1 . . . . 155 B3
Christ Church Sq NR32 . . 113 E1
Christchurch St IP4 . . . . 155 C3
Christmas La
  Lowestoft NR32 . . . . 112 C1
  Metfield IP20 . . . . 23 D3
Christopher Ct **15** CO10 . 148 C5
Christopher Rd CO10 . . . 148 C5
Church Ave NR32 . . . . . . 112 C2
Church Cl
  Aldeburgh IP15 . . . . 130 E4
  Bucklesham IP10 . . . . 98 A5
  Carlton IP17 . . . . 128 D7
  4 Cavendish CO10 . . . . . 76 E1
  Creeting St Mary IP6 . . . 125 F8
  Dullingham CB8 . . . . 59 F4
  Exning CB8 . . . . 120 C8
  Fornham St Martin IP28 . . 48 D5
  Hepworth IP22 . . . . 35 A5
  Ipswich IP5 . . . . 141 B8
  Kenton IP14 . . . . 54 B4
  Pulham St Mary IP21 . . . . 22 A8
  Rede IP29 . . . . 62 E3
  Risby IP28 . . . . 47 E5
  1 Roydon IP22 . . . . 20 A3
  15 Stanton IP31 . . . . 34 E4
  Wangford NR34 . . . . 26 B2
  Wilby IP21 . . . . 39 C3
  Wortwell IP20 . . . . 22 F7
Church Cres IP8 . . . . 138 A6
Church Dr IP13 . . . . 71 E5
CHURCH END 106 F7
Church Farm Cl IP21 . . . . 38 F3
Church Farm La IP19 . . . 118 A3
Church Farm Rd
  Aldeburgh IP15 . . . . 130 E5
  Bramfield IP19 . . . . 41 F4
Church Field
  Monks Eleigh IP7 . . . . 79 C2
  Walberswick IP18 . . . . . . 119 A2
Church Field Rd CO10 . . 148 F7
Churchfields Dr **1** CB9 . . 88 D3
Church Fm Rise IP15 . . . 130 F5
Churchgate CO10 . . . . . . 77 B3
Churchgate St
  Bury St Edmunds IP33 . . 154 B2
  15 Soham CB7 . . . . 28 D4
Church Gdns
  1 Barningham IP31 . . . . 34 E7
  6 Beck Row, Holywell Row &
  Kenny Hill IP28 . . . . . . 29 F6
Church Gn
  Bramford IP8 . . . . 134 B1
  Normanston NR32 . . . . . 113 C3
Church Hill
  Benhall IP17 . . . . 72 C8
  Burstall IP8 . . . . 95 D7
  Cookley IP19 . . . . 41 C5
  Helions Bumpstead CB9 . . 88 B4
  Hoxne IP21 . . . . 38 C8
  Kersey IP7 . . . . 94 A6
  Lawford CO11 . . . . 104 C2
  Monks Eleigh IP7 . . . . 79 C2
  Pakenham IP31 . . . . 49 E6
  Ramsey & Parkeston
  CO12 . . . . 106 D1
  Saxmundham IP17 . . . . . 128 D2
  Starston IP20 . . . . 22 C7
  Westhall IP19 . . . . 25 D3
  Whepstead IP29 . . . . 63 B5
  Wyverstone IP14 . . . . 51 E6
Churchill Ave
  Hadleigh IP7 . . . . 149 D7
  Haverhill CB9 . . . . 132 F7
  Ipswich IP4 . . . . 140 B5

Churchill Ave continued
  Newmarket CB8 . . . . 120 D5
Churchill Cl
  3 Lawshall IP29 . . . . . . 63 D1
  Lowestoft NR32 . . . . 113 C4
  7 Woodbridge IP12 . . . 146 E4
Churchill Cres IP13 . . . . 127 C7
Churchill Ct CB8 . . . . . . 120 F3
Churchill Dr
  Mildenhall IP28 . . . . 116 B5
  Sudbury CO10 . . . . 148 C8
Churchill Rd
  Halesworth IP19 . . . . . . 118 B5
  5 Southwold IP18 . . . . 119 C8
  Thetford IP24 . . . . 16 C6
Church La
  Aldeby/Wheatacre/Burgh St
  Peter NR34 . . . . 2 B1
  Aldham IP7 . . . . 94 D7
  Aldringham cum Thorpe
  IP16 . . . . 129 E1
  Alpheton CO10 . . . . 77 F5
  Arwarton IP9 . . . . 106 C5
  Barnham IP24 . . . . 16 C2
  Barton Mills IP28 . . . . . . 116 D1
  Bayham IP6 . . . . 81 E6
  Beck Row, Holywell Row & Kenny
  Hill IP28 . . . . 29 F6
  Bedfield IP13 . . . . 54 E5
  Birds End IP29 . . . . 62 A7
  Blo' Norton IP22 . . . . 18 E2
  Blythburgh IP19 . . . . 42 E6
  Brantham CO11 . . . . 104 F5
  Bressingham IP22 . . . . . . 19 E3
  Brockdish IP21 . . . . 21 F2
  Bromeswell IP12 . . . . 85 A5
  Broome NR35 . . . . 8 B7
  Brundish IP13 . . . . 55 C8
  Bucklesham IP10 . . . . 98 A5
  Burrough Green CB8 . . . . 59 F2
  15 Burwell CB5 . . . . 44 A5
  Carlton IP17 . . . . 128 D7
  1 Cheveley CB8 . . . . . . 60 E7
  Claydon IP6 . . . . 134 E8
  Clopton IP13 . . . . 83 E8
  Cockfield IP30 . . . . 64 C1
  Copdock & Washbrook IP8 142 A7
  Corton NR32 . . . . 3 C4
  Creeting St Mary IP6 . . . 125 D7
  Dalham CB8 . . . . 46 C1
  Ditchingham NR35 . . . . . . 7 F7
  Dullingham CB8 . . . . 59 F4
  Earl Soham IP13 . . . . 55 A2
  Exning CB8 . . . . 120 B8
  Felixstowe IP11 . . . . 152 E6
  Finningham IP14 . . . . 52 A8
  Fritton & St Olaves NR31 . . 2 C7
  Frostenden NR34 . . . . 26 C4
  Harkstead IP9 . . . . 106 B6
  3 Harwich CO12 . . . . . . 107 B3
  Hemingstone IP6 . . . . 82 C8
  Hemley IP12 . . . . 98 E5
  Henley IP6 . . . . 82 E5
  Hepworth IP22 . . . . 35 A5
  Hitcham IP7 . . . . 79 E6
  Hockwold cum Wilton IP26 . . 5 A2
  Hoo IP13 . . . . 70 B6
  Iken IP12 . . . . 72 F3
  Kennett CB8 . . . . 45 F6
  Kenton IP14 . . . . 54 A4
  Kirton IP10 . . . . 98 E2
  Levington IP10 . . . . 145 E3
  Lowestoft NR33 . . . . 114 B2
  Martlesham IP12 . . . . 84 B1
  Mistley CO11 . . . . 104 F2
  3 Mundford IP26 . . . . . . 6 B8
  Nayland CO6 . . . . 102 D5
  Newmarket CB8 . . . . 121 A3
  Norton IP31 . . . . 50 C4
  2 Occold IP23 . . . . 37 F1
  Playford IP6 . . . . 137 B4
  Preston St Mary CO10 . . . 79 A5
  Redenhall with Harleston
  IP20 . . . . 22 E7
  Rendlesham IP12 . . . . 85 C7
  Rickinghall Superior IP22 . 36 A5
  Ridgewell CO9 . . . . 89 D3
  Semer IP7 . . . . 79 F1
  Shottisham IP12 . . . . 99 C3
  Somersham IP8 . . . . 81 D3
  Spexhall IP19 . . . . 24 F3
  Sproughton IP8 . . . . 138 B6
  Stetchworth CB8 . . . . 60 A5
  St James, South Elmham
  IP19 . . . . 23 F4
  St Mary, South Elmham
  otherwise Homersfield
  IP20 . . . . 23 B8
  Stoke Ash IP23 . . . . 37 B1
  Stonham Earl IP14 . . . . . 67 E6
  Stuston IP21 . . . . 37 D8
  Swilland IP6 . . . . 83 A7
  Thelnetham IP22 . . . . 18 E1
  Thwaite IP23 . . . . 52 F7
  Timworth IP31 . . . . 48 E8
  Troston IP31 . . . . 33 E3
  9 Ufford IP13 . . . . 84 F7
  Walberswick IP18 . . . . . . 43 C5
  Wenhaston with Mells Hamlet
  IP19 . . . . 42 C6
  Westerfield IP6 . . . . 135 F4
  Westley Waterless CB8 . . 59 D3
  Weston NR34 . . . . 9 E2
  Winfarthing IP22 . . . . 20 B8
  Worlington IP28 . . . . 30 B4

Church La *continued*
Yaxley IP23 . . . . 37 C4
Church La Cl IP28 . . . . . 116 D2
Churchman Cl IP12 . . . 147 B8
Church Meadow
Barton Mills IP28 . . . . 116 D2
Rickinghall Inferior IP22 . . 35 F6
Church Meadows
1 Henley IP6 . . . . 82 D6
Waldingfield IP12 . . . . 98 D7
Church Pk CO10 . . . . . . 89 E6
Church Rd
Alburgh IP20 . . . . 7 A2
Ashbocking IP6 . . . . 68 E1
Bacton IP14 . . . . 51 F6
Bardwell IP31 . . . . 34 B4
Barningham IP31 . . . . . . 34 E7
Barrow IP29 . . . . 47 A3
Battisford IP14 . . . . 66 E1
Bedfield IP13 . . . . 54 E5
Bentley IP9 . . . . 142 A1
Beyton IP30 . . . . 49 F1
6 Bildeston IP7 . . . . . . 79 F4
Blaxhall IP12 . . . . 71 F4
Blundeston NR32 . . . . 3 A4
Boxted CO4 . . . . 102 F3
Bradfield Combust with
 Stanningfield IP29 . . . . 63 F3
Bradfield St George IP30 . 64 D6
Brandon IP27 . . . . 5 E1
Brettenham IP7 . . . . 65 C1
Brockdish IP21 . . . . 21 F2
Bruisyard IP17 . . . . 56 C5
Bulmer CO10 . . . . 91 C2
Butley IP12 . . . . 86 B5
Carlton CB8 . . . . 74 A8
Chevington IP29 . . . . . . 62 C6
Combs IP14 . . . . 124 E2
Cotton IP14 . . . . 52 B5
Cratfield IP19 . . . . 40 D5
Crowfield IP6 . . . . 68 C4
Dallinghoo IP13 . . . . . . 70 C1
Denham IP21 . . . . 38 C5
Dickleburgh & Rushall IP21 . 20 F3
Earsham NR35 . . . . 7 F3
Ellingham NR35 . . . . 8 D7
Ellough NR34 . . . . 111 F1
Elmswell IP30 . . . . 50 E2
Felixstowe IP11 . . . . . . 153 C6
Felsham IP30 . . . . 65 A4
Flixton NR35 . . . . 7 E1
Friston IP17 . . . . 72 F7
Garboldisham IP22 . . . . 18 D4
Gillingham NR34 . . . . 9 C7
Gisleham NR33 . . . . 11 A3
Great Barton IP31 . . . . . 49 A5
1 Great Finborough IP14 . 66 B4
Great Yeldham CO9 . . . . 89 F1
Hasketon IP13 . . . . 146 B7
Hedenham NR35 . . . . 7 E8
Henstead with Hulver Street
 NR34 . . . . 26 E8
Heveningham IP19 . . . . . 40 E3
Holbrook IP9 . . . . 105 F6
Honington IP31 . . . . 33 F5
Kessingland NR33 . . . . . 11 B1
Kettleburgh IP13 . . . . . . 70 C7
Kirby Cane NR35 . . . . 8 E8
Knodishall IP17 . . . . 58 A1
Leiston IP16 . . . . 129 B6
Lindsey IP7 . . . . 93 D7
Little Glemham IP13 . . . . 71 E5
Little Thurlow CB9 . . . . . 74 D6
Little Waldingfield CO10 . 92 E8
Lowestoft NR32 . . . . . . 113 C3
Market Weston IP22 . . . . 18 C1
Marlesford IP13 . . . . . . 71 C5
Mendlesham IP14 . . . . . 52 E4
Milden IP7 . . . . 79 B1
Monewden IP13 . . . . . . 69 F5
5 Moulton CB8 . . . . . . 45 F3
Mutford NR34 . . . . 10 D3
Nacton IP10 . . . . 145 B4
Newton CO10 . . . . 92 D3
North Lopham IP22 . . . . 19 A5
Old Newton with Dagworth
 IP14 . . . . 51 F1
Otley IP6 . . . . 69 C1
Pettaugh IP14 . . . . 68 E6
Playford IP6 . . . . 137 B5
Redlingfield IP23 . . . . . . 38 C1
Rushbrooke with Rougham
 IP30 . . . . 49 C1
Shelfanger IP22 . . . . 20 B6
Snape IP17 . . . . 72 D5
Stambourne CO9 . . . . . 89 B1
Stowmarket IP14 . . . . . 124 D3
Stowupland IP14 . . . . . . 67 B7
Stutton IP9 . . . . 105 D5
Sudbury CO10 . . . . 148 E3
Sutton IP12 . . . . 85 A1
Tattingstone IP9 . . . . . . 105 B7
Theberton IP16 . . . . 58 B4
Thistley Green IP28 . . . . 29 F6
6 Thorpeness IP16 . . . . 73 F6
Thurston IP31 . . . . 49 E4
Tostock IP30 . . . . 50 B2
Uggeshall NR34 . . . . . . 26 A3
Weybread IP21 . . . . 22 D2
Wheatacre NR34 . . . . 2 A1
Wicken CB7 . . . . 28 B1
Wilby IP21 . . . . 39 C3
Wingfield IP21 . . . . 39 A7
Worlingworth IP13 . . . . . 54 E7
Wormingford CO6 . . . . . 101 F2

Church Rd *continued*
Wortham IP22 . . . . 19 F1
Wrabness CO11 . . . . . . 105 F2
Church Rd N IP21 . . . . . 21 F3
Church Row
Bury St Edmunds IP33 . . 154 B3
Framsden IP14 . . . . 69 C6
Church Sq 4 CO8 . . . . 101 C4
Church St
2 Ashley CB8 . . . . 60 F8
Belchamp Otten CO10 . . 90 D5
1 Boxford CO10 . . . . . 93 C3
Boxted CO4 . . . . 103 A4
5 Chelmondiston IP9 . . 106 C8
6 Clare CO10 . . . . 90 A8
Diss IP22 . . . . 20 C2
Exning CB8 . . . . 120 C8
Eye IP23 . . . . 117 D2
Fordham CB7 . . . . 29 B1
Framlingham IP13 . . . . 126 D3
2 Fressingfield IP21 . . . 39 E8
Gestingthorpe CO9 . . . . 90 F1
Groton CO10 . . . . 93 C5
1 Hadleigh IP7 . . . . . . 149 D5
23 Harleston IP20 . . . . 22 D6
5 Harwich CO12 . . . . 107 C3
Hundon CO10 . . . . 75 D3
10 Isleham CB7 . . . . . . 29 C5
Lavenham CO10 . . . . . . 78 D3
Orford IP12 . . . . 131 C2
Peasenhall IP17 . . . . . . 56 F8
Saxmundham IP17 . . . . 128 D3
12 Southwold IP18 . . . . 119 D5
Steeple Bumpstead CB9 . 88 D4
Stoke-by-Nayland CO6 . . 102 E6
Stradbroke IP21 . . . . . . 39 B4
Sudbury CO10 . . . . . . 148 B4
Wangford NR34 . . . . . . 26 B2
Wetherden IP14 . . . . . . 51 A1
Wetheringsett-cum-Brockford
 IP14 . . . . 53 A4
Withersfield IP21 . . . . . 74 A2
Woodbridge IP12 . . . . . 147 A5
Worlingworth IP13 . . . . . 54 F7
CHURCH STREET 90 D6
Church Terr IP13 . . . . 127 C6
Church View
Halesworth IP19 . . . . . 118 E4
Harleston IP20 . . . . 22 E6
1 Haughley IP14 . . . . . 51 C1
Leiston IP16 . . . . 129 B6
Stowlangtoft IP31 . . . . . 50 B7
Wyverstone IP14 . . . . . . 51 E6
Church View Cl IP12 . . 147 C7
Church Walks IP33 . . . 154 C1
Churchway 3 IP22 . . . . 36 A8
Church Wlk
Aldeburgh IP15 . . . . . . 130 E4
Hadleigh IP7 . . . . 149 C5
3 Laxfield IP13 . . . . . . 40 B3
Long Melford CO10 . . . . 77 E1
Mildenhall IP28 . . . . . . 116 B4
Shelfanger IP22 . . . . . . 20 B6
Stowmarket IP14 . . . . . 124 D6
Sturmer CB9 . . . . 133 C2
2 Sudbury CO10 . . . . . 148 C5
Church Wood IP19 . . . 118 E4
Churchyard IP33 . . . . 154 C2
Churchyard The IP28 . 116 B4
Cinnabar Cl 11 IP8 . . . . 142 E8
Civic Dr IP1 . . . . 155 A2
Clacton Rd CO11 . . . . 104 E1
Clapgate La IP3 . . . . . 140 A1
Clapham Rd Central 3
 NR32 . . . . 113 D1
Clapham Rd S NR32 . . 113 D1
CLARE 90 B8
Clare Ancient House Mus★
 CO10 . . . . 90 A8
Clare Ave IP12 . . . . . . 146 E4
Clare Castle Ctry Pk★
 CO10 . . . . 90 A8
Clare Castle (remains of)★
 CO10 . . . . 90 A8
Clare Cl
2 Bury St Edmunds
 IP33 . . . . 122 D4
Mildenhall IP28 . . . . . 116 D5
Stowmarket IP14 . . . . . 124 E3
Clare Cty Prim Sch CO10 . 90 A8
Clare Mid Sch CO10 . . . 90 B8
Claremont Pier NR33 . . 115 C6
Claremont Rd 1 NR33 . 115 C6
Clarence Rd
7 Clare CO10 . . . . 76 A1
Ipswich IP3 . . . . 140 B1
1 Lowestoft NR32 . . . . 113 D2
Sudbury CO10 . . . . . . 148 C6
Clarendale Est CB9 . . . 74 C7
Clarendon Rd CB9 . . . 132 D5
Clare Pl CB8 . . . . 121 B2
Clare Priory (remains of)★
 CO10 . . . . 90 B7
Clare Rd
Hundon CO10 . . . . 75 C2
Ipswich IP4 . . . . 139 F8
2 Kessingland NR33 . . . 11 C1
Poslingford CO10 . . . . . 76 A2
Sudbury CO10 . . . . . . 148 D6
3 Tattingstone IP9 . . . 105 B8
Clark Dr 10 IP26 . . . . . . 4 E5
Cloutings Cl IP17 . . . . 128 C6
Clovelly Cl IP4 . . . . . . 140 F4
Clovelly Rise NR32 . . . 113 B3
Clover Cl
Ipswich IP2 . . . . 138 F4
Needham Market IP6 . . 125 D3
Clover Field CB9 . . . . . 132 B6

Claude St IP1 . . . . 155 B3
Claudian Cl CB9 . . . . . 133 B5
Claverton Way IP4 . . . 140 D5
CLAY COMMON 26 B4
CLAYDON 134 C8
Claydon Dr NR32 . . . . 112 F3
Claydon High Sch IP6 . . 134 C8
Claydon Prim Sch IP6 . . 82 B5
Clayhall La CO10 . . . . . 92 C7
Clayhall Pl CO10 . . . . . 92 C7
Clay Hill
Dennington IP13 . . . . . 55 F5
Hintlesham IP8 . . . . . . 95 B5
Monks Eleigh IP7 . . . . . 79 D2
Ubbeston IP19 . . . . 40 E3
Clayhill La
Hitcham IP7 . . . . 79 F6
Wattisham IP7 . . . . 80 A6
Clayhill Rd IP17 . . . . . 128 E5
Clayhills 8 IP19 . . . . . 118 A3
Clayhive Dr 4 CB9 . . . 132 D5
Clay La
Bacton IP14 . . . . 51 F6
Hadleigh IP7 . . . . 94 F4
Henley IP6 . . . . 82 E7
Hepworth IP22 . . . . 35 B5
Ixworth IP31 . . . . 34 A2
Lavenham CO10 . . . . . . 78 E4
Stoke Ash IP23 . . . . 37 B1
CLAYPITS 109 B4
Claypits Ave 1 CO8 . . 101 D4
Claypits La CO10 . . . . . 91 B7
Clay Rd
20 Bury St Edmunds IP32 . 48 C5
Bury St Edmunds IP32 . . . 122 E8
Fornham All Saints IP32 . . 48 B5
Clay St
Soham CB7 . . . . 28 D4
Thornham Magna IP23 . . 36 F1
CLAY STREET 35 D2
Clayton Ct IP12 . . . . . 146 D3
Clayton Rd 2 CO12 . . . 106 E1
Clearwing Cl 15 IP8 . . 142 E8
Clematis Cl 4 IP28 . . . 30 B1
Clemence St NR32 . . . 113 C1
Clementine Gdns IP4 . 140 A5
Clement Prim Sch CB9 . 132 D5
Clement Rd NR33 . . . . 115 B6
Clements Cl
1 Haverhill CB9 . . . . . 132 D5
8 Scole IP21 . . . . 20 F1
Clements Dr 2 CB9 . . 132 D5
Clements La CO10 . . . . 91 B7
Clement Sq NR33 . . . . 115 B6
Clements Rd 4 IP12 . . . 84 E6
Clement's Way 11 IP28 . 30 B8
Clench Cl IP4 . . . . 155 C3
Clench Rd IP9 . . . . . . 105 E8
Clerk's Piece NR34 . . . 111 D3
Clermont Ave CO10 . . 148 C8
Cleveland Rd NR33 . . . 115 C7
Cleves Rd CB9 . . . . . . 132 B4
Cley Ct 1 CB9 . . . . . . 132 A7
Clicket Hill CO8 . . . . . 101 D4
Cliff La
Great Yarmouth NR31 . . . 3 B8
Ipswich IP3 . . . . 139 E3
Cliff La Prim Sch IP3 . . 139 E3
Clifford Dr NR33 . . . . 114 C5
Clifford Rd IP4 . . . . . . 139 F5
Clifford Rd Air Raid Shelter
 Mus★ IP4 . . . . 139 F5
Clifford Rd Prim Sch
 IP4 . . . . 139 F6
Cliff Quay IP3 . . . . . . 139 D2
Cliff Rd
Felixstowe IP11 . . . . . 153 D6
Harwich CO12 . . . . . . 107 B2
Ipswich IP3 . . . . 139 E3
Lowestoft NR33 . . . . . 115 C6
Waldringfield IP12 . . . . 98 E7
Cliffs The NR33 . . . . . 115 F5
Clifton Rd NR33 . . . . . 115 C7
Cliftonville NR33 . . . . 115 B4
Cliftonville Rd NR33 . . 115 B3
Clifton Way IP2 . . . . . 138 D2
Clifton Wood 2 IP9 . . 105 E7
Clink The IP19 . . . . . . 41 C5
Clint Hill IP31 . . . . . . 33 F6
Clint Rd IP23 . . . . 37 D1
Clive Ave IP1 . . . . 135 B2
Clockhall La CO10 . . . . 75 D3
Clockhouse La IP14 . . . 67 F7
Cloncurry Gdns IP11 . 152 D3
CLOPTON CORNER . . . 69 E1
Clopton Dr 2 CO10 . . . 91 E7
Clopton Gdns IP7 . . . 149 E4
CLOPTON GREEN
Wickhambrook 62 A1
Woolpit 65 D7
Clopton Pk CB8 . . . . . 62 A1
Clopton Rd IP6 . . . . . 136 C7
Close The
Corton NR32 . . . . 3 D4
9 Harwich CO12 . . . . 107 A2
Kennett CB8 . . . . 45 F7
North Lopham IP22 . . . . 19 A6
Sudbury CO10 . . . . . . 148 D6

Cloverfield Dr CB7 . . . . 28 C5
Cloverfields 2 IP31 . . . 49 E4
Clovers Ct IP14 . . . . . 124 C6
Clover Way
Lowestoft NR32 . . . . . 113 C5
1 Red Lodge IP28 . . . . 30 C1
Clowes Ct NR34 . . . . . 111 B5
Clowes's Cnr IP14 . . . . 54 D2
Cluanie Orch CO10 . . . 76 F1
Clumps The IP12 . . . . 86 A4
Coach La CB8 . . . . 60 E7
Coachman's Cl IP1 . . . 155 B2
Coachman's Paddock 3
 IP9 . . . . 105 E7
Coakers La IP13 . . . . . . 70 A1
Coalpit La IP29 . . . . . . 46 F4
Coastguard La 22 NR33 . 11 C1
Coast Guards The 8 IP16 73 F6
Coast Rd NR32 . . . . 3 C5
Coates Dro 1 CB7 . . . . 29 C5
Cobbler's Cnr IP8 . . . . 95 B5
COBBLER'S GREEN 7 C6
Cobbold Cl IP14 . . . . . 66 C1
Cobbold Mews IP4 . . . 155 C3
Cobbold Rd
Felixstowe IP11 . . . . . 153 A4
Woodbridge IP12 . . . . 146 E7
Cobbold St
Diss IP22 . . . . 20 B2
Ipswich IP4 . . . . 155 C3
Cobden Pl IP4 . . . . . . 155 C3
Cobham Rd IP3 . . . . . 140 C2
Coblers Way 3 CO10 . . 92 B7
Cock & Bel La CO10 . . . 91 E8
COCK & END 75 C8
COCKFIELD 64 C1
Cockfield CE Prim Sch
 IP30 . . . . 64 C1
Cockfield Hall La IP6 . . 135 E7
Cockfield Rd IP30 . . . . 65 A3
Cock La CO10 . . . . 78 F2
Cockpen Rd CB7 . . . . . 28 F1
Cock Rd IP14 . . . . 52 A6
Cockrell's Rd CO6 . . . . 102 A2
Cocks Gn La IP30 . . . . 64 A5
COCKS GREEN 64 A5
Cock's Rd IP23 . . . . . . 117 F1
COCK STREET 102 C7
CODDENHAM 68 C1
CODDENHAM GREEN . . 67 F2
Coddenham Rd IP6 . . . 67 E1
Coddington Way 8 IP31 . 34 B1
Codling Rd IP32 . . . . . 123 E6
Cody Rd IP3 . . . . 140 C1
Coggeshall Rd
Dedham CO7 . . . . 104 A2
Foxash Estate CO7 . . . . 103 F1
Colbeck Rd CB9 . . . . . 132 C8
Colchester Ct IP27 . . . . 13 F2
COLCHESTER GREEN . . 64 C2
Colchester Rd
Bures CO8 . . . . 101 C4
Dedham CO7 . . . . 103 E2
Ipswich IP4 . . . . 135 F1
10 Manningtree CO11 . . 104 E2
Wormingford CO6 . . . . 102 A1
Coldfair Cl IP17 . . . . . 129 B3
Coldfair Gn Prim Sch
 IP17 . . . . 129 B2
COLDFAIR GREEN 129 B2
Coldham La IP23 . . . . . 36 D2
Cold Store Rd IP11 . . . 152 B2
Coleman Cl IP24 . . . . . 20 C1
Cole Ness Rd IP3 . . . . 144 A8
Coleridge Rd IP1 . . . . 134 F3
Coles Croft IP19 . . . . . 42 C6
COLES GREEN 95 D4
COLE'S GREEN 126 E1
Coles Hill IP19 . . . . . . 42 C7
Coles La CB8 . . . . 59 E1
Coles Oak La CO7 . . . . 103 E3
Cole St IP21 . . . . 39 B2
Coles View IP19 . . . . . 42 C6
Colethorpe La IP29 . . . 46 F3
College Cl 8 IP29 . . . . 63 A8
College Gn IP11 . . . . . 153 C5
College Heath Mid Sch
 IP28 . . . . 116 C6
College Heath Rd IP28 . 116 D6
College La
Bury St Edmunds IP33 . . 154 B1
Worlingham NR34 . . . . 111 F2
College Meadows 2
 NR32 . . . . 113 A3
College Rd
Framlingham IP13 . . . . 126 C4
Hockwold cum Wilton IP26 . 4 F3
Lowestoft NR33 . . . . . 115 C6
2 Soham CB7 . . . . 28 D3
College St
Bury St Edmunds IP33 . . 154 B1
Ipswich IP3 . . . . 155 B2
Colletts Chase CO6 . . . 101 F2
Collett's Wlk IP12 . . . . 146 E5
Collimer Cl 2 IP9 . . . . 106 C8
Collings Pl CB8 . . . . . 120 E5
Collingwood Ave 6 IP3 . 140 B3
Collingwood Fields CO7 . 151 B6
Collingwood Rd IP12 . . 146 F7
Collins Cl IP17 . . . . . . 128 B3
Collin's Hill CB7 . . . . . 29 B1
Collinson's Fp IP22 . . . 138 D5
Colman Rd 4 NR32 . . . . 3 D4
Colneis Jun Sch IP11 . . 153 B6
Colneis Rd IP11 . . . . . 153 B6
Colne Rd CO8 . . . . . . 101 C4
Colne Springs CO9 . . . 89 D4
Colne Valley Rd CB9 . . 132 E5

Colneys Cl CO10 . . . . . 148 B7
Colsterdale NR33 . . . . 114 D3
COLTON 48 F5
Coltsfoot Cl
7 Ixworth IP31 . . . . . 34 B1
8 Lowestoft NR33 . . . 114 F3
7 Wickhambrook CB8 . . 61 E2
Coltsfoot Cnr IP32 . . . 123 F5
Coltsfoot Rd IP2 . . . . 138 E4
Columbia Cl IP5 . . . . . 141 A7
Columbine Cl 7 NR33 . 114 F3
Columbine Gdns IP2 . . 138 E5
Columbines The CO10 . 76 F1
Columbine Way 3 IP23 . 36 D2
Columbyne Cl IP14 . . . 67 A7
Colville Rd NR33 . . . . . 114 E6
Colville Way NR33 . . . . 114 C3
Comber Cl IP21 . . . . . . 21 A4
Combers The IP5 . . . . 141 E7
COMBS 124 C1
COMBS FORD 124 D4
Combs Ford Prim Sch
 IP14 . . . . 124 E4
Combs Gn IP14 . . . . . . 66 D2
Combs La IP14 . . . . . . 124 D4
Combs Mid Sch IP14 . . 124 F3
Combs Wood Dr IP14 . 124 D3
Combs Wood Nature
 Reserve★ IP14 . . . . . 124 E2
Comet Way IP28 . . . . 116 B5
Comfrey Way IP24 . . . . 16 D6
Commerce Way 3 CO11 . 104 E3
Commercial Rd
Ipswich IP1 . . . . 155 A1
Lowestoft NR32 . . . . . 115 C8
Commister La 14 IP31 . . 34 B1
Commodore Rd NR32 . 112 E1
Common Gate Dro CB7 . 29 A5
Common La
Beccles NR34 . . . . 111 C5
Bromeswell IP12 . . . . . 147 F7
Syleham IP21 . . . . 22 A2
Troston IP31 . . . . 33 E3
Common La Ind Est
 NR34 . . . . 111 C6
Common La N NR34 . . 111 B6
Common Rd
Aldeby NR34 . . . . 10 D7
Botesdale IP22 . . . . . . 36 B5
Bressingham IP22 . . . . 19 F4
Hopton IP22 . . . . 18 C2
Scole IP21 . . . . 21 B4
Shelfanger IP22 . . . . . . 19 F7
St James, South Elmham
 IP19 . . . . 23 D4
Common St 3 CO10 . . . 90 A8
Common The
Beccles NR34 . . . . 111 E5
Claydon IP8 . . . . 134 A6
1 Harleston IP20 . . . . 22 D5
Knodishall Common IP17 . 129 A1
Leiston IP16 . . . . 129 F7
Southwold IP18 . . . . . 119 C5
Compass Cl IP27 . . . . 109 D4
Compass St NR32 . . . . 113 C2
Compiegne Way IP33 . 154 B3
Conach Rd IP12 . . . . . 146 E5
Coney Cl IP24 . . . . 16 A6
Coney Hill NR34 . . . . . 111 D3
CONEY WESTON 17 E1
Coney Weston Rd
Coney Weston IP31 . . . . 34 D8
Fakenham Magna IP31 . . 33 F6
Sapiston IP31 . . . . 34 A6
Congreve Rd IP1 . . . . 135 A3
Conifer Cl IP28 . . . . . 116 D6
Coniston Cl IP11 . . . . 153 E7
Coniston Rd IP3 . . . . . 140 B2
Coniston Sq E IP3 . . . 140 B2
Coniston Sq W IP3 . . . 140 B2
Connaught Rd
Haverhill CB9 . . . . . . 132 C5
Ipswich IP1 . . . . 134 D2
Conrad Cl NR33 . . . . . 114 D6
Conrad Rd NR33 . . . . 114 D6
Consent La IP7 . . . . . . 79 E4
Constable Cl
Halesworth IP19 . . . . . 118 A2
Lowestoft NR32 . . . . . 112 F1
3 Manningtree CO11 . . 104 D2
Nayland-with-Wissington
 CO6 . . . . 102 A5
Constable Ct 15 IP20 . . 22 D6
Constable Rd
Bury St Edmunds IP33 . . 122 C4
Felixstowe IP11 . . . . . 153 B4
Haverhill CB9 . . . . . . 132 B7
Ipswich IP4 . . . . 155 C4
Sudbury CO10 . . . . . . 148 C6
Constable Way IP14 . . 124 B7
Constantine Rd IP1 . . 155 A2
Constitution Hill
Ipswich IP1 . . . . 139 B8
2 Needham Market IP6 . 125 D5
Southwold IP18 . . . . . 119 D4
Sudbury CO10 . . . . . . 148 C6
Convalescent Hill IP11 . 153 A3
Conway Cl
Felixstowe IP11 . . . . . 153 C7
4 Haverhill CB9 . . . . 132 C6
Ipswich IP2 . . . . 139 B2
Conway Rd 2 IP32 . . . . 48 C5
CONYERS GREEN 49 B3
Conyers Way IP31 . . . . 49 A6
Cooke Cl NR33 . . . . . . 114 F2
Cooke Rd NR33 . . . . . 114 F2
COOKLEY 41 A6
COOKLEY GREEN 40 F6

Cookley La IP23 . . . . 38 B5
Cookley Rd
  Cookley IP19 . . . . 41 B5
  Eye IP23 . . . . 38 A5
Cookley & Walpole CE Prim
  Sch IP19 . . . . 41 B5
Cooks Cl IP5 . . . . 141 E8
Cook's Dro IP28 . . . . 12 D2
COOK'S GREEN 79 D8
Cooks Hill
  Boxted CO4 . . . . 103 A4
  Letheringham IP13 . . . . . 70 D4
Cook's La
  Hawkedon IP29 . . . . 62 E1
  Wortwell IP20 . . . . 22 F6
Cooks Rd IP30 . . . . 50 E2
Coombers IP9 . . . . 150 D3
Cooper Cl 2 IP17 . . . . 128 C4
Cooper La IP29 . . . . 63 E8
Cooper Rd IP6 . . . . 68 C1
Coopers Cl IP6 . . . . 83 A6
Cooper's Cl CB8 . . . . 60 A5
Coopers Dr 27 NR33 . . . . 11 C1
Coopersfield 6 IP14 . . . . 53 F2
Coopers La NR33 . . . . 11 B1
Cooper's La CO7 . . . . 103 F3
Coopers Rd 30 IP5 . . . . . 98 A8
Cooper's Rd IP6 . . . . 82 C6
Coopers Way 4 IP6 . . . . . 82 A5
COPDOCK 95 F4
Copdock Intc IP8 . . . . . . 138 B2
Copdock Prim Sch IP8 . . . 95 F4
Copellis Cl CB9 . . . . 132 E8
Copeman Rd 3 IP22 . . . . 20 A3
Copland Way NR34 . . . . . 10 B8
Copleston High Sch IP4 . 140 C5
Copleston Rd IP4 . . . . . . 140 B5
Coplow Dale 12 NR33 . . . 114 E3
Copper Beech Dr 5
  NR33 . . . . 114 D4
Copperfield Rd IP2 . . . . . 138 E5
Copperfield Way 11 CB5. . 44 B5
Copper Gr 14 IP8 . . . . . . 142 E8
Coppers Cl IP33 . . . . . . 154 C1
Copperwheat Ave IP18 . . 119 B8
Coppice Cl IP12 . . . . 147 A6
Coppice Ct NR33 . . . . . . 115 A6
Coppice The IP31 . . . . . . 49 A6
Copplestone Cl 12 NR34 . .9 F4
Coprolite St IP3 . . . . 139 E5
Copse Cl IP33 . . . . 123 B1
Copswood Cl IP5 . . . . . . 141 F7
Copy Hill CB9. . . . . 132 C1
Coral Dr IP1 . . . . 134 D1
Coram St IP7 . . . . 149 A6
Cordell Pl CO10 . . . . 91 E8
Cordell Rd CO10 . . . . 91 E8
Corder Rd IP4 . . . . 139 D8
Cordwinders CO7 . . . . . . 151 F3
Cordy's La IP11 . . . . 152 B6
Coriander Dr IP24 . . . . . . 16 D6
Corks La IP7 . . . . 149 C6
Corkway Dro IP26 . . . . 4 A4
Cormorant Dr IP14 . . . . . 124 F5
Cornard Rd CO10 . . . . . . 148 D5
CORNARD TYE 92 C4
Cornerth Cres CO10 . . . . 148 F4
Cornfield Ave IP27 . . . . . 109 D7
Cornfield Cres 5 NR32. . . 3 D4
Cornfield Rd IP33 . . . . . 154 A3
Cornfields IP21. . . . . 21 B5
Cornflower Cl IP2 . . . . . 138 E4
Cornford Way 13 CO11 . . 104 D2
Corn Hatches La IP7 . . . . 80 E1
Cornhill
  Bury St Edmunds IP33. . . 154 B2
  Ipswich IP1 . . . . 155 B3
Cornhill Wlk Sh Ctr IP33 154 B2
Cornish Hall End Rd CO9 . 89 A1
Cornish Wlk IP2 . . . . 122 E8
Cornmill Gn 9 IP30. . . . . 50 D1
Cornmills Rd CB7 . . . . . . 28 E2
Cornwall Cl 25 CO11 . . . 104 D2
Cornwallis Cl IP28 . . . . . 32 C1
Cornwallis Ct IP33 . . . . . 154 A1
Cornwallis Rd CB9 . . . . . 132 D4
Cornwall Rd IP11 . . . . . 152 F5
Cornwell Cl CB7 . . . . 29 B4
Coronation Ave IP2 . . . . 99 D6
Coronation Dr IP11 . . . . 152 D3
Coronation Rd IP4 . . . . . 140 B5
Coronation Rise 1 CO10 . 92 C6
Corporation Ave IP2 . . . 139 B1
Corsbie Cl IP33 . . . . 154 B1
Corsican Pine Cl CB8. . . 120 F5
CORTON 3 C4
Corton CE VC Prim Sch
  NR32. . . . . 3 D4
Corton Long La NR32. . . 113 B8
Corton Rd
  Ipswich IP3 . . . . 140 B1
  Lowestoft NR32. . . . . . . 113 D6
Cosford Rd IP7 . . . . 94 C7
Cotes The CB7 . . . . 28 B6
Cotman Ave 8 CO10 . . . 104 D2
Cotman Cl 3 NR32. . . . . 113 B6
Cotman Rd IP3 . . . . 140 A1
Cotmer Rd NR33 . . . . . . 114 D7
Cotswold Ave IP1 . . . . . 135 B1
Cotswold Dr 1 CO10 . . . 91 E7
Cotswold Way NR32. . . . 112 C2
Cottesford Cl IP7 . . . . . 149 E5
Cottingham Rd IP8 . . . . 138 B2
COTTON. 52 B6
Cotton End Rd CB8. . . . . 120 C8
Cotton La
  Bury St Edmunds IP33. . . 154 C1
  Cotton IP14. . . . . 52 A6

Cotton La Flats IP33 . . . . 154 C3
Coucy Cl IP13 . . . . 126 C4
Coulson La 1 IP27 . . . . . . .5 F1
Coupals Cl CB9 . . . . 133 A4
Coupals Prim Sch CB9 . . 133 B5
Coupals Rd CB9 . . . . 133 C4
Courier Cl IP28 . . . . 116 B5
Courtenay Cl CO10 . . . . 148 B8
Court Knoll (Earthworks)★
  CO6. . . . . 102 D4
Court St CO6 . . . . 102 D5
Courts The
  Felixstowe IP11 . . . . 153 B4
  Playford IP6 . . . . 137 B5
COVE BOTTOM. 26 E3
Covehite Ct 4 CB9. . . . . 132 C4
COVEHITHE. 27 B4
Covell Cl IP33 . . . . 122 C4
Coverdale 6 NR33. . . . . 114 E3
Covert Cl CB9. . . . . 132 E7
Covert Rd IP18 . . . . 119 C8
Covert Sycamore 5 IP26. 16 D6
Covey Dr IP27 . . . . 109 E6
Covey Way IP27 . . . . . . 109 E6
Cow and Sheep Dro IP28. 29 E7
Cowell St IP2 . . . . 139 C3
Cow Fair 7 IP30. . . . . . . 50 D1
COW GREEN 51 F4
Cowle's Dro IP26 . . . . 4 D1
Cowley Rd IP11 . . . . 153 A4
COWLINGE 61 B1
Cowper St IP4 . . . . 140 B6
Cowslip Cl
  Bury St Edmunds IP32. . . 123 F5
  Ipswich IP2 . . . . 138 E4
Cowslip Cres NR33 . . . . 114 C5
Cowslip Way IP6. . . . . . 125 D3
Cox Cl IP5 . . . . 141 B6
COX COMMON 25 A5
Coxhall Rd IP9. . . . . 142 E1
Cox Hill CO10 . . . . 93 C3
Cox La
  Great Barton IP31. . . . . . 49 B6
  Ipswich IP4 . . . . 155 C2
Cox's Cl CB9 . . . . 132 A5
Cox's Cl NR34. . . . . 111 C3
Cox's Hill CO11 . . . . 104 D2
Cox's La IP18 . . . . 119 C8
Coytes Gdns IP1 . . . . . . 155 B2
Crabbe's Cl 8 IP26 . . . . .4 C1
Crabbe St
  Aldeburgh IP15 . . . . 130 F4
  Ipswich IP4 . . . . 140 A6
Crabtree Cl IP19 . . . . . . 118 B2
Crabtree La
  Aldeby NR34 . . . . .9 F8
  Little Horkesley CO6 . . . 102 B1
Crabtree Meadow 5 IP30 50 F2
Crabtree Rise IP21. . . . . 21 F2
Cracks La IP12 . . . . 85 C6
CRACKTHORN CORNER. . . 19 A1
Crag Farm Rd IP12 . . . . 131 E7
Crag Path IP15 . . . . 130 F3
Craig Cl 7 IP11 . . . . 107 D8
Craig's La CO8. . . . . 101 B3
Cramswell Cl CB9. . . . . . 132 B4
Cranberry Sq 2 IP3 . . . 144 C7
Cranborne Chase 1 IP4 136 A1
Cranbrook La CO10 . . . . . 77 C1
Crane Cl IP12 . . . . 146 D3
Crane Hill London Rd
  IP2. . . . . 138 E4
Cranesbill Dr IP32 . . . . . 123 E5
Cranesbill Rd NR33 . . . . 114 F3
Cranes Meadow 31 IP20. 22 D6
Cranfield Cl 4 NR33 . . . 115 A3
Cranfield Pk IP8 . . . . . . 95 D7
Cranleigh Rd NR33 . . . . 114 F3
CRANLEY. 37 F3
Cranley Gn Rd IP23 . . . . 117 D2
Cranley La IP23. . . . . . . 117 F1
CRANMER GREEN 35 E2
Cranmoregreen La CO10 . 77 C1
CRANSFORD. 56 B3
Cranwell Cres IP3 . . . . . 140 C1
Cranwell Gr 1 IP5. . . . . 141 C7
Cranworth Gdns 1
  NR32. . . . . 112 F4
Cranworth Rd IP7 . . . . . 149 E4
CRATFIELD 40 D6
Cratfield La IP19. . . . . . . 40 C4
Cratfield Rd
  Bury St Edmunds IP32. . . 123 E4
  Fressingfield IP21. . . . . . 39 F8
  Huntingfield IP19 . . . . . . 40 E5
Craven Way CB8 . . . . . . 120 E6
Crawford Ave IP14. . . . . 66 D8
Crawford Cl 5 IP14. . . . . 51 A1
Crawford La 2 IP5 . . . . 141 C7
Crayford Rd CO10 . . . . . 148 B8
Creed Wlk IP32 . . . . 122 D7
CREETING BOTTOMS. . . . 67 F5
Creeting Hills IP6. . . . . . 125 F6
Creeting La IP14. . . . . . . 67 B7
Creeting Rd IP14. . . . . . 124 E6
Creeting Rise 20 IP14 . . 67 A5
CREETING ST MARY 125 F8
Creeting St Mary Prim Sch
  IP6 . . . . 125 F8
CREETING ST PETER. 67 C5
Crepping Hall Dr IP9. . . . 105 C5
Crescent Rd
  Aldeburgh IP15 . . . . 130 E4
  Felixstowe IP11 . . . . 153 A4
  Ipswich IP1. . . . . 155 A3
Crescents The IP18 . . . . 119 B8
Crescent The
  Dullingham CB8. . . . . . . 59 D5

Crescent The continued
  East Harling NR16. . . . . . 18 C8
  Great Horkesley CO6. . . . 102 D1
  6 Soham CB7. . . . . 28 D3
  7 Thurstow IP31. . . . . . . 49 D4
  Wicken CB7. . . . . 28 A1
  Wickham Market IP13. . . 127 B6
Cresmedow Way IP30. . . 50 F2
Crespigny Rd IP15 . . . . . 130 E3
Cresslands La IP29. . . . . 76 D8
Crestland Bsns Pk CO10. . 92 A8
Crestview Dr NR32. . . . . 113 A4
CRETINGHAM 69 F7
Cricketers Cl CO10 . . . . 148 C4
Cricket Field Rd CB8 . . . 121 B2
Cricket Hill Rd IP11 . . . 152 D5
Crick's Rd
  Beck Row, Holywell Row &
    Kenny Hill IP28 . . . . . 30 A6
  Thistley Green IP28. . . . . 29 F6
Crimbold's La IP30. . . . . 64 D1
Crimp Cramp La NR34. . . 10 B8
Crisp Cl 3 NR32 . . . . . . 113 B4
Crispin Cl CB9 . . . . 132 B5
Crisp Rd NR35 . . . . .8 E7
Crockatt Rd IP7 . . . . . . 149 E8
Crockfords Rd CB8. . . . . 121 A1
Crocus Cl IP2. . . . . 138 F4
Croft Cl
  Beccles NR34. . . . . 111 E4
  Diss IP22 . . . . 20 C2
  10 Harleston IP20. . . . . . 22 D6
  8 Wickhambrook CB8. . . 61 E2
Croft Ct 13 CO10 . . . . . 148 C5
Croft La
  Diss IP22 . . . . 20 C2
  Haverhill CB9. . . . . 132 F4
  Trimley St Martin IP10 . . 98 C2
Croft Lea CO10 . . . . 92 E8
Crofton Rd IP4 . . . . 140 B7
Croft Pl IP28 . . . . 116 C4
Croft Rd
  15 Isleham CB7. . . . . . . 29 C5
  Newmarket CB8. . . . . . . 120 F5
  Sudbury CO10. . . . . 148 C6
Croft Rise IP33 . . . . 123 B1
Croft St IP2 . . . . 139 C3
Croft The
  6 Bures CO8 . . . . 101 C5
  1 Glemsford CO10. . . . . 77 A2
  Great Yeldham CO9 . . . . 90 A1
  1 Lowestoft NR32. . . . . 113 C1
  2 Sudbury CO10. . . . . . 148 C6
Cromarty Rd IP4. . . . . . 140 B8
Cromer Rd IP1 . . . . 134 F1
Crome Wlk NR32 . . . . . . 113 B6
Crompton Rd
  Ipswich IP2 . . . . 138 F7
  Lowestoft NR33. . . . . . . 114 E7
Cromwell Ave NR34 . . . 111 B3
Cromwell La NR34. . . . . 111 B3
Cromwell Ct NR33 . . . . 114 D2
Cromwell Rd
  Ringsfield NR34 . . . . .9 C2
  Weeting IP27 . . . . .5 E4
  Weston NR34. . . . . 111 B1
Cromwell Sq 1 IP1. . . . . 155 B2
Crooked House Gall The★
  CO10. . . . . 78 D4
Cropley Cl IP32. . . . . . . 123 E4
Cross Cl CB9. . . . . 132 E7
Crossfields CO6. . . . . . . 102 E7
Cross Field Way CO4. . . . 103 A3
Crossgate Field 3 IP11 . 152 E5
CROSS GREEN
  Cockfield 64 B2
  Hartest 77 A7
  Hitcham 79 E7
Crossing Rd IP22 . . . . . . 20 C1
Cross La Cl IP27 . . . . . . 109 D6
Crossley Gdns IP1 . . . . . 134 C2
Cross Rd IP20 . . . . 22 C6
Cross St
  1 Bungay NR35. . . . . . . 110 B4
  Drinkstone IP30 . . . . 65 C7
  Elmswell IP30 . . . . 50 E2
  Eye IP23 . . . . 117 C2
  Felixstowe IP11. . . . . . . 152 E6
  Hoxne IP21 . . . . 38 C7
  Leiston IP16 . . . . 129 C5
  Sudbury CO10. . . . . 148 B4
CROSS STREET. 38 C7
Cross The IP23 . . . . 117 C2
Cross Ways IP30. . . . . . . 50 E2
Crotchets Cl 2 IP9 . . . . 150 E3
Croutel Rd IP11. . . . . . . 153 B5
Crowbrook Pl IP30. . . . . 78 C8
Crowcroft Glebe IP7. . . . 80 B5
Crowcroft Rd IP7. . . . . . 80 B5
Crowe Hall La IP9 . . . . . 105 D5
Crowe St IP14 . . . . 124 D6
CROWFIELD 68 D4
Crowfield Rd IP14 . . . . . 68 C6
Crowfoot Com Prim Sch
  NR34. . . . . 111 D4
Crowfoot Gdns 7 NR34 . 111 B5
Crowhurst Cl 4 NR33 . . 114 D4
Crow La IP14 . . . . 124 D5
Crowland Cl 1 IP2 . . . . 139 A2
Crowland Rd CB9 . . . . . 132 B6
Crown Cl 10 IP12 . . . . . . 84 A1
Crown Cnr IP6. . . . . 68 B1
CROWN CORNER. 39 D1
Crown Cres 15 IP31. . . . . 34 B1
Crownfield Rd 8 CO10 . . 77 A3
Crownfields 2 IP13. . . . . 84 F7

Crescent The continued
Crown Gn IP22 . . . . 20 E6
Crown La
  Coney Weston IP31 . . . . 17 E1
  Ixworth IP31. . . . . 34 B1
  Orford IP12 . . . . 131 C2
  Wickham Market IP13. . . 127 C6
CROWNLAND 35 D1
Crownland Rd IP31 . . . . 35 C1
Crown Meadow Wlk 3
  NR32. . . . . 113 C2
Crown Mill 3 IP30. . . . . 50 F2
Crown Pl IP12 . . . . 147 A4
Crown Rd IP26 . . . . .6 B8
Crown St E 5 NR32 . . . . 113 E2
Crown St W NR32 . . . . . 113 D2
Crown St
  Brandon IP27 . . . . 14 E8
  Bury St Edmunds IP33. . . 154 C1
  Dedham CO7. . . . . 103 F3
  Felixstowe IP11 . . . . 152 E5
  Ipswich IP1. . . . . 155 B3
  Leiston IP16 . . . . 129 D6
  Needham Market IP6 . . . 125 D5
  Stowmarket IP14. . . . . . 124 D7
Crown Swimming Pool
  IP1. . . . . 155 B3
Crown Wlk CB8 . . . . 121 A4
Crow St IP31 . . . . 34 D8
Crowswell Ct 6 IP11 . . . 107 D8
Croxton Cl IP32 . . . . 98 E2
Croxton Rd IP24 . . . . . . 16 C7
Crunch Croft CB9 . . . . . 133 C3
Cryspen Ct IP33 . . . . . . 154 B3
Cuckfield Ave IP3. . . . . . 140 E3
CUCKOLD'S GREEN 26 C5
CUCKOO GREEN 3 A6
Cuckoo Hill CO8 . . . . . . 101 C5
Cuckoo Hill (Tumulus)★
  IP28 . . . . 47 C8
Cuckoo La IP20. . . . . . . 22 F6
CUCKOO TYE 92 A7
Cucumber La NR34. . . . . 111 D1
CULFORD 32 D1
CULFORDHEATH 32 F1
Culford Rd
  Bury St Edmunds IP28. . . 48 C6
  Ingham IP31 . . . . 32 F1
Culford Sch IP28 . . . . . . 32 D1
Culford Terr IP33 . . . . . 154 A1
Culford Wlk IP11 . . . . . 152 C3
Culley Way 2 NR31. . . . . .3 B6
Cullingham Rd IP3 . . . . 139 A6
Cullum Rd IP33. . . . . . . 154 B1
Culpho. 137 A7
Culvers Meadow 4 IP31. 34 E4
Culzean Gdns 1 NR32. . 113 A4
Cumberland Cl
  4 Felixstowe IP11. . . . . . 153 D6
  5 Southwold IP18 . . . . . 119 C6
Cumberland Mews IP12. 147 A4
Cumberland Pl 13 NR32 . 113 E2
Cumberland Rd IP18 . . . 119 C6
Cumberland St
  Ipswich IP1 . . . . 155 A4
  Woodbridge IP12. . . . . . 147 A4
Cundle Gn La IP17 . . . . . 72 C5
Cundys Marsh 5 IP15. . 130 E5
Cunningham Way NR33 . 115 B3
Curlew Cl IP27 . . . . 109 D5
Curlew Gn NR32 . . . . . . 112 C1
CURLEW GREEN 128 C7
Curlew Rd IP2 . . . . 138 D4
Curlews The IP33 . . . . . 123 C1
Curriers' La IP1 . . . . . . 155 A2
Curtis Cl IP8. . . . . 138 C1
Curtis Dr 1 IP26 . . . . 4 D5
Curtis Way IP5 . . . . 141 D7
Curwen Rd IP14 . . . . . . 124 C6
Curzon Rd CO10 . . . . . . 148 F6
Cuthbert Cl 2 IP24. . . . . 16 D6
Cutler Rd 5 NR32. . . . . 112 D2
Cutlers La CO7. . . . . . . 151 D7
Cutler St IP1 . . . . 155 B2
Cutter's La IP14 . . . . 66 A6
Cutler St IP1 . . . . 155 B2
Cutter's La IP31 . . . . 49 E8
Cutting's Rd IP21 . . . . . . 21 E4
Cypress Cl IP28. . . . . . . 116 D6
Cypress Way 4 NR33 . . 114 F7

D

Dad's Army Mus★ IP24 . 16 C6
Daffodil Cl IP2. . . . . 138 E3
Daffodil Wlk NR33 . . . . 114 C5
DAGWORTH 66 E8
Dagworth La IP14. . . . . . 66 D8
Daimler Rd IP1 . . . . 134 C2
Dains Pl IP11 . . . . 152 C7
Daires La IP12. . . . . 147 C7
Dairy Dr 4 IP28 . . . . 48 B6
Dairy Hill IP19 . . . . 118 D3
Dairy La
  Ixworth IP31 . . . . 34 A2
  Mutford NR34 . . . . 10 C3
Dairy Rd IP7. . . . . 80 A1
Daisy Ave IP32 . . . . 123 F5
Daisy Gn La IP23. . . . . . 52 D7
DAISY GREEN
  Great Ashfield 51 A6
  Wickham Skeith 52 D7
Daisy Hill IP21 . . . . 39 F8
DAKING AVE
  Daking Ave CO10 . . . . . . 93 B3
  Daking's Drift 6 IP19. . . 118 A3
Dakota Rd 6 IP28 . . . . . 30 A8
Dale End NR33 . . . . 114 E2
Dale Hall La IP1 . . . . . . 135 B1
Dale Hall Prim Sch IP1 . 135 B2
Dale Haven NR33 . . . . . 114 D3
Dale Hill IP14. . . . . 53 A6
Dale Rd
  Fressingfield IP21. . . . . . 22 C1
  Stanton IP31. . . . . 34 E5
Dales Rd IP1 . . . . 135 A1
Dales View IP8. . . . . 95 F4
Dales View Rd IP1. . . . . 135 A1
Dale Tree Rd 11 IP29. . . 47 A2
DALHAM 61 C8
Dalham Pl CB9. . . . . . . 132 F6
Dalham Rd
  Ashley CB8. . . . . 61 B8
  Moulton CB8 . . . . 45 F2
DALLINGHOO 70 D1
Dallinghoo Rd IP13 . . . . 127 A6
Dalton Rd IP1 . . . . 155 A3
Damask Cl 5 NR33 . . . . 114 E4
DAM GREEN 19 C8
Dam La
  Burgate IP22. . . . . 36 E7
  Kessingland NR33 . . . . . 11 A1
Damselfly Rd 5 IP3 . . . 144 C8
Dandalan Cl IP1 . . . . . . 138 E8
DANDY CORNER. 52 B6
Dane Cl CB9 . . . . 133 E8
Dane Comm CB9 . . . . . 133 D8
Dane Hill Rd CB8 . . . . . 45 E8
Danes Cl IP14 . . . . 124 C5
Danescourt Ave IP14. . . 124 C5
Danes Ct CO10 . . . . 148 F2
Daneway Gdns IP16. . . . 129 C4
Danforth Cl IP13. . . . . . 126 B4
Daniel Gdns IP23 . . . . . 117 C3
Daniels Cl 8 CO10 . . . . . 92 B7
Daphne Rd IP12 . . . . . . 131 C2
Darby Cl IP32. . . . . 123 F6
Darby Rd NR34. . . . . . . 111 B3
Darcy Cl IP32. . . . . 123 E4
Darkings La IP30 . . . . . . 64 F2
Dark La
  Dickleburgh & Rushall
    IP21 . . . . 20 E2
  Easton IP13. . . . . 70 E7
DARMSDEN. 125 F1
Darrell Rd 1 IP11 . . . . 153 H11
Darrow Gn Rd IP20 . . . . . 7 A4
Darrow Wood La IP22. . . 20 A5
DARSHAM 42 C1
Darsham St 19 IP11 . . . 152 D5
Darsham Marshes Nature
  Reserve★ IP17 . . . . 57 F8
Darsham Rd IP17 . . . . . . 58 B8
Darsham Sta IP17. . . . . . 57 F8
Darsham Vale 8 NR32 . . 112 F4
Darter Cl 4 IP3 . . . . . . 144 C8
Darwin Cl IP28 . . . . 116 C6
Darwin Pl CB8 . . . . 121 B1
Darwin Rd IP4. . . . . 139 F5
Dash End CB9 . . . . 133 F8
Dash End La CB9. . . . . . 133 F8
Dashwood Cl IP8 . . . . . 138 C1
Daundy Cl IP2. . . . . 138 D5
Davall Cl 16 CO12 . . . . 106 E1
Davey Cl
  Bungay NR35. . . . . 110 E4
  Ipswich IP3 . . . . 139 F1
Davey La IP13 . . . . 70 B4
Davey's La IP31. . . . . . . 34 C4
Davidson Cl CO10 . . . . . 92 B2
Davoren Wlk IP32. . . . . 122 D7
Dawes Cl IP9 . . . . 150 D4
Dawson Dr IP11 . . . . . . 152 C8
Dawson Drift 3 IP5 . . . . 141 C7
Dawson Mews NR32. . . . 113 A6
Daw St CO9. . . . . 89 A3
Days Gn IP9 . . . . 150 D3
Day's La IP31. . . . . 34 E8
Days Rd IP9 . . . . 150 D3
Dazeley's La CO7 . . . . . 151 F2
Deacon Ct 8 IP11 . . . . . 153 D6
Deacon's Cl 2 CO10 . . . . 78 D4
Dead La
  Ardleigh CO7. . . . . 103 E1
  Bures St Mary CO8 . . . . 101 F5
  Lawford CO11. . . . . 104 E1
Deadman's La
  Benhall IP17 . . . . 128 A2
  Combs IP14. . . . . 66 E1
  Rendham IP17 . . . . 57 A3
  Stoke Ash IP23 . . . . 53 A8
  Woolpit IP30 . . . . 50 C1
Deanery Cl CO10. . . . . . 148 B8
Deane's Cl 1 CO12 . . . . 107 A1
Deans Cl CB9 . . . . 132 E7
DEBACH. 70 A1
Debach Airfield Mus★
  IP13. . . . . 69 F1
Deben Ave
  Ipswich IP5 . . . . 141 F8
  Martlesham IP5. . . . . . . 137 F1
Deben Dr CO10 . . . . . . 148 E6
DEBENHAM 53 E2
Debenham CE High Sch
  IP14. . . . . 53 E2
Debenham Rd
  Crowfield IP6. . . . . 68 E5
  Winston IP14. . . . . 53 F1
Debenham Sports Ctr
  IP14. . . . . 53 E2
Deben High Sch IP11 . . 152 E6
Deben La
  Waldringfield IP12 . . . . . 98 E7
  6 Woodbridge Airfield
    IP12 . . . . 85 B3

Deben Mill Bsns Ctr
IP12...................147 B6
Deben Pool IP12.......147 A4
Deben Rd
  Haverhill CB9.........132 F6
  Ipswich IP1...........134 F1
  Saxmundham IP17......128 C4
  Woodbridge IP12......147 B5
Deben Rise IP14.........53 F1
Debenside The IP12....147 C7
Deben Valley Dr IP5...141 C7
Deben Way IP11........152 E3
De Burgh Pl 6 CO10....76 A1
Deck Wlk IP32..........122 E7
Decoy Rd IP27..........12 F8
DEDHAM................103 F4
Dedham Dr 4 NR32....112 F3
DEDHAM HEATH.........103 F2
Dedham Meade CO7....103 F2
Dedham Rd
  Ardleigh CO7..........103 E1
  Boxted CO4...........103 A3
  Lawford CO11.........104 C2
Dedham Vale Family Farm★
CO7...................151 A1
Deepdale NR33.........114 E2
Deepdale Rd 6 CO12...107 A2
Deer Row NR35...........8 D5
Defoe Rd IP1...........135 A4
Degas Gdns 1 NR32...113 B6
De Greys Cl 8 CO10....92 B3
De Havilland Ct 7 IP28.116 B5
Delbrig Dro CB7........29 A5
Delf Cl IP7.............149 E7
Delius Cl
  Lowestoft NR33........115 A6
  1 Stowmarket IP14...124 C7
Dell Ct NR33...........114 E7
Dell Prim Sch NR33....114 E7
Dell Rd NR33...........114 E7
Dell Rd E NR33........114 F7
Dellview NR33..........114 D6
Dellwood Ave IP11.....153 B5
Delph Dro IP28.........12 D1
Delph Rd IP27.........109 D7
Demesne Gdns 6 IP5...98 A8
Dene Rd NR32..........113 D4
Denes High Sch The
NR32.................113 D4
DENHAM
  Denham..............61 F8
  Hoxne...............38 D5
Denham Cl IP33........122 D5
Denham Cnr IP21.......38 D3
DENHAM END...........46 F2
Denham La IP29........47 A2
Denham Low Rd IP21...38 C5
Denham Rd
  Dalham CB8...........61 C8
  Denham IP29..........47 A1
  Hoxne IP21...........38 D6
Denmark Gdns 1 IP9..105 E7
Denmark Hill IP22......20 C2
Denmark La IP22........20 B2
Denmark Rd
  Beccles NR34.........111 B6
  9 Lowestoft NR33...115 D8
Denmark Rise 1 IP22...20 C2
Denmark St IP22........20 C2
Denney's La IP17......128 D7
DENNINGTON...........55 E5
Dennington CE Prim Sch
IP13.................55 D6
DENNINGTON CORNER..126 C8
Dennington Rd
  Dennington IP13......55 F8
  Framlingham IP13.....126 B5
  Laxfield IP13.........40 B1
Denny Ave IP14........66 D8
Denny's Hill IP20......23 A6
DENSTON...............76 A7
DENTON................7 A3
Denton Cl IP2.........138 D2
Denton Dr NR33.......114 F5
Denton Rd IP20..........7 C2
DEPDEN................62 B3
DEPDEN GREEN.........62 B4
Depden La IP29........62 C5
Depot Rd CB8..........120 E6
Derby Cl IP4...........140 A5
Derby Pl 8 IP31........49 A5
Derby Rd IP3..........140 A4
Derby Rd Sta IP3......140 A4
Derby Way CB8........120 D5
Dereham Ave IP3......139 F3
Dereham Cl 17 IP27....13 F2
Derry Brook La 1 IP14..53 F2
Derwent Gdns 5 NR32.113 A4
Derwent Rd
  15 Bury St Edmunds IP32.48 C5
  Ipswich IP3..........139 F3
Desmond Cl 9 NR32...112 E2
Dettingen Way IP33...122 D5
Devereaux Ct IP4......155 C3
De Vere Cl IP13.......126 C3
Devils Dyke Nature Reserve★
CB5...................44 A3
Devil's La IP17.........42 C1
Devlin Rd IP8..........138 B1
Devon Cl IP32.........122 E8
Devon Rd
  Felixstowe IP11......152 F5
  7 Stowupland IP14...67 A6
Devon Way 10 CO12...106 E1

Dewar La IP5..........141 C7
Dewarrene Dr IP27......5 E3
Dhobi Pl IP1...........138 F7
Dial La IP1............155 B3
Diamond Cl IP1........134 D1
Dickens Ct 6 NR32......3 A4
Dickens Rd IP2........138 E6
Dickinson Terr 8 IP5..141 D7
DICKLEBURGH............21 B5
DICKLEBURGH MOOR......21 D6
Dickleburgh Prim Sch
IP21..................21 B5
Dickleburgh Rd IP21...21 A5
Dicks Mount NR34.....10 D7
Dicky Hill IP20.........22 D7
Didsbury Cl IP2.......138 D2
Digby Cl 5 IP5.........98 A7
Digby Rd IP4..........140 C7
Dillistone Ct CB8......133 C3
Dillwyn St W IP1......155 A3
Dinsdale Pl IP16.......129 C6
Diomed Dr IP31........49 A5
Diprose Dr NR32.......113 A6
Dip The CB8...........121 D2
Dirty La IP21...........21 F7
DISS...................20 C4
Diss Church Jun Sch
IP22..................20 C3
Diss High Sch IP22....20 D3
Diss Inf Sch IP22......20 D2
Diss Mus★ IP22........20 C3
Diss Rd
  Burston & Shimpling IP22..20 E5
  Garboldisham IP22....18 D4
  3 Scole IP21.........20 F1
  South Lopham IP22....19 C4
  Wattisfield IP22.......35 D5
Diss Sta IP22..........20 D2
DITCHINGHAM...........110 C7
Ditchingham Dam NR35.110 B5
Ditchingham Gr IP4....140 F6
Ditton Cl CB8..........121 A1
Ditton Gn CB8..........60 B5
DITTON GREEN..........60 B4
Ditton Lodge Fst Sch
CB8...................121 B2
Dixon Cl 11 CO11.....104 D2
Dixon Dr NR33........114 E7
Dobbs Drift IP5.......141 F7
Dobbs La IP5..........137 E1
Dobson Way NR34.....111 C5
DOCKENEY..............8 F6
Dockfield Ave 5 CO12.106 F2
Dockings La CB7......29 C5
Dock La IP12..........147 C7
Dock St IP2...........155 B1
Doctors La IP21........39 B4
Doctor's La
  Ashen CO10..........89 E5
  Orford IP12...........131 C3
  Pulham St Mary IP21..22 A6
Doctor Watson's La IP5.137 A1
Dodmans IP30.........150 E3
Dodson Vale IP5.......141 C7
Does Field IP14........68 C6
Dog La
  Shelfanger IP22.......20 A8
  Tannington IP13.......55 A4
Dogs Head St IP4.....155 B2
Dogs La NR34...........9 C7
Dogwood Cl IP3.......140 D2
Dogwood Wlk 31 IP27.13 F2
Doit La IP22...........20 A3
Doit The IP22...........19 F2
Dolphin Cl IP3 NR33..115 B4
Dombey Rd IP2........138 E5
Dome Leisure Ctr IP28.116 E4
Donegal Rd IP1........134 D2
Donkey La
  Bradfield Combust with
   Stanningfield IP29....63 F2
  Friston IP17..........72 F7
Dooley Rd IP11........152 C3
Dorchester Rd
  Bury St Edmunds IP33.122 D3
  Ipswich IP3..........140 D3
Doric Pl IP12..........147 A4
Doris St CB8..........120 F3
Dorking Rd NR32.......3 A6
DORKING TYE..........101 D7
Dorley Dale NR33.....114 E3
DORLEY'S CORNER.....128 D8
Dorothy Hodgkin Ct
NR34.................111 B2
Dorset Cl IP4..........135 F1
Doubleday Cl IP22.....20 C2
Double St IP13........147 B8
Doughty Wylie Cres IP16.58 B4
Douglas Cl
  Halesworth IP19......118 C5
  Lowestoft NR33.......114 D3
Douglas Rd 11 CO12...107 A2
Doug Smith Cl CB8....120 F6
Doune Way 9 IP20.....22 D6
Dove Cl
  15 Debenham IP14....53 F2
  9 Harleston IP20.....22 D5
  Saxmundham IP17.....128 C4
Dove Cres 9 CO12.....106 E1
Dovedale
  Felixstowe IP11......152 D3
  2 Lowestoft NR33....114 F3
Dove Gdns 2 IP14.....67 A5
Dovehouse Hill IP29...77 D7
Dove House Rd CB9...132 F5

Dove La IP23..........117 D2
DOVERCOURT...........107 B2
Dovercourt Sta CO12..107 B2
Dovercourt Swimming Pool
CO12.................107 B1
Dove Rd IP18..........119 B7
Dover Rd IP3..........140 B4
Dove St
  Ipswich IP4..........139 E5
  Lowestoft NR32......113 D2
Dowes Hill Cl NR34...111 C4
Dowling Rd CO8.......101 C2
DOWN FIELD............28 F2
Downham Bvd IP3.....144 C7
Downham Way IP27.....6 A1
Downing Cl
  Bury St Edmunds IP32.123 E5
  Ipswich IP2..........138 F2
  Mildenhall IP28......116 D5
  Newmarket CB8.......121 B2
  2 Woodbridge IP12...146 E4
Downing Dr 4 IP31....49 A6
Downing Prim Sch IP2.138 F2
Downlands 5 IP7......80 F1
Downs Cres CB9.......132 D6
Downs Farm La IP20...23 B7
Downside IP14.........124 B6
Downside Cl IP2.......142 F8
Downs Pl CB9.........132 D6
Downs The
  Felixstowe IP11......152 D5
  Rushbrooke with Rougham
   IP30...............49 C2
Downton Dr CB9.......132 C6
Dowson Dr 2 NR33....11 B1
Drab's La IP13..........83 E7
Drake Cl IP14.........124 A6
Drake Inf Sch 3 IP24..16 C7
Drake Rd CO10........148 E7
Drake's Heath NR32..113 B2
Drake Sq S IP3........140 B2
DRAKESTONE GREEN....93 F8
Drapers Cl 1 IP7......149 E6
Drapers Hill IP21......39 B5
Drapers La
  Ditchingham NR35......8 A7
  Helions Bumpstead CB9.88 A5
Drapery Comm 3 CO10.77 A2
Draymans Way IP3....139 E3
Drays The CO10........91 D7
Drift Cl IP6...........125 D4
Drift Rd IP27.........109 C8
Drift The
  Botesdale IP22.......36 A7
  2 East Bergholt CO11.104 A4
  Exning CB8...........120 A8
  Fornham St Martin IP31.48 D5
  Holbrook IP9.........105 C5
  Ipswich IP3..........140 C1
  Ipswich IP4..........140 A6
  Levington IP10.......145 C3
  24 Martlesham Heath IP5..98 A8
  Middleton IP17........58 B6
  Polstead CO6..........93 D2
  Sudbury CO10.........92 B3
  Tostock IP30..........50 B2
  Wickham Market IP13..127 D8
Driftway The
  15 Grundisburgh IP13.83 E5
  Ipswich IP14.........140 B6
DRINKSTONE...........65 C8
Drinkstone Gn Cl IP30.65 B7
DRINKSTONE GREEN....65 B7
Drinkstone Mills★ IP30.50 C1
Drinkstone Rd
  Beyton IP30..........49 F2
  Gedding IP30.........65 B5
Drinkwater Cl CB8....120 E4
Drive The
  Harwich CO12........107 A1
  Heveningham IP19....41 B3
  Hitcham IP7..........80 A8
  Lowestoft NR32......112 F2
  Martlesham Heath IP5.98 B8
  Rushbrooke with Rougham
   IP30...............64 B8
  Southwold IP18......119 B7
Drout's La IP31........34 E7
Drove La IP14..........51 A3
Drovers Ave IP32.....123 F5
Drover's Ct IP11......152 B8
Drove The IP27.........14 D8
Druids La IP22.........20 B6
Druids' La IP22.........20 A7
Drum Field 5 CO7.....103 E4
Drummond Ct IP33....154 A1
Drury Cl 19 NR33......11 C1
Drury Dr CO10........148 D8
Drury La
  Milden IP7............79 B1
  Ridgewell CO9........89 D3
  Wicken CB7..........28 B1
Drury Pk IP17.........72 D5
Drury Rd IP6..........134 C4
Drybridge Hill IP12...146 E4
Dryden Rd IP1........135 A3
DUBLIN................53 E8
Dublin Rd IP23........53 E8
Duchess Dr
  Newmarket CB8.......121 D2
  Woodditton CB8......60 C8
Duckamere IP8........134 A1
Duck Dro CB7..........12 A6
Ducksen Rd IP14.......52 E4
Ducks La CB8..........120 C7
Duddery Hill CB9......132 E5
Duddery Rd 6 CB9....132 E5
Dudley St IP27........109 F1

Duffs Hill CO10........77 A4
Dukes Cl IP11.........153 D6
Duke's Dr IP19........118 A2
Dukes Head St 6 NR32.113 E2
Dukes Meadow
  1 Beccles NR34.....111 C4
  Cockfield IP30........64 D3
Duke's Meadow IP12..146 D3
Duke's Pk IP12........146 D2
Duke's Rd NR35.......110 C2
Duke St
  Beccles NR34........111 D3
  4 Bildeston IP7......79 F4
  Hadleigh IP7.........149 D5
  Haughley IP14........51 C1
  Hintlesham IP8.......95 C5
  Ipswich IP3..........139 E4
  7 Stanton IP31.......34 E4
DUKE STREET..........95 B5
Dukesway 1 NR35......7 F4
Dulgate Rd NR35.......7 B7
DULLINGHAM...........59 F5
DULLINGHAM LEY......60 A3
Dullingham Rd
  Newmarket CB8......120 F1
  Woodditton CB8......59 D5
Dullingham Sta CB8...59 D5
Dumbarton Rd 3 IP4..136 C1
Dumfries Rd 2 IP4....136 C1
Dumplingbridge La IP27.109 C6
Dunburgh Rd NR34.....9 A6
Duncan Rise CO9......89 F1
Dunche's La IP6........67 E4
Dun Cow Rd NR34.....10 B8
Dunhill La IP22........35 B5
Dunlin Rd IP2.........138 E2
Dunlop Rd IP2........138 F6
Dunn Cl IP7...........149 E6
Dunnock Cl 18 IP14...67 A5
Dunsey Wood Cl CB9.132 C7
Dunstall Gn Rd CB8....61 E6
DUNSTALL GREEN......61 E7
Dunster Dr 15 CB9....132 C6
Dunston Dr NR32.....112 E4
Dunston's Cnr IP6.....82 B8
Dunton Gr IP7.........149 E4
DUNWICH...............43 B1
Dunwich Ct 5 CB9....132 A6
Dunwich Heath Nature
  Reserve★ IP17.......58 F7
Dunwich La IP17.......41 A2
Dunwich Mus★ IP17...43 B1
Dunwich Pl 2 IP31....49 A5
Dunwich Rd
  Blythburgh IP19......42 F5
  4 Southwold IP18....119 D5
  Westleton IP17.......58 D8
Dunwich Underwater
  Exploration Ex★ IP12.131 B3
Dunwich Way 11 NR32.112 F4
Durban Cl IP19........118 B2
Durban Rd NR33......115 B7
Durbar Terr IP33......154 A3
Durbidge's Hill IP22....20 E5
Durham Cl 22 IP32....48 C5
Durham Rd IP27.......14 A3
Durham Way CB8.....120 E5
Durrant Rd IP7........149 D7
Durrant's Cl 8 NR33...11 C1
Durrant View IP5......141 E7
Dutchman Ct NR33....114 D7
Dux St IP7.............65 B1
Dyer Ct IP7...........149 F5
Dyers La CO10........92 E2
Dyers Rd CO9.........89 C1
Dyke St IP1...........155 B3
Dyson's Dro CB5......44 A7

E

Eades Wlk NR33.......114 C5
Eagle Ct NR34.........26 E5
Eagle Dr IP15.........130 C6
Eagle La CB8..........59 E5
Eagles Cl IP11........152 F4
Eagle St IP4..........155 C2
Eagle Way IP5.........98 A8
Eagle Wlk IP32.......122 E8
Earlsbrook IP14.......51 E6
Earls Cl IP11.........153 D6
Earl's Cl IP19.........118 A2
Earlsfield IP27.........13 F2
Earlsford Rd
  Mellis IP23...........36 F5
  Thornham Parva IP23..37 A4
Earls Gn 6 CB9.......132 A6
EARL'S GREEN.........51 D5
EARL SOHAM...........54 E2
Earl Soham Prim Sch
IP13..................54 F2
EARL STONEHAM.......67 E5
EARSHAM..............7 E4
Earsham CE VA Fst Sch
NR35..................7 F4
Earsham Dam NR35...110 A4
Earsham Rd NR35......7 E6
Earsham St NR35.....110 A4
EARSHAM STREET.....22 C1
Eartha La NR32........2 F5
Easdale NR33.........114 E2
Easlea Rd IP32.......123 E4
East Anglia Transport Mus★
NR33.................114 A3
EAST BARTON..........49 C4
East Barton Rd IP31...49 B5
EAST BERGHOLT........151 C4

East Bergholt CE Prim Sch
CO7..................151 B5
East Bergholt High Sch
CO7..................151 D6
EASTBRIDGE............58 D4
East Church St NR16...19 B8
East Cl IP33..........123 C6
Eastcliff IP11.........153 E7
East Cliff IP18.......119 E5
East Dock Rd CO12...106 F3
EAST END
  East Bergholt........104 E6
  Stonham Aspal........68 D6
East End La CO7.......104 E6
East End Rd
  East Bergholt CO7....151 F4
  Stonham Aspal IP14...68 C6
Eastern Ave
  Haverhill CB9........132 D6
  18 Soham CB7.......28 D4
Eastern Cl IP4........140 F4
Eastern Way
  Bury St Edmunds IP32.123 C6
  Elmswell IP30........50 F2
  Lowestoft NR32......113 B1
Eastfen Dro IP26.......5 B2
East Fen Dro CB7......28 F4
East Fen Rd CB7......29 D5
Eastfield Gdns 3 NR33.114 E4
Eastgate Sh Ctr IP4..155 C3
Eastgate St IP33......154 C2
East Gn IP18..........119 D5
EAST GREEN
  Great Bradley........74 E8
  Kelsale cum Carlton...57 E4
East Harling Rd NR16..18 F8
East La
  Bawdsey IP12.........99 F2
  Dedham CO7.........104 A2
  Middleton IP17........58 B6
  Ufford IP13..........85 A7
Eastland Ct IP11......152 D7
Eastlands IP21.........39 B4
Eastlands La IP23.....52 B8
Eastlands Rd IP16.....129 E6
East Lawn IP4.........140 C8
Eastlowhill Rd IP30...64 B8
Eastlow Hill (Tumulus)★
IP30...................64 C8
East Mill Gn IP9......104 F7
EASTON................70 E5
Easton Farm Pk★ IP13.70 D5
Easton La
  Hacheston IP13......70 F5
  Reydon IP18.........27 A1
Easton Prim Sch IP13..70 E5
Easton Rd
  Hacheston IP13......71 A4
  Woodbridge Airfield IP12.85 B3
East Point Academy
NR33.................115 A6
East Point Pavilion Visitor
  Ctr★ NR33..........115 D8
East Rd CB7...........29 C5
East Side CO4.........103 A2
East St
  6 Harwich CO12....107 A2
  Southwold IP18......119 D5
  Sudbury CO10.......148 D5
East View
  Carlton IP17.........128 D6
  Freckenham IP28.....29 E3
Eastward Ho IP16.....129 D5
Eastward Pl IP14......124 C7
Eastwood Ave NR33..114 F6
Eaton Cl IP11.........152 C7
Eaton Gdns IP11......152 E2
Eccles Rd IP2.........138 D2
Economy Rd NR33....115 C7
Eddies The NR33......114 E4
Eddowes Rd 6 IP6....82 B5
Edelweiss Cl 1 NR33..114 C4
Edendale NR32........112 D2
Eden Rd
  5 Haverhill CB9.....132 E5
  Ipswich IP4..........140 B5
Edes Paddock 9 IP31..49 A6
Edgar Ave IP14.......124 D3
Edgar Sewter Prim Sch
IP19..................118 B5
Edgeborough Cl CB8...46 A5
Edgecomb Rd IP14....124 D3
Edgefield Ave 15 CO11.104 C4
EDGE GREEN...........19 B8
Edgerton Rd NR33....115 A7
Edgworth Rd CO10...148 C4
Edies La CO6..........102 B7
Edinburgh Cl
  6 Barnham IP24....16 C2
  Stowmarket IP14.....124 E6
Edinburgh Gdns IP6...82 B5
Edinburgh Rd
  Lowestoft NR32......113 D3
  Newmarket CB8......120 E4
Edith Cavell Way CB9.88 E3
Edmonton Cl IP5.....141 A7
Edmonton Rd IP5.....141 A7
Edmund Cl CB9.......132 D6
Edmund Moundford Rd 11
IP26...................4 E5
Edmund Rd IP27......14 D8
Edmunds Rd IP14.....65 F4
Edward Cl IP1........138 F7
Edward Fitzgerald Ct
IP12..................146 E6
Edwards La IP19......41 F5
Edward St 6 CO12....106 F3
EDWARDSTONE.........93 A5

Edwin Ave IP12 . . . . 146 F7
Edwin Panks Rd IP7 . . . 149 E6
Edwin Terr IP12 . . . . . . 146 F6
Egglestone Cl IP2 . . . . 138 F1
Eggshell La IP28 . . . . 88 F1
Eglantine Way 2 CO6 . . 102 A7
Egremont Cl NR32 . . . . . . 77 A2
Ehringshausen Way CB9. 132 F5
El Alamein Rd NR32 . . . 113 A4
Elderberry Rd 6 IP3 . . 144 C7
Elder Crescen 2 IP7 . . . 80 D6
Elders The IP27 . . . . . . 109 E5
Elderstub La IP30 . . . . . 49 B1
Edith Ave CB7 . . . . 29 C1
Eldo Gdns 8 IP28 . . . . . 29 F6
Eldon La IP28 . . . . 30 D8
Eldo Rd IP28 . . . . 29 F6
Eldred Cl
  Bury St Edmunds IP32. . 123 E4
  Westbourne IP1 . . . . . 138 D8
Eldred Dr CO10 . . . . 92 B2
Eleanor Pl 6 IP31 . . . . . 49 A6
Electric Picture Palace★
  IP18 . . . . 119 C5
Eley's Cnr IP7 . . . . 94 E8
Elgar Cl NR33 . . . . 115 A6
Elim Terr 11 NR32 . . . . . 113 D2
Eliot Way 4 IP14 . . . . . 124 B8
Elizabeth Ave CB8 . . . . 120 E5
Elizabeth Bonhote Cl 3
  NR35 . . . . 110 C2
Elizabeth Cl NR32 . . . . 113 A3
Elizabeth Ct 8 CO10 . . 148 D6
Elizabeth Dr IP29 . . . . . 62 D5
Elizabeth Par CB8 . . . . 120 E5
Elizabeth Rd
  Brandon IP27 . . . . 5 F1
  15 Harwich CO12 . . . . 107 A2
Elizabeth Way
  Burrough Green CB8 . . . 59 F2
  Eye IP23 . . . . 117 C3
  Felixstowe IP11 . . . . . 152 D3
  Stowmarket IP14 . . . . 124 E6
  Sudbury CO10 . . . . . . 148 A3
Elizabeth Wlk 27 IP20 . . 22 D6
Ellenbrook Gn IP2 . . . . 138 D1
Ellenbrook Rd
  Ipswich IP2 . . . . 138 D1
  Pinewood IP9 . . . . . . 142 E8
ELLINGHAM 8 D7
Ellingham VC Prim Sch
  NR35. . . . . 8 D7
Ellington Rd 1 IP24 . . . 16 C2
Elliott Ave IP18 . . . . . . 119 C8
Elliott Cl CB8 . . . . 121 A6
Elliott St IP1 . . . . 139 A6
Ellis Rd CO4 . . . . 102 F2
Ellis St CO10 . . . . 93 C3
Elliston Cl 4 IP30 . . . . . 50 F2
ELLOUGH 9 F1
ELLOUGH HILL 111 D3
Ellough Ind Est NR34. . . 10 A3
Ellough Rd
  Beccles NR34. . . . . . . 111 D4
  Worlingham NR34 . . . . 111 F2
Ellwood Cl NR34 . . . . . 111 B7
Ellwoods Cl 2 CB7 . . . . 29 C5
Elm Cl
  10 Bentwaters Airfield
    IP12 . . . . 85 E8
  6 Brantham CO11 . . . 104 E4
  Dullingham CB8 . . . . . 59 E5
  Haverhill CB9. . . . . . . 132 D6
  Lakenheath IP27 . . . . 109 C7
  Lowestoft NR33 . . . . . 114 C3
Elm Coppice 6 NR33 . . 114 E4
Elmcroft Cl 12 IP28 . . . 30 A8
Elmcroft La IP11 . . . . . 153 C2
Elmcroft Rd IP1 . . . . . . 135 A2
Elm Ct CB9 . . . . 133 C3
Elmdale Dr
  Lowestoft NR33 . . . . . 114 D4
  28 Mistley CO11 . . . . 104 E2
Elmdon Pl CB9. . . . . . . 132 F6
Elm Dr IP30 . . . . 49 F1
Elmers La IP5 . . . . 141 D7
Elm Est CO7 . . . . 151 C5
Elm Gdns IP11 . . . . 152 C7
Elm Gr
  Garboldisham IP22 . . . . 18 C4
  5 Nayland CO6 . . . . . 102 C5
Elmham Dr IP10 . . . . . . 145 B8
Elmhurst Ave NR32. . . . 112 E1
Elmhurst Cl CB9 . . . . . 132 F5
Elmhurst Dr IP3 . . . . . . 139 F3
Elmhurst Rd 17 CO12 . . 107 B2
Elm La
  Capel St Mary IP9 . . . . 150 E3
  Copdock & Washbrook IP8 . 95 F4
Elm Lodge Rd 7 IP13 . . 40 B3
Elms Cl
  6 Earsham NR35 . . . . . 7 F4
  Great Barton IP31 . . . . 49 B6
ELMSETT 80 F1
Elmsett CE Prim Sch IP7 . 80 F1
Elmsett La IP14 . . . . . . 124 F3
Elm St IP8 . . . . 81 B3
Elms La NR34 . . . . 26 B2
Elmsley Way IP17 . . . . . 57 C8
Elms Rd
  Cowlinge CB8. . . . . . . 75 B7

Elms Rd continued
  Freckenham IP28 . . . . . 29 F2
Elm St IP1 . . . . 155 B3
Elms The
  Framlingham IP6 . . . . 126 C4
  4 Horringer IP29 . . . . . 63 A8
ELMSWELL 50 E2
Elmswell Prim Sch IP30. 50 F2
Elmswell Rd
  Great Ashfield IP31. . . . 50 F6
  Wetherden IP14 . . . . . . 51 A1
  Elmswell Stn NR32 . . . . 50 E3
Elmtree Bsns Pk IP30 . . 50 E3
Elm Tree Cl 1 IP14 . . . . 51 E1
Elm Tree CP Sch NR33. . 114 E5
Elm Tree La 5 CO6 . . . 102 A7
Elm Tree Rd NR33. . . . . 114 E5
Elm Tree Rd W NR33. . . 114 E5
Elm Way IP14. . . . . 51 F6
Elm Wlk 30 IP27 . . . . . . 13 F2
Elsey's Yd IP33 . . . . . . 154 B3
Elsmere Rd IP1 . . . . . . 139 C8
Elton Pk IP2 . . . . 138 D6
ELVEDEN 15 D3
Elveden CE Prim Sch
  IP24 . . . . 15 C2
Elveden Rd IP24 . . . . . . 15 C2
Elvedon Way CB8 . . . . . 120 E5
Ely Cl IP33 . . . . 123 B3
Ely Rd
  5 Claydon IP6 . . . . 82 B5
  Ipswich IP4 . . . . 135 F1
  Soham CB7 . . . . 28 B6
Embry Cres 10 IP7 . . . . . 80 D6
Emerald Cl IP5 . . . . 141 C8
Emily Frost Cl 4 CB8 . . . 61 E2
Emlen St IP1 . . . . 155 A3
Emmanuel Cl
  Ipswich IP2 . . . . 138 F2
  Mildenhall IP28 . . . . . 116 D5
Emmerson Way IP7 . . . . 149 D7
Emperor Circ IP3 . . . . . 144 C8
Emsworth Cl 2 IP32 . . . 123 D6
Endway The CB9 . . . . . . 88 E4
Engine Rd CB7. . . . . 28 B5
Ennerdale Cl 2 IP11 . . . 153 D6
Ensign Way IP22 . . . . . . 20 E2
Enstone Rd NR33 . . . . . 115 B6
Enterprise Bsns Pk IP33 154 C4
Entry The IP23. . . . . 52 D8
Epsom Dr IP1 . . . . 135 A4
Erbury Pl CO10 . . . . 90 A8
ERISWELL 13 F1
Eriswell Dr IP27 . . . . . 109 D5
Eriswell Rd
  Beck Row, Holywell Row &
    Kenny Hill IP28. . . . . 13 E1
  Haverhill CB9. . . . . . . 132 F6
  Lakenheath IP27 . . . . 109 D4
Ernleigh Rd IP4. . . . . . . 140 B6
Erratts Hill CB8 . . . . 61 B1
Errington Way IP30 . . . . 50 B2
Erskine La 14 CO11 . . . 104 E2
Erskdale Way NR32 . . . 113 A4
Esplanade NR33 . . . . . 115 D7
Essex Ave CO10 . . . . . . 148 D7
Essex Rd NR32 . . . . . . 113 B1
Essex Way IP3. . . . . . . 140 E1
Estuary Cres 5 IP9 . . . 107 A4
Estuary Dr IP11. . . . . . 153 D7
Estuary 7 IP9. . . . . . . 107 A4
Ethel Mann Rd 5 NR35. 110 C2
Ethel Rd NR32 . . . . 113 D1
Ethelreda Dr 1 IP24 . . . 16 D7
Etna Rd IP33 . . . . 154 B4
Europa Rd NR32 . . . . . 113 C4
Europa Way
  9 Harwich CO12 . . . . 106 F2
  Ipswich IP1 . . . . 138 E1
Euro Ret Pk IP3 . . . . . . 140 E1
Euroscope★ NR32 . . . . 113 E2
Eustace Rd IP1 . . . . . . 138 E8
EUSTON. 16 F1
Euston Ave IP4 . . . . 140 F6
Euston Cl IP33 . . . . 154 A1
Euston Ct 4 IP11 . . . . . 152 C4
Euston Hall★ IP24 . . . . 16 E1
Evans Cl IP18. . . . . 119 C7
Evans' Rd NR32 . . . . . . 113 B2
Evans' Heath CO10 . . . . 93 F4
Eve Balfour Way IP14 . . 66 D8
Evelyn Cl IP21 . . . . 38 C7
Everard Cl 5 IP32 . . . . 122 E8
Evergreen La CB8. . . . . 74 C8
Evergreen Rd NR32 . . . 113 B2
Evergreen Way IP28 . . . 116 D6
Everitt Rd NR33. . . . . . 114 D8
Everton Cres IP1 . . . . . 134 F1
Everts Ct 12 CO12. . . . 106 E1
Evesham Cl 7 IP2 . . . . 139 A2
Exchange Sq 6 NR34 . . 111 B5
Exchange St 32 IP20 . . . 22 D6
Exeter Cres IP27 . . . . . 109 F1
Exeter Ct 6 CB9 . . . . . 132 C4
Exeter Rd
  9 Claydon IP6 . . . . 82 B5
  Felixstowe IP11. . . . . 152 F5
  Ipswich IP3 . . . . 140 B4
  Newmarket CB8 . . . . . 121 A4
Exeter Way IP24 . . . . . . 16 A6
Exmoor Rd IP11 . . . . . . 152 F6
EXNING 120 B8
Exning Prim Sch CB8 . . 120 B8
Exning Rd CB8 . . . . 120 D6
EYE 117 D3
Eye Airfield Ind Est IP23 117 A6

Eye Castle★ IP23 . . . . . 117 D2
Eye Hill Dro CB7 . . . . . . 28 B7
Eye Rd
  Brome IP23 . . . . 117 B7
  Yaxley IP23 . . . . 37 C5
EYKE 85 B6
Eyke CE Prim Sch IP12 . 85 B6
Eyke Rd IP12 . . . . 85 A5
Eyre Cl IP33 . . . . 154 B1

F

Factory La
  Brantham CO11 . . . . . 104 E4
  Chevington IP29 . . . . . 62 C5
  Diss IP22 . . . . 20 B3
Factory St NR32. . . . . . 113 D2
Fagbury Rd IP11 . . . . . . 152 A4
Faiers Cl IP33 . . . . 123 B2
Fairbairn Ave 1 IP5 . . . 141 D7
Fair Cl
  Beccles NR34. . . . . . . 111 B5
  14 Feltwell IP26 . . . . . . 4 E5
Fairey Fox Dr 2 IP28 . . 116 B5
Fairfax Ct NR34 . . . . . . 111 B3
Fairfax Dr IP27 . . . . 5 E4
Fairfax Gdns IP6. . . . . . 125 E4
Fairfield Ave IP11 . . . . . 153 A5
Fairfield Cres IP13 . . . . 126 C3
Fairfield Dr
  Lowestoft NR33 . . . . . 114 D6
  Saxmundham IP17. . . . 128 C3
Fairfield Hill IP14 . . . . . 124 D6
Fairfield House Gdns
  IP17 . . . . 128 C3
Fairfield Inf Sch IP11 . . 153 A5
Fairfield Rd
  Aldeburgh IP15 . . . . . 130 D5
  Bungay NR35 . . . . 110 C2
  Framlingham IP13 . . . . 126 D2
  Ipswich IP3 . . . . 140 A2
  Lowestoft NR33 . . . . . 114 D6
  Reydon IP18 . . . . 119 C8
  Saxmundham IP17. . . . 128 C3
Fairfields IP24 . . . . 16 C7
Fairfield Way 12 IP26 . . . 4 E5
Fairhaven Way CB8 . . . . 120 E5
Fairhead Loke NR33. . . . 114 B1
Fairlawns Rd CB8 . . . . . 120 F2
Fairlight Cl 2 IP4 . . . . 136 A1
Fairmead IP30. . . . . 50 F3
Fairmile Cl 2 NR34 . . . 111 F4
Fairstead House Sch
  CB8 . . . . 121 B4
Fairstead The IP22. . . . . 36 A7
Fair View Rd IP19. . . . . 118 C5
Fairways The IP4 . . . . . 140 E5
Fairway The
  Aldeburgh IP15 . . . . . 130 C6
  1 Great Yarmouth NR31 . 3 B8
  Lowestoft NR33 . . . . . 114 F5
Fakenham Hill IP31. . . . 33 F5
FAKENHAM MAGNA . . . 33 E7
Falcon Ave IP22 . . . . . . 20 D3
Falcon Cl CB9 . . . . 133 A6
Falcon Dr IP27 . . . . 6 A1
Falconer Ave 8 IP14. . . 51 E1
Falconer Rd CB9 . . . . . 133 A3
Falcon Inn Rd NR34 . . . 26 C7
Falcon La NR35 . . . . . . 110 B5
Falcon Rd 15 IP26. . . . . 4 E5
Falcon St
  Felixstowe IP11. . . . . 152 E6
  Ipswich IP1 . . . . 155 B2
Falcon Way IP28 . . . . . 13 B1
FALKENHAM 98 E2
Falkenham Rd IP10 . . . . 98 E2
FALKENHAM SINK 98 F2
Falklands Dr 21 CO11. . 104 E2
Falklands Rd CB9 . . . . 132 E7
Fallowfield 2 IP30 . . . . 49 F2
Fallowfield Ct 10 CB9 . . 132 C5
Fallowfields IP17 . . . . . 112 F5
Fallowfield Wlk IP33 . . 123 B1
Falmouth Ave CB8 . . . . 120 F3
Falmouth Cl IP5 . . . . . 141 B6
Falmouth Gdns CB8 . . . 121 A6
Falmouth St CB8 . . . . . 120 F3
Famona Rd NR33 . . . . . 114 C2
Faraday Rd IP3 . . . . . . 139 F5
Farford Field 5 CO10 . . 92 B3
Farina Cl IP1 . . . . 138 F7
FARLEY GREEN 75 D8
Farlingaye High Sch
  IP12 . . . . 146 E6
Farlingayes IP12. . . . . . 146 F7
Farm Cl
  Bungay NR35. . . . . . . 110 D3
  Bury St Edmunds IP33. . 123 B1
  5 Lowestoft NR33 . . . 114 D5
  Wissett IP19 . . . . 24 C2
Farm Ct St IP20. . . . . . . 23 A5
Farmerie Rd CO10 . . . . . 75 D3
Farmland Cl IP18 . . . . . 119 B8
FARNHAM 72 A7
Farnham Cl 5 NR32. . . 112 F4
Farnham Rd
  Blaxhall IP12 . . . . 71 F5
  Snape IP17 . . . . 72 D6
Farriers Cl
  15 Martlesham Heath IP5. . 98 A8
  Stradbroke IP21 . . . . . 39 A4
Farrier's Rd IP14 . . . . . 124 D6
Farriers Went IP11. . . . 152 D7
Farrow Cl IP16 . . . . . . 129 B6

Farthing Dro
  Beck Row, Holywell Row &
    Kenny Hill IP27. . . . . 12 E6
  Lakenheath IP27 . . . . . 13 A6
Farthing Rd IP1 . . . . . . 138 C7
Farthings The IP28 . . . . 31 D3
Farthings Went IP9 . . . . 150 E4
Fastnet Cl CB9 . . . . . . 133 B6
Fastolf St 4 NR32 . . . . 113 A3
Faulkeners Way IP11 . . . 152 C7
Faversham Ct NR33 . . . 115 A4
Fawcett Rd IP15 . . . . . . 130 E4
Fawley Cl IP4. . . . . 140 C7
Fayrefield Rd IP12 . . . . 147 B7
Feast Cl 7 CB7 . . . . 29 A1
Featherbroom Gdns
  IP13 . . . . 127 C5
Feathers Field 3 IP11 . 152 D5
Feilden Way CB8 . . . . . 120 E5
Felaw St IP2 . . . . 155 C1
Felix Cl IP5. . . . . 141 B7
Felix Rd
  Felixstowe IP11. . . . . 153 B4
  Ipswich IP3 . . . . 140 C2
  5 Stowupland IP14 . . . 67 A6
FELIXSTOWE 152 E4
FELIXSTOWE FERRY . . 108 C8
Felixstowe General Hospl
  IP11 . . . . 153 B4
Felixstowe Leisure Ctr
  IP11 . . . . 152 F3
Felixstowe Mus★ IP11 . 107 E2
Felixstowe Rd
  Ipswich IP3 . . . . 139 F4
  8 Martlesham IP5 . . . . 98 A8
Felixstowe Sta IP11 . . . 153 A5
Fellbrigg Ave IP5 . . . . . 140 F6
Fellows Cl IP21 . . . . . . 21 A1
Fell Rd CO9 . . . . 89 A4
Felnor Wlk IP11 . . . . . . 153 B3
FELSHAM 65 A3
Felsham Chase CB5 . . . 44 B5
Felsham Ct IP14 . . . . . 124 F3
Felsham Rd
  Bradfield St Clare IP30 . 64 D4
  Rattlesden IP30. . . . . . 65 C5
Felsham Rise IP17 . . . . 128 C3
Feltons 6 CB7. . . . . 29 A1
Felton Wlk IP32 . . . . . . 122 D8
FELTWELL 4 D5
Feltwell Elementary Sch
  IP26 . . . . 4 E6
Feltwell Pl CB9 . . . . . . 132 F6
Feltwell Prim Sch IP26. . 4 D5
Feltwell Rd IP26 . . . . . . 4 F3
Fen Alder Carr Nature
  Reserve★ IP6 . . . . . 125 D8
Fen Bank CB7 . . . . 29 C6
Fenbridge La CO7 . . . . 151 B3
Fen Bright Circle IP3 . . 144 C7
Fen Ct NR33 . . . . 115 A6
Fengate Dro IP27 . . . . . 5 E2
Fen La
  Ardleigh CO7 . . . . 103 E1
  Beccles NR34. . . . . . . 111 B7
  Beck Row, Holywell Row & Kenny
    Hill IP28. . . . . 13 D1
  Braiseworth IP23 . . . . 37 D3
  Creeting St Peter or West
    Creeting IP6 . . . . . 125 D8
  Ditchingham NR35 . . . . 7 E7
  Garboldisham IP22 . . . 18 D3
  Hitcham IP7 . . . . 79 E5
  Rickinghall Inferior IP22. . 36 A4
  Roydon IP22 . . . . 19 F3
  Stonham Earl IP6. . . . . 67 D4
  Thelnetham IP22. . . . . 18 E1
Fenlands Cres NR33. . . . 114 F6
Fen Meadow IP11. . . . . 152 C8
Fenn Cl
  Halesworth IP19 . . . . 118 A5
  Stowmarket IP14. . . . 124 D4
Fenn La IP12 . . . . 98 D6
Fen Pk CP Sch NR33 . . 115 B6
Fen Rd
  Blo' Norton IP22 . . . . 18 F2
  Pakenham IP31 . . . . . 49 F6
Fen St
  Boxford CO10 . . . . 93 C3
  Hinderclay IP22. . . . . . 18 F1
  Nayland CO6 . . . . 102 D5
FENSTEAD END 76 E5
FEN STREET
  Hopton 18 B2
  Redgrave 19 C2
Fenstreet Rd IP17 . . . . 58 A7
Fenton Rd CB9 . . . . . . 132 F6
Fentons Way IP5 . . . . . 141 C7
Fen View
  Copdock & Washbrook IP8 . 95 F4
  Thorndon IP23 . . . . . . 53 B8
Fen Way IP33. . . . . 154 A4
Fen Wlk IP12 . . . . 146 F4
Ferguson Way IP5 . . . . 141 B8
Fern Ave NR32 . . . . . . 112 D2
Ferndale Ave NR32 . . . 113 B3
Ferndale Cl CB8 . . . . . . 121 B6
Ferndown Rd 3 IP11 . . 153 C6
Ferneley Cres CB8 . . . . 121 A4
Fern Gn Cl 1 NR32 . . . 112 E4
Fern Gr CB9 . . . . 132 C6
Fernhayes Cl IP2 . . . . . 139 A3
FERN HILL 77 B4
Fern Hill CO10 . . . . 77 A4
Fernhill Cl IP12. . . . . . . 147 A7
Fernlea Rd 4 CO12 . . . 107 B3

Ferry La
  Beck Row, Holywell Row &
    Kenny Hill IP28. . . . . 29 F5
  Felixstowe IP11. . . . . 152 C3
Ferry Quay IP12 . . . . . 147 A4
Ferry Rd
  Bawdsey IP12 . . . . . . 99 D1
  Felixstowe IP11. . . . . 153 D7
  Southwold IP18 . . . . . 119 C3
  Sudbourne IP12. . . . . 131 C6
  Walberswick IP18 . . . . 119 B2
FERSFIELD 19 D6
Fersfield Rd IP22 . . . . . 19 D5
Festival Cl 4 IP17 . . . . 72 C8
Festival Rd 14 CB7 . . . . 29 C5
Feveryears Yd 4 IP21 . . 39 D8
Fiddlers La CO7 . . . . . . 151 C5
Fiddlers La IP23. . . . . . 117 F2
Field Cl 3 IP30 . . . . 49 F2
Field Fuller's IP6 . . . . . 135 E4
Field Grange NR32. . . . 112 F5
Field House Gdns IP22 . 20 D2
Field La NR33. . . . . 11 B1
Field Rd IP28 . . . . 116 C5
Field Stile Rd 2 IP18 . . 119 D5
Fields View CO10 . . . . 148 D6
Field Terr Rd CB8 . . . . 120 F5
Field View
  Buckenham IP10. . . . . 98 A4
  8 Thurstow IP31 . . . . 49 E4
Field View Cl IP18 . . . . 119 B8
Field View Dr NR32 . . . 113 A1
Field View Gdns NR34. . 111 D3
Field Way
  Debenham IP14. . . . . . 53 F1
  18 Stanton IP31 . . . . . 34 E4
Field Wlk IP28 . . . . . . 116 C5
Fife Rd IP4 . . . . 136 B1
Finbars Wlk IP4 . . . . . . 139 F5
Finborough Cl IP4 . . . . 140 F6
Finborough Rd IP14 . . . 124 B6
Fincham Rd IP28 . . . . . 116 B5
Finch Cl 7 IP14 . . . . . . 67 A5
Finch Hill CO10 . . . . . . 91 D4
Finchingfield Rd
  Stambourne CO9 . . . . . 89 B1
  Steeple Bumpstead CB9 . 88 E3
Finchley Ave IP28. . . . . 116 B6
Finchley Rd IP4. . . . . . . 139 E6
Findley Cl IP9 . . . . 105 C5
Fingal St IP13 . . . . 39 A1
FINKLE GREEN 89 A2
Finney's Drift IP10 . . . . 145 C3
FINNINGHAM 52 B8
Finningham Rd
  Gislingham IP23 . . . . . 36 D1
  Old Newton with Dagworth
    IP14 . . . . 51 F2
  Rickinghall Superior IP22. . 36 A4
  Walsham le Willows IP31 . 35 D2
Finsbury Pl IP23 . . . . . 154 B1
Finsbury Sq IP33 . . . . . 154 C1
Fir Cl
  Barnby NR34 . . . . 10 C4
  Mundford IP26 . . . . 6 B8
  Wickham Market IP13 . . 127 C6
Fircroft Rd IP1 . . . . 135 A2
Firebrass La IP12 . . . . . 85 C2
Firebronds Rd 7 IP9 . . 105 E7
Firecrest Dr 2 IP14. . . . 124 F7
Firefly Way 1 IP3 . . . . 144 C8
Firfield Cl NR34. . . . . . 111 B3
Fir La NR32. . . . . 113 A2
Firmin Cl IP1 . . . . 139 A6
Fir Rd IP24 . . . . 16 B4
First Ave
  4 Glemsford CO10. . . . 77 B3
  Sudbury CO10 . . . . . . 148 E7
First Dro
  Burwell CB5. . . . . 44 B8
  Lakenheath IP27 . . . . 109 A8
Firs The
  Beccles NR34. . . . . . . 111 F4
  Lakenheath IP27 . . . . 109 E6
  Lowestoft NR33 . . . . . 114 C3
  Southwold IP18 . . . . . 119 B8
Firtree Cl IP32. . . . . . . 122 D7
Fir Tree Cl
  Mildenhall IP28 . . . . . 116 D6
  Weybread IP21 . . . . . . 22 D2
Fir Tree Hill IP9 . . . . . 105 F7
Fir Tree La IP14 . . . . . . 51 C3
Fir Tree Rise IP8. . . . . . 138 C2
Fir Wlk 29 IP12 . . . . . . 13 F2
Fishbane Cl 9 IP3. . . . . 144 A8
Fisher Cl
  Haverhill CB9. . . . . . . 133 B5
  2 Saxmundham IP17. . 128 C2
Fisherman's Way 13 NR33 11 C1
Fisher Rd IP22 . . . . 20 D2
Fisher Row
  Carlton Colville NR32. . 114 B8
  Lowestoft NR33 . . . . . 112 B1
Fisher's Dro IP28 . . . . . 12 D3
Fisher's La
  East Bergholt CO7 . . . 104 E6
  Hoxne IP21 . . . . 38 C8
Fishers The IP5. . . . . . 141 C7
Fisher Theatre★ NR35. . 110 B4
Fish Pond Hill IP9 . . . . 106 B6
Fishpond Rd IP12. . . . . 98 D3
Fishponds Hill CO6 . . . 102 C3
Fishponds La IP9 . . . . . 105 F3
Fishponds Way IP14 . . . 66 C8

Fiske Cl IP32 . . . . **123** E6
Fison Way IP24 . . . . **16** B7
Fitches La IP16 . . . . **129** D1
Fitches The IP17 . . . . **129** A2
Fitzgerald Cl ⁴ CO11 . . . . **104** D2
Fitzgerald Rd
   Bramford IP8 . . . . **134** A1
   Woodbridge IP12 . . . . **147** A6
Fitzgerald Wlk IP33 . . . . . . **122** B6
Fitzmaurice Rd IP3 . . . . . . **140** B3
Fitzroy St
   Ipswich IP1 . . . . **155** B3
   Newmarket CB8 . . . . **121** A1
Fitzwilliam Cl
   Ipswich IP2 . . . . **138** F2
   ⁶ Woodbridge IP12 . . . . . **146** E4
Five Acre La NR35 . . . . **7** E3
Five Acres ⁔ IP9 . . . . **105** E7
Five Cross Ways
   Butley IP12 . . . . **86** B4
   Sudbourne IP12 . . . . **131** B6
   Wetheringsett-cum-Brockford
   IP23 . . . . **53** A7
Fiveways IP28 . . . . **116** F3
Flatford Cl IP14 . . . . **124** E3
Flatford La CO7 . . . . **151** D1
Flatford Mill★ CO7 . . . . . . **151** D1
Flatford Rd
   East Bergholt CO7 . . . . **151** D2
   Haverhill CB9 . . . . **132** A6
Flatts La IP30 . . . . **50** B2
Flavian Cl CB9 . . . . **133** B5
Flax La CO10 . . . . **77** B2
Fleet Dyke Dr NR33 . . . . . . **114** E5
Fleetwood Ave IP11 . . . . . . **153** B5
Fleetwood Rd IP11 . . . . **153** B5
Fleming Ave IP28 . . . . **116** C5
FLEMPTON **47** F8
Flempton Rd IP28 . . . . **47** D5
Flemyng Rd IP33 . . . . **122** A5
Fletcher Cl ³ IP6 . . . . **82** A5
Fletcher Rd IP3 . . . . **140** A1
Fletchers La IP5 . . . . **141** E8
Fletcher's La IP17 . . . . **58** B6
Flindell Dr IP8 . . . . **134** A2
Flint Cl IP2 . . . . **139** B2
FLIXTON **7** D1
Flixton Marsh La NR32 . . **112** B6
Flixton Rd
   Blundeston NR32 . . . . **112** C8
   Bungay NR35 . . . . **110** A1
   Flixton NR35 . . . . **7** E2
   Somerleyton, Ashby &
   Herringfleet NR32 . . . . **2** F4
   St Mary, South Elmham
   otherwise Homersfield
   IP20 . . . . **23** B8
Flora Rd NR33 . . . . **115** A3
Flordon Rd IP6 . . . . **125** E5
Florence Rd NR33 . . . . **115** B3
Florence Way NR35 . . . . **8** D7
Flowerday Cl ⁴ NR31 . . . . **3** B7
FLOWTON **81** C1
Flowton Rd
   Elmsett IP7 . . . . **81** A1
   Flowton IP8 . . . . **95** B8
   Somersham IP8 . . . . **81** C3
Floyd Rd IP32 . . . . **122** D8
Foal's Gn Rd IP21 . . . . **39** D2
FOALS GREEN **39** D2
Fodderfen Dro
   Beck Row, Holywell Row &
   Kenny Hill IP28 . . . . **12** C1
   Feltwell PE38 . . . . **4** A3
Foden Ave IP1 . . . . **134** C2
Folly End IP15 . . . . **130** D5
Folly La
   Bressingham IP22 . . . . **19** F4
   Copdock & Washbrook IP8 . . **95** E2
   Lawshall IP29 . . . . **63** C3
Folly Rd
   Great Waldingfield CO10 . . **92** C6
   Hundon CO10 . . . . **75** F3
   Mildenhall IP28 . . . . **116** A7
Folly The
   Harleston IP14 . . . . **66** C8
   Haughley IP14 . . . . **51** C1
Fonnereau Rd IP1 . . . . **155** B3
Forbes Dr NR34 . . . . **111** B3
Ford Cl
   Beck Row, Holywell Row &
   Kenny Hill IP28 . . . . **29** F7
   Stowmarket IP14 . . . . **124** E4
FORDHAM **29** B1
Fordham Moor CB7 . . . . **29** A3
Fordham Pl
   ⁴ Ipswich IP4 . . . . **140** F5
   ²⁴ Ixworth IP31 . . . . **34** B1
Fordham Rd
   Fordham CB8 . . . . **44** F7
   Freckenham IP28 . . . . **29** D2
   Mount Bures CO6 . . . . **101** C1
   Newmarket CB8 . . . . **120** F7
   Snailwell CB8 . . . . **45** A7
   ⁷ Soham CB7 . . . . **28** D3
   Soham CB7 . . . . **28** F2
   Wormingford CO6 . . . . **101** E2
Fordhams Cl ²¹ IP31 . . . . . . **34** E4
Ford Hill IP12 . . . . **99** B7
Fordley Rd IP17 . . . . **57** F6
Ford Rd IP13 . . . . **71** C5
Fordson Way NR33 . . . . **114** C3
Ford View Rd IP14 . . . . **124** E4
Fore Hamlet IP3 . . . . **139** E5

Fore St
   Framlingham IP13 . . . . **126** D3
   Ipswich IP4 . . . . **155** C2
Forest End CB8 . . . . **46** A7
Forester Cl ⁹ IP8 . . . . **142** E8
Foresters Wlk ⁶ IP6 . . . . . . **82** A5
Forest Gdns ⁹ IP8 . . . . **85** D8
Forest Glade CB9 . . . . **132** D8
Forest La ³ IP5 . . . . **98** A7
Forest Mount NR31 . . . . **2** B7
Forest Prim Sch The IP27 . . **5** F1
Forest Rd IP14 . . . . **66** B6
Forest Ret Pk IP24 . . . . **16** A5
Forest Way IP28 . . . . **116** E4
Forfar Cl
   ² Ipswich IP4 . . . . **136** B1
   Ipswich IP4 . . . . **140** B8
Forge Cl
   ² Benhall IP17 . . . . **72** C8
   Bucklesham IP10 . . . . **98** A4
   Palgrave IP22 . . . . **20** C1
Forge End IP28 . . . . **48** B6
Forge Gr NR34 . . . . **9** B6
Forge St CO7 . . . . **104** A3
Forge Way IP22 . . . . **18** D4
FORNHAM ALL SAINTS . . . **48** B6
Fornham La IP33 . . . . **122** A7
Fornham Rd
   Bury St Edmunds IP32 . . . . **154** B4
   Fornham St Martin IP31 . . . **48** D5
   Great Barton IP31 . . . . **49** A5
FORNHAM ST GENIEVIE . . **48** C6
FORNHAM ST MARTIN **48** C6
Forties Cl CB9 . . . . **133** B6
Fortress Rd NR33 . . . . **114** E3
FORWARD GREEN **67** E7
Foster Cl IP18 . . . . **119** D6
Foster Rd ⁷ CO12 . . . . **106** F3
Foundation St IP4 . . . . **155** B2
Foundry La IP1 . . . . **155** B2
Fountain La CB7 . . . . **28** D4
Fountain Rd ⁴ IP12 . . . . **85** D8
Fountain's La NR34 . . . . **10** C4
Fountains Rd
   Bury St Edmunds IP33 . . . . **122** D2
   Ipswich IP2 . . . . **139** A1
Fountain Way IP18 . . . . **119** C8
FOUR ASHES **35** C1
Four Ash Hill CO9 . . . . **89** C4
Four Elms Residential Sch
   IP14 . . . . **68** A8
Fourth Ave ⁵ CO10 . . . . **77** A3
Four Wheel Dr IP30 . . . . **49** B2
Fowe's La CO10 . . . . **90** D4
Fowler's Cres ² NR32 . . . . . . **3** D4
Fox And Pin La IP29 . . . . **63** E8
FOXASH ESTATE **104** B1
Foxborough Rd NR32 . . . . . **113** A4
Foxburrow Cl CB9 . . . . **132** D7
Foxburrow Farm Nature
   Reserve★ IP12 . . . . **84** D6
Foxburrow Hill NR32 . . . . . **113** A6
Foxburrow Rd ⁶ IP3 . . . . . . **140** F1
Foxburrow Wood Nature
   Reserve★ NR32 . . . . **113** B6
Fox Ct IP14 . . . . **124** D6
FOXEARTH **91** B7
Foxes La
   Ashen CO10 . . . . **89** E5
   Mendham IP20 . . . . **23** B4
Foxes Rd CO10 . . . . **89** E5
Foxes Wlk NR32 . . . . **113** A6
Foxglade NR32 . . . . **112** C2
Foxglove Ave IP6 . . . . **125** D3
Foxglove Cl
   Lowestoft NR33 . . . . **115** A2
   ⁣ Worlingham NR34 . . . . . **111** E3
Foxglove Cres IP3 . . . . **140** E1
Foxglove Rd IP24 . . . . **16** D6
Foxhall Cl CO7 . . . . **151** C6
Foxhall Fields CO7 . . . . **151** C5
Foxhall Rd
   Foxhall IP10 . . . . **98** A6
   Ipswich IP3 . . . . **139** F5
Foxhall Stadium IP4 . . . . . . **141** A5
Fox Hill
   Hollesley IP12 . . . . **99** F7
   St Cross, South Elmham
   IP20 . . . . **23** C7
Fox La IP17 . . . . **42** B1
Fox Lea IP5 . . . . **141** E8
Foxtail Rd IP3 . . . . **144** D8
Foxwood Cl CO11 . . . . **104** B1
Foxwood Cres IP4 . . . . **140** F5
Fox Wood N ⁷ CB7 . . . . **28** D5
Fox Wood S ⁣ CB7 . . . . **28** D5
Fox Yd IP18 . . . . **119** D5
Framfield Rd NR33 . . . . **114** C4
FRAMLINGHAM **126** D2
Framlingham Cl ⁴ IP12 . . . . **85** B3
Framlingham Coll IP13 . . . **126** C4
Framlingham Mere Nature
   Reserve★ IP13 . . . . **126** C4
Framlingham Rd
   Dennington IP13 . . . . **39** F2
   Easton IP13 . . . . **70** E5
   Laxfield IP13 . . . . **40** A2
**Framlingham Castle (remains
   of)★** IP13 . . . . **126** C4
Framlinham Coll Prep Sch
   IP13 . . . . **70** A7
Frampton Cl CB8 . . . . **121** A5
Frampton Rd IP3 . . . . **144** A8
FRAMSDEN **69** B6

Framsden Rd IP14 . . . . **69** E7
Framsden Windmill★
   IP14 . . . . **69** B6
Franciscan Way IP1 . . . . . . **155** B2
Francis Cl
   Haverhill CB9 . . . . **132** D6
   Ipswich IP5 . . . . **141** E8
Francis Rd
   Aldeburgh IP15 . . . . **130** C5
   Ipswich IP3 . . . . **140** B2
Fraser Rd
   Bramford IP8 . . . . **134** B2
   Ipswich IP1 . . . . **138** F7
FRECKENHAM **29** F3
Freckenham Rd
   Freckenham CB7 . . . . **29** E2
   Worlington IP28 . . . . **30** A3
Fred Archer Way CB8 . . . . . **121** A3
Fred Dannatt Rd IP28 . . . . **116** A6
Frederick's Rd ³ NR34 . . . . **111** C4
Frederick Talbot Cl ⁣⁴
   CB7 . . . . **28** D4
Freehold Rd
   Ipswich IP4 . . . . **140** A6
   Needham Market IP6 . . . . . **125** C6
Free La NR35 . . . . **110** A8
Freelands IP14 . . . . **52** E4
Freeman Ave ⁴ IP6 . . . . **82** D6
Freeman Cl IP7 . . . . **149** D7
Freeman Prim Sch The
   IP14 . . . . **67** B7
Freemantle Rd NR33 . . . . . **115** C7
Freewood St IP30 . . . . **64** D6
Freezes Barns CB9 . . . . **88** D4
FRENZE **20** F3
Frenze Hall La IP22 . . . . **20** D3
Frenze Rd IP22 . . . . **20** D2
Frere Cnr ⁷ IP22 . . . . **20** A3
Frere Rd ³⁰ IP20 . . . . **22** C6
Freshfields
   ⁔ Harwich CO12 . . . . **106** F1
   Newmarket CB8 . . . . **120** F4
FRESSINGFIELD **39** D8
Fressingfield CE Prim Sch
   IP21 . . . . **39** D8
Fressingfield Rd IP20 . . . . . **23** C1
FRESTON **143** D3
Freston Hill IP9 . . . . **143** D3
Freston St IP9 . . . . **143** D3
Freston Twr★ IP9 . . . . **143** F4
Friar Cl CB9 . . . . **132** D7
Friars IP9 . . . . **150** F7
Friars Bridge Rd IP1 . . . . . **155** A2
Friars Cl
   Bury St Edmunds IP33 . . . . **154** B1
   ⁷ Felixstowe IP11 . . . . **153** D6
Friars Croft IP21 . . . . **22** D3
Friars Ct
   Melton IP12 . . . . **147** C7
   Sudbury CO10 . . . . **148** C4
Friar's La IP33 . . . . **154** B1
Friars Meadow IP21 . . . . . . **22** D3
Friars Rd IP7 . . . . **149** C6
Friars St
   Ipswich IP1 . . . . **155** B2
   Sudbury CO10 . . . . **148** C5
Friary Meadow IP28 . . . . . . **48** D5
Friday St Farm Maize Maze★
   IP17 . . . . **72** B7
Friday's Orch IP16 . . . . **129** C5
Friday St
   Beck Row, Holywell Row &
   Kenny Hill IP28 . . . . **29** F6
   Rendlesham IP12 . . . . **85** D7
FRIDAY STREET
   Benhall **72** B7
   Brandeston **70** A6
   Rendlesham **85** D7
Friends Field ⁷ CO8 . . . . . . **101** C5
Friends Wlk IP5 . . . . **141** D8
FRISTON **72** F7
Fristonmoor La
   Knodishall IP17 . . . . **57** E1
   Sternfield IP17 . . . . **72** E8
Friston Rd IP12 . . . . **85** C2
Fritillary Cl ⁸ IP8 . . . . **142** E8
FRITTON **2** B7
Fritton Cl
   Ipswich IP2 . . . . **139** A1
   ⁣² Oulton NR32 . . . . **112** F4
Fritton Ct ⁵ CB9 . . . . **132** C4
Fritton Lake & Visitor Ctr★
   NR31 . . . . **2** C6
FRIZZELER'S GREEN **47** C1
Frobisher Rd
   ²¹ Harwich CO12 . . . . **106** F1
   Ipswich IP3 . . . . **139** E1
Frog Hall La IP7 . . . . **149** F6
Frogmore CB8 . . . . **120** B7
Frogs Alley IP9 . . . . **106** F6
Frogs Alley Vineyard★
   IP9 . . . . **106** F7
Frogs Hall Rd CO10 . . . . **78** D5
Frogs Hole NR32 . . . . **2** C5
Fronk's Ave ³ CO12 . . . . **107** B1
Fronk's Rd CO12 . . . . **107** A1
Front Rd IP3 . . . . **144** D8
Front St
   Mendlesham IP14 . . . . **52** E4
   Orford IP12 . . . . **131** B3
   Ousden CB8 . . . . **61** E6
FROSTENDEN **26** C4
FROSTENDEN CORNER **26** D3

Frostenden Cres ⁢
   NR32 . . . . **113** B4
Frowd Cl CB7 . . . . **29** B1
Fryatt Ave ⁷ CO12 . . . . **107** A2
Fryth Cl CB9 . . . . **132** E7
Fuchsia La IP4 . . . . **140** A5
Fulcher Cl IP33 . . . . **123** D2
Fulchers Field IP13 . . . . . . **126** B4
Fulford Cl ⁸ IP28 . . . . **48** C6
Fuller Rd IP4 . . . . **22** D5
Fullers Cl ² IP27 . . . . **149** E6
Fullers Teasle NR33 . . . . . . **114** A3
Fulmar Way NR33 . . . . **114** C5
Fulmerston Rd IP24 . . . . . . **16** B5
Furness Cl IP2 . . . . **142** F8
Further St CO10 . . . . **92** E2
Furthest Dro IP27 . . . . **4** D1
Furze Cl ⁴ IP31 . . . . **49** D4
Furze Way IP22 . . . . **36** D5
Fyffe Way ⁓ NR33 . . . . **115** D8
Fynn La IP6 . . . . **136** C5
Fynn Rd IP12 . . . . **146** D3

G

Gables The CB9 . . . . **133** D3
Gaell Cres ⁵ IP7 . . . . **149** D5
Gage Cl IP33 . . . . **154** A4
Gage's Rd CO10 . . . . **90** C4
GAINSBOROUGH **144** B8
Gainsborough Ctr IP3 . . . . **144** B8
Gainsborough Dr
   Halesworth IP19 . . . . **118** A2
   Lowestoft NR32 . . . . **113** B6
   Manningtree CO11 . . . . **104** D2
Gainsborough La IP3 . . . . . **143** F8
Gainsborough Rd
   Bury St Edmunds IP33 . . . . **122** D5
   Felixstowe IP11 . . . . **153** A4
   Haverhill CB9 . . . . **132** B7
   Ipswich IP3 . . . . **155** C4
   Stowmarket IP14 . . . . **124** B6
   Sudbury CO10 . . . . **148** C5
Gainsborough St CO10 . . . **148** C5
Gainsborough's House★ ⁲⁰
   CO10 . . . . **148** C5
Galley Cl NR33 . . . . **114** B4
Galley Rd CO10 . . . . **75** D3
Gallow La IP30 . . . . **78** C7
Gallows Hill IP7 . . . . **149** B7
Gallows La IP14 . . . . **66** C7
Galway Ave IP1 . . . . **134** E1
Gandish Cl CO7 . . . . **151** D3
Gandish Rd CO7 . . . . **151** E4
Ganges Rd ⁔ IP9 . . . . **107** A4
Gannet Cl CB9 . . . . **133** A6
Gannet Rd IP2 . . . . **138** E3
Ganwick Cl CB9 . . . . **132** D8
Ganymede Cl IP2 . . . . **138** D7
Gaol La
   Beccles NR34 . . . . **111** B5
   Sudbury CO10 . . . . **148** C5
Gap The NR33 . . . . **114** F6
GARBOLDISHAM **18** D4
Garboldisham Rd
   Harling NR16 . . . . **18** C7
   Kenninghall NR16 . . . . **18** C7
Garboldisham VC Prim Sch
   IP22 . . . . **18** D4
Garden Cl
   Bungay NR35 . . . . **110** C3
   ⁵ Great Barton IP31 . . . . . . **49** A6
   Normanston NR32 . . . . **113** B2
   Shotley IP9 . . . . **106** F6
Garden Ct ² CB5 . . . . **44** B6
Gardeners La ²¹ CB7 . . . . . **28** D4
Gardeners Rd IP14 . . . . **53** F1
Gardeners Wlk IP30 . . . . **50** E2
Garden Field ² IP11 . . . . . . **152** E5
Garden Fields IP31 . . . . **33** D3
Gardenhouse La IP22 . . . . . **36** A6
Garden House La IP30 . . . . **65** C6
Garden La
   Beccles NR34 . . . . **111** F4
   Westley IP33 . . . . **122** A5
Garden Pl CO10 . . . . **148** B5
Garden Sq IP12 . . . . **85** D8
Gardens The
   ⁴ Beyton IP30 . . . . **49** F2
   Lowestoft NR33 . . . . **114** C2
Gardiner Cl IP33 . . . . **122** C4
Gardner Rd IP18 . . . . **119** D5
Garfield Cl IP11 . . . . **152** F3
Garfield Rd IP11 . . . . **152** F3
Garland Rd ⁵ CO12 . . . . **106** F3
Garlands CB9 . . . . **132** A6
Garland St IP33 . . . . **154** B3
Garlic St IP21 . . . . **22** A6
GARLIC STREET **22** A6
Garnons Chase ³ CO6 . . . . **101** F2
Garrard Pl ⁣² IP31 . . . . **34** B1
Garrards Rd ³ IP7 . . . . **80** F1
Garrett Cl IP17 . . . . **72** D5
Garrett Cres IP16 . . . . **129** D5
Garrick Way IP1 . . . . **135** A3
Garrison La
   Felixstowe IP11 . . . . **152** F4
   ⁵ Great Waldingfield CO10 **92** C6
Garrod App IP12 . . . . **84** E7
Garrods IP9 . . . . **150** F3
Garrods End CO10 . . . . **29** C5
Gascoigne Dr ³ IP6 . . . . **82** D6
Gashouse Dro IP27 . . . . **5** F1
GASTHORPE **18** A4
Gaston End CO7 . . . . **151** C5
Gaston St CO7 . . . . **151** C4
Gas Works Rd NR32 . . . . . . **113** E2

Gatacre Rd IP1 . . . . **139** A7
Gate Farm Rd ² IP9 . . . . . . **107** A5
Gatesbury's La IP29 . . . . **62** C2
Gateway The IP33 . . . . **123** C3
Gavell St IP19 . . . . **24** D5
Gawdy Cl ² IP20 . . . . **22** D6
Gaye Cres IP23 . . . . **117** B3
Gaye St IP1 . . . . **155** A3
Gayfer Ave IP5 . . . . **141** F8
Gayford Sq IP7 . . . . **80** C6
Gaymers La IP11 . . . . **152** B8
GAZELEY **46** B3
Gazeley Rd
   Ashley CB8 . . . . **46** A1
   Kentford CB8 . . . . **46** A5
Gdn Room The★ IP6 . . . . . **125** D5
GEDDING **65** A5
Gedding Hill IP30 . . . . **65** B4
Gedding Rd IP30 . . . . **65** B7
Gedge Cl IP33 . . . . **122** C4
Gedgrave Rd IP12 . . . . **131** A1
GELDESTON **8** F7
Geldeston Hill NR34 . . . . **8** F6
Geldeston Rd
   Ellingham NR35 . . . . **8** D6
   Geldeston NR34 . . . . **8** F7
General Castle Way IP30 . . **49** B2
Generals Mews ⁣² IP11 . . . **152** D5
GENESIS GREEN **61** F4
Genesta Dr ² IP31 . . . . **49** D4
Geneva Gdns ⁴ NR31 . . . . . . **3** C6
Geneva Rd IP1 . . . . **155** A4
Gentle Ct ³ IP27 . . . . **5** F1
Gents La IP29 . . . . **77** F7
George Baldry Way ²
   NR35 . . . . **110** C2
George Brown Way
   NR34 . . . . **111** C3
George Cl NR32 . . . . **112** E1
George Frost Cl IP4 . . . . . . **155** C4
George Gent Cl ⁷ CB9 . . . . . **88** D3
George Gibson Cl CB8 . . . . **120** C8
George Hill IP31 . . . . **34** A4
George La ³ CO10 . . . . **77** B2
George Lambton Ave
   CB8 . . . . **120** F5
George Rd ³ IP24 . . . . **16** C6
George St
   Brandon IP27 . . . . **5** F1
   Hadleigh IP7 . . . . **149** E6
   ² Harwich CO12 . . . . **107** A5
   Hintlesham IP8 . . . . **95** C6
George Westwood Way
   NR34 . . . . **111** C6
Geralds Ave IP4 . . . . **140** A5
GESTINGTHORPE **90** F1
Gestingthorpe Rd CO10 . . . **90** F2
Gibbon Cl IP32 . . . . **123** E5
Gibraltar Cl IP33 . . . . **122** C6
Gibraltar Rd IP6 . . . . **69** B1
Gifford Cl ⁶ IP9 . . . . **105** E7
Giffords Pl IP4 . . . . **140** F6
Giggle Factory The★
   IP7 . . . . **148** F7
Gilbert Cl IP6 . . . . **125** C5
Gilbert Rd ² CO10 . . . . **90** A8
Giles Way
   Risby IP29 . . . . **47** E5
   ⁴ Witnesham IP6 . . . . **83** A5
GILLINGHAM **9** C6
Gillingham Rd NR34 . . . . **9** A6
Gillngham Dam NR34 . . . . . **111** C5
Gilpin Rd IP22 . . . . **112** D1
Gilray Rd IP22 . . . . **20** D2
Gilstrap Rd IP31 . . . . **48** D5
Gimbert Rd ⁷ CB7 . . . . **28** D4
Gin La IP13 . . . . **40** C2
Gippeswyk Ave IP2 . . . . . . **139** A4
Gippeswyk Rd IP2 . . . . **155** A1
GIPPING **52** B2
Gipping Cl CB9 . . . . **132** C4
Gipping Pl IP14 . . . . **124** D7
Gipping Rd
   Claydon IP6 . . . . **82** A5
   Stowupland IP14 . . . . **67** A5
Gippingstone Rd IP8 . . . . **134** A1
Gipping Way
   Bramford IP8 . . . . **134** B2
   Sproughton IP8 . . . . **138** B6
   Stowmarket IP14 . . . . **124** D7
Gipsy La
   Aldringham cum Thorpe
   IP16 . . . . **129** D1
   Frostenden NR34 . . . . **26** D4
   Needham Market IP6 . . . . . **125** C4
GIPSY ROW **150** A4
Girling St CO10 . . . . **148** C6
Girton Cl
   Mildenhall IP28 . . . . **116** C6
   Woodbridge IP12 . . . . **146** D4
   Woodditton CB8 . . . . **121** B1
Girton Rd CB9 . . . . **132** F5
Girton Way IP2 . . . . **138** F1
GISLEHAM **11** A3
Gisleham Rd NR33 . . . . **114** B1
GISLINGHAM **36** D2
Gislingham CE Prim Sch
   IP23 . . . . **36** C2
Gislingham Rd IP14 . . . . **36** C1
GISSING **20** F8
Gissing Rd IP22 . . . . **20** F6
Glade Prim Sch The IP27 . . **5** F1
Glades The IP32 . . . . **112** D2
Glade The IP24 . . . . **16** C7
Gladstone Rd
   ⁣ Corton NR32 . . . . **3** C4
   Ipswich IP3 . . . . **139** F5
   ⁶ Woodbridge IP12 . . . . . . **147** A5

Glamis Cl CB9 . . . . 132 B6
Glamis Ct 26 IP20 . . . . 22 C6
Glamorgan Rd IP2 . . . . 139 B1
Glanely Gdns CB8 . . . . 120 C8
Glanfield Wlk IP33 . . . . 122 C4
Glanville Pl IP5 . . . . 141 B6
Glanville Rd IP7 . . . . 149 E4
Glassfield Rd IP31 . . . . 34 C4
Glastonbury Cl IP2 . . . . . . 138 F1
Glastonbury Rd IP33 . . . . . 122 C3
Glebe Cl
  Bayham IP6 . . . . 81 E6
  Horringer IP29 . . . . 63 A7
  Ingham IP31 . . . . 32 F1
  Lowestoft NR32 . . . . 113 C5
  Sproughton IP8 . . . . 138 B6
  1 Tattingstone IP9 . . . . . 105 B8
  2 Thetford IP24 . . . . 16 C6
Glebe End IP9 . . . . 150 F4
Glebe La IP9 . . . . 144 B1
Glebe Meadow IP13 . . . . . . 54 F2
Glebe Rd
  Bredfield IP13 . . . . 84 C7
  Gissing IP21 . . . . 21 A8
  Weeting IP27 . . . . 5 E3
Glebe Rd E 15 NR32 . . . . . . 11 C1
Glebe Rd W 18 NR33 . . . . . . 11 B1
Glebes The IP17 . . . . 72 D5
Glebe The
  Haverhill CB9 . . . . 132 E7
  Lavenham CO10 . . . . 78 D3
Glebe View NR34 . . . . 111 C3
Glebe Way
  1 Claydon IP6 . . . . 82 B5
  Mendlesham IP14 . . . . 52 E4
Glemham Dr IP4 . . . . 140 F4
Glemham Hall* IP13 . . . . . 71 E6
Glemham Rd IP17 . . . . 56 E2
GLEMSFORD 77 B2
Glemsford Cl IP11 . . . . 152 D3
Glemsford Com Prim Sch
  CO10 . . . . 77 A3
Glemsford Pl 7 CB9 . . . . . 132 F6
Glemsford Rd
  Lowestoft NR32 . . . . 112 F4
  Stowmarket IP14 . . . . 124 E4
Glenavon Rd IP4 . . . . 140 D7
Glenbourne Wlk 2
  NR33 . . . . 114 C3
Glencoe Rd IP4 . . . . 136 C1
Gleneagles Cl
  4 Bury St Edmunds IP28 . . 48 C6
  1 Felixstowe IP11 . . . . . . 153 C6
Gleneagles Dr IP4 . . . . 140 D5
Glenfield Ave IP11 . . . . . . 153 A6
Glenhurst Ave IP4 . . . . 140 B8
Glenside CO10 . . . . 148 E4
Glenwood Ct CB8 . . . . 120 F3
Glenwood Dr NR34 . . . . . . 111 E4
Globe Yd 3 CO10 . . . . 148 C6
Gloster Rd IP5 . . . . 98 A8
Gloucester Ave NR32 . . . . . 112 F3
Gloucester Pl 4 CO10 . . . . 76 A1
Gloucester Rd
  4 Bury St Edmunds
  IP32 . . . . 122 E8
  Haverhill CB9 . . . . 132 D5
  Ipswich IP3 . . . . 140 A2
Gloucester Way CO10 . . . . 148 B8
Go Ape* IP27 . . . . 15 C8
Gobbets La IP22 . . . . 35 E7
Gobbett's Rd IP22 . . . . 35 E8
Gobbitts Yd IP12 . . . . 147 A4
Godbold Cl 3 IP5 . . . . 141 D7
Goddard Pl IP14 . . . . 66 B7
Goddard Rd IP1 . . . . 134 C3
Goddard Rd E IP1 . . . . 134 D3
GODDARD'S CORNER 55 E7
Godetia Ct 6 NR32 . . . . . . 113 B4
Godfrey's Ct 12 NR32 . . . . 113 C7
Godfrey's Hill IP19 . . . . 40 F8
Godfrey's Wood IP12 . . . . 147 A7
Godolphin Cl IP33 . . . . . . 122 C3
Godyll Rd IP18 . . . . 119 C5
Goldcrest Rd IP2 . . . . 138 C5
Golden La IP29 . . . . 63 C2
Golden Lion La 5 CO12 . . 107 B3
Goldenlond CO6 . . . . 102 E7
Golden Miller Cl CB8 . . . . 120 D7
Goldings Cl CB9 . . . . 132 E8
Golding's La IP16 . . . . 129 C4
Golding Way 1 CO10 . . . . . 77 A2
Goldsmith Cl IP32 . . . . . . 122 D7
Goldsmith Rd IP1 . . . . 134 C3
Goldsmith Way IP21 . . . . . . 21 F8
Golf La IP15 . . . . 130 C6
Golf Links Rd
  Barton Mills IP28 . . . . 30 C3
  Worlington IP28 . . . . 116 A1
Golf Rd IP11 . . . . 153 D5
Gondree NR33 . . . . 114 E3
Gonville Cl
  Mildenhall IP28 . . . . 116 D6
  1 Woodbridge IP12 . . . . 146 E4
Goodall Terr IP11 . . . . 141 E8
Goodchilds Gdns 8 CB7 . . 29 C5
Goodlake Cl 6 CO12 . . . . . 106 F1
Goodman Gr IP5 . . . . 141 E7
Goodwood Cl IP1 . . . . 135 B4
Goosander Rd IP24 . . . . . . 124 F6
Goose Gn E NR34 . . . . 111 C5
Goose Gn W NR34 . . . . 111 C5
Gorams Mill La IP13 . . . . . . 40 B3
Gordon Rd
  California IP4 . . . . 140 A6
  5 Harwich CO12 . . . . . . 107 A1
  Ipswich IP4 . . . . 140 A7
  Lowestoft NR32 . . . . 113 D1

Gordon Richards Cl CB8 . 120 F6
Goring Rd IP4 . . . . 140 C6
Gorleston Rd
  Blundeston NR32 . . . . . . 112 F8
  Corton NR32 . . . . 3 B4
Gorse Cl
  Lakenheath IP27 . . . . 109 E4
  6 Red Lodge IP28 . . . . . . 30 C1
Gorse Gn NR32 . . . . 113 B3
Gorsehayes IP2 . . . . 139 B3
Gorse Ind Est IP24 . . . . 16 A3
Gorse La IP18 . . . . 119 C7
Gorseland Prim Sch IP5 . . 141 E8
Gorselands IP12 . . . . 99 F7
Gorse Rd
  Ipswich IP3 . . . . 140 B2
  Southwold IP18 . . . . 119 C6
Gorse View IP17 . . . . 58 C8
Gorst Cl 7 IP32 . . . . 122 E8
GOSBECK 68 D2
Gosford Cl 4 CO10 . . . . . . 90 A8
Gosford Rd NR34 . . . . 111 C5
Gosford Way IP11 . . . . 153 C6
GOSLAND GREEN 76 A5
GOSLING GREEN 93 C5
Gostling Cl 2 IP22 . . . . 20 B2
Gostling Pl IP5 . . . . 141 E8
Gothic Cl IP2 . . . . 22 D5
Gotsfield Cl 1 CO10 . . . . . . 92 B7
Gough Pl 9 IP31 . . . . 34 B1
Governors Mews IP33 . . . . 123 C2
Gowers Cl IP5 . . . . 141 E7
Gowers End 6 CO10 . . . . . . 77 B3
Gower St IP2 . . . . 155 B1
Gowle Rd IP14 . . . . 124 C8
Goyfield Ave IP11 . . . . 152 F4
Gracechurch St IP14 . . . . . . 53 E2
Graften Way IP1 . . . . 155 A2
Grafton Cl IP33 . . . . 122 D5
Grafton Rd 2 CO12 . . . . . . 107 B2
Grafton Way IP1 . . . . 155 B2
Graham Ave IP1 . . . . 139 B8
Graham Rd
  Felixstowe IP11 . . . . 152 F5
  Ipswich IP1 . . . . 155 A1
Grainger Cl IP32 . . . . 123 F5
Granby St CB8 . . . . 121 B2
Granary Crafts* IP14 . . . . . 66 A5
Granary Rd CB8 . . . . 121 B2
Granary The
  Clare CO10 . . . . 90 A7
  Hadleigh IP7 . . . . 149 E5
Granby St CB8 . . . . 121 B2
Grand Ave NR33 . . . . 115 B3
Grange Cl
  Felixstowe IP11 . . . . 152 E5
  Ipswich IP5 . . . . 141 E6
Grange Ct IP12 . . . . 147 B6
Grange Farm Ave IP11 . . . 152 D5
Grange La
  Barton Mills IP28 . . . . . . 116 D2
  Burgh St Peter NR34 . . . . . 10 C8
  Cockfield IP30 . . . . 64 D2
  Creeting St Mary IP14 . . . . 67 F5
  Ditchingham NR35 . . . . . . 110 C7
  6 Feltwell IP26 . . . . 4 E5
  Frostenden NR34 . . . . 26 C4
  Great Barton IP31 . . . . 49 B5
  Hundon CB9 . . . . 75 D2
  Kessingland NR33 . . . . 11 C1
  3 Martlesham IP12 . . . . . . 84 A1
  Pettistree IP13 . . . . 127 D5
  Redenhall with Harleston
  IP20 . . . . 22 E6
  Reydon IP18 . . . . 26 E1
  Shipmeadow NR34 . . . . 8 F5
  Somerleyton, Ashby &
  Herringfleet NR32 . . . . . . 2 E4
  Southwold IP18 . . . . 119 B8
  Starston IP20 . . . . 22 D8
  Stratford St Mary CO7 . . . 103 E6
  Syleham IP21 . . . . 38 E8
  2 Tattingstone IP9 . . . . . 105 B8
  Thelnetham IP22 . . . . 35 C6
  Thetford IP24 . . . . 16 C6
  Thrandeston IP21 . . . . 37 B6
  Troston IP31 . . . . 33 D6
  Tuddenham St Martin IP6 . 136 C4
  Wetheringsett-cum-Brockford
  IP14 . . . . 53 A6
Green La Cl IP18 . . . . 119 B8
Green Man Pl IP12 . . . . 71 F2
Green Man Way IP12 . . . . 147 B6
Green Oak Glade IP8 . . . . 142 D8
Green Pk
  Brinkley CB8 . . . . 59 E1
  42 Harleston IP20 . . . . . . 22 D6
Green Rd
  Brandon IP27 . . . . 6 A1
  Newmarket CB8 . . . . 121 A2
  Thorpe Morieux IP30 . . . . . 64 F1
  Woolpit IP30 . . . . 50 D1
Greensmill 2 CO11 . . . . . . 104 C3
Greenspire Gr IP8 . . . . 138 B2
Green St IP21 . . . . 38 C8
Greens The
  Aldeburgh IP15 . . . . 130 C6
  Ipswich IP4 . . . . 140 F4
GREENSTREET GREEN . . . 80 D5
Green The
  4 Ashley CB8 . . . . 60 F8
  Beck Row, Holywell Row & Kenny
  Hill IP28 . . . . 29 E7
  Chedburgh IP29 . . . . 62 C4
  8 Earsham NR35 . . . . 7 F7
  Fornham All Saints IP26 . . 48 B6
  1 Grundisburgh IP13 . . . . 83 E5

Great Cornard Sports Ctr
  CO10 . . . . 148 F2
Great Cornard Upper Sch
  CO10 . . . . 148 F2
Great Dro CB7 . . . . 28 A4
Great Eastern Rd CO10 . . . 148 D5
Great Eastern Sq IP11 . . . . 153 A5
Great Fen Rd CB7 . . . . 28 D8
Great Field IP11 . . . . 152 C8
GREAT FINBOROUGH 66 B4
Great Finborough Prim Sch
  IP14 . . . . 66 A4
Great Gipping St IP1 . . . . . 155 A2
GREAT GLEMHAM 71 D8
GREAT GREEN
  Burgate 36 D7
  Cockfield 64 D7
  Denton 7 A4
  Thrandeston 37 C8
Great Harlings IP9 . . . . . . 107 A5
Great Heath Prim Sch
  IP28 . . . . 116 D6
GREAT HORKESLEY 102 E1
GREAT LIVERMERE 33 C2
Great Oak Ct CO9 . . . . 90 A1
GREAT SAXHAM 47 C1
GREAT THURLOW 74 E5
Great Tufts IP7 . . . . 150 F3
GREAT WALDINGFIELD . . . 92 C6
Great Waldingfield VCE Prim
  Sch CO10 . . . . 92 C6
GREAT WELNETHAM 63 F6
GREAT WENHAM 150 A3
Great Whelnetham CE Prim
  Sch IP30 . . . . 63 F6
Great Whip St IP2 . . . . 155 B1
GREAT WRATTING 74 E3
GREAT YELDHAM 90 A1
Grebe Cl
  Ipswich IP2 . . . . 138 E2
  Mildenhall IP28 . . . . 116 D3
  Stowmarket IP14 . . . . . . 124 A6
Green Acre 2 CO10 . . . . . . 92 C6
Greenacre Cres 1 NR32 . . 113 B2
Greenacres IP14 . . . . 51 F1
Greenbank IP19 . . . . 118 C5
Green Cres IP10 . . . . 98 A4
Green Dr NR33 . . . . 115 A4
Greene King Brewing Mus*
  IP33 . . . . 154 C1
Greene Rd IP33 . . . . 122 C6
Green Farm La 5 IP29 . . . . 47 A2
Greenfield Rd NR33 . . . . . 114 F5
Greenfields CB8 . . . . 121 C5
Greenfields Way CB9 . . . . 132 C5
Greenfinch Ave IP2 . . . . . . 138 D3
Greenfinch Cl IP14 . . . . . . 124 F7
Green Fleet Dr NR32 . . . . . 112 E4
Green Hill IP6 . . . . 68 B1
Greenhills CB7 . . . . 28 E3
Green La
  Boxted CO4 . . . . 102 E3
  Burgh St Peter NR34 . . . . . 10 C8
  Cockfield IP30 . . . . 64 D2
  Creeting St Mary IP14 . . . . 67 F5
  Ditchingham NR35 . . . . . . 110 C7
  6 Feltwell IP26 . . . . 4 E5
  Frostenden NR34 . . . . 26 C4
  Great Barton IP31 . . . . 49 B5
  Hundon CB9 . . . . 75 D2
  Kessingland NR33 . . . . 11 C1
  3 Martlesham IP12 . . . . . . 84 A1
  Pettistree IP13 . . . . 127 D5
  Redenhall with Harleston
  IP20 . . . . 22 E6
  Reydon IP18 . . . . 26 E1
  Shipmeadow NR34 . . . . 8 F5
  Somerleyton, Ashby &
  Herringfleet NR32 . . . . . . 2 E4
  Southwold IP18 . . . . 119 B8
  Starston IP20 . . . . 22 D8
  Stratford St Mary CO7 . . . 103 E6
  Syleham IP21 . . . . 38 E8
  2 Tattingstone IP9 . . . . . 105 B8
  Thelnetham IP22 . . . . 35 C6
  Thetford IP24 . . . . 16 C6
  Thrandeston IP21 . . . . 37 B6
  Troston IP31 . . . . 33 D6
  Tuddenham St Martin IP6 . 136 C4
  Wetheringsett-cum-Brockford
  IP14 . . . . 53 A6

Green The continued
  Hadleigh IP7 . . . . 149 E6
  Hessett IP30 . . . . 64 F8
  Kersey IP7 . . . . 94 A7
  Kirtling CB8 . . . . 60 E3
  Lound NR32 . . . . 2 F6
  Lowestoft NR33 . . . . 114 F6
  Mendlesham IP14 . . . . 52 D2
  2 Mistley CO11 . . . . 104 F2
  North Lopham IP22 . . . . . . 19 A6
  Snailwell CB8 . . . . 45 A6
  Walberswick IP18 . . . . . . 119 B2
Greenview IP29 . . . . 77 B7
Greenway 4 IP31 . . . . 49 A5
Greenways IP12 . . . . 85 C2
Greenways Cl IP1 . . . . 139 B8
Greenways Cres IP32 . . . . 123 D6
Greenway The NR34 . . . . . 111 B4
GREENWICH 139 E1
Greenwich Bsns Pk IP3 . . 139 E2
Greenwich Cl IP3 . . . . 139 E2
Greenwich Rd IP3 . . . . . . 139 D2
Green Willows CO10 . . . . . 78 C2
Greenwood Cl CB9 . . . . . . 132 C5
Greenwoods The IP31 . . . . 49 E6
Greenwood Way 1
  NR32 . . . . 113 A6
Gregory Rd IP28 . . . . 116 A6
Gregory St CO10 . . . . 148 C5
Grenadier Rd CB9 . . . . 132 A6
Grenville Rd CO10 . . . . . . 148 D8
Gresham Ave NR32 . . . . . . 112 F2
Gresham Cl NR32 . . . . 112 F2
Gresham Rd NR34 . . . . . . 111 C6
Gresley Gdns IP3 . . . . 139 C3
Gretna Gdns 1 IP4 . . . . . . 136 B1
Greville Starkey Ave
  CB8 . . . . 121 A5
Greyfriars* IP17 . . . . 43 B1
Greyfriars*
  Ipswich IP1 . . . . 155 A2
  Woodbridge IP12 . . . . . . 146 D4
Greyfriars Rd IP32 . . . . . . 123 E4
Grey Friars Rd IP1 . . . . . . 155 B2
Greyhound Hill CO4 . . . . . 103 C2
Greyhound La IP22 . . . . 18 B1
Greyhound Rd 7 CO10 . . . . 77 A2
Greys Cl 5 CO10 . . . . 76 E1
Greys Cl B 75 A3
Grice Cl 3 NR33 . . . . 11 C1
Griffith Cl 4 NR33 . . . . 11 C1
Grime's Graves (Flint
  Mines)* IP27 . . . . 6 C4
Grimsey Rd IP16 . . . . 129 D5
Grimsey's La IP16 . . . . 129 E5
GRIMSTONE END 49 F8
Grimston La IP11 . . . . 107 C8
Grimwade Cl 2 CO11 . . . . 104 E4
Grimwade St IP4 . . . . 155 C2
Grinder's La IP21 . . . . 22 D4
Grindle Gdns IP33 . . . . . . 123 B3
Grindle The IP8 . . . . 95 F8
Grinstead Gdns IP6 . . . . . 125 E3
GRINSTEAD HILL 125 E3
Grinstead Hill IP6 . . . . 125 E3
GROMFORD 72 C5
Gromford La IP17 . . . . 72 C5
Groomes Cl 6 NR31 . . . . . . 3 B7
Grosvenor Cl IP4 . . . . 139 E8
Grosvenor Gdns IP33 . . . . 122 F3
Grosvenor House Ct 9
  IP28 . . . . 116 B5
Grosvenor Rd
  Lowestoft NR33 . . . . 115 C7
  Sudbury CO10 . . . . 148 B8
Grosvenor Yd CB8 . . . . . . 121 A3
GROTON 93 B4
Groton St CO10 . . . . 93 B5
Groton Wood Nature
  Reserve* CO10 . . . . 93 D6
Grove Ave IP28 . . . . 92 E8
Grove City Prim Sch
  NR33 . . . . 114 C4
Grove End IP17 . . . . 39 B5
Grove Gdns
  Carlton Colville NR33 . . . . 114 C4
  Fordham CB7 . . . . 29 A2
  Woodbridge IP12 . . . . . . 146 E6
Grove; Henley Rd The
  IP1 . . . . 135 C2
Grove Hill
  Belstead IP8 . . . . 142 C7
  Dedham CO7 . . . . 103 E2
  Langham CO4 . . . . 103 C3
Grove La
  Ashfield cum Thorpe IP14 . . 54 C2
  Elmswell IP30 . . . . 51 A3
  Harkstead IP9 . . . . 106 C7
  Ipswich IP4 . . . . 139 E5
  Mendham IP20 . . . . 23 A2
  Stanton IP31 . . . . 34 F4
  Thetford IP24 . . . . 16 C6
Grove Mews 4 NR34 . . . . . 111 C4
Grove Pk
  Bury St Edmunds IP33 . . . 154 A3
  Fordham CB7 . . . . 29 A2
  5 Walsham le Willows
  IP31 . . . . 35 C2
Grove Rd
  Beccles NR34 . . . . 111 B5
  2 Brantham CO11 . . . . . . 104 E4
  Brockdish IP21 . . . . 21 F3
  Bury St Edmunds IP33 . . . 154 A3
  Felixstowe IP11 . . . . 153 A6
  Gissing IP21 . . . . 21 A8
  Knodishall IP17 . . . . 72 F7
  Lowestoft NR33 . . . . 114 C4
  Pettistree IP13 . . . . 127 A4

Grove Rd continued
  Starston IP20 . . . . 22 C6
  Walsham le Willows IP31 . . 35 C2
  Woodbridge IP12 . . . . . . 146 E6
Grove Rd N IP33 . . . . 114 D5
Grove The
  Great Glemham IP17 . . . . . 56 F1
  12 Martlesham Heath IP5 . . 98 A8
  Mildenhall IP28 . . . . 29 F8
  Stowmarket IP14 . . . . . . 124 E5
  5 Woodbridge IP12 . . . . 147 B6
Grove Wlk IP8 . . . . 142 D8
Grub La IP19 . . . . 24 E5
GRUNDISBURGH 83 D5
Grundisburgh Cty Prim Sch
  IP13 . . . . 83 E5
Grundisburgh Rd
  Clopton IP13 . . . . 83 D8
  Great Bealings IP13 . . . . . 137 C6
  Tuddenham St Martin IP6 . 136 D6
Grundle Cl 6 IP31 . . . . 34 E4
Guildhall Feoffment Cty Prim
  Sch IP33 . . . . 154 C1
Guildhall La NR34 . . . . 26 D5
Guildhall of Corpus Christi
  The* CO10 . . . . 78 D4
Guildhall St IP33 . . . . 154 B2
Guineas Cl CB8 . . . . 120 C8
Guineas Sh Ctr The CB8 . . 121 A4
Gules Gn IP21 . . . . 22 F1
Gullemot Cl IP14 . . . . 124 F6
Gull Hill IP19 . . . . 25 C3
GULLING GREEN 63 A3
Gull La
  Grundisburgh IP13 . . . . . . 83 D6
  Thornham Magna IP23 . . . 37 A2
Gull Rd IP17 . . . . 128 B3
Gull's La CO7 . . . . 104 A2
Gull The IP13 . . . . 70 C2
Gulpher Bsns Pk IP11 . . . . 152 F8
Gulpher Rd IP11 . . . . 152 E6
Gun Hill
  Dedham CO7 . . . . 103 D4
  Southwold IP18 . . . . 119 D4
Gun La NR32 . . . . 113 E2
GUNTON 113 C6
Gunton Ave NR32 . . . . 113 A7
Gunton Church La NR32 . . 113 C5
Gunton Cliff NR32 . . . . . . 113 D5
Gunton Com Prim Sch
  NR32 . . . . 113 C6
Gunton Dr NR32 . . . . 113 D5
Gunton St Peter's Ave
  NR32 . . . . 113 C5
Guntons 3 CB7 . . . . 28 D4
Gunton Warren Nature
  Reserve* NR32 . . . . 113 D6
Gurdon Rd 5 IP13 . . . . 83 E5
Gurlings CB9 . . . . 132 E8
Guscot Cl NR32 . . . . 113 A6
Gusford Prim Sch IP2 . . . . 138 D1
Guston Gdns IP10 . . . . 98 E2
Guthrum Rd IP7 . . . . 149 D6
Guyatt Ct 8 CB5 . . . . 44 A5
Guy Cook Cl CO10 . . . . . . 92 B2
Gwendoline Rd IP4 . . . . . . 140 E4
Gwynne Rd 4 CO12 . . . . . . 107 B2
Gymnasium St IP1 . . . . . . 155 A3

H

HACHESTON 71 A6
Hacheston Rd IP13 . . . . 70 F5
Hackney Rd
  Peasenhall IP17 . . . . 56 E8
  Woodbridge IP12 . . . . . . 147 B6
Hackney's Cnr IP6 . . . . 81 F5
Hackney Terr IP12 . . . . . . 147 B6
Haddiscoe Sta NR31 . . . . . . 2 A5
Hadenham Rd NR33 . . . . . 114 F1
HADLEIGH 149 F6
Hadleigh Bsns Pk IP7 . . . . 94 E4
Hadleigh Dr IP33 . . . . 112 F3
Hadleigh Guildall* IP7 . . . 149 D5
HADLEIGH HEATH 93 F4
Hadleigh High Sch IP7 . . . 149 F5
Hadleigh Prim Sch IP7 . . . 149 D6
Hadleigh Railway Walk*
  IP7 . . . . 94 E3
Hadleigh Rd
  Aldham IP7 . . . . 94 A4
  Bildeston IP7 . . . . 79 F3
  Boxford CO6 . . . . 93 D2
  East Bergholt CO7 . . . . . . 151 B4
  Elmsett IP7 . . . . 80 F1
  Higham CO7 . . . . 103 D7
  Ipswich IP2 . . . . 138 C4
Hadleigh Rd Ind Est IP2 . . 138 F7
Hadleigh Swimming Pool
  IP7 . . . . 149 D6
Hadrian Cl CB9 . . . . 133 B5
Haggars Mead IP14 . . . . . . 67 D7
HAGMORE GREEN 93 B2
Hague Cl NR33 . . . . 114 C6
Halcyon Cres NR32 . . . . . . 113 C1
Hale Cl IP12 . . . . 138 D2
Hales Barn Rd CB9 . . . . . . 132 C8
Halesowen Cl IP2 . . . . 142 F8
HALESWORTH 118 A4
Halesworth & District Mus*
  IP19 . . . . 118 B4
Halesworth Sta* IP19 . . . . 118 B3
Halesworth (Holton) Airfield
  Mus* IP19 . . . . 118 D6

Halesworth Mid Sch IP19 118 C5
Halesworth Millennium Green IP19 118 B3
Halesworth Rd
Brampton with Stoven IP19 25 E3
Heveningham IP19 40 F3
Linstead Parva IP19 40 F8
Reydon IP18 119 B7
Sibton IP17 41 B1
St Andrew, Ilketshall NR34 25 A6
St Lawrence, Ilketshall NR34 24 E8
Uggeshall NR34 25 F3
Walpole IP19 41 C5
Wenhaston with Mells Hamlet IP19 41 F6
Halesworth Sta IP19 118 B4
Halfar Rd 2 IP31 33 D5
Halfmoon La IP27 109 C7
Half Moon La
6 Grundisburgh IP13 83 E5
Redgrave IP22 36 A8
Half Moon St IP30 65 D5
Halford Ct 6 IP8 138 C2
Halford La IP22 19 D3
Halifax Prim Sch IP2 139 A2
Halifax Rd
Ipswich IP2 139 B2
9 Mildenhall IP28 30 A8
Halifax St IP27 109 F1
Halifax Way CB8 120 E5
Haling Way IP24 16 A6
Hall Barn Rd CB7 29 B5
Hall Cl IP29 62 B4
Hall Cl The IP28 31 D4
Hall Dr
17 Feltwell IP26 4 E5
Lakenheath IP27 109 C7
Lowestoft NR32 112 C1
Santon Downham IP27 6 C2
Hall Farm Cl IP12 147 B8
Hall Farm La NR34 10 E1
Hall Farm Rd
Boot Street IP13 137 E6
Woodbridge IP12 147 B8
Hall Field 1 IP11 152 E5
Hallfields IP27 109 C7
HALL GREEN 90 C2
Hallifax Pl IP29 77 F7
Halliwell Rd IP4 140 B6
Hall La
Blundeston NR32 3 A4
Bressingham IP22 19 D5
Brinkley CB8 59 F1
Burston & Shimpling IP21 21 A6
Burwell CB5 44 A5
Claydon IP6 134 E8
Harwich CO12 107 A1
Hawkedon CO10 76 C7
Otley IP6 69 C2
Oulton NR32 112 C4
Redgrave IP22 36 A8
Ridgewell CO9 89 D3
Risby IP28 47 D5
Roydon IP22 20 A3
Scole IP21 21 C4
Shelfanger IP22 20 B6
Somersham IP8 81 C3
Spexhall IP19 24 E4
Wetheringsett-cum-Brockford IP14 53 B4
3 Witnesham IP6 83 A5
Yaxley IP23 37 B4
Hall Pond Way IP11 152 D5
Hall Rd
Barnardiston CB8 75 B5
Barsham NR34 8 F3
Bedingfield IP23 54 A7
Bedingham NR35 7 C7
Belchamp Walter CO10 91 A3
Blundeston NR32 112 C8
Borley CO10 91 D5
Brent Eleigh CO10 79 A3
Brockdish IP21 22 A3
Burston & Shimpling IP22 20 E7
Carlton Colville NR33 114 B2
Charsfield IP13 69 F3
Chelsworth IP7 79 E2
Cowlinge CB8 75 A7
Earsham NR35 7 E4
Ellingham NR35 8 C7
Foxhall IP10 141 E4
7 Hopton on Sea NR31 3 B7
Hundon CO10 75 E4
9 Kessingland NR33 11 C1
Lavenham CO10 78 D4
Little Bealings IP5 137 E2
Lowestoft NR32 112 D1
Marlesford IP13 71 C5
Mount Bures CO8 101 C3
Parham IP13 71 B7
Pulham St Mary IP21 22 A8
Stowmarket IP14 124 B8
Thorndon IP23 53 C7
Wenhaston with Mells Hamlet IP19 42 D5
Hall Rise CO10 148 A3
Halls Drift IP5 141 B6
Hall's La IP31 50 B5
Hall St
Long Melford CO10 91 E8
Soham CB7 28 D4
Hall Wlk IP8 81 F1
Hallwong La IP20 22 D7
Hallwyck Gdns CB8 120 F2
Halton Cres IP3 140 C1
Hambling's Piece NR16 18 C8
Hamblin Rd IP12 147 A5
Hamblin Wlk IP12 147 A5
Hambrook Cl IP30 63 F7
Hambros The 3 IP31 49 D4
Hamilton Ct CB8 120 E2
Hamilton Gdns IP11 153 A3
Hamilton Rd
Felixstowe IP11 153 A4
Ipswich IP3 140 B3
Lowestoft NR32 113 E1
Newmarket CB8 120 D5
7 Sudbury CO10 148 C5
Hamilton St
6 Felixstowe IP11 152 E5
4 Harwich CO12 106 F3
Hamiltons The CB8 120 F2
Hamilton Way
Ditchingham NR35 110 C8
Stowmarket IP14 124 D7
Hamlet Ct 2 CO8 101 C4
Hamlet Rd CB9 132 F5
Hammond Cl CB8 120 E6
Hammond's Cnr IP14 67 C6
Hammonds Wlk IP19 42 C6
Hampstead Ave IP28 116 B6
Hampton Rd IP1 138 F7
HANCHET END 132 A8
Hanchet End CB9 74 A1
Hanchett End CB9 132 A7
Hancocks Cl 4 IP16 129 D5
Handford Cut IP1 139 A6
Handford Hall Prim Sch IP1 139 A6
Handford Rd IP1 155 A3
Hankin Ave 13 CO12 106 E1
Hanmer Ave IP28 116 C5
Hanmer Wlk IP33 122 B6
HANNINGFIELDS GREEN 63 F1
Hanover Cl
5 Bury St Edmunds IP32 123 A8
Exning CB8 120 E8
Oulton Broad NR33 114 F5
Hanover Ct CO10 148 B4
Ha'penny Field 8 IP9 105 E7
Ha'penny Pier Visitor Ctr* CO12 107 B3
Harbourage The NR34 111 C5
Harbour Cres 7 CO12 107 C3
Harbour La IP22 18 D3
Harbour Rd NR32 112 E1
Harcourt Ave 1 CO12 107 A2
Harding's La IP31 50 E4
Hardwick Cl IP4 140 E5
Hardwick La IP33 122 F2
Hardwick Mid Sch IP33 123 B1
Hardwick Pk Gdns IP33 123 A1
Hardwick Prim Sch IP33 123 B2
Hardwick Rd
Haverhill CB9 132 F6
Starston IP20 22 C7
Hardwick Sh Ctr IP33 123 F4
Hardy Cl
8 Brantham CO11 104 E4
Lowestoft NR33 115 A7
Hardy Cres IP1 134 F4
Hardy Ct 1 CO10 148 D8
Harebell Rd
Ipswich IP8 138 F4
Red Lodge IP28 30 C1
Harebell Way NR33 114 C5
Harefield CO10 77 E1
Hare & Hounds Cnr IP6 82 F8
Hares La IP19 25 B4
Hares Rd IP7 65 D1
Hares Wlk 1 CO10 148 D6
Harewood Terr 7 CB9 132 C5
HARGRAVE 62 B6
Hargrave Ave IP6 125 D3
Hargrave Rd IP29 62 B6
HARKSTEAD 106 B5
Harkstead La
Freston IP9 105 F8
Woolverstone IP9 144 A1
Harkstead Rd 3 IP9 106 A5
Harland St IP2 139 C3
HARLESTON
Harleston 66 B7
Rendenhall with Harleston 22 E5
Harleston Hill IP21 39 E8
Harleston Mus* IP20 22 D6
Harleston Prim Sch IP20 22 D6
Harleston Rd
Metfield IP20 23 B3
Pulham Market IP21 21 E8
Scole IP21 21 D5
Weybread IP21 22 D4
Harling Dro IP27 6 E3
Harling Rd
Garboldisham IP22 18 C6
North Lopham IP22 19 A6
Harling Way IP16 129 B6
Harman's La IP20 22 C5
Harold Rd NR33 115 C6
Harpclose Rd 2 CO10 148 D6
Harper's Est 9 CO6 102 C5
Harper's Hill CO6 102 C5
Harpers La IP17 128 D3
Harp's Cl Rd NR32 113 B3
Harpur's Rd 2 CO10 77 A2
Harrier Cl IP3 140 B1
Harriers Wlk IP13 70 E5
Harrier Way IP14 67 A5
Harrington Ave NR32 113 C6
Harrington Cl IP33 154 C1
Harris Ave NR32 113 C4
Harris Ct 12 IP14 53 F2
Harrison Gn 3 IP18 119 C8
Harrison Gr IP5 141 C8
Harrison Rd NR32 112 E1
Harrisons La IP19 118 C5
Harrison Way IP26 4 F3
Harrod Cl NR33 115 C7
Harrop Dale 10 NR33 114 E3
Harrow Cl IP4 140 A5
Harrow Gn 2 IP29 63 D1
HARROW GREEN 63 D1
Harrow La
Benhall IP17 72 A7
Theberton IP16 129 A8
Harrow Rd
Haverhill CB9 132 C5
Troston IP31 33 D4
Harrow St CO6 102 B8
Harry Palmer Cl 1 CB7 29 A1
Hart Cl CB9 132 D8
HARTEST 77 A7
HARTEST HILL 77 C7
Hartest Hill IP29 77 C6
Hartest La IP29 63 C1
Hartest Prim Sch IP29 77 A7
Hartest Rd IP29 63 A1
Hartest Way
Stowmarket IP14 124 F3
Sudbury CO10 148 F4
Hartfield Rd CB8 59 F2
Hartington Rd IP15 130 E3
Hartismere High Sch IP23 117 B3
Hartismere Hospl IP23 117 C3
Hartley St IP2 155 B1
Hartree Way IP5 141 E7
HART'S GREEN 63 E2
Hart's La CO7 103 E1
Harvard Rd 6 IP26 4 D5
Harvest Cl IP14 51 D1
Harvest Dr NR33 114 F2
Harvesters Way
2 Martlesham Heath IP5 98 A7
Martlesham IP5 141 F6
Harvey Cl 7 CO11 104 E2
Harvey La IP21 21 C5
Harvey's La IP6 82 C6
HARWICH 107 A3
Harwich Int Port CO12 106 F3
Harwich Rd
Foxash Estate CO11 104 A1
Mistley CO11 105 A2
Ramsey & Parkeston CO11 106 A1
Wrabness CO11 105 F1
Harwich Town Sta CO12 107 B3
Harwood Ave IP24 16 C7
Hascot Hill
Barking IP6 125 A1
Battisford IP14 81 A8
Haselmere Cl 5 IP32 123 D6
HASKETON 146 C8
Hasketon Rd
Burgh IP13 83 F6
Woodbridge IP13 146 E6
Haskins Wlk IP5 141 E7
Haslemere Dr IP4 139 E7
Hasse Rd CB7 28 E8
Hasted Cl IP33 122 C4
Hatchley Cl IP12 85 C3
Hatfield Rd IP3 140 A3
Hatley Dr CB5 44 A6
Hatter St IP33 154 B2
Haughgate Cl IP12 146 F6
Haugh La
Great Ashfield IP31 50 F5
Haughley IP14 51 D1
Woodbridge IP12 146 F6
HAUGHLEY 51 C1
Haughley Crawfords CE Prim Sch IP14 51 C1
Haughley Dr IP4 140 F6
HAUGHLEY GREEN 51 C3
HAUGHLEY NEW STREET 51 B1
Haughley Pk* IP14 51 A1
Haughley Rd IP14 66 B7
Hauliers Rd IP11 152 D2
Haven Ave NR32 113 B3
Haven Cl IP11 152 D4
Haven Nature Reserve The* IP16 130 F6
Haven Rd IP16 129 D5
Havens The IP10 144 E7
Haven The IP16 73 F6
Havergate Island National Nature Reserve* IP12 86 F2
Havergate Rd 3 IP3 144 D8
HAVERHILL 132 C6
Haverhill Arts Ctr* CB9 132 E5
Haverhill Bsns Pk CB9 132 F3
Haverhill & District Local History Ctr* CB9 132 E5
Haverhill Leisure Ctr CB9 132 F6
Haverhill Railway Walks Nature Reserve* CB9 133 B4
Haverhill Rd
Haverhill CB9 132 F8
Helions Bumpstead CB9 88 B5
Kedington CB9 133 E8
Steeple Bumpstead CB9 88 D5
Haverhill Trade Pk CB9 132 F3
Haward St NR32 113 C1
Hawbridge IP9 150 E4
Hawe's La
Norton IP31 50 B4
Wicken CB7 28 A2
Hawes St IP2 155 C1
HAWKEDON 76 D7
Hawk End La IP30 50 E2
Hawke Rd IP3 139 E1
Hawker Dr IP5 98 A8
Hawkes La IP11 152 D6
Hawkins Ct 2 CO10 148 D8
Hawkins Rd CO10 148 E8
Hawk's La IP29 63 A2
Hawks Mill St IP6 125 D5
HAWSTEAD 63 D6
HAWSTEAD GREEN 63 E5
Hawstead La IP29 63 E6
Hawthorn Ave NR33 115 A7
Hawthorn Cl
Beccles NR34 111 E4
Bury St Edmunds IP32 122 D8
Knodishall IP17 129 B2
8 Stowupland IP14 67 A6
Hawthorn Dr
9 Horringer IP29 63 A8
Ipswich IP2 138 D2
Hawthorn La 25 IP27 13 F2
Hawthorn Pl IP12 146 E6
Hawthorn Rd
Haverhill CB9 132 B7
Middleton IP17 58 A5
Sudbury CO10 148 F5
Theberton IP16 57 F4
Hawthorns The 8 IP31 49 D4
Hawthorn Way CB5 44 B6
Hawthorn Wlk 10 IP28 30 B8
Hay Barn Meadow 2 IP30 50 D1
Haycocks Rd CB9 132 A7
Haygate IP23 117 C3
Hayhill Rd IP4 139 E7
Hayland Dro IP28 29 D7
Haylings Gr IP16 129 C4
Haylings Rd IP16 129 C4
Hayman Rd IP3 139 F1
Haynings Mill IP13 126 D4
Haysborder Rd IP29 46 F3
Haythill La IP26 4 D6
Hayward Cl IP23 117 D2
Haywards Fields IP5 141 D8
Hazel Cl
9 Bentwaters Airfield IP12 85 E8
Haverhill CB9 132 C5
Mildenhall IP28 116 E4
Hazel Covert 4 IP24 16 D6
Hazelcroft Rd IP1 135 B2
Hazel Ct 6 CO10 148 D6
Hazel Dr
10 Horringer IP29 63 A8
Ipswich IP3 140 E1
Hazel Rise IP6 134 C8
Hazels La IP17 42 D5
HAZEL STUB 132 A5
Hazelville Cl 11 CO12 106 F1
Hazelwood 1 IP7 80 F1
Hazelwood Cl 10 IP31 49 D4
Hazelwood Marshes Nature Reserve* IP15 73 B4
Hazelwood St IP17 130 A7
Hazlitt Rd 6 IP1 135 A3
Headingham Cl 13 IP2 139 A2
Head La CO10 148 F2
Headland Ave CB9 132 C5
Headland Dro IP26 4 A1
Head Way CO10 148 B8
Healey Cl NR32 113 A5
Heasman Cl CB8 120 F5
Heathbell Rd CB8 121 C3
Heath Cl
East Bergholt CO7 151 D5
Hessett IP30 64 F8
Polstead CO6 93 F3
Heath Ct 12 IP11 107 D8
Heath Dr IP12 99 C7
Heather Ave IP3 140 C2
Heather Cl
1 Great Barton IP31 49 D4
Martlesham Heath IP5 141 F6
Heathercroft Rd IP1 135 A3
Heatherhayes IP2 139 A3
Heather Rd NR32 113 D4
Heatherset Way IP28 30 C1
Heather Way
Brandon IP27 6 A1
Worlingham NR34 111 F3
Heath Farm Rd IP28 30 B1
Heathfield IP5 141 F6
Heathfield Mews IP5 141 F6
Heathfield Rd 9 IP9 105 E7
Heathfields IP11 98 D1
Heathgate Piece IP11 152 C8
Heath La
Blundeston NR32 3 A4
Ipswich IP4 140 C5
Pakenham IP31 49 D8
Heathlands Pk IP4 140 E4
Heathland Way IP28 116 D6
Heath Prim Sch IP5 141 B7
Heath Rd
Burwell CB5 44 C2
East Bergholt CO7 151 D5
Exning CB8 120 A4
Fritton & St Olaves NR31 2 B5
Geldeston NR34 9 A7
Hessett IP30 64 F8
Ipswich IP4 140 C7
Ixworth IP31 33 E2
Kenninghall NR16 19 A7
Lowestoft NR33 114 F8
Mildenhall IP28 116 E5
Mistley CO11 105 A2
Heath Rd *continued*
Newmarket CB8 121 C3
Norton IP31 50 B4
Polstead CO6 93 F2
Sapiston IP31 34 B7
Swaffham Prior CB5 44 A1
Thurston IP31 49 D4
Troston IP31 33 D4
Wenhaston with Mells Hamlet IP19 42 B7
Woolpit IP30 50 D1
Heathside Specl Sch IP4 140 D6
Heath The
Dedham CO7 104 A2
Great Waldingfield CO10 92 C6
Woolpit IP30 65 F8
Heath View
Ipswich IP5 141 A6
Leiston IP16 129 E5
Heath Way CO10 92 C6
Heath Wlk IP12 72 A4
HECKFIELD GREEN 38 D7
HEDENHAM 7 E8
Hedley La NR33 114 A3
Heigham Dr NR33 114 F5
Heights The NR34 111 C4
Heldhaw Rd IP32 123 E5
Helena Rd IP3 139 E4
Helens Cl 2 IP22 36 A8
HELIONS BUMPSTEAD 88 B4
Helions Bumpstead Rd CB9 132 D3
Helions Pk Ave CB9 132 E5
Helions Pk Gdns 8 CB9 132 E5
Helions Pk Rd 7 CB9 132 E5
Helions Rd CB9 88 D4
Helions Service Rd 3 CB9 132 E5
Helions Wlk CB9 132 E5
HELMINGHAM 69 B4
Helmingham Hall & Gdns* IP14 69 A4
Helmingham Prim Sch IP14 69 B6
Helmingham Rd IP6 69 C2
Helston Cl IP5 141 B7
HEMINGSTONE 82 C8
HEMLEY 98 E5
Hemmant Way NR34 9 B7
HEMP GREEN 57 C8
Hemplands The 2 NR32 113 D2
Hempnall Rd NR35 7 A8
Hempstead Rd CB9 132 A7
Hencote La
Horringer IP29 63 C8
Nowton IP33 123 B1
Henderson Cl
Bramford IP8 134 A1
Haverhill CB9 132 A7
HENGRAVE 48 A7
Hengrave Cl 11 IP2 139 A2
Hengrave Hall* IP28 48 A7
Hengrave Rd IP28 48 B6
Henham Park* NR34 25 F1
Henham Rd NR32 113 A5
HENLEY 82 D6
Henley Ave IP1 135 B3
Henley Cl IP17 128 C3
Henley Prim Sch IP6 82 E6
Henley Rd
Henley IP6 82 D5
Ipswich IP1 155 B4
Henniker Rd
3 Debenham IP14 53 F2
Ipswich IP1 138 C8
Henny Rd CO8 101 A7
HENNY STREET 91 F1
Hen Reed Bed Nature Reserve* IP18 43 B8
Henry Cl CB9 132 B4
Henry Rd IP3 140 B1
Henry St IP14 53 E2
Henry Ward Rd 1 IP20 22 D6
Henry Watson's Potteries* IP22 35 D5
Henslow Rd IP4 140 B5
HENSTEAD 26 E8
Henstead Arts & Crafts Ctr* NR34 10 F1
Henstead Exotic Gdn* NR34 26 E8
Henstead Gdns IP3 140 A2
HEPWORTH 35 A6
Hepworth Ave IP33 122 D5
Hepworth Rd
Barningham IP31 34 F7
Hepworth IP22 35 A7
Stanton IP31 34 E4
Thelnetham IP22 35 B7
Herbert Cl CO10 148 E8
Herbert Human Cl 3 CB7 28 D4
Herbert Rd IP5 141 E8
Hereford Dr 14 IP6 82 B5
Hereward Ave IP28 116 C5
Hereward Way
5 Feltwell IP26 4 D5
Littleport CB7 12 B7
Weeting-with-Broomhill IP27 5 E3
Heritage Gn 6 NR33 11 B1
Heritage Workshop Ctr* NR32 113 E3
Herivan Cl NR32 112 E4
Herivan Gdns 6 NR32 112 E4
Hermitage Ct IP13 126 B3
Hermitage Meadows CO10 76 B1
Herolf Way 11 IP20 22 D6

Heron Cl
 5 Mildenhall IP28 . . . . 13 B1
Stowmarket IP14 . . . . 124 B1
Heron Ct CB7 . . . . 28 C5
Heron Hill IP14 . . . . 66 C6
Heron Rd
Bury St Edmunds IP33 . . . . 123 B2
Ipswich IP2 . . . . 138 E3
Saxmundham IP17 . . . . . . 128 B3
Herons Cl NR32 . . . . 112 D2
Herring Fishery Score 2
NR32 . . . . 113 E1
HERRINGFLEET 2 D4
Herringfleet Drainage Mill*
NR32 . . . . 2 B4
Herringfleet Rd NR31 . . . . . . 2 B5
Herring Mkt 14 NR32 . . . . . 115 D8
HERRINGSWELL 46 C8
Herringswell Rd
Herringswell IP28 . . . . 30 D2
Kentford CB8 . . . . 46 A6
Hertford Cl 19 IP32 . . . . 48 C5
Hertford Pl IP15 . . . . 130 E3
Hertford Rd 5 CO10 . . . . . . 76 A1
Hertfords Pl IP12 . . . . 86 D7
Hervey Cl 6 IP9 . . . . 107 A5
Hervey Rd IP33 . . . . 122 E3
Hervey St
Ipswich IP4 . . . . 155 C4
Lowestoft NR32 . . . . 115 C8
HESSETT 64 F8
Hessett Cl IP14 . . . . 124 F3
Hethersett Cl CB8 . . . . 120 E8
HEVENINGHAM 40 F3
Heveningham Long La
IP17 . . . . 41 A1
Heveningham Rd IP19 . . . . . 40 C5
Hewitt Rd
 15 Harwich CO12 . . . . 106 E1
 19 Ramsey CO12 . . . . 106 E1
Hexham Cl 3 IP2 . . . . 139 A2
Heycroft Way 4 CO6 . . . . . 102 C5
Heyford Ct 8 IP28 . . . . 116 B5
Heyford Rd 12 IP31 . . . . 33 D5
Heywood Ave IP22 . . . . 20 C3
Heywood Cl IP2 . . . . 138 D1
Heywood Rd IP22 . . . . 20 C4
Hibbard Rd IP8 . . . . 134 C2
HICKFORD HILL 90 C7
Hickford Hill CO10 . . . . 90 B7
Hickling Dr IP33 . . . . 123 B1
Hicks Way CB9 . . . . 133 C3
HIGHAM
Bury St Edmunds 46 E4
Stratford St Mary 103 D6
Higham Hill IP7 . . . . 103 D8
Higham Race Course
CO7 . . . . 103 D7
Higham Rd
Higham CO7 . . . . 103 D6
Tuddenham IP28 . . . . 31 A1
High Baxter St IP33 . . . . . . 154 B2
High Beach IP11 . . . . 153 C4
High Beech NR32 . . . . 113 B3
Highbridge Gravel Dro
IP27 . . . . 109 B7
Highbury Cres IP33 . . . . . . 122 E5
Highbury Rd IP33 . . . . 122 E5
Highbury Way CO10 . . . . . 148 F4
Highclere Cl CB8 . . . . 120 D8
High Comm Rd IP22 . . . . . . 18 F5
High Ct IP20 . . . . 22 E6
Higher Dr NR32 . . . . 112 F2
Highfield
Blythburgh IP19 . . . . 42 F6
Clare CO10 . . . . 90 B8
Eye IP23 . . . . 117 C3
Highfield App 1 IP1 . . . . . 134 F1
Highfield Ave CO12 . . . . . 107 A2
Highfield Cl NR33 . . . . 114 B1
Highfield Dr IP6 . . . . 134 D8
Highfield Rd
Felixstowe IP11 . . . . 153 A4
Halesworth IP19 . . . . 118 B2
Ipswich IP1 . . . . 134 F2
 6 Stowupland IP14 . . . . . . 67 A6
Sudbury CO10 . . . . 148 C8
Highfields
Bentley IP9 . . . . 104 F1
Great Yeldham CO9 . . . . . 90 A1
Lakenheath IP27 . . . . 109 E6
 1 Thetford IP24 . . . . 16 C6
Highfields Dr IP27 . . . . . . 109 D6
Highgate La IP13 . . . . 70 B2
High Gn IP16 . . . . 129 C6
HIGH GREEN 63 D7
Highgrove Cl NR32 . . . . . . 113 A3
High Hall Cl 2 IP11 . . . . . 107 D8
High House Farm Rd
IP12 . . . . 131 D8
High House La IP7 . . . . 79 B5
High La IP14 . . . . 53 B6
Highland Dr NR34 . . . . . . 111 E4
Highlands
Bury St Edmunds IP32 . . . 154 B4
Lakenheath IP27 . . . . 109 E6
Highlands Cl IP6 . . . . 125 C5
Highlands Rd
Hadleigh IP7 . . . . 149 E5
Monks Eleigh IP7 . . . . 79 C4
Highlands The CB8 . . . . . . 120 D8
Highland Way NR33 . . . . . 114 F6
High Leas NR34 . . . . 111 C3
High Leas NR34 . . . . 111 C3
High Lighthouse Wireless
Mus* CO12 . . . . 107 C3

High Lodge Forest Ctr
Thetford Forest Pk*
IP27 . . . . 15 C7
High London La IP22 . . . . . . 20 A8
High Rd
Badingham IP13 . . . . 56 C6
Bressingham IP22 . . . . 19 F4
Felixstowe IP11 . . . . 152 B8
Great Finborough IP14 . . . 66 A2
Kettleburgh IP13 . . . . 55 B2
Leavenheath CO6 . . . . . . 102 A7
Needham IP6 . . . . 22 B3
Roydon IP22 . . . . 20 A3
Swilland IP6 . . . . 83 A7
Trimley St Martin IP11 . . . . 98 C1
Wortwell IP20 . . . . 23 A7
High Rd E IP11 . . . . 153 B5
High Rd W IP11 . . . . 152 F5
HIGH ROUGHAM 49 E1
High Row Field IP11 . . . . . 153 C5
High St Ex Gall* IP1 . . . . . 155 B3
High St
Acton CO10 . . . . 92 B7
Aldeburgh IP15 . . . . 130 E4
Ashley CB8 . . . . 60 F8
Brandon IP27 . . . . 5 F1
Brinkley CB8 . . . . 59 F1
 5 Bures CO8 . . . . 101 C5
Burwell CB5 . . . . 44 A5
Cavendish CO10 . . . . 76 E1
Cheveley CB8 . . . . 60 E8
Chippenham CB7 . . . . 45 C8
Clare CO10 . . . . 90 A8
Debenham IP14 . . . . 53 F2
Dedham CO7 . . . . 103 F3
Dunwich IP17 . . . . 43 B1
Felixstowe IP11 . . . . 152 E6
Feltwell IP26 . . . . 4 E5
Flowton IP8 . . . . 81 C1
Gislingham IP23 . . . . 36 D2
Hadleigh IP7 . . . . 149 D6
Harwich CO12 . . . . 107 B2
Haverhill CB9 . . . . 132 E5
Hemingstone IP6 . . . . 68 C1
Hitcham IP7 . . . . 79 F4
Hopton IP22 . . . . 18 C2
Ipswich IP1 . . . . 155 B3
Ixworth IP31 . . . . 34 B1
Kessingland NR33 . . . . . . 11 B1
Lakenheath IP27 . . . . 109 C6
Langham CO4 . . . . 103 B2
Lavenham CO10 . . . . 78 D4
Laxfield IP13 . . . . 40 B3
Leiston IP16 . . . . 129 C6
Long Melford CO10 . . . . . . 77 E1
 7 Lowestoft NR32 . . . . . . 113 C2
Manningtree CO11 . . . . . . 104 E2
Mildenhall IP28 . . . . 116 C4
Nayland CO6 . . . . 102 D5
Needham Market IP6 . . . . 125 D5
Newmarket CB8 . . . . 120 F2
Orford IP12 . . . . 131 C2
Pettistree IP13 . . . . 127 C5
Rattlesden IP30 . . . . 65 D6
Saxmundham IP17 . . . . . . 128 D3
Soham CB7 . . . . 28 D4
Southwold IP18 . . . . 119 D5
Sproughton IP8 . . . . 138 A6
Stansfield CO10 . . . . 76 C6
Stetchworth CB8 . . . . 60 A5
St Margaret, Ilketshall
NR35 . . . . 24 D7
Thelnetham IP22 . . . . 18 E1
Thornden IP23 . . . . 53 C8
Tuddenham IP28 . . . . 30 F2
Tuddenham St Martin IP6 . 136 B5
Wangford with Henham
NR34 . . . . 26 B2
Wicken CB7 . . . . 28 A1
Wickham Market IP13 . . . . 127 C7
Wrentham NR34 . . . . 26 E5
Yoxford IP17 . . . . 57 D8
HIGH STREET
Darsham 42 B1
Iken 73 B2
St Margaret, Ilketshall 24 D7
HIGH STREET GREEN 64 B3
HIGHTOWN GREEN 65 D3
Highview CI CO10 . . . . . . 148 C8
High View Rd IP1 . . . . 134 D1
Highwood Cres CB8 . . . . . . 46 B2
Highwood La CO10 . . . . . . 92 C5
Highwood Rd CB8 . . . . 46 B2
Hildesley Ct NR33 . . . . . . 115 B4
Hillary Cl IP4 . . . . 140 A5
Hill Cl
 6 Long Melford CO10 . . . 91 E8
Newmarket CB8 . . . . 120 E3
Hill Cres CB9 . . . . 132 E2
Hillcrest IP17 . . . . 129 A3
Hillcrest App IP8 . . . . 134 B2
Hillcrest Cl 3 NR33 . . . . . 111 B3
Hillcrest Dr NR32 . . . . 113 B4
Hillcrest Gdns NR32 . . . . . 113 B3
Hillcrest Rd
Beccles NR34 . . . . 111 B3
Sudbury CO10 . . . . 148 C8
Hillcroft Prep Sch IP14 . . . 51 D2
Hill Farm La 9 IP9 . . . . . 106 C8
Hill Farm Rd
Grundisburgh IP13 . . . . . . 83 D6
Halesworth IP19 . . . . 118 C3
Playford IP6 . . . . 137 B4
Rendham IP17 . . . . 56 E4
Hill House Gdns NR33 . . . 115 C5
Hill House La IP6 . . . . 125 C6
Hill House Rd IP4 . . . . 139 E5

Hill La CB9 . . . . 133 D1
Hill of Health (Tumulus)*
IP28 . . . . 32 D2
Hill Rd
Lowestoft NR32 . . . . 113 C1
Southwold IP18 . . . . 119 C6
Wangford with Henham
NR34 . . . . 26 B1
Westley IP33 . . . . 122 A5
Hill Rise IP14 . . . . 124 D3
Hillrise Cl NR34 . . . . 111 E3
Hillside
Brandon IP27 . . . . 14 D8
Stowmarket IP14 . . . . 124 D3
Hillside Ave NR34 . . . . 111 E4
Hillside Com Prim Sch
IP2 . . . . 139 C3
Hillside Cres 5 IP3 . . . . . . 140 B3
Hillside Cl 1 NR35 . . . . . . 110 C2
Hillside Meadow CB7 . . . . . 29 B1
Hillside Rd
Southwold IP18 . . . . 119 C7
Sudbury CO10 . . . . 148 C5
Hillside Rd E NR35 . . . . . . 110 D3
Hillside Rd W NR35 . . . . . 110 D2
Hillside Specl Sch CO10 . . 148 D7
Hillside Way IP19 . . . . 118 B5
Hill St 10 IP26 . . . . 4 E5
Hill The
North Cove NR34 . . . . 10 C4
Shipmeadow NR34 . . . . 8 F4
Tuddenham St Martin IP6 . 136 C5
Westleton IP17 . . . . 58 C8
Hill Top IP31 . . . . 34 E5
Hilltop Gn NR32 . . . . 113 A4
Hilltop Rise 2 NR34 . . . . . 111 E3
Hilltop Way IP31 . . . . 34 E5
Hill View CB8 . . . . 61 C4
Hill View Bsns Pk IP6 . . . 134 D6
Hilly Cl IP31 . . . . 33 F5
Hilly Fields IP12 . . . . 146 E4
Hilton Cl 13 CO11 . . . . . . 104 E2
Hilton Rd
Ipswich IP3 . . . . 140 C1
Martlesham Heath IP5 . . . . 98 A8
HINDERCLAY 35 E7
Hinderclay La IP22 . . . . 18 E1
Hinderclay Rd
Redgrave IP22 . . . . 19 A1
Rickinghall Inferior IP22 . . . 35 F6
Hines Rd IP3 . . . . 140 A4
Hintesham Cl 6 IP4 . . . . . 140 F5
HINTLESHAM 95 C6
Hintlesham & Chattisham CE
VCP Sch IP8 . . . . 95 C6
Hintlesham Cl 3 IP14 . . . . 124 E3
Hintlesham Dr IP11 . . . . . 152 D4
Histon Cl IP5 . . . . 140 F7
HITCHAM 79 E6
Hitcham Cswy IP7 . . . . 79 E6
Hitcham Rd
 2 Debenham IP14 . . . . . . 53 F2
Wattisham IP7 . . . . 80 B6
Hitcham's La NR34 . . . . . . 26 E4
Hitchcock Pl CO10 . . . . . . 148 C7
HMS Ganges Mus* IP9 . . 107 B4
Hobart Cl NR32 . . . . 112 E3
Hobart Way NR32 . . . . . . 112 E3
Hobbies La IP14 . . . . 52 D4
HOBBLES GREEN 75 A8
Hobbs Dr CO4 . . . . 103 A3
Hobbs La CO10 . . . . 77 B2
Hobland Rd
Belton with Browston NR31 . 2 F8
Bradwell NR31 . . . . 3 A8
Hocket Cres IP12 . . . . 71 F2
Hockey Hill IP14 . . . . 53 A5
Hockney Gdns IP3 . . . . . . 144 A8
HOCKWOLD CUM WILTON . . 5 A3
Hockwold Prim Sch IP26 . . . 5 A2
Hodgkinson Rd IP11 . . . . . 152 C3
Hodson Cl 6 IP32 . . . . 122 E8
Hoe La CO10 . . . . 90 F8
Hogarth Rd IP3 . . . . 139 F1
Hogarth Sq IP3 . . . . 140 A1
Hogarth Wlk NR32 . . . . . . 113 B6
HOGGARD'S GREEN 64 C3
Hoggars Rd IP14 . . . . 52 C4
Hogg La
Bury St Edmunds IP33 . . . 154 B1
Earsham NR35 . . . . 7 C5
Hog La
St Lawrence, Ilketshall
NR34 . . . . 24 F6
Wenhaston with Mells Hamlet
IP19 . . . . 42 C5
Westhall NR34 . . . . 25 A6
Hogsty La IP21 . . . . 22 A5
Holbecks La IP7 . . . . 149 C4
Holbein Way 2 NR34 . . . . 113 B6
Holborn Ave IP28 . . . . 116 B6
HOLBROOK 105 C7
Holbrook Barn Rd 6
CO10 . . . . 93 C3
Holbrook Cl 11 CO10 . . . . . 92 C6
Holbrook Cres 2 IP11 . . . . 152 D4
Holbrook High Sch IP9 . . . 105 E8
Holbrook Prim Sch IP9 . . . 105 E7
Holbrook Rd
Haverhill CB9 . . . . 132 C4
Holbrook IP9 . . . . 106 A5
Ipswich IP3 . . . . 139 F1
Lowestoft NR32 . . . . 112 F4
Stutton IP9 . . . . 105 D5
Holcombe Cres IP2 . . . . . 138 D2
Holdans La IP17 . . . . 56 D2
Holdans Meadow IP17 . . . . 56 E2

Holden Cl
Ipswich IP2 . . . . 139 D3
Lowestoft NR32 . . . . 112 C1
Holden Rd IP28 . . . . 31 F1
Holderness Rd IP32 . . . . . 123 C4
Holeywall La IP31 . . . . 35 A1
Holfen CT IP12 . . . . 84 B1
Holkham Cl 7 IP4 . . . . 140 F5
Holkham Mead 1 CB5 . . . . 44 B5
Holland Pk CB8 . . . . 60 E8
Holland Rd
Felixstowe IP11 . . . . 152 F3
Ipswich IP4 . . . . 139 F6
Holland Rise IP19 . . . . 41 A4
Hollands Bsns Ctr The
CB9 . . . . 132 E4
Holland's La NR35 . . . . 7 C7
Hollands Rd CB9 . . . . 132 E4
Hollands Rd Ind Est CB9 . 132 E4
HOLLESLEY 99 F7
Hollesley Ave CB9 . . . . . . 132 E4
Hollesley Prim Sch IP12 . . . 99 F7
Hollesley Rd
Hollesley IP12 . . . . 99 D7
Rendlesham IP12 . . . . 85 D7
Holliday Cl IP32 . . . . 123 F7
Hollingsworth Rd
Lowestoft NR32 . . . . 113 C3
 3 Stowmarket IP14 . . . . . 124 C5
Hollowell Cl 1 NR32 . . . . . 112 E4
Hollow Gr Way NR33 . . . . 114 C4
Hollow Hill CB9 . . . . 74 A2
Hollow Hill Rd NR35 . . . . . 110 B7
Hollow La
Badingham IP13 . . . . 56 C6
Barningham IP31 . . . . 34 F8
Bures St Mary CO8 . . . . . 101 C6
Carlton Colville NR33 . . . . 114 C4
 6 Chelmondiston IP9 . . . 106 C8
Coney Weston IP31 . . . . . 18 A1
Earl Soham IP13 . . . . 54 F3
Mendham IP20 . . . . 23 A4
Thurston IP31 . . . . 49 F3
Tostock IP30 . . . . 50 A2
Hollow Rd
Ashen CO10 . . . . 89 F6
Bury St Edmunds IP32 . . . 123 C6
Copdock & Washbrook IP8 . 95 E4
Hollows The IP6 . . . . 67 F2
Hollow Way Hill NR34 . . . . . 9 D8
Holly Blue Cl 10 IP8 . . . . . 142 E8
Holly Bush Cnr CO7 . . . . . 103 E7
HOLLYBUSH CORNER 64 D6
Hollybush Dr IP11 . . . . . . 153 D7
Hollybush La IP30 . . . . 64 D6
Holly Cl
Beccles NR34 . . . . 111 E3
 5 Horringer IP29 . . . . 63 A8
Little Bealings IP13 . . . . . 137 D5
 6 Red Lodge IP28 . . . . . . 30 B1
Warren Heath IP3 . . . . . . 140 F1
Hollycroft Cl 5 IP1 . . . . . . 135 A3
Holly Ct 34 IP20 . . . . 22 D6
Hollydene Cl 4 NR32 . . . . 112 D2
Holly End IP5 . . . . 141 F6
Holly Gr NR34 . . . . 111 C4
HOLLY HILL 110 B8
Holly Hill NR32 . . . . 112 C3
Holly La
Belstead IP8 . . . . 142 C7
Great Horkesley CO6 . . . . 102 E2
Lakenheath IP27 . . . . 109 D5
Little Bealings IP13 . . . . . 137 D5
Mutford NR34 . . . . 10 E3
Rushmere St Andrew IP5 . 136 E2
Stutton IP9 . . . . 105 C6
Holly Oaks 2 CO6 . . . . . . 101 F2
Holly Rd
 4 Great Bricett IP7 . . . . . 80 D6
Ipswich IP1 . . . . 155 A4
Lowestoft NR32 . . . . 112 C1
Willisham IP8 . . . . 81 A5
Holly Wlk 8 IP28 . . . . 30 B8
Holm Cl 4 NR34 . . . . 9 F4
Holme Cl IP22 . . . . 18 C2
Holmere Dr IP19 . . . . 118 A3
Holme's Hill IP17 . . . . 41 A4
Holmes La 5 CB7 . . . . 28 D5
Holmsey Gn
Beck Row, Holywell Row &
Kenny Hill IP28 . . . . 13 C1
Mildenhall IP28 . . . . 30 B8
Holmsey Gn Gdns 7 IP28 . 30 B8
Holst Cl NR33 . . . . 115 A6
Holst Mead IP14 . . . . 124 C8
HOLTON 118 E4
Holton Ave NR32 . . . . 112 F4
Holton Rd IP19 . . . . 118 C5
HOLTON ST MARY 151 A8
Holton St Peter Postmill*
IP19 . . . . 118 E3
Holton St Peter Prim Sch
IP19 . . . . 118 C4
Holton Terr IP19 . . . . 118 C4
Holt Rd CO6 . . . . 93 E2
Holt's La IP6 . . . . 125 F6
Holt's Rd CO6 . . . . 102 A2
Holyhouse Drift 1 IP31 . . . 49 A6
Holyrood 4 CO12 . . . . . . 106 F1
Holyrood Cl IP2 . . . . 138 F1
Holystone Way NR33 . . . . 114 C4
Holywell Cl IP33 . . . . 123 A3
Holywell Dro IP28 . . . . 13 C2
HOLYWELL ROW 30 C8
Holywells Cl IP3 . . . . 139 E4
Holywells High Sch IP3 . . . 140 C1
Holy Wells Rd IP3 . . . . . . 139 E3
Home Cl CB9 . . . . 88 C4

Her—How 169

Home Farm La IP33 . . . . . 123 B1
Home Farm Rd NR35 . . . . . 8 C7
Homefield
Boxford CO10 . . . . 93 C3
Capel St Mary IP9 . . . . . . 150 F3
Homefield Ave
 5 Beccles NR34 . . . . 111 B5
Lowestoft NR33 . . . . 114 F6
Homefield Paddock
NR34 . . . . 111 B5
Homefield Rd CB9 . . . . . . 132 C4
Homefield Rd Ind Est
CB9 . . . . 132 D4
Home Meadow 4 IP13 . . . 40 B3
Home Piece IP22 . . . . 35 A8
Homeport NR32 . . . . 113 E3
Homer Cl IP1 . . . . 134 F4
HOMERSFIELD 23 B8
Homestall Cres CB9 . . . . . . 74 A2
Homestead Dr 2 IP20 . . . . 30 B8
Homestead The NR33 . . . . 114 D3
Homey Bridge Rd CO6 . . . . 93 E1
Honey Hill IP33 . . . . 154 C1
Honey La CO6 . . . . 102 B6
Honeymeade Cl 23 IP31 . . . 34 C4
Honeypot La
Kelsale cum Carlton IP17 . . 57 C4
Mendham IP20 . . . . 23 C4
Monewden IP13 . . . . 69 F4
Wattisfield IP22 . . . . 35 D4
Honeypot Meadow 2
NR35 . . . . 110 B3
Honeysuckle Cl
Haverhill CB9 . . . . 132 C7
 8 Lowestoft NR33 . . . . . 115 A3
 1 Red Lodge IP28 . . . . . . 46 A8
 4 Soham CB7 . . . . 28 D4
Honeysuckle Gdns IP2 . . . 138 C5
Honeysuckle Way 4
IP32 . . . . 123 E6
HONEY TYE 102 B6
HONINGTON 33 E5
Honington CE VC Prim Sch
IP31 . . . . 33 F5
Honington Rise IP31 . . . . . 33 E5
HOO 70 B5
Hood Dr IP6 . . . . 81 F5
Hood Rd IP3 . . . . 139 E1
Hood's La NR34 . . . . 25 F4
Hook La IP7 . . . . 149 F4
Hoo La IP12 . . . . 71 E4
Hooper Sq IP33 . . . . 122 C6
Hope Cres IP12 . . . . 147 A6
Hopelyn Cl 4 NR32 . . . . . 113 B4
Hop Meadow CO7 . . . . . . 151 B4
Hopper Way IP2 . . . . 20 E2
HOPTON 18 C2
Hopton CE VC Prim Sch
IP22 . . . . 18 C1
Hopton Fst Sch NR31 . . . . . 3 C6
Hopton Gdns NR31 . . . . . . 3 B7
HOPTON ON SEA 3 C7
Hopton Rd
Barningham IP31 . . . . 34 F8
Thelnetham IP22 . . . . 18 D1
Hopton Rise CB9 . . . . 132 A6
HORHAM 38 E3
Horham Rd IP21 . . . . 38 E1
Horkesley Hill CO6 . . . . . . 102 D4
Horkesley Rd CO6 . . . . . . 102 D4
Hornbeam Cl
Beccles NR34 . . . . 111 E4
Rosedale Park NR33 . . . . 114 F4
Hornbeam Dr IP29 . . . . . . 63 A8
Hornbeam Rd
Mildenhall IP28 . . . . 116 E5
 2 Stowupland IP14 . . . . . 67 A6
HORNER'S GREEN 93 C4
HORNESTREET 103 C3
Horn Hill NR33 . . . . 115 C7
Horn La CB8 . . . . 60 D3
HORRINGER 63 A8
Horringer Ct Mid Sch
IP33 . . . . 122 D3
Horringer Rd IP29 . . . . . . 122 D2
Horringer Rd IP29 . . . . . . 122 E1
Horsecroft Rd
Bury St Edmunds IP33 . . . 122 F2
Horringer IP29 . . . . 63 C8
Horsefair IP30 . . . . 50 D1
Horsefair Cl IP14 . . . . 52 E4
Horseheath Rd IP29 . . . . . 74 A2
Horseshoe La CB9 . . . . . . 132 C5
Horseshoe Rd IP28 . . . . . . 30 C1
Horsham Ave IP3 . . . . 140 D3
Horsham Cl CB9 . . . . 132 A7
Hospital Rd
Bury St Edmunds IP33 . . . 154 A1
Orford IP12 . . . . 131 B6
Hossack Rd IP3 . . . . 144 A8
Hotson Rd IP18 . . . . 119 D6
Houghton Dr
Hopton on Sea NR31 . . . . . 3 B6
Oulton NR32 . . . . 112 C4
Houghton Pl 5 IP4 . . . . . . 140 F5
Houghtons La CB7 . . . . . . 29 D5
Houldsworth Terr CB8 . . . 120 F3
Houldsworth Valley Prim Sch
CB8 . . . . 120 F3
Howard Cl
 6 Framlingham IP13 . . . . 126 C3
Harleston IP20 . . . . 22 E6
Lowestoft NR32 . . . . 132 B5
Howard Com Prim Sch
IP32 . . . . 122 E8

Howard de Walden Way
CB8 . . . .**121** A4
Howard Mid Sch
Bury St Edmunds IP32 . . . . . .**48** B5
Fornham All Saints IP28 . .**122** D8
Howard Rd **1** NR35 . . . .**110** D3
Howard St IP4 . . . .**140** B7
Howards Way IP5 . . . .**141** D8
Howe Ave IP3 . . . .**140** C3
Howe La
Cockfield IP30 . . . .**64** C1
Thornham Parva IP23 . . . . . .**37** A3
Howe Rd CB9 . . . .**132** D7
Howes Ave IP31 . . . .**49** D4
How Hill (Tumulus)★
IP27 . . . .**31** B7
Howlett Cl IP5 . . . .**141** E7
Howlett Way IP24 . . . .**16** B7
Howley Gdns NR32 . . . .**113** A6
HOXNE **38** B8
Hoxne Cl **5** IP14 . . . .**124** E3
Hoxne Rd
Eye IP23 . . . .**117** E2
Hoxne IP21 . . . .**38** D3
Syleham IP21 . . . .**21** F1
Upper Weybread IP12 . . . . . .**22** B2
Hoxter Way CO10 . . . .**148** C8
Hoylake Cl **6** IP28 . . . .**48** C6
Hubbard's Ave **2** NR32 . . . . .**113** C6
Hubbards Cl IP17 . . . .**128** B4
Hubbard's Hill IP17 . . . .**41** B1
Hubbard's La IP30 . . . .**64** F8
Hubbard's Loke NR32 . . . .**113** C6
Huckleberry Cres **7** IP3 . . . .**144** C7
Hudson Cl
10 Harwich CO12 . . . .**107** A1
Haverhill CB9 . . . .**133** A4
Hudsons La CO6 . . . .**103** A7
Hudson Way **6** IP29 . . . .**47** A2
Huggins La IP23 . . . .**37** B1
Hugh Ager Cl **5** IP14 . . . . . .**124** D3
Hughes Cnr CO7 . . . .**151** A6
Hughes Rd CO7 . . . .**151** B6
Hull St IP27 . . . .**109** F1
Hulver La IP17 . . . .**72** C6
Hulver Rd NR34 . . . .**9** F2
HULVER STREET **10** C1
Humber Doucy La IP4 . . . .**136** A2
Humber Doucy Sports Ctr
IP4 . . . .**140** D7
HUMBLE GREEN **92** F8
Hummingbird Cl IP32 . . . .**49** A3
Humphry Rd CO10 . . . .**148** C6
HUNDON **75** E3
Hundon Cl CB8 . . . .**75** B6
Hundon Pl **6** CB9 . . . .**132** F6
Hundon Prim Sch CO10 . .**75** D3
Hundon Rd
Hundon CO10 . . . .**75** B1
Kedington CB9 . . . .**133** F8
Hundred La
Boxted CO4 . . . .**103** B2
Old Newton with Dagworth
IP14 . . . .**51** F3
Hungate NR34 . . . .**111** B5
Hungate Ct NR34 . . . .**111** B5
Hungate La NR34 . . . .**111** B5
Hungerdown La CO11 . . . .**104** B1
HUNSTON **50** D7
HUNSTON GREEN **50** D5
Hunston Rd IP31 . . . .**50** E7
Hunt Cl
5 Redenhall with Harleston
IP20 . . . .**22** D4
Stowmarket IP14 . . . .**124** D3
Hunter Dr
19 Manningtree CO11 . . . .**104** D2
18 Thurstow IP31 . . . .**49** D4
Hunter Gall The★ CO10 . . . . .**91** E8
Hunter Rd
Bury St Edmunds IP32 . . . .**122** C4
Honington IP31 . . . .**33** D5
2 Ipswich IP3 . . . .**144** C8
Hunter's Chase CO7 . . . .**103** F1
Hunters End IP11 . . . .**152** C7
Hunters La IP20 . . . .**23** B2
Hunter's La IP20 . . . .**23** A3
Hunters Ride **21** IP5 . . . .**98** A8
Huntingdon Cl **9** NR33 . . . .**115** A3
HUNTINGFIELD **41** A5
Huntingfield Rd
Bury St Edmunds IP33 . . . .**122** C4
Cratfield IP19 . . . .**40** D5
Leiston IP16 . . . .**129** C5
Huntley Cres IP19 . . . .**118** C5
Hunts Hill CO10 . . . .**77** A2
Hurdle Dro IP28 . . . .**29** F8
Hurdle Makers Hill IP8 . . . . . .**95** F6
Hurn Crag Rd IP19 . . . .**119** C2
Hurricane Pl IP3 . . . .**140** B1
Hurstlea Ct IP6 . . . .**125** D5
Hurstlea Rd IP6 . . . .**125** C5
Hurth Way IP24 . . . .**16** C6
Hurts Croft **3** CB7 . . . .**29** A1
Hut Hill (Tumulus)★ IP31 **17** E3
Hutland Rd IP4 . . . .**139** F7
Hutton Ct IP23 . . . .**117** D3
Hyams La IP9 . . . .**105** E7
Hyam's La IP9 . . . .**105** C5
Hyde Rd CO10 . . . .**148** C5
Hydewood Rd CO9 . . . .**90** A2
Hyem's La IP11 . . . .**153** B7
Hyntle Cl IP2 . . . .**138** E5
Hyperion Way CB8 . . . .**120** D8
Hythe Cl **9** CB5 . . . .**44** A6

Hythe La CB5 . . . .**44** A6
Hythe Rd IP26 . . . .**4** E7

I

Ice House Quay NR32 . . . . . .**114** E8
Iceni Way CB8 . . . .**120** B8
Icepits Cl IP31 . . . .**49** C6
Icewell Hill CB8 . . . .**121** A4
Ickleton Pl **9** CB9 . . . .**132** F6
ICKLINGHAM **31** D4
Icklingham Rd IP28 . . . .**32** B2
Icknield Cl **3** CB8 . . . .**60** E7
Icknield Way IP24 . . . .**16** B5
Ickworth Cres NR4 . . . .**140** F5
Ickworth Ct **2** IP11 . . . .**152** C3
Ickworth Dr IP33 . . . .**154** A1
Ickworth House Pk & Gdn★
IP29 . . . .**62** F8
Ickworth Pk Prim Sch
IP29 . . . .**63** A8
Ickworth Vineyard★ IP29 .**62** E8
IKEN **72** F2
Ilex Cl IP33 . . . .**123** A3
Iliffe Way IP14 . . . .**124** D6
ILKETSHALL ST ANDREW **8** E2
ILKETSHALL ST
LAWRENCE **24** F6
ILKETSHALL ST
MARGARET **24** B8
Imperial Mews NR31 . . . .**3** B6
Impson Way NR26 . . . .**6** A8
Ingate NR34 . . . .**111** C4
Ingestre St **1** CO12 . . . .**107** B2
INGHAM **32** F1
Ingham Rd
Haverhill CB9 . . . .**132** E6
West Stow IP28 . . . .**32** C1
Ingram's Rd IP21 . . . .**21** F3
Ingram's Well Rd CO10 . . . . .**148** D5
Inkerman Cl **4** IP7 . . . .**149** D6
Inkerman Row **4** CO10 . . . .**148** C6
Inkerman Terr **3** IP7 . . . . . .**149** D6
Innes End **4** IP8 . . . .**138** C2
Interchange Ret Pk IP8 . .**138** A1
Inverness Rd IP4 . . . .**136** A2
Inworth La CO6 . . . .**101** B5
Ion Rd **1** IP32 . . . .**122** E8
IPSWICH **155** B3
Ipswich Ave **3** IP12 . . . .**85** B3
Ipswich Cl **1** IP12 . . . .**85** B3
Ipswich Ct IP3 . . . .**154** B3
Ipswich High Sch IP9 . . . .**144** C2
Ipswich Hospl IP4 . . . .**140** C7
Ipswich Mus★ IP1 . . . . . .**155** B3
Ipswich Pre Prep Sch
IP14 . . . .**68** B6
Ipswich Prep Sch IP1 . . . .**155** B4
Ipswich Rd
Brantham CO11 . . . .**104** E5
Charsfield IP13 . . . .**70** B2
Claydon IP6 . . . .**134** C8
Dedham CO4 . . . .**103** D3
East Bergholt CO7 . . . .**151** A6
Elmsett IP7 . . . .**95** A8
Grundisburgh IP13 . . . .**83** E5
Hadleigh IP7 . . . .**149** F7
Harkstead IP9 . . . .**106** A6
Holbrook IP9 . . . .**105** E8
Lowestoft NR32 . . . .**113** D3
Nacton IP10 . . . .**145** A5
Nedging-with-Naughton IP7 **80** C4
Needham Market IP6 . . . . .**125** E4
Newbourne IP12 . . . .**98** C6
Orford IP12 . . . .**131** B4
Otley IP6 . . . .**69** B2
2 Scole IP21 . . . .**20** F1
Scole NR15 . . . .**21** C7
Stowmarket IP14 . . . .**124** E4
Stratford St Mary CO7 . . . .**103** E4
Tattingstone White House
IP9 . . . .**142** D1
Waldringfield IP12 . . . .**98** D7
Willisham IP8 . . . .**81** B4
Winston IP14 . . . .**53** F1
Witnesham IP6 . . . .**136** A8
Woodbridge IP12 . . . .**146** B3
Yaxley IP23 . . . .**37** B4
Ipswich Sch IP1 . . . .**155** B4
Ipswich St
Bury St Edmunds IP33 . . . .**154** B3
Lakenheath IP27 . . . .**109** F1
Stowmarket IP14 . . . .**124** D6
Ipswich Sta **5** IP1 . . . . . .**155** A4
Ipswich Transport Mus★
IP3 . . . .**140** C2
Ipswich Way IP14 . . . .**68** E6
Ireland Rd IP3 . . . .**139** F1
Irex Rd NR33 . . . .**115** B3
Iris Cl IP2 . . . .**138** F5
Irlam Rd IP2 . . . .**138** D2
Isaacson Rd CB5 . . . .**44** B4
Isinglass Cl CB8 . . . .**121** E2
ISLEHAM **29** B5
Isleham Rd CB7 . . . .**29** B2
Ivry St IP1 . . . .**155** A4
Ivy Cl IP13 . . . .**54** E7
Ivy La N33 . . . .**114** C2
Ivy Lodge Rd IP12 . . . .**71** D1
Ivytree La IP7 . . . .**94** C7
Ixer La IP30 . . . .**64** B5
IXWORTH **34** B2
Ixworth Abbey IP31 . . . .**34** A1
Ixworth CE Prim Sch IP31 **34** B1
Ixworth Mid Sch IP31 . . . .**34** B1
Ixworth Rd
Haverhill CB9 . . . .**132** C4

Ixworth Rd continued
Honington IP31 . . . .**33** F5
Stowlangtoft IP31 . . . .**50** B6
Troston IP31 . . . .**33** D3
Walsham le Willows IP31 . . .**35** A1
IXWORTH THORPE **33** F4

J

Jack Jarvis Cl **5** CB8 . . . . . .**121** A3
Jacks Gn IP26 . . . .**125** E7
Jack's Gn Rd IP6 . . . .**125** E6
Jack's La IP14 . . . .**124** A2
Jackson Cl IP5 . . . .**141** F7
Jackson Rd IP12 . . . .**98** C5
Jackson Way IP6 . . . .**125** D4
Jacobs Cl **14** IP31 . . . .**34** E4
Jacobs Meadow IP30 . . . .**65** D5
Jacobs St **7** NR32 . . . .**113** D2
Jacob Way **11** IP12 . . . .**147** A3
Jacqueline Cl
Bury St Edmunds IP33 . . . .**154** A1
7 Grundisburgh IP13 . . . . .**83** E5
James Boden Cl **7** IP11 . . . .**152** E5
James Carter Rd CO10 . . . . . .**148** C6
Jameson Pl **6** CO10 . . . .**148** C6
Jamestown Bvd IP2 . . . .**139** D3
Janet Hadenham Cl **11**
NR34 . . . .**9** F4
Janus Cl CB9 . . . .**133** F4
Jaques Cl **3** CO10 . . . .**77** B3
Jarman Cl IP23 . . . .**123** C3
Jarman's La IP28 . . . .**29** F7
Jarrold Cl **1** IP31 . . . .**34** F7
Jarvis Way CB8 . . . .**120** E5
Jasmine Cl
9 Felixstowe IP11 . . . .**107** D8
Ipswich IP2 . . . .**138** F3
Jasmine Gn NR32 . . . .**113** C2
Java Lodge Rd IP13 . . . .**127** B3
Jay Cl CB9 . . . .**133** A5
Jay Dr IP14 . . . .**124** F7
Jay La NR32 . . . .**3** A6
Jays Croft Rd **2** IP12 . . . . . .**85** E8
Jay's Gn IP20 . . . .**22** E6
Jay's Hill Rd
Ellough NR34 . . . .**10** B2
Willingham St Mary NR34 . .**26** A8
Jaywick Rd **2** CB9 . . . .**132** E6
Jeaffresons Well IP6 . . . .**126** D4
Jeannie Mann Ct NR32 . . . . .**113** B3
Jeavons La IP31 . . . .**141** E7
Jefferies Rd IP4 . . . .**139** E6
Jellicoe Ave NR33 . . . .**114** D6
Jenkins Gn NR32 . . . .**113** A5
Jenkinsons Pightle NR35 . . . . .**7** B8
Jenner Cl NR35 . . . .**110** C2
Jenners Cl **1** IP12 . . . .**147** B6
Jennings Way IP22 . . . .**20** C3
Jermyn Ave IP32 . . . .**123** F5
Jermyns Cl IP9 . . . .**150** F4
Jermyns Rd IP18 . . . .**119** B8
Jermyn Way IP19 . . . .**118** A2
Jervis Cl **10** IP9 . . . .**105** E7
Jewell View IP5 . . . .**141** F8
Jim Mollison Cl **5** IP28 . . . .**116** B5
Jimmy's Farm★ IP9 . . . . .**142** E5
Jimmy's La CO11 . . . .**104** F5
Jocelyn Cl **16** IP32 . . . .**48** C5
Jockey's La
Combs IP14 . . . .**66** C2
Framsden IP14 . . . .**69** B7
Joes Rd CO10 . . . .**92** C3
John Childs Way NR35 . . . . . .**110** C2
John Lawrence Cl NR34 . . . . .**111** B2
John Russell Gall★ IP3 . .**155** C2
John Shepherd Rd **1**
IP21 . . . .**39** D8
Johnson Cl **5** IP2 . . . .**139** C3
Johnson Rd **7** IP29 . . . .**47** A2
Johnson Way NR32 . . . .**113** A5
John St
Leiston IP16 . . . .**129** C5
Lowestoft NR33 . . . .**115** C7
Rose Hill IP3 . . . .**139** E4
John Swain Cl IP6 . . . .**125** C5
John Tibauld Ct **4** CB9 . . . . .**88** D3
Jolly's Way IP31 . . . .**35** C1
Jones Rd CO10 . . . .**76** C3
Jordan Cl IP5 . . . .**125** E7
Jordayn Rise IP7 . . . .**149** E6
Joshua Ct **5** NR31 . . . .**3** B8
Josselyns The IP11 . . . .**152** B8
Jovian Way IP1 . . . .**138** E8
Joyce Rd NR35 . . . .**110** D3
Jubilee Ave IP14 . . . .**124** D4
Jubilee Cl
11 Claydon IP6 . . . .**82** B5
11 Felixstowe IP11 . . . . . .**107** D8
10 Harwich CO12 . . . .**106** F1
13 Isleham CB7 . . . .**29** C5
2 Laxfield IP13 . . . .**40** B3
4 Thetford IP24 . . . .**16** B5
Weeting IP27 . . . .**5** E3
Jubilee Cres IP14 . . . .**67** A7
Jubilee Ct CB8 . . . .**60** A5
Jubilee Ctr IP28 . . . .**116** C3
Jubilee End **5** CO11 . . . .**104** E3
Jubilee Rd
Bungay NR35 . . . .**110** B2
Lakenheath IP27 . . . .**109** C8
Lowestoft NR33 . . . .**115** A2
Sudbury CO10 . . . .**148** D6
Jubilee Terr **10** IP30 . . . .**50** F2
Jubilee Way
Lowestoft NR32 . . . .**113** E2
Mildenhall IP28 . . . .**116** C4

Jubilee Wlk CB9 . . . .**132** E5
Judas La IP23 . . . .**37** B5
Judith Ave IP17 . . . .**129** B2
Julian Cl CB9 . . . .**133** B5
Julian Rd IP28 . . . .**30** C1
Julian Way **12** NR31 . . . .**3** B7
Julius Martin La CB7 . . . .**28** C4
Junction Rd IP28 . . . .**116** B5
June Ave
Ipswich IP1 . . . .**135** B2
Lowestoft NR32 . . . .**113** B3
Juniper Cl IP28 . . . .**116** E5
Juniper Rd IP28 . . . .**30** C1
Jupes Hill CO7 . . . .**104** B3
Jupe's Hill CO6 . . . .**101** B1
Jupiter Cl CB9 . . . .**133** B4
Jupiter Rd
Bury St Edmunds IP32 . . . . .**49** A3
Ipswich IP4 . . . .**140** B7
Justinian Cl CB9 . . . .**133** B4

K

Karen Cl
Ipswich IP1 . . . .**135** B1
4 Scole IP21 . . . .**20** F1
Kate's La IP14 . . . .**51** A1
Katwijk Way **2** NR32 . . . . . .**115** D8
Keating Cl **2** CO11 . . . .**104** D2
Keats Cl IP17 . . . .**128** B4
Keats Cres IP1 . . . .**134** F3
Kebbles **9** CO10 . . . .**77** A3
KEDINGTON **133** E7
Kedington Prim Sch CB9 **133** E8
Kedington Rd CB9 . . . .**133** D3
Keebles Yd **5** CB9 . . . .**132** E6
Keel Cl NR33 . . . .**114** B4
Keens La IP18 . . . .**119** B7
Keeper's La
Marlesford IP13 . . . .**71** D5
Stoke-by-Nayland CO6 . . . .**102** C8
Trimley St Mary IP11 . . . . .**152** A7
Keep Rise **6** NR35 . . . .**110** B4
Keightley Way IP6 . . . .**136** B5
Kell's Acres NR34 . . . .**8** F7
Kell's Way NR34 . . . .**8** F6
Kelly-Pain Ct NR32 . . . .**113** D3
Kelly Rd IP2 . . . .**138** E5
KELSALE **128** C7
Kelsale CE VCP Sch
IP17 . . . .**128** C5
Kelso Rd IP33 . . . .**122** D2
Kelvedon Dr IP4 . . . .**140** F5
Kelvin Pl IP24 . . . .**16** A4
Kelvin Rd IP1 . . . .**134** F1
Kemball St IP4 . . . .**140** A5
Kembold CT IP32 . . . .**123** E5
Kempshorne Cl NR32 . . . . . .**112** E4
Kemps La NR34 . . . .**111** B3
Kempson Dr **7** CO10 . . . .**92** B3
Kempson Way IP30 . . . .**123** F4
Kempsters The IP11 . . . .**152** D7
Kempton Cl **4** IP11 . . . .**135** A3
Kempton Cross NR34 . . . .**111** A4
Kempton Rd IP11 . . . .**135** A3
Kemsley Rd IP11 . . . .**152** F5
Kendal Gn IP11 . . . .**153** D7
Kendall Cl IP32 . . . .**49** A3
Kendal Rd NR33 . . . .**115** B5
Kennedy Ave IP19 . . . .**118** A1
Kennedy Cl
Halesworth IP19 . . . .**118** B1
Ipswich IP4 . . . .**140** A6
Kennedy Rd CB7 . . . .**29** C5
Kennedy St IP27 . . . .**109** E1
Kennel Loke NR31 . . . .**3** B8
Kennels La IP3 . . . .**146** C8
Kennels Rd
Brightwell IP10 . . . .**98** A6
Foxhall IP10 . . . .**141** F2
Kennetside CB8 . . . .**61** B1
KENNETT **45** F7
Kennett Prim Sch CB8 . . . .**45** F6
Kennett Rd or Moulton
CB8 . . . .**45** F6
Kennett Sta CB8 . . . .**45** F3
Kenney Cl IP8 . . . .**95** D7
KENNINGHALL **19** B8
Kenninghall Prim Sch
NR16 . . . .**19** A8
Kenninghall Rd NR16 . . . .**19** A7
KENNY HILL **13** A3
Kennyhill Dro IP28 . . . .**13** A3
Kensington Rd
Ipswich IP1 . . . .**139** A8
Lowestoft NR33 . . . .**115** C5
Stowmarket IP14 . . . .**124** D5
KENTFORD **46** A5
Kentford Rd **5** IP11 . . . .**152** C4
KENTON **54** B5
KENTON CORNER **54** C4
Kenton Rd IP14 . . . .**53** F2
Kent Rd
Lackford IP28 . . . .**31** F1
Lowestoft NR32 . . . .**113** B1
Stowmarket IP14 . . . .**124** C7
Kents La
Bungay NR35 . . . .**110** D3
Soham CB7 . . . .**28** D4
Kentwell Cl IP4 . . . .**140** F4
Kentwell Hall & Gdns★
CO10 . . . .**77** E2
Kentwell Pl **7** CB8 . . . .**44** B5
Kenyon Dr **9** CO10 . . . .**92** C6
Kenyon Row NR34 . . . .**9** B6
Kenyon St IP2 . . . .**155** B1

Kerridges NR16 . . . .**18** C8
Kerridge's Cut **15** CO11 . . . .**105** A2
Kerridge Way **29** IP20 . . . . . .**22** D6
Kerrison Con Ctr IP23 . . . . . .**37** D1
Kerrison Rd NR35 . . . .**110** D2
Kerry Ave IP1 . . . .**134** D1
Kerrys Farm La IP14 . . . .**51** F4
KERSEY **94** A7
Kersey Ave CO10 . . . .**148** F4
Kersey CE Prim Sch IP7 . .**94** A6
Kersey Cl IP14 . . . .**124** E3
Kersey Pottery★ IP7 . . . . .**94** A7
Kersey Rd IP11 . . . .**152** D4
KERSEY TYE **93** E6
KERSEY UPLAND **93** F5
Kersley Hall La IP21 . . . .**39** A3
KESGRAVE **141** E8
Kesgrave Dr NR32 . . . .**112** F2
Kesgrave High Sch IP5 . .**141** C8
KESSINGLAND **11** C2
KESSINGLAND BEACH **27** C8
Kessingland CE VCP Sch
NR33 . . . .**11** C2
Kesteven Rd IP2 . . . .**155** A1
Kestrel Cl
1 Beck Row, Holywell Row &
Kenny Hill IP28 . . . .**13** B1
Thetford IP24 . . . .**16** C4
Kestrel Dr IP14 . . . .**67** A5
Kestrel Gn NR33 . . . .**114** C6
Kestrel Rd
Bury St Edmunds IP33 . . . .**123** B2
Haverhill CB9 . . . .**133** A5
Ipswich IP2 . . . .**138** D3
Keswick Cl IP11 . . . .**153** C6
KETTLEBASTON **79** C5
Kettlebaston Way **3**
IP1 . . . .**135** D1
KETTLEBURGH **70** C7
Kettleburgh Rd IP13 . . . .**126** C1
Kettlefields CB8 . . . .**59** F5
Kettlefields CP Sch CB8 . .**59** F5
Kettle La IP6 . . . .**67** E1
Kevington Dr NR32 . . . .**112** C2
Keynes Way **18** CO12 . . . . . .**106** F1
Key St IP3 . . . .**155** C2
Khartoum Rd IP4 . . . .**139** F7
Kids Play★ IP32 . . . .**154** B4
Kidz Kingdom★ IP5 . . . . .**98** A4
Kilbourn Rd **6** NR33 . . . . . .**115** A3
Kilbrack NR34 . . . .**111** C5
Kilbrack Gdns NR34 . . . .**111** C5
Kildare Ave IP1 . . . .**134** D2
Kilick Cres NR32 . . . .**114** C4
Kilmaine Rd **22** CO12 . . . . . .**106** F1
Kiln Bottom IP7 . . . .**149** E8
Kiln Cotts IP14 . . . .**124** C5
Kiln Dr CO10 . . . .**148** E4
Kiln Farm La IP22 . . . .**35** F5
Kiln Field **1** IP11 . . . .**152** D5
Kiln La
Benhall IP17 . . . .**128** C1
Boot Street IP13 . . . .**137** E6
Buxhall IP14 . . . .**65** F3
Dickleburgh & Rushall IP21 **21** C2
Elmswell IP30 . . . .**50** E1
Friston IP17 . . . .**72** D7
1 Mistley CO11 . . . .**104** F2
Needham IP20 . . . .**22** A4
Rede IP29 . . . .**62** E4
Stowlangtoft IP31 . . . .**34** E1
Kiln Rd NR34 . . . .**26** C3
Kilverstone Rd IP24 . . . .**17** A6
Kimberley Rd NR33 . . . .**115** A7
Kimms Belt IP24 . . . .**16** B5
King Edward Ave IP13 . . . . . .**127** C3
King Edward Rd
Ipswich IP3 . . . .**140** B3
Leiston IP16 . . . .**129** C6
King Edward VII Dr IP9 . . . . .**107** A4
King Edward VII Rd CB8 . . . .**120** E5
King Edward VI Sch
IP33 . . . .**154** A3
Kingfisher Ave IP2 . . . .**138** D3
Kingfisher Cl CB9 . . . .**133** A6
Kingfisher Cres IP18 . . . .**119** A7
Kingfisher Ct NR33 . . . .**114** C6
Kingfisher Dr
6 Burwell CB5 . . . .**44** A6
Claydon IP6 . . . .**81** F5
13 Harwich CO12 . . . .**106** F1
Kingfisher Leisure Ctr
CO10 . . . .**148** D4
Kingfisher Rd IP32 . . . .**123** C2
Kingfisher Rise IP17 . . . .**128** C4
Kingfishers CO10 . . . .**148** B4
Kingfisher Way
Mildenhall IP28 . . . .**116** D4
6 Stowmarket IP14 . . . . . .**67** A5
King George Ave CB8 . . . . . .**120** B8
King George's Ave
3 Harwich CO12 . . . .**107** A2
Leiston IP16 . . . .**129** E6
Kings Ave IP4 . . . .**139** E5
King's Ave IP13 . . . .**126** B5
Kingsbury Rd IP11 . . . .**152** D5
Kings Cl
7 Acton CO10 . . . .**92** B7
1 Manningtree CO11 . . . .**104** E2
Mildenhall IP28 . . . .**116** D5
Woodbridge IP12 . . . .**146** E4
King's Dam NR34 . . . .**9** B6
Kings Dr CB8 . . . .**121** B1
Kingsfield Ave IP1 . . . .**139** D8
Kings Fleet Prim Sch
IP11 . . . .**153** C6
Kings Fleet Rd IP11 . . . .**152** E3

Kingsgate Dr IP4 . . . . 139 F8
KINGSHALL GREEN 64 D7
Kingshall St IP30 . . . . 64 C8
KINGSHALL STREET 64 D8
Kings Head La IP22 . . . . . 19 A6
King's Head St [2] CO12 . 107 C3
Kings Hill CO10 . . . . 148 E4
King's Hill CB9 . . . . 133 E7
King's La
  Blyford IP19 . . . . 42 C8
  Gosbeck IP6 . . . . 68 D3
  Long Melford CO10 . . . . . 92 A7
  Sotherton NR34 . . . . 25 D2
  Tannington IP13 . . . . 55 B7
  Walsham le Willows IP31 . . 35 C3
  Weston NR34 . . . . 9 D1
Kingsland IP9 . . . . 106 F5
Kingsland La [3] CO6 . . . . 102 A7
Kingsley Cl [8] IP1 . . . . . 135 A3
Kings Mead CB8 . . . . 60 E8
Kingsmead Cl [3] IP14 . . 124 C7
Kings Meadow
  Great Cornard CO10 . . . . 148 E4
  Kedington CB9 . . . . 133 E7
Kingsmead Rd IP14 . . . . . 124 C7
Kings Parade CB7 . . . . 28 D3
Kings Pk IP29 . . . . 62 D5
Kings Rd
  Bungay NR35 . . . . 110 C2
  Glemsford CO10 . . . . 77 A3
  Leiston IP16 . . . . 129 C5
King's Rd
  Bury St Edmunds IP33 . . 154 A2
  Harwich CO12 . . . . 107 A2
  Topcroft NR35 . . . . 7 A8
King St
  Aldeburgh IP15 . . . . 130 E3
  Felixstowe IP11 . . . . 152 E6
  Ipswich IP1 . . . . 155 B3
  [1] Mildenhall IP28 . . . . 116 C4
  Sudbury CO10 . . . . 148 C5
  Weybread IP21 . . . . 22 D3
King's Theatre CB8 . . . . . 120 F3
KINGSTON 146 F2
Kingston Cl NR33 . . . . . . 115 A3
Kingston Ct NR34 . . . . . . 111 D5
Kingston Dr NR34 . . . . . . 111 C5
Kingston Farm Rd IP12 . . 147 A4
Kingston Pas [3] CB8 . . . 121 A3
Kingston Rd
  Ipswich IP1 . . . . 138 F8
  Woodbridge IP12 . . . . . . 147 A4
Kingsway
  [4] Earsham NR35 . . . . 7 F4
  [9] Harwich CO12 . . . . . 107 B2
  Mildenhall IP28 . . . . 116 C4
  Newmarket CB8 . . . . 120 F4
  Woodbridge IP12 . . . . . . 147 B5
Kingswood NR34 . . . . 114 D4
Kingsworth Rd IP32 . . . . 123 D6
King William St [3] IP6 . 125 D5
Kinross Rd IP4 . . . . 136 B1
Kipling Cl [5] NR33 . . . . . 11 C1
Kipling Rd IP1 . . . . 134 F3
Kipling Way IP14 . . . . . . 124 B8
KIRBY CANE 8 E8
Kirby Cane Wlk NR32 . . . 113 A3
Kirby Cl IP4 . . . . 140 A7
KIRBY ROW 8 E7
Kirby St IP4 . . . . 140 A7
Kirkdale Ct [4] NR33 . . . 115 B4
Kirkham Cl [2] IP2 . . . . . 139 A4
KIRKLEY 115 B5
Kirkley Cliff Rd NR33 . . . 115 C5
Kirkley Gdns NR33 . . . . . 115 B6
Kirkley Pk Rd NR33 . . . . 115 B6
Kirkley Run NR33 . . . . . . 115 A7
Kirkley Sports & Fitness Ctr
  NR33 . . . . 115 B6
Kirkley St NR33 . . . . 115 B6
Kirkstead Rd IP33 . . . . . . 122 D3
Kirkstone Way [4] NR32 . 113 A4
Kirkton Cl IP9 . . . . 107 A5
Kirkwood Dr [1] NR33 . . 114 C2
KIRTLING 60 E3
KIRTLING GREEN 60 E2
Kirtling Pl [3] CB9 . . . . . 132 F6
Kirtling Rd CB8 . . . . 60 E5
KIRTON 98 E2
Kirton Rd IP11 . . . . 107 D8
Kitchener Rd
  Ipswich IP1 . . . . 138 F8
  Leiston IP16 . . . . 129 C6
Kitchener Way [5] IP9 . . 107 A5
Kitchen Hill CO10 . . . . . . 91 D4
Kitson Meadows IP33 . . . 122 A5
Kittiwake Cl
  Ipswich IP2 . . . . 138 E3
  Lowestoft NR33 . . . . 114 D5
Kittiwake Ct IP14 . . . . . . 124 F6
Klondyke IP32 . . . . 122 F8
Knaves Acre Dro CB7 . . . . 29 B6
KNAVES GREEN 53 A5
KNETTISHALL 17 E3
Knettishall Heath Cntry Pk★
  IP31 . . . . 17 E3
Knight Rd IP12 . . . . 85 D8
Knights Cl
  [7] Debenham IP14 . . . . . 53 F2
  [10] Felixstowe IP11 . . . 153 D6
  [1] Manningtree CO11 . . 104 C2
  [4] Old Newton with Dagworth
    IP14 . . . . 51 E1
Knights Ct
  [19] Haverhill CB9 . . . . . 132 C5
  Roman Hill NR32 . . . . . . 113 C1
Knightsdale Rd IP1 . . . . . 135 A1

Knights La [5] IP5 . . . . . . 141 D7
Knightswood [3] NR32 . . 113 B5
Knights Yd NR34 . . . . 111 B6
KNODISHALL 73 A8
KNODISHALL COMMON . 129 A2
Knoll The IP13 . . . . 126 D3
Knowle The [17] IP31 . . . . 34 E4
KNOWL GREEN 90 C4
Knox La IP31 . . . . 34 C4
Knutsford Cl IP8 . . . . 138 C1
Kreswell Gr [7] CO12 . . . 107 A1
Kylborne Cl IP33 . . . . 122 C4
Kyson Hill★ IP12 . . . . . . 146 F2
Kyson Prim Sch IP12 . . . 146 D4

L

Laburnum Ave IP28 . . . . 116 E5
Laburnum Cl
  Ipswich IP3 . . . . 140 D2
  [3] Ipswich IP8 . . . . 138 C2
  Red Lodge IP28 . . . . 30 B1
  Worlingworth IP13 . . . . . . 54 E7
Laburnum Dr IP14 . . . . . . 80 C8
Laburnum Gdns IP5 . . . . 136 E1
Laburnum La [11] CB5 . . . 44 A6
Laburnum Rd IP3 . . . . . . 110 B3
Laburnum Way [2] CO6 . 102 C5
Lacewing Cl [13] IP8 . . . 142 E8
Lacey's La CB8 . . . . 120 B7
Lacey St IP4 . . . . 139 E6
Lachlan Gn IP12 . . . . 146 F7
LACKFORD 31 F1
Lackford La IP28 . . . . 47 D6
Lackford Pl [7] IP3 . . . . . 144 C8
Lackford Wildfowl Nature
  Reserve★ IP28 . . . . 31 F1
Lacon Rd [2] IP8 . . . . 134 A2
Ladbrook Cl IP7 . . . . 80 E1
Ladyfield IP14 . . . . 66 D8
Ladygate [1] CB9 . . . . . . 132 C4
Lady La
  Hadleigh IP7 . . . . 149 E7
  Ipswich IP1 . . . . 155 A3
Lady La Ind Est IP7 . . . . 149 E7
Lady Margaret Gdns
  IP12 . . . . 146 D4
LADY'S GREEN 61 F6
Lady's La IP22 . . . . 19 F5
Lady's Meadow NR34 . . . 111 B6
Lady St [13] CO10 . . . . . . 78 D4
Ladywell Rd IP14 . . . . 51 F7
Ladywood Rd IP4 . . . . . . 140 C7
Lagonda Dr IP1 . . . . 134 C1
Lake Ave IP32 . . . . 48 C5
Lakeland [3] IP26 . . . . 5 A3
Lakeland Dr NR32 . . . . . . 112 F1
LAKENHEATH 109 E7
Lakenheath Airfield IP27 . 14 B5
Lakenheath American High
  Sch IP27 . . . . 109 F1
Lakenheath Fen Nature
  Reserve★ IP27 . . . . 4 F1
Lakenheath Mid Sch IP26 . 4 D5
Lakenheath Prim Sch
  IP27 . . . . 109 D6
Lakenheath Sta IP27 . . . . . 4 F1
Lake Side IP14 . . . . 124 C6
Lakeside Ave IP16 . . . . . . 73 E6
Lakeside Cl IP18 . . . . 119 B7
Lakeside Pk Dr IP18 . . . . 119 B6
Lakeside Rd 138 C2
Lakeside Rise NR32 . . . . 112 C8
Lake View Rd IP14 . . . . . 114 E8
Lakforth [4] CO10 . . . . . . 91 E8
LAMARSH 101 A6
Lamarsh Hill [1] CO8 . . . 101 C5
Lamarsh Rd CO8 . . . . 101 A6
LAMB CORNER 103 C2
Lamb Ct IP28 . . . . 116 D2
Lambert Cl
  Halesworth IP19 . . . . . . 118 B3
  Weeting IP27 . . . . 5 E4
Lambert Dr CO10 . . . . 92 B7
Lamberts Cl [21] IP26 . . . . 4 E5
Lamberts La IP5 . . . . 136 D2
Lambert's La
  Mendlesham IP14 . . . . . . 52 B2
  Sudbourne IP12 . . . . 73 B1
Lambert's Way NR35 . . . 110 C6
Lambeth Cl [1] IP1 . . . . . 139 A7
Lambeth Way IP14 . . . . . . 67 F7
LAMBFAIR GREEN 75 A8
Lamble Cl IP28 . . . . 30 B8
Lambourne Cl [3] IP32 . . 123 E6
Lambourne Rd IP1 . . . . . 135 B4
Lambsale Meadow IP17 . 128 D4
Lambseth St IP23 . . . . . . 117 C3
Lambs La IP29 . . . . 63 D1
Lamdin Rd IP32 . . . . 48 C5
Lammas IP31 . . . . 34 C4
LAMPARDBROOK 70 E8
Lanark Rd IP4 . . . . 136 B1
Lancaster Ave IP32 . . . . . 122 F8
Lancaster Cl IP29 . . . . 62 C4
Lancaster Dr [8] IP5 . . . . 98 A7
Lancaster Rd
  [5] Feltwell IP26 . . . . 4 E5
  Ipswich IP4 . . . . 139 E6
  [7] Mildenhall IP28 . . . . . 30 A8
  Sudbury CO10 . . . . 148 B8
Lancaster Way
  [10] Claydon IP6 . . . . 82 B5
  Stradishall CB8 . . . . 75 C7
Lancers La IP31 . . . . 34 C4
Lancewood Wlk [27] IP27 . 13 F2
Lancing Ave IP4 . . . . 140 A8

Landguard Fort★ IP11 . . . 107 E2
Landguard Nature Reserve★
  IP11 . . . . 107 E2
Landguard Rd IP11 . . . . . 153 I11
Landsdown Rd CO10 . . . . 148 E7
Landseer Cl IP3 . . . . 140 A1
Landseer Ct [1] CB9 . . . . 132 D4
Landseer Rd IP3 . . . . 139 E2
Landspring La NR35 . . . . 114 E6
LANDWADE 44 D4
Landwade Rd CB8 . . . . . . 44 D6
Lanercost Way IP2 . . . . . 139 A1
Lane The
  Creeting St Peter or West
    Creeting IP6 . . . . 67 B5
  [3] Mistley CO11 . . . . . 104 F2
  Wrentham NR34 . . . . 26 E5
  Yoxford IP17 . . . . 57 C8
Langdale Cl [3] IP11 . . . . 153 D6
Langdale Pk NR32 . . . . . 113 A4
Langer Prim Sch IP11 . . . 152 E2
Langer Rd IP11 . . . . 152 E2
Langford Cl IP14 . . . . 124 B8
Lang Gate Way NR35 . . . . 7 D6
LANGHAM
  Bury St Edmunds IP33 . . . 50 D8
  Stratford St Mary 103 C2
Langham La CO4 . . . . . . 103 B1
Langham Rd
  Blaxhall IP19 . . . . 72 B4
  Boxted CO4 . . . . 102 F1
Langham Way CO9 . . . . . . 74 A1
Langley Ave IP11 . . . . . . 152 E4
Langley Cl IP11 . . . . 152 E5
Langley Gdns NR33 . . . . 114 F5
Langley Hill CO8 . . . . 101 B6
Langmere Rd IP21 . . . . . . 21 C4
Langridge The IP31 . . . . . 34 B2
Langstons IP11 . . . . 152 D7
LANGTON GREEN 117 C4
Langton Rd [4] IP33 . . . . 122 D4
Lanman Mus★ IP13 . . . . 126 D4
Lansbury Rd IP19 . . . . . . 118 B3
Lansdowne Rd
  Felixstowe IP11 . . . . 153 B6
  Ipswich IP1 . . . . 140 A5
  Lowestoft NR33 . . . . 114 F3
Lapwing Cl [17] IP31 . . . . 49 D4
Lapwing Ct [4] IP28 . . . . 116 D4
Lapwing Gr IP14 . . . . 124 F6
Lapwing Rd IP2 . . . . 138 D3
Lapwing Way CB7 . . . . . . 28 C5
Larch Cl IP27 . . . . 109 D7
Larchcroft Cl IP1 . . . . . . 135 B2
Larchcroft Rd IP1 . . . . . . 135 A2
Larches The NR34 . . . . . . 26 E5
Larch Gr [6] CO6 . . . . . . 102 C5
Larch Rd NR32 . . . . 113 B3
Larchwood Cl IP8 . . . . . . 138 C5
Largent Gr IP5 . . . . 141 E8
Lark Cl
  [4] Stowmarket IP14 . . . . 67 A5
  Worlington IP28 . . . . 30 B4
Larkhall Cl CB7 . . . . 28 F1
Lark Hill CB8 . . . . 45 F3
Larkhall Rise IP4 . . . . . . 140 E5
Larkhill Way [9] IP11 . . . 152 D5
Lark Rd IP28 . . . . 116 D4
Lark Cl
  [23] Martlesham Heath IP5 . 98 A4
  Sudbury CO10 . . . . 148 B3
Larks Cl CB9 . . . . 133 A5
Larksfield Cres [5] CO12 . 107 A2
Larksfield Rd IP9 . . . . . . 105 D5
Larks Gate IP28 . . . . 48 C6
Larks Rise IP19 . . . . 118 C3
Larksway IP11 . . . . 152 D5
Lark Valley Dr [9] IP28 . . 48 C6
Larters La IP14 . . . . 67 D8
La Salle Cl IP2 . . . . 139 B3
Lathbury Cl IP33 . . . . 154 B3
Lattens Sq [4] NR32 . . . . 113 C2
Lattice Ave IP4 . . . . 140 C6
LATTINFORD HILL 151 D8
Laud Mews IP3 . . . . 140 A2
Laundry La
  Bury St Edmunds IP33 . . 123 B3
  Huntingfield IP19 . . . . . . 41 A4
Laureate Com Prim Sch
  CB8 . . . . 120 E6
Laureate Gdns CB8 . . . . 120 E6
Laureate Paddocks CB8 . 120 E6
Laureate Sch Rd CB8 . . . 120 E6
Laurel Ave
  [1] Harwich CO12 . . . . . 106 F1
  Ipswich IP5 . . . . 141 A7
Laurel Cl
  Haverhill CB9 . . . . 132 B7
  [7] Red Lodge IP28 . . . . . 30 C1
  [19] Thurston IP31 . . . . . 49 D4
Laurel Ct [9] IP30 . . . . . . 50 F2
Laurel Dr
  [13] Claydon IP6 . . . . . . 82 A5
  [8] Long Melford CO10 . . 91 E8
Laurelhayes IP2 . . . . 139 A3
Laurel Rd NR33 . . . . 115 B6
Laurels The
  [8] Hopton on Sea NR31 . 3 B7
  Worlingham NR34 . . . . . 111 F3
Laurel Way [5] IP6 . . . . . 134 C8
Lavender Cl [3] IP28 . . . . 30 B1
Lavender Hill IP2 . . . . . . 138 F4

LAVENHAM 78 D4
Lavenham Guildhall of
  Corpus Christi★ CO10 . . 78 E4
Lavenham Prim Sch CO10 78 D4
Lavenham Rd
  Great Waldingfield CO10 . 78 D1
  Ipswich IP2 . . . . 138 E5
Lavenham Way
  [5] Lowestoft NR32 . . . . 112 F3
  [4] Stowmarket IP14 . . . 124 E3
LAWFORD 104 E2
Lawn Gr NR32 . . . . 112 F5
Lawns The IP4 . . . . 140 C8
Lawn Way IP11 . . . . 152 E5
Lawrence Dr NR32 . . . . . 113 B6
Lawrence Rd IP24 . . . . . . 16 D7
Law's Drift IP10 . . . . 98 C2
LAWSHALL 63 E1
LAWSHALL GREEN 77 F8
Lawshall Rd
  Hartest IP29 . . . . 77 B8
  Hawstead IP29 . . . . 63 D4
Lawshall Row IP29 . . . . . . 63 D2
Lawson Ct [2] NR33 . . . . 115 C7
Lawson Pl IP32 . . . . 123 E5
Lawson Rd NR33 . . . . 115 C7
LAXFIELD 40 C3
Laxfield & District Mus★
  IP13 . . . . 40 B3
Laxfield Rd
  Badingham IP13 . . . . 56 B8
  Dennington IP13 . . . . 55 E6
  Fressingfield IP21 . . . . . . 39 F7
  Laxfield IP13 . . . . 40 C1
  Stradbroke IP21 . . . . 39 E4
Laxfield Way NR33 . . . . . 114 F4
Layer Rd CB9 . . . . 132 C5
Layham Dr [4] IP32 . . . . 123 A8
Layham Gdns IP14 . . . . . 124 F3
Layham Rd IP7 . . . . 149 D4
Layhill IP32 . . . . 123 D5
Laywood Cl [1] IP32 . . . . 123 D6
Layzell Croft CO10 . . . . . 92 B2
Leabrook Cl IP32 . . . . . . 123 E6
Leader's Way CB8 . . . . . 120 E4
Lea's Drift [1] NR33 . . . . 114 C5
Leas The IP18 . . . . 112 F5
Lea The IP18 . . . . 119 B2
Leather La
  Great Yeldham CO9 . . . . . 90 A1
  Haverhill CB9 . . . . 132 C5
Leathes Cl NR32 . . . . 112 F1
Leathes Ham Nature
  Reserve★ NR32 . . . . . . 113 A1
LEAVENHEATH 102 B7
Leech Wlk IP32 . . . . 122 E8
Lee Cl CB9 . . . . 132 D8
Leeks Cl IP7 . . . . 149 D7
Leeks Hill IP12 . . . . 147 A7
Lee Rd
  Aldeburgh IP15 . . . . 130 E3
  Harwich CO12 . . . . 107 B2
  Ipswich IP3 . . . . 139 F3
Leggatt Dr IP8 . . . . 134 A2
Le Grice Wlk IP32 . . . . . 122 E7
Leicester Cl IP2 . . . . 138 F1
Leighton Rd IP3 . . . . 144 A8
Leighton Sq [8] IP3 . . . . 144 A8
LEISTON 129 B5
Leiston Abbey★ IP16 . . . . 58 C3
Leiston High Sch IP16 . . 129 E5
Leiston Leisure Ctr IP16 . 129 C5
Leiston Mid Sch IP16 . . . 129 C6
Leiston Prim Sch IP16 . . 129 E5
Leiston Rd
  Aldeburgh IP15 . . . . 130 D7
  Coldfair Green IP17 . . . . 129 B3
  Haverhill CB9 . . . . 132 C5
  [4] Lowestoft NR32 . . . . 113 D1
  Theberton IP16 . . . . 58 B5
Leisure Way NR32 . . . . . 113 B7
Lely Rd IP3 . . . . 143 F8
Lemons Hill IP9 . . . . 105 B8
Lentins The IP14 . . . . 68 E6
Leona Cres NR33 . . . . . . 114 C2
Leonard Dr [2] NR33 . . . 113 A6
Leonard's La IP26 . . . . 4 D5
Leopold Gdns IP4 . . . . . . 140 B8
Leopold Rd
  Felixstowe IP11 . . . . 153 A3
  Ipswich IP4 . . . . 140 B7
Leslie Rd IP3 . . . . 140 C1
Lester Piggott Way CB8 . 120 F6
LETHERINGHAM 70 C4
Letton Cl IP9 . . . . 150 E3
Leverett's La IP18 . . . . . . 119 B2
LEVINGTON 145 E3
Levington Ct NR33 . . . . . 115 D8
Levington La IP10 . . . . . . 98 A3
Levington Rd
  Felixstowe IP11 . . . . 152 E1
  Ipswich IP3 . . . . 140 A4
  Nacton IP10 . . . . 145 C4
Lewes Cl IP3 . . . . 140 D3
Lewis Cl
  Ditchingham NR35 . . . . 110 C8
  Hopton IP22 . . . . 18 C2
Lewis La IP9 . . . . 105 B5
Ley Rd
  Barrow IP29 . . . . 47 A2
  Stetchworth CB8 . . . . 60 A5
Leys La IP23 . . . . 37 B5
Leys Rd IP30 . . . . 50 B2
Leyton Ave IP28 . . . . 116 B6
Liberty Cl IP32 . . . . 123 F6
Liberty Intermediate Sch
  IP27 . . . . 14 A3
LIDGATE 61 C4

Lidgate Ct [1] IP11 . . . . . 152 C4
Lidgate Rd CB8 . . . . 61 C8
Lighthouse Score [2]
  NR32 . . . . 113 E3
Lilac Cl IP27 . . . . 14 D8
Lilac Dr
  Lakenheath IP27 . . . . . . 109 D6
  Lowestoft NR32 . . . . 113 B3
Lilac Wlk IP6 . . . . 125 D3
Lilley Cl IP33 . . . . 122 C3
Lily La NR34 . . . . 10 A7
Lily Way NR33 . . . . 114 C5
Lime Ave
  Harwich CO12 . . . . 107 A2
  Lowestoft NR32 . . . . 112 D2
Lime Cl
  Burwell CB5 . . . . 44 B5
  [7] Harleston IP20 . . . . . . 22 D5
  Lakenheath IP27 . . . . . . 109 D5
  Mildenhall IP28 . . . . 116 E5
  [6] Ufford IP13 . . . . 84 F7
  Wickham Market IP13 . . 127 B6
Limecroft Cl [1] IP1 . . . . 135 A3
Lime Gr CO10 . . . . 148 A3
Limekiln Cl [7] IP6 . . . . . 134 C8
Lime Kiln Quay IP12 . . . . 147 B5
Lime Kiln Quay Rd IP12 . 147 B5
Limerick Cl IP1 . . . . 134 E2
Limes Ave IP8 . . . . 134 C2
Limes The
  Framlingham IP6 . . . . . . 126 B4
  Halesworth IP19 . . . . . . 118 A3
  [6] Horringer IP29 . . . . . . 63 A8
  Long Melford CO10 . . . . . 91 E8
  Rushmere St Andrew IP5 . 136 D1
Limestone Cl [12] CB7 . . 29 C5
Lime Tree Ave IP16 . . . . . 129 C5
Limetree Cl IP6 . . . . 125 E4
Lime Tree Cl [3] IP30 . . . 64 F8
Limetree Dr IP3 . . . . 140 D2
Lime Tree Pl IP14 . . . . . . 124 E5
Lime Wlk IP30 . . . . 65 A3
Limmer Ave IP21 . . . . 21 C5
Lincoln Ave IP17 . . . . . . 128 B2
Lincoln Cl IP1 . . . . 135 B3
Lincoln Ct [11] NR33 . . . . 11 B1
Lincoln Gdns [8] IP6 . . . 82 B5
Lincoln Gn IP33 . . . . 123 B2
Lincoln La CO6 . . . . 102 E1
Lincoln Rd [10] IP28 . . . . 30 A8
Lincoln Terr IP11 . . . . . . 152 F3
Linda Cl [11] NR32 . . . . . . 3 D4
Lindbergh Rd IP3 . . . . . . 140 C1
Linden Cl
  Aldeburgh IP15 . . . . 130 D6
  [20] Manningtree CO11 . 104 D2
Linden Rd IP15 . . . . 130 C5
Linden Wlk [11] IP28 . . . . 13 B1
Lindisfarne Cl IP2 . . . . . 139 A1
Lindisfarne Rd IP33 . . . . 122 D2
LINDSEY 93 D7
Lindsey Ave CO10 . . . . . 148 F4
Lindsey Rd IP4 . . . . 140 C7
LINDSEY TYE 93 E8
Lindsey Way IP14 . . . . . . 124 E3
Lingfield Rd IP1 . . . . 135 B4
Lingheath Rd IP27 . . . . . . 6 A1
Ling Rd
  Palgrave IP22 . . . . 20 B2
  Wortham IP22 . . . . 19 F2
Lings Field IP13 . . . . 70 C7
Lingside [1] IP5 . . . . 98 A7
Ling's La IP9 . . . . 106 B7
Link La IP9 . . . . 104 E7
Link Rd
  Capel St Mary IP9 . . . . . 150 E3
  [5] Shotley Gate IP9 . . . 107 A5
Links Ave IP11 . . . . 153 B6
Links Cl
  Bury St Edmunds IP33 . . 123 B1
  Lowestoft NR33 . . . . 114 F5
  Worlington IP28 . . . . 30 B4
Linksfield IP5 . . . . 140 E7
Linksfield Gdns IP5 . . . . 140 E7
Links Rd
  Great Yarmouth NR31 . . . 3 B8
  Lowestoft NR32 . . . . 113 D5
Links The
  Flempton IP28 . . . . 32 B1
  Woodditton CB8 . . . . 59 E8
Links View CO10 . . . . 92 D3
Link The IP9 . . . . 104 E7
Linkwood Rd IP30 . . . . . . 64 B7
Linnet Dr [14] IP14 . . . . . 67 A5
Linnet Pl IP33 . . . . 154 C1
Linnet Rd
  Bury St Edmunds IP33 . . 122 E4
  Ipswich IP2 . . . . 138 D4
Linnetts La [3] IP9 . . . . . 133 E2
LINSTEAD PARVA 40 E8
Linstead Rd IP19 . . . . 40 F5
Linton Cl CB8 . . . . 120 F5
Linton Gdns IP33 . . . . . . 122 E3
Linton Pl [2] CB9 . . . . . . 132 F6
Linx The [6] IP13 . . . . . . 40 B3
Lionel Hurst Cl [15] CO10 . 92 B3
Lion La IP6 . . . . 125 C5
Lion Meadow CB9 . . . . . . 88 D4
Lion St
  Glemsford CO10 . . . . 77 A3
  Palgrave IP22 . . . . 20 B1
  Wortham IP22 . . . . 36 F8
Lion St IP1 . . . . 155 B3
Lisburn Rd CB8 . . . . 121 B3

Lister Rd
Hadleigh IP7 149 F5
Ipswich IP1 134 F1
LISTON 91 D7
Liston La CO10 91 D7
Lithgo Paddock 8 IP31 49 A6
Little Back La 8 IP14 53 F2
LITTLE BEALINGS 137 E5
LITTLE BLAKENHAM 81 F3
LITTLE BRADLEY 74 E6
LITTLE CORNARD 92 C2
LITTLE DITTON 60 C5
Little Fen Dro CB5 44 A7
LITTLE FINBOROUGH 66 B1
Little Gipping St IP1 155 A3
LITTLE GLEMHAM 71 E5
Little Gn
Cheveley CB8 60 E6
Earl Soham IP13 54 F1
Elmswell IP30 50 E2
Little Gn Cl IP23 36 C3
Little Gr IP9 150 E2
LITTLE GREEN
Burgate 36 D5
Gislingham 36 C3
Little Gulls IP9 150 D3
Little Hall Mus★ CO10 78 E4
Little Hasse Dro CB7 28 E6
LITTLE HORKESLEY 102 B3
Little Horkesley Rd CO6 102 A2
Little Hyde Cl CO9 90 A1
Little Hyde Rd CO9 90 A1
LITTLE KNOWLES GREEN 62 B5
LITTLE LONDON 66 E2
Little London Hill IP14 53 E3
Little London La CB7 29 B5
Little Lumpkid IP7 149 E8
Little Meadows Dr IP6 69 C2
Little Mill La IP29 47 A3
Littlemoor Rd IP17 57 E6
Little Oulsham Dro IP26 4 B6
Little St John's St 8
IP12 147 A5
Little St Mary's CO10 91 E7
LITTLE SAXHAM 47 D2
Little's Cres IP2 155 B1
Little St IP17 57 C8
LITTLE STONHAM 67 F6
LITTLE THURLOW 74 E5
LITTLE THURLOW GREEN 74 E6
Little Tufts IP9 150 F3
LITTLE WALDINGFIELD 92 D8
LITTLE WELNETHAM 64 B6
LITTLE WENHAM 150 B5
Little Whip St IP2 155 B1
LITTLE WHITTINGHAM GREEN 40 A8
LITTLE WRATTING 74 E2
LITTLE YELDHAM 90 B2
Little Yeldham Rd CO9 90 B2
Livermere Drift IP31 48 E6
Livermere Rd
Great Barton IP31 49 A6
Troston IP31 33 D2
Llewellyn Drift 8 IP5 141 C7
Lloyd Rd 3 IP9 107 A4
Lloyds Ave
Ipswich IP1 155 B3
15 Kessingland NR33 11 B1
Lloyds The IP5 141 C7
Loam Pit La IP19 118 C4
Locarno Rd 1 IP3 140 B3
Loch Rannoch Cl IP30 50 E2
Lock Cl 14 IP14 53 F2
Lockhart Rd NR35 8 D7
Lockington Cl 4 IP14 124 E5
Lockington Cres IP14 124 D5
Lockington Rd IP14 124 D5
Lockington Wlk IP14 124 D5
Lock's La
6 Leavenheath CO6 102 A7
Shipmeadow NR34 8 E5
Wrentham NR34 26 F6
Lock's Rd NR34 25 C5
Lockwood Cl 1 IP12 147 A5
Loddon Rd
Ditchingham NR35 110 C7
Gillingham NR34 9 B6
Kirby Cane NR35 8 E8
Lode Cl 1 CB7 28 D3
Lode La CB7 28 A1
Lodge Cl IP14 51 E1
Lodge Farm Dr IP11 153 C5
Lodge Farm La
Barsham NR34 9 B4
8 Melton IP12 84 E6
Lodge Farm Rd CO10 77 B1
Lodge La
Claydon IP6 134 A8
Riddlesworth IP22 18 A3
Shelfanger IP22 20 B5
Lodge Rd
Feltwell IP26 4 F6
Great Bealings IP13 137 E5
Hollesley IP12 99 D7
Holton IP19 118 E5
St John, Ilketshall NR35 110 F2
1 Ufford IP13 84 F7
Walberswick IP18 119 A2
Lodge Way IP24 16 B7
Lofft Cl 11 IP31 34 E4
Loftus Ave IP18 119 C7
Loganberry Rd 4 IP3 144 C7
Loggers La IP22 18 E1
Loke The
Blundeston NR32 3 A4
Ditchingham NR35 110 B7
Lombardy Rd CO10 148 B8
Lonbarn Hill CO11 105 D1
London City Rd IP21 39 C3
London La
Harleston IP14 66 C7
4 Mundford IP26 6 B8
London Rd
Beccles NR34 111 B2
Blythburgh IP19 42 E5
Brampton with Stoven NR34 25 E6
Brandon IP27 14 E8
Capel St Mary IP9 150 F2
Copdock & Washbrook IP8 138 A1
Elveden IP24 15 C2
Great Horkesley CO6 102 C1
Halesworth IP19 118 A2
Harleston IP20 22 D5
Icklingham IP27 31 E8
Ipswich IP1 155 A3
Kessingland NR33 11 B2
Lowestoft NR33 115 A2
Pinewood IP8 138 B2
Thetford IP24 16 A5
Westley Waterless CB8 59 A4
Weston NR34 9 D2
Wrentham NR34 26 E4
London Rd N NR32 113 D1
London Rd Pakefield
NR33 115 A2
London Rd S NR33 115 C5
Lone Barn Ct IP1 138 D8
Lonely Rd IP21 21 C6
Long Acre
Lowestoft NR33 115 B3
Southwold IP18 119 B7
Longacre Gdns IP33 122 E3
Long Ave IP17 128 B4
Longbeach Dr NR33 114 D3
Long Bessels IP7 149 D6
Long Brackland IP33 154 B3
Longcroft IP11 152 E6
Longden Ave NR32 112 F2
Long Dolver Dro CB7 28 D6
Long Field IP11 152 D6
Longfield Rd IP9 150 E4
Longfield Way 6 NR32 112 D2
Longfulans La NR31 3 B6
LONG GREEN 36 D8
Long La
Bawdsey IP12 99 E3
Burston & Shimpling IP22 20 E8
Feltwell IP26 4 D5
Long Marsh Cl IP18 119 C7
Longmeadow IP33 122 E3
Long Meadows 2 CO12 106 F1
Long Meadow Wlk NR33 114 D5
LONG MELFORD 77 F1
Long Melford CE Prim Sch
CO10 91 E8
Longmere La CB7 28 C5
Long Pastures 2 CO10 77 B2
Long Perry IP9 150 F3
Long Rd
Lowestoft NR33 114 E3
Manningtree CO11 104 D1
Long Rd E CO7 104 A2
Long Rd W CO7 103 F2
Longrigg Rd NR35 110 C7
Long Row IP16 129 D6
Long Shop Mus★ IP16 129 C6
Long St IP3 139 E5
LONG THURLOW 51 B7
Long Thurlow Rd IP31 51 A7
Lonsdale Cl IP4 139 F7
Looe Rd IP11 153 C5
Looms La IP33 154 B2
Lopham Rd NR16 18 D8
Lophams Cl CB9 132 D8
Loraine Way IP8 134 A1
Lord Rd IP22 20 D2
Lord's Croft La CB9 132 E5
Lord's Highway The IP14 67 E5
Lord's La CB8 61 E5
Lord's Wlk IP27 13 F2
Lorne Pk Rd NR33 115 C6
Lorne Rd
Lowestoft NR33 115 C6
Southwold IP18 119 D5
Lothingland Cl NR32 112 F5
Lothing St NR32 112 F1
Lotus Cl IP1 134 C1
Loudham Hall Rd IP13 127 D3
Loudham La IP13 85 A7
Louie's La IP22 20 C3
LOUND 2 F5
Lound Dam NR14 2 A3
Lound Rd
Belton with Browston NR31 2 E8
Blundeston NR32 3 A4
Louse La
Dedham CO7 103 F2
Rattlesden IP30 65 D3
Louvain Rd 13 CO12 107 A1
Lovat Cl IP20 22 E6
Love La
Lowestoft NR33 114 F4
Thorndon IP23 53 B8
Westleton IP17 58 C7
Love Rd NR32 113 C1
Lovers La IP9 106 B6
Lover's La IP16 129 E8
Lovetofts Dr IP1 134 D1
Lovewell Rd NR33 115 C6
Low Comm IP22 19 B3
Low Comm La NR34 2 A1
Low Comm Rd IP22 19 B3
Lower Barn Rd IP8 95 D5
Lower Baxter St IP33 154 B2
Lower Brook St IP4 155 B2
Lower Broom Rd IP30 50 C1
Lower Byfield IP7 79 C2
LOWER COMMON 25 B3
Lower Coney Gr IP8 81 A4
Lower Cres IP6 82 A6
Lower Dales View Rd
IP1 139 A8
Lower Downs Slade 5
CB9 132 E6
Lower Drag Way IP22 19 A4
LOWER FALKENHAM 98 F1
Lower Farm Rd
Boxted CO4 103 A4
Ringshall IP7 80 E6
LOWER GREEN 46 E4
LOWER HACHESTON 127 F8
Lower Harlings 4 IP9 107 A4
LOWER HOLBROOK 106 A6
Lower House La IP12 98 C5
Lower Houses Rd IP9 106 B5
LOWER LAYHAM 149 D1
Lower Marine Par CO12 107 B1
Lower N St CO10 75 D3
Lower Oakley IP21 37 F8
Lower Olland St NR35 110 B4
Lower Orwell St IP4 155 C2
Lower Pk Wlk IP19 118 E4
LOWER RAYDON 94 D1
Lower Rd
Borley CO10 91 D6
Coddenham IP6 68 B1
Falkenham IP10 98 F1
Glemsford CO10 77 B1
Grundisburgh IP13 83 E5
Hemingstone IP6 68 C1
Hundon CO10 75 D3
Lavenham CO10 78 D4
Little Blakenham IP8 81 D3
Melton IP13 84 F6
Mount Bures CO8 101 D3
Onehouse IP14 66 B5
Westerfield IP6 135 D4
Wicken CB7 28 A2
Lower Rose La IP21 20 D1
Lower St
Baylham IP6 81 E7
Cavendish CO10 76 E1
Great Bealings IP13 137 E6
Rattlesden IP30 65 D6
Sproughton IP8 138 A6
Stansfield CO10 76 C6
Stanstead CO10 77 C3
Stratford St Mary CO7 103 E5
Stutton IP9 105 D5
Ufford IP13 85 A6
Wickham Market IP13 127 C7
LOWER STREET
Stansfield 76 C6
Stutton 105 D5
Lower Ufford La IP13 127 D3
Lower Ufford Rd IP13 127 C1
Lowes Hill IP17 128 E7
LOWESTOFT 113 F1
Lowestoft Coll NR32 113 C2
Lowestoft Hospl NR32 113 D1
Lowestoft Maritime Mus★
NR32 113 E3
Lowestoft Mus★ NR33 114 D8
Lowestoft Porcelain★
NR32 113 E8
Lowestoft Rd
Beccles NR34 111 E4
Blundeston NR32 112 E8
Hopton on Sea NR31 3 B6
Lowestoft NR33 114 D3
Reydon IP18 119 C8
Worlingham NR34 10 A4
Lowestoft Sixth Form Coll
NR32 113 C2
Lowestoft Sta NR32 115 D8
Lowestoft War Meml
Musuem★ NR32 113 E3
Low Farm Dr NR33 114 C3
Lowgate St IP23 117 D2
LOW GREEN 63 E7
Low La
Brandeston IP13 70 A7
Creeting St Mary IP6 125 E8
Lowlands Cl 17 NR33 11 C1
Low Lighthouse Maritime
Mus★ CO12 107 C3
Low Rd
Alburgh IP20 7 A1
Bramfield IP19 42 A5
Brampton with Stoven NR34 25 D5
Burwell CB5 44 A5
Carlton IP17 128 D6
Cransford IP17 56 C4
Darsham IP17 57 F8
Debenham IP14 53 E1
Denham IP21 38 C2
Denton IP20 7 B1
1 Dickleburgh & Rushall
IP21 20 F2
Earl Soham IP13 54 E2
Eyke IP12 85 B7
1 Fressingfield IP21 39 E8
Friston IP17 72 F6
Great Glemham IP17 56 C1
Harwich CO12 106 F1
Hasketon IP13 146 B8
Hedenham NR35 7 D8
Marlesford IP13 71 C5
Mettingham NR35 110 F5
Low Rd *continued*
Monk Soham IP13 54 D3
Redenhall with Harleston
IP20 22 F5
Starston IP20 22 C7
St John, Ilketshall NR34 8 D2
Stratford St Andrew IP17 71 F7
Swefling IP17 56 E3
Ubbeston IP19 40 D3
Wenhaston with Mells Hamlet
IP19 42 C7
Wortham IP22 19 E2
Wortwell IP20 23 A7
Lowry Cl CB9 132 B7
Lowry Gdns 6 IP3 144 A8
Lowry Way
Lowestoft NR32 113 C5
Stowmarket IP14 124 B7
Low's La IP22 20 C1
Low St
Badingham IP13 56 A7
Bardwell IP31 34 C3
Glemsford CO10 77 B3
Hoxne IP21 38 B8
Kettleburgh IP13 70 B7
St Margaret, Ilketshall
NR35 24 B8
Lowther St CB8 120 F3
Low Wr La IP22 20 A1
Loxley Rd NR33 114 E6
Lucas Rd CO10 148 D5
Lucena Ct IP14 124 C6
Lucerne Cl
Lowestoft NR33 114 C5
5 Red Lodge IP28 30 B1
Ludbrook Cl IP6 125 C5
Ludgate Cswy IP23 117 E2
Ludlow Cl IP1 135 B4
Luff Meadow IP6 125 D5
Lugano Ave IP12 98 B8
Lulworth Ave IP3 140 D3
Lulworth Dr 14 CB9 132 C6
Lulworth Pk 8 NR32 113 A4
Lummis Vale IP5 141 C7
Lundy Cl CB9 133 B5
Lunnish Hill CO12 106 C2
Lupin Cl IP18 119 B6
Lupin Rd IP2 138 E4
Lupin Way IP6 125 D3
Lushington Rd 5 CO11 104 E2
Luther Rd IP2 155 B1
Lutus Cl CO10 90 A7
Lydgate Cl
11 Bury St Edmunds IP32 48 C5
14 Lawford CO11 104 D2
Lydgate Rd IP14 124 C7
Lyle Cl IP5 141 E7
Lymingster Cl 6 IP32 123 D6
Lymm Rd NR32 113 B5
Lyncroft Rd NR33 115 B3
Lyndhurst Ave IP4 140 C5
Lyndhurst Rd NR32 113 D4
LYNFORD 6 C5
Lyngate Ave NR33 114 F5
Lyng La IP22 18 F5
Lynnbrook Cl IP2 138 E1
Lynn's Hall Cl CO10 92 C6
Lynton Gdns NR32 113 C3
Lynwood Ave IP11 153 B5
Lynx Bsns Pk CB8 44 F7
Lyon Cl IP23 37 C4
Lysander Dr 3 IP3 144 C8

M

MacAulay Rd IP1 134 F3
McCalmont Way CB8 121 E2
MACE GREEN 95 E4
McIntyre Wlk IP32 122 E7
Mackenzie Dr IP5 141 B8
Mackenzie Pl IP30 78 C8
Mackenzie Rd IP24 16 A5
McLaren Ct 1 NR34 111 C3
McLean Dr 16 NR33 11 B1
Maconochie Way NR33 115 C7
Macpherson Robertson Way
3 IP28 116 B5
Mafeking Pl IP16 129 D6
Magdalen Cl 3 NR32 113 A3
Magdalen Ct IP23 117 C2
Magdalen Dr IP12 146 D3
Magdalene Cl IP2 138 F2
Magdalen Rd IP7 149 D6
Magdalen St IP23 117 C2
Magingley Cres IP4 140 F6
Magnolia Cl
9 Beck Row, Holywell Row &
Kenny Hill IP28 13 B1
2 Red Lodge IP28 30 B1
Magnolia Ct 3 NR32 113 B2
Magnolia Dr 7 IP12 85 D8
Magpie Cl
8 Ipswich IP8 138 C2
Ramsey CO12 106 F1
Magpie Ct 33 IP20 22 D6
MAGPIE GREEN 19 E1
Magpie Hill IP22 19 E1
MAIDENHALL 139 B1
Maidenhall App IP2 139 B2
Maidenhall Sports Ctr
IP2 139 C2
MAIDENSGRAVE 146 E3
Maiden Way IP7 149 D6
Maid Marion Ct IP33 122 F3
Maids Cross Hill IP27 109 E6
Maidscross Hill Nature
Reserve★ IP27 109 F5
Maids Cross Way IP27 109 D6
Maidstone Cty Inf Sch
IP11 152 E5
Maidstone Rd
Felixstowe IP11 152 E5
Lowestoft NR32 113 C1
Maine St 4 IP24 16 A5
Main Rd
Benhall IP17 72 C8
Bucklesham IP10 141 F1
Chelmondiston IP9 106 B8
Darsham IP17 42 A1
Hacheston IP13 127 D8
Harwich CO12 106 F1
Henley IP6 82 D6
Ipswich IP5 141 A8
Kelsale cum Carlton IP17 128 C8
Marlesford IP13 71 D4
Martlesham IP12 146 C1
Parham IP13 70 F8
Pettistree IP13 127 B3
3 Ramsey & Parkeston
CO12 106 D1
Somersham IP8 81 C3
Tuddenham St Martin IP6 136 B4
Woolverstone IP9 143 F2
Wormingford CO6 101 F2
Main St
Hockwold cum Wilton IP26 4 F3
Leiston IP16 129 C6
Maisie's Meadow IP13 54 D7
Maitland Rd IP6 125 E3
Major La IP23 37 A2
Major's Cl IP29 62 C5
Makins Rd 2 CO12 106 F3
Malcolm Way CB8 121 A5
Maldon Ct CO10 148 F5
Malin Cl CB9 133 B5
Mallard Rd IP18 119 B7
Mallards The IP27 109 D5
Mallard Way
Brandon IP27 6 A1
Hollesley IP12 99 F7
Ipswich IP2 138 F3
Stowmarket IP14 124 A6
Sudbury CO10 92 B3
Mallets La IP12 131 C2
Mallowhayes Cl IP2 139 B3
Mallow Rd 1 IP24 16 D6
Mallow Way NR33 114 C4
Mallow Wlk 4 CB9 132 A6
Malmesbury Cl IP2 139 A2
Malt Cl
5 Laxfield IP13 40 B3
Newmarket CB8 121 B3
Malthouse Ct 24 IP20 22 D6
Malthouse La
Bury St Edmunds IP32 154 B4
Gissing IP22 20 F8
Malthouse Rd 22 CO11 104 E2
Malting Cotts CB9 133 D2
MALTING END 61 E1
Malting End CB8 60 E2
Malting Farm La CO7 103 E1
Malting La
10 Clare CO10 90 A8
Isleham CB7 29 C5
Malting Row IP31 33 F5
Maltings IP14 52 D3
Maltings Cl
2 Bures Hamlet CO8 101 C5
1 Chevington IP29 62 C6
Halesworth IP19 118 B4
Moulton CB8 45 F3
Maltings Dr 6 IP20 22 D6
Maltings Garth 9 IP31 49 D4
Maltings La IP31 32 F1
Maltings Mews IP7 149 D5
Maltings The
Beccles NR34 111 B7
Bungay NR35 110 C4
Maltings Way IP33 154 B4
Malt Office Ave IP19 24 B4
Malt Office La IP19 24 A4
Malt's La IP26 4 F3
Maltsters' Way NR32 114 D8
Maltsters Wlk IP14 124 C3
Maltward Ave IP33 122 C5
Malvern Cl
Ipswich IP3 140 B3
Newmarket CB8 121 B2
Malvern Rd IP33 122 D3
Malvern Rise NR32 113 B3
Malyon Rd IP7 149 E8
Manchester Rd IP2 138 D2
Manderston Rd CB8 120 E3
Manderville Rd IP33 122 C4
Mandeville 14 CB5 44 A5
Mandy Cl IP4 140 A6
Mannall Wlk IP5 141 E8
Manners Rd IP31 48 D5
Manning Rd
Bury St Edmunds IP32 123 F7
Felixstowe IP11 152 E2
Manning's Amusement
Park★ IP11 152 F1
Mannings La IP9 144 A2
Manning's La IP22 35 D5
Mannington Cl 3 IP4 140 F6
MANNINGTREE 104 F2
Manningtree High Sch
CO11 104 D2
Manningtree Mus★
CO11 104 E2
Manningtree Rd
Dedham CO7 104 A3
East Bergholt CO7 151 F3
Stutton IP9 105 C5

Manningtree Sports Ctr CO11 104 D2
Manningtree Sta CO11 104 D3
Manor Ash Dr IP32 123 E6
Manor Cl
9 Beccles NR34 9 F4
3 Cavendish CO10 76 E1
Walberswick IP18 119 A2
Worlingham NR34 9 F4
Manor Farm Cl
Haverhill CB9 132 F5
11 Southwold IP18 119 D5
Manor Farm Rd
St John, Ilketshall NR34 8 D3
1 Thistley Green IP28 29 F6
Manor Garth IP31 49 E6
Manor Gdns
7 Hopton on Sea NR31 3 C6
Saxmundham IP17 128 E2
Manorhouse La 8 NR34 111 B6
Manor House Mus★ IP33 154 C1
Manor La
Gosbeck IP6 68 D2
14 Harwich CO12 107 A2
Horringer IP29 122 B1
Stutton IP9 105 C5
Manor Pk Rd
Corton NR32 3 C4
9 Southwold IP18 119 D5
Manor Rd
10 Bildeston IP7 79 F4
Brandon IP27 5 E1
Bungay NR35 110 B2
Clopton IP13 69 E1
Elmsett IP7 80 F2
Felixstowe IP11 152 B8
Harwich CO12 107 A2
Hasketon IP13 146 D6
Haverhill CB9 132 F5
Hessett IP30 64 F7
Hopton on Sea NR31 3 B6
Ipswich IP4 139 D8
11 Martlesham Heath IP5 98 A8
Mildenhall IP28 116 B4
Roydon IP22 20 B3
Sudbury CO10 148 C7
Trimley St Martin IP11 153 I11
Manor Terr IP11 107 F3
Manor View IP28 116 D2
Manor Wlk 20 NR33 11 B1
Mansbrook Bvd 5 IP3 144 C7
MAN'S CROSS 89 F2
Manse La IP19 40 C6
Mansfield Ave IP1 134 F2
Manthorp Cl IP12 147 B8
Manwick Rd IP11 152 E2
Maple Cl
6 Great Bricett IP7 80 D6
Ipswich IP2 139 A3
12 Lakenheath IP27 13 F2
Rendlesham IP12 85 D8
Yaxley IP23 37 B5
Maple Covert 5 NR32 112 F5
Maple Gn 3 IP31 49 A6
Maple Gr IP6 82 A6
Maple Hill CO10 75 E1
Maple Rd
5 Lowestoft NR33 114 F7
Stowupland IP14 67 A6
Sudbury CO10 148 F3
Maples The IP5 140 E8
Maple Way
Beccles NR34 111 C5
Eye IP23 117 D3
Leavenheath CO6 102 B7
Marbella Gn NR33 114 E5
Marbled White Dr IP9 142 E8
March Pl 2 CO10 76 A1
Marcus Cl CB9 133 B5
Marcus Rd IP11 153 D5
Mardle Rd
Reydon NR34 43 B8
Wangford with Henham NR34 26 C1
Mardle The NR33 114 C2
Mare Hill CO10 75 D3
Margaret Rd 2 IP14 124 C7
Margaret St IP11 152 E5
Margate Rd IP3 140 B3
Marham Rd 4 NR32 113 B2
Maria St 7 CO12 107 B3
Marigold Ave IP2 138 E3
Marigold Dr 3 IP28 46 A8
Marina 6 NR32 113 E1
Marina Gdns IP11 152 E2
Marina Theatre★ 11 NR32 113 D1
Marine Cl 3 NR31 3 B8
Marine Par
12 Harwich CO12 107 B2
Lowestoft NR33 115 D7
Mariner's Cl 2 NR31 3 B8
Mariners Pk Cl 11 NR31 3 B7
Mariners St NR32 113 E2
Mariners Way IP15 130 D5
Marion Cl 5 NR34 111 C3
Markant Cl IP32 123 E6
Market Cross Pl IP15 130 F4
Market Gr CO9 90 A1
Market Hill
8 Clare CO10 90 A8
Clopton IP13 83 D8
Framlingham IP13 126 C3
Haverhill CB9 132 E6
Orford IP12 131 C2
6 Sudbury CO10 148 C5
Market La
Blundeston NR32 3 B4
Burston & Shimpling IP22 20 E5
Somerleyton, Ashby & Herringfleet NR32 2 D6
Market Pl
11 Bildeston IP7 79 F4
Hadleigh IP7 149 D5
2 Halesworth IP19 118 A3
22 Harleston IP20 22 D6
8 Kessingland NR33 11 B1
11 Lavenham CO10 78 D4
Saxmundham IP17 128 D3
Southwold IP18 119 D5
Stowmarket IP14 124 D6
Market Row NR34 111 B5
Market Sq CB8 121 A3
Market St
1 Beccles NR34 111 B5
Fordham CB7 29 A1
3 Harwich CO12 107 C3
Laxfield IP13 40 B3
3 Mildenhall IP28 116 C4
2 Newmarket CB8 121 A3
16 Soham CB7 28 D4
Market Thoroughfare IP33 154 B2
MARKET WESTON 35 A8
Market Weston Rd IP22 35 A7
Markhams Cl CB9 132 D7
Mark Jennings La IP33 154 C3
Mark La IP27 6 C2
Marlborough Ct
4 Haverhill CB9 132 C5
Lowestoft NR32 112 F1
Marlborough Dr 4 CO10 148 D6
Marlborough Rd
Ipswich IP4 140 A5
Lowestoft NR32 112 F1
Saxtead IP13 55 A4
Southwold IP18 119 D6
MARLESFORD 71 C5
Marlesford Rd IP13 71 B5
Marlow Rd IP1 134 D1
Marriott's Wlk 5 IP14 124 D6
Marsden Cl 5 NR33 115 A3
Marshall Cl IP5 141 C8
Marshalls Meadow 3 IP14 67 A6
Marshams Piece 4 NR33 114 C5
Marsh La
Aldeby NR34 2 A2
Carlton Colville NR33 114 A4
3 Earsham NR35 7 F4
Felixstowe IP11 153 C8
26 Kessingland NR33 11 C1
Kessingland NR33 27 C8
North Cove NR34 10 B5
Reydon IP18 26 D2
Somerleyton, Ashby & Herringfleet NR32 2 C4
Worlingham NR34 9 F5
Wortham IP22 20 A1
Marsh Rd
Boxford CO10 93 C3
Fritton & St Olaves NR31 2 B7
Lowestoft NR33 114 D7
Stoke-by-Nayland CO6 103 C7
Marsh View NR34 111 D5
Marsh Way IP33 154 A4
Marshy La CO10 90 B4
Martello La IP11 153 D5
Martello Rd NR32 113 B4
Marten's La CO6 102 F8
Martin Cl
Brandon IP27 6 A1
Lowestoft NR33 114 D3
Mildenhall IP28 116 D3
8 Soham CB7 28 D5
Martinet Gn IP3 140 C1
Martin Rd
16 Burwell CB5 44 A6
Harleston IP20 22 E6
Ipswich IP2 155 B1
Martin's Ave NR33 115 B6
Martins La IP13 69 F2
Martins Meadow 6 IP23 36 D2
Martin's Meadow Nature Reserve★ IP13 69 E4
Martins Mews 2 CB9 132 A7
Martins Rd CO10 148 F7
Martinsyde 9 IP5 98 A8
MARTLESHAM 84 A1
Martlesham Beacon Hill Prim Sch IP12 84 A1
MARTLESHAM HEATH 98 B7
Martlesham Heath Control Twr Mus★ 31 IP5 98 A8
Martlesham Rd IP13 137 F3
Martyns Rise 5 CO10 91 E7
Maryday Cl IP6 68 B1
Mary La CO10 75 C3
Maryon Rd IP3 140 B1
Mary's La IP19 40 E6
Masefield Rd
Diss IP22 20 D2
Stowmarket IP14 124 B8
Mashay Rd CO9 90 B3
Maskell's La IP7 80 E4
Mason Cl CB9 132 D8
Mason Ct 1 IP6 82 A5
Mason Gdns 2 IP28 29 F6
Mason Rd CB5 44 A7
Masons Cl IP4 139 F6
Mason's La 5 IP30 50 D1
Mast Cl NR33 114 B4
Masterlord Ind Est IP16 129 B6
Masterson Gr IP5 141 C6
Mat Dawson Cl CB8 120 F6
Mather La IP20 22 B5
Mather Way IP2 155 C1
Matlock Cl 13 IP8 138 C2
Matlock Dale 11 NR33 114 E3
Matson Rd IP1 138 F8
Matthews La CB8 74 C7
Maude St IP3 139 E4
Maudslay Rd IP1 134 C2
Maulkin Cl IP32 123 F7
Mautby Way NR33 114 F5
Maybury Rd IP3 140 B1
Maybush La IP11 153 C5
Maycroft Cl 2 IP1 135 A3
Mayes La CO12 106 D1
Mayfair Rd NR35 110 C3
Mayfield CO6 102 B7
Mayfield Ave 12 NR33 11 C1
Mayfield La 7 IP5 98 A7
Mayfield Rd
Bury St Edmunds IP33 123 B1
Ipswich IP4 140 C7
Lowestoft NR33 114 C4
Mayfields
Lakenheath IP27 109 C7
6 Martlesham Heath IP5 98 A7
Mayfield Way IP14 52 E5
Mayflower Ave
8 Harwich CO12 107 C3
Saxmundham IP17 128 B2
Mayflower Way
14 Harleston IP20 22 D5
Sudbury CO10 148 D8
Mayfly Cl 12 IP8 142 E8
Mayhem Adventure Play Area★ NR33 115 E8
Maynewater La IP33 154 C1
Maynewater Sq IP33 154 C1
MAYPOLE GREEN
Bradfield St George 64 D6
Dennington 55 D6
Maypole La CB8 60 C6
May Rd
Ipswich IP3 140 C2
Lowestoft NR32 113 C1
May's La CO7 103 F2
Mead Dr IP5 141 C7
Meadow Barn IP14 66 C2
Meadow Cl
Bury St Edmunds IP33 122 E3
8 Felixstowe IP11 107 D8
Felsham IP30 65 A4
Lavenham CO10 78 D3
8 Soham CB7 28 D3
Westhall IP19 25 B4
Meadow Cres IP3 140 F1
Meadow Ct
4 Great Yarmouth NR31 3 B8
16 Stanton IP31 34 E4
Meadow Dr
Horringer IP29 63 A8
Lakenheath IP27 109 D7
MEADOWEND 89 E3
Meadow Gdns NR34 111 A3
Meadow La
Newmarket CB8 121 D1
Sudbury CO10 148 C4
Thurston IP31 49 E4
Meadowlands
1 Blundeston NR32 3 A4
11 Burwell CB5 44 A5
Kirton IP10 98 D2
4 Woolpit IP30 50 D1
Meadowlands Cl IP17 57 C8
Meadow Prim Sch NR33 115 B6
Meadow Rd
8 Barrow IP29 47 A2
Bungay NR35 110 D2
Lowestoft NR32 112 F4
Meadow Rise IP16 129 D2
Meadow Sh Ctr The IP14 124 D6
Meadowside
Blo' Norton IP22 18 E2
Wickham Market IP13 127 C7
Meadowside Gdns IP4 140 E8
Meadows The
Drinkstone IP30 65 B7
Worlington IP28 30 B4
Meadows Way IP7 149 D6
Meadowsweet Cl
Haverhill CB9 132 C7
3 Lowestoft NR33 114 D5
Meadowvale Cl
Beccles NR34 111 B2
Ipswich IP4 139 F8
Meadow Valley IP7 80 D5
Meadow View
Needham Market IP6 125 C5
Woolpit IP30 65 E8
Meadow View Rd CO10 148 B4
Meadow Way
Assington CO10 92 F1
Lowestoft NR33 114 C2
Meadow Wlk 3 IP17 72 C8
Mead Rd IP32 49 A3
Meads The NR32 113 D5
Mead The CO10 148 F2
Meadway 22 CO11 104 D2
Mead Way IP14 52 E5
Mear Cl IP12 85 C2
Mechanical Music Mus & Bygones★ IP14 52 A6
Medway Rd IP3 139 F2
Meekings Rd CO10 148 F6
Meeting Field 10 CO10 91 E8
Meeting La
Grundisburgh IP13 83 E5
Ridgewell CO9 89 D4
Meeting Wlk CB9 132 F5
Melbourne Dr IP28 116 B5
Melbourne Rd
Ipswich IP4 140 D7
Lowestoft NR32 113 D3
Melford Cl
2 Burwell CB5 44 B5
8 Ipswich IP4 140 F5
Melford Hall★ CO10 77 E1
Melford Rd
Acton CO10 92 A8
Cavendish CO10 76 F1
Lavenham CO10 78 C3
Lawshall IP29 63 D1
Stowmarket IP14 124 F4
Sudbury CO10 148 B7
Melford Way IP11 152 C3
MELLIS 37 A5
Mellisash Rd IP23 36 F5
Mellis Cl CB9 74 A1
Mellis Ct 18 IP11 152 D5
MELLIS GREEN 36 F5
Mellis Rd
Gislingham IP23 36 D3
Thrandeston IP21 37 B6
Wortham IP22 36 E7
Yaxley IP23 37 B5
MELLS 118 E2
MELON GREEN 63 C4
Melplash Cl IP3 140 E4
Melplash Rd IP3 140 E4
Melrose Cl NR32 112 F5
Melrose Gdns
Ipswich IP4 140 B8
Newmarket CB8 120 E4
MELTON 147 C8
Melton Cl CB8 121 B2
Melton CP Sch IP12 147 C7
Melton Grange Rd IP12 147 A6
Melton Hill IP12 147 B6
Melton Meadow Rd 4 IP12 147 B6
Melton Rd
Hollesley IP12 99 F8
Woodbridge IP12 147 B6
Melton Sta IP12 147 D7
Melville Rd IP4 139 F5
MENDHAM 23 A6
Mendham Cl 36 IP20 22 D6
Mendham La
38 Harleston IP20 22 D6
St Cross, South Elmham IP20 23 C6
Mendham Prim Sch IP20 23 A6
Mendham Rd IP20 23 A4
Mendip Dr IP5 140 F6
Mendip Rd NR32 112 E2
MENDLESHAM 52 E4
MENDLESHAM GREEN 52 D2
Mendlesham Prim Sch IP14 52 D4
Mendlesham Rd IP14 52 B5
Mercers Rd IP32 123 D7
Mere Cl IP31 49 C6
Meredith Rd IP1 134 E2
Mere Gdns IP4 140 F4
Mere La IP28 48 A6
Mere Manor Ct IP22 20 C2
Mere Side CB7 28 C4
Meriton Rise IP7 149 F4
Merivale Rd 17 CO11 104 D2
Merlewood IP21 21 C5
Merlin Rd IP2 138 C3
Mermaid Cl IP32 123 A8
Merriam Cl 5 CO11 104 E4
Merrifield Rd NR33 114 F3
Merrion Cl 12 IP8 138 C2
Merrylees NR34 111 C4
Mersey Rd IP3 139 F2
Merville 9 NR33 114 E3
Messenger Cl NR35 110 B2
METFIELD 23 C3
Metfield Rd IP20 23 D3
Metfield St IP20 23 C3
METHERSGATE 84 E1
Methersgate Hall Dr IP12 84 E1
METTINGHAM 8 D4
Meynell Gdns CB8 121 A5
Micawber Mews 4 NR32 3 A4
Michaelhouse Way 12 IP31 34 E4
Michaels Mount IP13 137 D5
Michaelstowe Cl 1 CO12 106 E1
Michigan Cl IP5 141 B7
MICKFIELD 68 B8
Mickfield Mews 16 IP11 152 D5
Micklegate Rd IP11 152 E2
Micklemere Nature Reserve★ IP31 49 F8
Micklesmere Dr 23 IP31 34 B1
MICKLEY GREEN 63 B4
Middle Dro CB7 28 B4
Middlefield Dr 3 IP14 66 B4
Middlefield Rd 10 CO11 105 A2
Middle Gn CO6 101 B1
MIDDLE GREEN 46 E4
MIDDLE HARLING 18 B8
Middle La NR34 10 D8
Middle Rd
Blo' Norton IP22 18 F2
Earsham IP20 7 C4
MIDDLETON
Leiston 58 B6
Sudbury 148 C2
Middleton Cl IP2 138 D2
MIDDLETON MOOR 58 A6
Middleton Prim Sch IP17 58 B6
Middleton Rd
Sudbury CO10 148 B4
Yoxford IP17 57 E7
Middle Way CO10 91 E8
Middle Wlk NR32 113 C5
MIDDLEWOOD GREEN 67 D8
Midhurst Cl 3 IP32 123 D6
Midmeadow 4 NR34 111 B5
Mid Suffolk Leisure Ctr IP14 124 B7
Mid-Suffolk Light Rly Mus The★ IP14 53 B4
Mights Rd IP18 119 C6
Milano Ave IP12 98 B8
Milburn Dro CB8 45 F3
MILDEN 79 B1
Milden Cl 6 IP14 124 E3
MILDENHALL 116 D6
Mildenhall Airfield IP28 30 B7
Mildenhall Coll of Tech IP28 116 E4
Mildenhall Dro IP28 12 F3
Mildenhall Ind Est IP28 116 B6
Mildenhall Mus★ IP28 116 C4
Mildenhall Pl 1 CB9 132 F6
Mildenhall Rd
Barton Mills IP28 116 C2
Beck Row, Holywell Row & Kenny Hill IP28 116 C8
2 Bury St Edmunds IP32 123 A8
Fordham CB7 29 C1
Icklingham IP28 31 A5
Littleport CB7 12 A8
Mildenhall Stadium IP28 29 D8
Milden Rd
Brent Eleigh CO10 79 A2
Ipswich IP2 138 E5
Mildmay Rd IP3 140 B1
MILE END 77 A7
Mile End IP27 14 E8
Mile End Rd CB7 12 A7
Miles Hawk Way IP28 116 A5
Miles Paddock IP14 52 A6
Military Rd CB7 28 E2
Military Way 5 CO12 106 E1
Millbank CB8 120 F4
Mill Bank 1 NR32 112 F2
Mill Broadway IP12 131 C4
Mill Chase CB9 88 E3
Mill Cl
6 Burwell CB5 44 B5
Capel St Mary IP9 150 C3
Exning CB8 120 B8
Felixstowe IP11 152 D4
Kirby Row NR35 8 E7
1 Walsham le Willows IP31 35 C2
Woolpit IP30 50 D1
Mill Cnr CB7 28 C3
MILL COMMON 25 C4
Mill Croft 9 CB7 28 D3
Mill Drift IP26 5 A3
Mill Dro CB7 28 C3
MILL END 60 F3
Mill End La IP14 67 C7
Millennium Grandstand CB8 120 C1
Millennium Way
Kesgrave IP5 141 E7
Lowestoft NR32 113 A4
Miller Cl
Elmswell IP30 50 F2
Lowestoft NR33 115 B5
Millers Cl
Bungay NR35 110 C3
Hadleigh IP7 149 E6
Stowmarket IP14 124 C3
Millers Ct 5 IP6 82 A5
Millers Dr IP21 21 B5
Millers Gn 44 IP20 22 D6
Millers View IP1 138 F7
Millfield IP23 117 B3
Mill Field
3 Aldeburgh IP15 130 E5
Bramford IP8 134 B2
Pettaugh IP14 68 E6
Millfield Ave IP14 124 C5
Millfield Cl
Ditchingham NR35 110 C8
1 Saxmundham IP17 128 C2
Millfield Dr IP14 65 F4
Millfield Gdns IP4 140 A7
Millfield Rd
2 Barningham IP31 34 F7
Walberswick IP18 119 A2
Millfields
2 Peasenhall IP17 56 F8
Wangford NR34 26 B2
Mill Fields IP14 51 D1
Millfields Way CB9 132 F6
Mill Gdns
Bedingham NR35 7 B8
Elmswell IP30 50 F2
MILL GREEN
Burston and Shimpling 20 E7
Buxhall 65 F4
Edwardstone 93 B5
Stoneham Aspal 68 B7
MILL HILL 77 E6
Mill Hill
Burgh IP13 83 F6
Capel St Mary IP9 150 C3

Mill Hill continued
Cotton IP14 . . . . **52** A6
Earl Soham IP13 . . . . **54** E1
Hadleigh IP7 . . . . **94** B7
Haverhill IP19 . . . . **132** D5
Lawford CO11 . . . . **104** B2
Leiston IP16 . . . . **129** C2
Manningtree CO11. . . . . . **104** E2
Mettingham NR35 . . . . **8** D5
Newmarket CB8. . . . . **121** A4
Peasenhall IP17 . . . . **56** F8
Rattlesden IP30 . . . . **65** D6
Sudbury CO10 . . . . **148** B5
Wormingford CO6 . . . . . **101** F3
Mill Hill Dr IP19 . . . . **118** A4
Mill Hill Est IP16 . . . . . . **129** C2
MILL HILLS **147** A6
Mill Hill (Tumulus)★ NR31. **2** C8
Mill Hoo IP12 . . . . **99** E4
Mill La
All Saints & St Nicholas, South
Elmham IP20 . . . . **23** E5
Barnham IP24 . . . . **16** B2
Barrow IP29 . . . . **47** A2
Baylham IP6 . . . . **81** F7
Benhall IP17 . . . . **72** C8
Boyton IP12. . . . . **86** B2
Bradfield CO11 . . . . **105** B1
Bramford IP8. . . . . **134** B1
Brandeston IP13 . . . . **70** A7
Bruisyard IP17 . . . . **56** C5
7 Burwell CB5. . . . . . . **44** B5
Butley IP12 . . . . **86** B6
Campsey Ash IP13 . . . . . **127** F6
Cavendish CO10. . . . . **90** D8
Chelmondiston IP9 . . . . . **106** B8
Coddenham IP6. . . . . **68** B1
Combs IP14. . . . . **124** B1
Copdock & Washbrook IP8 **138** A1
Corton NR32 . . . . **3** D4
Cowlinge CB8. . . . . **75** B8
Creeting St Peter or West
Creeting IP6. . . . . **125** D8
Dedham CO7 . . . . **103** F4
Dennington IP13 . . . . **55** D5
Ellingham NR35 . . . . **8** E7
Exning CB8. . . . . **120** B8
Felixstowe IP11. . . . . **152** F4
Fordham CB7. . . . . **29** B1
Garboldisham IP22 . . . . . . **18** D3
9 Great Blakenham IP6. . **82** A5
Great Yeldham CO9 . . . . . **90** A2
Hasketon IP13. . . . . **146** A7
Henley IP6. . . . . **82** D6
Hockwold cum Wilton IP26 . . **5** A3
Hoo IP13 . . . . **70** C6
Hopton IP22 . . . . **18** C3
Hundon CO10. . . . . **75** D3
Kersey IP7. . . . . **94** A7
Layham IP7 . . . . **149** C2
Leiston IP16 . . . . **129** C2
18 Manningtree CO11. . **104** E2
Marlesford IP13 . . . . **71** C5
Metfield IP20. . . . . **23** C3
North Cove NR34. . . . . **10** C4
Polstead CO6. . . . . **102** E8
Pulham St Mary IP21 . . . . . **21** F8
4 Redgrave IP22. . . . . . . **36** A8
Shadingfield NR34 . . . . **25** D7
Somersham IP8. . . . . **81** C3
Southwold IP18. . . . . **119** D5
Stetchworth CB8 . . . . **59** F5
St John, Ilketshall NR34 . . . . **8** E2
Stoke Ash IP23 . . . . **52** F8
Stonham Earl IP14. . . . . . . **67** D5
Stradbroke IP21 . . . . **39** C5
Sudbury CO10 . . . . **148** B5
Thetford IP24 . . . . **16** B5
Thurston IP31 . . . . **49** D5
Tunstall IP12 . . . . **72** B1
Weybread IP21 . . . . **22** C3
Wickham Market IP13. . . . **127** C6
2 Witnesham IP6. . . . . . . **83** A5
Woodbridge IP12. . . . . . . **147** A5
Woolpit IP30. . . . . **50** D1
Wrentham NR34 . . . . **26** F5
Millmarsh Dro IP27 . . . . . **109** A7
Mill Piece IP10 . . . . **145** C6
Mill Pk Gdns IP28. . . . . . **116** B3
Mill Pool La NR35. . . . . **8** D6
Mill Pouch IP11 . . . . **152** C8
Mill Rd
Aldeby/Wheatacre/Burgh St
Peter NR34. . . . . **10** B8
Ashley CB8. . . . . **45** F1
Badingham IP13 . . . . **56** A7
Barningham IP31. . . . . **34** E7
Battisford IP14 . . . . **80** B8
Beccles NR34. . . . . **111** C2
Birdbrook CO9. . . . . **89** C5
Botesdale IP22 . . . . **36** B6
Boxted CO4 . . . . **102** F2
Brockdish IP21 . . . . **21** E3
Brockley IP29 . . . . **63** A1
Burston & Shimpling IP22. . **20** E6
Bury St Edmunds IP33. . . . **154** A2
Buxhall IP14 . . . . **65** F4
Chevington IP29 . . . . **62** C6
Clare CO10 . . . . **90** B8
Coldfair Green IP17. . . . . . **129** A2
Cotton IP14. . . . . **52** A6
East Bergholt CO7. . . . . . **151** E4
Ellingham NR35. . . . . **8** D7
Foxearth CO10. . . . . **91** B7
Friston IP17. . . . . **72** E6

Mill Rd continued
Gazeley CB8. . . . . **46** B3
Great Barton IP31. . . . . . . **49** A6
Halesworth IP19 . . . . **118** E3
Haverhill CB9. . . . . **132** E5
Hemley IP12 . . . . **98** E5
Hengrave IP28 . . . . **48** A7
Honington IP31. . . . . **33** F5
Hundon CO10. . . . . **75** D4
Ipswich IP3 . . . . **140** F1
Kedington CB9 . . . . **133** E8
Kirtling CB8 . . . . **60** F3
Lakenheath IP27 . . . . **109** D6
Laxfield IP13 . . . . **40** B2
Lowestoft NR33. . . . . **115** C7
Mendlesham IP14 . . . . **52** D4
Moulton CB8 . . . . **46** A1
Mutford NR34. . . . . **10** D3
Newbourne IP12. . . . . **98** D5
Occold IP23. . . . . **37** F1
Peasenhall IP17 . . . . **56** E8
Redlingfield IP23. . . . . **38** C2
Ridgewell CO9 . . . . **89** D3
Rumburgh IP19 . . . . **24** B4
Saxmundham IP17. . . . . . **128** C3
Stambourne CO9 . . . . **89** B2
Swefling IP17 . . . . **56** E3
Thelnetham IP22 . . . . **18** E1
Westleton IP17 . . . . **58** C7
Weybread IP21 . . . . **22** C4
Winfarthing IP22. . . . . **20** B8
Wissett IP19 . . . . **118** A5
Worlingworth IP13 . . . . . . **54** D7
Wyverstone IP14. . . . . **51** D6
Mill Rd S IP22 . . . . **36** B6
Mill Rd (South) IP33 . . . . **154** A1
Mill Reef Cl CB8 . . . . **120** D7
Mill Rise
11 Holbrook IP9 . . . . . . **105** E7
Saxmundham IP17. . . . . . **128** C2
Mills Dr NR32. . . . . **3** D4
Millside IP23 . . . . **37** C4
Mills La CO10 . . . . **91** E6
Mills Meadow IP13 . . . . . **126** D3
Mills Rd CO10. . . . . **148** E6
Mill St
Gislingham IP23 . . . . **36** B2
Isleham CB7 . . . . **29** C5
Middleton IP17 . . . . **58** A6
Mildenhall IP28 . . . . **116** B3
Nayland CO6 . . . . **102** D5
Stowupland IP14 . . . . **67** A6
Westleton IP17 . . . . **58** C7
Mills The
Framlingham IP13. . . . . . . **126** C3
Ipswich IP4. . . . . **140** E8
MILL STREET **102** E8
Mill Tye CO10 . . . . **148** E2
Mill View CB8 . . . . **46** B3
Mill View Cl IP12 . . . . **146** E5
Millway NR34 . . . . **10** C4
Millway Ave IP22 . . . . **20** C3
Millway La
Palgrave IP22 . . . . **20** A1
Wortham IP22. . . . . **19** F1
Millwood Rd CO6 . . . . **94** A3
Milner La
Chilton CO10 . . . . **92** B4
Sudbury CO10 . . . . **148** F6
Milner St IP4 . . . . **139** E6
Milnes Way NR33 . . . . **114** B3
Milnrow **10** IP8 . . . . **138** C2
Milton Cl IP17 . . . . **128** B4
Milton Rd CO11 . . . . **104** D1
Milton Rd E NR33 . . . . . . **113** D1
Milton Rd N **4** IP14. . . . . **124** D6
Milton Rd S IP14. . . . . . . **124** E6
Milton Rd W NR32 . . . . . . **113** D1
Milton St IP4 . . . . **140** B7
Mimosa Wlk NR32 . . . . . . **113** B2
Mincarlo Trawler★
NR33. . . . . **115** D8
Minden Cl IP33 . . . . **154** C2
Minden Dr
Bury St Edmunds IP33. . . . **122** D5
Leiston IP16 . . . . **129** D5
Minden Rd
Lowestoft NR32. . . . . **113** C2
Sudbury CO10 . . . . **148** D5
Minerva Cl CB9 . . . . **133** B4
Minos Rd NR32 . . . . **113** C4
Minos Way IP1 . . . . **138** D3
Minsmere House Hospl
IP4 . . . . **140** C6
Minsmere Nature Reserve★
IP17. . . . . **58** E6
Minsmere Rd IP17 . . . . **58** F8
Minsmere Rise IP17. . . . . . **58** A6
Minsmere Way CO10 . . . . . **92** B3
Minster Rd CB9 . . . . **132** D7
Minton Ent Pk CB8. . . . . . **120** E7
Mirbeck's Cl **6** NR34. . . . . . **9** F4
Misburgh Way NR31. . . . . . **3** C6
Mission La CO7 . . . . **104** D6
Mission Rd IP22 . . . . **20** D2
MISTLEY **105** A2
MISTLEY HEATH. **105** A1
Mistley Sta CO11. . . . . . . **104** F2
Mistley Way IP12 . . . . **146** F6
Mitchell Ave IP32. . . . . **48** C5
Mitchery La IP14. . . . . **65** E4
Mitford Cl IP1 . . . . **135** A4
Mitford Rd IP17 . . . . **72** B8
Mitre Cl **6** IP30 . . . . **50** D1
Mitre Way IP3 . . . . **139** E4
Moat Farm Cl IP4 . . . . **139** F8
Moat La
Alphamstone CO8 . . . . . . **101** A6

Moat La continued
Rushbrooke with Rougham
IP30 . . . . **49** D1
Moat Rd
Birdbrook CO9. . . . . **89** B4
Theberton IP16 . . . . **57** F4
MOATS TYE. **66** E2
Moat Wlk **2** CB9. . . . . . . **132** C6
Mobbs Way NR32. . . . . . . **112** E3
Mockbeggars Hall★ IP8 **134** C6
Moffat Ave IP4 . . . . **136** B1
Moles La NR34. . . . . **8** D1
Moll's La NR34. . . . . **25** D5
Monarch Cl CB9 . . . . **132** A6
Monarch Way
Carlton Colville NR33. . . . . **114** A3
Pinewood IP8 . . . . **142** D8
Monastery Ct IP7 . . . . **149** E7
Monastery Hill IP17. . . . . . **43** B1
Monckton Ave NR32. . . . . **112** F2
Monckton Cres NR32. . . . **112** F2
Monet Sq **1** NR32 . . . . . . **113** B5
MONEWDEN **69** F5
Monewden Rd IP13 . . . . . . **70** A3
Moneyhole Cnr CO10. . . . . **78** E5
Moneypiece Cl CB9 . . . . . **132** D7
Moneypot La IP22 . . . . **19** B1
Monks Cl IP11 . . . . **153** D6
MONKS ELEIGH **79** B2
Monks Eleigh CE VC Prim
Sch IP7 . . . . **79** B2
Monksgate IP24 . . . . **16** B6
Monks Gate IP8 . . . . **138** A6
Monkshood Cl NR34 . . . . . **114** F2
Monk's La CO7. . . . . **103** E2
MONK SOHAM **54** D4
Monmouth Cl IP2. . . . . . . **139** B1
Montagu Dr IP27 . . . . **5** E4
Montague Rd IP11. . . . . . . **153** A4
Montana Rd IP3 . . . . **141** A7
Montessori Sch The IP7. . . . **94** E6
Montford Cl CB5 . . . . **44** B6
Montfort Ct **11** CB9. . . . . **132** D5
Montgomery Ave NR32. . . **113** B4
Montgomery Rd IP2 . . . . . **139** B1
Monton Rise IP2. . . . . **138** D2
Montpelier Dr **1** IP24. . . . . **16** A5
Monument Farm La
IP10. . . . . **141** C3
Monument Farm Rd
IP10. . . . . **141** B4
Moon Hall La CB9 . . . . **132** E3
Moorbridge La IP14. . . . . . **66** B8
Mooreland Dr IP31. . . . . . . **49** C6
Moore Rd
Ipswich IP1. . . . . **134** F3
Rushbrooke with Rougham
IP30 . . . . **49** B2
Moore's Cl **17** IP14. . . . . . **53** F2
Moorfield Rd IP12 . . . . **146** E5
Moorhall Cswy IP23. . . . . . **117** C1
Moor Rd
Burston & Shimpling IP21. . **21** B6
Langham CO4. . . . . **103** B2
Middleton IP17 . . . . **57** F6
Moorsfield CO10. . . . . **148** F2
Moor's Way IP12 . . . . **146** E5
Moreton Hall Prep Sch
IP32. . . . . **123** D5
Moreton Hall Ret Pk
IP32. . . . . **123** F4
Morgan Ct **3** IP6 . . . . **134** C8
Morgan Dr IP1 . . . . **134** C1
Morgan Meadow IP14. . . . **124** C2
Morland Prim Sch IP3 . . . . **144** A8
Morland Rd **1** IP3. . . . . . . **144** A8
Morley Ave IP12 . . . . **146** F4
Morley Cl **3** IP28. . . . . **30** B8
Morleys La IP23 . . . . **36** D2
Mormor La IP21 . . . . **21** F4
Mornington Ave **2** IP1. . **134** F1
Morris Way IP6 . . . . **125** D4
Mors End **2** CO7. . . . . **103** E5
Morston Hall Rd IP11 . . . . . **98** B1
Mortimer La IP28 . . . . **29** E3
Mortimer Pl **3** CO10 . . . . . **76** A1
Morton Peto Cl NR32. . . . . . **2** D3
Morton Rd NR33 . . . . **115** B4
Moss La IP6. . . . . **135** F4
Mother Quy's IP24. . . . . . . **15** C5
Mottram Ct **14** IP8 . . . . . . **138** C2
MOULTON. **45** F3
Moulton Ave CB8 . . . . **46** B5
Moulton CE Prim Sch CB8 **45** F3
Moulton Cl CO10 . . . . **148** D6
Moulton Packhorse Bridge★
CB8. . . . . **45** F3
Moulton Paddocks CB8 . **121** F7
Moulton Rd
Cheveley CB8. . . . . **121** D4
Gazeley CB8. . . . . **46** B3
Kentford CB8. . . . . **46** A5
Moulton CB8. . . . . **45** F1
Mountbatten Cl CO10 . . . . **148** D8
Mountbatten Ct IP1. . . . . . **139** A7
Mountbatten Rd
Bungay NR35. . . . . **110** B2
Lowestoft NR32. . . . . **113** B4
Sudbury CO10 . . . . **148** D8
MOUNT BURES. **101** C3
Mount Cl **5** IP30 . . . . **64** F8
Mount Dr IP3 . . . . **140** F1
MOUNT PLEASANT. **75** D2
Mount Pleasant
Framlingham IP13. . . . . . . **126** B4
Halesworth IP19 . . . . **118** B5
Lowestoft NR32. . . . . **113** C3

Mount Pleasant continued
1 Peasenhall IP17. . . . . . **56** F8
Southwold IP18. . . . . **119** C8
Mount Rd
Bury St Edmunds IP32. . . . **123** D6
Haverhill CB9. . . . . **132** E5
Rushbrooke with Rougham
IP30 . . . . **49** A3
Mount St IP22 . . . . **20** C3
Mounts The IP17 . . . . **56** F8
Mouse La IP30. . . . . **49** C2
Moverley Way **1** IP15. . . . **130** E5
Mowbrays The IP13. . . . . . **126** D3
Mow Hill IP6 . . . . **83** A5
Mowlands IP9. . . . . **150** F3
Mowness Hall La IP14. . . . . **68** A6
Moyes Rd NR32. . . . . **112** D1
Moyse Ave **4** IP18. . . . . . **119** C8
Moyse's Hall Mus★ IP33 **154** B2
Mulberry Cl
Beccles NR34. . . . . **111** C5
18 Feltwell IP26 . . . . **4** E5
Mildenhall IP28 . . . . **116** E4
Mulberry Gdns **11** IP6. . . **82** A5
Mulberry Rd **3** IP3 . . . . . **144** C7
Mumford Rd IP1. . . . . **138** E8
Munday's La IP12 . . . . **131** B3
MUNDFORD. **6** B8
Mundford Prim Sch IP26 . . **6** A8
Mundford Rd
Brandon IP27 . . . . **5** F2
Thetford IP24 . . . . **16** B7
Weeting-with-Broomhill IP27 **6** A4
Mundy's Rd IP20. . . . . **23** A5
Munnings Cl
Haverhill CB9. . . . . **132** B7
3 Lowestoft NR33. . . . . . **114** C3
Newmarket CB8. . . . . **121** A5
Munnings Way CO11 . . . . . **104** D3
Munson's La IP26 . . . . **4** E6
Munson's Pl IP26 . . . . **4** E6
Murfitt's La CB7 . . . . **29** A2
Muriel Cl **4** IP7 . . . . **149** E6
Murillo Dr **1** NR32. . . . . . **113** C6
Murrayfield Prim Sch
IP3 . . . . **140** A3
Murray Rd IP3. . . . . **140** A3
Murrills Rd IP3 . . . . **140** E1
Murton Cl **10** CB5. . . . . . . **44** A6
Museum of E Anglian Life★
IP14 . . . . **124** D5
Museum St IP1 . . . . **155** B3
Musgrave Cl **22** CO12. . . . **106** F1
Mustards Gapp CB9 . . . . . **133** A5
Mustow St IP33. . . . . **154** C2
Mutford NR32 . . . . **112** F1
MUTFORD. **10** D2
Mutford Cl NR32. . . . . **112** F1
Mutford Gn IP27. . . . . **109** C7
Mutford Wood NR33 . . . . . **10** D4
Mutfordwood La NR33 . . . . **114** A2
Mutton La IP13 . . . . **70** A8
Mylford Cl IP32. . . . . **123** D4
Mylodon Rd NR32. . . . . . . **113** C4
Myrtle Cl
Bury St Edmunds IP33. . . . **154** A3
26 Eriswell IP27 . . . . **13** F2
Lowestoft NR32. . . . . **113** B2
Myrtle Rd IP3 . . . . **139** E4

N

NACTON **145** C5
Nacton CE VC Prim Sch
IP10. . . . . **145** C5
Nacton Cl **5** IP12. . . . . **85** B3
Nacton Cres IP3. . . . . **140** B2
Nacton La **2** IP31 . . . . **49** A6
Nacton Rd
Felixstowe IP11. . . . . **152** E1
Ipswich IP10. . . . . **144** D7
Levington IP10 . . . . **145** E3
Nan Hazle's La IP22. . . . . . **36** B4
Nansen Rd IP3. . . . . **140** B2
Napier Pl IP24 . . . . **16** B5
Naples Cl **5** NR31. . . . . **3** C6
Narrow Way IP19 . . . . **42** C6
Nash Cl CO11 . . . . **104** D3
Nash Gdns **2** IP3. . . . . . . **144** B8
Nat Flatman St CB8. . . . . . **121** B3
National Horseracing Mus★
CB8. . . . . **121** A3
National Stud★ CB8. . . . . . **59** B8
Nato Pl IP27. . . . . **109** F1
NAUGHTON. **80** C3
Naughton Gdns **8** IP14 . . **124** E3
Naughton Rd IP7 . . . . **80** C1
Naunton Rd IP12 . . . . **146** E5
Navarre St IP1. . . . . **155** B3
Naverne Meadow IP12 . . . . **147** A5
NAYLAND. **102** D4
Nayland Prim Sch CO6 . . . **102** D5
Nayland Rd
Bures St Mary CO8 . . . . . **101** D4
1 Felixstowe IP11. . . . . . **152** C3
Great Horkesley CO6. . . . . **102** D2
Haverhill CB9. . . . . **132** C4
Little Horkesley CO6 . . . . . **102** C3
Naylor Ct IP14. . . . . **124** B7
Neale Cl IP16 . . . . **129** B6
Neale St IP1. . . . . **155** B3
Neath Dr IP2 . . . . **139** A1
Neaves La IP21 . . . . **39** B4
NEDGING **79** F3
Nedging Rd IP7. . . . . **79** F3
NEDGING TYE. **80** B4
NEEDHAM. **22** B4
Needham La IP7. . . . . **79** F4

Needham Lake Nature★
Reserve & Visitor Ctr★
IP6 . . . . **125** E4
NEEDHAM MARKET. **125** E5
Needham Mkt Mid Sch
IP6 . . . . **125** D4
Needham Mkt Sta IP6. . **125** E4
Needham Rd
Coddenham IP6. . . . . **67** F1
Needham IP20. . . . . **22** C5
Stowmarket IP14. . . . . . . **124** E4
Needham Rd W IP14 . . . . . **124** F4
NEEDHAM STREET. **46** B4
Needle Cnr IP9 . . . . **106** B5
Nelson Cl IP6. . . . . **83** A8
1 Lowestoft NR33. . . . . . **115** A3
Sudbury CO10 . . . . **148** E7
Nelson Cres **2** IP24. . . . . . **16** B5
Nelson Rd
Bury St Edmunds IP33. . . . **154** A2
Ipswich IP4. . . . . **140** A7
1 Lowestoft NR33. . . . . . **115** A3
Sudbury CO10 . . . . **148** E7
Nelson Way
Beccles NR34. . . . . **111** A4
Woodbridge IP12. . . . . . . **146** F7
Nelson Wharf NR33. . . . . . **114** F7
Nene Dr IP3 . . . . **144** D7
Neptune Quay IP4 . . . . **155** C2
Neptune Sq IP3. . . . . **155** C2
Neptune St NR32. . . . . **115** C8
Ness Rd
Arwarton IP9. . . . . **106** D5
Burwell CB5. . . . . **44** B7
Nethergate St
Bungay NR35. . . . . **110** A5
Clare CO10 . . . . **90** A7
Hopton IP22 . . . . **18** B2
Netherhall Cl IP14. . . . . **52** A1
Nether Hall CO9. . . . . **90** E2
Nether Hall Mus & Gall★
CO10. . . . . **76** E2
Nether Hill CO9. . . . . **90** E2
Nether Rd **2** CO10. . . . . . . **76** E1
NETHER STREET **64** E8
Netley Cl IP27 . . . . **142** F8
Netley Rd IP33. . . . . **122** D3
NETTLESTEAD **81** C4
Nettlestead Rd IP8. . . . . . . **81** D4
Neve Gdns IP28. . . . . **30** A6
Newall Rd **2** IP24. . . . . **16** C2
Newark Cl IP2. . . . . **138** F1
Newark Rd
3 Lakenheath IP27 . . . . . . **13** C4
Lowestoft NR33. . . . . **115** B6
Newberry Rd **7** IP7. . . . . . **79** F4
NEWBOURNE. **98** C5
Newbourne Gdns IP11 . . **152** D3
Newbourne Rd
Brightwell IP10 . . . . **98** A6
Martlesham IP12. . . . . **84** B1
Waldringfield IP12. . . . . . . **98** C7
Newbourne Springs Nature★
Reserve★ IP12 . . . . **98** D6
Newbourn Rd IP10. . . . . . . **98** C4
Newbury Rd IP4 . . . . **140** C6
Newby Cl IP19 . . . . **118** A3
Newby Dr IP4 . . . . **140** F5
New Cangle Com Prim Sch
CB9. . . . . **132** D7
New Cardinal St IP1 . . . . . **155** A2
Newcastle Cl **6** IP27. . . . . . **13** C2
New Cheveley Rd CB8. . . . **121** C3
Newcombe Dr **16** IP26 . . . . . **4** E5
Newcombe Rd NR32 . . . . . **113** E1
New Comm Rd IP22. . . . . . **35** B8
New Cut
5 Bures CO8 . . . . **101** C4
8 Glemsford CO10. . . . . . **77** A2
Hadleigh IP7. . . . . **149** E6
Halesworth IP19 . . . . **118** B4
Newmarket CB8. . . . . **121** B3
Saxmundham IP17. . . . . . **128** C3
New Cut E IP3. . . . . **155** C1
New Cut W IP2 . . . . **155** C1
Newdelight Rd IP22. . . . . . **35** F2
New Dro
Beck Row, Holywell Row &
Kenny Hill IP28. . . . . **12** E1
Soham CB7 . . . . **28** A4
Newell Rise IP6. . . . . **134** C8
NEW ENGLAND. **89** A5
New England Way **2**
IP24. . . . . **16** A5
Newfen Gravel Dro IP27. **109** A8
Newgate
Beccles NR34. . . . . **111** B5
Kirby Row NR35. . . . . **8** E7
Newgate La NR35 . . . . **8** E7
New Gn Ave **13** IP31. . . . . . **49** C4
New Hampshire Way **5**
IP24. . . . . **16** A5
Newhaven Way IP7 . . . . . . **149** E7
New House La CO10 . . . . . . **76** B3
New La IP9. . . . . **105** F6
Newland Ave NR34. . . . . . **111** E4
Newlands
2 Elmsett IP7 . . . . **80** F1
Otley IP6. . . . . **69** D2
Newlands Cl
40 Harleston IP20. . . . . . . **22** D6
Lowestoft NR33. . . . . **114** F3
Newlands La CO6 . . . . **102** D5
NEWMAN'S GREEN **92** A6
Newman's Rd CO10. . . . . . **148** C6
NEWMARKET **121** B4
Newmarket Coll CB8. . . . **120** F4
Newmarket Com Hospl
CB8. . . . . **120** F5
Newmarket Lawn Tennis
Club CB8 . . . . **120** E3

Newmarket Leisure Ctr
CB8 120 F4
Newmarket Racecourse
CB8 120 B1
Newmarket Rd
1 Ashley CB8 60 F8
Barton Mills IP28 116 D1
Burwell CB5 44 B5
Bury St Edmunds IP33 122 D6
Cowlinge CB8 61 B2
Fordham CB7 44 E8
Moulton CB8 45 F3
Newmarket CB8 121 B8
Red Lodge IP28 30 C2
Risby IP28 47 C5
Snailwell CB8 45 A5
Newmarket Sports Ctr
CB8 121 A4
Newmarket Sta CB8 121 A2
Newmarket Swimming Pool
CB8 120 F3
Newmarket Upper Sch
CB8 120 F4
Newmill La CO11 105 A5
NEW MISTLEY 105 A2
New Mkt NR34 111 B5
Newnham Ave IP12 146 D4
Newnham Cl IP28 116 D5
Newnham Ct IP2 138 E1
Newnham Dro CB5 44 A6
Newnham La 14 CB5 44 A6
New Path 4 CB7 29 A1
Newport Ave CB7 29 C1
Newport Cl 7 IP27 13 F2
Newquay Cl IP5 140 F6
New Quay Ct IP12 147 B5
New Quay La IP12 147 B6
New Quay Terr IP12 147 B6
New Queens Rd CO10 148 C7
New Rd
Ampton IP31 33 A1
Aspall IP14 53 E4
Badingham IP13 56 B8
Barnby NR34 10 C4
Barrow IP29 47 B3
Beccles NR34 111 B7
Brettenham IP24 17 B6
5 Burwell CB5 44 A6
Chevington IP29 62 C7
Dickleburgh & Rushall IP21 21 A4
Elmswell IP30 50 E2
Exning CB8 120 B8
Felixstowe IP11 152 C7
Framlingham IP13 126 C5
Fritton & St Olaves NR31 2 B7
Gissing IP22 20 F8
Great Glemham IP17 71 E8
Helmingham IP14 69 A5
19 Ixworth IP31 34 B1
Little Livermere IP31 33 A2
Long Melford CO10 91 D8
Manningtree CO11 104 E2
Marlesford IP13 71 C6
Melton IP12 84 D6
Mettingham NR35 110 F2
Nedging-with-Naughton IP7 80 C3
Rumburgh IP19 24 C4
Rushbrooke with Rougham
IP30 49 D1
Sibton IP17 41 D1
St Cross, South Elmham
IP20 23 D5
Thelnetham IP22 35 B7
Thrandeston IP21 37 C8
Timworth IP31 48 E8
Tivetshall St Mary NR15 21 B8
Tostock IP30 50 B2
Troston IP31 33 D4
Worlingworth IP13 54 F8
New River Gn CB8 120 B8
Newry Ave IP11 152 F4
New St Cl IP21 39 A4
Newson Ave NR34 10 C3
Newson's Meadow 1
NR32 113 C2
Newson St IP1 155 A4
New St
Chippenham CB7 29 E1
Framlingham IP13 126 A4
Fressingfield IP21 39 D8
Glemsford CO10 77 A3
4 Mildenhall IP28 116 C4
Stradbroke IP21 39 A4
Sudbury CO10 148 C6
9 Woodbridge IP12 147 A5
Newthorpe IP30 49 C1
NEWTON 92 D3
Newton Croft CO10 148 E5
Newton Pl 4 CB9 132 F6
Newton Rd
17 Harwich CO12 107 A2
Ipswich IP3 140 A4
Stowupland IP14 124 D8
Sudbury CO10 148 D5
Newton St IP4 155 C3
NEWTOWN 54 D7
New Way IP2 138 F6
New Wolsey Theatre★
IP1 155 A3
Nicholas Dr IP18 119 C7
Nicholas Everitt Pk
NR33 114 D8
Nicholas Rd IP11 152 C4
Nicholas's St 2 IP22 20 C2
Nicholls Cl 7 IP13 84 F7
Nichols Cl 24 CO11 104 D2
Nicholson Dr NR34 111 C2
Nicholsons Ct CO10 92 D3
Nicholson Sq 2 NR32 113 C2
Nick's La IP23 117 B6
Nidderdale 8 NR33 114 E3
Nightall Rd 5 CB7 28 D4
Nightingale Ave IP18 119 B7
Nightingale Cl
Bury St Edmunds IP33 154 A1
19 Harwich CO12 106 F1
5 Mildenhall IP28 116 D4
5 Stowmarket IP14 67 A5
Nightingale Hill CO4 103 C3
Nightingale La 9 IP26 4 E5
Nightingale Piece IP12 131 C3
Nightingale Rd
Ipswich IP3 144 A8
Lowestoft NR33 115 B3
Nightingale Sq 5 IP3 144 A8
Nimbus Way CB8 120 E8
Nine Acres IP2 138 D6
Ninfield Cl NR33 114 D4
Noahs Ark Pl CO10 148 B5
Noahs Dr 5 NR33 11 B1
Noaks Rd IP7 94 F1
Nock Gdns IP5 141 C6
Noel Cl NR31 3 B7
Noel Murless Dr CB8 120 F6
Noel Rd NR32 112 C1
Noel's Wlk NR34 111 B6
Noller's La IP19 24 F4
No Man's Meadow★
IP33 123 C4
Nonsuch Meadow 2
CO10 148 C4
Norbury Rd IP4 140 B7
Nordalls The 16 NR33 11 C1
Norfolk Ave CB8 120 E5
Norfolk Cres 1 IP13 126 C3
Norfolk Rd
Bury St Edmunds IP32 123 A8
9 Honington IP31 33 D5
Ipswich IP4 155 C3
Thetford IP24 16 C6
Wangford NR34 26 B2
Norfolk St NR32 113 B1
Norfolk & Suffolk Aviation
Mus★ NR35 7 D2
Norgate La IP21 21 B2
Norman Cl
Felixstowe IP11 153 D6
Woodbridge IP12 147 A7
Norman Cres IP3 140 A2
Normandie Way 8 CO8 101 C4
Normandy Cl IP14 124 D3
Normandy Rd NR32 113 B4
Normanhurst Cl NR32 113 A2
Norman Rd
6 Bury St Edmunds IP32 48 C5
Bury St Edmunds IP32 122 F8
23 Manningtree CO11 104 E2
NORMANSTON 113 B3
Normanston Dr 5 NR32 113 B2
Norman Way 1 CO10 78 D4
Nornea La CB7 28 A8
Norse Ave IP29 64 A3
Northacre 12 NR33 11 B1
North Acres IP8 81 A6
North Ave CB9 132 C6
North Cl
Bacton IP14 51 F6
Ipswich IP4 135 E1
9 Stanton IP31 34 E4
NORTH COMMON 34 F6
NORTH COVE 10 C4
North Cres CB9 88 D4
Northcroft 1 CO10 148 C5
North Dr
Newmarket CB8 120 F5
1 Soham CB7 28 D5
NORTH END 90 C2
North End CB8 120 B8
North End Ave IP16 73 F6
North End Rd CO9 90 C2
North Entrance IP17 128 D3
Northern Rd CO10 148 F7
Northern Rose Cl IP32 123 F7
Northern Way IP32 48 C5
North Field Cl 3 NR32 112 F5
Northfield Ct IP15 130 E5
Northfield La IP15 130 E5
Northfield Pk CB7 28 C5
Northfield Rd
Onehouse IP14 66 C6
Soham CB7 28 C5
Northfield St Nicholas CP
Prim Sch NR32 113 C3
Northgate
Beccles NR34 111 B6
11 Harleston IP20 22 D5
Lowestoft NR32 113 B2
Northgate Ave IP32 154 B4
Northgate Cty High Sch
IP4 136 A1
Northgate Lodge IP33 154 B3
Northgate St Bsns Pk
IP33 154 C3
Northgate Sports Ctr
IP4 136 A2
Northgate St
Bury St Edmunds IP33 154 C3
Ipswich IP4 155 B3
North Gn IP18 119 D6
North Gn Rd
Cratfield IP19 40 C7
Pulham St Mary IP21 22 A8
NORTH GREEN
Cratfield 40 C7
Kelsale cum Carlton 57 D5
Parham 56 B1
North Hill IP12 146 F6
North Hill Gdns IP4 139 E6
North Hill Rd IP4 139 E6
North Lawn IP4 140 B8
NORTH LOPHAM 19 A5
North Lopham Rd NR16 19 A7
North Parade
Lowestoft NR32 113 D4
Southwold IP18 119 E5
North Par Gdns IP18 119 E6
North Pl IP28 116 C4
North Quay Ret Pk NR32 113 B1
North Rd
Great Yeldham CO9 90 A1
Lakenheath IP27 109 E4
Southwold IP18 119 D6
North Rise CO10 148 E4
North St Parade 5
CO10 148 C5
North St
Burwell CB5 44 A6
Freckenham IP28 29 E3
Hundon CO10 75 D4
11 Manningtree CO11 104 E2
Steeple Bumpstead CB9 88 D4
Sudbury CO10 148 C6
Wicken CB7 28 A1
North Terr IP28 116 C5
Northumberland Ave
IP32 122 E8
North Warren IP15 130 C8
North Warren Nature
Reserve★ IP15 73 D6
Northwood Cl NR33 114 F6
NORTON 50 B4
Norton CE Prim Sch IP31 50 B5
NORTON LITTLE GREEN 50 D5
Norton Rd
Haverhill CB9 132 C4
Hunston IP31 50 E5
11 Thurstow IP31 49 D4
Tostock IP30 50 B2
Norway Cres 2 CO12 106 F2
Norwich La
Bardwell IP31 34 C8
Coney Weston IP31 17 E2
Norwich Rd
Barham IP6 82 A6
Claydon IP6 134 C8
Denton IP20 7 B3
5 Dickleburgh & Rushall
IP21 20 F1
Ditchingham NR35 110 A8
Earsham NR35 7 E5
Gillingham NR34 111 A8
Halesworth IP19 118 C5
Ipswich IP1 155 A3
5 Lakenheath IP27 13 F2
Lakenheath IP27 109 F1
Lowestoft NR32 113 C1
Newmarket CB8 121 D6
Pulham St Mary IP21 21 F8
Scole IP21 21 B5
Stockton NR34 9 A8
Thetford IP24 16 C6
Norwich Rd Sch IP24 16 C6
Norwood Rd IP27 14 E8
Notcutts CO7 151 E3
Notley Dr CB9 132 A7
Notley Ent Pk CO7 95 A2
Notley Rd NR33 115 A7
Nottidge Rd IP4 139 E6
Nova Scotia La IP7 79 B4
NOWTON 63 E7
Nowton Ctry Pk★ IP33 63 E8
Nowton Pk IP29 123 D1
Nowton Rd
Bury St Edmunds IP33 123 C1
Nowton IP29 63 E8
Noyes Ave IP13 40 B3
Nuffield Hospl (Private)
IP33 154 C1
Nunn Cl 1 IP12 84 A1
Nunnery Gn 2 CB8 61 E2
Nunn's Hill IP19 24 C3
Nunn's La IP19 23 E1
Nunn Sq IP32 122 D8
Nuns' Bridges Rd IP24 16 B5
Nuns Wlk CO9 89 F1
Nursery Cl
Isleham CB7 29 B4
Mildenhall IP28 116 D4
Nursery La IP26 5 A2
Nursery Rd CO10 148 F2
Nursery Wlk IP11 152 F4
Nursey Cl NR35 8 D7
Nuttery Vale IP23 38 B6

O

Oak Ave NR34 111 F5
Oak Cl
Bury St Edmunds IP28 48 C6
Felixstowe IP11 152 E4
4 Great Finborough IP14 66 B4
Oak Cres IP23 117 C3
Oakdene IP10 98 D2
Oak Dr
Diss IP22 20 E2
6 Mildenhall IP28 30 B8
Oak Eggar Chase IP8 142 D8
Oakes Cl IP32 122 E7
Oakes Rd IP32 122 E7
Oakey Field Rd 6 IP31 49 E4
Oakey Ley IP30 64 D6
Oak Farm La IP14 52 D6
Oakfield Rd
Bacton IP14 52 A6
Copdock & Washbrook IP8 142 A6
Oakfield Wood Nature
Reserve★ CO11 105 E3
Oak Gn IP19 118 B2
Oak Gr
Fornham St Martin IP31 48 D5
Sproughton IP8 138 A6
OAK HILL 100 A8
Oak Hill Cl NR34 26 E5
Oak Hill La IP2 139 B3
Oak La
Beccles NR34 111 D2
Cheveley CB8 60 E6
Elmswell IP30 50 F3
Ipswich IP1 155 B3
Lakenheath IP27 13 F2
Rushbrooke with Rougham
IP30 64 D8
Woolpit IP30 65 E8
Oakland Rd 15 CO12 107 B2
Oaklands CO6 102 B8
Oaklands Dr IP27 14 D8
OAKLEY 38 A8
Oakley Church La IP21 37 F8
Oakley Rd 11 CO12 106 E1
Oakley Sq IP15 130 E4
Oak Meadow Cl IP19 42 C6
Oak Rd
3 Sudbury CO10 92 B3
Sudbury CO10 148 F4
Oaks Bsns Pk CB8 120 E7
Oaks Com Prim Sch
Chantry IP2 138 E4
Ipswich IP2 138 E3
Oaks Dr CB8 120 F7
Oaks La NR34 2 B1
Oaksmere Gdns 8 IP2 139 A2
Oak St IP26 4 E5
Oaks The
7 Horringer IP29 63 A8
Martlesham Heath IP5 141 F6
Soham CB7 28 D3
Wattisfield IP22 35 C5
Woolpit IP30 65 F8
Oak Tree Way 8 IP20 22 D5
Oak Way IP19 118 A1
Oakwood Pk IP17 57 D7
Oakwood Rd NR33 114 F5
Oasis Camel Ctr★ IP19 40 C8
Oast Ct IP33 154 C1
Oatfields 6 IP21 39 D8
Oatlands Cl 4 NR33 114 E4
Oban St IP1 155 A4
OCCOLD 37 F1
Occold Prim Sch IP23 37 F1
Occold Rd IP23 38 B2
O'feld Terr IP11 153 C6
Off Sea View Rd IP18 119 C7
OFFTON 81 A4
Offton Rd
Elmsett IP7 81 A2
Great Bricett IP7 80 F5
Ohio Cl 4 NR33 114 E3
Old Barningham Rd 1
IP31 34 E4
Old Barn Rd CO8 101 C3
Old Barrack Rd IP12 146 E4
Old Brandon Rd IP26 4 F5
Old Brewery Yd IP19 118 A3
Old Buckenham Hall Sch
IP7 79 B7
Old Bungay Rd NR35 8 D8
Old Bury Rd
Alpheton CO10 78 A6
Lackford IP28 31 F1
Palgrave IP22 37 A8
Stanton IP31 34 E4
Stuston IP21 20 D1
Wortham IP22 36 F8
Old Cattle Mkt IP1 155 B2
Old Church La
Bulmer CO10 91 C1
Westley IP33 122 A6
Old Church Rd 1 NR31 3 B6
Old Clements La 5 CB9 132 D5
Old Coll Cl NR34 111 B5
Old Convent Orch IP33 154 B1
Old Dairy Bsns Pk IP31 49 B5
Old Farm Rd
Beccles NR34 111 C5
4 Lowestoft NR33 114 D5
OLD FELIXSTOWE 153 C6
Oldfield Rd IP8 138 B1
Old Forge Cl IP22 36 D8
Old Forge Ct IP21 22 A2
Old Foundry Pl IP16 129 C6
Old Foundry Rd IP4 155 C3
Old Gram La NR35 110 B3
Old Hall Cl 2 IP6 82 D6
OLDHALL GREEN 64 C3
Old Hall La
Bentley IP9 95 F2
Bury St Edmunds IP28 48 D5
Cockfield IP30 64 B3
Westleton IP17 58 B8
Old Hall Meadow IP30 65 D6
Oldhall Rd IP9 106 F6
Old Hall Rd IP13 56 C8
Old Harleston Rd NR35 7 E3
Old Haverhill Rd CB9 74 F2
Old High Rd
Roydon IP22 20 B3
Yoxford IP17 57 D7
Old Homes Rd 7 IP16 73 F6
Old House La CO4 103 A1
Old House Rd CO6 102 D1
Olding Rd IP33 122 D6
Old Ipswich Rd IP6 134 C7
Old Kirton Rd IP11 107 D8
Old La
Bradfield Combust with
Stanningfield IP29 63 F3
Corton NR32 113 B8
Thelnetham IP22 35 C6
Old London Rd IP9 150 D1
Old Maids' La IP13 70 A7
Old Maltings App IP12 147 B6
Old Maltings Ct IP12 147 B5
Old Methwold Rd IP26 4 E6
Old Mill Dr IP21 21 F8
Old Mill La
Barton Mills IP28 116 F2
Beccles NR34 111 B4
Old Mill Rd CO4 103 B3
Old Mill Terr 2 NR34 111 B6
Old Mkt 6 NR34 111 B6
Old Mkt Pl
21 Harleston IP20 22 D6
19 Sudbury CO10 148 C5
Old Mkt Plain 8 NR32 113 E2
Old Mkt St IP14 52 E4
Old Nelson St 4 NR32 113 E1
OLD NEWTON 51 F1
Old Newton CE Prim Sch
IP14 52 A1
Old Norwich Rd
Whitton IP1 134 D5
Yaxley IP23 37 C5
Old Orch IP7 149 F1
Old Orch Cl IP19 118 A2
Old Paper Mill La 8 IP6 134 C8
Old Post Office La
Blaxhall IP12 72 A4
Kirby Row NR35 8 E7
Sutton IP12 99 A8
Old Post Office Rd IP29 62 C6
Old Priory Gdns NR34 26 B2
Old Rd The CO6 102 B8
Old Rectory Cl
2 Claydon IP6 82 B5
6 Roydon IP22 20 A3
Old Rectory Gdns 3 IP23 37 F1
Old Rectory La IP29 77 E6
Old Rectory Rd IP13 56 A6
Old Rectory Sch The IP7 65 C1
Old Rectory Wlk IP9 150 D3
Old Rly Rd
Alburgh IP20 7 B1
Bungay NR35 110 A4
Old Rope Wlk CB9 132 C5
Old St The IP9 150 F3
Old Sch Cl
Brampton with Stoven
NR34 25 E5
5 Burwell CB5 44 B6
Leiston IP16 129 C6
4 Soham CB7 28 D5
Old Sch Dr IP28 26 E1
Old Sch Hall The★ IP33 154 B3
Old Sch La CB8 59 F1
Old Schools Ct IP30 50 E2
Old Sch Rd IP29 63 A5
Old Sch The NR34 10 E1
Old St IP14 51 C1
Old Sta Rd
Ellingham NR35 8 D6
Halesworth IP19 118 B5
Mendlesham IP14 52 E3
Newmarket CB8 121 B4
Old Stores Cl IP13 54 E7
Old Stowmarket Rd IP30 50 D1
Old Town La IP33 123 C1
Old Vicarage Dr IP31 50 E7
Old Vicarage Rd 13
CO12 107 A2
Olive Cl 2 IP27 13 F2
Olive Ct NR32 113 B3
Oliver Cl NR33 114 D2
Oliver Ct IP27 5 E4
Oliver Rd IP33 122 C6
Olivers Cl CO10 91 E8
Olland Ct 5 NR35 110 B3
Olle Cl IP33 123 C1
Olympus Cl IP1 134 C2
One Eyed La IP21 22 D3
ONEHOUSE 66 C6
Onehouse La IP1 135 C1
Onehouse Rd IP14 124 B6
Onner's La IP16 58 C4
Ontario Rd NR33 115 C6
Opal Ave
1 Ipswich IP1 134 D1
Ipswich IP1 138 D8
Orchard Ave NR33 114 E6
Orchard Cl
Beyton IP30 49 F1
2 Blundeston NR32 3 A4
Elmswell IP30 50 F3
Great Livermere IP31 33 C2
6 Haverhill CB9 132 D5
Lidgate CB8 61 C4
2 Ramsey & Parkeston
CO12 106 D1
Ridgewell CO9 89 D3
Risby IP28 47 D5
Rushbrooke with Rougham
IP30 64 D8
Woodbridge IP12 147 A7
Orchard Croft 2 NR33 114 E4
Orchard Dr IP14 65 F4
Orchard End 16 IP13 83 E5

Orchard Farm Barns **2**
　IP29. . . . . 47 A2
Orchard Farm Bsns Pk
　CB7. . . . . 28 C7
Orchard Gate
　Ipswich IP2. . . . . 138 C5
　1 Needham Market IP6. .125 D5
Orchard Gdn NR33 . . . . . . 114 E7
Orchard Gn NR34 . . . . 111 C4
Orchard Gr
　Claydon IP6. . . . . 134 C7
　Ipswich IP5 . . . . 141 A7
Orchard La
　3 Blundeston NR32 . . . . . . 3 A4
　Thurston IP31. . . . . 49 E5
Orchard Pl
　Sudbury CO10 . . . . 148 B4
　Wickham Market IP13. . . 127 B6
Orchard Rd
　6 Bramford IP8. . . . . 134 A2
　Leiston IP16 . . . . 129 C5
Orchard Rise
　Badingham IP13 . . . . 56 A7
　Beccles NR34. . . . . 111 F4
Orchard Row CB7 . . . . 28 E2
Orchard St
　Bury St Edmunds IP33. . . 154 B3
　Ipswich IP4. . . . . 155 C3
Orchards The **1** IP13 . . . . 40 B3
Orchard Terr **4** NR33 . . . 115 C7
Orchard The
　5 Ashley CB8. . . . . 60 F8
　Felsham IP30. . . . . 65 A4
　Redisham NR34. . . . . 25 B7
Orchard Valley IP19. . . . . 118 D4
Orchard Way
　Badwell Ash IP31. . . . . 50 F7
　12 Barrow IP29. . . . . 47 A2
　4 Burwell CB5. . . . . 44 A6
　4 Glemsford CO10. . . . . . 77 A3
　Scole IP21. . . . . 21 A2
Orchard Way The **2** IP29 63 A8
Orchid Cl
　Halesworth IP19 . . . . 118 C4
　Ipswich IP2. . . . . 138 E4
Orchids IP NR35 . . . . 110 D3
Orchid Way IP6. . . . . 125 D3
Oregon Rd IP5. . . . . 141 A6
ORFORD. 131 C2
Orford Castle Mus & Visitor
　Ctr★ IP12. . . . . 131 B2
Orford CE VA Prim Sch
　IP12. . . . . 131 B3
Orford Dr NR32 . . . . 112 E4
Orford Ness★ IP12. . . . . . 131 C1
Orford Ness National Nature
　Reserve★ IP12 . . . . 87 C3
Orford Rd
　Bromeswell IP12. . . . . 147 F7
　Butley IP12 . . . . 86 A6
　Felixstowe IP11. . . . . 152 E1
　Haverhill CB9. . . . . 132 D4
　Tunstall IP12 . . . . 71 F2
Orford St IP1. . . . . 155 A4
Oriel Cl CO10. . . . . 148 F4
Original Factory Shop The
　IP32. . . . . 123 D7
Orkney Cl CB9 . . . . 133 B5
Orkney Rd **4** IP4 . . . . 136 A1
Orttewell Rd IP32. . . . . . . 123 E6
Orvis La CO7. . . . . 151 E3
Orwell Ave IP17 . . . . 128 C4
Orwell Ct IP12. . . . . 146 E3
Orwell Ctry Pk★ IP3 . . . . . 139 F3
Orwell Dr **1** NR32 . . . . . . 112 F3
Orwell High Sch IP11 . . . . . 152 E5
Orwell Pk Sch IP10 . . . . . . 145 B3
Orwell Pl IP4 . . . . 155 C2
Orwell Rd
　Felixstowe IP11. . . . . 152 F3
　10 Harwich CO12 . . . . 107 B2
　Ipswich IP3. . . . . 140 A4
　Stowmarket IP14. . . . . . . 124 D4
Orwell Ret Pk IP2 . . . . 139 A5
Orwell Rise **10** IP9 . . . . . 106 C8
Orwell View Rd IP9 . . . . . 106 F6
Osborne Dr IP3. . . . . 140 A4
Osborne St **4** NR32 . . . . 113 E3
Osier Cl IP12. . . . . 147 B6
Osier Rd IP33. . . . . 154 B3
Osiers The IP14. . . . . 124 D7
Osmund Wlk IP33. . . . . . . 122 C4
Osprey Gn NR33 . . . . 114 C6
Osprey Rd CB9. . . . . 133 A5
Oswyn Cl IP33 . . . . 123 D4
OTLEY. 69 C2
Otley Coll
　Otley IP6. . . . . 69 C1
　Rendlesham IP12 . . . . 85 E8
Otley Ct **5** IP11 . . . . 152 D5
Otley Hall★ IP6. . . . . 69 C3
Otley Prim Sch IP6 . . . . 69 C2
Otley Rd IP12. . . . . 85 C2
Otten Rd CO10 . . . . 90 D5
Otter Trust The★ NR35. . . . 7 E3
OULTON. 112 F5
OULTON BROAD. 114 C8
Oulton Broad N Sta
　NR32. . . . . 112 F1
Oulton Broad Prim Sch
　NR32. . . . . 112 C2
Oulton Broad S Sta
　NR33. . . . . 114 D7
Oulton Broad Wr Sports Ctr
　NR33. . . . . 114 D7

Oulton Cl **6** CO12. . . . . . 106 F2
Oulton Ct NR32 . . . . 112 E4
Oulton Ind Est NR32. . . . . 112 E3
Oulton Marshes Nature
　Reserve★ NR32. . . . . 112 B3
Oulton Rd
　Flixton NR32 . . . . 112 F7
　Ipswich IP3. . . . . 139 F2
　Lowestoft NR32. . . . . 113 A4
Oulton Rd N NR32. . . . . . . 112 F5
Oulton St NR32 . . . . 112 F4
Ound Farm Nature Reserve★
　IP17. . . . . 56 C1
OUSDEN. 61 E6
Ousden Rd IP29 . . . . 62 A6
Outney Meadow Cvn Pk
　NR35. . . . . 110 A5
Outney Rd NR35. . . . . 110 A4
Out Northgate IP33 . . . . . 154 B4
Out Risbygate IP33. . . . . . 122 E6
Out Westgate IP33. . . . . . 154 B1
Overbury Hall Rd IP7 . . . . 149 D1
OVINGTON. 90 A5
Ovington Pl **5** CB9 . . . . . 132 F6
Owell The IP31. . . . . 49 E6
Oxer CI IP30. . . . . 50 F2
Oxford Cl
　Mildenhall IP28 . . . . 116 A4
　Sudbury CO10. . . . . 148 E4
Oxford Dr
　Hadleigh IP7 . . . . 149 D8
　Woodbridge IP12. . . . . . . 146 D3
Oxford Rd
　2 Feltwell IP26 . . . . 4 E5
　Ipswich IP4. . . . . 139 E5
　Lowestoft NR32. . . . . 113 D3
　25 Manningtree CO11. . . . 104 E2
Oxford St CB8 . . . . 120 B8

Packard Ave IP3. . . . . 140 B2
Packard Pl IP8 . . . . 134 B2
Packards La
　Fordham CO6. . . . . 102 A1
　Wormingford CO6 . . . . . . 101 F1
Packway La IP31. . . . . 50 A5
Packway The IP20 . . . . 23 A7
Paddock Farm IP31. . . . . . 34 D8
Paddock Hill **2** NR33 . . . 114 E7
Paddock Rd **13** IP20. . . . . 22 D6
Paddocks Cty Prim Sch
　CB8. . . . . 120 E4
Paddocks Cl CB8 . . . . 121 A2
Paddocks Gn NR34. . . . . . 111 F4
Paddock St CB7. . . . . 28 D4
Paddocks The
　Ashen CO10. . . . . 89 C5
　Badwell Ash IP31 . . . . 50 F7
　6 Bures CO8 . . . . 101 C4
　12 Burwell CB5. . . . . 44 A5
　Halesworth IP19 . . . . 118 C4
　3 Martlesham Heath IP5. 98 A8
　Tuddenham St Martin IP6 136 B5
　Worlington IP28 . . . . 30 B4
Paddock The **16** IP31. . . . . 34 B1
Paddock Way
　Chedburgh IP29. . . . . 62 C4
　Troston IP31 . . . . 33 D3
Paddock Wood Cl **8**
　NR33 . . . . 114 C4
Padstow Rd IP5 . . . . 141 A6
Pageant Pl IP13 . . . . 126 E3
Page Gdns IP5. . . . . 141 E8
Page's Cl IP14. . . . . 124 C6
PAGE'S GREEN. 53 C4
Pages Hill Rd IP29 . . . . . . 63 B6
Paget Cl IP6. . . . . 125 C5
Paget Pl CB8 . . . . 121 A6
Paget Rd IP1 . . . . 155 A4
Pains Cl **2** NR34. . . . . 9 F4
Pains Hill IP14. . . . . 67 F6
PAKEFIELD. 115 B3
Pakefield High Sch
　NR33. . . . . 115 A3
Pakefield Prim Sch
　NR33. . . . . 115 A3
Pakefield Rd NR33. . . . . . 115 C5
Pakefield St NR33. . . . . . . 115 B4
PAKENHAM. 49 E6
Pakenham Pl CB9 . . . . 132 F5
Pakenham Rd IP31. . . . . . . 49 D6
Pakenham Watermill★
　IP31. . . . . 49 F8
Pakenham Windmill★
　IP31. . . . . 49 F8
Palace La CB7. . . . . 45 B8
Palace St **4** CB8. . . . . 121 A3
PALE GREEN. 88 B5
Palfrey Height CO11. . . . . 104 E4
PALGRAVE. 20 C1
Palgrave VC Prim Sch
　IP22. . . . . 20 C1
Palmcroft **10** IP1. . . . . 135 A3
Palmcroft Rd IP1. . . . . . . 135 A3
Palmer Cl NR32. . . . . 113 B6
Palmer Dr IP27. . . . . 109 C7
Palmer's La IP18. . . . . 119 A2
Palmer St IP31. . . . . 35 C1
Palmerston Rd IP4. . . . . . 139 E6
Palmerswent Cl CO10. . . . 91 F8
Pamment's La **5** IP28 . . . . 29 F4
Pannels Cl **5** CO10 . . . . . . 77 A2
Pantile La **12** CB5. . . . . . . 44 A6
Papeley Meadow IP29 . . . . 47 B2
Paper Mill La IP8. . . . . . . 134 B4

Parade Dr **6** CO12. . . . . . 106 E1
Parade Rd IP4. . . . . 139 F7
Parade Rd N **18** NR33 . . . . 115 D8
Parade Rd S NR33. . . . . . . 115 D7
Parade The CB9 . . . . 133 F8
Paradise Pl IP16. . . . . 129 D2
Pardoe Pl IP4 . . . . 140 E5
PARHAM. 71 A7
Parham Airfield Mus★
　IP13. . . . . 71 C7
Parish Bush Dro CB7. . . . . . 12 A1
Park Ave
　Felixstowe IP11. . . . . 153 B5
　3 Fornham St Martin IP28 48 C6
　Newmarket CB8. . . . . 121 B3
　Saxmundham IP17. . . . . . 128 C3
Park Cl
　3 Bentwaters Airfield
　　IP12 . . . . 85 D8
　1 Lowestoft NR33 . . . . . . 114 D4
　5 Martlesham Heath IP5. 98 A8
　4 Moulton CB8. . . . . 45 F3
　Sudbury CO10 . . . . 148 E6
Park Cotts CB8 . . . . 121 B2
Park Dr NR34. . . . . 111 E4
Park End IP17 . . . . 128 C2
Parker Ave IP11 . . . . 152 B4
Parker's Dro **3** IP28. . . . . 29 F6
Parker's Rd IP14. . . . . 52 A5
Parker's Way CO6. . . . . . 102 D5
Parkers Wlk CB8. . . . . 120 E8
PARKESTON. 106 F3
Parkeston Rd
　Felixstowe IP11. . . . . 152 D4
　Harwich CO12 . . . . 107 A2
Park Farm Dr
　Barton Mills IP28 . . . . 30 C2
　Stanton IP31 . . . . 34 E3
Park Farm La
　Euston IP24. . . . . 33 E8
　Hoxne IP21 . . . . 38 E6
PARK GATE. 61 E3
PARK GREEN. 53 B3
Parkhill NR32. . . . . 112 F5
Park Hill IP16. . . . . 129 C6
Parkington Wlk IP32. . . . . 122 D7
Park La
　Aldeburgh IP15 . . . . 130 E4
　Bulmer CO10. . . . . 91 C2
　Charsfield IP13 . . . . 70 C3
　Eye IP23 . . . . 117 D1
　Glemsford CO10 . . . . 77 B2
　Hawstead IP29 . . . . 63 D7
　Kirton IP10 . . . . 98 E3
　Langham CO4. . . . . 103 C2
　Newmarket CB8. . . . . 121 B3
　Southwold IP18. . . . . 119 D4
　Thornham Parva IP23 . . . . 37 A3
Parklands **5** IP13 . . . . 84 F7
Parklands Cl **9** CO10 . . . . 77 B3
Parklands Gn **2** IP28 . . . . 48 C6
Parklands The NR32. . . . . 114 D4
Parklands Way **41** IP20. . . 22 D6
Park Meadows NR32. . . . . 112 F6
Park N IP1 . . . . 139 D8
Park Pl IP17. . . . . 57 D7
Park Rd
　Aldeburgh IP15 . . . . 130 D4
　Benhall IP17 . . . . 72 A7
　Boot Street IP13 . . . . 137 D8
　Burwell CB5. . . . . 44 A5
　Bury St Edmunds IP33. . . 122 D4
　Cheveley CB8. . . . . 60 D7
　Combs IP14. . . . . 124 B2
　Diss IP22. . . . . 20 C2
　Drinkstone IP30 . . . . 50 B1
　East Bergholt CO7. . . . . . 104 D5
　Great Horkesley CO6. . . . 102 D4
　Grundisburgh IP13 . . . . . . 83 E5
　Halesworth IP19 . . . . 118 A5
　3 Harwich CO12 . . . . 107 B2
　Haverhill CB9. . . . . 132 B7
　Ipswich IP1. . . . . 139 C8
　Lavenham CO10. . . . . 78 D4
　Letheringham IP13 . . . . . . 70 D4
　Lowestoft NR32. . . . . 113 D3
　Needham Market IP6 . . . . 125 D4
　Southolt IP23. . . . . 54 A8
　St Cross, South Elmham
　　IP20. . . . . 23 C7
　Stoke-by-Nayland CO6. . . 102 F6
　Sudbury CO10. . . . . 148 E6
　Wetherden IP14 . . . . 51 A1
Parkside
　Chippenham CB7 . . . . 45 C8
　Haverhill CB9. . . . . 132 D4
　Mildenhall IP28 . . . . 30 C8
　3 Stanton IP31 . . . . 34 E4
Parkside Ave IP4. . . . . . . 155 C4
Parkside Dr NR32. . . . . . . 113 A2
Park St CO6 . . . . 102 E7
Park The
　3 Great Barton IP31 . . . . 49 A5
　Tannington CO11 . . . . 104 E2
Park View
　Botesdale IP22 . . . . 36 B7
　Weeting IP27. . . . . 5 E3
　Wetherden IP14 . . . . 51 A1
Park View Rd IP1 . . . . 135 B1
Parkway
　Bury St Edmunds IP33. . . 154 A2
　Wickham Market IP13. . . 127 C4
Parkway Mid Sch CB9. . . . . 132 B6
Parkwood Dr CO10. . . . . . 148 C5
PARLIAMENT HEATH. 93 C6
Parliament Rd IP4 . . . . . . 140 B5

Parmenter Dr **13** CO10 . . . 92 B3
Parnell Cl IP1 . . . . 134 F3
Parnell La IP30. . . . . 50 D3
Parnell Rd IP1. . . . . 134 F3
PARNEY HEATH. 103 D2
Parnham Pl **2** IP4. . . . . . . 140 F5
Parrington Way **26** CO11 104 D2
Parr Rd CB9. . . . . 132 B4
Parry Cl IP19 . . . . 118 B5
Parsonage Cl
　5 Burwell CB5. . . . . 44 A5
　3 Felixstowe IP11. . . . . . 152 D4
Parsonage Farm La CB8. . 60 C3
Parsonage Gdns **16** CB9 . 132 C5
Parsonage Gr **7** CO8 . . . . 101 C4
Parsonage La
　Burwell CB5. . . . . 44 A5
　Chelsworth IP7 . . . . 79 E3
Parsons Ct IP33. . . . . 154 B3
Parsons Field **4** IP15. . . . 130 E5
Parson's Field CO7. . . . . . 104 A3
Parsons Hill IP12 . . . . 99 F7
Parson's La IP6. . . . . 125 B2
Parsons Yd **24** CO11. . . . . 104 E2
Partridge Cl
　Boxford CO10 . . . . 93 C4
　Stowmarket IP14. . . . . . . 124 F6
　15 Thurston IP31 . . . . 49 D4
Partridge Rd IP2. . . . . 138 D3
Pashford Cl IP27. . . . . 109 D6
Pashford Pl **6** IP3 . . . . . . 144 C8
Paske Ave CB9. . . . . 132 D5
Pastures The
　Ipswich IP4. . . . . 140 F5
　Oulton NR32 . . . . 112 F6
Patricia Cl NR32 . . . . 112 D2
Patrick Stead Hospl
　IP19 . . . . 118 C5
Patten La NR15. . . . . 21 B7
Patterdale Gdns **3**
　NR32. . . . . 113 A4
Pattern Bush Cl **4** CO11. . 104 E4
Patteson Rd IP3 . . . . 139 E4
Patticroft **7** CO10 . . . . . . 77 A3
Pauline St IP2. . . . . 155 B1
Pavilion Ct CB9. . . . . 132 F5
Paxton Chadwick Cl **1**
　IP16 . . . . 129 D5
Payne's La IP26. . . . . 4 E5
Payne St NR33. . . . . 115 C7
Peacock Cl
　Hockwold cum Wilton IP26 . 4 F3
　5 Ipswich IP8 . . . . 138 C2
　Lowestoft NR33. . . . . 114 C2
Peacock Rise **18** IP31 . . . . 34 B1
Peacocks Cl **1** CO10. . . . . 76 E1
Peacocks Rd CO10 . . . . . . 76 E2
Peacock St IP5 . . . . 141 E7
Peak Dale NR33. . . . . 114 E3
Pearce Rd IP3. . . . . 140 A4
Pearce's Cl **2** IP26 . . . . . . 5 A3
Pearcroft Rd IP1. . . . . 135 B3
Pearl Cl IP6 . . . . 69 C2
Pearl Rd IP3. . . . . 138 D8
Pearmain Wlk **8** CB9 . . . . 132 A6
Pearse Way IP3. . . . . 140 E1
Pearson Rd IP4. . . . . 140 C5
Pearsons Way IP8 . . . . 95 F5
Peart Gr IP5. . . . . 141 D6
Peartree Cl IP17 . . . . 128 C6
Peartree Hill CO8 . . . . 101 D2
Peasecroft Rd **3** IP31. . . . 34 B1
PEASENHALL. 56 E8
Peasenhall Cl **2** IP12. . . . . 85 B3
Peasenhall Prim Sch
　IP17 . . . . 56 E8
Peasenhall Rd IP19 . . . . . . 41 C3
Peasey Gdns IP5. . . . . 141 C6
Peasey La IP5 . . . . 141 C6
PEATS CORNER. 69 B7
Pebble Cl NR32 . . . . 113 A3
Pebble View Wlk **8** NR31 . 3 C6
Peckham St IP33 . . . . 154 B3
Pecockes Cl **10** CO10. . . . . 92 B3
Peddars Cl **1** IP31. . . . . . . 34 B1
Peddars La NR34. . . . . 111 B4
Peddars Way NR32. . . . . . 113 B4
Peel St IP1. . . . . 155 B3
Peel Yd **2** IP5. . . . . 98 A8
Peewit Hill IP11. . . . . 152 D3
Peewit Rd IP2. . . . . 138 F5
Pegasus Mews **1** NR32 . 112 D1
Pegg's Hill IP20 . . . . 22 F2
Pelham Cl **21** CO12. . . . . . 106 F1
Pelican Cl IP2. . . . . 138 E3
Pemberton Rd **6** IP20 . . . . 22 D5
Pemberton Wlk IP33. . . . . 123 A2
Pembroke Ave IP12. . . . . . 146 E4
Pembroke Cl
　Ipswich IP2. . . . . 139 B3
　Mildenhall IP28 . . . . 116 C5
　Newmarket CB8. . . . . 121 B2
Pembroke Pl CO10. . . . . . 148 B8
Pembroke Rd
　Bury St Edmunds IP33. . . 122 D3
　Framlingham IP13. . . . . . 126 B4
Pembrooke Way **1**
　NR32. . . . . 113 A3
Pendleton Rd IP2. . . . . . . 138 D1
Penfold Rd IP11. . . . . 153 A4
Penn Cl IP9. . . . . 150 F4
Pennine Way NR32. . . . . . 112 E2
Pennings Nature Reserve
　The★ IP23 . . . . 117 E2
Pennycress Dr **4** IP24 . . . . 16 D7

Pennyfields NR35. . . . . . . 110 B2
Pennygate Dr NR33. . . . . . 114 E6
Penny La
　5 Ipswich IP3. . . . . 140 F1
　Lowestoft NR33. . . . . 113 A4
Penny Meadow **3** IP9 . . . . 150 E3
Pennyroyal Gdns IP2. . . . . 138 E4
Penryn Rd IP5. . . . . 141 A7
Penshurst Rd IP3 . . . . 140 D4
Pentland Wlk **9** NR32. . . . 113 A4
PENTLOW. 76 E1
Pentlow Dr CO10. . . . . 76 F1
Pentlow Hawke Cl NR33. . 133 A5
Pentlow Hill CO10. . . . . . . 91 A8
PENTLOW STREET. 91 A8
Penzance Rd IP5. . . . . 141 A6
Peppercorn Way **2** IP2 . . . 139 C3
Pepper La IP31. . . . . 49 E3
Pepper Pl IP5. . . . . 141 D6
Peppers Cl IP27 . . . . 5 E3
Pepper's Rd CO4. . . . . 102 F1
Peppers Wash IP13 . . . . . . 126 B6
Pepys Ave **1** NR34. . . . . . . 9 F4
Percy Ruse Cl CO10 . . . . . 148 F5
Peregrine Dr IP14 . . . . 124 F7
Peregrine Way **18** NR33 . . 11 C1
Periman Cl CB8. . . . . 121 A5
Periwinkle Cl **8** NR33. . . . 114 C5
Perkins Rd IP30 . . . . 49 B2
Perkins Way
　Ipswich IP5 . . . . 139 F1
　Tostock IP30 . . . . 50 B3
Perrydown La IP30. . . . . . . 64 C1
Perryfields CO10. . . . . 148 F2
Perry La CO4. . . . . 103 D2
Persimmon Wlk CB8. . . . . 120 E7
Pesthouse La IP6. . . . . 82 A6
Petch Cl IP33. . . . . 154 B3
Peter Dr **3** IP24 . . . . 16 D7
Peterhouse Cl
　Ipswich IP2. . . . . 138 E7
　Mildenhall IP28 . . . . 116 D4
Peterhouse Cres IP12. . . . 146 D4
Peterhouse Dr CB8. . . . . . 121 A2
Peter's Gr **4** IP9 . . . . 150 E3
Petingo Cl CB8 . . . . 120 D7
Petit Couronne Way
　NR34. . . . . 111 D3
Peto Way NR32. . . . . 113 A1
Pets Cnr★ NR33 . . . . 114 D7
PETTAUGH. 68 E6
Pettaugh La IP6. . . . . 68 E2
Petticoat La
　9 Barrow IP29 . . . . 47 A2
　Bury St Edmunds IP33. . . 154 A1
PETTISTREE. 127 B4
Pettits La IP21. . . . . 20 F3
Petunia Way IP27. . . . . . . 14 E8
Pheasant Cl **14** IP31. . . . . 49 D4
Pheasant Rd IP2. . . . . 138 E3
Pheasant Rise IP8 . . . . 95 F4
Pheasants Wlk NR35. . . . . 7 E4
Pheasant Way IP27 . . . . . . 6 A1
Philip Ave IP11. . . . . 152 E3
Philipps Cl CB8. . . . . 120 D4
Philip Rd
　Bury St Edmunds IP32. . . 122 F8
　Ipswich IP2. . . . . 155 B1
Phillipps Rd **3** IP6. . . . . . 82 B5
Phillips Cres IP6. . . . . 125 E4
Phillips Field Rd CO10. . . . 148 B3
Phoenix Day Hospl IP33 . . 154 A1
Phoenix Rd IP4. . . . . 140 A7
Phoenix Way IP14. . . . . . . 124 F7
Phoenix Yd CB9. . . . . 132 E3
Picketts Rd IP11. . . . . 153 C5
Pickwick Cres IP33 . . . . . 154 C3
Pickwick Dr **5** NR32. . . . . . 3 A4
Picton Ave **5** IP1. . . . . 135 D1
Pier Ave IP18. . . . . 119 D6
Pier Terr NR33. . . . . 115 D8
Pigeon La IP28 . . . . 48 B6
Pigeon's La IP8. . . . . 138 A3
Pightle Cl IP30 . . . . 50 E2
Pightle The
　Capel St Mary IP9 . . . . . . 150 F4
　Haverhill CB9. . . . . 132 E6
　4 Needham Market IP6. . 125 D5
　North Cove NR34. . . . . . . 10 B4
Pig La NR34 . . . . 111 B6
Pilgrims Way
　Bungay NR35. . . . . 110 C3
　6 Great Finborough IP14 . 66 B4
　1 Thorpeness IP16 . . . . . 73 F6
Pilgrim's Way **7** IP20. . . . . 22 D6
Pimpernel Rd IP2. . . . . . . 138 F3
Pinbush Cl IP33. . . . . 114 F2
Pinbush Rd NR33. . . . . . . 114 F2
Pine Ave IP1 . . . . 135 B1
Pine Bank IP5 . . . . 141 F6
Pine Cl
　1 Brantham CO11. . . . . . 104 C4
　Eye IP23 . . . . 117 D3
　4 Harleston IP20. . . . . . . 22 D5
　9 Lakenheath IP27 . . . . . 13 F2
　Rendlesham IP12 . . . . 85 D8
Pinecroft Rd IP1. . . . . 135 A2
Pinecroft Rise CO10. . . . . 148 B3
Pinecroft Way IP6. . . . . . . 125 E4
Pine Gr **14** IP13 . . . . 83 E5
Pine Leys IP32. . . . . 122 F8
Pines Ind Est The CB8. . . . . 44 F6
Pine Sq IP7. . . . . 80 C6
Pines The
　Claydon IP6. . . . . 134 C8
　Felixstowe IP11. . . . . 153 E6
Pinetree Cl IP5. . . . . 140 F7

Pine Tree Cl NR34 ..... 111 F4
Pine Tree Ct IP22 ..... 18 C2
Pinetrees NR31 ..... 2 B7
Pine Trees Ave IP28 ..... 116 E4
Pine View IP14 ..... 52 A6
Pineview Cl IP14 ..... 124 D5
Pine View Rd IP1 ..... 139 B8
Pineway Cl **1** IP29 ..... 63 A1
Pinewood IP12 ..... 146 E3
Pinewood Ave NR33 ..... 114 F6
Pinewood Dr IP27 ..... 14 F8
Pinewood Gdns NR34 ..... 10 B4
PINFORD END 63 D6
Pinhoe Dr **1** IP8 ..... 132 A6
Pinkney's La **19** IP18 ..... 119 D5
Pinkuah La CO10 ..... 90 F7
Pin Mill Cl IP8 ..... 138 C1
Pin Mill Cliff★ IP9 ..... 106 D8
Pinmill Rd IP9 ..... 106 C8
Pinners La IP13 ..... 146 B7
Pinners Way IP33 ..... 122 E4
Pintail Cl IP2 ..... 138 E3
Pintail Rd IP14 ..... 67 A5
Pinza Cl CB8 ..... 120 E8
Piperell Way CB9 ..... 132 E3
Pipers Cl CB9 ..... 133 A4
Pipers Meadow IP13 ..... 54 E7
Pipers Vale Cl IP3 ..... 139 E1
Pipers Vale Com Prim Sch
　Gainsborough IP3 ..... 139 F1
　Ipswich IP3 ..... 139 F1
Pipers Vale Nature Reserve★
　IP3 ..... 143 F7
Pipney Hill IP17 ..... 56 F4
Pippin Cl **2** IP32 ..... 123 E6
Pippin Post Cl CO10 ..... 76 C6
Pippins The
　Blundeston NR32 ..... 3 A4
　Glemsford CO10 ..... 77 B2
Pipp's La IP6 ..... 135 E6
Pirnhow St NR35 ..... 110 D5
Pitcairn Rd IP1 ..... 138 E8
PITCHER'S GREEN 64 D5
PITMAN'S CORNER 53 C5
Pitman's Gr IP19 ..... 42 A4
Pitmire La CO8 ..... 101 A7
Pit Rd NR34 ..... 10 B8
Pits The CB7 ..... 29 C4
Pitts End CO7 ..... 151 D5
Place Farm Com Prim Sch
　CB9 ..... 132 D6
Place for Plants The★
　CO7 ..... 151 F3
Plampin Cl CO10 ..... 92 D3
Plantation The IP15 ..... 130 D5
Plantation Way IP14 ..... 66 C1
Planters Gr **3** NR33 ..... 114 F7
Plash Rd IP23 ..... 53 F7
Plashwood Rd IP14 ..... 51 B1
Platers Wlk IP16 ..... 129 C5
Platten Cl IP6 ..... 125 C5
Platters Cl IP3 ..... 144 A7
Platters Rd IP11 ..... 152 E2
Playfield Rd IP9 ..... 150 F3
PLAYFORD 137 B5
Playford La IP5 ..... 136 E2
Playford Mount IP13 ..... 137 C6
Playford Rd
　Ipswich IP4 ..... 140 E8
　Playford IP5 ..... 137 B2
Pleasant Pl NR34 ..... 111 B3
Pleasant Row IP4 ..... 155 C2
Pleasurewood Cl **5**
　NR32 ..... 113 B5
Pleasurewood Hill NR32 ..... 113 A7
Pleasurewood Hills Leisure
　Pk★ NR32 ..... 113 C8
Plough Hill CO10 ..... 76 C7
Plough La
　Leavenheath CO6 ..... 102 B7
　Sudbury CO10 ..... 148 B5
Ploughman's Dro IP26 ..... 4 B5
Plough Rd
　Capel St Mary IP9 ..... 150 D3
　Woolpit IP30 ..... 50 D1
Plough St IP3 ..... 139 E4
Plover Cl
　4 Mildenhall IP28 ..... 13 B1
　11 Stowmarket IP14 ..... 67 A5
Plover Rd IP2 ..... 138 E2
Plovers Way
　Bury St Edmunds IP33 ..... 123 C1
　Hockwold cum Wilton IP26 ..... 4 F3
　Lowestoft NR33 ..... 114 D5
Plummer Cl **22** IP31 ..... 34 B1
Plummers Dell **10** IP6 ..... 82 A5
Plumpton Ave IP28 ..... 116 C5
Plum St CO10 ..... 77 A3
Plum Tree Rise **3** IP7 ..... 80 D6
Plumtrees **8** NR32 ..... 112 D2
Plymouth Rd
　Felixstowe IP11 ..... 152 F6
　4 Troston IP31 ..... 33 D5
Pole Hill (Tumulus)★
　IP10 ..... 141 F5
Police Sta Rd **5** NR32 ..... 113 D1
Pollard Piece NR33 ..... 114 C5
Pollards La IP28 ..... 29 F7
Polls La NR34 ..... 9 C2
POLSTEAD 93 F1
Polstead Cl IP14 ..... 124 F4
POLSTEAD HEATH 93 F2
Polstead Hill CO6 ..... 93 F1
Polstead St CO6 ..... 102 E7
Pond Cl IP11 ..... 152 D5
Pond End IP6 ..... 82 E6
Pond Gn CB7 ..... 28 A1
Pond Gr Cl IP32 ..... 123 E6

Pond Hall Rd IP7 ..... 149 F5
Pond Piece IP13 ..... 70 A7
Ponds End La IP22 ..... 35 A8
Poole Cl IP3 ..... 140 D3
Poole St CO10 ..... 76 E1
Pooley St IP22 ..... 19 C3
POOLEY STREET 19 D4
Popes Ct CB9 ..... 133 C3
Pope's Gn La IP7 ..... 94 B2
Poplar Cl
　1 Barrow IP29 ..... 47 A2
　4 Claydon IP6 ..... 134 C8
　Haverhill CB9 ..... 132 B7
　Mildenhall IP28 ..... 116 C6
Poplar Farm La IP31 ..... 49 E5
Poplar Farm Rd IP12 ..... 73 A2
Poplar Hill IP14 ..... 124 E4
Poplar La IP8 ..... 138 B3
Poplar Rd
　Lowestoft NR33 ..... 114 D3
　Sudbury CO10 ..... 148 F5
Poplars Cl **1** CB5 ..... 44 A5
Poplars CP Sch The
　NR32 ..... 113 D3
Poplars The
　Beck Row, Holywell Row &
　　Kenny Hill IP28 ..... 13 D1
　3 Brantham CO11 ..... 104 E5
　Spexhall IP19 ..... 24 F5
Poppy Cl
　Bury St Edmunds IP32 ..... 123 E5
　Ditchingham NR35 ..... 110 B7
　Ipswich IP2 ..... 138 F5
　Worlingham NR34 ..... 111 F3
Poppy Fields IP6 CB7 ..... 28 D5
Popson St NR35 ..... 110 A4
Portal Ave IP5 ..... 84 A1
Portal Cl
　4 Barnham IP24 ..... 16 C2
　7 Feltwell IP26 ..... 4 D5
Porter Rd **3** IP3 ..... 140 F1
Porthole Cl NR33 ..... 114 B4
Port La IP23 ..... 37 C3
Portland Ave **16** CO12 ..... 107 B2
Portland Cl **18** IP27 ..... 13 F2
Portland Cres **4** IP12 ..... 146 E4
Portland Gn CB8 ..... 120 E3
Portland Pl **3** IP24 ..... 16 A5
Portland Rd CB8 ..... 120 E3
Portlight Cl **3** CO11 ..... 105 A2
Portman Rd IP1 ..... 155 A2
Portman's Wlk IP1 ..... 139 A5
Port of Felixstowe Rd
　IP11 ..... 152 C3
Portsch Rd NR33 ..... 114 E3
Portsmouth Cl **19** IP27 ..... 13 F2
Portsmouth Rd **3** IP31 ..... 33 D5
POSLINGFORD 76 A3
Posters La IP31 ..... 35 A2
Posting House Pottery The★
　CO10 ..... 91 D8
Post Mill Cl IP4 ..... 139 F6
Post Mill Cres **12** IP13 ..... 83 E5
Post Mill Gdns **10** IP13 ..... 83 E5
Post Office La
　Glemsford CO10 ..... 77 A3
　Martlesham IP12 ..... 146 C1
Post Office Rd IP17 ..... 129 A3
POTASH 104 F8
Potash La
　Bentley IP9 ..... 104 F8
　Eye IP23 ..... 117 B5
　Polstead CO6 ..... 93 F4
　Wyverstone IP14 ..... 51 D7
Pot Kiln Chase CO9 ..... 90 F1
Pot Kiln Prim Sch CO10 ..... 148 E4
Pot Kiln Rd CO10 ..... 148 F4
Pot Kilns The CO10 ..... 92 B3
Potkins La IP13 ..... 131 B3
Potland La **15** CO10 ..... 78 D4
Potters Brook IP6 ..... 126 B3
Potters Dr NR31 ..... 3 B7
Potter's La
　Rickinghall Superior IP22 ..... 36 B5
　Stanton IP31 ..... 34 E4
Potter's St IP16 ..... 58 C4
Potters Vale IP22 ..... 35 E7
Pott Hall Rd IP28 ..... 30 A6
Pouch Mill IP11 ..... 152 B8
Poulter's La IP29 ..... 62 F6
Poultry Rd IP27 ..... 13 A7
Pound Cl
　8 Burwell CB5 ..... 44 A5
　Halesworth IP19 ..... 118 B3
　4 Harleston IP20 ..... 22 D6
　4 Walsham le Willows
　　IP31 ..... 35 C2
Pound Farm Dr
　8 Harwich CO12 ..... 107 A2
　Lowestoft NR32 ..... 112 F4
Pound Farm Parade **7**
　NR32 ..... 112 F4
Pound Fm Nature Reserve★
　IP17 ..... 56 C1
Pound Gn Rd IP13 ..... 56 C7
POUND GREEN 61 B5
Pound Hill
　Bacton IP14 ..... 51 F6
　Dallinghoo IP13 ..... 70 C1
Pound Hill Cl IP14 ..... 51 F6
Pound La
　Blundeston NR32 ..... 3 A4
　Bramford IP8 ..... 81 F3
　Capel St Mary IP9 ..... 150 D1
　Dallinghoo IP13 ..... 70 C1
　Ditchingham NR35 ..... 7 E6
　Hadleigh IP7 ..... 149 C6
　Isleham CB7 ..... 29 C5

Pound La continued
　Stowmarket IP14 ..... 124 D7
Pound Meadow **3** IP28 ..... 48 B6
Pound Pl NR34 ..... 111 B6
Pound Rd
　3 Beccles NR34 ..... 111 B6
　Creeting St Peter or West
　　Creeting IP6 ..... 67 B4
　Sotterley NR34 ..... 26 A7
Pound Wlk NR34 ..... 111 B6
Pouy St IP17 ..... 41 B1
Powling Rd IP3 ..... 140 A2
Powney St IP7 ..... 93 B8
POYSTREET GREEN 65 E5
Pratt's La IP9 ..... 144 A2
Pratt St CB7 ..... 28 D4
Prentice Rd IP14 ..... 124 E6
Prentices La IP13 ..... 146 B6
Prentice St **8** CO10 ..... 78 D4
Prescott Dr **11** IP30 ..... 50 F2
Presland Ct IP27 ..... 109 B7
Presmere Rd IP13 ..... 127 A4
Preston Dr IP1 ..... 134 F2
Preston Rd CO10 ..... 78 D4
PRESTON ST MARY 79 A5
Prestwick Ave **2** IP11 ..... 153 C6
Pretty Dr IP21 ..... 21 A2
Pretty Rd IP16 ..... 58 A4
Pretyman Ave IP14 ..... 51 F6
Pretyman Rd
　Felixstowe IP11 ..... 152 E1
　Ipswich IP3 ..... 140 B3
Prevetts Way IP15 ..... 130 E5
Prickwillow Rd CB7 ..... 12 A2
Priestly Cl IP14 ..... 124 B8
Priestly Rd IP6 ..... 125 D4
Prigg Wlk IP32 ..... 122 E7
Primack Rd IP32 ..... 49 A3
Primes La
　Blyford IP19 ..... 42 B8
　Holton IP19 ..... 118 F5
Primrose Alley IP18 ..... 119 D4
Primrose Cl NR33 ..... 114 F2
Primrose Hill
　Haverhill CB9 ..... 132 D5
　Ipswich IP2 ..... 138 F4
　Royal Hospital School IP9 ..... 105 E6
Primrose La
　Frostenden NR34 ..... 26 B4
　Ramsey & Parkeston CO11 ..... 106 A1
　10 Soham CB7 ..... 28 D5
Primrose Rise NR34 ..... 111 E3
Primrose Way IP6 ..... 125 D3
Prince Charles Ave **17**
　IP32 ..... 48 C5
Prince Charles Cl CO10 ..... 148 D6
Prince Cl CB8 ..... 120 B8
Princedale Cl IP1 ..... 135 A1
Princel La CO7 ..... 103 F4
Prince of Wales Cl IP33 ..... 122 C5
Prince of Wales Dr **9**
　IP2 ..... 139 A2
Princes Gdns IP11 ..... 152 F4
Princes' Gdns **5** IP8 ..... 81 C3
Princes Gn IP19 ..... 118 A2
Princes Rd
　Felixstowe IP11 ..... 152 F4
　13 Harwich CO12 ..... 107 A2
　Lowestoft NR32 ..... 113 C2
Prince's Rd NR35 ..... 110 B2
Princess Rd **2** IP18 ..... 119 C8
Princes St
　Bury St Edmunds IP33 ..... 154 A2
　Ipswich IP2 ..... 155 A1
Princess Way
　5 Earsham NR35 ..... 7 F4
　Haverhill CB9 ..... 132 B6
　Newmarket CB8 ..... 120 E4
Prince St CO10 ..... 148 C6
Princes Wlk NR32 ..... 113 A2
Princethorpe Rd IP3 ..... 140 C4
Prior's Ave IP33 ..... 122 E4
Priors Cl
　Lowestoft NR32 ..... 113 C5
　Rushbrooke with Rougham
　　IP30 ..... 64 D8
Priors' Hill Rd IP15 ..... 130 D3
Prior Stephen Way IP24 ..... 16 B5
Priors Way IP15 ..... 130 E4
Priory Cl
　7 Burwell CB5 ..... 44 A5
　Ingham IP31 ..... 32 F1
　Palgrave IP22 ..... 20 C1
　St Olaves NR31 ..... 2 A6
　Stradbroke IP21 ..... 39 B4
Priory Cres IP21 ..... 39 D8
Priory Gdns
　Isleham CB7 ..... 29 C5
　St Olaves NR31 ..... 2 A6
　Sudbury CO10 ..... 148 B4
PRIORY GREEN 92 F6
PRIORY HEATH 140 D1
Priory La
　Bungay NR35 ..... 110 B4
　Carlton Colville NR33 ..... 114 A2
　Darsham IP17 ..... 42 B1
　Debenham IP14 ..... 53 F2
Priory Pk IP10 ..... 144 C6
Priory Rd
　Beccles NR34 ..... 111 B4
　Blythburgh IP19 ..... 42 E6
　Felixstowe IP11 ..... 153 C5
　Fressingfield IP21 ..... 39 D7
　Fritton & St Olaves NR31 ..... 2 A6
　Palgrave IP22 ..... 20 C1
　Snape IP17 ..... 72 E5
　Sudbury CO10 ..... 148 B7

Priory Rd continued
　Wrentham NR34 ..... 26 E5
Priory Specl Sch IP32 ..... 123 C5
Priory Stadium CO10 ..... 148 C4
Priory Wlk CO10 ..... 148 C4
Prittlewell Cl IP2 ..... 138 F1
Private Rd
　Earsham NR35 ..... 7 D4
　Mutford NR34 ..... 10 B2
　4 Oulton Broad NR33 ..... 114 E7
Privet Gn NR33 ..... 115 A7
Progress Way IP23 ..... 117 B5
Promenade
　Harwich CO12 ..... 107 A1
　Southwold IP18 ..... 119 D4
Prospect Hill CO10 ..... 92 B2
Prospect Pl
　Leiston IP16 ..... 129 D6
　Lowestoft NR33 ..... 115 B3
Prospect Rd
　Ipswich IP1 ..... 139 A6
　Lowestoft NR32 ..... 112 C1
　Norton IP31 ..... 50 C4
Prospect Row IP33 ..... 154 B2
Prospect Terr CB9 ..... 133 F8
Providence La **5** IP1 ..... 139 A4
Providence Stree IP1 ..... 155 B3
Provost Rd IP26 ..... 4 D5
Prussia La IP33 ..... 154 C1
Puddingmoor NR34 ..... 111 A5
Puddleduck La NR34 ..... 111 F3
Pug St IP21 ..... 21 A6
PULHAM ST MARY 21 F8
Pump Cl IP13 ..... 84 C7
Pump Ct **9** CO10 ..... 78 D4
Pump House La IP17 ..... 57 A8
Pump La IP33 ..... 154 B2
Pump St
　Needham Market IP6 ..... 125 E4
　Orford IP12 ..... 131 C2
Punchard Way IP11 ..... 152 C8
Purcell Rd IP14 ..... 124 B8
Purdis Ave IP3 ..... 140 F2
Purdis Farm La
　Foxhall IP10 ..... 141 C2
　Ipswich IP3 ..... 140 F2
　Purdis Farm IP10 ..... 141 B2
Purdis Rd IP10 ..... 141 D2
Purplett St IP2 ..... 155 C1
Putney Cl IP27 ..... 14 E8
Putticks La CO7 ..... 151 E5
PUTTOCK END 90 E3
Pyes Meadow **1** IP30 ..... 50 F2
Pykenham Way IP7 ..... 149 D6
Pytches Cl **2** IP12 ..... 147 B6
Pytches Rd IP12 ..... 147 A6

Q

Quadling St IP1 ..... 155 B2
Quail Cl **9** IP14 ..... 67 A6
Quaker La
　Bardwell IP31 ..... 34 C4
　Beyton IP30 ..... 49 F1
Quaker's La **2** CB9 ..... 132 E5
Quakers' Rd IP28 ..... 116 F5
Quakers Way **3** IP16 ..... 129 D5
Quantock Cl IP5 ..... 140 F7
Quantrill Terr IP5 ..... 141 D6
Quarries Cross IP14 ..... 66 C8
Quaves La NR35 ..... 110 B4
Quay La
　Reydon IP18 ..... 26 D1
　Sudbury CO10 ..... 148 C4
Quay Side IP12 ..... 147 A4
Quayside Ct IP27 ..... 109 C7
Quay's Rd IP28 ..... 47 E5
Quay St
　Halesworth IP19 ..... 118 B4
　13 Manningtree CO11 ..... 104 E2
　Orford IP12 ..... 131 C2
　Woodbridge IP12 ..... 147 A4
Quay The IP12 ..... 107 B3
Quay Theatre The★
　CO10 ..... 148 C4
Quay View NR32 ..... 113 A1
Quebec Dr IP5 ..... 141 B8
Queech La IP9 ..... 105 A4
Queech The IP9 ..... 150 F4
Queen Edith Dr CB9 ..... 88 D3
Queen Elizabeth Cl IP16 ..... 129 C4
Queen Elizabeth Dr
　NR34 ..... 111 D3
Queens Ave **5** IP12 ..... 146 E4
Queensberry Rd
　1 Ipswich IP3 ..... 144 B8
　Newmarket CB8 ..... 121 A3
Queens Cl
　Combs IP14 ..... 124 A1
　Halesworth IP19 ..... 118 A2
　Saxmundham IP17 ..... 128 C3
　Sudbury CO10 ..... 148 C6
Queen's Cl IP33 ..... 122 E5
Queenscliffe Rd IP2 ..... 139 A3
Queens Ct CB9 ..... 132 C6
Queensdale Cl IP1 ..... 135 B1
Queensdale Rd IP1 ..... 135 B1
Queens Dr IP19 ..... 118 A2
Queen's Dr IP28 ..... 116 B4
Queensgate Dr IP4 ..... 139 F8
Queen's Head La IP21 ..... 21 A2
Queen's Head Rd CO4 ..... 102 F1
Queen's Highway NR32 ..... 112 C2
Queens La IP29 ..... 62 D5
Queensland IP9 ..... 106 F5
Queens Rd
　Brandon IP27 ..... 14 E8

Queens Rd continued
　1 Southwold IP18 ..... 119 C8
　Sudbury CO10 ..... 148 C6
Queen's Rd
　Beccles NR34 ..... 111 B6
　Bungay NR35 ..... 110 B2
　Bury St Edmunds IP33 ..... 154 A2
　Felixstowe IP11 ..... 153 A3
　4 Harwich CO12 ..... 107 A1
　Lowestoft NR32 ..... 113 D3
　Southwold IP18 ..... 119 D4
Queens Sq **7** CB9 ..... 132 E6
Queens St CB9 ..... 74 B2
Queen St
　Cowlinge CB8 ..... 61 B1
　Felixstowe IP11 ..... 152 E5
　6 Hadleigh IP7 ..... 149 D6
　Haverhill CB9 ..... 132 E6
　Ipswich IP1 ..... 155 B2
　Newmarket CB8 ..... 121 B3
　Southwold IP18 ..... 119 D5
　Stradbroke IP21 ..... 39 B5
Queens View CB8 ..... 120 A8
Queensway
　4 Acton CO10 ..... 92 B7
　1 Earsham NR35 ..... 7 F4
　Exning CB8 ..... 120 B8
　Haverhill CB9 ..... 132 C6
　3 Manningtree CO11 ..... 104 E2
　2 Mildenhall IP28 ..... 116 B4
　6 Soham CB7 ..... 28 D4
　Sudbury CO10 ..... 148 F3
　Thetford IP24 ..... 16 B5
Queen's Way IP21 ..... 140 B2
Queensway Com Jun Sch **7**
　IP24 ..... 16 B5
Queensway Inf Sch IP24 ..... 16 B5
Quendon Pl CB9 ..... 132 F6
Quentin Cl IP1 ..... 138 E8
Quilter Dr
　Ipswich IP8 ..... 138 C1
　Pinewood IP8 ..... 142 C8
Quilter Rd IP11 ..... 153 B4
Quince Cl CO11 ..... 104 E5
Quinnell Way **5** NR32 ..... 113 A6
Quinton Rd IP6 ..... 125 C4
Quintons Cnr CO7 ..... 151 D6
Quinton's La IP11 ..... 153 C5
Quintons Rd CO7 ..... 151 C5
Quoits Field **2** IP6 ..... 134 C8
Quoits Meadow IP14 ..... 68 B6

R

RACECOURSE 140 B2
Rackham Cl **1** NR31 ..... 3 B7
Radcliffe Dr IP2 ..... 138 D2
Radcliffe Rd IP27 ..... 14 A2
Radiator Rd CO10 ..... 148 E3
Radleys La CO6 ..... 102 B6
Radnor Cl IP32 ..... 123 E6
Raeburn Rd IP3 ..... 139 F1
Raeburn Rd S IP3 ..... 139 E1
Raedwald Dr IP14 ..... 123 D5
Raedwald Way IP14 ..... 53 F1
Raglan Rd **2** NR32 ..... 113 D1
Raglan St NR32 ..... 113 D1
Rag's La IP30 ..... 50 D1
Raile Wlk CO10 ..... 91 E8
Railway App IP11 ..... 153 A5
Railway Cl CB5 ..... 44 A5
Railway Hill IP20 ..... 22 C6
Railway St **19** CO11 ..... 104 E2
Railway Terr CB9 ..... 133 E7
Raine Ave CB9 ..... 132 B6
Rainey Ct **37** IP20 ..... 22 D6
Raingate St IP33 ..... 154 C1
Raleigh Cl CO10 ..... 148 E8
Raleigh Inf Sch **1** IP24 ..... 16 C7
Raleigh Rd CO10 ..... 148 E8
Ram La NR15 ..... 21 C8
Rampart Way IP24 ..... 16 C5
Rampling Cl IP7 ..... 149 D7
RAMSEY 106 C1
Ramsey Cl IP2 ..... 139 A1
Ramsey Rd
　Hadleigh IP7 ..... 149 F7
　Harwich CO12 ..... 106 D1
Ramsgate Dr IP3 ..... 140 B3
RAMSHOLT 99 A4
Randall Cl
　2 Hopton on Sea NR31 ..... 3 B7
　Ipswich IP5 ..... 141 E7
Randolph Cl IP4 ..... 140 B5
Rands Rd IP7 ..... 149 B1
Rands Way IP3 ..... 140 B2
Randwell Cl IP4 ..... 140 B5
Ranelagh Prim Sch IP2 ..... 138 F5
Ranelagh Rd
　Felixstowe IP11 ..... 153 A4
　Ipswich IP2 ..... 155 A1
Ransome Ave IP21 ..... 21 A2
Ransome Cl IP4 ..... 138 A6
Ransome Cres IP3 ..... 140 B2
Ransome Rd IP3 ..... 140 B2
Ransomes Europark
　IP10 ..... 144 F7
Ransomes Way IP3 ..... 140 D1
Ransom Rd IP12 ..... 146 E6
Ranson Rd IP6 ..... 125 C4
Rant Score NR32 ..... 113 E2
Ranville CB8 ..... 114 E3
Ranworth Ave NR33 ..... 114 E5
Raphael Wlk **10** NR32 ..... 113 B6

Rapier St **6** IP2 . . . . .139 C3
Rat Hill IP9 . . . . .106 C5
Rattla Cnr IP16 . . . . .58 C5
Rattlerow Hill IP21 . . . . .39 B6
Rattler's Rd IP27 . . . . .5 F1
RATTLESDEN 65 E6
Rattlesden CE Prim Sch
    IP30 . . . . .65 D6
Rattlesden Cl **2** IP14 . . . .124 D3
Rattlesden Rd IP30 . . . . . . .65 C6
Raven Cl
    Mildenhall IP28 . . . . . . .116 D3
    Stowmarket IP14 . . . . . .124 F7
Raveningham Rd NR34 . . . . .9 C8
Raven Rd IP33 . . . . .123 C1
Ravensfield Rd IP1 . . . . . .134 E1
Ravens La IP8 . . . . .134 A2
Ravensmere NR34 . . . . . . .111 B6
Ravensmere Cty Inf Sch
    NR34 . . . . .111 B7
Ravensmere E NR34 . . . . . .111 B6
Ravens Way **6** IP12 . . . . . .84 A1
Ravenswood Ave IP33 . . . . .144 B8
Ravenswood Com Prim Sch
    IP3 . . . . .144 C8
Raven Way IP7 . . . . .149 D4
Ravenwood Mews NR33 . . .115 A5
Ravine NR32 . . . . .94 F1
Rawlings Way **22** IP26 . . . . . .4 E5
Ray Ave CO12 . . . . .107 A2
RAYDON 94 E1
Raydon Croft IP14 . . . . . .124 F3
Raydon La IP12 . . . . .131 D3
Raydon Rd CO7 . . . . .150 A4
Raydon Way CO10 . . . . . . .92 B3
Rayes La CB8 . . . . .121 A4
Ray La **8** IP12 . . . . .106 F3
Rayleigh Rd IP1 . . . . .134 E1
Rayment Drift **5** IP5 . . . . .141 C7
Rayner's La NR35 . . . . .8 D8
Raynham Rd IP32 . . . . . . .154 A4
Raynsford Rd IP30 . . . . . . .63 F7
Reach Rd CB5 . . . . .44 A5
Reade Rd **5** IP9 . . . . .105 E7
Reading Gn IP21 . . . . .38 D4
READING GREEN 38 E5
Reading Rd IP4 . . . . .140 B7
Reading's La IP31 . . . . .35 A2
Rebow Rd **9** CO12 . . . . . .107 A1
Reckford Rd IP17 . . . . .58 B6
Recreation La IP11 . . . . . .152 F6
Recreation Rd
    Haverhill CB9 . . . . .132 D5
    Stowmarket IP14 . . . . . .124 C6
Recreation Way
    Ipswich IP3 . . . . .140 C2
    Mildenhall IP28 . . . . . . .116 C4
Recreation Wlk CO10 . . . . .148 F3
Rectory Cl
    Beccles NR34 . . . . .111 F4
    3 Glemsford CO10 . . . . .77 A3
    Ousden CB8 . . . . .61 E6
    Raydon IP7 . . . . .94 F1
Rectory Field **4** IP9 . . . . .106 C8
Rectory Gdns IP30 . . . . . . .49 F1
Rectory Gn IP19 . . . . .118 A4
Rectory Gr IP29 . . . . .63 B5
Rectory Hill
    Botesdale IP22 . . . . .35 F6
    East Bergholt CO7 . . . . .151 C3
    Polstead CO6 . . . . .102 E8
    Rickinghall Superior IP22 . .36 A5
Rectory La
    Beccles NR34 . . . . .9 F4
    Brantham CO11 . . . . . . .104 F5
    Hedenham NR35 . . . . . . .7 D8
    Hintlesham IP8 . . . . .95 C6
    Kettlebaston IP7 . . . . . . .79 B5
    Kirton IP10 . . . . .98 D2
    Mettingham NR35 . . . . .110 F3
    4 Ramsey & Parkeston
        CO12 . . . . .106 D1
    Scole IP21 . . . . .21 C5
    Stuston IP21 . . . . .37 D8
    Whatfield IP7 . . . . .80 C1
    3 Woolpit IP30 . . . . . . .50 D1
Rectory Meadow **5** IP28 . .48 B6
Rectory Pk **3** CO10 . . . . . .93 C3
Rectory Pl IP29 . . . . .47 A1
Rectory Rd
    Aldeby/Wheatacre/Burgh St
        Peter NR34 . . . . .10 A8
    Bacton IP14 . . . . .51 E5
    Blaxhall IP12 . . . . .71 F4
    Brome & Oakley IP23 . . .117 B7
    Broome NR35 . . . . .8 B7
    Burston & Shimpling IP22 . .20 E6
    Dickleburgh IP21 . . . . . . .21 B5
    Gillingham NR34 . . . . . . .9 B7
    Gissing IP22 . . . . .20 F8
    Great Waldingfield CO10 . . .92 D6
    Harkstead IP9 . . . . .106 B6
    Hemingstone IP6 . . . . . . .68 C1
    Hollesley IP12 . . . . .99 F7
    Ipswich IP2 . . . . .155 B1
    Kedington CB9 . . . . . . .133 F8
    Langham CO4 . . . . .103 C3
    7 Lowestoft NR33 . . . . .115 C6
    Mellis IP23 . . . . .36 F5
    Middleton CO10 . . . . . .148 C2
    Newton CO10 . . . . .92 D2
    Orford IP12 . . . . .131 C3
    Shelfanger IP22 . . . . .20 B6
    Sotterley NR34 . . . . .26 A7
    Tivetshall St Mary NR15 . . .21 C8
Rendham Rd
    Bruisyard IP17 . . . . .56 D4
    Kelsale cum Carlton IP17 . .128 A6

Rectory Rd *continued*
    Whepstead IP29 . . . . . . .63 B4
    Wortham IP22 . . . . .19 F1
    Wrabness CO11 . . . . . . .106 A2
    Wyverstone IP14 . . . . . . .51 D6
Rectory St IP19 . . . . .118 B4
Redan St IP1 . . . . .155 A4
Red Barn Dr **4** CO6 . . . . .102 A7
Redbarn La IP17 . . . . .72 D7
Red Barn Piece **11** IP13 . . .83 E5
Redcastle Furze Prim Sch **6**
    IP24 . . . . .16 B5
Reddells Cl CO10 . . . . . . .148 D5
Red Dock La CB8 . . . . .61 C1
REDE 62 E2
Rede La IP6 . . . . .134 F8
REDENHALL 22 E7
Redenhall Rd IP20 . . . . . . .22 D6
Rede Rd IP29 . . . . .62 F4
Rede Way CO10 . . . . .92 B3
Rede Wood Nature Reserve★
    IP6 . . . . .82 D5
Redgate IP24 . . . . .16 C6
Redgate La IP9 . . . . .143 D5
REDGRAVE 36 A8
Redgrave & Lopham Fen
    National Nature Reserve★
    IP22 . . . . .19 C2
Redgrave & Lopham Fen
    Visitor Ctr★ IP22 . . . . . . .19 C3
Redgrave Rd IP22 . . . . .19 B3
Red Hall Ct IP11 . . . . .153 C4
Red Hill IP7 . . . . .94 D7
Red Hill Rd IP7 . . . . .149 E8
Red House Cl
    3 Felixstowe IP11 . . . . .107 D8
    Lowestoft NR32 . . . . . . .112 F5
Redhouse Gdns **5** CB7 . . . .28 D3
Redhouse La
    Bawdsey IP12 . . . . .99 E3
    Boxted CO4 . . . . .102 E1
    9 Sudbury CO10 . . . . . .148 C5
Red House La
    Leiston IP16 . . . . .129 D4
    Sudbury CO10 . . . . .148 E2
Redhouse Rd IP13 . . . . . . .56 B8
Red House Way **5** IP15 . . .130 C6
Red House Wlk IP10 . . . . . .145 E4
REDISHAM 25 B7
Redisham Cl NR32 . . . . . . .113 A5
Redisham Rd
    Redisham NR34 . . . . .25 B6
    Weston NR34 . . . . .9 C1
Red La
    Capel St Mary IP9 . . . . . .150 E2
    Sternfield IP17 . . . . .72 D8
REDLINGFIELD 38 D2
Redlingfield Rd
    Horham IP21 . . . . .38 D2
    Occold IP23 . . . . .37 F2
Red Lion Ct IP21 . . . . .38 C7
RED LODGE 30 B1
Red Rose Cl IP12 . . . . .99 E4
Redshank Cl CB9 . . . . .133 A5
Red Sleeve IP9 . . . . .150 D3
Redwald Rd IP12 . . . . .85 E8
Redwing Cl IP2 . . . . .138 D3
Redwing Rd IP33 . . . . .123 C1
Redwings Horse Sanctuary
    (Caldecott)★ NR31 . . . . . .2 C8
Redwings Horse Sanctuary
    (Stonham)★ IP14 . . . . . . .68 C6
Redwold Cl IP12 . . . . .146 C1
Redwood Gdns IP33 . . . . . .154 C2
Redwood La **23** IP27 . . . . . .13 F2
Reedland Way **4** IP11 . . . .152 D5
Reed's Bldgs IP33 . . . . . . .154 C3
Reeds La CB9 . . . . .132 E6
Reeds Way IP14 . . . . .67 A7
Reet **1** NR32 . . . . .115 D8
Reeve Cl
    12 Bury St Edmunds IP32 . .48 C5
    Scole IP21 . . . . .21 A2
Reeve Gdns IP5 . . . . .141 C8
Reeve's Cl NR35 . . . . .110 C3
Reeves La IP26 . . . . .5 A3
Reeve St NR32 . . . . .113 D2
Refinery Rd CO12 . . . . . . .106 F3
Regal Dr CB7 . . . . .28 E3
Regal La CB7 . . . . .28 E3
Regal Theatre★ IP14 . . . . .124 E5
Regan Ct NR32 . . . . .113 A5
Regent Pl **3** CB7 . . . . . . .28 D3
Regent Rd NR32 . . . . .113 D1
Regents Ct **8** CB8 . . . . . .121 A4
Regent St
    20 Manningtree CO11 . . . .104 E2
    Stowmarket IP14 . . . . . .124 D7
Regent Theatre★ IP4 . . . . .155 C3
Regimental Mus★ IP33 . . .122 E6
Regimental Way
    18 Harwich CO12 . . . . . .106 E1
    18 Ramsey CO12 . . . . . .106 E1
Regina Cl IP4 . . . . .140 B5
Reigate Cl IP3 . . . . .140 B3
Rembrandt Cl **3** NR32 . . . .113 C6
Rembrandt Gdns **4**
    IP33 . . . . .122 F3
Rembrandt Way IP33 . . . . .123 A3
Rembrow Rd IP7 . . . . .150 E3
Rememberance Rd IP16 . . . .73 F6
Remercie Rd **7** CO11 . . . .105 A2
Rendall La IP14 . . . . .67 A8
RENDHAM 56 E3
Rendham Hill IP17 . . . . . . .56 F7
Rendham Rd

Rendham Rd *continued*
    Peasenhall IP17 . . . . .56 F7
RENDLESHAM 85 C8
Rendlesham Est★ IP12 . . . .85 D6
Rendlesham Forest Ctr★
    IP12 . . . . .85 F3
Rendlesham Rd
    15 Felixstowe IP11 . . . . .152 D5
    9 Ipswich IP1 . . . . .139 A7
Renfrew Rd IP4 . . . . .136 B1
Renoir Pl **2** NR32 . . . . . .113 B5
Renson Cl **6** IP30 . . . . . . .64 F8
REYDON 119 C7
Reydon Bsns Pk IP18 . . . . .119 D8
Reydon Cl **2** IP28 . . . . . .132 A6
Reydon La IP18 . . . . .26 D1
Reydon Mews IP18 . . . . . . .119 A6
Reydon Prim Sch IP18 . . . .119 C8
REYDON SMEAR 26 F1
Reydon Wood Nature
    Reserve★ IP34 . . . . .26 C2
Reynolds Ave **2** IP3 . . . . .144 A8
Reynolds Ct **10** IP11 . . . . .152 D5
Reynolds Rd IP3 . . . . .140 A1
Reynolds Way CO10 . . . . . .148 E8
Reynolds Wlk
    Bury St Edmunds IP33 . . .122 B6
    Gunton NR32 . . . . .113 B6
Ribblesdale NR33 . . . . .114 E3
Riby Rd IP11 . . . . .152 F3
Richard Burn Way CO10 . . .148 C8
Richard Crampton Rd
    NR34 . . . . .111 B3
Richard Easter Rd IP24 . . . . .16 C7
Richards Dr IP13 . . . . .137 D5
Richardson Rd CO7 . . . . . . .151 D5
Richardsons La IP9 . . . . . . .106 B8
Richard's Cl NR33 . . . . . . .114 C6
Richer Cl IP31 . . . . .50 E7
Richer Rd IP31 . . . . .50 F7
Richmond Cres **8** CO12 . . .107 A1
Richmond Pl **8** NR33 . . . .115 C6
Richmond Rd
    Brandon IP27 . . . . .14 E8
    Ipswich IP1 . . . . .138 F7
    Lowestoft NR33 . . . . . . .115 C6
RICKINGHALL 36 A6
Riddlesworth Hall Sch
    IP22 . . . . .17 F4
Rider Haggard La **7**
    NR33 . . . . .11 C1
Rider Haggard Way
    NR35 . . . . .110 C7
Ridgeville **9** NR33 . . . . . .114 F3
Ridgeway IP14 . . . . .124 B6
Ridgeways The NR33 . . . . .114 D5
Ridgeway The **10** CO12 . . .107 A2
RIDGEWELL 89 D4
Ridgewell Rd CO10 . . . . . . .89 D5
Ridings The
    3 Beccles NR34 . . . . . .111 F4
    Leavenheath CO6 . . . . . .102 B8
Ridley Rd IP33 . . . . .122 C6
Rigbourne Hill NR34 . . . . .111 C3
Rigbourne Hill La **6**
    NR34 . . . . .111 C2
Rigby Ave CO11 . . . . .105 A2
Riley Cl IP1 . . . . .134 C1
Rimmer Cl CO10 . . . . .148 E8
Ringham Rd IP4 . . . . .140 A6
RINGSFIELD 9 B3
Ringsfield CE VCP Sch
    NR34 . . . . .9 B2
RINGSFIELD CORNER 9 B2
Ringsfield Rd
    Beccles NR34 . . . . .111 A4
    6 Lowestoft NR32 . . . . .113 A3
    Ringsfield NR34 . . . . .9 A1
RINGSHALL 80 E7
Ringshall Prim Sch IP14 . . . .80 E6
RINGSHALL STOCKS 80 F6
Rio Cl **3** NR33 . . . . .114 C5
Risbridge Dr CB9 . . . . .133 E8
RISBY 47 D5
Risby Barn Antique & Craft
    Ctr★ IP28 . . . . .47 D5
Risby CE VC Prim Sch
    IP28 . . . . .47 D5
Risby Cl IP4 . . . . .140 B6
Risbygate St IP33 . . . . .154 B2
Riseway Cl IP33 . . . . .123 B1
RISHANGLES 53 D7
Rishton Rd **7** NR30 . . . . . .113 D1
Rising Sun Hill IP30 . . . . . .65 D5
Rissemere La E IP18 . . . . . .119 C8
Ritabrook Rd IP2 . . . . .138 E1
Rivendale **4** NR33 . . . . . .114 D3
Riverbank Cl CO10 . . . . .90 B8
River Gdns IP14 . . . . .124 E4
River Hill IP8 . . . . .138 C8
River La
    Fordham CB7 . . . . .29 A1
    Halesworth IP19 . . . . . . .118 B3
Riverside
    4 Framlingham IP13 . . . .126 C3
    Hasketon IP13 . . . . .146 A7
    Palgrave IP22 . . . . .20 B2
Riverside Ave E **6** CO11 . .104 E3
Riverside Ave W **4**
    CO11 . . . . .104 E3
Riverside Bsns Ctr NR33 . .115 C8
Riverside Cl IP28 . . . . .116 B4
Riverside Ct IP32 . . . . .123 A8
Riverside Ind Est IP13 . . . .127 C7
Riverside Ind Pk IP28 . . . .116 B4
Riverside Mid Sch IP28 . . .116 B4
Riverside Rd
    Ipswich IP1 . . . . .138 F7

Rendham Rd *continued*

Riverside Rd *continued*
    Lowestoft NR33 . . . . . . .115 B8
Riverside Theatre The★
    IP12 . . . . .147 A4
Riverside View IP13 . . . . . .127 C8
Riverside Way IP27 . . . . .5 F2
Rivers St IP4 . . . . .139 F7
Riverview IP12 . . . . .147 C7
River View NR34 . . . . .111 B7
River View Rd **1** IP9 . . . .106 A5
Riverwalk Sch IP33 . . . . . .154 A1
Rivish La CO10 . . . . .91 E8
Rixon Cres **3** IP12 . . . . . . .84 E6
Roamwood Gn La IP14 . . . . .53 E3
Robeck Rd IP3 . . . . .139 E1
Robert Boby Way IP33 . . . .154 B2
Robertsbridge Wlk **6**
    NR33 . . . . .114 D4
Robert's Hill CO8 . . . . .101 C2
Roberts Rd IP16 . . . . .129 D6
Robin Cl
    Haverhill CB9 . . . . .133 A5
    Mildenhall IP28 . . . . . . .116 D4
    15 Stowmarket IP14 . . . . .67 A5
    12 Thurstow IP31 . . . . . .49 D4
Robin Dr IP2 . . . . .138 D3
Robin Hill NR32 . . . . .113 A2
Robin Rd IP33 . . . . .123 C1
Robins Cl **16** CB7 . . . . . . .29 C5
Robinson Cl IP33 . . . . .122 D6
Robinson Rd **7** IP21 . . . . . .20 F1
Robinson Wlk IP32 . . . . . . .122 D7
Robin Way CO10 . . . . .148 A3
Robletts IP13 . . . . .84 D7
Robletts Way **1** CO6 . . . .101 F2
Rochdale **3** NR33 . . . . . .114 F3
Rochester Rd **1** NR33 . . . .115 B4
Rochester Way CO10 . . . . . .148 B8
Rochfort Ave CB8 . . . . .120 E5
Rock Rd NR32 . . . . .112 D1
Rockstone La IP19 . . . . .41 C7
Rodber Way NR32 . . . . .113 A6
RODBRIDGE CORNER 91 E6
Rodbridge Hill CO10 . . . . . .91 D6
Rodney Ct IP12 . . . . .146 F7
Roebuck Dr IP27 . . . . .109 E4
Roebuck The IP27 . . . . . . .109 E1
Rogeron Cl CO10 . . . . .75 D3
Rogers Cl IP11 . . . . .152 F6
Roger's Cl NR31 . . . . .3 B7
Roger's La CO10 . . . . .92 F4
Rogue's La IP13 . . . . .127 C5
Rokewood Pl IP29 . . . . .64 A3
Roman Cl **3** CB5 . . . . .44 A5
ROMAN HILL 113 C1
Roman Hill Prim Sch
    NR32 . . . . .113 C1
Roman Rd NR32 . . . . .113 C1
Roman Way
    Felixstowe IP11 . . . . . . .153 D6
    Halesworth IP19 . . . . . . .118 A3
    Haverhill CB9 . . . . .133 B4
    Long Melford CO10 . . . . .91 E7
Romany La IP33 . . . . .11 B3
Romany Rd NR32 . . . . .114 C8
Romany Way IP33 . . . . . . .123 D3
Romney Pl **6** NR32 . . . . .113 B6
Romney Rd IP3 . . . . .140 A1
Romsey Rd IP33 . . . . .122 D3
Ronald La IP17 . . . . .128 D5
Ronden Cl NR34 . . . . .111 B2
Rookery Chase CO7 . . . . . .103 F1
Rookery Cl NR33 . . . . .114 F7
Rookery Dro **2** IP28 . . . . . .13 B1
Rookery La IP19 . . . . .23 F4
Rookery Rd
    Elmsett IP7 . . . . .80 E2
    Monewden IP13 . . . . . . .69 F5
Rookery Sh Ctr CB8 . . . . . .121 A4
Rookery The
    Brandon IP27 . . . . .5 D1
    Eye IP23 . . . . .117 D2
    4 Manningtree CO11 . . . .104 E2
    Newmarket CB8 . . . . . . .121 B3
Rookery Way IP14 . . . . .51 F1
Rookery Wlk IP27 . . . . .109 B7
ROOKSEY GREEN 78 E6
Rook's La **7** NR34 . . . . . . .111 B5
Rookwood La CO10 . . . . .78 F6
Rookwood Way CB9 . . . . . .132 E4
Roosevelt Wlk **5** NR33 . . .114 C5
ROOST END 133 E2
Roper's Ct **3** CO10 . . . . . .78 D4
Ropers La CO10 . . . . .91 D7
Ropes Dr IP5 . . . . .141 B8
Rope Wlk
    Carlton Colville NR33 . . . .114 B4
    Ipswich IP4 . . . . .155 C2
Rosbrook Cl **1** IP33 . . . . .122 D4
Rose Acre CO7 . . . . .103 F7
Rose Ave IP22 . . . . .20 A3
Rosebay Gdns **1** CB7 . . . .28 D4
Rosebery Rd
    Felixstowe IP11 . . . . . . .153 B4
    Ipswich IP4 . . . . .139 F5
Rosebery Way CB8 . . . . . . .120 E5
Rosecroft Rd IP1 . . . . .135 A2
Rosecroft Way IP24 . . . . . . .16 D6
Rose Ct
    Lowestoft NR32 . . . . . . .113 B2
    Shotley IP9 . . . . .106 C6
Rosedale Gdns **9** NR33 . .114 E4
ROSEDALE PARK 114 E4
Rosefinch Cl CB9 . . . . .133 A5

Rose Gn CO10 . . . . .101 F8
Rose Gn La **4** IP28 . . . . . . .30 B8
ROSE GREEN
    Assington 101 F8
    Lindsey 93 D7
Rose Hall Gdns NR35 . . . . .110 B3
ROSE HILL 139 F4
Rose Hill
    Grundisburgh IP13 . . . . . .83 E5
    Withersfield CB9 . . . . . . .74 B3
    Witnesham IP6 . . . . .135 F7
Rosehill Cres IP3 . . . . .139 F4
Rose Hill Prim Sch IP3 . . . .140 A4
Rosehill Rd IP3 . . . . .139 F4
Rose La
    Botesdale IP22 . . . . .36 A7
    Bungay NR35 . . . . .110 B3
    Diss IP22 . . . . .20 D1
    Elmswell IP30 . . . . .50 E2
    Ipswich IP4 . . . . .155 B2
    Wickham Skeith IP23 . . . . .52 D8
Rose La Cl IP22 . . . . .20 C1
Rosemary Ave IP11 . . . . . .153 B5
Rosemary Cl **4** IP28 . . . . . .30 C1
Rosemary Gdns CO10 . . . . .148 D8
Rosemary La
    Ipswich IP4 . . . . .155 B2
    Kelsale cum Carlton IP17 . .128 C6
Rosemary Musker Cty High
    Sch IP24 . . . . .16 C7
Rosemary Rd **5** IP32 . . . . .48 C5
Rosery La IP13 . . . . .137 F6
Rose Wlk IP6 . . . . .125 D3
Rosewood NR33 . . . . .115 A5
Rosewood Cl **22** IP27 . . . . .13 F2
Ross Cl CB9 . . . . .133 B5
Ross Peers Sports Ctr The
    CB7 . . . . .28 D3
Ross Rd IP4 . . . . .136 B1
Rosyth Rd **5** IP31 . . . . . . .33 C5
ROTCHFORDS 101 F1
Rotheram Rd **9** IP7 . . . . . .79 F4
Rotten Row CO10 . . . . .92 D2
Rotterdam Rd NR32 . . . . . .113 B1
ROUGHAM 64 D8
Rougham CE Prim Sch
    IP30 . . . . .49 D1
Rougham Control Twr
    Musuem★ IP30 . . . . .49 B3
ROUGHAM GREEN 64 C8
Rougham Hill IP33 . . . . . . .123 B3
Rougham Ind Est IP30 . . . . .49 B2
Rougham Rd
    Bradfield St George IP30 . . .64 D7
    Bury St Edmunds IP33 . . .123 C3
Roughlands IP27 . . . . .109 D6
Roundingham Rd IP9 . . . . .150 F4
Roundwood Rd IP4 . . . . . . .140 A7
Rousies Cl IP7 . . . . .149 E6
Rous Meml Ct CB8 . . . . . . .121 B3
Rous Rd CB8 . . . . .121 B3
Routh Ave **4** IP3 . . . . . . .140 F1
Rowan Cl
    Haverhill CB9 . . . . .132 C7
    Priory Heath IP3 . . . . . . .140 D2
Rowan Dr
    Brandon IP27 . . . . .14 F8
    Bury St Edmunds IP32 . . .123 F6
Rowan Gn **7** IP30 . . . . . . .50 F2
Rowanhayes Cl IP2 . . . . . . .139 B3
Rowans Way **1** CO6 . . . . .102 A7
Rowan Way
    Beccles NR34 . . . . .111 E3
    Lowestoft NR33 . . . . . . .114 D6
    5 Thurstow IP31 . . . . . . .49 D4
Rowan Wlk IP28 . . . . .116 C5
Rowarth Ave IP5 . . . . .141 C7
Rowell Cl CB9 . . . . .132 E8
Rowell's La IP14 . . . . .51 D4
Rowe's Hill IP13 . . . . .40 C2
Rowley Cl **7** CO11 . . . . . .104 E4
Rowley Ct
    Newmarket CB8 . . . . . . .120 E3
    Sturmer CB8 . . . . .133 C3
Rowley Dr CB8 . . . . .120 F3
Rowley Hill CB9 . . . . .133 B3
Rowntree Cl **6** NR32 . . . . .113 A6
Rows The CB8 . . . . .120 E3
Row The
    Bramford IP8 . . . . .134 A2
    Gipsy Row CO7 . . . . . . .150 A4
    Stratford St Mary CO7 . . .103 E5
Roxburgh Rd IP4 . . . . .136 B1
Royal Ave NR32 . . . . .113 D3
Royal Hospl Sch IP9 . . . . . .105 E6
Royal Naval Patrol Service
    Mus★ NR32 . . . . .113 D4
Royal Pal Cl CB8 . . . . .120 D7
Royal Plain NR33 . . . . .115 D8
Royal Terr NR33 . . . . .115 D7
Roy Ave IP4 . . . . .140 B5
Roy Cl IP5 . . . . .141 B7
ROYDON 20 A3
Roydon Fen IP22 . . . . .20 B2
Roydon Prim Sch IP22 . . . . .20 B3
Roydon Rd IP22 . . . . .20 C3
Roydon Way **10** NR32 . . . .112 F4
Roylands La CO10 . . . . .93 D3
Royston Dr IP2 . . . . .138 D2
Rozlyne Cl **8** NR33 . . . . . .114 E4
Rubens Ct IP3 . . . . .140 A1
Rubens Wlk
    Gunton NR32 . . . . .113 B6
    Sudbury CO10 . . . . .148 E8
Ruby Cl **9** NR32 . . . . .3 D4
Rudlands IP8 . . . . .138 C1
Rudlands Cl **6** CB7 . . . . . .29 C5
Rue's La IP11 . . . . .153 C8

Ruffles Rd CB9. . . . . .133 A5
Rugby Rd CO10 . . . . .148 F2
RUMBURGH 24 B4
Rumburgh La NR35 . . .24 D6
Rumburgh Rd
  Lowestoft NR32. . . . . . . .113 B5
  Rumburgh IP19 . . . . .24 B3
Runce's La NR33. . . . . . .114 C3
Run Meadow NR33. . . . .114 C6
Runnacles Way IP11 . . .152 D5
Runnymede Gn IP33 . . .123 A3
Run The NR34 . . . . .26 A7
RUSHALL 21 F5
Rushall Rd IP20. . . . . .22 B6
RUSHBROOKE 64 B8
Rushbrooke La IP33 . . .123 D3
Rushbury Cl IP4 . . . . .140 B8
Rush Cl IP4. . . . . .140 E4
RUSHFORD 17 B4
Rushford Rd
  Coney Weston IP31 . . . . . .17 E1
  Euston IP24 . . . . .16 E2
Rushlake Way [7] NR33 . .114 D4
Rushmeadow Way [1]
  IP11 . . . . .153 D7
RUSHMERE 10 D1
Rushmere Hall Prim Sch
  IP4 . . . . .136 A1
Rushmere Pl CB9 . . . . . .132 F6
Rushmere Rd
  Gisleham NR33 . . . . .114 B1
  Ipswich IP4. . . . . .140 A7
  Rushmere NR33. . . . . .10 F3
RUSHMERE ST
  ANDREW 136 E1
Rushmere St IP5 . . . . . . .136 E1
RUSHMERE STREET. . . .136 E2
Rushton Dr NR33 . . . . . .114 B3
Ruskin Cl [3] IP14 . . . . . .124 E8
Ruskin Rd IP4 . . . . .139 F5
Russell Baron Rd IP31 . .48 D5
Russell Cl IP12 . . . . .146 E6
Russell Rd
  Felixstowe IP11. . . . . . . .152 F2
  Ipswich IP1. . . . . .155 A2
Russell's Gn NR34. . . . . . . .9 C2
RUSSEL'S GREEN 39 C3
Russet Cl
  [4] Beccles NR34. . . . . . .111 C3
  Great Barton IP32. . . . . . .123 E7
Russett Cl CB9. . . . . .132 C5
Rutland Ct [15] CB9. . . . . .132 C5
Rutland Sq IP33 . . . . . . .154 C1
Rydal Ave IP11 . . . . .153 D7
Rydal Cl IP14 . . . . .124 B6
Rydal Wlk IP3 . . . . .140 C2
Ryders Way [2] IP22 . . . . .36 A6
Ryeburn Cl [1] NR33 . . . . .11 B1
Rye Cl
  Ipswich IP3 . . . . .140 D4
  [3] Lowestoft NR33 . . . . .114 D4
Rye Ct [8] CB9. . . . . .132 C5
Ryedale [1] NR33 . . . . . . .114 F3
Ryefields [9] IP31 . . . . . . .49 E4
Ryes La CO10 . . . . .91 D1
Ryes Sch The
  Bulmer Tye CO10. . . . . . . .91 E1
  Kesgrave IP5. . . . . .137 E1
Rylands IP9 . . . . .150 E4
Rylands Cl [1] IP31. . . . . . .49 E4

S

SACKERS GREEN 92 D2
Sackville St CB8 . . . . . . .121 B4
Sackvylle St IP11 . . . . . . .53 E1
Saddlemakers La IP12 . .147 C8
Saddlers Meadow [2] IP13 83 E5
Saddlers Pl [19] IP5 . . . . . .98 A8
Saddlers Yd [17] IP31. . . . .34 E1
Saffrons Cl IP30 . . . . .50 D1
Saffron Sq NR33 . . . . . . .115 A2
Sagehayes Cl IP2 . . . . . .139 B3
Sages End Rd CB9. . . . . . .88 A4
St Agnes Way IP5. . . . . . .140 F6
St Albans CB8 . . . . .121 A4
St Alban's Cath High Sch
  IP4 . . . . .140 D7
St Andrew [2] CB8. . . . . .121 A4
St Andrew Cl [1] NR31 . . . .3 C7
St Andrews CE VA Prim Sch
  IP22 . . . . .19 A5
St Andrew's Church Cl
  IP5. . . . . .136 D1
St Andrews Cl
  [2] Barningham IP31 . . . . .34 E7
  [2] Great Finborough IP14 . .66 B4
  Ipswich IP4. . . . . .140 D1
  [3] Isleham CB7. . . . . .29 C5
St Andrew's Cl IP12. . . . .147 D7
St Andrew's Ct [4] IP33 . .154 B1
St Andrews Dr [7] IP8 . . . .48 C6
St Andrew's Dr [3] IP9. . .106 C8
St Andrews Mead IP14 . . .68 B8
St Andrew's Pl IP12. . . . .147 D8
St Andrews Rd
  Scole IP21 . . . . .21 A1
  Sudbury CO10 . . . . .148 E4
St Andrew's Rd
  Beccles NR34. . . . . .111 C2
  Coldfair Green IP17. . . . . .129 B2
  Felixstowe IP11. . . . . . . .153 A5
St Andrew's St N IP33 . .154 B3
St Andrew's St S IP33 . .154 B2
St Andrew's St IP28. . . . .116 C4
St Annes Cl IP12. . . . . . .146 D3
St Anne's Cl NR34. . . . . .111 C4

St Anne's Dr IP28. . . . . .116 B4
St Anne's Rd NR34 . . . . .111 C4
St Anthony [3] CB8. . . . . .121 A4
St Anthonys Cres IP4 . . .139 F6
St Aubyns Rd IP4 . . . . . .140 A5
St Aubyn's Rd [6] NR33 . .115 C6
St Audrys Pk Rd [5] IP12. .84 E6
St Audrys Rd IP12. . . . . . .84 E6
St Augustine Rd IP3 . . . .140 D4
St Augustine's Gdns IP3. .140 C3
St Austell Cl IP5 . . . . . . .141 A6
St Austin's La [1] CO12 . . .107 C3
St Barbara's Ct [18] CO10 .148 C5
St Bartholomews La
  CO10 . . . . .148 B7
St Benedicts Cath Sch
  IP32. . . . . .122 F8
St Benedicts Rd IP27. . . . . .6 A1
St Benedict's Rd NR34 . .111 B6
St Benet's Dr NR34. . . . . .111 C3
St Benet's RC Minst
  NR34 . . . . .111 A4
St Benets RC Prim Sch
  NR34. . . . . .111 A5
St Botolphs CE VC Prim Sch
  IP22 . . . . .36 B7
St Botolph's La IP33 . . . .154 C1
St Botolphs Pl [18] CB9 . .132 D5
St Botolph's Way CB9 . . .132 D6
St Catherines Cl IP28 . . .116 D6
St Catherine's Cl NR33 . .114 C4
St Catherine's Ct IP2. . . .138 E1
St Catherine's Rd [11] CO10 91 E8
St Clare Ct [15] NR31 . . . . . .3 B7
St Clement Mews [13] NR31. .3 B7
St Clements Church La
  IP4. . . . . .155 C2
St Clement's Hospl IP3 . .140 C4
St Cross Rd IP20. . . . . . . .23 B8
ST CROSS SOUTH
  ELMHAM 23 D7
St David [4] CB8. . . . . . . .121 A4
St David's Cl [5] NR34 . . .111 C2
St David's Rd [7] IP3 . . . .140 B3
St Denis Ct [11] CO12 . . . .107 A1
St Denys [5] CB8 . . . . . . .121 A4
St Domonic's Dr IP27 . . . . .6 A1
St Edmund Cl [6] IP31 . . . .34 B1
St Edmund Rd IP27 . . . . . . .5 E4
St Edmundsbury Cath★
  IP33 . . . . .154 C2
St Edmundsbury CE VA Prim
  Sch IP33 . . . . .154 A3
St Edmundsbury Mews
  IP33. . . . . .154 B1
St Edmundsbury Ret Pk
  IP32 . . . . .123 E4
St Edmunds Cl
  [2] Beccles NR34. . . . . . .111 C2
  [12] Harwich CO12 . . . . . .107 A1
  Stowmarket IP14. . . . . . . .124 C8
  [3] Woodbridge IP12. . . . .146 E4
St Edmund's Cl [1] IP12 . . .85 A5
St Edmunds Cres [1] NR33 .11 C1
St Edmund's Dr IP30. . . . .50 F3
St Edmunds Gate [1] IP31. .33 D5
St Edmunds La CO8 . . . . .101 D5
St Edmunds Pl IP33 . . . .154 B3
St Edmund's Pl IP11 . . . .139 C8
St Edmunds Prim Sch
  IP21 . . . . .38 C6
St Edmunds RC Prim Sch
  NR35. . . . . .110 B4
St Edmunds RC VA Prim Sch
  IP33 . . . . .154 B1
St Edmunds Rd IP14 . . . .124 C7
St Edmund's Rd
  Felixstowe IP11. . . . . . . .152 E2
  Ipswich IP3. . . . . .139 B8
  Southwold IP18. . . . . . . .119 D6
St Edmunds Sq [10] IP31. . .33 D5
St Etienne IP14 . . . . .69 B6
St Fabians Cl CB8 . . . . . .120 F5
St Fabians Cl Sch CB8. . .120 E5
St Felix CE VE Mid Sch
  CB8. . . . . .120 F6
St Felix Cl [2] CB7 . . . . . . .28 D5
St Felix RC Prim Sch
  CB9. . . . . .132 B5
St Felix Sch IP18 . . . . . . .119 A6
St George [1] CB8 . . . . . . .121 A4
St George's Ave [2] CO12 107 B1
St George's La IP18 . . . . .119 A6
St George's Rd
  Beccles NR34. . . . . .111 B4
  Felixstowe IP11. . . . . . . .153 C6
  Lowestoft NR33. . . . . . . .115 B4
  Stowlangtoft IP31. . . . . . . .50 B7
St Georges Sq IP18 . . . . .119 A7
St George's Sq IP1 . . . . .155 B3
St Gotthards Ave IP12. . . .98 B8
St Gregory Ct CO10 . . . . .148 B6
St Gregorys CE VC Prim Sch
  CO10. . . . . .148 B5
St Gregorys Cl [1] IP12 . . . .85 E8
St Helena Wlk IP28 . . . . .116 C6
St Helens Prim Sch IP4 . .139 E6
St Helen's St IP4 . . . . . . .155 C3
St Helens Way IP24 . . . . .16 B7
St Isidores IP5. . . . . .141 E7
St Ives Cl IP5. . . . . .141 A6
St James [6] CB8. . . . . . . .121 A4
St James Ct [3] CB8 . . . . .132 C6
St James' Gn [7] IP18. . . .119 D5
St James La IP33 . . . . . . .154 A2
St James' La
  Chediston IP19 . . . . .24 A3

St James' La continued
  St James, South Elmham
  IP19 . . . . .23 F4
St James Mid Sch IP33 .123 C5
St James Rd
  All Saints & St Nicholas, South
  Elmham IP19 . . . . .24 A5
  St James, South Elmham
  IP19 . . . . .23 F4
ST JAMES SOUTH
  ELMHAM 23 F4
St James's St IP17 . . . . . .43 B1
St Johns Ave CB8 . . . . . .121 A1
St Johns CE Prim Sch
  IP4. . . . . .140 A7
St John's Cl IP28 . . . . . . .116 D6
St Johns Ct IP11 . . . . . . .153 A4
St John's Hill
  Bungay NR35. . . . . .110 C2
  [4] Woodbridge IP12. . . . .147 A5
St Johns Meadow IP20. . . .23 C3
St John's Pl IP33 . . . . . . .154 B3
St John's Rd
  Bungay NR35. . . . . .110 B3
  Ipswich IP4. . . . . .140 A6
  Lowestoft NR33. . . . . . . .115 D7
  Saxmundham IP17. . . . . . .128 C3
St John's Terr [5] IP12. . . .147 A5
St John's Way
  [13] Feltwell IP26 . . . . .4 E5
  Thetford IP24 . . . . .16 A5
St Josephs Coll IP2. . . . .139 A3
St Josephs RC Prim Sch
  CO10. . . . . .148 B6
St Lawrence Cl NR34. . . .111 C2
St Lawrence Gn IP5. . . . .141 A7
St Lawrence Prim Sch
  NR34 . . . . .24 F6
St Lawrence St IP1 . . . . .155 B3
St Lawrence Way IP5 . . .141 B8
St Leonards Cl IP21. . . . . .21 A1
St Leonards Rd IP5. . . . . .148 D5
St Leonards Rd [2] IP3. . .140 B3
St Leonard's Rd [1] NR33 115 C7
St Leonards St IP26. . . . . .6 B8
St Louis Cath Mid Sch
  IP33 . . . . .154 B1
St Louis RC Prim Sch
  CB8. . . . . .121 A4
St Margarets CE VA Prim Sch
  IP4 . . . . .155 C3
St Margarets Com Prim Sch
  NR32. . . . . .113 C3
St Margaret's Cres
  Leiston IP16 . . . . .129 B6
  [3] Thetford IP24 . . . . .16 B5
St Margaret's Gn IP4. . . .155 C3
ST MARGARET SOUTH
  ELMHAM 23 E6
St Margaret's Pl CB8 . . . .75 E7
St Margarets Plain IP4. . .155 B3
St Margaret's Rd
  Bungay NR35. . . . . .110 B1
  [3] Lowestoft NR32. . . . . .113 E3
St Margaret's St IP4 . . . .155 B3
St Margaret's Way [3] NR31 3 B7
St Marks RC Prim Sch
  IP2 . . . . .138 F3
St Martin's Cl CB8 . . . . . .120 C7
St Martins Ct IP5 . . . . . . .141 E7
St Martins Gn [14] IP11. . .107 D8
St Martin's La IP24 . . . . . .16 B2
St Martin's Pl IP33 . . . . .154 B3
St Martin's Rd NR34 . . . .16 B5
St Mary's Ave [5] IP14. . . .51 C1
St Marys Cath Prim Sch
  IP4 . . . . .139 F6
St Marys CE Aided Prim Sch
  IP12 . . . . .146 E5
St Marys CE VA Prim Sch
  IP28 . . . . .116 C5
St Marys Cl [1] IP23 . . . . .36 D2
St Mary's Cl
  Bacton IP14. . . . . .51 F6
  Bramford IP8. . . . . .134 B1
  Felixstowe IP11. . . . . . . .152 B7
  Flixton NR35. . . . . .7 E1
  Harleston IP20 . . . . .22 E6
  Horham IP21. . . . . .38 F3
  Mildenhall IP28 . . . . .116 C3
  Sudbury CO10 . . . . .148 F8
St Mary's Cres
  Badwell Ash IP31 . . . . .50 E7
  Felixstowe IP11. . . . . . . .152 F6
St Mary's Gdns IP6 . . . . .125 E6
St Marys Pk IP10 . . . . . . .98 A4
St Marys Prim Sch IP7. . .149 E6
St Marys RC Prim Sch
  NR33. . . . . .115 C5
St Mary's Rd IP4 . . . . . . .139 F6
St Mary's Rd
  Aldeby NR34. . . . . .10 A7
  Beccles NR34. . . . . .111 A5
  Creeting St Mary IP6. . . . .125 E5
  Stowmarket IP14. . . . . . . .124 B7
St Marys Sq [9] CB8 . . . . .121 A4
St Mary's Sq IP33 . . . . . .154 C1
St Mary's St [2] NR35. . . .110 B4
St Marys View IP31 . . . . .49 E6
St Marys Way IP6. . . . . . .135 C4
St Mary's Wlk [2] CB9. . . .88 D3
St Mathew's St Service Rd
  IP1. . . . . .155 A3

St Matthew's Ave [3]
  NR34 . . . . .111 C2
St Matthew's CE VA Prim Sch
  IP1 . . . . .155 A3
St Matthew's St IP1 . . . .155 A3
St Michaels CE VA Prim Sch
  NR34. . . . . .9 B6
St Michaels Cl IP6 . . . . . .126 C4
St Michael's Cl
  [1] Beccles NR34. . . . . . .111 C2
  Ipswich IP5. . . . . .141 A6
  Lowestoft NR33. . . . . . . .112 C1
St Michaels Ct [16] CO11. .104 E2
ST MICHAEL SOUTH
  ELMHAM 24 A6
St Michael's Rd [4] CO12. .107 B1
St Michael's Way IP19 . . .42 C6
St Nicholas Cl
  Bury St Edmunds IP32. . . .123 C6
  Rattlesden IP30. . . . . .65 D5
St Nicholas Ct [1] NR34. . .111 C2
St Nicholas Dr [23] IP26. . . .4 E5
ST NICHOLAS SOUTH
  ELMHAM 23 E6
St Nicholas St IP1 . . . . . .155 B2
ST OLAVES 2 A6
St Olaves Prec IP32. . . . .122 D8
St Olaves Precinct IP32 . .122 E8
St Olaves Rd
  Bury St Edmunds IP32. . . .122 E8
  Herring Fleet NR32. . . . . . . .2 D4
  Ipswich IP5. . . . . .141 C8
St Osyth Cl IP2 . . . . .142 F8
St Pancras Cath Prim Sch
  IP1 . . . . .134 F2
St Patrick [7] CB8 . . . . . . .121 A4
St Pauls Cl IP15 . . . . . . .130 E5
St Paul's Cl
  [4] Beccles NR34. . . . . . .111 C2
  Brockdish IP21 . . . . .22 D3
St Peter & Paul CE VA Prim
  Sch IP23 . . . . .117 D2
St Peters Ave CB8. . . . . . .45 F2
St Peter's Ave [1] IP6. . . .134 C8
St Peter's Brewery & Visitor
  Ctr★ NR35. . . . . .24 A8
St Peters Cl
  Charsfield IP13 . . . . .70 B3
  [6] Moulton CB8. . . . . .45 F3
St Peter's Cl
  Brockdish IP21 . . . . .21 F2
  [8] Claydon IP6. . . . . .82 A5
  Stowmarket IP14. . . . . . . .124 B6
St Peters Ct IP33 . . . . . . .154 B1
St Peter's Ct [16] CO10. . .148 C5
St Peter's Hall★ NR35. . . .24 A8
ST PETER SOUTH
  ELMHAM 24 A7
St Peters Path IP19 . . . . .118 E4
St Peters Pl CB7 . . . . .29 B1
St Peters Rd
  Aldeburgh IP15 . . . . .130 E5
  Lowestoft NR33. . . . . . . .114 C3
St Peter's Rd
  Lowestoft NR33. . . . . . . .115 C6
  Stowmarket IP14. . . . . . . .124 B6
St Peter's St
  Ipswich IP4. . . . . .155 B2
  [4] Lowestoft NR32. . . . . .113 D2
St Peters Way [11] IP31. . . .49 E4
St Peter's Wlk IP26 . . . . . .4 F3
St Philips Rd CB8 . . . . . .120 F5
St Quinton's Ct NR33 . . . .115 B3
St Stephens Cl IP33 . . . . .123 C6
St Stephens La IP1. . . . . .155 B2
St Vincent Wlk [14] NR31 . . .3 B7
St Wendred's Way CB8 . .120 B7
Salehurst Rd IP3. . . . . . . .140 E3
Salisbury Ct [12] CB9 . . . .132 C5
Salisbury Gn IP3 . . . . . . .123 B3
Salisbury Rd
  Ipswich IP4. . . . . .140 A3
  Lowestoft NR33. . . . . . . .115 C7
  [1] Southwold IP18. . . . . .119 D5
Salisbury Terr [1] CO10 . .148 C6
Sallows Cl IP1. . . . . .138 F7
Sally Wood's La IP6. . . . .125 C4
Salmet Cl IP2. . . . . .139 A3
Salmond Dr [5] IP24. . . . . .16 C2
Salmon Wlk IP32 . . . . . . .122 D7
Salter Cl IP32. . . . . .123 E4
Salters Gdns IP13 . . . . . . .83 E5
Salters Hall Mews CO10 .148 B5
Saltgate [5] NR34. . . . . . .111 B6
Salthouse La IP4 . . . . . . .155 C2
Saltwater Way NR33 . . . .114 E8
Samford Cl IP9 . . . . .105 E8
Samford Ct [5] NR34. . . . .111 F4
Samford Pl IP8 . . . . .138 B6
Sampson Dr [5] CO10. . . . .91 E8
Samson Cl [14] IP32. . . . . .48 C5
Samson's La IP22 . . . . . . .19 F4
Samuel Cl IP4. . . . . .155 C3
Samuel St Wlk IP33 . . . . .154 C2
Samuel Vince Rd [2] IP21. 39 C1
Samuel Ward Arts & Tech
  Coll CB9. . . . . .132 F2
Sancroft Way
  [5] Fressingfield IP21 . . . . .39 D8
  Wortwell IP20 . . . . .23 A7
Sancroft Wlk IP33 . . . . . .122 B6
Sanctuary Gdns [4] NR32. 112 F5
Sanctuary The IP16 . . . . . .73 F6
Sanctuary Way [9] NR33 . . .11 B1
Sand Acre Cl IP28 . . . . . .116 D5
Sandbank Rd [1] NR33. . .114 C4
Sandbanks Ct IP17. . . . . .128 C3

Sanderling Cl [3] IP28 . . .116 D4
Sanders Cl [2] NR32 . . . . .112 F4
Sandford Rd IP14. . . . . . . .52 A1
Sandgalls Rd IP27 . . . . . .109 D6
Sand Hill CO10. . . . . .93 C3
Sandholme Cl IP33 . . . . .123 B2
Sandhurst Ave IP4 . . . . . .139 F4
Sandling Cres IP4 . . . . . .140 E5
Sandlings Prim Sch IP12 . .85 C3
Sandlings The
  Aldeburgh IP15 . . . . .130 C6
  Ipswich IP3. . . . . .140 D1
Sandown Cl [3] IP1. . . . . .135 A3
Sandown Rd IP1. . . . . . . .135 A3
Sandpath [5] IP21 . . . . . . .39 E8
Sandpiper Cl CB9 . . . . . .133 A6
Sandpiper Rd
  Bury St Edmunds IP33. . . .123 C2
  Ipswich IP2. . . . . .138 E2
  [1] Stowmarket IP14. . . . .124 F7
Sandpit Cl IP4 . . . . .140 F5
Sandpit Dr [3] IP31. . . . . . .49 E4
Sandpit Hill IP20. . . . . . . .23 B3
Sandpit La
  Thurstow IP31. . . . . .49 E4
  Worlingham NR34 . . . . .9 F4
Sandringham Cl IP2 . . . .138 F2
Sandringham Rd NR32 . .113 C1
Sands Cl [9] NR31. . . . . . . .3 C6
Sands La NR32. . . . . .112 D2
Sand St CB7 . . . . .28 D3
Sandy Cl [5] IP15 . . . . . . .107 D8
Sandy Dro IP28 . . . . .30 F3
Sandy Hill
  Barham IP6. . . . . .82 B7
  Wormingford CO6 . . . . . . .101 E3
Sandyhill La IP3 . . . . .139 E1
Sandy La
  Barham IP6. . . . . .82 A6
  Barningham IP31 . . . . .34 C3
  Barsham NR34. . . . . .9 A4
  [2] Bromeswell IP12 . . . . . .85 A5
  Bulmer CO10 . . . . .91 D3
  Diss IP22 . . . . .20 D2
  Gisleham NR33 . . . . .11 A1
  Holton IP19 . . . . .118 E4
  Hoo IP13 . . . . .70 B4
  Iken IP12 . . . . .72 F2
  Little Bealings IP13. . . . . .137 D4
  Marlesford IP13 . . . . .71 C5
  Rendham IP17 . . . . .56 F3
  Ringshall IP14 . . . . .80 D8
  Sternfield IP17 . . . . .72 C8
  St Mary, South Elmham
  otherwise Homersfield
  IP20 . . . . .23 B7
  Stowlangtoft IP31. . . . . . . .50 A7
  Sudbury CO10 . . . . .148 A4
  Sutton IP12 . . . . .99 B8
  Waldringfield IP12. . . . . . .98 E8
  Westerfield IP6. . . . . .135 C4
  Wickham Market IP13. . . . .127 D5
  Witnesham IP6 . . . . .136 B8
  Woodbridge IP12. . . . . . . .146 D2
San Francisco Wlk [3]
  NR33 . . . . .114 C5
SANTON DOWNHAM 6 C2
SAPISTON 33 F6
Sapiston Rd IP31 . . . . . . .33 F5
Sapling Pl IP4 . . . . .140 E5
Saracens House Bsns Ctr
  IP4 . . . . .155 C3
Sarah Ct CB9 . . . . .132 E3
Sarsen Cl [2] IP19 . . . . . .118 C4
Sascombe Vineyard★
  CB8. . . . . .60 F2
Saturn Cl NR32 . . . . .113 C4
Saturn Rd IP2 . . . . .138 D8
Sawmill La IP10 . . . . .145 B6
Sawmills Rd IP22 . . . . . . .20 E2
Sawston Cl [10] IP2 . . . . .139 A2
Sawyers IP7. . . . . .80 F1
Sawyers Cl IP9 . . . . .150 E2
Saxham Bsns Pk IP29 . . . .47 E4
SAXHAM STREET. 67 C8
SAXMUNDHAM 128 D3
Saxmundham Mid Sch
  IP17 . . . . .128 C2
Saxmundham Mus★
  IP17 . . . . .128 D3
Saxmundham Prim Sch
  IP17 . . . . .128 C3
Saxmundham Rd
  Aldeburgh IP15 . . . . .130 C5
  Framlingham IP13 . . . . . . .126 E3
  Friston IP17. . . . . .72 E7
  Knodishall IP17 . . . . .57 F1
  Theberton IP16 . . . . .58 A2
Saxmundham Sports Club
  IP17 . . . . .128 C4
Saxmundham Sta IP17 . .128 C3
Saxon Cl
  Exning CB8. . . . . .120 D8
  [11] Felixstowe IP11. . . . . .153 D6
Saxon Cres [7] IP31 . . . . .33 D5
Saxon Dr [9] CB5 . . . . . . .44 A5
Saxonfields IP17 . . . . .72 D5
Saxon La IP8 . . . . .95 E4
Saxon Pl
  [1] Thetford IP24. . . . . . . .16 B5
  Weeting IP27. . . . . .5 E3
Saxon Rd
  Lowestoft NR33. . . . . . . .115 B3
  Saxmundham IP17. . . . . . .128 B3
Saxon Rise IP33 . . . . . . .122 E3

Saxon St Rd CB8 60 E6
SAXON STREET 60 D6
Saxons Way IP19 118 B4
Saxon Way IP12 147 A7
Saxon Wlk IP26 6 A8
SAXSTEAD BOTTOM 55 C5
Saxstead Gn Postmill★ IP13 55 B3
SAXTEAD 55 C4
SAXTEAD GREEN 55 B3
SAXTEAD LITTLE GREEN 55 B5
Saxtead Rd
Dennington IP13 55 D5
Framlingham IP13 126 A5
Scalesbrook La IP19 118 E7
Scales St NR35 110 A4
Scaltback Cl CB8 120 E6
Scaltback Mid Sch CB8 120 E5
Scama La IP22 36 C6
Scarlin Rd IP33 122 C3
Schneider Rd 3 IP11 153 H11
Scholars Wlk IP22 20 C3
School Ave IP30 50 E2
School Cl
1 Capel St Mary IP9 150 E3
Cheveley CB8 60 E8
Hadleigh IP7 149 E5
Kenninghall NR16 19 A8
North Cove NR34 10 C4
Norton IP31 50 B4
20 Stanton IP31 34 E4
School Cres CB9 133 E8
School Farm La CO10 78 C2
Schoolhall La IP33 154 B3
School Hill
Boxford CO10 93 C3
Copdock & Washbrook IP8 95 F4
Kettleburgh IP13 70 C7
Nacton IP10 145 B4
School La
Bardwell IP31 34 C4
Bawdsey IP12 99 E2
Benhall IP17 72 C8
5 Brantham CO11 104 E5
16 Burwell CB5 44 A5
Dedham CO7 103 F4
East Bergholt CO7 151 B5
Easton IP13 70 E5
Fornham St Martin IP31 48 D6
Great Barton IP31 49 B6
Great Horkesley CO6 102 C1
Halesworth IP19 118 A4
17 Harleston IP20 22 D6
Haverhill CB9 132 B5
Hollesley IP12 99 F7
Little Horkesley CO6 102 B3
Long Melford CO10 77 E1
Manningtree CO11 104 D1
Martlesham IP12 146 C1
Metfield IP20 23 C3
4 Mistley CO11 104 F2
Reydon IP18 26 E1
Stratford St Mary CO7 103 E5
Thelnetham IP22 18 E1
7 Thurstow IP31 49 E4
Ufford IP13 84 F7
School Meadow
1 Stowmarket IP14 124 E3
4 Wetherden IP14 51 A1
School Rd
Alburgh IP20 7 A1
Bedingham NR35 7 B7
Blaxhall IP12 72 A3
Bressingham IP22 19 E4
Coddenham IP6 68 B1
Coldfair Green IP17 129 A3
Earsham NR35 7 F4
Elmswell IP30 50 E2
Great Ashfield IP31 50 F6
Great Barton IP31 49 B6
Great Wratting CB9 74 F3
Hinderclay IP22 35 E7
Hollesley IP12 99 F7
Kedington CB9 133 E8
Kirby Cane NR35 8 E8
Knodishall IP17 73 A8
Langham CO4 103 C2
Little Horkesley CO6 102 B2
Little Yeldham CO9 90 B2
Lowestoft NR33 114 F8
Monk Soham IP13 54 D4
Pentlow CO10 90 F7
Ringsfield NR34 9 B1
Risby IP28 47 E5
9 Shotley Gate IP9 107 A4
St Andrew, Ilketshall NR34 8 E2
Sudbourne IP12 87 A8
Tattingstone IP9 142 D1
Thurstow IP31 49 E4
Tunstall IP12 71 F2
Waldringfield IP12 98 D7
Woodditton CB8 60 D6
School St
Foxearth CO10 91 B7
Needham Market IP6 125 D4
Stoke-by-Nayland CO6 102 E7
Sudbury CO10 148 C5
School View NR34 24 F5
Schreiber Rd IP4 140 B7
Scofield Ct CO10 148 E4
SCOLE 21 A2
Scole Comm IP21 20 F3
SCOLE COMMON 20 F3
Scole Comm Rd IP21 21 A2
Scole Prim Sch IP21 21 A2
Scole Rd IP21 21 F2
Sconch Beck Rd IP20 23 A6
Scopes Rd IP5 141 C8
Scotland End CB7 29 E1
Scotland St CO6 103 A7
SCOTLAND STREET 102 F7
Scotred Cl CB5 44 A4
Scott Ave IP28 116 C5
Scott La 2 IP12 84 E6
Scott Rd
Ipswich IP3 140 B1
13 Ixworth IP31 34 B1
Scotts Cl 14 NR33 11 B1
Scott's Hill IP14 68 B6
Scott's La IP13 84 C7
Scrivener Dr IP8 138 B2
Scudamore Pl NR35 110 B7
Scuffin's La IP14 52 A6
Seabreeze Rd IP14 124 D5
Seafield Ave 5 CO11 105 A2
Seafield Rd 6 CO12 107 A1
Seafields Dr 3 NR31 3 B6
Seago St NR32 113 D1
Sea Lake Rd NR32 114 E8
Sealodes Rd CB7 28 A5
Seaman Ave IP17 128 B2
Sea Rd IP11 152 F2
Seaton Cl 18 CO11 104 D2
Seaton Rd IP11 152 E5
Seavert Cl 3 NR33 114 E3
Sea View NR33 11 C1
Seaview Rd IP18 119 C7
Sea View Rise NR31 3 C6
Sea View Wlk NR33 115 B4
Seaward Ave 2 IP16 129 D5
Sebert Rd IP32 123 E5
Sebert Wood Cty Prim Sch IP32 123 D5
Seckford Almshouses IP12 146 F5
Seckford Cl 1 IP4 140 F5
Seckford Hall Rd IP12 146 D3
Seckford St IP12 146 F5
Second Ave
Felixstowe IP11 152 B7
2 Glemsford CO10 77 B3
Sudbury CO10 148 E7
Second Dro IP27 13 C7
Sedan Wlk IP1 155 A2
Sedgefen Rd IP27 12 F7
Sedge Way IP33 154 A4
Sedlescombe Rd 8 NR33 114 D5
Sefton Way CB8 120 D5
Selby St NR32 113 C1
Self's La IP22 18 F3
Selkirk Rd IP4 136 C1
Selvale Way IP11 152 E4
Selway Dr IP32 49 A3
Selwyn Cl
Ipswich IP2 155 B1
Mildenhall IP28 116 D6
Newmarket CB8 121 A1
SEMER 79 F1
Semer Cl IP14 124 E3
Semere Gn La IP21 21 D6
Semere La IP21 21 D8
Sergeants Wlk IP33 154 B3
Serpentine Rd IP3 140 B2
Seven Acres NR33 115 A2
Seven Cotts La IP5 136 C1
Seven Gdns Rd IP13 83 F6
Seven Hills (Barrow Cemetery)★
Brettenham IP24 16 F4
Little Livermere IP31 33 A4
Sevenhills La IP31 33 A4
Severalls La IP13 55 D6
Several Rd IP13 55 B3
Severals The CB8 121 B4
Severn Rd
Bury St Edmunds IP32 48 C5
Ipswich IP3 139 F3
Sewells IP7 79 E6
Sewell's La CO10 90 D5
Sewells The IP33 123 A2
Sewell Wontner Cl IP5 141 C8
Sexton Rd NR35 7 D6
Sextons Manor Prim Sch IP33 122 C6
Sextons Md IP33 154 C1
Sextons Meadow IP33 123 B3
Sextons Mews IP33 154 C1
Seymore Dr CB9 132 B5
Seymour Ave IP27 14 D8
Seymour Cl CB8 121 C3
Seymour Rd IP2 155 B1
Shackleton Cl 20 CO12 106 F1
Shackleton Rd IP3 140 B3
Shackleton Sq 3 IP3 140 B3
Shaddick Rd IP18 119 B8
Shade The CB7 28 C5
SHADINGFIELD 25 E7
Shadingfield Cl NR32 113 A5
Shadowbush Cl CB9 132 D7
SHADWELL 17 C6
Shadwell Cl IP27 5 E3
Shadwell Wlk IP33 122 B6
Shaftesbury Ave 4 CO12 107 A2
Shaftesbury Sq IP4 155 C2
Shafto Rd IP1 134 E1
Shaker's La IP33 123 C5
Shaker's Rd IP29 47 B4
Shakers' Rd
Brandon IP27 15 A5
Wangford IP27 14 E4
Shakespeare Rd
Ipswich IP1 134 E3
Stowmarket IP14 124 B8
Shamrock Ave IP2 138 E4
Shannon Cl CB9 133 B5
Shannon Rd 4 IP3 144 A8
Shardlow Cl CB9 132 A7
Sharman's Rd CB7 29 A1
Sharon Dr NR32 113 B3
Sharon Rd IP33 122 D5
Sharper's Cnr IP27 109 B8
Sharpes Cnr IP27 109 C7
Sharpe's Hill IP29 47 B2
Sharpe's La IP29 63 A7
Sharpe's Row IP30 65 E8
Sharp Rd IP33 122 F2
Sharp's Gn 11 IP29 63 A8
Shaw Ave NR33 114 D3
Shawlands Ave CO10 148 F5
Shaw Rd CO10 91 E8
Shawsgate Vineyard★ IP13 126 F6
Shaw Valley Rd 7 IP12 84 A1
Shearman Rd IP7 149 F5
Sheepdrift Rd IP12 85 B5
Sheepgate NR34 111 B5
Sheepgate La
Badwell Ash IP31 51 B7
Falkenham IP10 98 F1
Sheepshead Hill 2 CO10 92 B3
Sheepwash La IP17 58 E6
Sheerwater 9 IP14 67 A5
Sheerwater Cl IP30 123 F6
Shelbourne Cl 7 IP5 141 D7
Sheldrake Dr IP2 138 E1
Sheldrick's Rd CB7 29 D5
SHELFANGER 20 C6
SHELLAND 66 A7
SHELLEY 94 C1
Shelley Ave CO10 148 F4
Shelley Cl IP14 124 F3
Shelley Rd
3 Bury St Edmunds IP32 48 C5
Layham IP7 149 E1
Shelley St IP2 155 B1
Shelley Way
Bacton IP14 51 E5
Thetford IP24 16 C7
Shelterhouse Cnr IP24 32 C8
Shelton Hill IP21 39 B5
Shelton Rd 4 NR33 114 F3
Shenley Rd IP3 140 B1
Shenstone Dr IP1 135 A3
Shepherd Dr IP8 138 C2
Shepherds Ct 9 CB9 132 C5
Shepherds Dr 1 IP29 63 D1
Shepherds Gr Ind Est IP22 35 B4
Shepherds La
Burgate IP22 36 D7
Glemsford CO10 77 A3
Onehouse IP14 124 A8
Sheppards Way 6 IP5 141 D7
Sherborne Ave IP4 136 A2
Sherborne Rd IP33 122 D3
Sherbourne St CO10 93 B4
SHERBOURNE STREET 93 B4
Sheridan Cl IP14 124 A8
Sheridan Wlk NR34 111 E4
Sheriffs Ct CB8 59 F2
Sherrington Rd IP1 139 A8
Sherwood Fields 4 IP5 141 C7
Shetland Cl
5 Ipswich IP4 136 A1
Ipswich IP4 140 A8
Shetland Rd CB9 133 B5
Shetlands 13 IP31 34 E4
Shickle Pl IP22 18 C2
Shilling St 14 CO10 78 D4
Shillitoe Cl IP33 154 A2
SHIMPLING
Burston and Shimpling 21 A6
Shimpling 77 E6
Shimpling Cl 7 IP14 124 E3
Shimpling Rd IP21 21 B5
SHIMPLING STREET 77 E8
Shingle Hill IP21 38 C4
SHINGLE STREET 100 A5
Ship Gdns IP28 116 B3
Ship La
Bradfield CO11 105 C2
Bramford IP8 134 B1
Ship Launch Rd IP3 139 E3
SHIPMEADOW 8 F4
Shippea Hill Sta CB7 12 C7
Ship Rd NR33 115 A3
Shire Ct 11 CB9 132 C5
Shire Hall Yd IP4 155 C2
Shires The NR32 113 B8
Shirley Cl 9 IP1 135 A3
Shoals Wlk NR33 114 E6
Shoebridge's Hill CO7 103 F3
Shoe Devil La NR35 24 C8
SHOP CORNER 106 C5
Shop Hill CB8 61 E1
Shop La IP13 71 E5
Shop Rd IP13 69 E1
Shop St IP13 54 D7
Shore La
Bradfield CO11 105 C2
Harkstead IP9 106 A5
Nacton IP10 145 B3
Shores Cl IP28 29 E2
Short Beck 19 IP26 4 E5
Short Brackland IP33 154 B2
Short La
Feltwell IP26 4 D5
Lowestoft NR33 114 C2
Short La *continued*
Walberswick IP18 43 C5
Shortlands IP2 138 D1
Short Rd
Belton with Browston NR31 2 D8
Blundeston NR32 3 A4
Snailwell CB8 45 A5
Short St 2 NR33 115 B4
SHOTFORD HEATH 22 D4
Shotford Rd IP20 22 D5
SHOTLEY 106 F6
Shotley Cl
1 Felixstowe IP11 152 D4
Ipswich IP8 138 C2
SHOTLEY GATE 107 A4
Shotley Mews 8 IP12 85 B3
Shotley Prim Sch IP9 106 F5
Shotley Wlk IP9 106 E7
SHOTTISHAM 99 C7
Shrimpling Rd IP29 77 C6
Shrubberies The CB8 121 D1
Shrubbery Cl IP11 152 F4
Shrubbery Rd IP13 146 B7
Shrub House Cl 1 IP28 30 B8
Shrubland Ave IP1 134 E1
Shrubland Dr IP4 140 F5
Shrubland Pk Gdns★ IP6 82 A6
Shrubland Rd 11 CO11 105 A2
Shrublands 2 IP28 116 C4
Siamhall La CO10 92 F3
Siam Pl 4 CO10 148 C5
SIBTON 57 A8
SIBTON GREEN 41 D2
SICKLESMERE 63 F7
Sicklesmere Rd
Bury St Edmunds IP33 123 D2
Nowton IP30 63 E8
Sidegate Ave IP4 140 A8
Sidegate La IP4 136 A1
Sidegate La W IP4 135 F1
Sidegate Prim Sch IP4 140 A8
Sidegate Rd NR31 3 A8
Siding Rd NR34 10 C5
Silent St IP4 155 B2
Silhalls Cl 7 CB8 60 F8
Silk Mill Cl 2 IP7 149 D5
Silverdale Ave IP14 124 C7
Silverdale Cl IP1 135 A1
Silver Dr IP15 130 C6
Silver Hill IP8 95 D6
SILVERLACE GREEN 71 C7
Silver Leys IP9 104 F7
SILVERLEY'S GREEN 40 B6
Silverley Way 6 CB8 60 F8
Silver St
Burwell CB5 44 A6
Kedington CB9 133 F7
Old Newton with Dagworth IP14 51 E2
South Lopham IP22 19 C3
Withersfield CB9 74 A2
Silverwood Cl NR33 115 A4
Simon's Cross IP13 127 B7
Simons Rd IP12 147 A7
Simpers Drift IP17 56 D1
Simpson Cl IP3 139 F1
Sim's La CB9 133 F7
Sinclair Dr IP2 139 C3
Singleton Ct CO10 148 E3
Sir Alf Ramsey Way IP4 155 A2
Sirdar Rd IP1 139 A6
Sir John Leman High Sch NR34 111 A4
Sir John Leman Rd NR34 111 D2
Sir Robert Hitcham CE VA Prim Sch IP14 53 E2
Sir Robert Hitchams CE VAP Sch IP13 126 B4
Siskin Gn 1 NR33 114 D5
Sitwell Cl 12 CO11 104 D2
Sitwell Gdns 7 IP13 126 C3
SIZEWELL 58 F1
Sizewell Belts Nature Reserve★ IP16 58 E2
Sizewell Gap IP16 58 F1
Sizewell Power Sta IP16 58 F2
Sizewell Rd IP16 129 D5
Skamacre Cres NR32 113 B2
Skate's Hill CO10 77 A2
Skeaping Cl CB8 121 A5
Skelton Cl 9 CO11 104 E2
Skelton Rd IP22 20 D2
Skelton's Dro IP28 13 A2
Skilman Hill IP18 119 D4
Skinner's La
Metfield IP20 23 C3
Starston IP20 22 B8
Skinner St IP33 154 B2
Skipper Cl 3 IP8 142 E8
Skipper Rd 4 IP2 138 D1
Skipper's La CB9 74 A3
Skoulding Cl 1 NR33 114 F7
Sky Hall Hill CO4 103 B4
Skylark Cl IP32 49 A4
Skylark La IP8 138 C2
Skylark Way IP14 124 F6
Slade La IP22 19 E2
Slades Cl 7 CO10 77 B3
Slade St IP4 155 C2
Slade The IP6 134 D8
Slaters Dr CB9 132 C8
Slaughden Rd IP15 130 E2
Sleaford Cl IP2 139 A3
Sloeberry Rd IP3 144 C7
Sloe La IP17 129 A2
SLOUGH HILL 77 E7
Slough Hill IP29 77 E7
Slough La
Acton CO10 78 C1
Horringer IP29 122 A2
Slough Rd
Botesdale IP22 36 C5
Brantham CO11 104 E5
Slugs La NR32 2 C4
Sluice Dro IP26 4 E3
Slushy La IP9 106 A6
Smaley La 1 CO10 91 E8
Smallbridge Entry CO8 101 E4
Smallbridge Hall★ CO8 101 E4
SMALLWOOD GREEN 64 F5
SMALLWORTH 18 D3
Smallworth La IP22 18 E3
Smart St IP4 155 C2
Smear La IP18 26 D2
Smear La E IP18 26 F1
Smeetham Hall La CO10 91 C3
Smithbrook La IP29 77 A8
Smith Cres 17 NR33 11 B1
Smithers Cl 9 IP9 150 E3
Smithfield IP12 147 B6
Smiths Cl IP14 54 E7
Smiths Dr IP21 21 B5
SMITH'S GREEN 88 C3
Smiths Pl 9 IP5 141 D7
Smith's Wlk NR33 114 C6
Smith Wlk IP33 123 D2
SMITHWOOD GREEN 78 C7
Smithy Cl
Bradfield Combust with Stanningfield IP29 64 A3
Rushbrooke with Rougham IP30 64 D8
Smock Meadow 8 IP7 79 F4
Snab Hill NR33 11 A1
SNAILWELL 45 A6
Snailwell Rd
Fordham CB8 44 F7
Newmarket CB8 121 B7
Snailwell Short Rd CB8 44 F5
Snakes and Ladders★ IP3 139 E5
Snake's La
Lound NR32 2 F6
Topcroft NR35 7 A8
SNAPE 72 D4
Snape Com Prim Sch IP17 72 D5
Snape Dr NR32 113 A4
Snape Hill IP22 35 F6
Snape Maltings IP17 72 D4
Snape Maltings Concert Hall★ IP17 72 D4
Snape Marshes Nature Reserve★ IP17 72 D4
Snape Rd
Friston IP17 129 A2
Sudbourne IP12 131 A7
Tunstall IP12 72 A2
Snare Dro IP28 12 E3
Snipe Farm Rd IP13 69 E1
Snowberry Way 6 CB7 28 D5
Snowcroft IP9 150 E3
Snowdens Yd 14 IP18 119 D5
Snowdon Ct 7 CB9 132 C4
Snowdon Hill IP13 127 C7
Snowdon Rd IP2 139 B2
Snowdrop Cl IP32 123 F5
Snow Hill CO10 76 A1
Snow Hill La CO6 103 B7
SNOW STREET 20 A4
Soames Cl IP14 124 C7
Soane St IP4 155 C3
Soft Rd CO10 90 F3
SOHAM 28 D4
SOHAM COTES 28 B6
Soham Rd CB7 28 A8
Soham Town Cnr IP13 54 F3
Solace Cl NR35 110 D3
Solomon Rd 10 NR33 11 C1
Somerleyton Hall & Gdns★ NR32 2 E4
Somerleyton Prim Sch NR32 2 D4
Somerleyton Rd NR32 112 F4
Somerleyton Sta NR32 2 C3
Somerset Ct 12 CB9 132 C5
Somerset Rd IP4 139 F8
SOMERSHAM 81 C3
Somersham Prim Sch IP8 81 C3
Somersham Rd IP8 81 F2
SOMERTON 76 F8
Somerton Ave NR32 113 C3
Somerton Rd IP29 77 A7
Somerville Lea 2 IP15 130 E5
Sorrel Cl IP2 138 F3
Sorrell Gn IP14 51 D6
Sorrell Wlk IP5 141 F7
Sorrel Wlk CB9 132 B7
SOTHERTON 25 E2
SOTHERTON CORNER 25 E1
SOTTERLEY 26 A7
Sotterley Cl 7 NR32 113 A6
Sotterley Rd
6 Lowestoft NR32 112 F4
Sotterley NR34 10 C1
Willingham St Mary NR34 25 F7
Sound The NR33 114 E5
South Cl
Beccles NR34 111 A3
Bury St Edmunds IP33 154 A1
Ipswich IP4 139 E8
Leiston IP16 129 D5
9 Melton IP12 84 E6

S. Elmham Hall

South Coast National Nature Reserve★ IP17 43 B4
SOUTH COVE 26 F4
South Dr CB8 120 F4
South Elmham Hall★ IP20 23 D6
South Elmham Terr NR33 114 E8
Southend Rd 4 NR35 110 B3
South Entrance IP17 128 D2
Southern Belle Cl IP32 123 F7
Southern La IP22 19 A1
Southery Rd IP26 4 B6
Southfield Dr IP16 129 C5
Southfield Gdns NR33 114 F6
Southfields CO7 103 F3
Southfields Cl CB8 120 E4
Southgate 12 IP20 22 D5
Southgate Ave IP28 116 B7
Southgate Gdns
  Bury St Edmunds IP33 123 C3
  3 Long Melford CO10 91 E7
Southgate Rd IP8 138 B1
Southgate St
  Bury St Edmunds IP33 154 C1
  4 Long Melford CO10 91 E7
South Gn IP19 119 D4
SOUTH GREEN
  Hoxne 38 B5
  Pulham St Mary 21 F6
South Hill IP11 152 F3
South Lee Sch IP33 123 C2
South Leet Cl 4 NR32 112 E4
South Lodge Dr 1 IP28 48 C6
SOUTH LOPHAM 19 B4
South Lowestoft Ind Est NR33 114 E2
SOUTHOLT 54 B7
Southolt Rd
  Athelington IP21 38 F1
  Bedfield IP13 54 D6
South Pier Leisure Complex NR33 115 E8
South Pk IP27 5 E3
South Rd
  Beccles NR34 111 A3
  Lakenheath IP27 109 E3
South St
  Hockwold cum Wilton IP26 4 F2
  Ipswich IP1 155 A4
  12 Manningtree CO11 104 E2
  Risby IP28 47 D4
South Strand 1 CO11 104 E3
South View Cl 8 NR32 113 B2
South View Gn IP9 104 F7
Southwell La NR34 26 A6
Southwell Rd NR33 115 B7
SOUTHWOLD 119 C5
Southwold & District Hospl IP18 119 D6
Southwold Lighthouse★ 20 IP18 119 D5
Southwold Maze★ IP18 43 C7
Southwold Mus★ 21 IP18 119 D5
Southwold Pier★ IP18 119 E6
Southwold Prim Sch IP18 119 D5
Southwold Rd
  Blyford IP19 42 B8
  Brampton with Stoven NR34 25 E5
  Holton IP19 118 F3
  Wrentham NR34 26 E5
Southwold Sailors Reading Rm★ IP18 119 D5
Southwood Cl IP17 128 D2
SOWLEY GREEN 75 A5
Spalding's Chair Hill IP24 17 B3
Spanbies Rd 3 CO7 103 E5
Sparhawk St IP33 154 C1
Sparkes Cl 5 CB7 29 C5
Sparks La CO9 89 D3
Sparrow Ct 11 IP14 53 F2
Sparrowhawk Rd IP19 118 C7
Sparrow Rd CO10 148 F4
Sparrows Croft Rd 5 IP12 85 E8
Spartan Cl 3 CB9 132 A6
Spashett Rd 2 NR32 113 B4
Speckled Wood Cl IP8 142 D8
Speed La CB7 28 D4
Speedwell Cl 7 NR33 115 A3
Speedwell Rd IP2 138 F4
Speedwell Way 13 IP20 22 D5
Spencer Dr NR32 113 B6
Spencer Dro CB7 28 C4
Spencer Rd 4 IP12 85 E8
Spencer Way IP14 124 B7
Spenser Rd IP1 134 E3
Sperling Dr CB9 132 C8
SPEXHALL 24 F3
Spexhall Way NR32 113 B5
Spicers La 2 CO10 91 E8
Spiers Way 1 IP22 20 B2
Spike's La IP14 66 E7
Spindler Cl IP5 141 D7
Spindle Rd CB9 132 B7
Spinks' La NR35 7 D6
Spinnel's Hill CO11 105 D1
Spinnel's La CO11 105 E1
Spinner Cl IP1 138 D8
Spinners La 3 IP18 119 D5
Spinney Cl NR34 10 B4
Spinney Gdns NR33 114 C4
Spinney Hill IP7 81 A1
Spinney Rd IP31 33 B3
Spinney The
  Beccles NR34 111 D4
  Ipswich IP4 140 F4
Spinning Cl IP17 128 D5
Spire Chase CO10 148 E8
Spirkett's La IP20 22 D5
Spitfire Cl IP3 140 B1
Spong La IP30 50 E2
Spong The IP20 23 C3
Spooners Cl CB8 59 F4
Spooners La 5 IP7 149 D6
Spooner's La NR34 26 E2
Spout La CO10 101 B8
SPRATT'S STREET 85 D5
Springbank Ave 16 CO11 104 D2
Spring Cl
  3 Bentwaters Airfield IP12 85 D8
  Burwell CB5 44 A5
Springett's Hill CO8 101 B5
Springfield IP18 119 A7
Springfield Ave
  Bury St Edmunds IP33 154 A3
  Felixstowe IP11 153 A5
Springfield Dr IP27 109 D6
Springfield Gdns NR33 114 F5
Springfield Inf Sch IP1 138 F8
Springfield Jun Sch IP1 138 F8
Springfield La IP1 138 F8
Springfield Rd
  Aldeburgh IP15 130 C5
  Bury St Edmunds IP33 154 A3
  4 Somersham IP8 81 C3
  Sudbury CO10 148 C7
Springhurst Cl IP4 139 F6
Spring La
  Bury St Edmunds IP33 154 A3
  Crowfield IP6 68 B3
  Dennington IP13 55 B5
  5 Lavenham CO10 78 D4
  Polstead CO6 93 D2
  Ufford IP13 127 B1
  Wickham Market IP13 127 D7
Springland Cl IP4 140 A6
Springlands Way CO10 148 D8
Spring Meadow
  10 Glemsford CO10 77 A3
  Playford IP6 137 B4
Spring Pk IP6 69 C2
Spring Rd
  Bardwell IP31 34 C5
  Copdock & Washbrook IP8 95 E5
  Ipswich IP4 139 F6
Spring Row IP14 124 D7
Spring St 6 CO10 78 D4
Springtail Rd IP8 142 E8
Spring Wood Nature Reserve★ IP9 142 E7
Sprites End IP11 152 D7
Spriteshall La IP11 152 D7
Sprites La IP8 138 C1
Sprites Prim Sch IP2 138 C2
SPROUGHTON 138 A7
Sproughton Bsns Pk IP1 138 D7
Sproughton CE Prim Sch IP8 138 B6
Sproughton Ct IP8 138 A6
Sproughton Rd IP1 138 C7
Spruce Cl 14 IP27 13 F2
Spruce Ct NR32 113 C3
Spruce Dr IP27 5 F1
Spur End IP12 147 C7
Spurgeon Score 12 NR32 113 E2
Spurling Cl 2 CB8 60 E7
Square The IP14 124 E4
Squires Ct 21 CB9 132 C5
Squires La 4 IP5 98 A8
Squires Wlk NR32 113 C5
Squirrells Mill Rd 3 IP7 79 F4
Squirrells The IP9 150 E4
Stackwood Rd CO6 93 F3
STACKYARD GREEN 93 C8
Stafford Ct NR32 112 E4
Staithe Cl 4 NR35 110 B4
Staithe Rd
  Bungay NR35 110 B4
  Burgh St Peter NR34 10 C7
Staithe The NR33 114 E6
STAMBOURNE 89 B1
STAMBOURNE GREEN 89 A1
Stambourne Rd CO9 89 E2
Stamford Cl IP2 142 F8
Stamford Ct 3 IP33 122 F3
Stamford St CB8 121 B2
Stammers Pl IP5 141 E8
Stanford St 3 NR32 113 C1
Stanhope Cl IP17 72 D5
Stanley Ave IP3 140 A4
Stanley Drapkin Prim Sch 8 CB9 88 D3
Stanley Rd
  Diss IP22 20 B2
  Felixstowe IP11 153 A3
  Lowestoft NR33 114 E7
  Newmarket CB8 121 C3
  Sudbury CO10 148 C6
Stanley St NR32 113 D1
Stanley Wood Ave CO10 148 D7
Stannard Way CO10 148 E4
STANNINGFIELD 64 A4
Stanningfield Rd IP30 63 F5
STANSFIELD 76 C7
Stansfield Cl NR33 114 E6
STANSTEAD 77 C4
STANTON 34 D4
STANTON CHARE 34 D5
Stanton Cl
  Beccles NR34 111 C3
  Lowestoft NR32 113 C5
Stanton Com Prim Sch IP31 34 E4
Stanton Hughes Way 10 CO11 104 D2
Stanton Pl 12 CB9 132 F6
Stanton Postmill★ IP31 34 F4
Stanton Rd IP31 34 C4
STANTON STREET 50 B5
Stanway Cl CO10 77 B3
STANWAY GREEN 39 C1
Staple Cl IP31 35 C1
Staplehurst Cl 7 NR33 114 C4
Staples La CB7 28 D3
Star And Garter La CB8 60 E8
Starfield Cl IP4 140 B6
Starhouse La IP14 66 C5
Star La IP4 155 C2
Starling Way IP14 124 F7
Starre Rd IP33 122 C5
STARSTON 22 C7
Starston La IP20 22 C5
Station App
  Newmarket CB8 121 A2
  Saxmundham IP17 128 D3
Station Gate CB5 44 A4
Station Hill
  1 Bures CO8 101 C4
  Bury St Edmunds IP33 154 B4
  Harleston IP20 22 D6
  Little Whelnetham IP30 64 B6
  Thurston IP31 49 D4
Station La 13 CO12 107 B2
Station Rd
  Alburgh IP20 7 A1
  Bacton IP14 52 A6
  Barnham IP24 16 B2
  Beccles NR34 111 B5
  Bentley IP9 104 E7
  Birdbrook CO9 89 B4
  Blaxhall IP12 71 E3
  Bradfield CO11 105 B2
  Brampton with Stoven NR34 25 C5
  Burston & Shimpling IP21 20 F6
  Clare CO10 90 B8
  Claydon IP6 134 B8
  8 Corton NR32 3 D4
  Corton NR32 113 C8
  Diss IP22 20 D2
  Ditchingham NR35 110 C6
  Dullingham CB8 59 E5
  2 Earsham NR35 7 F4
  Ellingham NR35 8 D7
  Elmswell IP30 50 F2
  Felixstowe IP11 152 C7
  Fordham CB7 29 A1
  Framlingham IP13 126 C2
  Geldeston NR34 8 F6
  Haddiscoe NR31 2 A5
  Hadleigh IP7 149 E5
  Halesworth IP19 118 B4
  Harleston IP20 22 D6
  1 Harwich CO12 106 F3
  Haughley IP14 51 D1
  4 Haverhill CB9 132 E6
  Hopton on Sea NR31 3 B6
  Isleham CB7 29 C4
  Kennett CB8 45 F7
  Lakenheath IP27 109 C7
  Laxfield IP13 39 F4
  Leiston IP16 129 C6
  Long Melford CO10 91 E7
  Lowestoft NR32 113 D4
  Manningtree CO11 104 E3
  Mildenhall IP28 116 B3
  Pulham Market IP21 21 E8
  Pulham St Mary IP21 22 A8
  Ramsey & Parkeston CO12 106 F3
  Soham CB7 28 C4
  Somerleyton, Ashby & Herringfleet NR32 2 C3
  Southwold IP18 119 C6
  Sudbury CO10 148 C5
  Tattingstone IP9 105 A7
  Thetford IP24 16 B6
  Wetheringsett-cum-Brockford IP14 53 B4
  Woodbridge IP12 147 A4
  Wrabness CO11 105 F2
Station Rd E IP14 124 E6
Station Rd W IP14 124 D6
Station Sq 11 NR32 115 D8
Station St IP2 139 C3
Station Terr IP13 126 C2
Station Yd
  Hadleigh IP7 149 E5
  Mildenhall IP28 116 B3
  Needham Market IP6 125 E4
Staverton Cl IP12 85 B6
Stayngate Wlk 7 NR32 112 E4
Stearn Dr IP14 66 C6
Stearn's La IP14 67 D6
Stebbings La IP12 99 E7
Stedman Terr IP18 119 C8
Steeds Meadow 7 CO10 91 E8
Steeles Rd IP30 50 D1
STEEPLE BUMPSTEAD 88 D4
Steeple Bumpstead Pottery★ CB9 88 D3
Steeple Bumpstead Rd CB9 88 B4
Steeplechase CO10 75 C4
Steeple End IP19 118 B3
Steggall Cl IP6 125 C6
Stella Maris IP2 138 D5
Stennetts Cl IP11 152 B8
Stephen Cl
  Haverhill CB9 132 D6
  Long Melford CO10 91 D7
Stephen Rd IP5 141 E8
Stephen's Ct IP4 140 B6
Stephenson Pl IP32 122 F8
Stephensons Wlk NR32 113 D4
Stephenson Way IP24 16 A4
Stepping Hill 3 NR34 111 B5
STERNFIELD 72 D8
STETCHWORTH 60 A5
Stetchworth Rd
  Dullingham CB8 59 F4
  Stetchworth CB8 60 B4
Stevenson Rd IP1 155 A3
Stevens St NR32 113 C1
Steward Rd IP33 123 C2
Stewards Field CB7 29 A1
Stewart Young Gr IP5 141 D7
Stimpson Cl 3 NR32 113 A6
Stirling Cl
  Lowestoft NR32 112 F4
  7 Thistley Green IP28 29 F6
Stirling Dr 13 CB9 132 C6
Stirling Gdns CB8 120 E4
Stirling Rd 3 IP26 4 E5
Stirrups La NR32 3 C5
Stobart Cl NR34 111 D3
STOCK HILL 50 E8
Stockley Cl CB9 133 A5
Stockmers End 8 IP9 150 E3
Stocks La IP18 119 A2
Stockton Cl IP7 149 F4
Stockton Rd NR34 9 A7
STOKE 155 B1
STOKE ASH 37 B1
Stoke Ash Prim Sch IP23 52 F8
STOKE BY CLARE 89 E6
STOKE-BY-NAYLAND 102 E6
Stoke-by-Nayland CE VC Prim Sch CO6 102 E7
Stoke-by-Nayland Mid Sch CO6 102 D7
Stoke Coll CO10 89 E6
Stoke Hall★ IP2 155 B1
Stoke Hall Rd IP2 155 B1
Stoke High Sch IP2 139 C3
STOKE PARK 138 F1
Stoke Pk Dr IP2 139 A1
Stoke Quay IP2 155 C1
Stoke Rd
  Clare CO10 90 A7
  Layham IP7 149 D1
  Leavenheath CO6 102 B8
  Nayland-with-Wissington CO6 102 D5
  Stoke Ash IP23 37 D1
  Stoke-by-Clare CO10 89 F7
Stoke St IP2 155 B1
Stollery Cl IP5 141 B7
Stonalls IP30 50 C1
Stonebridge Ave IP33 122 F3
Stonebridge La IP14 67 A8
Stonechat Rd IP2 138 C3
Stonegrove Rd IP11 152 D1
Stone Hall Rd IP23 36 A2
Stonehouse Rd IP7 149 D6
Stone La
  Bressingham IP22 19 F6
  Wrabness CO11 105 F2
Stone Lodge La IP2 139 A3
Stone Lodge La W IP2 138 F3
Stone Lodge Wlk IP2 139 B3
Stone Pl 12 IP12 147 A5
Stone St Rd 2 CO10 93 C3
Stone St
  Boxford CO6 93 C3
  Crowfield IP6 68 C3
  Hadleigh IP7 149 B8
  Spexhall IP19 118 C8
STONE STREET
  Boxford 93 C2
  Spexhall 24 F5
Stonewell Hill IP6 68 D1
Stoney La
  Barrow IP29 47 B2
  Thurston IP31 49 F4
Stoney Rd IP13 83 D6
STONHAM ASPAL 68 A6
Stonham Aspal CE Prim Sch IP14 68 B6
Stonham Barns Leisure Complex★ IP14 68 C6
Stonham Rd IP14 52 B4
Stony La
  2 Aldringham cum Thorpe IP16 73 F6
  Debenham IP14 53 D2
  Wortwell IP20 22 F8
Stopford Ct 8 IP1 139 A7
Store St IP22 20 C3
Stour Ave IP11 152 E3
Stour Cl
  Glemsford CO10 77 B1
  4 Harwich CO12 106 E1
  Saxmundham IP17 128 C4
Stourdale Cl 27 CO11 104 D2
Stour Gdns CO10 148 E2
Stourmead Cl CB9 133 E8
Stour Rd CO12 107 B3
Stourside IP9 107 A4
Stour St
  Cavendish CO10 90 D8
  17 Manningtree CO11 104 E2
  Sudbury CO10 148 B5
Stour Vale CO9 89 B5
Stour Valley Rd CB9 132 F5
Stourview Ave 4 CO11 105 A2
Stourview Cl 6 CO11 105 A2
Stour Wood Nature Reserve★ CO12 106 B2
STOVEN 25 F4
Stoven Cl NR32 113 B5
Stoven Rd NR34 25 F3
Stow La IP31 50 A8
STOWLANGTOFT 50 C7
STOWMARKET 124 E6
Stowmarket High Sch IP14 124 B7
Stowmarket Mid Sch IP14 124 C6
Stowmarket Rd
  Badley IP6 125 A8
  Great Blakenham IP6 81 F6
  Old Newton with Dagworth IP14 51 E1
  Rattlesden IP30 65 E6
  Stonham Aspal IP14 68 A6
  Wetherden IP14 51 A1
Stowmarket Sta IP14 124 E6
Stow Rd IP31 34 B1
STOWUPLAND 67 B6
Stowupland High Sch IP14 67 A7
Stowupland Rd IP14 124 F7
Stowupland St IP14 124 D6
STRADBROKE 39 A5
Stradbroke CE Prim Sch IP21 39 A5
Stradbroke High Sch IP21 39 B4
Stradbroke Rd
  Fressingfield IP21 39 D7
  Ipswich IP4 140 A7
  Lowestoft NR33 115 A4
  Southwold IP18 119 D5
STRADISHALL 75 F7
Stradishall Rd CO10 75 E5
Straight La 19 IP20 22 D6
Straight Rd
  Battisford IP14 66 D1
  Boxted CO4 102 F1
  Bradfield CO11 105 B1
  Foxhall IP10 141 C1
  Polstead CO6 93 F3
  Whepstead IP29 63 C4
Strand The IP2 143 C8
Strasbourg Sq 11 CB9 132 F6
Stratford Rd
  Dedham CO7 103 E4
  Ipswich IP1 134 F2
STRATFORD ST ANDREW 71 F7
STRATFORD ST MARY 103 D5
Stratford St Mary Prim Sch CO7 103 E5
Strattonhall Drift IP10 145 F2
Strawberry Fields CB9 132 B5
Strawberry La IP19 25 D3
Straw La CO10 148 B5
Street Farm La 4 IP31 34 B1
Street Farm Rd IP17 128 D3
Streetfield Cl IP29 77 F7
Street The
  Aldeby NR34 9 F8
  Alderton IP12 99 E3
  Aldham IP7 94 E8
  Ashen CO10 89 E5
  Ashfield cum Thorpe IP14 54 C1
  Assington CO10 92 F1
  Bacton IP14 51 E5
  Badwell Ash IP31 50 E7
  Barnham IP24 16 B2
  Barrow IP29 47 A2
  Barton Mills IP28 116 E2
  Bawdsey IP12 99 E3
  Beck Row, Holywell Row & Kenny Hill IP28 30 C8
  Belchamp Otten CO10 90 E4
  Belstead IP8 142 C6
  Benacre NR34 27 A7
  Birdbrook CO9 89 A3
  Blo' Norton IP22 18 E2
  Blundeston NR32 3 A4
  Botesdale IP22 36 A6
  Boxted IP29 77 A6
  Bradfield CO11 105 C1
  Bradfield Combust with Stanningfield IP30 64 B4
  Bramfield IP19 41 F5
  Bramford IP8 134 A2
  Brampton with Stoven NR34 25 E4
  Brandon IP27 5 E1
  Brantham CO11 105 A5
  Bredfield IP13 84 C8
  Bressingham IP22 19 D6
  Brettenham IP7 65 C1
  Bridgham NR16 17 E8
  Brockdish IP21 21 E2
  Brome & Oakley IP23 117 D8
  Bruisyard IP17 56 D4
  Brundish IP13 39 D1
  Bulmer CO10 91 C3
  Burrough Green CB8 59 E3
  12 Bury St Edmunds IP28 48 C6
  Butley IP12 86 A6
  Capel St Mary IP9 150 D3
  Cavenham IP28 47 A8
  Charsfield IP13 70 B3
  Chattisham IP8 95 C4
  Chedburgh IP29 62 C4
  Chelsworth IP7 79 D3
  Coney Weston IP31 17 E1
  Copdock & Washbrook IP8 95 F5
  Corton NR32 3 D4
  Cratfield IP19 40 D5
  Cretingham IP13 69 E7

Street The continued
Culford IP28 . . . . 48 B8
Dalham CB8 . . . . 61 B8
Darsham IP17 . . . . 42 B1
Dennington IP13 . . . . 55 E6
Dickleburgh IP21 . . . . 21 B5
Drinkstone IP30 . . . . 65 B8
Earl Soham IP13 . . . . 54 F2
Earsham NR35 . . . . 7 F4
East Bergholt CO7 . . . . 151 B4
Easton IP13 . . . . 70 E5
Elmsett IP7 . . . . 80 F1
Eriswell IP27 . . . . 13 F1
Eye IP21 . . . . 38 B4
Eyke IP12 . . . . 85 B6
Farnham IP17 . . . . 72 A7
Flixton NR35 . . . . 7 E2
Foxearth CO10 . . . . 91 B7
Framsden IP14 . . . . 69 B6
Freckenham IP28 . . . . 29 E3
Gazeley CB8 . . . . 46 B3
Geldeston NR34 . . . . 9 A7
Great Barton IP31 . . . . 49 B5
Great Bricett IP7 . . . . 80 D5
Great Livermere IP31 . . . . . . 33 C2
Great Waldingfield CO10 . . . . 92 D6
Great Wratting CB9 . . . . 74 F3
Grundisburgh IP13 . . . . 83 E5
Hacheston IP13 . . . . 71 A6
Halesworth IP19 . . . . 118 E3
Harkstead IP9 . . . . 106 A5
45 Harleston IP20 . . . . 22 D6
Hessett IP30 . . . . 64 F8
Hinderclay IP22 . . . . 35 E7
Holbrook IP9 . . . . 105 E7
Hollesley IP12 . . . . 99 F7
Horham IP21 . . . . 38 E3
Horringer IP29 . . . . 122 B1
Huntingfield IP19 . . . . 41 A4
Icklingham IP28 . . . . 31 D4
Kersey IP7 . . . . 93 F7
Kettleburgh IP13 . . . . 70 C7
Kirtling CB8 . . . . 60 E3
Lawshall IP29 . . . . 63 E1
Layham IP7 . . . . 149 E2
Letheringham IP13 . . . . 70 D4
Lidgate CB8 . . . . 61 B4
Little Bealings IP13 . . . . . . 137 D4
Little Thurlow CB9 . . . . 74 D5
Little Waldingfield CO10 . . 92 E8
Lound NR32 . . . . 2 F6
Lowestoft NR33 . . . . 114 C2
Market Weston IP22 . . . . 35 A8
Martlesham IP12 . . . . 146 C1
Middleton CO10 . . . . 148 C1
Mildenhall IP28 . . . . 30 B8
Monks Eleigh IP7 . . . . 79 C2
Moulton CB8 . . . . 45 F3
Nacton IP10 . . . . 145 C5
Newbourne IP12 . . . . 98 D6
North Cove NR34 . . . . 10 B4
North Lopham IP22 . . . . 19 A6
Norton IP31 . . . . 50 B4
Occold IP23 . . . . 37 F1
Pakenham IP31 . . . . 49 E6
Parham IP13 . . . . 71 A7
Peasenhall IP17 . . . . 56 F8
Pettistree IP13 . . . . 127 C4
Poslingford CO10 . . . . 76 A3
Preston St Mary CO10 . . . . . 79 A5
Ramsey & Parkeston
   CO12 . . . . 106 D1
Raydon IP7 . . . . 94 E1
Redenhall with Harleston
   IP20 . . . . 22 F5
1 Redgrave IP22 . . . . 36 A8
Riddlesworth IP22 . . . . 18 A3
Rumburgh IP19 . . . . 24 C4
Rushmere NR33 . . . . 10 E1
Shotley IP9 . . . . 106 F6
Shottisham IP12 . . . . 99 B7
Snailwell CB8 . . . . 45 A6
Somerleyton, Ashby &
   Herringfleet NR32 . . . . . . 2 B4
South Lopham IP22 . . . . 19 B4
Southolt IP23 . . . . 54 B7
Stanton IP31 . . . . 34 E4
Starston IP20 . . . . 22 C7
Sternfield IP17 . . . . 72 D8
St James, South Elmham
   IP19 . . . . 23 F4
Stoke Ash IP23 . . . . 52 F8
Stoke-by-Clare CO10 . . . . . . 89 D6
Stonham Aspal IP14 . . . . . . 68 B6
Stowlangtoft IP31 . . . . 50 B6
Stradishall CB8 . . . . 75 E6
Stratford St Mary CO7 . . . . 103 E4
Sturmer CB9 . . . . 133 D3
Thorndon IP23 . . . . 53 B8
Thornham Magna IP23 . . . . . 37 A2
Troston IP31 . . . . 33 D3
Tuddenham St Martin IP6 . 136 C5
Ubbeston IP19 . . . . 40 F3
Walberswick IP18 . . . . 119 A2
Wattisfield IP22 . . . . 35 C4
Wenhaston IP19 . . . . 42 C6
Westleton IP17 . . . . 58 C7
Wetheringsett-cum-Brockford
   IP14 . . . . 52 F6
Weybread IP21 . . . . 22 D2
Whatfield IP7 . . . . 80 C1
Wherstead IP9 . . . . 143 A6
Winfarthing IP22 . . . . 20 B8
Wissett IP19 . . . . 24 D2
Witnesham IP6 . . . . 136 A8

Street The continued
Woodbridge IP12 . . . . 147 C7
Woodditton CB8 . . . . 60 D5
Woolpit IP30 . . . . 50 D1
Worlington IP28 . . . . 30 B4
Stretham Rd CB7 . . . . 28 A2
Stretton Ave CB8 . . . . . . 121 B2
Strickland Manor Hill
   IP17 . . . . 57 C8
Strickland Pl 18 IP18 . . . 119 D5
Stricklands Rd 1 IP14 . . 124 E5
Strickmere CO7 . . . . 103 E5
Strollers Way CB8 . . . . . . 60 A5
Strowger's Way 6 NR33 . . 11 C1
Struggler's La IP6 . . . . . 136 A8
Stuart Cl
   5 Felixstowe IP11 . . . . 153 D7
   Ipswich IP4 . . . . 139 F7
Stuart Dr NR34 . . . . 111 C4
STUBBING'S GREEN 36 C5
Stubbing's La IP21 . . . . . . 22 E3
Stubbin's La CB8 . . . . 46 B3
Stubbs Cl
   Ipswich IP3 . . . . 140 A1
   9 Manningtree CO11 . . 104 D2
Stubbs Wood NR32 . . . . . 113 B6
Studio Cl IP17 . . . . 58 C8
Studlands Pk Ave CB8 . . . 120 D6
Studlands Ret Pk CB8 . . . 120 F7
Stump's Cross CO9 . . . . . . 89 D1
Stump St IP13 . . . . 127 A3
Sturdee Ave IP3 . . . . 140 B3
Sturgeon Way 22 IP31 . . . . 34 E4
STURMER 133 C2
Sturmer End Ind Est
   CB9 . . . . 133 A3
Sturmer Rd CB9 . . . . 133 D5
Sturston Cl IP24 . . . . 16 C7
STUSTON 20 E1
Stuston La IP21 . . . . 117 B8
Stuston Rd IP21 . . . . 20 E1
STUTTON 105 D6
Stutton CE Prim Sch
   IP9 . . . . 105 D5
Stutton Cl IP9 . . . . 105 D5
Stutton Gn IP9 . . . . 105 E5
Stutton La IP9 . . . . 105 B7
Stutton Rd CO11 . . . . 105 A5
Sub-station Rd IP11 . . . . 152 D2
Sucklings Yd CB9 . . . . 88 E4
SUDBOURNE 86 F8
Sudbourne Rd
   14 Felixstowe IP11 . . . 152 D5
   Orford IP31 . . . . 131 B5
SUDBURY 148 C4
Sudbury Arts Ctr CO10 . . 148 D7
Sudbury Common Lands
   Nature Reserve★ CO10 . 148 B6
Sudbury Rd
   Acton CO10 . . . . 92 B7
   Bulmer CO10 . . . . 91 C3
   Bures St Mary CO8 . . . 101 C5
   3 Felixstowe IP11 . . . . 152 C4
   Gestingthorpe CO9 . . . . 90 F1
   Great Whelnetham IP30 . 64 A6
   Lavenham CO10 . . . . . . 78 D3
   Long Melford CO10 . . . . 91 D6
   Newton CO10 . . . . 92 C4
   Stoke-by-Nayland CO6 . 102 D7
Sudbury Ret Pk CO10 . . . 148 F6
Sudbury Sports Ctr
   CO10 . . . . 148 D7
Sudbury Sta CO10 . . . . . 148 D5
Sudbury Upper Sch & Arts
   Ctr CO10 . . . . 148 D7
Sue Ryder Foundation Mus★
   CO10 . . . . 76 C1
Suffolk Apple Juice & Cider
   Place The★ NR34 . . . . . 24 C7
Suffolk Ave IP31 . . . . 33 D5
Suffolk Bsns Pk IP30 . . . 123 F4
Suffolk Coast National
   Nature Reserve★ IP19 . . 43 A5
Suffolk Coll IP4 . . . . 139 E5
Suffolk Ct 2 IP27 . . . . 5 F1
Suffolk Dr IP12 . . . . 85 D8
Suffolk Horse Mus★
   IP12 . . . . 147 A5
Suffolk Nuffield Hospl The
   IP10 . . . . 141 B4
Suffolk Odyssey Llamas★
   IP19 . . . . 41 D5
Suffolk Owl Sanctuary★
   IP14 . . . . 68 C6
Suffolk Pl IP12 . . . . 147 B5
Suffolk Punch Trust Colony
   Stud The★ IP12 . . . . . 100 A8
Suffolk Rd
   2 Bury St Edmunds
      IP32 . . . . 122 E8
   Ipswich IP4 . . . . 155 C4
   Lowestoft NR32 . . . . . 115 D8
   Sudbury CO10 . . . . . . 148 C6
Suffolk Ret Pk IP1 . . . . . 139 A6
Suffolk Ski Ctr★ IP12 . . . 143 B7
Suffolk Sq 5 CO10 . . . . . 148 C5
Suffolk Way CB8 . . . . . . 120 E5
Suffolk Wildlife Pk★
   NR33 . . . . 11 B1
Suffolk Wr Pk★ IP8 . . . . 134 A5
Sulleys Hill IP7 . . . . 103 D8
Sullivan Rd IP2 . . . . 98 D7
Summerfield Cl IP4 . . . . 140 D8
Summerfield Gdns NR33 . 115 A6
Summerhill Sch IP16 . . . . 129 C7
Summer La IP12 . . . . 85 A6
Summer Rd 8 NR32 . . . . 113 D1
Summers Rd NR32 . . . . . 122 E8

Summit Bsns Pk IP11 . . . . 152 E1
Sumner Rd IP22 . . . . 35 B4
Sunbeam Cl NR33 . . . . . . 114 A3
Suncrest Rise 21 IP14 . . . . 67 A5
Sunderland Rd 2 IP11 . . 153 H11
Sunfield Cl IP4 . . . . 140 B6
Sun La
   Newmarket CB8 . . . . . 121 A3
   Woodbridge IP12 . . . . 147 A5
Sunley Cl NR35 . . . . 110 E8
Sunningdale Ave
   Ipswich IP4 . . . . 140 D5
   Lowestoft NR33 . . . . . 115 B4
   Mildenhall IP28 . . . . . . 116 B4
Sunningdale Dr IP11 . . . . 153 B6
Sunnyfields NR33 . . . . . . 115 A7
Sunnyhill IP12 . . . . 98 D7
Sunnyside
   Bedingham NR35 . . . . . . 7 C8
   Diss IP22 . . . . 20 C3
Sunray Ave IP11 . . . . . . 153 B6
Sun Rd NR35 . . . . 110 D8
Sun St 4 CB7 . . . . 29 C5
Surbiton Rd IP1 . . . . 138 F7
Surrey Cl 8 IP13 . . . . . . 126 C3
Surrey Rd
   Felixstowe IP11 . . . . . 152 F4
   Ipswich IP1 . . . . 139 A6
Surrey St
   6 Lowestoft NR32 . . . 113 D1
   4 Lowestoft NR32 . . . 115 D8
Sussex Crof 9 IP12 . . . . . 85 B3
Sussex Rd NR32 . . . . 113 D3
Sutherland Dr NR32 . . . . 113 B5
SUTTON 85 A1
Sutton Cl
   Bury St Edmunds IP32 . 123 E5
   Woodbridge IP12 . . . . 147 B5
Sutton Hoo★ IP12 . . . . . 147 D5
Sutton Hoo Maze Adventure
   Pk★ IP12 . . . . 146 D5
Sutton Rd IP12 . . . . 147 F5
Suttons Rd 10 NR34 . . . . . 9 F4
SUTTON STREET 99 A7
Swaffham Heath Rd CB8 . 59 A7
Swaffham Rd
   Burwell CB5 . . . . 44 A3
   Mundford IP26 . . . . 6 B8
Swainston Way IP13 . . . . 55 D5
Swallow Cl
   Felixstowe IP11 . . . . . 153 C7
   12 Harwich CO12 . . . 106 F1
Swallow Dr
   Brandon IP27 . . . . 6 A1
   3 Stowmarket IP14 . . 67 A5
Swallowfields NR33 . . . . 114 D3
Swallow Rd IP2 . . . . 138 C3
Swallowtail Cl 1 IP8 . . . 142 E8
Swamp La IP22 . . . . 20 A3
Swan Cl
   Halesworth IP19 . . . . . 118 B3
   29 Martlesham Heath IP5 . 98 A8
   Stowmarket IP14 . . . . 124 A6
Swan Ct 12 CO11 . . . . . . 105 A2
Swanfield CO10 . . . . 91 E8
Swan Gn La IP19 . . . . 40 C5
Swan Gr CB8 . . . . 120 B8
SWAN GREEN 40 B5
Swan Hill IP8 . . . . 138 A2
Swan La
   Bury St Edmunds IP33 . . 154 C1
   Coney Weston IP31 . . . . 34 D8
   Cretingham IP13 . . . . . . 69 E8
   Exning CB8 . . . . 120 B8
   Halesworth IP19 . . . . . . 118 B3
   Haverhill CB9 . . . . 132 E6
   9 Long Melford CO10 . . 91 E8
   North Cove NR34 . . . . . 10 C4
   Redenhall with Harleston
      IP20 . . . . 22 D6
   Westerfield IP6 . . . . . . 135 E4
Swan Meadow CO7 . . . . . 103 E5
Swan Rd IP13 . . . . 54 E7
Swansea Ave IP2 . . . . . . 139 B1
Swan St CO10 . . . . 93 B3
Swatchway Cl 3 IP3 . . . . 144 B8
Swaynes 1 CO7 . . . . 103 E5
Sweden Cl 1 CO12 . . . . . 106 F2
SWEFFLING 56 E2
Swift Cl NR33 . . . . 114 D3
Swift Dr IP14 . . . . 67 A5
SWILLAND 83 A7
Swilltub La IP14 . . . . 52 A4
Swinburne Rd IP1 . . . . . 134 E3
Swine's Gn NR34 . . . . . . 111 C4
SWINGLETON GREEN 79 C2
Swingleton Hill IP7 . . . . . 79 C2
Swinton Cl IP2 . . . . 138 D1
Swonnells Ct NR32 . . . . . 114 D8
Swonnell's Wlk 2 NR32 . 112 D1
Sycamore Ave NR33 . . . . 114 D7
Sycamore Cl
   Beccles NR34 . . . . 111 E3
   7 Great Bricett IP7 . . . 80 D6
   Ipswich IP8 . . . . 138 C1
   Leiston IP16 . . . . 129 C5
Sycamore Dr
   8 Beck Row, Holywell Row &
      Kenny Hill IP28 . . . . 13 B1
   Bury St Edmunds IP32 . . 49 A3
   5 Mildenhall IP28 . . . . 30 A8
   Rendlesham IP12 . . . . . 85 D8
Sycamore Rd
   Stowupland IP14 . . . . . 67 A6
   Sudbury CO10 . . . . . . 148 F4
Sycamore Way
   Brantham CO11 . . . . . . 104 E5
   Diss IP22 . . . . 20 D3

Sycamore Wlk 20 IP27 . . . 13 F2
SYLEHAM 22 A1
Syleham Hall La IP21 . . . . 22 C1
Syleham Rd
   Brockdish IP21 . . . . . . 22 A2
   Syleham IP21 . . . . 38 D8
Sylvester Rd IP16 . . . . . 129 D5
Symonds Rd IP33 . . . . . . 123 C4

T

Tacket St IP4 . . . . 155 C2
Tacon Cl IP23 . . . . 117 C2
Tacon Rd IP11 . . . . 152 E1
Takers La IP14 . . . . 124 E4
Talbot Rd CO10 . . . . 148 D7
Tallboys Cl IP5 . . . . 141 C8
Tallyho Cnr 8 CO7 . . . . . 103 E5
Talmash Gdns IP2 . . . . . 139 A4
Tamage Rd CO10 . . . . 92 B7
Tan House La CB5 . . . . . . 44 A4
Tannersfield Way CB8 . . . 120 F4
Tanners La CB7 . . . . 28 D3
Tanners View IP1 . . . . . . 138 F7
Tannery Bsns Ctr The
   IP14 . . . . 66 E2
Tannery Dr IP33 . . . . 123 B3
Tannery Rd IP14 . . . . 124 C1
TANNINGTON 55 A6
Tannington Long Rd IP13 . 39 D1
Tanns La IP22 . . . . 19 A6
TAN OFFICE 52 F2
TAN OFFICE GREEN 62 C6
Tan Office La
   Chevington IP29 . . . . . 62 C5
   Mendlesham IP14 . . . . . 52 E1
Tansy Cl 5 NR33 . . . . . . 114 F3
Tansy Meadow 3 IP21 . . . 39 D8
Target Hill IP20 . . . . 23 B6
Tarn Hows Cl 1 IP11 . . . 153 D6
Tasmania Rd IP4 . . . . . . 140 D6
Tasman Rd CB9 . . . . 133 A5
Tassel Rd IP32 . . . . 123 F6
TATTINGSTONE 105 B8
Tattingstone CE Prim Sch
   IP9 . . . . 105 B8
TATTINGSTONE WHITE
   HORSE 142 D1
Taunton Cl IP1 . . . . 135 B4
Taunton Rd IP11 . . . . . . 152 F5
Tavern La IP33 . . . . 154 B2
Tavern St
   Ipswich IP1 . . . . 155 B3
   Stowmarket IP14 . . . . 124 D6
Tawneys Ride 2 CO8 . . . 101 D4
Tayberry Pl IP3 . . . . 144 C7
Tayfen Rd IP33 . . . . 154 B3
Tayfen Terr IP33 . . . . 154 B4
Tayler Cl 4 IP7 . . . . 149 D5
Tayler Rd IP7 . . . . 149 E5
Taylor Dr 8 CO11 . . . . . 104 E2
Taylor Rd 3 IP22 . . . . 20 B2
Taylors Farm IP14 . . . . . . 66 C1
Taylors Farm Rd CB9 . . . . 75 A2
Taylors Field CB8 . . . . . . 59 F4
Tea Kettle La CB8 . . . . . . 59 F5
Teal Ave CB7 . . . . 28 C5
Teal Cl IP2 . . . . 138 D3
Teal Wlk IP27 . . . . 6 A1
Teasel Cl CB9 . . . . 132 B7
Tedder Cl 3 IP24 . . . . . . 16 C2
Tedder Rd NR32 . . . . . . 113 B4
Teesdale NR33 . . . . 114 E3
Telesia Ct NR32 . . . . 113 B4
Temperance Pl 8 NR34 . . 111 B5
Templars Ct CB9 . . . . . . 132 C5
Temple Cl IP28 . . . . 31 C4
TEMPLE END
   Foxearth 91 A6
   Little Thurlow 74 C5
Temple End CB9 . . . . 74 C5
Temple Pattle 11 CO11 . . 104 E4
Temple Rd
   Ipswich IP3 . . . . 140 C4
   Isleham CB7 . . . . 29 B4
   Stowmarket IP14 . . . . 124 D5
Ten Bell La 10 CB7 . . . . . 28 C4
Tenby Rd IP2 . . . . 139 B1
Tennyson Cl IP12 . . . . . . 146 E6
Tennyson Rd
   13 Bury St Edmunds IP32 . 48 C5
   Lowestoft NR32 . . . . . 113 D2
   Saxmundham IP17 . . . . 128 B4
Tennyson Way IP24 . . . . . 16 C2
Tenterden Cl 6 NR33 . . . 114 D5
Tenter Field 4 CO7 . . . . 103 E5
Tenter Piece 16 CO10 . . . . 78 D4
Tenth Rd IP10 . . . . 98 A3
Tentree Rd CO10 . . . . 92 C7
Terence Airey Ct 25 IP20 . 22 D6
Tern Cl CB9 . . . . 133 A5
Tern Rd
   Ipswich IP2 . . . . 138 E2
   Stowmarket IP14 . . . . 124 F6
Terr The
   Aldeburgh IP15 . . . . . . 130 E4
   Newmarket CB8 . . . . . 121 A3
   Snape IP17 . . . . 72 D5
Terry Gdns IP5 . . . . 141 E7
Tewkesbury Pl 7 IP31 . . . 49 A5
Thackeray Gr IP14 . . . . . 124 B7
Thackeray Rd IP1 . . . . . 134 E3
Thanet Rd IP4 . . . . 140 B6
Tharp Way CB7 . . . . 29 E1
Thatchers Wlk 4 IP14 . . . 124 D3
Theatre Royal★ IP33 . . . 154 C1
Theatre St IP12 . . . . 146 F5

THEBERTON 58 B4
Theberton Rd IP3 . . . . . . 140 B1
THE BROOK 36 E7
The Buntings 19 IP14 . . . . 67 A5
THE COMMON 81 F3
Thedwastre Cl 8 IP30 . . . 50 F2
Thedwastre Rd IP31 . . . . 49 E3
THE HEATH 105 A7
Theinetham Fen Nature
   Reserve★ IP22 . . . . . . 18 E1
Thellusson Rd 3 IP12 . . . 85 E8
THELNETHAM 18 D1
Thelnetham Rd IP22 . . . . 18 E2
Thelnetham Windmill★
   IP22 . . . . 18 E1
THELVETON 21 A4
THE MARSH 36 E8
Theobald Cl 5 IP6 . . . . . 125 D5
THE PORT OF
   FELIXSTOWE 152 C1
The Sidings 5 IP24 . . . . . 16 C6
THETFORD 16 D5
Thetford Adult Ed Ctr 5
   IP24 . . . . 16 B5
Thetford Cl 16 IP27 . . . . 13 F2
Thetford Cottage Hospl
   IP24 . . . . 16 C6
Thetford Gram Sch IP24 . . 16 B6
Thetford Heath National
   Nature Reserve★ IP24 . 16 A2
Thetford Rd
   Brandon IP27 . . . . 5 F1
   Coney Weston IP31 . . . 34 D8
   Euston IP24 . . . . 16 E2
   Fakenham Magna IP24 . . 33 E8
   Fornham St Martin IP31 . 48 D5
   Garboldisham IP22 . . . 18 C4
   2 Ipswich IP27 . . . . . 139 A7
   Ixworth IP31 . . . . 34 A2
   Ixworth Thorpe IP31 . . . 33 F3
   Mildenhall IP28 . . . . . . 116 E4
   Santon Downham IP27 . . 6 B1
   South Lopham IP22 . . . 19 A4
Thetford Sta IP24 . . . . . . 16 B6
THE WOODLANDS 95 A3
Thieves La IP31 . . . . 49 F8
Thingoe Hill IP32 . . . . . . 154 B4
Third Ave CO10 . . . . 77 B3
Thirlmere Ct IP11 . . . . . 153 D6
Thirlmere Dr IP14 . . . . . 124 B6
Thirlmere Wlk NR32 . . . . 113 A4
Thirlwall Dr CB7 . . . . 29 C1
Thistle Cl IP7 . . . . 138 F4
Thistledown NR33 . . . . . 114 D4
Thistledown Dr IP31 . . . . 34 B2
THISTLEY GREEN 29 E7
Thixendale NR33 . . . . . . 114 E2
Thomas Arne Cl IP14 . . . 124 C8
Thomas Ave IP11 . . . . . . 152 C8
Thomas Bardwell Dr 4
   NR35 . . . . 110 C2
Thomas Bole Cl IP22 . . . . 18 D4
Thomas Cl 20 IP31 . . . . . 34 B1
Thomas La IP33 . . . . 154 B1
Thomas Mills High Sch
   IP13 . . . . 126 A5
Thomas Walls Cl 3 IP13 . 83 E5
Thomas Wolsey Specl Sch
   IP1 . . . . 134 E3
Thomas Young Cl 3
   IP14 . . . . 124 D3
Thompson Cl IP14 . . . . . . 51 D1
Thompson Rd IP1 . . . . . 138 F8
Thompson Wlk IP32 . . . . 122 D7
Thomsons La IP6 . . . . . . 69 A2
Thong Hall Rd IP13 . . . . 127 A5
THORINGTON 42 C4
Thorington Rd IP19 . . . . . 42 A5
THORINGTON STREET . . . 103 A6
Thornbush La IP8 . . . . . . 138 A8
Thorn Cl CB7 . . . . 28 C5
THORNDON 53 B8
Thorndon CE Prim Sch
   IP23 . . . . 53 B8
Thorney Gn Rd IP14 . . . . 67 A6
THORNEY GREEN 67 A7
Thorney Hall Cl IP14 . . . 124 E6
Thorney Rd IP9 . . . . 150 E4
Thornham Cl 5 NR33 . . . 114 F4
THORNHAM MAGNA 37 A2
THORNHAM PARVA 37 B3
Thornham Rd IP23 . . . . . . 36 D2
Thornham Walled Gdn★
   IP23 . . . . 37 A2
Thornhayes Cl IP2 . . . . . 139 A3
Thornhill Rd IP6 . . . . 82 B5
Thornley Dr IP4 . . . . 140 C8
Thornley Rd IP11 . . . . . . 153 C4
Thorns Cl 6 CB8 . . . . 61 E2
Thornton Cl 15 IP27 . . . . 13 F2
Thornton Rd IP33 . . . . . . 122 E2
Thorn Way IP11 . . . . 152 E4
Thorn Wlk IP12 . . . . 85 C2
Thornycroft Gdns NR33 . 114 A3
Thoroughfare IP19 . . . . . 118 B3
Thoroughfare The
   Brundish IP13 . . . . 55 C8
   Harleston IP20 . . . . . . 22 D6
   Wilby IP21 . . . . 39 D1
   10 Woodbridge IP12 . . 147 A5
Thorpe Abbots Rd IP21 . . . 21 D4
THORPE ABBOTTS 21 E2
THORPE COMMON 107 C8
THORPE GREEN 64 F1
Thorpe Hall Rd IP21 . . . . 38 F4
Thorpe La
   Ashfield cum Thorpe IP14 . 69 C8
   Debenham IP14 . . . . . . 53 F1

Thorpe La *continued*
Trimley St Martin IP11 . . . 107 C8
THORPE MORIEUX 79 A8
THORPENESS 73 E6
Thorpeness Windmill★
IP16 . . . . 73 E6
Thorpe Rd
Aldeburgh IP16 . . . . 130 F6
Aldringham IP16 . . . . 129 D2
Thorpe's Hill IP8 . . . . 95 E6
THORPE STREET 35 D8
THRANDESTON 37 B7
Thrandeston Rd IP23 . . . 117 F7
Threadneedle St
Dedham CO7 . . . . 103 F4
🖪 Hadleigh IP7 . . . . 149 D6
Three Marsh La IP18 . . . 119 B6
Throckmorton Rd NR35 . 110 D3
Through Duncans IP12 . . 146 E3
Through Jollys IP5 . . . . . 141 D8
Thunderbird Way IP27 . . 109 F1
Thurleston High Sch
IP1 . . . . 135 A4
Thurleston La IP1 . . . . . . 134 F5
Thurlow CE Prim Sch
CB9 . . . . 74 D6
Thurlow Cl IP17 . . . . 128 B3
Thurlow Ct 🛛 IP14 . . . . . 124 D6
Thurlow Pl 🔢 CB9 . . . . . 132 F6
Thurlow Rd CB9 . . . . 74 D7
Thurmans La IP11 . . . . . . 152 B8
Thurne Rd NR33 . . . . 114 F5
THURSTON 49 E3
Thurston CE Prim Sch
IP31 . . . . 49 E4
Thurston Com Coll IP31 . 49 D4
Thurston Ct 🖪 IP11 . . . . 152 C4
THURSTON END 76 D6
Thurston La CO10 . . . . . . 76 C7
Thurston Rd
🖪 Beyton IP30 . . . . 49 F2
Lowestoft NR32 . . . . 113 D2
Thurston IP31 . . . . 49 E3
Thurston Sta IP31 . . . . . . 49 D3
THWAITE 52 F7
Thwaite Rd
Ditchingham NR35 . . . . . 110 C7
Thorndon IP23 . . . . 53 B8
Wickham Skeith IP23 . . . 52 D7
Tibbenham's Score 🖪
NR32 . . . . 3 D4
Tiberius Cl CB9 . . . . 133 B5
Tide Mill★ IP12 . . . . 147 B4
Tide Mill Way IP12 . . . . . 147 A4
Tideway NR32 . . . . 114 E8
Tidys Ct IP33 . . . . 154 B1
Tiger Hill Nature Reserve★
CO8 . . . . 101 E6
Tiggins La IP17 . . . . 128 D8
TILBURY GREEN 89 E4
TILBURY JUXTA CLARE . . . 90 A3
Tilbury Rd
Great Yeldham CO9 . . . . . 90 A2
Ridgewell CO9 . . . . 89 E4
Tile Barn La CO11 . . . . . . 104 B1
Tillbrooks Hill CB8 . . . . . 61 B1
Timperley Cl IP7 . . . . 149 D7
Timperley Rd IP7 . . . . . . 149 E7
Timperleys IP8 . . . . 95 C6
TIMWORTH 48 D8
TIMWORTH GREEN 48 D7
Tinabrook Cl IP2 . . . . 138 E1
Tinker Brook IP13 . . . . . . 71 F5
Tinkers La NR34 . . . . 10 D1
Tinker's La Hadleigh IP7 . 149 D5
Tivetshall St Mary NR15 . 21 C3
Tinker St CO12 . . . . 106 C1
Tintern Cl 🖪 IP2 . . . . . . 139 A2
Tippet Ave IP14 . . . . 124 C8
Titchwell Dr 🛛 IP3 . . . . 144 D8
Tithe Ave IP28 . . . . 30 B8
Tithe Cl CB8 . . . . 46 C3
Title Rd IP17 . . . . 58 A6
Titlow Rd 🔢 IP20 . . . . . . 22 D6
TOAD ROW 10 F1
Toad Row NR34 . . . . 10 F1
Todd Way IP32 . . . . 49 A3
Todhunter Ave NR34 . . . . .9 B6
Tog La CO6 . . . . 102 D2
Tokio Rd IP4 . . . . 140 A6
Tollemache Bsns Pk IP7 . 80 E4
Toller Cl IP21 . . . . 131 C3
Toller Rd IP3 . . . . 139 E3
Tolley Cobbold St 🖪
IP28 . . . . 30 A8
Tollgate La 🖪 IP32 . . . . 123 A8
Tollgate Prim Sch IP32 . 122 F8
Toll Gate Rd 🖪 IP9 . . . . 150 E3
Tolworth Rd IP14 . . . . . . 140 A6
Tom Jennings Cl CB8 . . . 120 F5
Tomline Ct IP10 . . . . 145 C5
Tomline Rd
Felixstowe IP11 . . . . 153 A3
Ipswich IP3 . . . . 140 A5
Tomline Wlk IP33 . . . . . . 122 B6
Tommy Flowers Dr IP5 . . 141 E7
Tomo Bsns Pk IP14 . . . . 124 F6
Tomo Ind Est IP14 . . . . . 124 E6
Tomtit's La IP14 . . . . 51 B2
Tonning St NR32 . . . . 113 C1
Tooks Comm La NR34 . . . .8 F1
Toper La IP33 . . . . 154 C1
Toppesfield Cl 🖪 IP7 . . 149 D5
Toppesfield Gdns IP7 . . 149 D5
Top Rd Hasketon IP13 . . 146 B8
Rattlesden IP30 . . . . 65 D5
St Andrew, Ilketshall NR34 . . 8 E1
Wingfield IP21 . . . . 39 A7

Top St IP12 . . . . 146 C2
Tortoiseshell Cl 🖪 IP9 . 142 E8
TOSTOCK 50 B2
Tostock Rd IP30 . . . . 49 F2
Tottington La IP22 . . . . . . 20 B2
Tovells 🖪 IP13 . . . . 84 F7
Tovell's Rd IP4 . . . . 139 F6
Tower Ct 🔢 CB9 . . . . . . 132 C5
Tower Field Rd IP12 . . . . 85 D7
TOWER HILL 107 C3
Tower Hill NR34 . . . . 111 C3
Tower Mill La IP7 . . . . . . 149 E6
Tower Mill Rd
Bungay NR35 . . . . 110 B3
Ipswich IP1 . . . . 138 F7
Tower Ramparts IP1 . . . . 155 B3
Tower Ramparts Sh Ctr
IP1 . . . . 155 B3
Tower Rd Felixstowe IP11 . 152 F4
Lowestoft NR33 . . . . 115 A2
Tower St IP1 . . . . 155 B3
Town End Cl CB9 . . . . . . 132 D7
Town Farm Cl IP20 . . . . . 23 C3
Town Farm Est IP12 . . . . 131 B3
Town Gn IP14 . . . . 124 C6
Town Hall Galleries★
IP1 . . . . 155 B3
Town House Cnr IP14 . . . 68 F7
Town House La IP22 . . . . 35 D6
Townhouse Rd IP31 . . . . 35 C1
Town La IP14 . . . . 53 A3
Townlands Dr NR34 . . . . 111 B3
Townlane Rd IP33 . . . . . 123 B1
Townsend CB7 . . . . 28 C5
Townsend Way NR32 . . . 113 A6
Town Stps IP15 . . . . 130 E4
Toyse Cl 🖪 CB5 . . . . 44 B6
Toyse La CB5 . . . . 44 A6
Trafalgar Cl IP4 . . . . 139 F6
Trafalgar Rd CO10 . . . . . 148 E2
Trafalgar St
🖪 Lowestoft NR32 . . . . 113 C1
Lowestoft NR32 . . . . 115 C8
Sudbury CO10 . . . . 148 E8
Trafford Cl 🛛 IP14 . . . . 51 E1
Tramere Gr IP1 . . . . 134 F2
Traveller's Hill (Tumuli)★
IP28 . . . . 32 E5
Travellers Rd IP13 . . . . . . 69 E5
Traverse The IP33 . . . . . 154 B2
Treetops IP11 . . . . 152 E7
Treeview IP14 . . . . 124 B6
Trefoil Cl IP2 . . . . 138 F4
Tremlett La IP5 . . . . 141 F7
Trenchard Sq 🛽 IP26 . . . . 4 D5
Trent Rd
🖪 Bury St Edmunds IP32 . . 48 C3
Ipswich IP3 . . . . 139 F2
Trevethan Cl IP32 . . . . . . 122 E7
Triangle Yd 🖪 NR32 . . . 113 E2
TRIMLEY LOWER
STREET. 107 C7
Trimley Marshes Nature
Reserve★ IP11 . . . . 107 B6
Trimley Rd IP10 . . . . 98 D2
TRIMLEY ST MARTIN 107 C8
Trimley St Martin Prim Sch
IP11 . . . . 98 D1
TRIMLEY ST MARY 152 C8
Trimley St Mary Prim Sch
IP11 . . . . 152 C8
Trimley Sta IP11 . . . . 152 C7
Trinity Ave
Felixstowe IP11 . . . . 152 B3
Mildenhall IP28 . . . . 116 C5
Trinity Cl Fordham CB7 . . 29 B1
Ipswich IP5 . . . . 140 F7
🔢 Manningtree CO11 . . 104 E2
🔢 Southwold IP18 . . . . 119 D5
Woodbridge IP12 . . . . . . 146 D3
Trinity Distribution Pk
IP11 . . . . 152 B4
Trinity Dr CB8 . . . . 121 D3
Trinity Gdns 🖪 NR35 . . 110 B4
Trinity Gild 🖪 CO10 . . . 78 D7
Trinity Link CB9 . . . . 132 E7
Trinity Mews IP33 . . . . . 154 A3
Trinity Rd
Lowestoft NR32 . . . . 113 E1
Manningtree CO11 . . . . . 104 E2
Trinity St Bungay NR35 . . 110 B4
Rose Hill IP3 . . . . 139 E4
🔢 Southwold IP18 . . . . 119 D5
Trinity Wlk IP14 . . . . 67 A7
Triple Plea La NR35 . . . . . .7 B3
Triple Plea Rd NR35 . . . . .7 B3
Troon Ct 🖪 IP28 . . . . 48 C6
Troon Gdns 🖪 IP4 . . . . 136 B1
Trossachs The 🖪 NR32 . 112 D2
TROSTON 33 D3
Troston Rd IP31 . . . . 33 D3
Trotting Horse La CB8 . . . 75 A8
Trott's La CO10 . . . . 92 F3
Trunch Hill IP20 . . . . 7 A3
Trunch Rd IP20 . . . . .7 B2
Trundley Cl CB9 . . . . 132 D7
Tubby Walk NR32 . . . . . . 112 F5
TUDDENHAM 30 F2
Tuddenham Ave IP4 . . . . 139 E7
Tuddenham CE Prim Sch
IP28 . . . . 30 F2
Tuddenham Cnr IP28 . . . 46 E6
Tuddenham La IP5 . . . . . 136 B2
Tuddenham Rd
Barton Mills IP28 . . . . . . 116 F2
Ipswich IP4 . . . . 155 C4

Tuddenham Rd *continued*
Westerfield IP4 . . . . 136 A3
TUDDENHAM ST MARTIN . 136 C5
Tudor Ave IP22 . . . . 20 B3
Tudor CE VC Prim Sch
CO10 . . . . 148 C7
Tudor Cl Chedburgh IP29 . 62 D5
🖪 Framlingham IP13 . . 126 C3
🖪 Shotley Gate IP9 . . . 107 A5
Sudbury CO10 . . . . 148 C7
Tudor Ct Ipswich IP4 . . . 155 C3
🖪 Occold IP23 . . . . 37 F1
Westhorpe IP14 . . . . 51 E7
Tudor Gn CO10 . . . . 148 C8
Tudor Rd CO10 . . . . 148 C8
Tudor Wlk
🖪 Honington IP31 . . . . . 33 D5
🔢 Lowestoft NR33 . . . . 114 E4
Tuffen La IP22 . . . . 35 D8
Tuffields Rd IP29 . . . . 63 B3
Tuffs Rd IP23 . . . . 117 D4
Tumbril La IP21 . . . . 22 A3
Tunbeck Cl IP20 . . . . 23 A7
Tunbeck Rd IP20 . . . . 23 A8
Tunbridge Cl 🛛 CB5 . . . 44 A5
Tunneys La NR35 . . . . . . 110 C8
Tuns La IP33 . . . . 154 C1
TUNSTALL 71 F2
Tunstall Dr NR32 . . . . . . 112 F4
Tunstall Gn IP12 . . . . 71 F2
Turino Ave IP12 . . . . 98 B8
Turin St IP2 . . . . 155 B1
Turin Way 🛛 NR31 . . . . . 3 C6
Turkentine Cl 🔢 CO10 . . 92 B3
Turkeyhall La IP14 . . . . . . 51 F6
Turnberry Cl 🖪 NR33 . . 114 F4
Turnberry Dr 🔢 IP28 . . . 48 C6
Turnbull Cl IP5 . . . . 141 E7
Turner Ave 🖪 CO11 . . . . 104 D2
Turner Cl
Ditchingham NR35 . . . . . 110 C7
Haverhill CB9 . . . . 132 B7
🖪 Lowestoft NR32 . . . . 113 C6
Sudbury CO10 . . . . 148 E8
Turner Gdns IP12 . . . . . . 146 D3
Turner Gr IP5 . . . . 141 D8
Turner La 🖪 IP14 . . . . . . 51 C1
Turner Rd Ipswich IP3 . . 144 A8
Stowmarket IP14 . . . . . . 124 B7
Turn La IP12 . . . . 147 A4
Turnpike Cl CB9 . . . . 74 B2
Turnpike Rd
Chippenham CB8 . . . . . . 45 F8
Red Lodge IP28 . . . . 30 B1
Woodbridge IP12 . . . . . . 147 B6
Turnstile La 🔢 NR35 . . . 110 B4
Turnstone Cl 🛛 IP28 . . . 116 D4
Turnstone Dr IP32 . . . . . . 49 A3
Turret La IP4 . . . . 155 B2
Tutelina Rd IP30 . . . . 64 A6
Tut Hill IP28 . . . . 48 B5
Tutt Hill (Tumulus)★
IP24 . . . . 16 D4
Tuyar Wlk CB8 . . . . 120 E8
Tweed CB8 . . . . 45 F3
Twelve Acre App IP5 . . . 141 B7
Twinnings The IP14 . . . . 124 C3
Twin Oak Dr IP13 . . . . 56 B7
Twiss Cl 🖪 IP22 . . . . 20 A3
Two Acres IP5 . . . . 150 F4
Two House Cl IP13 . . . . . 127 C4
Two Pole Dro CB7 . . . . . . 28 A7
Tydemans Ct 🖪 IP14 . . . 124 D6
Tye Gn CO10 . . . . 77 A3
Tye La IP8 . . . . 81 D2
Tylers Gn IP11 . . . . 152 C7
Tyler St
🖪 Harwich CO12 . . . . . 106 F3
Ipswich IP2 . . . . 155 B1
Tylers Way 🖪 IP14 . . . . 124 C5
Tymmes Pl IP13 . . . . 146 C8
Tyrone Cl IP1 . . . . 134 D2

U

UBBESTON 40 E4
UBBESTON GREEN 40 D3
Ubbeston Way NR33 . . . 114 F4
UFFORD 84 F7
Ufford Pl
🔢 Haverhill CB9 . . . . . . 132 F6
🖪 Ufford IP13 . . . . 84 F7
Ufford Rd Bredfield IP13 . 84 D7
Eyke IP12 . . . . 85 B6
UGGESHALL 25 F3
Uggeshall Cl NR32 . . . . . 113 A5
Ullswater NR32 . . . . 114 D2
Ullswater Ave 🛛 IP11 . . 153 D7
Ullswater Rd IP12 . . . . . . 71 C2
Ulster Ave IP1 . . . . 134 D1
Una Rd CO10 . . . . 106 F2
Uncle's La IP19 . . . . 24 B6
Undercliff Rd E IP11 . . . 153 C4
Undercliff Rd W IP11 . . . 153 A3
Underhill IP14 . . . . 124 C5
Underwood Cl NR32 . . . 113 A6
UNDLEY 13 C4
Undley Cl IP27 . . . . 109 B5
Undley Rd IP27 . . . . 109 B4
Unicorn Pl IP33 . . . . 123 C6
Union Hill IP7 . . . . 79 A8
Union La Lowestoft NR32 . 112 F5
Wortham IP22 . . . . 20 A1
Union Pl 🖪 NR33 . . . . . 115 C7
Union St Lowestoft NR32 . 113 C1
Onehouse IP14 . . . . 66 C1
Stowmarket IP14 . . . . . . 124 A7

Union St E IP14 . . . . 124 D6
Union St W IP14 . . . . . . 124 D6
Union St IP14 . . . . 155 C3
Unitarian Meeting House★
Bury St Edmunds IP33 . . 154 B2
Ipswich IP1 . . . . 155 B2
Unity Rd IP14 . . . . 124 D5
Unity St IP3 . . . . 139 E4
UPEND 60 F5
UPGATE STREET 7 B6
Upland Rd
🖪 Occold IP23 . . . . 37 F1
Thorpe IP16 . . . . 73 F6
Uplands Cl CO10 . . . . . . 148 C7
Uplands Cres CO10 . . . . 148 C7
Uplands Mid Sch CO10 . 148 D7
Uplands Rd 🖪 Aldringham cum
Thorpe IP16 . . . . 73 F6
Sudbury CO10 . . . . 148 C7
Uplands Rd N NR33 . . . . 114 D5
Uplands Rd S NR33 . . . . 114 C3
Uplands The Aldringham cum
Thorpe IP16 . . . . 73 E6
Beccles NR34. . . . . 111 D4
Uplands Way Diss IP22 . . 20 C3
Halesworth IP19 . . . . . . 118 B5
Upper Ave IP19 . . . . 118 B5
Upper Barclay St 🖪 . . . 155 C2
Upper Brook La IP20 . . . 22 B4
Upper Brook St IP4 . . . . 155 B3
Upper Burnthouse La
IP20 . . . . 22 A5
Upper Cavendish St IP3 . 140 A5
Upper E St CO10 . . . . . . 148 D6
Upper Farm Rd CO10 . . . 89 E4
Upperfield Dr IP11 . . . . . 153 C6
Upper Grange Rd NR34 . 111 A4
UPPER GREEN 46 E3
Upper Harmans La IP20 . 22 B5
Upper High St IP1 . . . . . 155 B3
UPPER HOLTON 118 E7
UPPER LAYHAM 149 F2
Upper Melton Terr 🔢
IP12 . . . . 84 E6
Upper Moorfield Rd
IP12 . . . . 146 F6
Upper Oakley IP23 . . . . . 117 F8
Upper Olland St NR35 . . 110 B3
Upper Orwell St IP4 . . . . 155 C2
Upper Rd CO10 . . . . 101 C8
Upper Rose La IP22 . . . . 20 C1
Upper St
Brome Street IP23 . . . . . 117 F8
Gissing IP22 . . . . 20 F8
Layham IP7 . . . . 149 F1
Stansfield CO10 . . . . 76 C6
Stratford St Mary CO7 . . 103 E5
UPPER STREET Baylham . . 81 E6
Dickleburgh and Rushall . 21 C2
Stansfield 76 C6
Stutton 105 B5
UPPER TOWN 49 E7
Upper Tumbril La IP20 . . 22 A4
UPPER WEYBREAD 22 B2
Upsher Green IP28 . . . . . 92 D6
Upsons Way IP5 . . . . 141 E8
Up St IP31 . . . . 34 C4
UPTHORPE 34 F3
Upthorpe Rd IP31 . . . . . . 34 F4
Upton Cl IP4 . . . . 139 E6
Upton Pl IP16 . . . . 129 C5
Urban Rd IP16 . . . . 129 D6
Uvedale Gdns IP6 . . . . . 125 E4
Uxbridge Cres IP3 . . . . . 140 C1

V

Vale Ct IP27 . . . . .5 E4
Vale La
Bury St Edmunds IP33 . . 123 C3
Kersey IP7 . . . . 94 A6
Stutton IP9 . . . . 105 A6
Valentine Way IP30 . . . . . 64 F7
Valerian Rise 🖪 IP24 . . . 16 D6
Valiant Rd IP31 . . . . 33 D4
Valiant St 🖪 IP28 . . . . . 13 B1
Valley Cl
🛛 Brantham CO11 . . . . 104 C4
Halesworth IP19 . . . . . . 118 E4
Ipswich IP1 . . . . 135 C1
Valley Farm Camargue
Horses★ IP13 . . . . 127 A8
Valley Farm La IP7 . . . . . . 94 E5
Valley Farm Rd IP12 . . . 147 B8
Valley Farm Vineyards★
IP19 . . . . 24 C2
Valley La Battisford IP14 . 80 F8
Buxhall IP14 . . . . 65 F3
Wherstead IP9 . . . . 143 A3
Valley Rd Battisford IP14 . 66 E1
Chilton CO10 . . . . 92 C5
Great Bricett IP7 . . . . 80 D6
Harwich CO12 . . . . 106 E1
Ipswich IP1 . . . . 135 B1
Leiston IP16 . . . . 129 E6
Little Blakenham IP8 . . . 81 E4
Valley View CO10 . . . . . 77 C4
Valleyview Dr IP4 . . . . . . 140 F4
Valley Wash CO10 . . . . . . 75 D4
Valley Way CB8 . . . . 120 E3
Valley Wlk IP11 . . . . 152 F5
Vallibus Cl 🖪 NR32 . . . . 112 E4
Van Dyck Cl 🖪 NR32 . . 113 B6
Vandyck Rd 🛽 IP3 . . . . 144 A8
Vanners Rd CB9 . . . . 132 E5
Vaughan St IP2 . . . . 155 B1
Vaunces La IP21 . . . . 21 E4
Vaunce's La IP21 . . . . 21 E4
Vaux Ave 🔢 CO12 . . . . . 106 F1

Velda Cl NR33 . . . . 114 F4
Ventris Cl IP2 . . . . 138 D5
Verdons La IP21 . . . . 39 E4
Verdure Cl 🛛 NR32 . . . . 112 F5
Vere Gdns IP1 . . . . 135 C2
Vermeer Cl 🖪 NR32 . . . 113 B6
Vermont Cres IP4 . . . . . . 155 C4
Vermont Rd IP4 . . . . 155 C4
Verneuil Ave IP14 . . . . . . 124 D3
Vernon St 🖪 IP2 . . . . . . 155 B1
Vetch Wlk CB9 . . . . 132 B7
Veyses End 🖪 CO7 . . . . 103 E5
Viburnum Gn NR32 . . . . 113 C2
Vicarage Cl CB8 . . . . 59 E5
Vicarage Field CO10 . . . 148 F3
Vicarage Gdns
🔢 Debenham IP14 . . . . 53 F2
🖪 Mildenhall IP28 . . . . 116 A4
Vicarage Hill 🖪 IP12 . . . 147 A5
Vicarage La Acton CO10 . 92 A6
Bramford IP8 . . . . 134 B1
Bungay NR35 . . . . 110 E3
Wherstead IP9 . . . . 143 B5
Woodditton CB8 . . . . 60 B6
Vicarage Rd
Belcham St Paul CO10 . . 90 D5
Felixstowe IP11 . . . . 152 D4
Laxfield IP13 . . . . 40 E3
Newmarket CB8 . . . . 121 B3
Thetford IP24 . . . . 16 C6
Wingfield IP21 . . . . 39 A3
Winston IP14 . . . . 54 A1
Victor Charles Cl IP27 . . . .5 E3
Victoria Cl 🖪 IP31 . . . . . 49 E4
Victoria Cres 🛛 CO11 . . 104 E2
Victoria Hill IP23 . . . . . . 117 C4
Victoria Mill Rd IP13 . . . 126 B2
Victoria Rd
Aldeburgh IP15 . . . . 130 E4
Diss IP22 . . . . 20 D2
Felixstowe IP11 . . . . 152 F3
Haverhill CB9. . . . . 132 B5
🖪 Lowestoft NR33 . . . . 114 E7
Stowmarket IP14 . . . . . . 124 C7
Woodbridge IP12 . . . . . . 147 A5
Victoria St
Bury St Edmunds IP33 . . 154 A2
Felixstowe IP11 . . . . 153 A4
🖪 Harwich CO12 . . . . . 107 B2
Ipswich IP1 . . . . 139 A6
🔢 Southwold IP18 . . . . 119 D5
Victoria Terr
🖪 Fressingfield IP21 . . . 39 E8
Lowestoft NR33 . . . . 115 D7
Victoria Way CB8 . . . . . . 120 E7
Victor Rd IP31 . . . . 33 D4
Victory Cl IP33 . . . . 123 C2
Victory Ct IP14 . . . . 124 D4
Victory Rd Ipswich IP4 . . 140 A7
Leiston IP16 . . . . 129 C5
View Point Rd IP13 . . . . 153 H10
Viking Cl IP12 . . . . 84 B1
Viking Hts IP12 . . . . 84 B1
Viking Rd IP14 . . . . 124 C5
Village Way
Lowestoft NR32 . . . . 113 B5
Waldringfield IP12 . . . . . . 98 D7
Villa Hill IP12 . . . . 99 B7
Vincent Cl Exning CB8 . . 120 E7
🖪 Feltwell IP26 . . . . 4 E5
Ipswich IP1 . . . . 138 E8
Vincent Drift IP5 . . . . . . 141 F7
Vince's Rd IP22 . . . . 20 D2
Vine Cl IP31 . . . . 17 E1
Vinefields The IP33 . . . . 154 C3
Vine Rd IP6 . . . . 69 C2
Vinery Cl IP13 . . . . 127 C5
Vinery Rd IP33 . . . . 122 F3
Vinesse Rd CO6 . . . . 102 B2
Vines The IP17 . . . . 128 D7
Vineway The 🛛 CO12 . . 107 A2
Vine Wlk IP9 . . . . 150 E3
Violet Cl
Bury St Edmunds IP32 . . 123 F5
Ipswich IP7 . . . . 138 F4
Violet Hill Rd IP14 . . . . . 124 C7
Virginia Rd 🔢 IP28 . . . . 30 A8
Virginia St IP2 . . . . 139 D3
Viscount Cl IP22 . . . . 20 E2
Vyces Rd IP13 . . . . 126 B3

W

Wacker Field Rd 🛽 IP12 . 85 E8
Waddesdon Rd 🖪 CO12 . 107 B2
Wadd La IP17 . . . . 72 C6
Waddlegoose La IP14 . . . 54 D2
Waddling La NR32 . . . . . 112 A7
Wade Cres CO10 . . . . 92 E8
Wades Gr IP5 . . . . 141 E7
Wade's La Raydon IP7 . . 94 E1
Shotley IP9 . . . . 106 E2
Wades Wood 🖪 IP30. . . . 50 D1
Wadgate Rd IP11 . . . . . . 152 E4
Wadhurst Rd IP3 . . . . . . 140 D3
Waggoners Ct IP12 . . . . 146 F5
Wagtail Dr IP32 . . . . 123 F7
WAINFORD 110 D5
Wainford Cl 🖪 NR34 . . . .9 C4
Wainford Rd NR35 . . . . . 110 E5
Wainwright Cl 🛛 NR32 . 113 A6
Wainwright Gdns IP6 . . . 81 F5
Wainwright Way IP5 . . . 141 D8

Wake Ave IP28 . . . . 116 C5
Wakeshall La CO10. . . . . . . 90 B4
WALBERSWICK. 119 A2
Walberswick Visitor Ctr★
IP18 . . . . 119 B2
Walberswick Way 8
NR32 . . . . 113 A3
WALCOT GREEN. 20 D4
Walcot Rd IP22. . . . . 20 D3
Walcot Rise IP22. . . . . 20 D3
Walcott Wlk NR33. . . . . . . 115 B5
Waldegrave Cl 23 CO11. . . . 104 C3
Waldegrave Rd CO11. . . . . 104 D2
Waldingfield Rd
10 Acton CO10. . . . . 92 B7
Chilton IP7. . . . . 148 F8
WALDRINGFIELD 98 D7
WALDRINGFIELD HEATH . . 98 C7
Waldringfield Prim Sch
IP12 . . . . 98 D7
Waldringfield Rd IP12. . . . . 84 C1
WALES END 76 D4
Walker Chase IP5. . . . . 141 C6
Walker Cl IP4 . . . . 140 C5
Walker Gdns NR34 . . . . 26 E5
Walks The NR34 . . . . 10 A8
Walk The Bacton IP14. . . . . 51 D5
Beccles NR34. . . . . 111 B6
Ipswich IP1. . . . . 155 B3
Walton IP11. . . . . 152 C6
Wallace Rd IP1. . . . . 138 E8
Walled Gdn The★ IP17 . . . 72 B8
Waller's Gr IP22. . . . . 138 F4
Wall La CO11 . . . . 105 E2
Wallow La IP7. . . . . 80 D4
Walls The CO11. . . . . 104 E2
Walmer Cl NR33 . . . . 115 A5
Walmer Rd NR33. . . . . 115 A5
Walnut Cl Acton CO10. . . . . 92 B8
Felixstowe IP11. . . . . 153 D7
Hopton IP22. . . . . 18 C1
13 Lakenheath IP27 . . . . . 13 F2
Walnut Gr IP28 . . . . 30 A4
Walnuts La IP13 . . . . 127 B5
Walnuts The
Beccles NR34. . . . . 111 E4
3 Ufford IP13. . . . . 84 F7
Walnut Tree Ave IP12. . . . . 85 D8
Walnut Tree Cl 4 IP8. . . . 134 A2
Walnuttree Hospl CO10. . . 148 B5
Walnut Tree La
2 Harkstead IP9 . . . . 106 A5
Sudbury CO10 . . . . 148 B5
Walnut Tree Meadow
IP14. . . . . 68 B6
Walnut Tree Wlk IP14. . . . 124 C6
WALPOLE 41 C5
Walpole Cl NR35. . . . . 110 D7
Walpole La IP19 . . . . 41 D5
Walpole Rd
Bramfield IP19. . . . . 41 E4
Halesworth IP19 . . . . 118 A1
WALSHAM LE WILLOWS . . 35 C2
Walsham Le Willows CE VC
Prim Sch IP31. . . . . 35 C2
Walsham Rd
Finningham IP14 . . . . 36 A1
6 Ixworth IP31. . . . . 34 B1
Wattisfield IP22. . . . . 35 B5
Walsingham Cl 11 CO10. . . 92 B3
Walsingham Rd IP33. . . . . 122 D3
Walters Cl 9 NR31. . . . . . . .3 B7
Waltham Cl IP2. . . . . 139 A2
WALTON 152 F6
Walton Ave IP11. . . . . 152 C3
Walton Cl
5 Fordham CB7. . . . . 29 A1
1 Stowmarket IP14. . . . . 124 B8
Walton Rd NR32 . . . . 113 D1
Wamil Rd IP28. . . . . 30 B5
Wamil Way IP28 . . . . 116 B4
WANGFORD 26 B2
Wangford Rd
Lakenheath IP27 . . . . 13 F7
Reydon IP18 . . . . 26 D1
Southwold IP18 . . . . 119 B8
Uggeshall NR34. . . . . 26 A3
Westhall IP19 . . . . 25 B4
Wannock Cl NR33. . . . . . . 114 D4
Wantisden Cnr IP12. . . . . . 86 A6
Ward Cl IP7. . . . . 149 D8
WARD GREEN. 51 E3
Wardlaw Ct 10 IP14. . . . . . 53 F2
Wardley Cl IP2. . . . . 138 D1
Wardley Hill Rd NR35 . . . . . 8 D8
Ward Rd IP8. . . . . 138 B2
Ward's View IP5. . . . . 141 E8
Wareham Ave IP3. . . . . 140 D3
Warene Cl 3 IP13 . . . . 126 C3
Ware Rd IP7. . . . . 80 B6
Warham Rd CO12. . . . . 106 F1
Warner Way CO10. . . . . . . 148 E6
Warren Chase IP5. . . . . 141 E7
Warren Cl Elmswell IP30. . . 50 E2
Lakenheath IP27 . . . . 109 D5
Warren Ct 14 CB9. . . . . . . 132 C5
WARREN HEATH 140 D2
Warren Heath Ave IP3. . . . 140 D2
Warren Heath Rd IP3 . . . . . 140 D2
Warren Hill La IP15. . . . . . 130 D7
Warren Hill Rd IP12. . . . . . 130 C7
Warren La Arwarton IP9. . . 106 D6
Elmswell IP30. . . . . 50 E2
27 Martlesham Heath IP5. . 98 A8
Woolpit IP30. . . . . 50 F1

Warren Loke NR31. . . . . .2 B7
Warren Rd
Great Yarmouth NR31 . . . . .3 B8
Herringswell CB8. . . . . . . 46 A8
Hopton on Sea NR31. . . . . 3 C7
Lowestoft NR32. . . . . 113 D4
Red Lodge IP28. . . . . 30 C1
Warren Sch NR33. . . . . . . 114 C6
Warren's La NR34. . . . . 10 A2
Warren The IP18 . . . . 119 E8
Warrington Rd IP1. . . . . . . 155 A4
Warrington St CB8. . . . . . . 121 A2
Warwick Ave
Halesworth IP19 . . . . 118 C5
Woodbridge IP12. . . . . . . 146 F6
Warwick Ct 10 CB9. . . . . . 132 C6
Warwick Rd IP4 . . . . 139 E6
WASHBROOK 95 F5
WASHBROOK STREET. 95 F6
Washington St 4 IP28. . . . 30 A8
Wash La
Beccles NR34. . . . . 111 B4
Boxford CO10. . . . . 93 D2
Burgh St Peter NR34. . . . . 10 C8
Dennington IP13. . . . . 55 E6
Frostenden NR34. . . . . . . 26 C3
Great Finborough IP14 . . . 124 A5
Hinderclay IP22. . . . . 35 E8
Kessingland NR33. . . . . . . 11 C1
Mendlesham IP14 . . . . . . 52 E3
Redgrave IP22. . . . . 19 D1
Reydon IP18 . . . . 26 D2
Shelfanger IP22. . . . . 20 B6
Spexhall IP19. . . . . 118 A7
Stanton IP31 . . . . 34 F3
St Peter, South Elmham
NR35. . . . . 23 F7
Topcroft NR35. . . . . 7 A8
Wenhaston with Mells Hamlet
IP19 . . . . 118 E1
Westleton IP17 . . . . 58 B8
Witnesham IP6 . . . . 83 A6
WASHMERE GREEN 78 D2
Wassicks La IP14. . . . . 51 E3
Watch House Hill NR35. . . 110 E4
Watercourse The CB8. . . . . 121 A4
Water Farm Dr IP7. . . . . . . 94 E1
Waterford Rd IP1. . . . . 134 D2
Waterhead La IP12 . . . . . . 147 D8
Watering Cl 1 IP8. . . . . 81 C3
Watering La IP17 . . . . 72 C7
Watering Rd IP21. . . . . 38 D5
Water La
Athelington IP21. . . . . . . 38 F1
Barnardiston CB9. . . . . . . 75 B4
Barnham IP24 . . . . 16 C2
Botesdale IP22. . . . . 35 F5
3 Bures CO8. . . . . 101 C5
Cavendish CO10. . . . . 76 E1
Debenham IP14. . . . . 53 F2
Denston CB8. . . . . 75 F7
Garboldisham IP22. . . . . . 18 D4
Great Bradley CB8. . . . . . 74 C8
Great Horkesley CO6. . . . 102 C4
Great Whelnetham IP30 . . 64 A6
Helions Bumpstead CB9. . . 88 B4
Kersey IP7. . . . . 94 A6
Layham IP7. . . . . 149 E1
Lowestoft NR32. . . . . 113 C2
Polstead CO6. . . . . 102 F8
Steeple Bumpstead CB9. . . 88 D3
Sturmer CB9 . . . . 133 D3
Thelnetham IP22. . . . . . . 18 E1
Thornham Magna IP23 . . . 37 A1
Weybread IP21. . . . . 22 D4
Worlingworth IP13 . . . . . . 54 D8
WATERLOO
Aldeby 9 E8
Dickleburgh and Rushall. . . 20 F2
Waterloo Ave
Leiston IP16 . . . . 129 B6
4 Roydon IP22. . . . . 20 A3
Waterloo Cl CB8. . . . . 120 D8
Waterloo Rd
4 Ipswich IP1. . . . . 139 A7
Lowestoft NR33. . . . . 115 D7
Sotterley NR34. . . . . 26 A7
Watermill Cl IP7. . . . . 149 E2
Water Mill La IP21. . . . . . . 38 C8
Watermill Rd IP12. . . . . . . 98 C5
Water Run The IP7. . . . . . . 79 F7
Waters Ave NR33 . . . . 114 C3
Waterside CB7. . . . . 29 C5
Water Steet CO10. . . . . 78 D4
Waterworks Rd 12 IP28. . . 30 A8
Waterworks St IP4. . . . . . . 155 C2
Watery La IP13 . . . . 146 A8
Watson Cl IP33 . . . . 123 B2
Watsons Cl 3 NR31. . . . . . 3 C7
Watson's Hill IP7 . . . . 79 F1
Watson Way IP12. . . . . 99 E4
Watt Cl IP12. . . . . 99 E4
WATTISFIELD 35 D5
Wattisfield Rd IP31. . . . . . . 35 C2
WATTISHAM 80 B6
Wattisham Airfield IP7. . . . 80 C6
Wattisham Airfield Mus★
IP7. . . . . 80 C6
Wattisham Rd IP7. . . . . 79 F4
WATTISHAM STONE 80 A6
Waveney Cl 3 IP17. . . . . . 128 C4
Waveney Cres NR33. . . . . 115 B7
Waveney Dr NR33. . . . . . . 115 A7
Waveney Hill
Carlton Colville NR32. . . . 114 B8
Lowestoft NR32. . . . . 112 B1
Waveney Hts IP21. . . . . 21 F2

Waveney Rd
Beccles NR34. . . . . 111 B4
Bungay NR35. . . . . 110 D3
10 Bury St Edmunds IP32. . 48 C5
Ditchingham NR35. . . . . . 110 C8
Felixstowe IP11. . . . . 152 E3
Ipswich IP1. . . . . 138 E8
10 Lowestoft NR32. . . . . . 115 D8
Waveney Sports & Leisure
Ctr NR32. . . . . 113 C3
Waveney Terr 4 CB9 . . . . . 132 E5
Waveney Valley Swimming
Pool NR35. . . . . 110 D2
Way Bank La CO9. . . . . 89 C7
Wayne Cl NR32 . . . . 113 B5
Wayside Cl IP14 . . . . 124 D3
Weald The NR32. . . . . 112 E2
Weatheralls Cl 9 CB7. . . . . 28 D4
Weaver Cl IP1. . . . . 138 D8
Weavers Cl
2 Hadleigh IP7 . . . . 149 D6
4 Lavenham CO10. . . . . . 78 D4
Stowmarket IP14. . . . . . . 124 C3
Weavers Croft 8 IP20. . . . . 22 D6
Weavers Ct 12 CO10. . . . . 148 C5
Weavers Dr 6 CO10. . . . . . 77 A2
Weavers La CO10 . . . . 148 C5
Weavers Marsh La IP17 . . . 41 E2
Weavers Way 2 IP6 . . . . . . 82 A5
Webb Rd IP14 . . . . 124 D3
Webb's Cl IP14 . . . . 124 C1
Webbs Ct IP5. . . . . 141 C7
Webb St 1 IP22. . . . . 139 C3
Webster St NR35. . . . . 110 A4
Weddell Rd CB8 . . . . 133 A4
WEETING. 5 E3
Weeting Castle★ IP27. . . . . 5 E4
Weeting Heath Nature
Reserve★ IP27 . . . . 5 C3
Weeting Heath Visitor Ctr★
IP27 . . . . 6 C4
Weeting Prim Sch IP27 . . . . 5 E3
Weir Pl IP10. . . . . 98 D2
Weirs Dr CB5. . . . . 44 A6
Welbeck Cl
Felixstowe IP11. . . . . 152 C7
North Grove NR34. . . . . . 10 C4
Welbourne Way NR34. . . . 10 C4
Welch Cl NR34. . . . . 10 D3
Welham La IP28. . . . . 47 D5
Well Bottom CB8 . . . . 45 D4
Wellesley Rd Ipswich IP3. . 139 F5
Troston IP31 . . . . 33 D4
Wellington Cl
Hadleigh IP7 . . . . 149 D7
Thistley Green IP28. . . . . . 30 A6
Wellington Espl NR33 . . . . 115 C6
Wellington Rd Eye IP23. . . 117 D3
4 Feltwell IP26 . . . . 4 E5
6 Harwich CO12. . . . . . . 107 C3
2 Lowestoft NR33 . . . . . . 115 A3
8 Mildenhall IP28 . . . . . . 30 A8
13 Troston IP31. . . . . 33 D5
Wellington St
7 Ipswich IP1. . . . . 139 A7
1 Newmarket CB8. . . . . . 121 A3
Wellington Terr 5 CB9 . . . . 132 C5
Well La 9 CO10 . . . . 90 A8
Wells Cl IP4. . . . . 139 E6
Wells Cnr IP13. . . . . 39 F2
Wells Ct IP28. . . . . 116 B5
Wells Hall Com Prim Sch
CO10. . . . . 148 F2
Wells Hall Rd CO10. . . . . . 148 F3
Wells' La IP20. . . . . 22 C5
Wells Rd IP20. . . . . 22 C5
Well St IP33. . . . . 154 B2
Wells Way IP14. . . . . 53 F1
Wellum Cl 13 CB9. . . . . . . 132 C5
Wembley Ave NR34 . . . . . . 111 B4
Wendy Cl 7 IP9 . . . . 106 C8
Wenham La
East Bergholt CO7. . . . . . 151 D8
Wenham Magna CO7. . . . . 150 A2
Wenham Rd IP8 . . . . 150 B8
WENHASTON 42 C6
Wenhaston La IP19 . . . . . . 42 D5
Wenhaston Prim Sch
IP19 . . . . 42 C6
Wenhaston Rd IP19 . . . . . . 42 B5
Wenhaston Way 2 NR32 . . 112 F3
Wensleydale 5 NR33 . . . . . 114 E3
Wensum Gdns NR32. . . . . 113 C3
Wentford St 7 CB9. . . . . . 132 A6
Wentford View 1 CO10. . . . 76 A1
Wentworth Cl
14 Fornham All Saints
IP28. . . . . 48 C6
Hadleigh IP7 . . . . 149 F5
Weeting IP27. . . . . 5 E4
Wentworth Dr
Felixstowe IP11. . . . . 153 C6
Ipswich IP4. . . . . 138 C2
10 Mildenhall IP28. . . . . . 116 B5
Wentworth Rd IP15. . . . . . 130 F4
Wentworth Terr 5 CB9 . . . 132 C6
Wentworth Way 2 NR33 . . 114 F4
Wesel Ave IP11. . . . . 152 D3
Wesley Cl NR34. . . . . 111 B2
Wesley End Rd CO9 . . . . . . 89 B2
Wesley Way IP1. . . . . 138 F8
WESTBOURNE 138 F7
Westbourne Ct 6 CB9 . . . . 132 E6
Westbourne High Sch
IP1. . . . . 134 E1
Westbourne Rd IP1. . . . . . 134 F1
WESTBROOK GREEN 20 C4
Westbury Ave IP33. . . . . . 122 D5

Westbury Rd IP4. . . . . 140 B8
West Dock Rd CO12. . . . . . 106 F3
West Dr Mildenhall IP28. . . 116 B4
Soham CB7 . . . . 28 C4
West Dr Cres CB7. . . . . 28 C4
West Dr Gdns CB7. . . . . 28 C4
WEST END. 26 B6
West End CB8 . . . . 60 B5
Westend La CB9 . . . . 133 F8
West End La
Great Thurlow CB9 . . . . . . 74 B4
16 Harwich CO12 . . . . 107 A1
West End Rd IP1. . . . . 155 A2
WESTERFIELD. 135 E4
Westerfield La IP6. . . . . . . 136 A5
Westerfield Rd
Ipswich IP1. . . . . 155 C4
Westerfield IP6. . . . . 135 E4
Westerfield Sta IP6. . . . . . 135 E4
Westerings The 1 CO6. . . . 102 C5
Western Ave
Felixstowe IP11. . . . . 153 D6
Haverhill CB9. . . . . 132 C5
Western Cl
4 Feltwell IP26 . . . . 4 D5
Ipswich IP4. . . . . 140 F4
Western's End 6 CO11. . . . 104 E4
Western Way IP33 . . . . 122 D6
Westfield CO10. . . . . 90 A7
Westfield Com Prim Sch
CB9. . . . . 132 F5
Westgarth Gdns IP33. . . . . 122 E3
Westgate 5 IP16. . . . . 73 F6
Westgate Prim Sch IP33 . . 154 A1
Westgate St Service Rd
IP1. . . . . 155 B3
Westgate St
Bury St Edmunds IP33. . . 154 C1
Ipswich IP1. . . . . 155 B3
Long Melford CO10 . . . . . . 77 L1
West Gr NR33. . . . . 115 A3
WESTHALL 25 C4
Westhall IP21 . . . . 39 B5
West Hall Dr IP10. . . . . 6 A8
Westhall Rd NR32. . . . . . . 113 B5
West Hall Rd
1 Mundford IP26. . . . . 6 B8
Walsham le Willows IP22. . 35 F3
WEST HARLING. 18 B8
West Harling Rd NR16. . . . . 18 B8
West Herne La IP22. . . . . . . 19 A1
West Hill IP16 . . . . 129 C2
Westholme Cl IP12 . . . . . . 146 F4
Westholme Rd IP1 . . . . 135 A1
WESTHORPE 51 D8
Westhorpe 3 CB5 . . . . 44 A6
Westhorpe Rd
Finningham IP14 . . . . 52 A8
Wyverstone IP14. . . . . 51 E6
West La IP15 . . . . 130 E3
Westland 26 IP5. . . . . 98 A8
Westland Rd NR33 . . . . . . 114 E6
West Lawn IP4 . . . . 140 C8
WESTLETON. 58 B7
Westleton Heath National
Nature Reserve★ IP17. . . . 58 B8
Westleton Rd IP17. . . . . 57 E8
Westleton Way 17 IP11. . . 152 D5
WESTLEY. 122 A6
Westley Bottom Rd CB8 . . . 59 A4
Westley La IP29 . . . . 122 C5
Westley Mid Sch IP33. . . . 122 C5
Westley Rd IP33. . . . . 122 D5
WESTLEY WATERLESS 59 E3
Westley Way IP31. . . . . 50 E7
West Meadows IP1 . . . . . . 134 C4
West Mill Gn IP9. . . . . 104 F7
Westminster Cl IP4. . . . . . 140 B5
Westminster Dr IP33. . . . . 122 C6
Westmorland Cl 8
CO11 . . . . 105 A2
Westmorland Rd IP11. . . . 153 D7
WESTON 9 D1
Weston Colville Rd CB8 . . . 59 F7
WESTON DITCH. 29 F7
Weston Rd NR32. . . . . 113 B5
Weston Way CB8. . . . . 120 F6
West Rd
Bury St Edmunds IP33. . . 122 E4
Ipswich IP3. . . . . 140 E1
Westropps 6 CO10 . . . . 91 E7
WEST ROW. 29 F6
West Row Prim Sch IP28 . . 29 F7
West Row Rd IP28. . . . . . . 116 A5
West Side Cl NR32. . . . . . . 113 C5
West St Harwich CO12. . . . 107 B3
Icklingham IP28. . . . . 31 C4
Isleham CB7 . . . . 29 B5
Rickinghall Inferior IP22. . . 35 E3
WEST STOW 32 B1
West Stow Anglo-Saxon
Village★ IP28. . . . . 31 F2
West Stow Ctry Pk★ IP28 . 31 F2
West Stow Rd IP28. . . . . . . 32 B1
WEST STREET
Rickinghall Inferior 35 A1
Walsham-le-Willows. 35 B5
West Suffolk Coll IP33. . . . 122 E6
West Suffolk Hospl The
IP33. . . . . 123 A2
WEST TOFTS. 6 E7
West Tofts Rd IP26 . . . . 6 D7
West View Burstall IP8. . . . 95 F7
Carlton IP17. . . . . 128 D6
Stowmarket IP14. . . . . . . 124 B6
West View Gdns 4 IP23. . . 36 D2
Westward Deals CB9. . . . . 133 F8
Westward Ho IP16. . . . . . . 129 C6

West Wood 9 IP31. . . . . 49 A5
Westwood Ave
Ipswich IP1. . . . . 139 A8
Lowestoft NR33. . . . . 114 E6
Wetherby Cl IP1. . . . . 135 B3
WETHERDEN. 51 B1
Wetherden Rd
Elmswell IP30 . . . . 50 F2
Great Ashfield IP31. . . . . . 51 B6
WETHERDEN UPPER
TOWN 51 B4
WETHERINGSETT. 53 A5
Wetheringsett CE Prim Sch
IP14 . . . . 53 A5
WETHERUP STREET. 53 C3
Wet La CB4. . . . . 102 F3
Wexford Rd IP1. . . . . 134 D2
WEYBREAD. 22 D3
Weyland Rd IP6 . . . . 83 A6
Weylands Cl IP14 . . . . 67 D7
Whalebone Cnr CO4 . . . . . 103 C4
Whaplload Rd NR32 . . . . . 113 E1
Wharfedale NR33 . . . . 114 F3
Wharfedale Rd IP1. . . . . . . 135 A1
Wharf La 3 CO8. . . . . 101 C4
Wharton St 5 NR35. . . . . . 110 B4
WHATFIELD 80 C1
Whatfield CE Prim Sch
IP7. . . . . 80 C1
Whatfield Rd
Aldham IP7 . . . . 94 C7
Elmsett IP7. . . . . 80 F1
Whatfield Way IP14. . . . . . 124 E3
WHEATACRE. 2 B1
Wheatacre Dr 3 NR32 . . . . .3 C4
Wheatfield Rd NR33. . . . . 114 D4
Wheatfields
3 Botesdale IP22. . . . . . . 36 A6
4 Thurston IP31. . . . . 49 E4
Whatfield IP7. . . . . 80 C1
Wheatsheaf Cl CO11 . . . . . 105 E2
Wheatsheaf La CO11 . . . . . 105 E2
Wheelbarrow La IP20. . . . . 23 F5
Wheeler's La IP31 . . . . 51 A5
Wheelwright Cl IP30. . . . . . 49 C2
Wheelwrights The IP11. . . 152 C8
WHELP STREET 79 B4
WHEPSTEAD. 63 B5
Whepstead Rd
Hawstead IP29 . . . . 63 B7
Horringer IP29 . . . . 122 D1
Wherry La IP4. . . . . 155 C2
Wherry Quay IP4 . . . . 155 C2
Wherry Rd
3 Bungay NR35. . . . . 110 D3
3 Dunnis Hill NR35 . . . . 110 D3
WHERSTEAD. 143 B6
Wherstead Rd IP2 . . . . 155 B1
Whights Cnr IP8. . . . . 138 A1
Whinchat Cl IP2. . . . . 138 D3
Whinfield 13 IP5. . . . . 98 A8
Whinfield Ave 23 CO12. . . 106 F1
Whinfield Cl 16 IP5. . . . . . 98 A8
Whin Marsh 6 IP15. . . . . . 130 E5
Whinneys The IP5. . . . . . . 141 D8
Whinyard Way 3 IP11. . . . 153 D7
Whiskin Cl 7 NR32. . . . . . 112 D2
Whistle Dro IP28. . . . . 12 D5
Whitby Rd
Bury St Edmunds IP33. . . 122 D3
Ipswich IP4. . . . . 139 F8
Whiteacres 4 IP24. . . . . . . 16 C6
Whitedike Dro IP26. . . . . . . 4 B4
White Elm Rd IP30. . . . . . . 50 C1
White Elm St IP3 . . . . 139 E4
White Foot La IP13 . . . . 83 E6
Whitegates CB8. . . . . 121 B3
White Hall Cl CO10. . . . . . . 92 C5
Whitehall Rd IP14 . . . . 51 F1
White Hart La IP7. . . . . . . 155 C2
White Hart La 20 CB7. . . . . 28 C4
White Horse Cl 4 IP11. . . . 153 C6
White Horse Hill IP9 . . . . . 142 D1
White Horse La IP30. . . . . . 64 D7
White Horse Rd
Capel St Mary IP9. . . . . . 150 F3
East Bergholt CO7. . . . . . 151 D3
Kedington CB9. . . . . 133 E8
White Horse St 4 NR32 . . . 113 E2
Whitehouse Com Inf Sch
IP1. . . . . 134 E1
White House Farm La
IP21. . . . . 22 B6
White House Gdns NR34. . 111 A4
Whitehouse Ind Est IP1. . . 134 C3
Whitehouse Jun Sch
IP1. . . . . 134 D2
Whitehouse La
Belchamp Otten CO10. . . . 90 D5
Earsham NR35. . . . . 7 C5
Stowupland IP14. . . . . . . 67 D8
White House Rd IP1. . . . . . 134 D2
White Lion Ct IP7. . . . . 149 D6
White Lion Rd NR34. . . . . . 10 B8
White Meadow 3 IP14. . . . 51 A1
Whitepost Cnr IP14. . . . . . . 54 C1
Whites IP21. . . . . 39 B4
Whites Field CO7 . . . . 151 B5
White's La NR33 . . . . 11 B1
WHITESTREET GREEN. 93 D2
Whitethorn Rd 2 IP3. . . . . 140 F1
White Womans La IP21 . . . . 85 B7
Whitewood Wlk 8 IP21. . . . 13 F2
Withersfield Rd CB9 . . . . . 132 C8
Whiting Rd NR32. . . . . 112 C2
Whiting St IP33. . . . . 154 B1
Whitland Cl IP2. . . . . 143 A8
Whitlands 6 CO10. . . . . 77 A3
Whitlock Dr CO9. . . . . 89 F1

Whittle Rd IP2 . . . . 138 F6
WHITTON 134 F3
Whitton Church La IP1 . . 134 F4
Whitton Cl NR33 . . . . . . 114 E6
Whitton Com Prim Sch
 IP1 . . . . 134 E3
Whitton Ct NR33 . . . . . . 115 A3
Whitton Gn Prim Sch
 NR33 . . . . 114 F5
Whitton La IP1 . . . . 134 D4
Whitton Leyer IP8 . . . . 134 C2
Whitton Sports Ctr IP1 . . 134 E4
Whitworth Cl IP2 . . . . . . 138 D2
Whyteway IP19 . . . . . . 24 B4
WICKEN 28 B1
Wicken Rd CB7 . . . . . . 28 D1
WICKER STREET GREEN . 93 E5
Wickhambrook 61 E2
Wickhambrook Ct [2]
 IP11 . . . . 152 A5
Wickhambrook Prim Sch
 CB8 . . . . 61 E2
Wickhambrook Rd IP29 . . 62 A5
Wickham Com Prim Sch
 IP13 . . . . 127 B6
WICKHAM GREEN 52 C8
Wickham La IP14 . . . . . . 52 A6
WICKHAM MARKET 127 B6
Wickham Mkt Sta IP12 . . 71 C2
Wickham Rd IP23 . . . . . . 52 F7
WICKHAM SKEITH 52 E8
WICKHAM STREET
 Wickhambrook 61 F1
 Wickham Skeith 52 C8
Wick La CO12 . . . . 107 A1
Wicklow Rd IP1 . . . . . . 134 D2
Wick Rd Langham CO4 . . 103 C2
 Stoke-by-Nayland CO6 . . 103 A6
Wicks La IP14 . . . . 67 D7
Widgeon Cl IP2 . . . . . . 138 F3
WIDGHAM GREEN 60 B2
WIGGENS GREEN 88 C5
Wiggin Cl IP28 . . . . . . 116 D2
Wiggs Acre NR34 . . . . . . 10 C4
Wigg's Way [3] NR32 . . . 3 D4
Wigmore Cl
 Ipswich IP2 . . . . 138 F1
 Stoke Park IP2 . . . . . . 139 A1
Wignall St CO11 . . . . . . 104 C2
Wigston Rd IP33 . . . . . . 122 C3
Wigwam Hill IP21 . . . . . 19 F1
Wilberforce St IP1 . . . . 139 A6
WILBY 39 C2
Wilby CE Prim Sch IP21 . . 39 B2
Wilbye Cl IP32 . . . . . . 123 E4
Wilby La IP13 . . . . 39 E2
Wilby Rd IP21 . . . . 39 A4
Wild Acres [13] CB5 . . . . 44 A5
Wilderness Cl [3] IP20 . . 22 D5
Wilderness Hill IP8 . . . . . 95 B6
Wilderness La
 Harleston IP20 . . . . 22 D6
 Woodbridge IP12 . . . . . 147 A6
Wilde St Est IP28 . . . . . 13 D1
Wildes St NR32 . . . . . . 113 E2
WILDE STREET 13 D2
Wildflower Way NR35 . . 110 B7
Wilding Dr IP5 . . . . . . 141 D7
Wilding Rd IP8 . . . . . . 138 C1
Wildmere La IP28 . . . . . . 13 D1
Wild Tracks Offroad Activity
 Pk★ CB7 . . . . 45 E7
Wilford Bridge Rd IP12 . . 147 D7
Wilford Bridge Spur
 IP12 . . . . 147 C7
Wilfred Hurry Cl IP8 . . . 134 A1
Wilfred Sherman Cl CB8 . . 121 A4
Wilkes Ct IP5 . . . . 141 E7
Wilkes Way IP12 . . . . . 124 C6
Wilkinson Dr IP5 . . . . . 141 C6
Wilkinson Way IP12 . . . 147 A6
Wilks Rd IP33 . . . . 123 B2
Willbye Ave IP22 . . . . . . 20 D3
Willcox Ave IP33 . . . . . 122 C6
William Armstrong Cl [6]
 IP30 . . . . 50 F2
William Blake Ct CB9 . . 132 C7
William Booth Way [11]
 IP11 . . . . 152 D5
William Groom Ave [2]
 CO12 . . . . 107 A1
WILLIAM'S GREEN 93 E5
Williamsport Way IP6 . . 125 F3
William St IP1 . . . . 155 B3
William's Way [4] IP28 . . 29 F6
Willie Snaith Rd CB8 . . 120 F6
WILLINGHAM 25 E7
WILLISHAM 81 A5
WILLISHAM TYE 81 A6
Willoughby Cl IP13 . . . 71 A7
Willoughby Rd IP1 . . . 155 A1
Willowbrook Cl NR33 . . 114 A3
Willow Cl
 Badwell Ash IP31 . . . . . 50 F8
 [6] Claydon IP6 . . . . . . 134 C8
 Haverhill CB9 . . . . 132 B1
 Stradbroke IP21 . . . . . 39 B5
 [1] Sudbury CO10 . . . . 148 C4
 Worlington NR34 . . . . . 111 F3
 Wortwell IP20 . . . . 23 A8
Willow Cres CB8 . . . . . 121 B2
Willowcroft Rd IP1 . . . 135 A2
Willow Gn IP13 . . . . 54 E7
Willow Gr [3] CO6 . . . 102 C5
Willow La
 Bedingham NR35 . . . . . . 7 B7
 Broome NR35 . . . . 8 C7
 Cotton IP14 . . . . 52 B6

Willow Marsh La
 Darsham IP17 . . . . 42 A1
 Yoxford IP17 . . . . 41 F7
Willow Rd NR33 . . . . . . 115 A2
Willow Tree Cl IP13 . . 127 B6
Willowvale NR32 . . . . . 112 F6
Willow Way
 Bury St Edmunds IP33 . . 154 A3
 [9] Great Bricett IP7 . . 80 D6
 [1] Harwich CO12 . . . . 106 F1
 [8] Rendlesham IP12 . . 85 D8
Willow Wlk
 [5] Harleston IP20 . . . 22 D5
 Needham Market IP6 . . 125 D6
Willrede Cl NR34 . . . . 111 B3
Wilmslow Ave IP14 . . 146 E5
Wilmslow Dr IP8 . . . . 138 C2
WILNEY GREEN 19 D4
Wilson Rd
 Hadleigh IP7 . . . . 149 E5
 Ipswich IP8 . . . . 138 B1
 Lowestoft NR33 . . . . . 115 C5
Wilton Rd IP26 . . . . 4 E5
Wimbledon Ave IP27 . . 14 E8
Wimborne Ave IP3 . . . 140 D4
Wimpole Cl IP5 . . . . . . 140 F6
Wincanton Cl IP4 . . . 136 A1
Winchester Cl IP14 . . 124 B6
Winchester Gdns [4] IP6 . . 82 B5
Winchester Rd IP33 . . 122 D4
Winchester Way IP4 . . 142 F8
Windermere Cl IP3 . . 144 B8
Windermere Pk NR32 . . 113 A4
Windermere Rd
 [6] Felixstowe IP11 . . 153 D7
 Stowmarket IP14 . . . . 124 C6
 Sudbury CO10 . . . . 148 E6
Windgap La IP14 . . . . . . 51 D1
Windham Rd CO10 . . . 148 E6
Winding Piece [5] IP9 . . 150 E3
Windings Rd [4] IP7 . . . 80 F1
Windmill Ave IP30 . . . 50 C1
Windmill Cl
 Boxted CO4 . . . . 102 F2
 Ramsey & Parkeston
 CO12 . . . . 106 C1
 [3] Soham CB7 . . . . . . 28 E2
 [3] Somersham IP8 . . . 81 C3
Windmill Gn
 Ditchingham NR35 . . . 110 C7
 [19] Stanton IP31 . . . 34 E4
Windmill Hill
 Capel St Mary IP9 . . . 150 C3
 Exning CB8 . . . . 120 C8
 Long Melford CO10 . . . 77 D1
Windmill La IP21 . . . . . 38 F8
Windmill Rd IP20 . . . . 23 A7
Windmill Rise
 Bury St Edmunds IP33 . . 154 A1
 Hundon CO10 . . . . 75 D4
 [1] Wetherden IP14 . . 51 A1
Windmill Row [5] CO10 . . 77 B3
Windrush Rd IP5 . . . . 141 C8
Windsor Circ
 Lakenheath IP27 . . . . . 14 A3
 Lakenheath IP27 . . . . . 109 F1
Windsor Cl
 [7] Barnham IP24 . . . . 16 C2
 Lawshall IP29 . . . . 63 D2
WINDSOR GREEN 64 B2
Windsor Pl CO10 . . . . 148 E5
Windsor Rd
 Felixstowe IP11 . . . . . 152 E3
 Ipswich IP1 . . . . 138 F7
 Lowestoft NR33 . . . . . 115 C7
 Newmarket CB8 . . . . . 120 E4
 Southwold IP18 . . . . . 119 B8
Windsor Terr [12] CB9 . . 132 C6
Windward Way NR33 . . 114 E5
Windyridge Rd IP30 . . 65 D5
WINFARTHING 20 B8
Winfarthing Rd IP22 . . 20 B6
Winfrith Rd IP3 . . . . . . 140 D4
WINGFIELD 39 B8
Wingfield Ave IP27 . . 109 D7
WINGFIELD GREEN 38 F8
Wingfield Meadows IP14 . . 68 B6
Wingfield Old Coll & Gdns★
 IP21 . . . . 39 A7
Wingfield Rd
 Lakenheath IP27 . . . . 109 D7
 Syleham IP21 . . . . 21 F1
 Weybread IP21 . . . . 22 C2
Wingfield St
 Bungay NR35 . . . . 110 B3
 [4] Ipswich IP4 . . . . . 155 C2
Wings Rd IP27 . . . . . . 109 D6
Wings Rd Cl IP27 . . . 109 D6
Winnipeg Rd NR32 . . 113 D2
Winsford Rd IP32 . . . 123 E6
WINSTON 68 F8
Winston Ave
 Ipswich IP4 . . . . 140 C8
 Lowestoft NR33 . . . . . 114 E7
Winston Cl
 [5] Felixstowe IP11 . . 152 D5
 [11] Kessingland NR33 . . 11 C1
Winston Rd
 Southwold IP18 . . . . . 119 C7
 Winston IP14 . . . . 53 F1
Winthrop Rd IP33 . . . 122 D4
Winthrops The CO10 . . 93 B4
WISSETT 24 D2
Wissett Cl IP19 . . . . . 118 B4
Wissett Rd
 Chediston IP19 . . . . . . 41 B8
 Halesworth IP19 . . . . 118 A5
 Wissett IP19 . . . . 24 D1

Wissett Way NR32 . . . 113 B4
Wissey View [2] IP26 . . 6 B8
Wissington Uplands
 CO6 . . . . 102 A5
Wiston Rd CO6 . . . . . . 102 B4
WITHERMARSH GREEN . . 103 A8
Withersdale Rd
 Mendham IP20 . . . . 23 A5
 Weybread IP21 . . . . 22 D4
WITHERSDALE STREET . . 22 F4
WITHERSFIELD 74 B2
Withersfield Rd
 Haverhill CB9 . . . . 132 C7
 Withersfield IP9 . . . . 74 C4
Withers Pl [2] CB7 . . . 29 A1
Withingdale Gall The★
 CO10 . . . . 91 D7
Withipoll St IP4 . . . . 155 C3
WITNESHAM 83 A6
Witnesham Church La
 IP6 . . . . 82 F5
Witnesham La IP6 . . . 136 C7
Witnesham Prim Sch IP6 . . 83 A7
Witney Gn NR33 . . . . . 115 A3
Witney Rd [3] NR33 . . 115 A3
Wittons La IP21 . . . . . . 38 C7
WIXOE 89 B6
Wix Rd CO12 . . . . 106 C1
Wollaston Cl IP32 . . . 122 D8
Wollaston Rd NR32 . . 115 D2
Wolsey Art Gall★ IP1 . . 155 C4
Wolsey Gdns IP11 . . . 153 A3
Wolsey Rd [4] IP14 . . 124 C7
Wolsey St IP1 . . . . 155 B2
Wolton Rd IP5 . . . . . . 141 C7
Wolves Farm La IP7 . . 94 E6
Wolves Wood Nature
 Reserve★ IP7 . . . . 94 F6
WOODBRIDGE 146 F6
Woodbridge Gall★ IP12 . . 146 F5
Woodbridge Mus The★
 IP12 . . . . 147 A5
Woodbridge Prim Sch [15]
 IP12 . . . . 147 A5
Woodbridge Rd
 Alderton IP12 . . . . 99 D5
 Bredfield IP13 . . . . . . 84 C7
 Butley IP12 . . . . 86 A5
 Framlingham IP13 . . . 126 C1
 Grundisburgh IP13 . . . 83 E6
 Ipswich IP4 . . . . 155 C3
 Sutton IP12 . . . . 85 A1
 Tunstall IP12 . . . . 71 E1
 Waldringfield IP12 . . . 98 D6
 Wantisden IP12 . . . . . 85 E5
Woodbridge Rd E IP4 . . 140 C7
Woodbridge Rd W IP4 . . 140 B7
Woodbridge Sch IP12 . . 146 F5
Woodbridge Sta 147 B4
WOODBRIDGE WALK 99 F8
Woodchurch Ave [6]
 NR33 . . . . 114 C4
Wood Cl
 [1] Bentwaters Airfield
 IP12 . . . . 85 D8
 Kenninghall NR16 . . . 19 A8
 Tostock IP30 . . . . 50 B3
Woodcock Cl CB9 . . . 133 A5
Woodcock Rd IP2 . . . 138 E2
Woodcock Rise IP26 . . 6 A1
Woodcote IP14 . . . . . . 124 B6
Woodcrofts Cl [2] IP29 . . 63 A1
Woodcutters Way IP27 . . 109 D7
WOODDITTON 60 C5
Woodditton Rd
 Kirtling CB8 . . . . 60 D3
 Newmarket CB8 . . . . . 121 A1
 Woodditton CB8 . . . . . 60 B6
Wood Farm La IP18 . . . 26 C2
Wood Farm Rd IP13 . . 83 C5
Woodfield Cl NR34 . . . 25 E7
Woodfield Dr IP14 . . 124 E5
Woodfield La
 Stowmarket IP14 . . . . 124 D4
 Stutton IP9 . . . . 105 C5
Woodfields IP21 . . . . . 39 A4
Woodgates Rd CO7 . . . 151 D7
Woodhall Bsns Pk CO10 . . 148 D8
Woodhall Cl CO10 . . . 148 C7
Woodhall Com Prim Sch [3]
 CO10 . . . . 148 D8
Wood Hall La IP23 . . . 37 B1
Woodhall Rd CO10 . . . 148 C7
Woodhouse La IP10 . . 141 C2
Woodhouse Sq IP4 . . 155 C2
Wood La
 Bedingham NR35 . . . . . . 7 C6
 Bressingham IP22 . . . 19 E6
 Dallinghoo IP13 . . . . . 70 B1
 Dickleburgh & Rushall
 IP21 . . . . 21 C2
 Fressingfield IP21 . . . 40 A8
 Henstead with Hulver Street
 NR34 . . . . 26 E7
 Hepworth IP22 . . . . . . 35 A6
 Oulton NR32 . . . . 112 C3
 Reydon IP18 . . . . 26 C1
 Scole IP21 . . . . 21 C4
 Thelnetham IP22 . . . . 35 C6
Woodland Ave NR34 . . 111 F4
Woodland Cl
 Onehouse IP14 . . . . . . 66 C6
 Risby IP28 . . . . 47 D5
 Thurston IP31 . . . . 49 E3
Woodland Dr
 Bungay NR35 . . . . 110 B1
 Ellingham NR35 . . . . . . 8 E7
WOODLAND GREEN 133 C5
Woodland Pl [7] IP31 . . 49 A4

Woodlands
 [1] Chelmondiston IP9 . . 106 C8
 Hadleigh IP7 . . . . 149 B7
 [35] Harleston IP20 . . 22 D6
 Lakenheath IP27 . . . . 109 D8
 Leiston IP16 . . . . 129 C4
Woodlands Ave [4] NR33 . . 114 C3
Woodlands Bsns Pk IP30 . . 49 B3
Woodlands Dr IP24 . . 16 C7
Woodlands Rd
 Holbrook IP9 . . . . 105 E8
 Raydon IP7 . . . . 94 F2
 Rushbrooke with Rougham
 IP30 . . . . 49 B3
Woodlands Rise IP27 . . 14 D8
Woodlands The NR32 . . 113 B8
Woodlands Way
 Bramford IP8 . . . . 134 C4
 Mildenhall IP28 . . . . 116 F5
Woodlane Rd IP23 . . . 38 C1
Woodlark Cl IP23 . . . 138 E1
Woodlark Dr [4] IP14 . . 124 F7
Woodley Com Sch IP14 . . 124 B7
Woodleys Yd IP18 . . . 119 D5
Woodpecker Ave [2]
 NR33 . . . . 114 D5
Woodpecker Cl [16] IP14 . . 67 A5
Woodpecker Rd IP2 . . 138 D3
Wood Rd Badingham NR35 . . 56 B6
 Woolpit IP30 . . . . 65 F8
Woodrush Rd IP3 . . . 140 E2
Woods Cl
 Ditchingham NR35 . . . 110 B7
 Sturmer CB9 . . . . 133 C3
Woodside
 Beccles NR34 . . . . . . 113 C1
 Brampton with Stoven NR34 25 E5
 Martlesham Heath IP5 . . 98 B8
Wood Side IP14 . . . . . 124 B5
Woodside Bsns Pk IP31 . . 32 F2
Woodside Cl
 Bury St Edmunds IP33 . . 123 B6
 Lowestoft NR33 . . . . . 114 C3
Woods La IP12 . . . . . . 147 B7
Woods Loke E NR32 . . 113 A3
Woods Loke Prim Sch
 NR32 . . . . 112 F3
Woods Loke W NR32 . . 112 F3
Woodspring Cl [12] IP2 . . 139 A2
Woodstone Ave IP1 . . 135 C1
Woodthorpe Cl IP7 . . 149 F5
Woodthorpe Rd IP7 . . 149 E5
WOODTON 7 C8
Wood View [4] IP17 . . . 56 F8
Woodville Rd IP4 . . . 139 F5
Woodward Ave IP14 . . 51 F6
Woodward Cl IP2 . . . 138 D5
Woolhall St [2] IP33 . . 154 B2
Woollards Cl IP1 . . . . 114 D4
Woollards Gdns [3] CO10 . . 91 E8
Woolmers IP14 . . . . . 124 D4
Woolner Cl [7] Claydon IP6 . . 82 A5
 [5] Hadleigh IP7 . . . . 149 E6
Woolnough Cl [6] CB9 . . 88 D3
Woolnough Rd IP12 . . 146 F6
Woolnoughs The [2] IP5 . . 141 D7
WOOLPIT 50 D1
Woolpit & District Musuem★
 IP30 . . . . 50 D1
WOOLPIT GREEN 65 D8
WOOLPIT HEATH 65 E8
Woolpit Prim Sch IP30 . . 50 D1
Woolpit Rd IP31 . . . . . 34 C2
WOOLVERSTONE 144 B1
Woolverstone Cl IP2 . . 138 D1
WOOTTEN GREEN 39 B3
Worcester Cl [5] IP32 . . 123 E6
Worcester Rd IP3 . . . 144 A8
Wordsell Cl IP2 . . . . . 139 C3
Wordsworth Cl IP7 . . 128 B4
Wordsworth Cres IP1 . . 134 C3
Wordsworth Rd
 [4] Bury St Edmunds IP32 . . 48 C5
 [2] Stowmarket IP14 . . 124 B8
WORDWELL 32 D3
Worell Dr NR34 . . . . . . 111 E4
WORKHOUSE GREEN . . . 101 C8
WORKHOUSE HILL 102 F2
Workhouse Hill
 Boxted CO4 . . . . 102 F3
 Hartest IP29 . . . . 77 B8
Workhouse La IP17 . . . 57 E2
Workhouse Rd
 Little Horkesley CO6 . . 102 B2
 Thornham Magna IP23 . . 37 A1
Workshop La IP10 . . 145 C5
WORLD'S END 65 F2
World's End La IP14 . . 65 F2
World's End Rd IP13 . . 55 B4
WORLINGHAM 111 F3
Worlingham Mid Sch
 NR34 . . . . 111 F3
Worlingham Prim Sch
 NR34 . . . . 9 F5
WORLINGTON 30 A4
Worlington Rd
 Barton Mills IP28 . . . 30 E3
 Worlington IP28 . . . . 116 A3
WORLINGWORTH 54 F8
Worlingworth CE Prim Sch
 IP13 . . . . 54 D7
Worlingworth Rd IP21 . . 38 F3
WORMINGFORD 101 F2
WORTHAM 36 D8
Wortham Ling Nature
 Reserve★ IP22 . . . . . . 19 F2
Wortham Pl [1] CB9 . . 132 E6
Wortham Prim Sch IP22 . . 36 E1

Whi–Zur 185

Worthing Rd NR32 . . . 113 D3
WORTWELL 23 B8
WRABNESS 105 F2
Wrabness Local Nature
 Reserve★ IP9 . . . . . . 105 E2
Wrabness Rd [1] CO12 . . 106 D1
Wrabness Sta CO11 . . 106 D1
Wragg Dr CB8 . . . . 121 A6
Wratting Rd
 Great Thurlow CB9 . . . 74 D5
 Haverhill CB9 . . . . . . 132 E7
Wren Ave IP2 . . . . 138 D3
Wren Cl
 Bury St Edmunds IP32 . . 49 A4
 Mildenhall IP28 . . . . 116 D4
 [1] Stowmarket IP14 . . 67 A5
 [13] Thurstow IP31 . . . 49 D4
Wrens Pk [2] IP11 . . . 153 D7
WRENTHAM 26 E5
WRENTHAM WEST END . . 26 C7
Wriggle St IP13 . . . . . . 70 A7
Wright Cl IP14 . . . . . . 124 D3
Wright La IP5 . . . . 141 D8
Wright Rd IP3 . . . . . . 140 C2
Wrights Way
 Leavenheath CO6 . . . 102 A7
 Woolpit IP30 . . . . 50 C1
Wroxham Rd IP3 . . . . 139 D3
Wyatt Cl IP30 . . . . 50 F3
Wyatts La CO10 . . . . . 101 B8
Wyatt Way IP24 . . . . . 16 B7
Wye Rd IP3 . . . . 140 A2
Wyken Rd IP31 . . . . . . 34 D3
Wyken Vineyard & Gdns★
 IP31 . . . . 34 E2
Wykes Bishop St IP3 . . 139 E4
Wymering Rd [10] IP18 . . 119 D5
Wyncoll's La IP7 . . . . . 94 B2
Wyndham Way CB8 . . 121 A6
Wynterton Cl IP3 . . . 140 B1
Wynton Rise IP14 . . . 124 E4
Wytchwoods The IP14 . . 68 E6
Wyvern Rd IP3 . . . . . . 140 C1
WYVERSTONE 51 E6
WYVERSTONE GREEN . . 51 E6
Wyverstone Rd
 Badwell Ash IP31 . . . . 51 B7
 Wyverstone Green IP14 . . 51 E6
WYVERSTONE STREET . . 51 D6

Y

Yale Bsns Pk IP3 . . . . 144 F8
Yarmouth Pl [3] CB9 . . 132 E6
Yarmouth Rd
 Corton NR32 . . . . 113 A8
 Ditchingham NR35 . . 110 D7
 Geldeston NR34 . . . . . . 9 A7
 Ipswich IP1 . . . . 139 A6
 Kirby Cane NR35 . . . . . 8 E7
 Lound NR32 . . . . 2 F7
 Lowestoft NR32 . . . . . 113 B5
 Melton IP12 . . . . 84 E6
 Ufford IP13 . . . . 127 B1
 Woodbridge IP12 . . . . 147 C8
Yarrow Dr NR33 . . . . . 114 C4
YAXLEY 37 B5
Yaxley Hall La IP23 . . 37 C4
Yaxley Rd IP23 . . . . . . 37 C3
Yeldham Pl CB9 . . . . 132 E6
Yeoman Cres IP7 . . . 149 E5
Yeoman Rd IP11 . . . . 152 D3
Yeomanry Yd IP33 . . 154 A2
Yeoman's Cl NR35 . . 110 C3
Yeoman Way IP7 . . . . 149 E5
Yeovil Rd NR32 . . . . . 113 C2
Yerril Gdn CB9 . . . . . 132 C5
Yew Cl [1] IP27 . . . . . . 13 F2
Yew Ct IP2 . . . . 139 A3
Yewdale NR33 . . . . . . 114 D2
Yewlands Gr IP30 . . . 65 A4
Yew Tree Cl IP28 . . . 116 D6
Yew Tree Ct [1] IP33 . . 122 F3
Yewtree Gr IP5 . . . . . . 140 F7
Yewtree Rise IP18 . . . 138 C1
Yew Tree Rise IP13 . . 127 C7
York Cl
 Bury St Edmunds IP33 . . 122 E5
 [1] Mildenhall IP28 . . 30 A8
 Sudbury CO10 . . . . 148 C2
York Cres [12] Claydon IP6 . . 82 B5
 Claydon IP6 . . . . 134 C8
York Rd
 Bury St Edmunds IP33 . . 154 A2
 Felixstowe IP11 . . . . . 153 A4
 Foxhall IP5 . . . . 98 A7
 Haverhill CB9 . . . . 132 C5
 Ipswich IP3 . . . . 140 A4
 Lowestoft NR32 . . . . . 113 C1
 Southwold IP18 . . . . . 119 B5
 Sudbury CO10 . . . . 148 C6
York Terr IP33 . . . . . . 154 A2
YOXFORD 57 D7
Yoxford Gdns★ IP17 . . 57 D7
Yoxford Mews [7] IP12 . . 85 B3
Yoxford Prim Sch IP17 . . 57 D8
Yoxford Rd Middleton IP17 . . 57 F6
 Sibton IP17 . . . . 57 A8

Z

Zanetta Ct NR32 . . . . 113 C1
Zurich Cl [3] NR31 . . . 3 C6